JOHNNY MERCER

JOHNNY MERCER

SOUTHERN SONGWRITER FOR THE WORLD

Glenn T. Eskew

THE UNIVERSITY OF GEORGIA PRESS • ATHENS AND LONDON

© 2013 by the University of Georgia Press
Athens, Georgia 30602
www.ugapress.org
All rights reserved

Designed by April Leidig
Set in Garamond Premier Pro by Copperline Book Services
Manufactured by Thomson-Shore, Inc.

The paper in this book meets the guidelines for permanence
and durability of the Committee on Production Guidelines
for Book Longevity of the Council on Library Resources.

Printed in the United States of America

17 16 15 14 13 C 5 4 3 2 1

Library of Congress Cataloging-in-Publication Data
Eskew, Glenn T.
Johnny Mercer : southern songwriter for the world / Glenn T. Eskew.
       pages   cm.
Includes bibliographical references and index.
ISBN 978-0-8203-3330-4 (hardcover : alk. paper)
ISBN 0-8203-3330-1 (hardcover : alk.paper)
1. Mercer, Johnny, 1909–1976.
2. Lyricists — United States — Biography. I. Title.
ML423.M446E75 2013
782.42164092 — dc23
[B]   2013003506

British Library Cataloging-in-Publication Data available

FOR PAMELA

From Natchez to Mobile,
From Memphis to Saint Joe,
Wherever the four winds blow—

Contents

· ·

Acknowledgments

· ·

HAVING LONG ENJOYED jazz and the musical theater, when I discovered the rich life story of Johnny Mercer I decided to undertake a research project about the southern songwriter. Since the publication of my previous book on the civil rights movement, I had searched for a topic that might provide a different approach to the history of the South. Mercer offered that and more. The key role he played in the creation of American popular culture in the twentieth century offered a look at the integration of southern music into the national mainstream. In addition to having his papers at my home institution of Georgia State University (GSU) in Atlanta, his ancestral ties to Georgia and Virginia presented opportunities to learn more about these regions, thereby strengthening my own understanding of the South. Tapping these resources in the classroom, I designed research assignments using his papers for my introduction to history course. Over the past decade, undergraduates explored Johnny Mercer's life and the Great American Songbook while writing essays for class. To them I owe a debt of gratitude for indulging me and offering many insightful observations, some of which appear in this narrative.

For nearly fifteen years now I have worked with Mercer materials, principally from the Popular Music Archives in the Pullen Library at GSU. Many archivists have assisted me (and my students), including several heads of the department beginning with Julia Marks Young, then Pam Harris, and now Stephen Zeitz, while several archivists oversaw the collection beginning with Chris Paton, Christine de Catanzaro, Laura Botts, and now Kevin Fleming, and still others helped out as archival assistants, including my former students Amanda Brown, Casey Cater, and especially David Bradley, for whom I offer a special word of thanks for providing invaluable aid on numerous occasions. I also recognize the assistance of the deans of the library, Charlene Hurt and Nancy H. Seamans. Colleagues in the Department of History offered support in a variety of ways, including the chairs Tim Crimmins, Diane Willen, and Hugh Hudson, as well as colleagues Clifford Kuhn, Michelle Brattain, Krystyn Moon, Wendy Venet, Alecia Long, Christine Skwiot, Richard Laub, and Mary Rolinson, and friends from the Department of English, John Burrison, Pearl and Tom McHaney, and Brennan Collins. History department staff, especially the late Elizabeth Adams, as well as Paula Sorrell and Carolyn Whiters, supplied needed resources. A GSU Research Initiation Grant followed by the buying out of my teaching obligation for a semester off for research purposes paid for by the Johnny Mercer Foundation chaired by Margaret Whiting and facilitated by university attorney John Marshall helped start the process just as a semester off from teaching from the College of Arts and Sciences approved by Dean Lauren Adamson brought the manuscript to completion. For this and all other assistance received from my colleagues at GSU, I offer thanks.

Scholarships from the Episcopal Women's History Project helped subsidize research in Savannah, for which I thank Dr. Jane Harris of Hendrix College and her colleagues on the awards committee. Many times I have used the collections of the Georgia Historical Society, being assisted by a variety of archivists over the years including Frank Wheeler, Mandy Johnson, Susan Dick, Jewell Anderson, Alison Bentley, and Rana Edgar, and I value the support I have received from Senior Historian Dr. Stan Deaton and President and Chief Executive Officer Dr. W. Todd Groce. The archivist in the Minis Room, Special Collections at Armstrong-Atlantic State University, Caroline Hopkinson, as well as my dear friend on the history faculty, Professor Michael Price, gave invaluable help when using the Mercer and related papers housed there. Georgia Spellman of the Savannah Roman Catholic Church Archives as well as the archivist Gillian Brown assisted me with the many Ciucevich connections, as did Mary Giles of the Charleston Roman Catholic Church Archives. Similarly Father Michael Spurlock tracked down records for me at Saint Thomas Church (Episcopal) in Manhattan. Two ladies in the Bull Street Branch of the Live Oak Chatham County Public Library, Honey Ryan and Sharen Lee, always offered help when needed, as did Glenda Anderson of the City of Savannah Archives, Gary Arthur of the Beehive Foundation, and Julie E. Walet of the Office of Clerk Superior Court, Chatham County. Other Georgia repositories that have materials related to the subject include the University of Georgia in Athens and the Georgia Music Hall of Fame in Macon.

A special word of thanks to Savannahians Robert A. "Bob" Ciucevich of Quatrefoil, Katherine Knapp Keena of the Juliette Gordon Low Birthplace, Girl

Scouts of the USA, and Dr. John Duncan of V & J Duncan Antique Maps, Prints & Books, as well as Mr. Pearce W. Hammond of Bluffton, South Carolina, for their help in locating rare photographs of Mercer. Likewise, a similar word of thanks for Frank Driggs, Michael Owen of the Ira and Leonore Gershwin Trusts, and Daria Enrick of the Margo Feiden Galleries for their help with images. Clint Eastwood and Bruce Ricker of Rhapsody Productions made available to me the many interviews (especially helpful were those with Michael Feinstein, Stephen Holden, and Jonathan Schwartz) conducted on behalf of the Emmy-nominated film *Johnny Mercer: "The Dream's On Me,"* produced — with the assistance of independent filmmaker Becky Marshall — for the Johnny Mercer Foundation by Turner Classics Movies, Warner Home Video, and BBC/Arena. I appreciated the opportunity to serve as a consultant to the film and write the accompanying biographical essay that appears in the two-disc special edition. Habitual listening to such National Public Radio programs as George Harter's *A Night on the Town,* Terry Gross's *Fresh Air,* Jim Cullum's *Riverwalk Jazz,* and H. Johnson's *Jazz Classics* on WABE Atlanta supplemented my education in American popular music.

The receipt of an Andrew W. Mellon Fellowship from the Virginia Historical Society assisted my research in Richmond, for which I thank Dr. Nelson D. Lankford and John McClure. My former professor and his charming wife, Dr. Emory and Fran Thomas, allowed us to stay with them at their family farm outside Richmond, which made the evenings away from the archives most enjoyable, and kindly arranged for our accommodations on the lawn at the University of Virginia. A visit to Woodberry Forest School enabled work in the Norfleet Archives assisted by Karen Culbertson. A stop in Winston-Salem on the return drive to Georgia afforded a visit with dear friends Dr. Michele Gillespie, Kevin Pittard, and family at Wake Forest.

A variety of trips taken to attend academic conferences, workshops on standards funded by then GSU provost Ron Henry, consultations with museums, review panels of the National Endowment for the Humanities, and even foreign exchange programs, led to research in far-flung archives. Over the years I have tracked down clues regarding Johnny Mercer in such varied holdings as those of the New York Public Library, the Maryland Historical Society in Baltimore, the Newberry Library and Chicago Historical Society, the Academy of Motion Picture Arts and Sciences in Los Angeles, and such academic institutions as the archives at the University of California, Los Angeles; University of California,

Berkeley; Stanford University; and the film archives at the University of Southern California. In Washington, D.C., the various archivists in the Music Department at the Library of Congress pulled the numerous collections I consulted, as did the staff at the National Portrait Gallery and the Martin Luther King Jr. Public Library. Work at the Children's Museum in Indianapolis allowed for a drive to Bloomington and the use of the Archives of Traditional Music at Indiana University assisted by Suzanne Mudge.

Participation in the 2009 Tri-National Summer Program hosted by Johannes Gutenberg University, Mainz, Germany, in collaboration with Peking University and the University of International Business and Economics, both in Beijing, China, and GSU in Atlanta, enabled me to present research on Mercer to the assembled international faculty and graduate students that resulted in a rethinking of the songwriter's context within a framework of the Global South. In addition to the fruitful exchange held with Professors Oliver Scheiding, Alfred Hornung, Zhao Baisheng, and Xu Dejin of the Tri-National institutions, I benefited from discussions with Dr. Katie McKee of the University of Mississippi, who held a Fulbright in Mainz that summer, as well as her colleague — the star attraction of the two-week seminar — Dr. Charles Reagan Wilson. My time in Germany included an excursion down to Baden-Baden, where I found materials in the Stadtmuseum/Stadtarchiv on Kuferstrase, for which I thank the archivist Dagmar Rumpf. A visit to the University of Northumbria in Newcastle, England, hosted by Dr. Allan Ingram facilitated a trip up to Scotland and the use of the national archives and the Edinburgh Public Library. No matter where my travels have taken me, inevitably Mercer's music surfaces, as when "Autumn Leaves" came over the speakers at the Internet café adjacent to Sunchon National University, South Korea, or when on the busy streets of Accra, Ghana, I spied a conveyance where the driver had painted across the back of his bus "And the Angels Sing," or discovering in Havana, Cuba, the Choral of Ninos Cantores Liricos under the direction of Malena D. Torres singing "Moon River." The southern songwriter had indeed given his music to the world.

Perhaps living memories offered the greatest insight as I talked with numerous people close to the subject, in particular such family members as Johnny Mercer's daughter, Amanda Mercer Neder, and her son, James "Jim" Corwin; Johnny's niece Nancy Mercer Keith Gerard, and her husband, Steve Gerard; Johnny's cousins Frank Ciucevich and Julie Ciucevich Paige; and Mercer friends Nick Mamalakis and Margaret Whiting. Others in Savannah, including film producer Stratton Leopold, Emma and Leopold Adler II, and especially David Oppenheim of the Friends of Johnny Mercer, provided valuable insights on the man and his family. Early in the process I received an invitation to speak before the members of the Bonaventure Historical Society, for which I thank Laurice E. Fetzer and Terry Shaw. Visits with Emma Kelly helped re-create the excitement of Mercer's music, and I thank Pat Kelly Alley for donating her mother's papers to GSU.

A variety of scholars have listened to and read ideas presented in this biography and offered their suggestions, often sharing with me materials of great value that helped me explain some aspect of the story. Charles W. Joyner, professor emeritus of Coastal Carolina State University, encouraged my project for years. Charles Reagan Wilson of the University of Mississippi; James Gavin Campbell, associate dean of American Studies at Doshisha University in Kyoto, Japan; John C. Inscoe of the University of Georgia, and his former colleague professor emeritus William F. Holmes — both mentors of mine — all read the whole manuscript and offered insightful criticism. Another Georgia mentor, Professor Emeritus William S. McFeely, encouraged me to write biography. Other scholars who talked over some of these ideas with me include William Fitzhugh Brundage of the University of North Carolina, Chapel Hill; Karen Cox of the University of North Carolina, Charlotte; David L. Chappell of the University of Oklahoma; Patrick Huber of the Missouri University of Science and Technology; and Brian Ward of the University of Manchester, England. Also my friends from Georgia Southern University, Jonathan Bryant and Lisa Denmark, shared resources with me from their own scholarship on Savannah, and I appreciate the comments of Stephen Corey, editor of The Georgia Review. Two historians with whom I discussed the subject but who I regret did not live to see the work in print include Numan V. Bartley and Bennett H. Wall, both formerly of the University of Georgia.

The staff at the University of Georgia Press patiently waited for this manuscript to be completed. My sincere appreciation goes out to executive editor Nancy Grayson, the former director of the press Nicole Mitchell and current director Lisa Bayer, project editor John Joerschke, assistant acquisitions editor Beth Snead, and acquisitions editor Reagan Huff, as well as copy editors Deborah Oliver and Maria DenBoer and marketing director John McLeod. Financial assistance to reproduce the photographs came from the Johnny Mercer Foundation. Colleen Hall designed the map of Mercer sites in Savannah. Sandi

Schroeder compiled the index. I appreciate the care with which the press selected readers that resulted in helpful evaluations. The book is much better because of the thoughtful suggestions generated by the juried review process. Any errors that exist are my fault entirely.

In addition to all the professional debts created by the writing of a scholarly work, there are numerous personal debts demanding recognition. At the forefront of this list are the names of my in-laws, Robert and Susie Hall, who generously allowed me to stay in their Tybee House on numerous occasions while I undertook research in Savannah. My now deceased Uncle Jerry McIntosh — a native of New Orleans — shared with me as a youngster his love of jazz as we played recordings of "Tiger Rag" and "Caravan" with my Aunt Margie. I have tried to do the same with my boys as Will, my older son born shortly after the project began, and Tom, my younger son, have both grown up listening to the Great American Songbook. My parents, Robert L. and Martha Bonner Eskew, arranged the foundation for this study by overseeing my schooling and promoting my varied interests all the while offering love and support, as they continue to do today. An outstanding debt I owe is to my teachers at Vestavia Hills High School in suburban Birmingham, Alabama, and two in particular who instilled in me a love for jazz and the musical theater. Having the good fortune to attend an exceptional public school in the late 1970s, I also had the good luck to get to participate in a variety of extracurricular activities overseen by stellar faculty. Beverly Braswell headed the theater department and saw something in a nervous freshman boy who showed up at fall tryouts by casting him in his first of eight shows over four wonderful years. From such dramas as *The Diary of Anne Frank* to such musicals as *Oklahoma* and *Annie Get Your Gun*, she directed quality productions that instilled in her students an appreciation for what she called the most "ephemeral of the arts." The acting, singing, and dancing required of the musical theater — to say nothing of memorizing all those lines and staying in character — prepared me for later life. Ted Galloway directed the high school band and tolerated this terrible trombone player for four years who benefited immensely from his seat in the jazz ensemble. Every spring, Galloway took these neophyte jazz musicians to New Orleans to play in a competition hosted by Loyola College. Afterward he turned them loose unchaperoned in the French Quarter, where the proximity of Pat O'Brian's and Preservation Hall made for an evening of fun. The hours of band practice nurtured in me a lifelong love of music.

Finally, throughout the entire process of researching and writing this book, I have had the support of my wife of twenty years, Pamela G. Hall. During that time she attended medical school, had two children, completed her residency, and assumed a private medical practice. All the while she suffered through this project and my many distractions such as the Teaching American History Grants and NEH Summer Workshops with Schoolteachers, the restoration of historic homes in Eatonton and Madison, and the start of the Georgia Literary Festival. Therefore this book is dedicated to her. As Johnny Mercer would say, "Here's to My Lady."

Take Bay Street West to Augusta Road and Five Mile Bend

Take Bay St. East To Tybee Island

Take M.L.K., Jr. Blvd. to Anderson West and Laurel Grove Cemetery

Take Abercorn St. to Victory Dr. East

N

SAVANNAH RIVER

WILLIAMSON

<Augusta Rd

BAY

Tybee Beach >

BRYAN

Washington Square

Franklin Square

Ellis Square

Johnson Square

Reynolds Square

Warren Square

ST. JULIAN

CONGRESS

BROUGHTON

Liberty Square

Telfair Square

Wright Square

Oglethorpe Square

Columbia Square

Green Square

STATE

PRESIDENT

YORK

< U.S. 17A & I-95

OGLETHORPE

HULL

Crawford Square

Elbert Square

Orleans Square

CHIPPEWA SQUARE

Colonial Park Cemetery

E. MCDONOUGH

PERRY

LIBERTY

W

E

HARRIS

Pulaski Square

Madison Square

Lafayette Square

Troup Square

MACON

CHARLTON

JONES

TAYLOR

BERRIEN

Chatham Square

Monterey Square

Calhoun Square

Whitfield Square

WAYNE

GORDON

PRICE

ALICE

GASTON

Forsyth Park

HUNTINGDON

HALL

GWINNETT

BOLTON

WALBURG

PARK

S

To I-16 & I-95

MARTIN LUTHER KING, JR. BLVD.

GREEN

MONTGOMERY

TATTNALL

BARNARD

WHITAKER

BULL

DRAYTON

ABERCORN

LINCOLN

HABERSHAM

E. BROAD

E. BROAD

Map of Johnny Mercer Sites in Savannah

1) 113 Congress St., "the castle," home of Andersons and Mercers, #4 Tyrconnel Tything (demolished)

2) 28 Bull St., Christ Church (Episcopal)

3) 23 Abercorn St., Planter's Bank, now the Pink House Restaurant

4) 501 Whitaker St., Georgia Historical Society

5) 803 (817) Whitaker St., George Anderson Mercer (demolished)

6) 1007 Whitaker St. Apartments, built by G. A. Mercer, the first to overlook Forsyth Park

7) 121 Barnard St., Telfair Academy of Arts and Sciences

8) 402 - 410 East Bay St., Anderson Warehouses and Wharf Lot 4

9) 210 East Taylor St., duplex of G. A. & Mary Walter Mercer, Robbie & Katharine Mercer

10) 207 East Gordon St., Massie School

11) 17 East Park Ave., Telfair Hospital, birthplace of Johnny Mercer

12) 20 East Macon St., home of infant Johnny Mercer

13) 118 East Hall St., childhood home of Johnny Mercer (demolished)

14) 302 East Hall St., home of Aunt Nannie Mercer and Joseph Muir Lang and Cousin Joe

15) 301 East Charlton St., home of Julia Ciucevich, Annie Rivers, and Cousin Walter

16) Abercorn at East Harris St., Cathedral of St. John the Baptist (Roman Catholic)

17) 207 East Charlton St., childhood home of Flannery O'Connor

18) 316 West Bryan St., grocery of John Ciucevich (demolished)

19) 226 East Gwinnett St., teenage home of Johnny Mercer

20) 7 - 9 East York St., G. A. Mercer Co.

21) 7 East Bay St., Mercer Insurance Agency

22) 22 Abercorn St., Lucas Theatre

23) 222 Bull St., Savannah Theatre

24) 20 East Broad St., Pirate's House Restaurant

25) Johnny Mercer Memorial Statue at City Market in Ellis Square

Take Abercorn St. to Victory Dr. East To:

1651 East Victory Dr., Johnny Harris's Restaurant

Bonaventure Cemetery

Bethesda Home for Boys

301 McAlpin St., G. A. Mercer house at Vernon View on Burnside Island

514 Moon River Ct., Johnny Mercer's Moon River House on Burnside Island

JOHNNY MERCER

Introduction

· ·

Two drifters
Off to see the world —
There's such a lot of world
To see

AS A SONGWRITER caught up in the southern diaspora, Johnny
Mercer joined a multiracial group of musicians in pushing music from the South
to the center of American popular culture. Born in Savannah, Georgia, on November 18, 1909, John Herndon Mercer remained rooted in the home ground
of his native region while living in New York City, Hollywood, London, and
Paris, where he worked with jazz bands, in radio, for film, on the stage, on television, and through Capitol Records until his death in Bel Air, California, on June
25, 1976. The thousands of lyrics, hundreds of recordings, scores of movies, and
nearly a dozen Broadway shows that made Johnny Mercer one of the twentieth
century's most popular songwriters kept him at the top of his profession throughout his career. Mercer crafted jazz-interpenetrated popular song that combined
the regionally distinctive rhythm and blues harmonic constructions with the old
Tin Pan Alley song format to create hot music that gained popularity in America
and abroad and influenced sounds worldwide. Like other jazz artists embracing
modernism, Johnny resisted the patriarchal and paternalistic attitudes of his ancestors, although their code of honor and belief in religion remained central tenets in his own life even while he struggled with alcohol abuse, marital infidelity,
and bouts of melancholy. His subtle references to place names, flora, and fauna
revealed a southern sensitivity to locale captured in his use of language, while jazz
singers liked how his syncopated lyrics could swing. Often Johnny composed his
own music for songs. At heart a jazz musician rather than a Tin Pan Alley lyricist,
Mercer followed the trajectory of the multiracial music from his native South,
and his role in creating the sounds challenges notions of racial essentialism used
to explain jazz, just like the performances of his fellow black and white diaspora

entertainers. Mercer composed popular songs for stage and screen while writing lyrics for Harlem singers and performing with jazz bands. A successful entertainer, he appeared regularly on radio and television, and his music remained among the most frequently played in the nation throughout his lifetime. Foreign broadcasts and the development of international markets for American records made Mercer's music global. As cofounder, president, and artists and repertoire (A&R) man at Capitol Records, Johnny captured in the studio performances by diaspora entertainers of the Great American Songbook, West Coast cool jazz, and hillbilly's evolution into country and western, commodifying these new sounds for sale to the public regardless of race. In the postwar era, he turned outward for inspiration, joining an international community of composers crafting transnational songs. Through his legacy of songwriting and performances, movie musicals and Broadway shows, records by himself and others on the Capitol label, Johnny Mercer helped remake popular culture in the twentieth-century United States. By the end of his life, the once-distinctive sounds of the South had transformed the music of the nation and the world.

Most people know a few words to at least a couple of Mercer's hits. Probably they have heard such movie music as "Hooray for Hollywood," "You Must Have Been a Beautiful Baby," "P.S. I Love You," and "Jeepers Creepers," or such torch songs as "I Wanna Be Around," "Travelin' Light," and "One for My Baby (And One More for the Road)," or such jazz standards as "Laura," "Skylark," "Early Autumn," and "Tangerine," or such popular songs as "Autumn Leaves," "I'm Old Fashioned," "That Old Black Magic," and "I Remember You." Of his record-setting eighteen nominations for the Academy Award for Best Original Song, he set another record when four received Oscars: "On the Atchison, Topeka, and the Santa Fe" (1946), "In the Cool, Cool, Cool of the Evening" (1951), "Moon River" (1961), and "Days of Wine and Roses" (1962). Such gems as "Satin Doll," "Day In — Day Out," and "Midnight Sun" provide opportunities to investigate his fundamental understanding of jazz as expressed through lyrics. Other songs such as "Moon Country," "Lazybones," "Ac-Cent-Tchu-Ate the Positive," and "Blues in the Night" reveal his debt to the South for poetic inspiration. Mercer contributed to legendary Hollywood musicals such as *Star Spangled Rhythm*, *Daddy Long Legs*, and *Seven Brides for Seven Brothers*. He also wrote the lyrics for a number of Broadway shows, including *St. Louis Woman*, *Top Banana*, and *Li'l Abner*. Mercer remained one of the most popular lyricists of his day, topping the Billboard charts. His music appeared regularly from the 1930s to the 1970s on *Your Hit Parade*, the weekly broadcast that showcased the nation's top ten hits. During his lifetime he set the record with fourteen of his songs reaching the number one spot, while he placed third for the most songs to make the top ten with thirty-six played on *Your Hit Parade*. When considering the singles he made of himself singing his own and other people's music, Mercer released thirteen recordings that made *Your Hit Parade*, four of which hit number one, something few singers — and no other songwriter — ever accomplished.

Many people remember the performers for whom Mercer wrote lyrics such as Bing Crosby, Billie Holiday, Judy Garland, Lena Horne, Betty Hutton, Jo Stafford, Pearl Bailey, Fred Astaire, and others, while Tony Bennett, Rosemary Clooney, Perry Como, Bobby Short, Dinah Shore, Johnny Mathis, Andy Williams, Nancy Walker, and Sarah Vaughan were among the hundreds of contemporary performers who added Mercer's lyrics to their repertoire. At Capitol Records he recruited and oversaw recording sessions of such discoveries as Nat "King" Cole, Margaret Whiting, and Stan Kenton, while his mentoring and music helped repackage older talents such as Peggy Lee and Frank Sinatra. Throughout his career Johnny regularly worked with the nation's leading jazz musicians such as Louis Armstrong, Paul Whiteman, and the Dorsey Brothers, while writing lyrics to accompany instrumentals by Duke Ellington, Benny Goodman, Benny Carter, and Lionel Hampton. The jazz aesthetic in his best songs made them standards played by such masters as Lester Young, Erroll Garner, Chet Baker, Coleman Hawkins, and Oscar Peterson and inspired riffs by bebop artists Charlie Parker, Stan Getz, and Dizzy Gillespie. Contemporary vocalists as diverse as Ella Mae Morse, Anita O'Day, Mabel Mercer, Kay Starr, Julia Lee, Julie London, and Blossom Dearie favored his work, as did such leading performers as Diana Krall, Michael Feinstein, Karrin Allyson, Jane Monheit, Audra McDonald, and Jamie Cullum at the end of the century. Mercer became the only lyricist honored by Ella Fitzgerald with an album in her Songbook series. Indeed, Johnny provided many of the twentieth century's most popular and gifted entertainers with material in the form of Great American Songs.

The public recalls the composers with whom Mercer collaborated while forgetting the man who put the words to the tune. Although Johnny admired his professional colleagues and they respected his talents, his southern style stood apart from that of other songwriters because it expressed the hybridity of the multiracial South. A handful of men dominated Tin Pan Alley in the golden age of the Great American Song. Irving Berlin stood at the forefront, followed by George and Ira Gershwin, Cole Porter, composers Jerome Kern, Harold Arlen, and Richard Rodgers, and lyricists Lorenz Hart, E. Y. "Yip" Harburg, and Oscar

Hammerstein II. With the exception of Porter, they were all Jewish New Yorkers whose understanding of America derived from their experiences in the metropolis and from books they read. With vivid imaginations they created heartfelt songs so elastic that they fit anywhere. Porter came from a privileged background in Indiana and an elite education at the Massachusetts prep school Worcester Academy and then Yale College, resulting in an urbane sophistication that largely established but somewhat limited his appeal to that of the art song. Critics tend to use such adjectives as "indoors" and "urban" to describe the music of these men. An Episcopalian like Porter from a similarly elite background and private education, nevertheless Mercer developed an uncanny ability to speak as if for all Americans, using language firmly grounded in the countryside and voiced in the vernacular. His lyrics expressed everyday happiness, the humor in life, or the gritty reality of unrequited love. Even at their utmost, Porter, Berlin and other leading songwriters never revealed with the same intensity the unbridled passion of desire or palpable sense of loss expressed in Mercer's best lyrics. Johnny paired most successfully with jazz arranger-composers such as Hoagy Carmichael, Bernie Hanighen, Harold Arlen, and Henry Mancini who shared his sense of harmony and rhythm by writing expressive melodies that captured the great outdoors. Mercer had more collaborators than any other songwriter of the period, working with all the great composers of popular song, among them, Walter Donaldson, Lewis Gensler, Richard Whiting, Harry Warren, Arthur Schwartz, Jimmy Van Heusen, Jimmy McHugh, Gordon Jenkins, and Johnny Green. No doubt the rich variety of his music derived from his exceptional assortment of partners. As a professional songwriter, Mercer contributed a particularly large body of work, writing 1,500 songs, including more than 100 hits.

John Herndon Mercer entered life at the moment southern vernacular forms of music — jazz, blues, and hillbilly — were breaking out of the region to influence the world. At the same time, the ready availability of sound recordings in the 1910s and then the national broadcasts over the airwaves in the 1920s instantly brought U.S. popular culture into the South. While Mercer loved the Tin Pan Alley tunes sung by family members and friends and played in the parlor on the piano, on gramophone records, and then on the radio, he was struck by the folk music he heard black and white southerners sing and, by extension, their blues and jazz recordings. His success in entertainment derived in part from his ability to turn these regional sounds into popular song. During the 1930s, radio shows regularly broadcast the recordings jazz artists made of Mercer's music. In the 1940s, nearly all of the jukeboxes in the United States contained records of

Johnny singing or someone else performing his songs. By the 1950s, his finger-prints were on many of the nation's top-selling albums. With American popular culture stretching worldwide by the 1960s, Mercer's songs circled the globe. Each decade found him working on at least two Broadway shows and appearing regu-larly on radio and television variety programs. Mercer and his regionally derived music appeared in nearly every popular entertainment format available.

At the time of Johnny's birth in 1909, he lived in a distinct section of the country that had a geographical boundary roughly dominated by the South's plantation-based political economy, in which a diverse people created a shared culture and ideology that constrained them all. Consisting for the most part of the former Confederate States of America and characterized by laws designed to maintain white supremacy, the South appeared as a separate nation within a nation.[1] As members of the southern ruling class, the Mercers subscribed to their forebears' patriarchal attitude toward women, paternalistic view of race, commit-ment to Protestant religion, and patrician sense of duty common among the elite. When considered alongside his personal behaviors and associations, such beliefs revealed an ideology of southern honor distinctive to the region. Identifying the code of conduct in the Mercer family like the one found in the Percy family of southern letters is one way to recognize the South in the songwriter.[2]

Journalists had no trouble seeing the region in the man. An AP reporter de-scribed Johnny as the "pixie from Dixie." Another noted, "sometimes a man's roots go so deeply into the soil of his own section of the country that . . . no mat-ter where he goes, he carries his homeland with him," then observing about Mer-cer that "he's never lost the touch of Dixie in his drawling voice or ambling gait. The Deep South is forever part of Johnny." Writer Henry Kane offered a more subtle analysis: "There is a soft-butter-burr in the voice, an ease, an unhurried, deliberate delivery. One is aware of the lingering vowels of a Southern accent; there is no click to the consonants." Yet Kane recognized that "all is leisurely, easygoing, but one is conscious of an inner strength, of words thought out before expressed, of a tumult of words held in leash, weighed, and then spun out slowly." About his songs Johnny understood, "I might be able to write Southern things a little better because I am a Southerner," but he emphasized "the Southern stuff got the attention first off because it was Southern in a different way. Nobody had brought in a song like 'Pardon My Southern Accent' or 'Lazybones' before. Up to then it had all been Tin Pan Alley Southern," that is, formulaic "Back to Dixie" songs written by nonsoutherners. Early in his career, Mercer's sense of being an exotic southerner in America led him to write such lyrics as "Pardon my southern accent, / Pardon my southern drawl." Early in his career, Mercer's sense of being an exotic southerner in America led him to write such lyrics as "Pardon my southern accent." After fifteen years in New York and Los Angeles, he had tempered that defensive attitude with the dismissive "They talk a different language." So comfortable in his own identity as a southerner, Mercer felt no "rage to explain" the South to others, and he revealed no guilt for being from a class-riddled, sexist, and segregated Savannah, although personally he promoted equality through his lyrics and actions. Neither did he publicly defend the region as a cause, despite having an active career that stretched from the era of H. L. Mencken's benighted South through the civil rights movement. Rather Mercer revealed historian Brian Ward's contention that "southern music was literally well grounded, that it was linked to a particular place — often expressed in terms of a passionate veneration of the land itself — and that it exhibited a laudable respect for its own traditions." Once his career took him abroad, Mercer displayed a "grounded globalism" that marked him as a native southerner at home in the larger world.[3]

Growing up in an elite Victorian household in the urban South, Johnny Mercer descended from as true an aristocracy as the United States produced; yet he embraced the modernism of the jazz age and displayed a modest everyman approach to life that advocated democracy and fairness in all dealings. Generations of extended family members had struggled to maintain a code of honor within the confines set by elite convention along the touchstones of race, class, and gender relations. Successfully maneuvering among the pitfalls of society revealed the hallmarks of the southern gentry. Most everyone knew of a relative who had stumbled along the way or failed to measure up to Victorian standards. As a member of a family that maintained such high expectations, Mercer both accepted and rejected these elite social conventions. While his progressive views rebelled against traditional attitudes toward gender and race, he remained doggedly devoted to a deep religious belief and sense of honor. As a gentleman, Johnny followed a code of honor handed down to him while, in what appears to be a contradiction, overindulging in alcohol as a way to lose self-control and allow his passions to run free. Through his own lyrics and by singing those written by others, he celebrated the cocktail culture of a society that promoted alcoholism and tolerated alcoholics. A patriarchal attitude that treated women as sexual objects dominated polite society in Mercer's lifetime, and Johnny followed the genteel conventions between the sexes but along with other jazz musicians emerged from the flapper era promoting sexual liberation. He remained married to the same woman for forty-five years but had numerous affairs, most notably a relationship with Judy Garland that lasted thirty years. Raised as a racial paternalist in a nation bound by white supremacy, Johnny accommodated to the unequal roles society created for the races under segregation while participating in integrated recording sessions where black and white musicians mingled and in making sure African Americans that he worked with received fair treatment. The South's patrician class structure, patriarchal gender roles, and paternalistic race relations informed the world that Johnny entered in 1909, but in many ways Mercer joined a generation of jazz musicians that rejected the Victorian past in favor of a more open and egalitarian modernism.[4]

In recent years writers have begun evaluating Mercer and his hundreds of songs, his letters, and his incomplete autobiography manuscript. In 1982, Mercer's widow, Ginger, and friend Bob Bach edited *Our Huckleberry Friend: The Life, Times and Lyrics of Johnny Mercer*, a memorial volume that included a biographical narrative, song lyrics, and photographs. In 2003, the literature professor Philip Furia, who had written several studies of Tin Pan Alley songwriters, published the first full-length biography of Mercer, *Skylark: The Life and Times of Johnny Mercer*. In 2004, the songwriter and jazz critic Gene Lees published his personal treatment of his friend's life, *Portrait of Johnny: The Life of John Herndon Mercer*. With great insights Furia's and Lees' accounts present the songwriter, using a Hollywood tell-all format to account for his life in entertainment. Often dwelling on his personal problems, both biographies outline Mercer's professional career. Furia pays special attention to Mercer's efforts for the stage while considering his lyrics as poetry, whereas Lees underscores Johnny's contributions to the catalogue of Great American Songs. Both men use oral interviews, quotations from Mercer's unpublished autobiography, and anecdotes extensively. In 2009, Robert Kimball, Barry Day, Miles Kreuger, and Eric Davis published *The Complete Lyrics of Johnny Mercer*, an attractive volume with choice illustrations that provides a thorough accounting of the man's music and attempts to document all his songs, presented as text with annotation. And Mercer remains a perennial favorite subject for music writers such as Stanley Booth.[5]

In several significant ways, *Johnny Mercer: Southern Songwriter for the World* marks a departure from these earlier efforts. This biography places the native Savannahian within what demographer James N. Gregory has called the southern diaspora — a movement of nearly thirty million people out of the South and into the North and West between 1900 and 1970 — roughly the span of Mercer's life. Gregory estimates eight million black, twenty million white, and one million Latino southerners left the region, and while much has been said about the African Americans caught up in the Great Migration, nearly three times as many white people left the South, with little known about them. This biography offers Mercer as one example of how white southerners responded to a new life in the North and West. And while Johnny's story appears unique, one need only recall that as a diaspora entertainer he, along with Louis Armstrong, Billie Holiday, Louis Prima, Rosemary Clooney, Harry James, Nat "King" Cole, Dinah Shore, and other southerners discussed in this work, helped transform American popular culture. Mercer joined these black, white, and Latino southern musicians cut loose from their native soil as they carried their regionally distinctive sounds to the center of the nation's popular culture scene, forever changing American song and influencing global sounds. The argument posited here suggests that the hybridity of the region's heritage as exemplified by its unique multiracial music — the vernacular jazz, blues, and hillbilly — provided an original contribution to the country's popular culture. Theorist Homi K. Bhabha's idea of liminality offers room to explore the synergies enjoyed by southern musicians as they made new sounds beyond the confines of old racial binaries. Such a "third space" opened up in the urban South at the turn of the century with jazz, nationally with jazz-infused popular song, and globally with transnational music.[6]

Using archival sources to corroborate oral interviews and the autobiography, *Johnny Mercer: Southern Songwriter for the World* thoroughly documents Mercer's personal life and professional career. Unlike earlier treatments, this biography explicates his family legacy, demonstrating — to borrow ideas from anthropologist James L. Peacock — the grounded nature of the global southerner's identity. It emphasizes Mercer's relationships with fellow jazz musicians and jazz arranger-composers to underscore his shared sympathies for the southern musical style. It explores the key role Mercer played at Capitol Records and considers his performances on radio and television. It suggests that with American hegemony, he looked abroad for inspiration in a bid to write transnational music. Through detailed analysis, this book recounts Johnny's many contributions to Broadway, Hollywood, the Great American Songbook, and popular culture. Mercer's story suggests how a talented southerner could excel in the American entertainment industry and contribute to global culture during the twentieth century. At the same time that a southern literary renaissance remade American letters and influenced world literature, so too the multiracial sounds from the South altered music made nationally and globally.[7]

The South's racial inequality expressed historically as white supremacy and demonstrated through Indian removal, slavery, and segregation failed to prevent cultural integration among Native American, black, white, Latino, and other ethnic southerners. While it is true that the legal structures of slavery and segregation codified the South as a land of black and white, the legacy of Indians should not be ignored any more than that of Latinos and other ethnic southerners who settled in the region and contributed to its multicultural heritage. In writing about the South's hybridity, historian George Tindall observed that "what in the colonial period may have been the most diverse population in America had fused into a new ethnic group — or rather two ethnic groups, black and white, that had much in common, however reluctant they were to acknowledge kinship." Blinded by segregation, Johnny's contemporary, the journalist W. J. Cash, saw only black and white southerners; yet he also understood that "the relationship between the two groups was, by the second generation at least, nothing less than organic. Negro entered into white man as profoundly as white man entered into Negro — subtly influencing every gesture, every word, every emotion and idea, every attitude." In the 1930s, folklorist B. A. Botkin described black and white southerners sharing "a homogeneous body of lore." Yet in a bid to document African retentions or British folkways, scholars have argued for separate black and white cultural traits, almost to the point of fetishism. Describing appropriation by racializing performances as reflections of blackness or whiteness suggests some inherently racial or genetic manner of singing, dancing, or otherwise engaging in entertainment. Such essentialist arguments result in efforts to ascribe racial authenticity in order to grant cultural legitimacy. Rather than defend old racial binaries, this study emphasizes the South's multiracial heritage, recognizing that whatever differences might have existed among black, white, Native American and ethnic southerners were more of degree than kind. Throughout the region a shared culture evolved that expressed an integrated culture despite the undemocratic exercise of power maintained by white supremacy.[8]

Southern music affords an opportunity to explore the region's hybrid culture. As historian Bill C. Malone suggested, in the antebellum era both black and white southerners "knew a common body of songs and instrumental pieces whose origins and 'racial identities' cannot always be determined." One is hard pressed to argue a racial basis for music when southerners of every stripe and hue contributed to everything from sacred harp singing to South Louisiana's swamp pop. Even in the changing Mississippi of the 1960s, the interviews conducted by William Ferris document shared cultural traits as black and white alike sang the blues and Dr. Watts's hymns or listened to black radio stations and the Grand

Ole Opry broadcasts. Fellow native Mississippian John A. Lomax, who a generation before began recording the region's folk music, understood that "Southerners have been swapping accents and attitudes, tales and tunes for three hundred years across the Jim Crow line." Recognizing that "musical styles are cultural rather than genetic," the historian and folklorist Charles Joyner argued that the "shared traditions" of the South resulted in a "racially mixed musical tradition." Regardless of the style — jazz, blues, or hillbilly — the South's hybrid culture created the new sounds. As modern music, jazz has little to do with the debates over folklore regarding "roots music" that try to parse between "traditional singers" and "singers of folk songs." Rather than emphasizing musical genealogies, jazz demonstrates a liminality of musical expression enjoyed by southerners from diverse backgrounds. Raised in the charged atmosphere of the urban South, Mercer drew on this rich multiracial heritage to create a catalogue of popular song permeated by jazz.[9]

The region had long disproportionately influenced the country's culture. By the antebellum era, interpretations of the South had inspired the nation's — and indeed the Atlantic world's — first commercially successful popular music. The white actors Thomas Dartmouth Rice and George Washington Dixon had independently created hurtful caricatures of African Americans that they marketed through song. Rice's mimicry of the rural black man as Jim Crow and Dixon's mimicry of the urban black dandy as Zip Coon provided demeaning stock images through which performers engaged in vitriolic and menacing commentary that exacerbated race and class divisions and threatened social order. Soon groups of white entertainers in blackface such as the Virginia Minstrels led by Daniel Decatur Emmett plied the country's stages, performing music inspired by the multiracial region. Emmett went on to write two of the most popular songs of the era, "I Wish I Was in Dixie's Land" and "Old Dan Tucker." Yet Stephen Foster won recognition as America's first great songwriter because of his ability to turn what he called "plantation" or "Ethiopian" melodies into popular songs consumed as sheet music across the United States, its territories, and indeed the world. Inspired by the hybridity he witnessed along the river ways of the Border States, Foster created a catalogue of songs that established the slaveholding South as romantic stereotype. In addition to the plantation melodies, Foster transformed European music — from traditional and folk songs to the latest opera arias — into sentimental parlor ballads, temperance, protest, war, and even comic songs, articulating such themes as rambling, lost love, and nostalgia that became staples of popular song. More than anyone else Foster wrote the music for what biographer Ken Emerson has called the first chapter in the Great American Songbook. Attuned to popular culture like Foster, Johnny Mercer shared several similarities with the earlier songwriter such as a limited formal education, an unfulfilling marriage, and dependency on alcohol.[10]

By the end of the nineteenth century, American popular music underwent another change. The success of Charles K. Harris's sentimental waltz, "After the Ball," published in 1892 and interpolated into a Broadway musical, sold five million copies as the nation's first modern hit and demonstrated the potential of mass-marketed sheet music by a national entertainment industry consolidated in New York City. The old minstrel melodies had degenerated into the hate-filled "coon songs" that dehumanized black people as violent beasts during what African American historian Rayford Logan described as the "nadir" for black America, that period around 1900 marked by lynching, disfranchisement, and segregation. Other songwriters focused on an exotic plantation South of moonlight and magnolias that might mention happy "darkies" while presenting a make-believe land of cotton free from modernity. Such "Back to Dixie" or "Tin Pan Alley Southern" songs sold well in an industrializing North and farming West torn by class divisions and social dislocation. By the arrival of ragtime from the South, the sounds of popular song changed with the addition of syncopation. Irving Berlin's incorporation of Scott Joplin's melodies to create the tune for "Alexander's Ragtime Band" in 1911 signaled a clear departure from the waltzes of old Europe. By infusing the ballads of Tin Pan Alley with the southern stylings of first ragtime and then jazz, songwriters such as Mercer contributed to another chapter in the Great American Songbook.[11]

The musicologist Henry Pleasants identified jazz as a progressive music created by southern black and white artists who took the indigenous sounds of their native South and turned them into something distinct and previously unheard. No more African than European, jazz was a sui generis music from multiracial America. To Pleasants the defining characteristic of jazz is the explicit rhythm of the music that the artist accentuates by playing either with the beat or against it, either ahead of the beat or behind it. Jazz also features the blue note — often the third or seventh in the scale — that is usually flattened for added contrast. Instruments mimic voices by bending notes, employing a falsetto break in solos, or adapting a choral call-and-response pattern for technical effect. Thus rhythm — derived from African musical traditions — joined with European melodies and harmonies that also include the flattened blue note, as well as shared strategies of improvisation, created the hybrid, and distinctly American, jazz.[12]

Black and white contemporaries recognized Johnny Mercer as a "rhythm singer" because of his innate ability to keep time — or, in the language of the day, to swing — thereby marking him as a jazz musician. Often he carried this talent into the writing of syncopated lyrics. Indeed, in Johnny Mercer's music, one may find what Pleasants observed as the interpenetration of musical styles, with "the pop song becoming the jazz vehicle — the jazz artist becoming the popular musician." Mercer admitted as much when late in life he confessed to André Previn that any song he sang began "to swing." While Mercer came from the urban South's upper class, his singing the latest popular sensation proved no less authentically southern than that of the Delta field hand who repeated a bluesy wail or of the Piedmont tenant farmer who imitated a hillbilly yodel — music's organic nature simply prevents it from existing in isolation. The type of music Alec Wilder documents in *American Popular Song* — the art song associated with jazz that the white middle class favored — does not include the contemporary hillbilly or blues tunes that many black and white people, especially in the working class, found similarly attractive. Yet, as Pleasants has argued, jazz was popular music and these jazz-infused Great American Songs dominated popular consumption from World War I until the outburst of rock 'n' roll in the postwar era. They appealed to a larger audience nationally than hillbilly and blues music, as demonstrated by record sales and radio broadcasts in the South and around the nation.[13]

Consequently, this book builds on the revisionist scholarship being published that challenges long-held assumptions regarding southern music. Previous understandings argued that the authentic blues and hillbilly sounds derived from rural black and white folk whose exceptional music remained racially distinct and somewhat isolated from the currents of mainstream America. Since jazz — and popular song — never fit neatly into that model, it was largely ignored. Also overlooked were the influences of Tin Pan Alley and the forces of commercialism — specifically, recording companies — on the blues and hillbilly performers. Such a definition of southern music made jazz virtually inauthentic and its performers American rather than southern. Reflecting this type of scholarship at its height, the seminal *Encyclopedia of Southern Culture* published 1,634 pages in 1989 without an entry on Johnny Mercer. Accounts of "Popular Music," "Jazz," and "Blues" mentioned dozens of Mercer's collaborators, and the volume contained a biographical sketch of Pennsylvania native Stephen Foster who never even traveled in the South but dismissed Mercer as reflective of "American popular song" and therefore not "southern culture." Instead, the massive volume featured black blues singers and white bluegrass bands. Upon revisiting the issue twenty years later, general editor Charles Reagan Wilson expanded the former section on music into a freestanding volume edited by Bill C. Malone that contained an entry on Mercer.[14]

Instead of seeing racially distinct music from a region in isolation, several books published since the millennium recognize national forces of commercialism extending into the South as part of a homogenizing of American popular culture. Historian Gavin James Campbell evaluates cultural events in Atlanta from 1909 to 1925 to reveal struggles for power among competing interests defined by race and class. He contrasts the southern elite using the international art of opera to show its control over society, with African Americans singing concert arrangements of slave spirituals to demand respectability, and white workers embracing fiddling contests to claim racial purity. Campbell's point — how individuals used music to relate to power in society — comes across clearly as the Atlanta of the New South demonstrates the ways audiences interpreted the playing of songs to either enforce or resist elite authority and white supremacy. By surveying a broad array of attractions, historian Steve Goodson documents how Atlanta revealed the cultural homogenization occurring around the nation through the consolidation of theater companies, which standardized stage productions using touring groups, mass-produced movies for the new motion picture palaces, and the availability of sound recordings made by national singing sensations — all the while finding that the region generated its own distinctive sounds that contributed to American popular culture. As a youth in Savannah, Johnny Mercer witnessed the process of homogenization taking place by participating in regional cultural activities while also consuming national entertainments.[15]

Several groundbreaking studies chart the evolution of hillbilly music out of the South and into a new national country music industry. Patrick Huber locates hillbilly musicians not in the mountains of Appalachia but in modern Piedmont cities, where they sang songs derived from experiences in the textile mills and addressed problems associated with technology and mass culture. He identifies Fiddlin' John Carson's 1923 popular recording of the songwriter Will S. Hays's 1871 minstrel hit, "The Little Old Cabin in the Lane," as a metaphor for the collapse of the rural South and the loss of traditional family values that helped establish "nostalgia for a bygone world" as a "central theme of American country music." During the 1930s, consumers in the South and those scattered by the diaspora to the North and West domesticated hillbilly music by adding western swing to the sound, so that by the postwar era such subgenres as honky-tonk, bluegrass, and country pop predominated in what had become a national music scene.

Historian Jeffrey J. Lange identifies two areas that vied for dominance as the capitals of country music: Nashville, with its Grand Ole Opry and recording studios, and Los Angeles, with its numerous dance hall radio broadcasts and Capitol Records. At the latter, Johnny Mercer played a leading role, promoting several of the West Coast country stars, including Tex Ritter, Jimmy Wakely, and Tennessee Ernie Ford.[16]

The blues followed a similar trajectory into the mainstream, first as rhythm and blues and then as rock 'n' roll. In his study of Robert Johnson, Elijah Wald challenges common understandings regarding blues singers and demonstrates their association with popular music. By busting the myth of "authenticity" and recognizing the romanticism surrounding critical analyses of the blues, Wald rewrites the history of the musical genre. Along similar lines, musicologist Peter Townsend describes the first meeting between blues singer Muddy Waters and folklorist John Lomax to underscore the reach of commercial music. By doing so he defamiliarizes old racial narratives that segregate music and academic arguments over authenticity and racial essentialism. Exploring the postwar mind-set of black and white youth, both Pete Daniel and Michael T. Bertrand find a new generation questioning old notions of race by embracing rock 'n' roll. Since black and white jazz musicians and popular song artists such as Mercer made covers of each other's music, the exaggerated significance of Elvis seems all the more contrived.[17]

Scattered throughout *Johnny Mercer: Southern Songwriter for the World* are references to musicians who like Johnny joined the southern diaspora, taking the region's multiracial music with them to the rest of America. In the biography, the black blues singer Muddy Waters and the white hillbilly singer Jimmie Rodgers intersect with Mercer's world, thereby demonstrating the region's musical heritage and providing multiple expressions of the southern diaspora. Similarly introduced are jazz artists who left their native soil to become nationally prominent performers with whom Mercer worked, including black southerners Louis Armstrong, Duke Ellington, Lena Horne, Fletcher Henderson, Lionel Hampton, Billie Holiday, Lester Young, Julia Lee, and Ella Fitzgerald, as well as white southerners Jack Teagarden, Dinah Shore, Wingy Manone, Ella Mae Morse, Charles "Pee Wee" Russell, Kay Starr, and Harry James. Mercer expressed a distinctive jazz aesthetic that he honed and crafted through years of study, performance, and composition. The hallmarks of jazz — swing, improvisation, and sonority in phrasing — distinguished the styles of these performers. Mercer's talents allowed him to provide them with music. He either wrote songs for and with them, performed with them, or had them personally select his music to record. By no means did all of

Mercer's work over the forty years of his career reflect a jazz aesthetic, but there remains a consistency of the style in his better music that these and many other jazz performers recognized and celebrated. At key moments in the history of jazz, Johnny worked with leading bands at the height of their popularity, such as Benny Goodman's, and contributed songs that helped push to the top the greatest singers, such as Billie Holiday. When searching for collaborators, Mercer preferred working with men whom Pleasants called "jazz arranger-composers" such as Hoagy Carmichael, Bernie Hanighen, Matty Malneck, Rube Bloom, Harold Arlen, Gene De Paul, Henry Mancini, Michel Legrand, and André Previn. Furthermore, his role as a founder, A&R man, and executive at Capitol Records assisting in recordings by Coleman Hawkins, Nat "King" Cole, Stan Kenton, Stan Getz, and Miles Davis underscored his evolving jazz aesthetic and kept his music fresh and popular.[18]

In several song lyrics Johnny Mercer recounts his understanding of the history of jazz. In "Mr. Crosby and Mr. Mercer," Johnny outlined its origins: "Is it true that swing's another name for jazz? / And the first place it was played / Was in a New Orleans parade, / And the southern Negro gave it all it has?" For Capitol in the 1940s, Johnny joined trumpeter Wingy Manone on a recording of their collaboration "Tailgate Ramble." After a spirited solo, the Louisiana native intones: "When the wagon starts, / Put the tailgate down. / Watch the band parade / All around the town." After Manone ends: "Wasn't long ago / I was in my teens / And we played that way / Way down in New Orleans," Johnny repeats the refrain, including the second lines, "Give the trombone man / Room to move his slide / And we'll march and play / 'Round the countryside." Then, sounding like Louis Armstrong, Johnny scats: "Wasn't long ago boy / Oh! The other day / That they played the same / In Savannah, GA." Mercer took the 1917 song "At the Jazz Band Ball" by the Original Dixieland Jazz Band and added new words that explained the origins of the music: "Four or five musicians in a small saloon / Inventin' a ragtime tune — / They kinda make up their own brand / Without a note up on the stand." Mercer's lyric emphasizes syncopation and the originality of the combo's improvisation — it not being written down — attracted audiences as jazz "moved from across the tracks / Into the society shacks," for "When the band plays J-A-double-Z, It's a B-A-double-LL!" With "The Old Music Master," Johnny has a black jazz singer tell a white classical composer: "You gotta jump it, music master, / You gotta play that rhythm faster." Then Mercer enumerates the evolution of the musical style: "Long about nineteen seventeen / Jazz'll come upon the scene; / Then about nineteen thirty-five, / You'll begin to hear swing, / Boogie woogie, and jive." In Mercer's song "The Waiter and the Porter and the Upstairs Maid," white guests at a party sneak off to meet the black help in the kitchen because "The waltzes and mazurkas, / We hate 'em, we spurn 'em. / We got a lot of rhythms / We wanna hear played." By combining the harmonies from Europe with the syncopation from Africa, the guests embrace the new American jazz that they then perform with the household staff: "And we know where to go to / If we want to learn 'em: / The waiter / And the porter / And the upstairs maid."[19]

Mercer understood that the shared musical heritage of black and white southerners created the integrated sounds. The example of jazz bandleader Paul Whiteman proved instructive; Whiteman once said, "I know as much about real Jazz as F. Scott Fitzgerald did about the Jazz Age." Like Fitzgerald's prose, Whiteman's jazz symbolized the era's music, taking what many considered to be disreputable and making it accessible — and even respectable enough — for mass public consumption. And like "the old music master" in Mercer's song, Whiteman might not have witnessed the birth of jazz in New Orleans, but he followed the advice of that "little colored boy" and quickly learned to "rock the spinet." Indeed, jazz turned on its ear the popular Tin Pan Alley standard, adding the syncopated styling to the novelty songs and love ballads of yore.[20]

Jazz confronted changing race relations throughout the twentieth century that influenced its production. Louis Armstrong described jazz as a rich gumbo because of its murky origins in the multiracial South. Yet around the time of the birth of jazz at the turn of the century, white supremacists successfully enacted new segregation laws that required the legal separation of the races, thereby reinforcing the creation of dual societies. Black and white musicians who had long played together confronted new irrational divisions that limited such opportunities. As diaspora entertainers, separate jazz bands — the black Creole and the white Dixieland — took the New Orleans sound to the nation. Recording industry executives exploited societal divisions by marketing "records" and "race records" separately to "whites" and "coloreds." Scholars have used this historical effort to create and enforce social "whiteness" and "blackness" through segregation as evidence of separate racial cultures, when in reality hybridity characterized the South's multiracial heritage. Nevertheless, determined academic writers focusing on racial binaries emphasize perceived or imagined racial differences, while black music ideologists embrace such distinctions for political reasons. Revisionist scholars have begun to recognize the historical nature of race relations and thereby reevaluate the centrality of multiracial jazz to popular music in the United States.[21]

The jazz that musicians such as Mercer made came out of the dynamic urban South around the turn of the century. A brief analysis of the history of jazz sets up the musical milieu in which Johnny thrived. While musicologists find the syncopated precursors to jazz appearing around 1900 in numerous places, the particular sounds from New Orleans captured the country's imagination and proved the strongest influence on the new music. In a definitive statement on the origins of jazz, veteran blues and jazz scholar Samuel Charters documents the complex background that gave birth to jazz, finding its multiracial roots in the city's black and white, mixed-race, and ethnic neighborhoods and musical traditions. Building on interviews he conducted in the 1950s, Charters traces the antecedents of jazz to numerous stimulants, such as the classical training among whites and Creoles in the antebellum era, the German brass bands playing funerals in the 1870s, and the ragtime orchestras at the Lake Pontchartrain resorts in the 1890s, all the while noting that "jazz in the city moved steadily though uneasily, back and forth across the racial barriers." Charters dismisses the argument for racial essentialism in jazz, concluding, "it seems virtually meaningless to give either of the two musical languages of early New Orleans syncopated ragtime precedence over the other." Describing a "continual cultural interchange between societies," Charters argues that "every musician in New Orleans in 1900, white, black, and Creole, was drawing from the same sources: the syncopated cakewalks and walk-around pieces of the minstrel show bands, the newly popular syncopated melodies of ragtime, the disciplined music of the ever-present marching bands, the popular songs that drifted into town like seeds in the wind with the traveling vaudeville shows, and the sheet music that was found in nearly every home in each of the city's social and ethnic groups." Charters demonstrates how the southern diaspora spread the multiracial music as "white" Dixieland and "black" Creole bands that left New Orleans for New York, Chicago, and San Francisco. There the syncopated sounds mingled with other music to make jazz a national phenomenon.[22]

Jazz musicians caught up in the southern diaspora as entertainers took the trains west to Kansas City and San Francisco or north to Chicago and New York City. Suggesting the regional reach of ragtime, one of its early progenitors — the Savannah-born pianist Tom Turpin — moved to St. Louis, Missouri, where he mentored the Texan Scott Joplin. The Alabama-born blues and jazz entrepreneur

W. C. Handy once called Turpin "the real father of jazz," whose influence on other ragtime composers cannot be discounted. Years later, New Orleans pianist and jazz bandleader Ferdinand "Jelly Roll" Morton arrogantly claimed the title, having played California before moving to Illinois. These and other black musicians ragged the music with an abandon that attracted audiences of dancers and musicians receptive to the syncopation, especially among white people thrilled by the free style of playing. During World War I, the Barbary Coast neighborhood in San Francisco rivaled the lively jazz scene in Storyville, New Orleans's red light district. Out of the hot musical climate in these two cities arose Paul Whiteman and Louis Armstrong. In comparing the two, jazz scholar Joshua Berrett recognized that marketers might have crowned the white Whiteman the "King of Jazz," but he understood the title also belonged to the black Armstrong. Johnny Mercer admired both men, eventually working with them. Given their roles in melding jazz and popular music — something Mercer assisted them with and likewise accomplished — an analysis of their careers helps explain the background of jazz prior to Johnny's arrival on the scene.[23]

Born of Scottish ancestry in Denver in 1890, Whiteman inherited his talent from his father, Wilberforce Whiteman, the music director of the public schools who taught the white Harry Barris (who with Bing Crosby and Al Rinker became the Rhythm Boys) and the black Jimmie Lunceford (whose swing style helped launch the big-band craze). After moving to San Francisco to play viola with the orchestra in 1914, Paul discovered the jazz that southerners made in the dance halls and beer dives on the Barbary Coast and organized a band to play the latest tunes. Dancing drove syncopation into popular music, bumping aside the old waltzes, two-steps, and ballads of Tin Pan Alley. Henceforth, as long as jazz set the tempo for dancing, its rhythms informed popular music. Just before World War I, the white partners Vernon and Irene Castle, who danced to accompaniment by the black bandleader James Reese Europe, launched a dance craze. This, followed by the northern tour of the Original Dixieland Jazz Band — a group of white musicians who became the first to record jazz for mass distribution — signaled the interplay of jazz and popular music on the national stage. Alert to the emerging style, Whiteman pioneered standardized settings of the songs, capturing the melodies on paper and leaving room for improvisation while making jazz appear "respectable" for dancing by using symphonic arrangements. Whiteman made recordings in 1920 of "Avalon" and "Whispering," songs that inspired Johnny Mercer. By 1924, in a bid to blend the "serious" with the "popular," Whiteman conducted his Palais Royal Orchestra in the world premiere of George Gershwin's *Rhapsody in Blue*, which revealed the omnipresence of syncopation. Indeed, Whiteman's various approaches to jazz gained him his crown, for he mastered a jazz-inflected light sweet music that while never the hot music of Armstrong nonetheless popularized the genre in the United States. From the cabaret to the symphony hall, musicians embraced the rhythm and blues style of playing as American audiences consumed Whiteman's liberating jazz.[24]

Louis Armstrong began life in New Orleans in 1901 as a poor black boy raised on the streets whose chances of success appeared slim. Kind people in his mixed-race neighborhood offered support. As a youth he worked for a Jewish junkman who bought him his first cornet. Arrested at age eleven, Louis entered the Colored Waif's Home, where he learned how to read music and conduct the brass band, joining a New Orleans tradition out of which the jazz ensemble emerged. Local jazz musicians such as clarinetist Sidney Bechet and trombonist Edward "Kid" Ory recognized the talent in the teenager who performed regularly at dance clubs in Storyville and on Mississippi riverboats. Seeking new opportunities after authorities shuttered the red light district, one of the city's best trumpet players, "Papa" Joe King Oliver, joined the southern diaspora and took a jazz band on the road in 1919, playing mostly in San Francisco and Chicago, summoning Armstrong to join his band in 1922. With Oliver, Armstrong helped standardize jazz around a theme — solo improvisation — theme format that jazz arrangements soon followed. Armstrong provided solos for some of the "race records" recorded by King Oliver's Creole Jazz Band. Companies marketed the releases to black consumers but Johnny Mercer and other white fans also bought them. Outperforming Oliver, Armstrong left his mentor to join the Fletcher Henderson Orchestra in 1924. The alcoholic Oliver returned to the South, dying in a Savannah boarding house in 1938.[25]

Armstrong and Whiteman joined other musicians in the center of the jazz age, New York City, where they found numerous refugees of the southern diaspora likewise seeking opportunities in entertainment. Having studied piano at Atlanta University, plugged songs for publisher W. C. Handy, and accompanied the blues singer Ethel Waters on her tours, the black Georgian Fletcher Henderson organized his own jazz orchestra that featured such players as Coleman Hawkins on tenor saxophone and that served as the house band at the Roseland ballroom at Fifty-first Street and Broadway. Henderson's arrangements as assisted by Don Redman — like those of Ferde Grofe's for Paul Whiteman — reflected the evolution of the music out of the informal Dixieland combo and into the fixed orchestrated sound by placing at counterpoint the reed and horn sections as choral groupings with a driving rhythm keeping it all together. From the 1920s to the 1940s, this structure predominated in jazz, providing the orchestration for many of Johnny Mercer's songs.[26]

Just as innovations in arrangements kept the band music fresh, so too did the addition of new players, often lured away from the competition. When the white Jean Goldkette Band broke apart after its famed "battle of the bands" with the black Fletcher Henderson Orchestra in 1927, Whiteman acquired from it the Dorsey brothers, Jimmy on reeds and Tommy on trombone. Already Whiteman had hired Bix Beiderbecke on cornet, Frankie Trumbauer on saxophone, Joe Venuti on violin, and Eddie Lang on guitar. The fluidity of the profession and the egos of the musicians made it a challenge to keep the players together in a band, but for the rest of the decade Whiteman used to great acclaim these and other white jazz artists. Similarly, Armstrong fidgeted under the organizational structure of Henderson's outfit, so after a year in New York he returned to Chicago, where he opened at the Dreamland in 1925 as Louis Armstrong and His Hot Five. The group made a series of seminal recordings on the Okeh label in a style reminiscent of New Orleans, such as "Heebie Jeebies," "Struttin' with Some Barbecue," and "Cornet Chop Suey." Gigs with Earl Hines and a series of broadcasts from the Chicago and Harlem Savoy Ballrooms gained Louis a national following. By 1930, the trumpet player appeared on the West Coast at Frank Sebastian's New Cotton Club in a house band that included Lionel Hampton on vibraphone. Within months of finally getting to hear Louis Armstrong live in Los Angeles, Johnny Mercer joined Paul Whiteman's orchestra in New York. The chapters that follow tell the life story of the southern songwriter who became world renowned for his musical melding of jazz with popular song.[27]

1 | Grounded Southerner

. . . .

Georgia, Georgia
Where do I start?
Words can sing,
But not like the heart —
There's no land in all this earth
Like the land of my birth!

TO APPRECIATE Johnny Mercer and his music fully, one must recognize how strong a sense of family and a sense of place remained with him throughout his life. From his paternal Mercer forebears, Johnny descended from a line of Scots linked to the Stuarts who fled to colonial America, settling in Virginia and then Georgia. With stories of his illustrious ancestors, his father handed down to the youngster a patrician code of honor with its patriarchal and paternalistic ideology. The Croatian heritage of Johnny's maternal Ciucevich forebears reflected the Eastern European immigrant experience in nineteenth-century America, with its values of family loyalty and hard work. Since generations of kinfolk had walked the streets of Savannah and dozens of extended family members still lived in the city during his lifetime, the old port forever retained a familiarity to Johnny, who valued every visit home. No matter where he resided — be it as a diaspora entertainer in New York City or Los Angeles or as a global citizen in Paris or London — Mercer remained a grounded southerner, for he cherished the legacies he received from his ancestors and the relationships they gave him to his hometown of Savannah.

Johnny Mercer joined an extended family of Mercers that stretched back in the records a thousand years and included a number of noted Church of Scotland ministers. Hugh, the first Mercer in Johnny's direct line to immigrate to America, became close friends with George Washington and other members of the Virginia gentry. Writing in 1910, a descendant noted that Hugh Mercer "was a man of modest, gentle, unassuming nature, content to do his duty faithfully as he saw it, without any undue regard either to the praise or blame of others," traits one finds in his descendants, including his great-great-great-grandson Johnny. As for the songwriter, the British Isles became his favorite haunt when traveling abroad.[1]

Baptized at Pitsligo, Scotland, in January 1726, Hugh Mercer trained as a surgeon at the University of Aberdeen. A Scottish nationalist, he tended the wounded during Charles Edward Stuart's Jacobite Rising to reclaim the British throne from the Hanoverians. With Bonnie Prince Charlie's defeat at the bloody Battle of Culloden Moor in 1746, Dr. Mercer fled for his life, joining a Scottish diaspora to the New World and briefly settling in western Pennsylvania. During the French and Indian War, Mercer befriended George Washington and afterward moved to Fredericksburg, Virginia, where he practiced medicine and managed an apothecary shop in which the future president maintained an office.[2]

With Fredericksburg in the thick of seditious talk against the king, Hugh Mercer cast his lot with the patriots' cause in the American Revolution. He had met and married Isabella Gordon, whose sister Catherine married George Weedon, the proprietor of the republican Rising Sun Tavern. At the Virginia Convention in 1775 Mercer volunteered to "serve his adopted country, and the cause of liberty, in any rank or station to which he may be assigned." Mustered in as a colonel in the Virginia militia, the Scottish doctor rose to the rank of brigadier general by June 1776. At the lowest point of the war he advised Washington to cross the Delaware River on Christmas and attack the British at Trenton, resulting in a much-needed victory that proved the resolve of the fledgling nation. Mercer planned and executed the Battle of Princeton on January 3, 1777. Initially his troops forced the British from the field, but returning redcoats shot his horse out from under him, and when he refused to surrender, stabbed him with bayonets. Nine days later he died of his wounds, an outcome that Washington bemoaned by saying he would have rather lost the battle than his friend. In addition to his wife and three children, General Mercer left behind a legacy of honor that family members cherished. Thirty thousand mourners attended the St. Andrew's Society funeral for him in Philadelphia's Christ Church Burial Ground. In 1962, Johnny Mercer paid homage to the hero by participating in a Daughters of the American Revolution ceremony that recognized the general's sacrifice. He also wrote a hit song with Bernie Hanighen for Paul Whiteman's Orchestra titled "Here Come The British, Bang! Bang!" and toyed with the idea of creating a Broadway musical about his illustrious ancestor.[3]

In patriotic fervor the public embraced General Mercer's children as wards of the state, and they remained among the propertied elite of the early republic in Virginia. Having no direct heirs, General George Weedon and his wife, Catherine, took in sister Isabella and her brood to raise as their own in their house called the Sentry Box, located on the banks of the Rappahannock in Fredericksburg. Daughter Anne married into the Patton family, which later produced General George Patton of World War II fame. Having lost his father at the age of six months, Hugh Tenant Weedon Mercer became "the foster child of the republic," and the Continental Congress arranged for him to attend William and Mary College in Williamsburg, from which he graduated in 1795. He married Louisa Griffin, whose father, Cyrus, had signed the Declaration of Independence and whose mother, Lady Christina Stuart, made Johnny Mercer a lineal descendant of Mary Queen of Scots. For generations a miniature portrait of the Stuart queen has sat on a mahogany secretary in the Mercer household, something Johnny would have seen in the parlor. When the National Bank opened a branch in Fredericksburg, authorities in Washington selected H. T. W. Mercer as president and he ran the bank for nearly fifty years.[4]

In memory of his father, H. T. W. Mercer enrolled his eldest son, Hugh Weedon Mercer, in the United States Military Academy in 1824. Military service reflected one aspect of an ethic of honor to which the Mercers subscribed. Immortalized valor — often embodied on the battlefield — helped define self-worth, as did the opinions of others, personal appearance, integrity, and one's word, all characteristics of primal honor. The elite embraced a gentility, too, a more refined form of honor that joined virtue with high social position in a vulnerable status that one struggled to maintain. Robert E. Lee — who shared with Mercer a Virginia heritage and Revolutionary War legacy — joined Hugh at West Point in 1825, and they became close friends. Following graduation in 1828, BVT Second Lieutenant Hugh W. Mercer first served in the Seminole War and then from 1829 to 1831 in Savannah, where his friend Robert E. "Bob" Lee was also stationed to help construct Fort Pulaski on Cockspur Island at the mouth of the Savannah River.[5]

While in Georgia, both Lee and Mercer courted the local ladies. Hugh took a fancy to Mary Stites Anderson, the attractive daughter of merchant and cotton factor George Wayne Anderson and Eliza Clifford Wayne, the sister of Savannah Mayor Richard Wayne Jr. and U.S. Supreme Court Justice James M. Wayne. The Nullification Crisis in 1832 sidelined the romance when the army assigned Mercer to the staff of General Winfield Scott at Charleston Harbor. Yet the passion persisted. On February 5, 1834, Hugh and Mary married in a ceremony

officiated by the Reverend Willard E. Preston of the Scottish Independent Presbyterian Church in Savannah. Mercer completed his military service as quarter-
master and then joined the local reserves, the Chatham Artillery, as first lieutenant. He assisted his brother-in-law, George Wayne Anderson, at the Planter's
Bank, rising to the rank of cashier in 1841. The Mercers had six children, five
of whom lived to adulthood, including Johnny's grandfather, George Anderson
Mercer, born in 1835. Although Hugh taught Sunday school at Independent Presbyterian, Mary and the children attended Christ Church (Episcopal). They lived
across Congress Street from this, Georgia's first church, on one side of a brick
federal-style mansion at 4 Derby Ward owned by the Andersons that Hugh referred to as the "Old Castle."[6]

The Georgia Mercers retained their ties to their ancestral homeland of Scotland through regular visits with their Virginia kin in Fredericksburg, where they
stayed with H. T. W. Mercer at the Sentry Box. When in town they socialized
with the Scottish immigrants who dominated banking such as the Gordons of
Kenmore and Dabney Herndon of the Chimneys, whose children gained fame
in finance, medicine, and the navy. One son, Dr. Brodie Strachan Herndon Sr.,
who married Lucy Ellen Hansbrough, won acclaim for performing in 1846
one of the first cesarean operations in the United States. The Mercers met the
Herndon children, including their four daughters. After the death of his father,
H. T. W. Mercer, in 1853, Hugh W. Mercer brought his widowed mother, Louisa
Griffin Mercer, to live with him in Savannah, where she died at the Old Castle
on December 28, 1859.[7]

Like other members of the coastal elite, the Mercers divided their time between Savannah and northern resorts that catered to the wealthy of the East
Coast, such as Saratoga Springs. To alleviate the pain she suffered from poor
health, Mary Stites Anderson Mercer sought experimental treatments from doctors in New Haven, Connecticut, traveling there with her brother's sister-in-law,
Sarah Anderson Stites Gordon, the wife of the Central of Georgia Railroad and
Banking Company founder William Washington Gordon; both women took
their sons, George Anderson Mercer and George Anderson Gordon. Like their
fathers, the boys would join Savannah's upper-class institutions, including the
Union Society (which oversaw America's oldest orphanage, the Bethesda Home
for Boys), the Scottish St. Andrew's Society, and the vestry of Christ Church.
They enjoyed the performances of the most beautiful and accomplished actors,
actresses, and singers touring the country when they stopped at the Savannah
Theatre on Chippewa Square. With his cousin, George Anderson Mercer ma-

triculated at a progressive gymnasium, the General Russell School at New Haven. Later, Mercer attended Princeton, joining the sophomore class at the College of New Jersey in 1853. Law courses at the University of Virginia and a grand tour of England and Scotland, across France and down the Rhine River, ending in Italy with his cousin E. C. Anderson Jr., completed his formal education. George Anderson Mercer returned to Savannah and, after his apprenticeship in the legal practice of Henry Rootes Jackson, received admission to the bar in 1859. By 1860, Mercer had formed a law partnership with his cousin George Anderson Gordon, the general counsel to his father W. W. Gordon's Central of Georgia Railroad and the uncle of Juliette Gordon Low, who later founded the Girl Scouts of America. With the railroad bringing Georgia's cotton harvest to the ships docked at the city's wharfs, Savannah grew wealthy as the world's leading exporter of cotton. To British novelist William Makepeace Thackeray, who enjoyed the "most comfortable quarters I have ever had in the United States" at his friend Andrew Low's house in 1855, Savannah appeared "a tranquil old city, wide-streeted, tree-planted, with a few cows and carriages toiling through the sandy road."[8]

In the waning years of the Old South, vanity got the better of Hugh W. Mercer, who embarked on the building of a mansion in Savannah still known as Mercer House. The banker and military man often complained to his wife and children of the drafty feel and dated look of the Old Castle on East Congress Street. The development of Monterey Square provided Mercer with an opportunity to buy property for a new residence. Named in celebration of the 1846 victory in the Mexican War and featuring in its center a monument erected by citizens in 1855 in memory of the Revolutionary War hero Casmir Pulaski, the ward celebrated American militarism. A number of army officers wanting grand edifices, such as Noble A. Hardee, purchased lots. Here Bull Street creates one last square before it empties into Forsyth Park a block away. After the 1853 death of his father, H. T. W. Mercer, and then his wife, Mary, at age forty-two in 1855, Hugh W. Mercer purchased in 1859 the full trust lot at 429 Bull Street that stretched all the way to Whitaker between West Wayne and Gordon streets. The wife's estate, including the Old Castle and half the Anderson wharf, legally belonged to their children. He used his income from the bank, his inheritance from his parents and wife, and the wharf rents to pay for the construction costs. Abandoning the modesty that had marked the behavior of his father and grandfather, an ambitious Hugh Mercer embraced visions of grandeur in his effort to erect the finest residence in the city commensurate with his status as a leading citizen. He hired New York architect John S. Norris to design the trophy house in an eclectic style that combined the Greek and Italianate with the Renaissance Revival. In 1860, work began on 429 Bull Street, the ill-fated Mercer House.[9]

At the outbreak of the Civil War, father and son supported the Confederacy. Both men had served in local militias — Hugh in the Chatham Artillery and George Anderson Mercer in the Republican Blues — and with war these and Savannah's other volunteer units mustered into the Confederate Army as the First Volunteer Regiment of Georgia. After enlisting as a colonel, Hugh W. Mercer served under Brigadier General Alexander R. Lawton, who commanded the Department of Georgia. For months Mercer tried to convince his superiors to withdraw troops from the indefensible Sea Islands and redirect efforts on the mainland. Then the Federals occupied Tybee Island and closed access to the port of Savannah. When the Union's new rifled cannon breached Fort Pulaski's seven-foot-thick brick walls, leading to its surrender on April 10, 1862, the Confederacy relieved Lawton of his command and installed Mercer in his place. As captain on his father's staff, George Anderson Mercer managed army bureaucracy. At the outset of the war he had received permission to travel to Virginia, where on October 23, 1861, George Anderson Mercer married his Fredericksburg sweetheart, Ann Maury "Nannie" Herndon. The couple returned to Savannah, where George's diary entries described wartime conditions in the port city. For the next year, Brigadier General Hugh W. Mercer oversaw the construction of earthen fortifications using impressed slave labor at Thunderbolt and Beaulieu and the Beulah Battery at the junction of the Burnside and Vernon rivers, where years later Johnny Mercer summered in the red-roofed house at Vernon View. Dug into the mainland along the coastline, these temporary bunkers held off a Federal invasion from the sea, for Savannah never suffered such an attack.[10]

As Union General William T. Sherman prepared a land invasion of North Georgia with ample armaments and a hundred thousand men, the Confederacy transferred the Mercers and their battalions to the Army of Tennessee under the command of Major General Joseph E. Johnston, whose total force numbered half that of the enemy. The battle-weary veterans in Johnston's army remarked on the size and inexperience of Mercer's 1,400 soldiers, whom some described as a silk-stocking brigade because of the wealth of its members. Some of the more seasoned officers whispered about General Mercer's struggles with gout and questioned his abilities. In one of the first skirmishes of what became known as the Atlanta Campaign, Mercer's men distinguished themselves at Rocky Face Ridge on May 8, 1864. Yet over the next two months they retreated with Johnston's army as Sherman's troops advanced along the Western and Atlantic Railroad line. When the opposing forces reached Atlanta, Confederate President Jefferson Davis replaced Johnston with the aggressive General John B. Hood. Quickly, in a series of rash attacks against the Union forces, Hood's army suffered terrible losses. In the devastating Battle of Atlanta on July 22, 1864, Mercer's Brigade took heavy fire with 168 casualties, including the Savannah brothers Joseph and Willie Habersham. Federals killed the Confederate Division Commander General W. H. T. Walker, too, and Mercer rose to replace him as the armies clashed on the eastern side of Atlanta between the old Georgia Railroad and present-day Interstate 20. Despite the valiant fighting, the Confederacy lost more than ten thousand men. Hood disbanded Mercer's decimated division and absorbed the surviving soldiers into his overall army. He reassigned General Mercer to reserves in Savannah, but kept Captain George Anderson Mercer on his staff. In September 1864, the Army of Tennessee abandoned Atlanta to Union forces.[11]

Father and son prepared for the inevitable outcome. Captain Mercer evacuated with the Confederates into Alabama, but at the Tennessee River he left to join General A. R. Wright's division in Savannah, which included his father's brigade of reserve forces. Having constructed the coastal defenses, the Mercers now joined in the scramble to prepare breastworks behind the city to fend off an attack by land anticipated from Sherman's March to the Sea. Once the 62,000 Union troops reached the outskirts of settlement in December 1864, the remaining 9,000 Confederates left to defend the port withdrew into South Carolina, thereby avoiding a bombardment but leaving Savannah in the hands of the invaders. The Mercers retreated across the river on pontoon boats with Wright's division as Lieutenant General William J. C. Hardee united his forces at Hardeeville from whence to rejoin General Joe Johnston in North Carolina for a last stand that never materialized. Union General J. H. Wilson captured the Mercers in April and paroled them in May 1865. At the outset of war Confederate patriotism had inspired Macon's Hermann L. Schreiner to write for piano the martial-sounding "Gen. Mercer's Grand March!" Yet the family stories of the steady retreat of the Rebel forces in Georgia — despite the heroism shown by his forebears — probably encouraged great-grandson Johnny Mercer's satirical verse in *Li'l Abner*. The songwriter lampoons a southern general named "Jubilation T. Cornpone" with the lyric, "When we fought the Yankees and / Annihilation was near, / Who was there to lead the charge / That took us safe to the rear?"[12]

With Confederate defeat the Mercers struggled to rebuild their lives. Hugh W. Mercer resumed his position as cashier of the Planter's Bank, but wartime investments in the Confederacy and the collapse of Georgia's economy had left the bank nearly insolvent, so he paid off what he could to the bank's shareholders and closed the accounts. Given the relationship of debt to honor in the South's economy, losing one's fortune made starting over difficult because southerners favored debtor relief strategies over the use of bankruptcy laws. Since the defeat in war resulted in unusual circumstances beyond human control, financial ruin did not necessarily signal a loss of honor unless it led to the loss of esteem in the eyes of others, perhaps brought about by the loss of property. In 1866, General Mercer sold his unfinished Monterey Square mansion, which occupying Union soldiers had ransacked and left as an uninhabitable brick shell. The Mercers never lived in the structure that Norris assistants Muller and DeWitt Bruyn completed in 1871, although the jewel retains the name Mercer House. In the twentieth century, the architectural triumph survived a variety of owners, including the Shriners, before being painstakingly restored and lavishly furnished by antiques dealer Jim Williams, the subject of the book *Midnight in the Garden of Good and Evil*. Under his stewardship the house both briefly fulfilled its destiny as Savannah's greatest residence and suffered as the site of a murder, which also clinched its reputation as the city's most famous domicile. On his last visit to Savannah in September 1975, Johnny Mercer sang several songs in front of the restored Mercer House for broadcast on *The Mike Douglas Show* in what became his final public performance.[13]

Postbellum Savannah's brief boom quickly went bust. Hugh W. Mercer joined his nephew, Edward C. Anderson Jr., in a new commission and banking business centered around a forty-five-thousand-dollar Central Cotton Press installed on the Anderson Wharf lot 4, but the investment failed to make the desired returns. It also revealed that the general had never settled his wife's estate, keeping the rents from the wharf that she had left to their children. With his world already turned upside down, he now confronted family scandals. In a bid to regain their inheritance, the four siblings, under the leadership of George Anderson Mercer, quietly forced Hugh W. Mercer to sign a settlement that obligated the general to turn over to them their mother's property. The children received the Anderson family home they called the Old Castle on Congress Street, valued at ten thousand dollars, and its furnishings. Also, the general surrendered to them his claim to the warehouse on the Bay Street wharf. Newly divested of his dead wife's estate, Hugh W. Mercer confronted a collapsing economy in Savannah. In late 1868, the general married in New York City a widow twenty-five years his junior, Elizabeth "Bessie" Steenbergen Cuyler of Savannah. Not surprisingly, the newlyweds found life around the general's children not entirely welcoming.[14]

During the war when the Federals had threatened the Herndon home known as the Chimneys, the mother-in-law and daughters fled Fredericksburg, living in the Old Castle as refugees with the Mercers. Dr. Brodie S. Herndon remained in Virginia assisting the Confederacy as chief surgeon in Richmond's hospitals, while his sons prosecuted the war as surgeons in Lee's army. After the Yankees looted and sacked Fredericksburg in December 1862, the Herndon women decided to remain in Savannah, where in 1863 grandmother Lucy assisted daughter Nannie and son-in-law George with their newborn. Following Confederate defeat, the parents returned to Fredericksburg, where Brodie Junior lived, but given the destruction to the city and the overall depression that gripped Virginia, they moved permanently to Georgia in November 1868. The four Herndon daughters had remained in Savannah, with two having married local men and a third, Lucy, marrying the Scottish publisher Robert Blackie in the parlor of the Old Castle in 1867 before moving to Glasgow. (Seventy years later, Johnny Mercer visited their daughter, Nell Herndon Blackie, in Edinburgh.) Henceforth the Herndons — who settled into the Old Castle on Congress Street with the good doctor joining the vestry of Christ Church — influenced the domestic life of the Mercers. Dr. Herndon's patriarchal presence in the household left a legacy on the Mercer children recognized in the naming of the great-grandson John Herndon Mercer. Indeed, given Johnny's occasional behavior later in life when drinking, one wonders if the songwriter inherited from the Herndons the traits of Edinburgh's Deacon Brodie, the real-life subject of Robert Louis Stevenson's *The Strange Case of Dr. Jekyll and Mr. Hyde.*[15]

While the Herndons' relocated to Savannah, the financially troubled General Hugh Mercer and his bride removed to the bustling port of Baltimore, which had become something of a postbellum haven for Confederate expatriates. In 1869, he started life over as a commission merchant in the Mercer and Johnston firm on Bowley's Wharf. They had a daughter, Alice. Yet Baltimore's Great Fire of 1873 literally burned them out of their residence. Having been twice reduced to ruin, the general chose more distant exile as the only way to sustain his honor. The Mercers decamped to the Black Forest resort in Baden-Baden, Germany, where the general sought relief from his gout and rheumatism with treatments at the Kurhaus. On June 9, 1877, he died there at the age of sixty-eight in rented rooms on Lichtentaler Strasse and was buried in the city cemetery. His obituary in the Savannah paper read, "No more high toned, honorable or honest officer was in the Confederate service." In his memory, mourners donated in 1886 to the Baden-Baden English Church of All Saints a stained glass window depicting

St. Andreas, the patron saint of Scotland. Meanwhile Bessie and Alice returned to the United States and settled in Orange, Virginia.[16]

Assuming the role of family patriarch, George Anderson Mercer watched as his family grew with each new addition provided by his wife, Nannie. The couple had seven children — six sons and one daughter — with two of the boys dying in childhood. Of the surviving children, the eldest son, Johnny Mercer's father, George Anderson Mercer, was born in 1868, Nannie Herndon Mercer in 1866, Lewis Herndon Mercer in 1870, Robert Lee Mercer in 1871, and Edward Clifford Anderson Mercer in 1873. George Anderson Mercer noted in the family Bible that toward the end of 1871 he had moved his wife and children into "my new house," a formal brick residence said to be "one of the finest homes" in the city. He had built it in Savannah's newly fashionable neighborhood along its municipal park designed in 1851 to honor the Orientalist William Brown Hodgson, whose Georgia Historical Society would soon anchor the adjacent corner of Whitaker and Gaston streets in a state-of-the-art library named in his memory. Today called Forsyth Park — with its distinctive 1858 cast-iron fountain and parterre gardens with their tropical plantings — its landscape was extended southward by the city to encompass the old militia drill field. Directly across from the upper center of this Forsyth Park Extension on the northern corner of West Bolton stood George Anderson Mercer's two-story mansion at 817 Whitaker Street.[17]

During Reconstruction, former Confederate Captain George Anderson Mercer played a key role in the Savannah low country. As militia leader of the Republican Blues, he joined soldiers in his old company mustered back into service to suppress the freedmen during the Ogeechee "insurrection" of 1868–69. (He remained in active command of the militia unit until 1886, when the state promoted him to colonel of the First Volunteer Regiment of Georgia.) He supported the restoration of white supremacy by joining with other elite Savannahians as founding members of the Chatham Conservative Club and by serving on the State Democratic Executive Committee. As a "Redeemer," Mercer won election to the seat in the Georgia General Assembly previously held by the black radical Republican, the Reverend James Meriles Simms of the First African Baptist Church. From the Georgia House of Representatives, Mercer assisted in the transition from Republican to Bourbon Democratic rule during the two Georgia General Assemblies, 1872–73 and 1873–74. At public addresses, Mercer expressed the Lost Cause. He had met with family friend Robert E. Lee during the venerated general's extended visit to Savannah in April 1870. Mercer supported Savannah's Ladies Memorial Association's effort to raise money for a monument to the Confederacy in Forsyth Park Extension. As the keynote speaker at the dedication of the cornerstone on June 16, 1874, Captain Mercer exalted the commitment to duty demonstrated by his fellow defeated veterans: "They espoused their cause with a unanimity and purity of purpose never exceeded — they maintained with a constancy and devotion never surpassed."[18]

The law dominated George Anderson Mercer's professional life. He headed the Georgia Bar Association and founded with others the American Bar Association on whose executive committee he served for several terms. His wife's first cousin had married Chester A. Arthur, who emerged as the nation's unexpected president in 1881 after the assassination of James A. Garfield. The Herndons and their kith and kin became occasional visitors to the White House. President Arthur offered George Anderson Mercer the position of U.S. judge of the Southern District of Georgia, but the Savannah attorney declined the federal appointment because of its low salary, although he hosted the president during his visit to Savannah in 1884.[19]

Recognizing civic duty as an obligation of honor but uninterested in rejoining state politics, George Anderson Mercer oversaw public education in Savannah. He began thirty years on the Chatham County Board of Education in 1876, holding the position of president for a quarter century. Through education, the white elite kept the civic peace as the class, race, and religious diversity of Savannah's neighborhoods mirrored the composition of the publicly funded schools segregated by race, gender, and religion. During his time on the Park and Tree Commission, which oversaw the city squares in Savannah's historic district, Mercer developed an appreciation for landscape gardening and made the cultivation "of everything that is beautiful in nature" a regular theme of his annual commencement addresses at Chatham Academy.[20]

A cosmopolitan, George Anderson Mercer assembled one of Savannah's great private libraries and turned to the writings of Montesquieu, Edmund Burke, and Herbert Spencer to rationalize his station in life. His personal journals — copies of which Johnny placed in the holdings of the Georgia Historical Society — reveal a man confined by the law. They also suggest he suffered from bouts of depression, something his grandson shared. A curator of the society and president of the venerated institution from 1900 to 1907, Mercer opened vine-covered Hodgson Hall to Savannah's white population for use as a public library until a new Carnegie library could be built farther up Bull Street in the Victorian district. Mercer assisted Director Carl L. Brandt and Henry R. Jackson, chair of the board of managers of Telfair Academy, in the selection of paintings for the galleries. The choices for the art museum made by the men revealed their shared tastes toward the Teutonic. From works of art and literature to books on history and biography, George Anderson Mercer promoted European civilization for "the advancement of his people," as noted by his peers, who identified him "with all that was best in the upbuilding of the city of Savannah."[21]

Given all the privileges of wealth, Mercer remained modest, for he "was not what is known as a club or society man," according to former Georgia governor William J. Northen in *Men of Mark*, despite the appearance of his name on the rosters of Savannah's most exclusive organizations. No doubt noblesse oblige underscored his public service, from which he derived gratification and public recognition. Mercer's contributions to the Union Society that managed the Bethesda Home for Boys reflected the paternalistic charity to poor whites that society expected of him, an obligation he derived from his forebears and one he conveyed to his sons. Likewise, his involvement in elite social organizations stemmed from similar expectations. The founders of the Oglethorpe Club extended membership to George as well as to his brother, Robert Lee Mercer, who would serve as secretary of the club from 1878 to 1898. Mercer descendants have remained members of the elite institution ever since. Likewise, George Anderson Mercer's name replaced his father's on the roster of the St. Andrew's Society in 1868, and in time the names of his sons and son-in-law J. M. Lang would be added to the list. These generations of Mercers socialized with generations of Andersons, Chisholms, Gordons, Joneses, Lawtons, Stoddards, and dozens of other aristocratic Savannah families, for whom wealth and social privilege expressed through membership in select private institutions provided a charmed avenue through life.[22]

During his childhood, George Anderson Mercer had summered with his mother at Newport, Rhode Island, where Savannah's George Noble Jones family kept a cottage, but during the Civil War he became more familiar with the Georgia coast when he inspected with his father the string of batteries from Causton's bluff to Thunderbolt, Rose Dhu, and Beaulieu. With money tight after hostilities ended but wanting to avoid the miasmas around Savannah with their supposed threat of fever, Mercer found it natural to revisit these breezy seaside villages. He took his growing family to White Bluff, a resort community located eight miles south of Savannah overlooking the Vernon River, where the Habershams and Chisholms kept summer houses. Here "on the salts" beside the marsh where the brackish river water approached the ocean, daughter Nannie and sons

G. A., Lewis, Robbie, and Ed went "bathing" at high tide, learned to sail, fished, crabbed, and engaged in other amusements. A plentiful supply of formerly enslaved African American labor made life easy for the white elite, who nonetheless shared with these black workers a hybrid southern culture. As commodore of the Savannah Yacht Club at Thunderbolt from 1888 to 1889, Colonel Mercer commanded the annual regattas in May, accessed the new boathouse, lounged around the large piazza of the clubhouse, and relaxed by the marble pool. The Mercer family enjoyed pleasant summers among the elite scattered in cottage communities on the higher ground above Georgia's salt marsh.[23]

As the children matured, George Anderson Mercer arranged for their education. After his eldest son, G. A., completed a course of study at Chatham Academy in Savannah, he attended Abbots' prep school in Fredericksburg. The father hoped to enroll his son at the University of Virginia to study law. He explained in a rational and loving letter addressed to "my dear boy" the reasoning behind his firm direction. "Your father is actuated only by an earnest desire to prosper you physically and intellectually." Implying his assent with Herbert Spencer's interpretation of Charles Darwin's theory as the survival of the fittest, Mercer observed: "In the wide diffusion of knowledge and the fierce competition of the present age, no man can expect to make real progress without a diligent and steady use and application of all his faculties, mental and physical. Now is the seed time of your life; employ it properly or you can reap no harvest." George Anderson Mercer demonstrated what Bertram Wyatt-Brown defined as true honor, the welding together of inner virtue and the desire for good with reason and outward action. Then the father revealed his aspiration: "To see you become an honest, able, and successful lawyer and to enjoy your assistance and co-operation as I grow older is the dearest wish of my heart." Mercer filled the letter with practical advice gleaned from years of encouraging Chatham Academy graduates at commencements, recommending that the reader "cultivate a power of expressing in appropriate words your own thoughts" and "cultivate the habit of reasoning, of getting at the true meaning and going to the bottom of things."[24]

In a frank exchange George Anderson Mercer lectured his son on the proper code of behavior expected of gentlemen. He focused on sexual matters, encouraging his son to avoid "that terrible habit of self-abuse, to which so many boys are addicted, and against which I have already warned you." He threatened that "one indulgence will lead to others until soon the habit becomes irresistible. Your future health and usefulness, your own capacity to contract marriage and become the parent of healthy children, depend upon control of your passions."

Mercer advised bearing in mind the ideals of gentility as a way to keep human desires in check, for "every son of Adam has been tempted in like manner. The weak and base nature yields; the noble nature conquers. It is usually the first struggle a young man encounters, and by his power to resist this, he may judge it his ability to resist the appetites and passions that will assail him in his future life. To yield means to abandon hope and success; to conquer means success, respect, and honor." Mercer burdened his son by casting desire within a social paradigm of self-control rewarded with honor and punished with shame. Yet he recognized that sexual desire might prove too strong and acknowledged the practice of "wenching"— intercourse with a willing woman — as an acceptable alternative to masturbation. Although referring specifically to the deadly sin of lust, Mercer's comments applied to any of the other attractive vices, such as gambling and drinking. The Mercer code, expressed here in the struggle over one's passions in defense of virtuous self-control, underpinned the family's reputation. Johnny Mercer kept a copy of his grandfather's letter in his own personal papers, understanding full well the measure of its demands.[25]

As the patriarch, George Anderson Mercer epitomized to his extended family the thoughtful and intelligent gentleman. As a contemporary noted: "His activity in all public affairs was guided by the great principle of right. He acted from principle and not from policy. He was a man of courage: he had convictions and never hesitated to express them. But, with all, he was a tender-hearted man, as gentle as a woman and as loveable as a child." While internationally gentlemen upheld a code of honor, the ideal Mercer embraced reflected a regional concept perhaps most widely recognized in the person of family friend Robert E. Lee, whose beliefs and behaviors symbolized southern honor and the ideal of the true gentleman. Lee refined the primal code of honor — defended through violence — by emphasizing gentility demonstrated through Christian duty and virtuous behavior. He practiced nonviolence by forgiving others and forgetting wrongs, he judiciously wielded power with mercy, and he modestly held to a personal dignity derived from self-control — all these behaviors are the hallmark of a gentleman. Indeed, wedded to the ancient obligations of the code of honor, Lee set a high standard many others tried to emulate.[26]

Certainly, George Anderson Mercer and other family members struggled to maintain the ideal of the gentleman as set forth by this southern icon. In his 1928 memoir, son Ed Mercer acknowledged that "General Robert E. Lee gave us his receipt for happiness: A sound mind, a healthy body, a firm belief in God, a loving wife and dutiful children — that is my idea of happiness." In his autobiography, grandson Johnny expressed the code: "So it behooved us to put our best foot forward, which usually meant taking time to be polite and kind to others, especially visitors. Children were truly seen, not heard, and seldom spoke unless spoken to. These old rules were valued very highly . . . and still are where people are civilized. In Savannah, they reigned supreme . . . right next to Robert E. Lee." Lee's actions revealed to his fellow southerners a nearly superhuman stoicism and disciplined devotion to duty that they might have found difficult to achieve. Yet all the Mercers strived to gain the standard set by Lee, for they all had been cast in the same mold, imbued with southern honor. As family friend Nick Mamalakis put it, "Johnny was a high-type person. His entire family was with that reputation, just honorable people, and he wouldn't veer away from that. His life recorded the fact that he respected the honorable issues of life." Johnny's friend, William "Bill" Harbach, said of Mercer, "He was a complete gentleman." As Johnny Mercer's drunken narrator sings succinctly in "One for My Baby (And One More for the Road)," "Could tell you a lot, / But that's not in a gentleman's code."[27]

The death of George Anderson Mercer's beloved wife, Nannie Herndon, at age forty-four in 1885 greatly affected the lives of her family members. George Anderson Mercer never remarried, leaving the housekeeping to Anna Taliaferro, who as mammy also helped raise the youngest sons. Returning from Virginia, G. A. enrolled in the law school at the University of Georgia in Athens in 1887. Enjoying an active social life in Sigma Alpha Epsilon fraternity, G. A. gained popularity on campus as a varsity baseball pitcher. With teams in Detroit and Cincinnati recruiting him, G. A. toyed with the idea of playing professional ball but instead dutifully returned to Savannah to practice law with his father. At first his siblings returned home, too. Lewis never married. Robbie took as his wife Katharine Mackay Stiles. In 1889, sister Nannie Herndon Mercer married a Scotsman, Joseph Muir Lang, suggesting the hold of the ancestral homeland over the Mercers. The brothers were in business together with their brother-in-law on Bay Street, with Lewis operating the Phosphate Mining Company and J. M. Lang and Robert Lee Mercer managing the J. M. Lang Company, which sold the phosphate rock as fertilizer to a hungry cotton economy farther inland.[28]

Just twelve when his mother died, Edward Clifford Anderson Mercer suffered immensely from her loss. Years later, George Anderson Mercer's youngest son remembered Nannie as "a very devout, sincere, beautiful Christian character," adding, "I will never cease being grateful to her memory for the seed of righteousness which she planted into my young boy heart, and which was never totally uprooted." Called "Ed" by the family but professionally and by friends as "Ted," the son recognized in his father "a kind and generous and loving parent, of the highest and finest sense of honor that I have ever known," but he felt his father's life lacked Christian direction. After his own religious conversion, Ed acknowledged his father regularly attended Christ Church but that "his mind from constant reading was saturated with the destructive philosophy of Voltaire, Darwin, Huxley, Herbert Spencer, and Napoleon, and at times he was very critical of God's Holy Word, and too freely expressed his doubts concerning some of the great fundamentals of the Christian faith. I am confident that he never realized for one moment the unconscious damage being done by his destructive criticisms and its possible offsetting in my tender life of the beautiful, sweet, simple faith of my dear mother." With no mother, with older brothers and a family doting on him as the baby, the spoiled Ed allowed his passions to control his behavior.[29]

Foreshadowing dilemmas Johnny would confront, Ed proved the problem for the widower as his behavior revealed the difficulties of meeting the code of honor. When elder brother G. A. failed to fulfill his father's wishes and attend the University of Virginia, George Anderson Mercer projected those dreams onto his youngest son. After graduating from Chatham Academy in 1889, Ed enrolled in Charlottesville. He joined the Georgia Crackers, a social club in which he held the office of Cork Puller. He pledged Beta Theta Pi Fraternity, later admitting that he made "the fraternity's too often petty interests my God." He entered the selective "ribbon" senior society known as TILKA. Playing varsity baseball as centerfielder, Ed helped the team with its winning season in 1891. Yet, as he wrote years later, "like thousands of other ignorant, foolish college boys, I took my first drink of intoxicating liquor, went into my very first act of impurity and lost my first five-cent piece at the gambling table, not because I actually craved these sinful things, but because I feared unpopularity by going contrary to such practices of older University associates." During initiation rites to join the private clubs and on other social occasions, Ed drank excessively because he thought it demonstrated his virility, validated his manliness, and secured friendship among other gentlemen. After his 1893 graduation, he moved back under his father's roof on Whitaker Street so that "nearly all of my income was spent on clothes." In a "fashionable society wedding," Ed married Josephine Peyton Freeland in 1898. On the surface he appeared to be the successful young professional, but the socially acceptable vices of drinking and gambling would slowly undermine his life.[30]

Unable to control his passions, Ed confronted dishonor. As his autobiography recalled, "gambling fever took hold" and he became an "absinthe fiend." Despair over a gaming debt led him in 1902 to down a quart of whiskey in preparation for a suicide jump from the Yacht Club boathouse into the receding tide, but he passed out before completing the deed. He owed thousands of dollars and death seemed the only escape from the shame he suffered. Made aware of the trouble, George Anderson Mercer gathered the family together to resolve the problem. Like other gentlemen, he interpreted the gambling loss as a debt of honor that had to be repaid immediately. As Ed remembered, "My dear, kind father mortgaged some of his property and paid every cent of my indebtedness, and cleared the family name of the public disgrace I had caused it." Then in a harsh decision, "I was advised to leave the city and start life over again in some distant town where I was not known. My father gave me a liberal check and advised my wife not to accompany me north, because if she went, he felt certain, it would only bring disgrace and shame upon her." Ed tried to get his life together again, but ended up on a spree that landed him in the Bowery of New York City in 1904. Again he contemplated suicide, but his uncle, the Wall Street broker Thomas Savage Clay, intervened, seeing that Ed entered the Jerry McAuley Water Street Rescue Mission under the Brooklyn Bridge. Shamed into finding religion, Ed swore off drinking and gambling and within a decade traveled the country as a popular evangelist, eventually reconciling with his father and with his wife.[31]

Johnny Mercer knew his Uncle Ed but never met his paternal grandfather, George Anderson Mercer. He heard stories about both men from his father, older brothers, and other relatives who recognized similarities between these forebears and the youngster. Like Uncle Ed, Johnny appeared on stage before thousands of people, although as an entertainer and not a charismatic morals crusader. And like his uncle — and others in the family — Johnny had a weakness for drink. But Johnny favored his grandfather, George Anderson Mercer, the most. He relished the comparison, adopting the nickname Little Colonel because of the character traits he perceived he shared with the Civil War veteran. Like George Anderson, Johnny read voraciously, and both men urged students "to use their education to advance the 'thought and wisdom of mankind.'" Echoing the advice his grandfather had given nearly a century before at a Georgia Historical Society anniversary dinner, Johnny Mercer answered a school girl's question, "What does it take to be a lyric writer?" with the comment, "Darlin' read, read, read. That's what it takes. Read a lot, and don't read just love stories. Read . . . the classics. Read about the Wild West . . . You must read and you must look up new words that you're not familiar with. But read a lot, and then be inquisitive about the meaning of words."[32]

All three men gained fame as public speakers. Ed's elite background, education, professional associations, and polish made him an ideal evangelist to the upper class. He worked with the Young Men's Christian Association and other Protestant church groups, often addressing college students "on the subject of morals." Within a decade of his conversion, he had spoken to more than 75,000 young men annually in churches and on campuses, often giving a talk he titled "Shattering Delightful Illusions Surrounding Vice." Acclaimed as "an effective speaker," Ed traveled across the United States to appear at hundreds of colleges, in thousands of factories, and before civic clubs in public auditoriums, in prisons, and in rescue missions, where he pleaded "for the better life." Although not as charismatic as his son, Ed, George Anderson Mercer had also gained fame for his formal declamations as an acolyte of the Lost Cause and "as an impromptu speaker," a reputation his grandson, Johnny, shared. More often than not, George Anderson's addresses occurred at dinners, such as the one hosted by the First Georgia Regiment for visiting Michigan troops shortly after the Spanish American War. Infirmities kept the old man seated as he spoke extemporaneously, but his words warmed the visitors, one of whom remarked, "If Col. Mercer could speak any better lying down than he could sitting, he hoped the attendants would bring in a cot at once." Johnny Mercer's ready tongue often served him well, as when he performed his "newsie bluesie" on Benny Goodman's radio show. No doubt his talents for public speaking derived in part from the traits he inherited from his uncle and grandfather.[33]

After his wife's death and with the boys grown, George Anderson Mercer, no longer contented with summers at White Bluff, sought the companionship of Princeton classmates and friends in New York City. He left domestic affairs in the hands of his black housekeeper, Anna Taliaferro, who, as he explained in his will, "has long been a faithful servant and true friend to me and to my family." With his bachelor son, Lewis Herndon Mercer, and his brother-in-law, Thomas Savage Clay, working on Wall Street, the old colonel spent every September and part of October in the metropolis. Pleasant afternoons found him sitting in a chair on the front sidewalk outside the Gilsey House, an elaborate seven-story hotel in the Flatiron District on the corner of Broadway and Twenty-ninth Street, or the nearby colonnade of the luxurious Fifth Avenue Hotel at Twenty-third. Perhaps he escorted along the Ladies' Mile — which stretched past the city's department stores — Mrs. Beatrice L. Childs, a New York resident whom he acknowledged in his will with a gift of three thousand dollars. He attended theaters in and around Union Square, perhaps catching performances at such venues as the birthplace of vaudeville, Tony Pastor's New Fourteenth Street Theatre. After the Metropolitan Opera House opened in 1883, he traveled farther uptown to hear the great singers. In the last decades of the nineteenth century, George Anderson Mercer consumed the cosmopolitan world of New York just as his grandson, Johnny, would absorb the city later in the twentieth century.[34]

With his father away, G. A. ran the thriving Mercer and Mercer law practice. In April 1892, he married Mary Ellis Walter, a native of Savannah with family ties to the W. W. Gordons. They began a family in 1893 with their first child, George Anderson Mercer, followed four years later by George Walter Mercer. The family lived in half of the 1855 duplex at 210 East Taylor Street, while brother Robbie and his wife, Katharine, lived in the other half. In 1900, both women got pregnant. On December 10, Katharine delivered Robert Lee Mercer, and two days later Mary gave birth to Hugh Mercer. The next week childbirth complications claimed Mary's life. At the time their mother died, George was nearly eight and Walter three and a half. At first Aunt Katharine helped the widower G. A. with the childcare for the newborn. She kept Hugh with her baby Robert those first two years until tragedy struck her family in late 1903 when her son died. By then G. A.'s older boys had attended Miss Mamie Woolhopter's private kindergarten on East Bolton Street that affiliated with the adjacent Pape School. Kindergarten prepared the boys for entering the elementary Massie School, a public institution located in an antebellum brick building across Calhoun Square from their East Taylor Street home. These three boys — Johnny Mercer's half-brothers George, Walter, and Hugh — also spent time with their grandfather and invalid great-uncle Robert and other kinfolk in the brick house on Whitaker Street.[35]

As with his father, the law proved less than rewarding for G. A., who, after the death of his wife in 1900, decided to leave practice and engage in enterprise. He reputedly owned the first automobile in Savannah. He did buy a Mercer raceabout and at one point invested in an electric automobile dealership with C. P. Reneau, who ran the business on State Street. Colonel Mercer frowned on such commercial ventures as trades unfit for a gentleman, and in July 1901 he revoked the clause in his will that bequeathed his office equipment, law library, and safe to his eldest son. Within a year G. A. resumed the practice of law and his father restored the codicil so that the professional equipment would descend to him separately from his share of the inheritance. Only after his father's death in 1907 did G. A. wander again from the law, concentrating on real-estate investments and sales, and even then he maintained a law practice that did title work and drew up wills. The ambitious G. A. invested in rental property and resold lots for profit. He built the first apartment building in Savannah overlooking Forsyth Park and purchased speculative ventures in the suburbs. With expanding industries seeking new employees, the city's population grew, increasing demands for housing that G. A. attempted to fill.[36]

After 1897, George Anderson Mercer's health began to decline, although he occasionally tended to legal affairs assisted by a staff that included by 1902 Lillian Ciucevich, a young stenographer. His annual trips to New York City ceased. After he suffered a stroke in 1906 that left him unable to walk, during good weather he held forth from the lobby of his garden gate seat on Whitaker Street, where neighbors passed by and children tarried to hear his recitations of poetry or listen to his tales of adventure and romance. As his physical state deteriorated, he suffered from what the newspaper called recurrent spells of dizziness that culminated in a severe case of vertigo on October 23, 1907. Taken to Savannah Hospital by the family physician, Dr. T. J. Charlton, he died several hours later from "acute congestion of the brain," possibly caused by a tumor, the malady that awaited his future grandson, Johnny. With George Anderson Mercer's death at the age of seventy-two, the city lowered its flags to half-mast. The *Savannah Morning News* bemoaned, "When a man of his mold dies, civilization itself sustains a loss. He stood for the beautiful in art, the ennobling in literature, the just and liberal in law, the gentle, refined and true in manhood. Such a code of principles believed in and lived up to made Col. Mercer a positive force in all of his associations and won for him the sincerest respect and esteem of all with whom he came in contact."[37]

As the family patriarch in life, George Anderson Mercer had arranged to keep his extended kinsmen together in death through burials in Savannah's necropolis, Bonaventure Cemetery. In 1877 he had joined his father-in-law in purchasing lots in section F on ground that lay near the bluff overlooking the St. Augustine Creek tributary of the Wilmington River. To reunite the family physically — perhaps in the hope of a spiritual reunion — he relocated previous family burials from the Anderson plot in Savannah's Laurel Grove Cemetery. In 1885, he had laid to rest his beloved wife, Nannie Herndon Mercer, in Bonaventure, placing beside her their dead sons removed from Laurel Grove. The next year the family buried Nannie's father, Dr. Brodie S. Herndon, next to his wife, their son, and other Herndon kin in the enclosure. Space remained for the

Mercer siblings, with sons and daughter buried in adjacent or nearby plots — everyone except for Ed, who lies beside his wife in Laurel Grove. Following the funeral in Christ Church, the family buried George Anderson Mercer in Bonaventure, erecting over the grave a large stone slab with an embossed Celtic cross.[38]

Though busy speculating in real estate, G. A. Mercer courted the twenty-five-year-old stenographer Lillian Barbara Ciucevich. Thirteen years her senior and the father of three young boys, G. A. began calling her "my little baby girl" out of affection. In 1906, she yielded to his wooing and married the widower. Sister Nannie Mercer Lang assured Lillian, "He is the best and dearest brother in the world and I know will make a loving and devoted husband." In becoming his second wife, Lillian made it clear she would not substitute as a nanny for the three stepsons, Hugh age six, Walter age nine, and George age thirteen, the last boarding at Woodberry Forest School in Orange, Virginia.[39]

Three years into their marriage, G. A. and Lillian announced the birth of John Herndon "Johnny" Mercer on November 18, 1909. Lillian's sister, the nurse Ann Ciucevich Rivers, assisted Dr. T. J. Charlton in the delivery at Telfair Hospital for Women; her other sister, Nora, witnessed the birth and signed Johnny's birth certificate. The arrival of the baby necessitated a larger house, so G. A. briefly moved his family to 20 East Macon Street in 1909 before settling in for the next decade at 118 East Hall Street, two blocks from sister Nannie and her husband, Joseph Muir Lang, at 302 East Hall Street (their son, Mercer Lang, had joined George at Woodberry). Johnny spent his childhood years from 1910 to 1919 in the now-demolished row house on Hall Street. While the Mercers lived along the eastern edge of Forsyth Park not far from the famous fountain, the Ciucevich clan held forth from its enclave at 301 East Charlton Street in Troup Ward a few blocks north up Lincoln Street.[40]

Years later, Johnny Mercer claimed that if he had any talent at all, he got it from his mother, Lillian. According to his daughter, Mandy, Lillian wrote beautiful poetry. From his mother Johnny inherited a family experience rooted in the lives of Roman Catholic children of an Eastern European immigrant in postbellum Savannah, a background vastly different from that of the Episcopalian Mercers. The story of "Captain" John Joseph Ciucevich and his descendants reflected a common narrative of hard work by newcomers to America determined to succeed that Johnny embraced in his own life and celebrated in song. His Austrian ancestry enabled him to relate to other children of immigrants, such as the Jewish songwriters of Tin Pan Alley, although it paradoxically also exposed him to the Old World prejudices Europeans brought with them to the New, such as his mother's anti-Semitism. The Ciucevich clan schooled the young boy in the importance of family commitment, a lesson that stayed with him the rest of his days.

Two Croatians—Lillian's father, John Joseph Ciucevich, and his brother, Francis Ciucevich—immigrated to the United States from the Austrian Empire sometime in the mid-nineteenth century. Family lore has John Joseph being born in Dalmatia in 1834, leaving the Adriatic Island of Lagosta as a fourteen-year-old, sailing the seas as a cabin boy, and settling in antebellum Charleston. His daughter claimed he piloted a sloop hauling rice down the Ashley and Cooper rivers before secession and captained the boat as a blockade-runner during the war, until Federals sank it off the Georgia coast in 1862. The family found naturalization papers dated July 2, 1866, for John Joseph Ciucevich when he applied for citizenship in Charleston. Whatever the accuracy of the oral accounts—and economic difficulties in Dalmatia led many to leave in the 1850s, especially after the failed 1848 revolutions in Europe—the story points to the fluidity of the global South.[41]

Through marriage the immigrant brothers strengthened their ties to the United States. The 1870 U.S. Census for Charleston includes "Jno. Cinciovik," a thirty-one-year-old native of Austria who listed his occupation as a seaman, his wife, Julia, a seventeen-year-old native of North Carolina, and in the household a seventeen-year-old seaman named Frank. Parish records show Julia A. Merritt marrying John Cucioci in Charleston's Roman Catholic Pro-Cathedral on May 1, 1870, in a ceremony witnessed by her sister, Catherine Merritt, and Angelo Garbaldi. The day before, the same priest, the Reverend Daniel J. Quigley, had baptized Julia Antonia Merit, a sixteen-year-old Methodist, whose sponsors were her sister, Lenora Ivanovitz, and Peter Jacobs. Julia's father worked for the railroad and raised his family in Charlotte. Brother Francis "Frank" Ciucevich later married Sarah Grogan, an Irish immigrant by way of Philadelphia.[42]

In the mid-1870s, court records put John and Frank in Georgia around the time their wives bought adjacent parcels of farmland carved out of the Savannah River Plantation Rae's Hall, which abutted the Charleston and Savannah Railroad. In 1880, the Chatham County commissioners gave John Ciucevich a license to sell liquor at the store he had opened at Five Mile Bend beside the Augusta Road. When grandson Johnny visited the farm located near the five-mile-wide arc of railroad track that splits off from the Augusta line and heads toward Charleston, the constant freight traffic he heard coming in and out of Savannah inspired a lyric in 1941. "Hear that lonesome whistle / Blowin' 'cross the trestle / Whooee! / (My mama done tol' me)," Mercer wrote in one of his more famous songs that ended with the song's title, "A Whoee-duh-whooee / Ol' clickety clack's / A-echoin' back, / The blues in the night." At the farm brother Frank helped John manage the growing business. The Ciucevich enterprises trucked foodstuffs into Savannah and sold supplies, liquor, and "near beer" to black sharecroppers and neighboring white tenants.[43]

Although the farming venture prospered, tragedy struck both Ciucevich families. Two sons of John and Julia's died within months of each other, and the priest of St. Patrick's Roman Catholic Church oversaw the burials in Savannah's cathedral cemetery. In 1888, Fred Roland, a sharecropper, robbed the Ciucevich store, savagely attacking clerk Domenico "Manigo" Cuiche. Police arrested Roland, who served time for the crime, and Manigo recovered. While Frank and Sarah had no children, John and Julia had eight more: Frank in 1878, Mary in 1879, Lillian Barbara in 1881, Edward John in 1883, Annie in 1886, Harriet in 1889, Katherine in 1891, and Lenora in 1893 — these became Johnny's Ciucevich aunts and uncles.[44] The growing family moved to Savannah proper. For several years John rented a frame building at 65 East Broad Street; his family lived upstairs, while he sold the fruits of the farm in a grocery located downstairs. In 1891, he paid Solomon Gardner four thousand dollars for the eastern half of lot 14, Franklin Ward, which contained a Federal-style brick building at 316 West Bryan Street, near the First African Baptist Church in Ellis Square. Here next to the city market the brothers opened a grocery store to sell their produce. The Ciucevich partnership prospered for four years. Then, in 1895, would-be murderer Roland escaped from prison and apparently returned to Five Mile Bend, where he mortally wounded Frank Ciucevich and brutally beat his wife, Sarah. John Ciucevich assumed his brother's affairs and took in his sister-in-law.[45]

The Ciucevich clan settled into life in Savannah. They attended St. Patrick's Catholic Church, a Romanesque brick building newly constructed at the intersection of Liberty and West Broad streets, where they associated with other immigrants living in the working-class neighborhood between the city market and railroad yards. The global network of immigration along the Atlantic coastline led numerous Austrians to seek the opportunities offered in postbellum Savannah. Family lore has them contacting "Captain John" on their arrival. As the grocery prospered, John sent sons Frank and Eddie to Belmont College in the Benedictine Abby near Julia's family in Charlotte, while the two oldest sisters, Lillie and Mary, matriculated at the Roman Catholic St. Joseph's Boarding School outside the Middle Georgia town of Washington. With the move to

Savannah, the younger children, Annie, Harriet, Kate, and Nora, took catechism at St. Patrick's Catholic School. By the 1890s, revealing their success and middle-class aspirations, the Ciucevich family transferred its membership to the Roman Catholic Cathedral of St. John the Baptist across town on Abercorn Street, where stained-glass windows made in Austria reflected the ties to the homeland. When John Ciucevich died from pneumonia at the age of sixty-five in 1899, the cathedral priest presided over the graveside service in the cemetery plot containing the remains of his first two sons. The death created a hardship on Julia. Daughter Kate remembered the family's move back to Five Mile Bend and her mother managing the truck farm. Manigo continued to sell goods at the Ciucevich store until his 1914 murder during another armed robbery.[46]

After Lillian's marriage to G. A. Mercer in 1906, the prominent attorney and his new wife advised her mother on business matters and legal affairs. Julia Ciucevich purchased in September 1908 at courthouse auction for $2,650 the townhouse at 301 East Charlton Street, cornering Lincoln Street and diagonal from the back entrance of the rectory to the Roman Catholic Cathedral of St. John the Baptist. The move to Troup Square placed Julia in a predominantly Roman Catholic neighborhood of middle-class residences, including the home a block away at 207 East Charlton in which writer Flannery O'Connor would later spend her childhood. In 1909, Julia added indoor plumbing to the 1855 three-story duplex, and converted the slave quarters at the rear of the back courtyard into a rental unit. Over the next twenty years Julia ruled her family as matriarch from the residence, often sharing her roof with her children and others in need, such as her sister-in-law, Sarah. Julia became Johnny's only living grandparent, until her death in 1929, while her daughter, Lillian, who had named her son John after her father but called him Bubba, outlived Johnny by one year, dying in Savannah at the age of ninety-five in 1977.[47]

On the advice of G. A. Mercer, Julia sold the West Bryan Street store in 1910 and used part of the proceeds to help Frank and Eddie Ciucevich get started in business. For a while Eddie lived in St. Augustine, Florida, where he met Louise Melcher and married, having several children there before returning to Savannah and moving his family into the 426 Lincoln Street apartment behind the courtyard of 301 East Charlton Street. He parlayed his share of inheritance into the ACME Plumbing Company. With improved city utilities, more residents elected to install indoor plumbing, often hiring Eddie to retrofit sewer and water lines into Savannah's older housing. On occasion G. A. Mercer got Eddie to maintain his rental properties and those of his late wife that belonged in trust to their three sons. Frank, who had married Sadie Hunthausen, took his share of inheritance and opened the Palace Pool Room and Café on West Broad Street in 1910. Prohibition laws adopted by the state of Georgia in 1907 had made it illegal to sell liquor, rendering the billiards business virtually unprofitable. Frank moved to Tybee Island in 1911 and opened the Ocean View Hotel on Savannah Beach. Tourists from town had flocked to the coast once the Savannah-Tybee Railroad reached the wide expanse of sand and water in the 1880s. By 1900, the Central of Georgia Railroad had taken over the short line and constructed as an added attraction to the beach the Tybrisa pier, with a large pavilion featuring a wraparound veranda; a dance floor and bandstand projected out over the waves. Frank sensed Tybee's need for accommodations, and the Ocean View Hotel provided them at reasonable rates along with hot meals of fried seafood and short-order dishes from its restaurant. On the side, Frank and Eddie began piloting a rum-runner to the Bahamas in which they smuggled choice illegal liquors to supply a select clientele, which years later apparently would include their teenage nephew, Johnny.[48]

The single daughters, Kate, Hattie, and Nora, lived with Julia in her East Charlton Street house as they trained as secretaries. Julia's other daughters married in 1906, and while Mary moved to Tampa, Lillie and Annie remained in Savannah and visited often. When Annie's husband, Paul Walter Rivers, from nearby Beaufort, South Carolina, died tragically about six weeks before the birth of their son, Julia took the expectant mother in and then helped raise the child named after his father. Annie apprenticed as a medical assistant at nearby Telfair Hospital for Women, often staying there overnight while Walter remained with his grandmother and aunts. According to the Ciucevich family oral history, Aunt Hattie basically raised Walter.[49]

The Ciucevich women might have ruled the roost at 301 East Charlton, but boy cousins filled the nest. Like stair steps the four boys lined up with about a year between each. The eldest of the bunch, Annie's Walter Rivers, born in October 1906, had two years on Eddie's Johnnie Ciucevich, born in July 1908. Lillian's son Johnny Mercer came in November 1909, while Frank's adopted son, Frank Ciucevich, born in August 1910, rounded out the bunch. No doubt when together these four boys ran roughshod in the house and tore up the courtyard. The family called them the "Musketeers." Walter took the lead as D'Artagnan, a role that might have helped prepare him for leadership in the Marines during World War II. Johnny Mercer would have settled for the gallant Athos, always the gentleman. The Ciucevich sisters and grandmother Julia took turns entertaining the boys by telling them stories about Captain John and singing songs, perhaps even ditties from Dalmatia. Expressing the same family loyalty, Johnny remained in contact with his Ciucevich aunts and cousins throughout his life.[50]

The character traits Johnny inherited from his Mercer and Ciucevich kin explain his behavior as a grounded southerner. He witnessed the commitment of his maternal grandmother to her brood at 301 East Charlton and internalized the importance of supporting family members. The code of honor by which the Mercers regulated themselves instilled beliefs in the boy that often clashed with the modern age. He could have followed the proscriptions of the day and remained confined by the private clubs and personal associations that accompanied a life of privilege. At times he acquiesced to the patriarchy with its paternalism as represented by these generations of Savannah's patrician class. Their example ingrained in him the expectations of a gentleman, which he demonstrated in all its contradictory fashion — remaining modest while seeking fame, defending marriage while "wenching" around, drinking excessively while being shamed for getting drunk, worshiping God while confessing stoicism, and defending the family honor by repaying others' debts. Throughout it all Johnny set his own course, sailing through the world by embracing the liberation of the jazz age, with its leveling views of race and gender and its celebration of modernism as expressed through music.

2 Early Years

. . . .

Games we used to play
While the rounds were sung
Only yesterday,
When the world was young!

ALTHOUGH REARED IN a conventional upper-class household, as a child Johnny received exposure to a wide variety of musical styles, a result of the extreme contrasts he confronted growing up in the South. From the urban bustle of Savannah to idyllic rural settings in Georgia and Virginia, from the Atlantic coast to the Blue Ridge Mountains, he enjoyed a breadth of natural environments that sustained a wealth of musical traditions derived from the region's multiracial cultural heritage. As an Episcopalian, Johnny experienced a liturgical Protestantism that varied sharply from the evangelical Baptist services he saw in the country and the charismatic Pentecostal performances he witnessed in the city. Johnny listened to sacred music ranging from organ-driven high-church hymns to a cappella spirituals and brass-band gospel. The blues and jazz he heard in the streets shared similarities with the hillbilly sounds of the mountains. These hybrid regional genres added to a distinctively commercial mass-produced national music promulgated from Tin Pan Alley and promoted by record companies and radio broadcasts. Thinking back on his childhood, Mercer recalled his musical background as being "largely Episcopalian hymns, minstrel shows, Harry Lauder records, and more than anything else, the popular songs of the day." He confessed music to be the "ruling passion of my life," placing it "first" above all else.[1]

The family recognized and encouraged Johnny's obvious musical talents. Mercer told a reporter, "I can remember what my mother says: that I could hum tunes when I was six months old." In his autobiography, Johnny claimed his Aunt Kate Ciucevich told him that at age six months he hummed back at her! He took piano as a child, although he hated his lessons and never mastered the keyboard, fearing his friends might call him a sissy. But Johnny learned to read music and play notes. "Not a Liberace, mind you," he joked to a reporter, "just a journeyman thumper, but I've never had the patience to practice. I always give up." Or as he explained to writer Henry Kane, "On the piano, I'm pretty lousy. Oh, I *can* bat out a tune, when I'm so inclined." He developed his own shorthand system to write music that identified the notes and meter and used a series of arrows to direct the tune while keeping "the rhythmic pattern in his mind," and he could jot it down on staff paper when necessary. Thus while not schooled in composition, Johnny knew his notes, could basically read sheet music, peck out songs on the piano, and sketch out tunes for arrangers to score.[2]

Johnny's formal musical training occurred at Christ Episcopal Church in Savannah, where generations of his family members had worshiped in services that reinforced the values they cherished. Lillie and her sister-in-law, Katharine, oversaw the altar guild, while Uncle Joseph Muir Lang sat on the vestry. By age six, John sang as a chorister in Christ Church's novel boys' choir, the first in Savannah. For the next eight years he studied and learned the beautiful hymns and carols for which the Church of England is justly known. Because of his love of the music, Mercer recalled that he "even went to choir practice assiduously." The adult and boys' choir and congregation performed the standards commonly heard in American Protestant sanctuaries as well as those peculiar to the worldwide Anglican Communion. Christ Church had a significant musical legacy in that brothers Charles and John Wesley, the founders of Methodism, had ministered there in 1736, and hymnist Lowell Mason had once served as rector of the parish. A massive pipe organ accompanied the singing of the harmonic hymns. The liturgical heritage of Anglican music Mercer experienced influenced his lyric writing just as the cantor's call and congregation's response in the Hebrew service appeared in the popular songs by George and Ira Gershwin, Jerome Kern, Harold Arlen, and other Jewish composers. In exploring the links between religious music and American popular song, poet and editor David Lehman noted, "Mercer was not Jewish, but I like to think of him as an honorary Jew."[3]

Certainly the lyricist's religious upbringing contributed to the frequency of angels in his imagery and the other biblical references that occasionally appear in his songs. In the days of Johnny Mercer's grandfather, when the Christ Church sanctuary boasted a circular nave, members had painted above the altar Charles Wesley's lyric, "Hark the Herald, The Angels Sing." Mercer probably knew the historic photograph of the interior and that might have inspired his "And the Angels Sing," with the line "We kiss, / And the angels sing / And leave their music ringing / In my heart." In "Dearly Beloved," the lover sings that "angel voices led me to you," just as in "I Remember You," the lover confesses, "When my life is through / And the angels ask me / To recall / The thrill of them all, / Then I shall tell them / I remember you." In "The Dixieland Band," Mercer has Gabriel as the "trumpet man who really can blast." Just as angels appeared in his lyrics, so too did the leading figures from the scriptures. Sunday school provided subject material for songs, as when the preacher recalled "Jonah in the whale, / Noah in the ark," in the lyric for "Ac-Cent-Tchu-Ate the Positive." At Christ Church, members — including children — participated in religious cantatas and pageants appropriate to the seasons of the liturgical year. Such musical lessons based on biblical stories introduced Johnny to the power of theatrical performances.[4]

Throughout his life he remained a committed Episcopalian, often attending divine services — sometimes weekly — in New York and California. His daughter, Amanda Mercer Neder, remembered Johnny might skip Sunday church but stop by later to pray, sitting on the right side of the sanctuary. She recalled, "Daddy had a Bible and read it all the time. We often read it together." Johnny's friend, the television producer William "Bill" Harbach, reported, "I hear he read the Bible. I never knew that. We never talked about that kind of stuff, but he knew the Bible." To observe Lent, Johnny quit drinking hard liquor and stuck to beer. When asked "Are you a religious man?" by a writer in the 1950s, Mercer answered, "Faith comes easy and natural to me. I don't pry; I'm not one of the modern-type looker-inners; I don't fix to examine; I don't search deeper and deeper, looking for the reasons — I just don't need any of that." Instead, he explained, "I have accepted my teachings, and my faith is pure. Yes, I'm a religious man. In a way, I'm all that goes with that." The cradle Episcopalian had heard of the global communion's missions in far-flung places and prayed for parishes in other parts of the world. As an adult, Mercer worshiped in churches wherever he traveled and particularly enjoyed touring the old cathedrals of Europe.[5]

Secular sounds filled the Mercer household, too. Johnny recalled listening to music all the time, sung by family, friends, and domestic workers, performed on the piano, or played on a record player. "I used to listen with awe and wonder to every kind of music I could get my hands on, Gypsy airs on the accordion or zither, harmonica blues, gems from Broadway, the yodels of Jimmie Rodgers, cowboy songs from the prairies, all reached my ears and touched my heart," Johnny noted in his autobiography. Thinking back, Mercer described music as "my sun on a dark day, my solace in time of pain and disappointment, and if not my life, my best friend." The family favored British culture, listening to the recordings of the D'Oyly Carte Company on the family gramophone. Johnny could quote whole verses of the Gilbert and Sullivan operettas, being particularly fond of *Iolanthe* and *The Mikado*. Mercer found the librettist W. S. Gilbert, with whom he shared a November 18 birthday, "so satirical and so intelligent" and later benefited in his own work from the wordplay he heard there. The traditional ballads of the Hebrides sung by Harry Lauder proved a family favorite, given the Mercer clan's Scottish heritage. Idealized images of England and Scotland colored the lad's perceptions as he viewed Great Britain from far-off Savannah.[6]

The most popular songs of Tin Pan Alley found their way into the household either as sheet music to be played on the square grand or as new pressings from Broadway shows to be spun on the gramophone. Johnny remembered recordings of "Evelyn, Oh, Evelyn, Won't You Kindly Quit Your Devilin'" and "When It's Apple Blossom Time in Normandie" as starting his "infatuation" with American popular song. He understood the importance of early popular songs on future songwriters such as himself: "Woody Guthrie was a boy same as I when they sang 'The Death of Floyd Collins' [about] the miner who was trapped in a cave-in for fifty some days. No Jimmy Rodgers record ever topped the sale of 'The Wreck of the Old '97' by Vernon Dalhart." As a young tot the towheaded boy climbed into the lap of his father, who sat by the fireplace softly singing turn-of-the-century favorites such as "In the Gloaming." On sunny Sunday afternoons, the Mercer family went for drives in the country, with G. A. booming boisterously "In The Good Old Summertime" and other personal favorites. Johnny recalled "being at my most impressionable when Walter Donaldson had his string of great hits: 'Mammy,' and 'How Ya Gonna Keep 'em Down on the Farm.'" Mercer's exposure to popular music proved remarkably similar to that experienced by other jazz musicians.[7]

With his Ciucevich kin Johnny explored Savannah's lowbrow entertainment. The Ciucevich sisters accompanied the boy cousins to the traveling vaudeville shows performing in the Keith Bijou and to the lectures and recitals of the Redpath Chautauquas. Johnny fondly recalled "the black-face comedians in Al G. Fields' minstrels at the old Savannah Theatre" and the carnival sideshows staged in Forsyth Park Extension. In Johnny's youth the Savannah Theatre presented all-black cast performances before segregated audiences of such shows as Noble Sissle and Eubie Blake's *Shuffle Along* or Irvin C. Miller's *Broadway Rastus*. When not offering black and white vaudeville shows, the Savannah Municipal Auditorium regularly hosted black musical groups such as W. C. Handy's Jazz Band, which 1,200 black and white patrons came out to hear in 1920. The crucial

Ciucevich connection exposed Johnny to a side of life he might otherwise have never seen.[8]

Wherever he went music seemed to surround the boy. Johnny recalled the impression made on him on first hearing the musical sensation "Ja Da" while riding with his Aunt Annie on a ferry piloted by her second husband, Morgan Pritchard. After singing the correct lyric "That's a funny little bit of melody / It's so soothing and appealing to me," it thrilled Johnny to add the saucy line, "I don't care if you don't like my ja da ja da jing, jing, jing." While visiting other Ciucevich kinfolk on Tybee, either at the Ocean View Hotel or after playing in the waves with his cousins, John heard the bands performing the latest Tin Pan Alley hits on the boardwalk at Savannah Beach. Likewise, when the Mercers traveled to Asheville to escape the heat of the summer, Johnny watched couples dancing to the tunes of the resort bands at the Grove Park Inn. Back in Savannah, party music filled the Oglethorpe Club on special occasions, and at Christmas most gatherings ended with the traditional singing of carols, a custom Mercer maintained throughout his life. Music promoted nationally through popular song sheets and recordings, sung in churches, or as common expressions of a multiracial southern culture provided the foundation on which Johnny developed his talents as a songwriter.[9]

As an accident-prone child, Johnny experienced painful incidents that created in him a lifelong fear of hospitals. On one occasion he bit his tongue nearly in two, requiring stitches from the doctor. On another he pulled a pot boiling a ham off the stove and suffered severe burns. Like other kids he received minor scrapes, but he also broke bones. When Johnny was forced to spend a summer with a leg in a cast, his mother hired an African American boy named Caesar to sit with him. When Caesar challenged Johnny's cheating at a game of go fish, Johnny irritably fired him.[10]

Deferential black servants helped make Johnny's childhood a happy one. A black nurse pushed Johnny in his perambulator around the fountain in Forsyth Park, just as other African Americans had done with generations of his ancestors. He remembered the kindness of his nanny, Sophie, whom he called "Soapy," and the cook Bertha Hall. Black maids kept the houses of family members, and black cooks prepared family meals. The writer William Dean Howells wintered in Savannah during Johnny's youth and described the domestic workers and African American hucksters who walked the streets with baskets of goods to sell calling out "A crab! Buyer! A crab!" With fondness Johnny recalled the former slave, Rachel, who worked for his maternal grandmother. He remembered her standing at the wood-burning stove frying for him a quail he had snitched from the game pouch of a hunter at Five Mile Bend, while he examined the newsprint that wallpapered her shack in the country. Decades later when following the dictates of paternalism he visited her, she remarked more than anything else she missed "walking along the big road" that stretched beside the Ciucevich land toward town. Similarly, his letters home always inquired about Big Nancy, his mother's black cook.[11]

As a white matron, Lillie interacted with African Americans on various levels. With house servants such as nurse Sophie or waiter Ben, she behaved familiarly. They appeared in family photos assisting with the children. With the black men who kept the yard and did odd jobs, however, Lillian limited her contact to giving them instructions and then leaving their pay and water on the back porch so as to have no direct physical contact with them. This racial etiquette that maintained levels of white supremacy took place around Johnny, who absorbed the meanings of deference and developed his own paternalism. Throughout his life he valued the civility expressed in the racial exchanges he saw under segregation, choosing to ignore the power relations that enforced the naked inequality. To Johnny, race "never made any difference as far as friendliness goes, never, because a mean person could be a mean white person, or a mean colored person. But a gentle person or a gentleman or a lady could be black or white." Johnny looked beyond skin color to the humanity of the individual. Although outside the Mercer household the threat of police brutality and lynching maintained white supremacy and segregation in Savannah, the South, and much of the United States, as a child Johnny would have known nothing of this inhumanity. His familiarity with black people derived from exchanges with individuals who were dependent on his family for their own well-being and who thereby showed deference to the Mercer paternalism.[12]

Lillie occupied her time overseeing the household on Hall Street and having children. The Roman Catholic–raised daughter of an Eastern European immigrant never had both feet within the magic circle of Savannah's high society. As Mrs. G. A. Mercer, she gained entrée to the events of the elite, but not having grown up with other matrons in the social set — or their debutante daughters — could prove limiting to the young and attractive second wife of the prominent businessman. She concentrated her intercourse on such activities as the church flower guild and the neighborhood garden club. On May 10, 1910, Lillie entered Johnny in a baby beauty pageant. The nearly six-month-old hazel-eyed and flaxen-haired boy won a blue ribbon. (Told of the story years later, Johnny's wife, Ginger, gave him the title for the song, "You Must Have Been a Beauti-ful Baby," and in return he gave her half of the royalties.) When Johnny was eighteen months old, G. A. and Lillie had their second child, Nancy Herndon Mercer, on July 11, 1911. Brothers Walter and Hugh attended the Massie School, while George, who had withdrawn from Woodberry Forest School to attend the Georgia Institute of Technology in Atlanta, returned home. Tragedy struck on May 11, 1914, when four-year-old Johnny's sister, Nancy, nearly three, died. The loss hit Lillie particularly hard according to her granddaughter, the dead girl's namesake. Nancy Mercer Keith Gerard recalled that her grandmother still mourned the child years after the death. The row house must have seemed empty to Lillie, for that fall Johnny started kindergarten at Miss Mamie Woolhopter's, while her stepsons, Walter and Hugh, left the Massie School for Woodberry For-est School in Virginia. Soon Lillie got pregnant, and she and G. A. had their last child, Juliana, on August 1, 1915. That year eldest son George, having remained in Savannah courting his future wife, married Bessie Wheless. G. A. watched one child leave the nest for good as his last child arrived.[13]

With the purchase on June 16, 1909, of Burnside Island, with its view of Green and Ossabaw islands and the open waters of the Atlantic Ocean beyond, the Mercers began spending summers on the Georgia coast. In the past they had visited the resorts southeast of the city that their grandfather had sailed around as commodore of the yacht club. The McAlpins had owned Burnside Island in the nineteenth century, growing sea island cotton on its three hundred acres. Now, however, the speculators intended to develop the back fields as suburban residen-tial housing for Savannah while saving the shoreline for family and friends. G. A. partnered with J. Ward Mott in purchasing the whole island, which came with a large frame cottage built in 1906 that overlooked the confluence of the Burnside and Vernon rivers above where they emptied into the Atlantic Ocean. Lillian named the spot Vernon View. G. A. reserved for family members the choice lo-cations beside the old house that he initially retained for himself, with brother Robert Lee Mercer and sister Nannie Herndon Mercer Lang taking the lots to the left and right of the structure on the bluff. By 1911 several cottages clustered at Vernon View, where brothers George, Walter, Hugh, and Johnny could cavort with cousins Joe Mercer and Mercer Lang.[14]

The development of Burnside Island expanded opportunities for specula-tion in real estate as G. A. Mercer's business took off in the early decades of the twentieth century. In 1912, he advertised the suburban Vernon View, "the ideal home spot where cooling breezes blow," as the choice location for cottages and bungalows. By 1913, the Savannah Bank and Trust Company — with resources valued at $1.2 million — named G. A. Mercer to its board of directors, on which served other family members. In 1915, he reorganized his holdings into several entities, including the new G. A. Mercer Company and the Burnside Island Development Company, which had as its secretary his friend, George W. Hunt. As the company graded construction sites for sale, real-estate speculation fueled bank profits that by 1917 had increased to $4.25 million. Through shrewd real-estate investments G. A. Mercer became a wealthy man.[15]

To reach Burnside Island the family traveled south on Abercorn Street to Victory Drive and east toward Thunderbolt before turning onto Ferguson Avenue, the same route used by the race cars in the famous competitions for the Vanderbilt Cup. All of Savannah remembered the excitement watching those early automobile races through which the city reached out to the world. Loziers made in the United States competed against Italian Fiats, German Benzes, French Renaults, and even Trenton, New Jersey, Mercer Raceabouts. Hugh and Walter shared with young John the stories of speeds reached on the straightaway down White Bluff Road and the harrowing twists and turns made by the drivers on the curve at Montgomery Cross Road and the bend at Sandfly. The retelling of the races in Johnny's autobiography reads as if he witnessed himself the derring-do of the stock car drivers who reached the fastest speeds yet clocked — some seventy miles per hour — but at the tender age of two when the city hosted the final race in 1911, it is unlikely he saw much and instead unconsciously embraced his older brothers' stories as his own.[16]

The house at Vernon View enabled the Mercers to spend idyllic summers enjoying the natural beauty of the Georgia coast. Johnny remembered with fondness the long twelve-mile drive from town down the crushed oyster shell road of Ferguson Avenue and past Bethesda Home for Boys, where G. A. served as treasurer of the Union Society. Once the car crossed the new plank causeway built by the Burnside Island Development Company to get over the tributaries and tidal marshes and onto the island, the boy felt as if he had landed in a different world. During part of the summer in these years before World War I the family remained ensconced in the red-tin-roofed white-frame cottage set high off the ground with its broad-screened porch and open vista. Only G. A. traveled to Savannah to go to his office and to bring back supplies. From this somewhat isolated outpost overlooking the river coursing through the marsh grass, the young boy confronted the splendor of nature. Forevermore he heard the wind whistling or a bird calling and saw the bright blue sky with a golden sun or the silvery moon sparkling on the water.[17]

Johnny became enamored with the black servants at Vernon View who helped with household chores by cooking, babysitting, and doing yard work. Coastal Georgia's Geechee people displayed a traditional folk culture that contrasted sharply with what Johnny witnessed among urban African Americans in Savannah. The domestic help lived a few miles up the Back River from Vernon View at Pin Point, an African American community in which U.S. Supreme Court Justice Clarence Thomas would be born in 1948. These black folks descended from the former slaves who had occupied nearby Ossabaw Island or had worked the rice and later sea island cotton plantations along the Back, Burnside, and Vernon rivers. Now they labored seasonally in the Pin Point cannery A. S. Varn and Son Company, where local workers shucked oysters and processed shrimp and crab. From black adults and their children, his playmates, Johnny learned to speak as a kind of second language Gullah-Geechee, with its African grammatical structures and peculiar words. Occasionally he accompanied servants to the Sweet Field of Eden Baptist Church in Pin Point, where the black congregation sang spirituals, humming and swaying to the sound of the music or joyously engaging in a call-and-response ring shout. At other times the boy listened as the servants quietly sang hymns, work songs from the fields and cannery, or lullabies. The exposure cultivated in him not only a tolerance for something different but also an eagerness to hear and appreciate something new. The young Johnny embraced the world of music with an open yet discerning mind.[18]

Visitors frequented Vernon View, as when the Ciucevich aunts came to call on Lillian. Often Annie Rivers brought Walter to stay with his cousin, Johnny. Instead of Savannah's hot, dusty squares and brick streets, the boys roamed the palmetto thickets and salt marshes of the low country. Cousin Walter remembered being accompanied by Eli, Caesar, and Tommy — the children of the house servants — to pick huckleberries that brother Walter blended with fresh cream from the cow borrowed from Bethesda to make into ice cream for Sunday dinner. Having the run of the island, the boys played in the tidal creeks and under the pine trees on the high ground. Here they came across the cottonmouth moccasin and the equally deadly eastern diamondback rattler. More than fifty years later, Walter shuddered thinking back on those snakes and their habitats under the brush that the boys crawled through.[19]

Voracious readers of such juvenile fiction as the Swift Brothers and Penrod, the boys imagined themselves in the adventure stories. On one occasion while at Vernon View, Johnny's Aunt Katharine Mercer entertained her sister, Caroline Couper Stiles Lovell, who later gained fame for publishing a collection of romantic anecdotes about the antebellum owners of the sea island plantations titled *The Golden Isles of Georgia*. The visit by the writer evolved into a challenge to the white and black youth around the houses on the Point to compose and illustrate their own stories. The black children wrote about animals in situations similar to the trickster tales they heard from their elders. Johnny and Walter described animals too, but as threats — sharks, rattlesnakes, raccoons, and bears to be killed. In talking about nature, though, Johnny could not omit songbirds, for in his prose he hears the trills of robins.[20]

The creative minds of the close cousins led them into literary pursuits as both Johnny and Walter wrote song lyrics, poetry, and prose. As a student at Benedictine Military School in 1924, Walter crafted personal histories for the class annual, *The Cadet*. Two years later at Woodberry Forest School, Johnny would do the same on its yearbook, *The Fir Tree*. The death of Walter's father, Paul Walter Rivers, before his birth left the boy with questions regarding his ancestry. Walter had inherited a collection of poetry written by his grandfather, the Confederate veteran G. W. O. Rivers from Walterboro, South Carolina. Drawing from this heritage, Walter began writing poems, as did Johnny, the cousins reading their work to each other. In the 1920s, Walter wrote a poem called "Long Search" that he dedicated to Johnny. The lines revealed a deep understanding of the future lyricist: "What ambition can make a man belong / To lonely roads, and steel him to each blow / That seeks to strike from his grim mouth his song, / And bruise the lips that sing — I do not know; / But this I know: he wears the flesh to bone / In his long search, and mostly walks alone." Johnny developed a similar theme for a *St. Louis Woman* song with the lines "Free an' easy, that's my style, / Howdy do me, watch me smile, / Fare-the-well me after a while, 'Cause I gotta roam / An' any place I hang my hat is home!"[21]

The boys rarely missed two annual events in Savannah that showcased urban culture. For years the African American community celebrated Easter with a parade on West Broad Street (now Martin Luther King Jr. Boulevard). Often G. A. and Lillian Mercer accompanied the Ciucevich aunts and the boys, joining other white people in cars, buggies, and carriages as they lined the wide street to watch the spectacle. Johnny particularly liked the energetic stepping of the Colored Elks Club members as they marched by. Walter recalled black ladies promenading in evening gowns and high heels with bright flowered hats and the gentlemen in tuxedoes, white ties and tails, and orange shoes — a subtle mocking of their white neighbors that Walter dismissed as inappropriate attire. Certainly Johnny and Walter appreciated the jazz they heard when individuals playing trumpets, clarinets, and banjos joined together in makeshift combos to entertain the crowd. The boys studied the buck dancers on the sidewalks of Liberty and Bull streets beside the brick walls and stone arches of the DeSoto Hotel. A reflection of the region's hybrid culture, the festive occasion brought black and white people together in an otherwise segregated Savannah.[22]

Another annual spectacle in Savannah that enthralled Johnny and Walter took place in the Ogeechee Road neighborhood of Brownville, where they and other boys followed the parade marking the annual return of Daddy Grace to his flock of followers at the United House of Prayer for All People. Bishop Charles "Sweet Daddy" Grace had twisted Pentecostalism into a cult of personality that through storefront churches had found converts up and down the Eastern Seaboard and in California. Periodically the Charlotte, North Carolina–based minister visited his congregations with annual pilgrimages through the streets of such towns as Savannah. The various groups of the denomination wore distinctive uniforms of vivid hues as they marched in procession announcing the arrival of Daddy Grace and escorting him into the church, setting off wild celebrations that combined ceremony with ecstasy to the beat of African drums. Inside the sanctuary, the congregation joined a gospel band in making lively music as the leader received the tributes of his followers. African Americans put on the event before a largely black audience, while some white people watched the festivities unfold and listened to the proceedings taking place in the United House of Prayer for All People. Jimmie McIntire remembered Daddy Grace as "a wonderful preacher" and that "he didn't object to you coming." To Johnny the sounds he heard differed from the ring shouts and spirituals sung in the Sweet Field of Eden Baptist Church in Pin Point. The urban gospel music with all the emotional carrying on stood at the polar opposite of the liturgical hymns sung at Christ Church.[23]

With George married and Hugh and Walter at Woodberry, the older brothers rarely saw Johnny, and the birth of sister Juliana in 1915 occupied his mother and left him to play with his cousins, Johnnie and Frank Ciucevich and Walter Rivers, and with neighborhood kids from the east side of Forsyth Park. Several of Savannah's most prominent citizens resided along these few blocks. The Mercers lived in 118 East Hall near the corner with Abercorn Street just steps from the fountain. A block north on Abercorn lived the C. G. Bell family with sons Charles and Malcolm "Mac" Bell. A block south on Abercorn lived the D. B. Hull family with their son Dudley. Family friend and local attorney Francis P. McIntire had moved his family into their newly built home at 220 East Hall Street in 1914. Johnny welcomed into the neighborhood gang the boys James W. "Jimmie" and Pope Barrow "P. B." and occasionally their sister, Cornelia McIntire. In the next block across Lincoln Street lived Uncle Joe and Aunt Nannie Mercer Lang and cousin Mercer Lang at 302 East Hall Street.[24]

These boys in the neighborhood became Johnny's close friends. They spent their spare change on Tutti Frutti ice cream at Leopold's, a fruit parlor that Greek immigrant brothers Peter, George, and Basil opened in 1919 on the corner of East Gwinnett and Habersham streets. The children roller-skated on the brick sidewalks or played in the swept square in front of the Massie School games like kick the can and hunter, holler, hero. The competitive half-rubber, or one-o-cat, involved pitching a bottle cap or half of the rubber insides of a golf ball at a batter wielding a broomstick. Indigenous to Savannah and similar to baseball, the sport required only three or four players and a linear trajectory. P. B. McIntire recalled the games being "played almost daily in Calhoun Square and I sweated many an hour cutting those damn sponge rubber balls in half—exactly in half—and also fiddling with broomsticks to get 'em just so." The boys rounded up stray golf balls at the country club and in time took up that sport too, with Johnny becoming an avid player as a young adult. They went on campouts as members of Boy Scout Troop 11. Sponsored by Christ Church under such scoutmasters as A. H. Stoddard, the boys gathered palmetto branches for the annual procession of the palms announcing the start of Holy Week. They volunteered to be "accident victims" for Juliette Gordon Low's Girl Guides to practice first aid on and received a "co'cola" for their efforts. Years later, Johnny remembered going on his first date wearing his Boy Scout uniform, and he wrote songs for his grandson's Cub Scout Den and for Savannah Boy Scout Troop 60.[25]

Boys throughout Savannah organized into neighborhood gangs that defended their turf in a chauvinistic manner. Johnny and the upper-class, mostly Protestant boys who went to Massie joined groups with sporting militia-sounding names like the Red Hussars and the Confederate Grays that roamed the area south of the school between Forsyth Park and East Broad Street, on whose other side stretched a railroad yard and a black community where similarly organized youth patrolled the streets. Running north of Massie School and east of Colonial Park Cemetery through the squares along Houston Street lived working-class Irish families with "rough" boys in gangs with names like the Old Fort

Bunch. Despite the admonitions of their parents, the Ciucevich cousins often played with their Irish classmates, as did middle-class Roman Catholics like Walter Rivers, who lived in Troup Square, which lay between the two neighborhoods. Johnny recalled in his autobiography that the boys often bullied outsiders and occasionally fought when the gangs clashed. A youth caught by the other side might wind up tied to a tree. The neighborhood gangs competed each New Year's Eve with the building of huge bonfires in several of Savannah's squares, fueled by old crates and wooden boxes the boys would have been stockpiling since Thanksgiving. Like those ancient Scots who lit the piers in the Highlands, Johnny participated in a centuries-old tradition that valued communal affirmation through celebration. In Savannah people walked the streets to see the fires and greet their neighbors on the festive occasion accompanied by singing and drinking. Just as Georgia's founder, General James E. Oglethorpe, had intended with his design for the first planned city in the United States, the wards around the squares functioned as intact communities.[26]

As a port city with a significant immigrant population for the South, Savannah observed a variety of celebrations every year. Within months of being established in 1733, the community welcomed Sephardic and Ashkenazi Jewish settlers who founded the congregation of Mickve Israel, later building its Gothic temple and assimilating into local life. German Lutherans reached the colony early too, with new arrivals founding a German Friendly Society. The Scots organized a St. Andrews Society just as the Irish established a Hibernian Society. They all celebrated distinctive religious holidays. Christmas topped the list for the boys because of the sweets and the gifts. Johnny enjoyed the caroling that took place on the streets and in private homes. At holiday parties, crowds gathered around the "flowing bowl" to drink the local favorite, Chatham Artillery Punch, and sing Christmas songs. At other times men broke out into barbershop quartets. With its large Irish community, Savannah observed St. Patrick's Day in style. A parade on Bull Street featured the city's leading citizens of Irish descent, numerous civic groups, and marching bands. On one occasion, so taken with the performance of Savannah's Irish Jasper Greens, young Johnny followed the marching band out of town to a picnic, where he stayed before returning home that evening to his worried parents.[27]

The perceived safety of what appeared to be an insular community actually masked a Savannah and a South operating in a global environment as World War I brought home to Johnny the reality of death. Not yet ten years old when the conflict began, the boy watched brother Walter, who had just graduated from Woodberry Forest School in 1917, enlist in the army. Brother Hugh still attended classes at the Virginia prep school. Thanks to the armistice signed in 1918, Walter avoided deployment overseas, so his tour of military duty proved short-lived. Instead, he retraced his father's footsteps to the University of Georgia, where he also pledged Sigma Alpha Epsilon. Yet the deaths of "old boys" from Woodberry made the bloodshed and military glory very real, as did the gold stars that Johnny remembered in the windows of Savannah houses where families had lost a loved one in the fighting. His Aunt Annie contributed to the war effort as a nurse on the U.S. Army's medical staff, processing recruits on Parris Island.[28]

During the heady postwar years the G. A. Mercer Company expanded with the growing economy by speculating in real estate, taking in the sons as employees. Eldest brother George had found employment outside the family as an engineer for the firm of his wife Bessie Wheless's family, the Savannah Blowpipe Company, from which he developed the Steel Products Company, soon turning out Great Dane truck trailers. His business acumen filling a void in goods transportation at just the right moment — the manufacture of truck trailers that could carry removable transfer containers shipped by the railroads — made him a multimillionaire. In 1921, the G. A. Mercer Company added a line of insurance when Walter, returning from Athens with a master's degree in business, partnered with F. G. Vinson as the subsidiary Mercer and Vinson Real Estate and Insurance Company, while Hugh worked for the firm as a stenographer. With offices at 7–9 East York Street next to the Chatham County Courthouse, the company managed rental properties and financed development in metropolitan resort areas in the growing South. G. A. Mercer advertised a full line of services, including "law, real estate and investment banking." As an investment concern, his business sold shares to raise capital with which it then bought property on speculation. The profits from the real-estate development enabled him to pay his shareholders dividends at rates higher than could be earned off interest at a bank. Investors joined G. A. Mercer in gambling over the potential value of land.[29]

Following generations of Mercer, Wayne, and Anderson ancestors, and as a measure of his financial success, in 1920 G. A. Mercer assumed the presidency of the Union Society, the charity that ran the Bethesda Home for Boys, America's oldest orphanage. Despite compulsory chapel services that followed a Protestantism favored by low-church Episcopalians, Bethesda emphasized being "nonsectarian." On its board sat Jewish and Gentile men drawn from the elite ranks of Savannah, demonstrating the success of assimilation and expressing a shared patrician "ideal of gentility." In 1920, the managers of the Union Society included

Leopold Adler, Frank G. Bell, Wymberly W. DeRenne, and East Hall Street neighbors Abram Minis and George J. Baldwin.[30]

Founded in 1740 by the evangelist George Whitefield, Bethesda took in white boys orphaned or abandoned by their parents and under a strict moral code taught them self-discipline and self-reliance to become honorable citizens adjusted for a productive life. The Union Society assumed responsibility for the buildings and five-hundred-acre farm located south of Thunderbolt along Ferguson Avenue. Here the young charges raised foodstuffs in vegetable gardens and produced fresh dairy products from a herd of cows. The wards received an education through the eighth grade, with the most capable being sent to Savannah for high school and the brightest then receiving scholarships to attend technical school or college. Through paternalism, a superintendent and his wife nurtured a homelike environment for the hundred boys who ranged in age from five to eighteen. Thankful for the opportunity, many of the young men recalled the bucolic institution with fondness.[31]

During the 1920s, Bethesda prospered, largely because of G. A. Mercer's contributions in support of the new superintendent, Ole Wycliff Burroughs. A Pittsburgh native hired in 1915, Burroughs initiated a series of changes at the institution such as arranging competitive sports for the boys. He inaugurated an annual minstrel show in 1916 in which the boys performed in blackface, possibly the first minstrels ever seen by seven-year-old Johnny. Burroughs promoted historical dramas and plays as ways to instill self-confidence and let the boys generate their own entertainment, with performances on the orphanage's Anniversary Day, April 23 — St. George's Day. An English Christmas featuring a boar's head processional, the bringing in of the Yule log on which sat the smallest boys, caroling around a wassail bowl, and a visit by Santa became a Bethesda institution after 1920. Rewarding adherence to the code of honor, G. A. Mercer sponsored two annual prizes for Bethesda boys — for courtesy and for reliability — giving the winners five-dollar gold pieces for the first time in April 1917.[32]

As president of the board Mercer solicited public support to shore up Bethesda's finances. He placed a large advertisement in the *Savannah Morning News* that featured Burroughs requesting donations in a pitch called "Heart to Heart," which ended with Mercer volunteering to write anyone's last will and testament for free as long as it included a bequest of more than a thousand dollars to Bethesda. The ads ran on Sundays for most of the decade and helped build the Union Society's meager endowment. As noted in the 1921 annual report, "For the first time in years, the income had been sufficient to cover maintenance."

Himself a member of the Order of the Cincinnati, Mercer encouraged the National Society of the Colonial Dames of Georgia to finish the construction of the Whitefield Chapel begun in 1916 and modeled after the 1748 All Hallows' Church in Maryland, where the evangelist had preached. Bethesda dedicated the chapel on Anniversary Day in 1925.[33]

Just as his father had demonstrated social rank by introducing him to the charity of the Union Society, G. A. brought his sons to Bethesda so that they might meet and assist others less fortunate than themselves. Johnny spent a lot of time on the sprawling rural campus, with its gardens, dairy, and pastures stretching to the Back River. The Mercers attended the festive processional every Christmas and watched theatrical performances, such as *Gammer Gurton's Needle*, as well as historical pageants, such as the *Spirit of the Savannah River* in 1919. Ole Burroughs nurtured in Johnny an interest in acting, and later both performed in the community theater. Johnny maintained a friendship with Bethesda boy Lee Jones, whose musical talents took him to NBC Radio, where he originated the quiz show format and worked with Bob Hope. These associations with Bethesda schooled Johnny in paternalistic gentility but also reinforced lessons of simple fairness, and he remained committed to the institution for life.[34]

Compared to Bethesda's disadvantaged youths, Johnny had it easy as a doted-on younger son of a much older father and an overly indulgent mother in a well-off family. Accustomed to having his way, he often did as he pleased. Acknowledging Mercer's "wonderful personality" and observing that "everybody that knew him liked him," friend Jimmie McIntire also recognized that Johnny "was a little bit wild, I would say," although "he never harmed anybody." Melancholia occasionally struck, and when such mood swings altered Johnny's behavior, his friends gave him a wide berth. As a teenager Mercer indulged in alcohol and tobacco; a photograph from the dedication of the Whitefield Chapel at Bethesda appears to show a fifteen-year-old Johnny smoking a cigarette behind the structure. Although he might have picked up some bad habits from the wards of the orphanage, it is perhaps more likely he got them from his older brothers and their prep-school chums. Whatever struggles he faced, Mercer's modest behavior and common outlook derived in part from these early contacts with Bethesda boys, from whom he learned the values of opportunity and charity as leavenings for the injustices of life. Lacking pretension, Johnny cultivated an everyman attitude that made him equally at ease on city sidewalks, in the stands at Little League games, in the parlors of high society, or on the sets with Hollywood stars. He took to heart his father's advice: "You need to have friends in all walks of life."[35]

By 1920, the Mercer family had changed addresses for the first time in a decade. With the older boys out of school but still living at home and with a six-year-old daughter, Juliana, G. A. Mercer moved the family out of the Hall Street house and into a new apartment in the complex he built at 1007 Whitaker Street between West Waldburg and West Park streets at the southern corner of Forsyth Park. The move took Johnny away from his playmates in the eastern neighborhood gang that congregated around the Massie schoolyard and Calhoun Square. To reach them, the ten-year-old had to cross the entire diagonal expanse of the grassy and overgrown park alone. These at times frightening journeys when members of opposing gangs might be hiding in the azaleas must have inspired him to write the lyric "Just like a child / Who, late from school, / Walks bravely home through the park," for Henry Mancini's 1969 tune, "Whistling Away the Dark." Perhaps Johnny's complaining convinced Lillie and G. A. Mercer to return to the east side of Forsyth; by 1922, the family occupied a duplex at 226 East Gwinnett Street. The Mercers lived in the right-hand side of the two-story frame duplex originally built in 1883 that ran along Lincoln Street. Savannahians regard this house as the childhood home of Johnny Mercer. While it is true his family lived here until after the death of his father, Johnny rarely stayed in the house, for shortly after its purchase, he matriculated at Woodberry Forest School in Virginia during nine months of the year and spent his summers on the Atlantic coast at Vernon View or in the Blue Ridge Mountains.[36]

Certainly the legacy of Scottish settlers in North Carolina and the number of challenging golf courses built into the highland terrain attracted the Mercers to Asheville, but its mountain climate proved to be the most enticing reason to visit: even in the hottest days of summer, the breezes kept the area temperate, with low humidity. Victims of tuberculosis found the high altitude helped their breathing. As a hypochondriac who often complained of his health, G. A. Mercer sought relief from asthma. For decades the beautiful scenery and summer retreats in the Blue Ridge Mountains had attracted wealthy southerners. The arrival of the railroad opened the area to cosmopolitan vacationers such as George W. Vanderbilt, who chose a view of Mount Pisgah for his French chateau–inspired Biltmore Estate. When G. A. arrived in Asheville, the rambling Queen Anne Battery Park Hotel had dominated the center of town since 1886. W. G. Raoul of Atlanta opened in 1899 the picturesque Manor with its English country house feeling and flower gardens tucked into the western slope of Sunset Mountain. Nearby, in 1913, Dr. E. W. Grove dedicated his rustic Grove Park Inn, catering to the wealthiest visitors with its Japanese-style rubble exterior walls, sweeping lobby supported by timbers, and rock grottoes. A handful of other hostelries operated in the area. In these resorts, Johnny heard live some of the nationally famous jazz bands as they traveled the summer circuit.[37]

Like his ancestors who had visited the hot springs in Virginia or the racetrack at Saratoga, G. A. Mercer began staying at the resorts in Asheville for several weeks each summer. He soon brought the family and rented rooms in a boarding house. Whether or not they lodged in the Old Kentucky Home managed by Julia Westall Wolfe, the novelist's mother, it is probable that she crossed the path of G. A. Mercer when engaging in real estate. One year the Mercers booked at the Manor and another year took rooms in the Battery Park Hotel, where Johnny recalled watching teenage girls preparing for the winter debutante season by learning the latest dance steps taught by a young instructor named Moses Teichman. (Decades later, Johnny crafted a playful lyric in honor of the by-then world-famous dancer who went by a professional name. After Kathryn Murray heard the song "Arthur Murray Taught Me Dancing in a Hurry," she wrote Johnny: "Arthur thinks that the special words that you wrote were a Christmas present just for him. Of course, I'm sure that you meant them for me since you told me yourself that you would rather dance with me than with Arthur any day." Mercer might take issue with her as he later suggested she liked to lead.) Perhaps Johnny read or had read to him the sentimental short stories with surprise endings written by O. Henry, who as William Sidney Porter summered in Asheville and was buried there in 1910. Those lazy weeks in the North Carolina mountains left memories that stayed with the fellow.[38]

Once familiar with the resort town, G. A. Mercer entered a hot real-estate market in 1923 primed by reports of Asheville's growing tourist trade. At the forefront stood Dr. E. W. Grove, who helped drive the boom by purchasing his competitors, the Manor, and the old Battery Park Hotel, which he bulldozed at the end of the 1923 season. Doctors built sanitariums for tuberculosis patients, while investors opened hotels that catered to patients' families and seasonal boarders. In June 1923, G. A. Mercer began construction on the Princess Anne Hotel, a three-story shingle-style L-shaped structure at the intersection of Chestnut Street and Furman Avenue. Its sixty rooms featured private telephones, big bay windows, and adjacent bathrooms with hot and cold water. The sharp lines and light interior of the hotel at 301 East Chestnut Street offered a bright, modern alternative to the older resorts.[39] After the Princess Anne opened in January 1924, the Mercers always stayed there when visiting the town that bustled with tourist activity. G. A. and Lillian bought several house lots near the golf course and some along Merrimon Avenue that within a year they flipped to other buyers. G. A. became an active member of the Asheville Real Estate Board and opened an office for the company in town.[40]

In *You Can't Go Home Again*, Thomas Wolfe captures the spirit of speculation that infused the Asheville of Johnny's youth. "The faces of natives and strangers alike appeared to be animated by some secret and unholy glee . . . drunk with an intoxication which never made them weary, dead, or sodden, and which never wore off . . . Everyone bought real estate . . . to buy, always to buy, to pay whatever price was asked, and to sell again within two days at any price one chose to fix. It was fantastic." After criticizing the destruction of the once grand Battery Park Hotel that graced the center of town, Wolfe goes on to observe, "They signed their names to papers calling for the payment of fabulous sums, and resold their land the next day to other madmen who signed away their lives with the same careless magnificence. On paper, their profits were enormous, but their 'boom' was already over and they would not see it. They were staggering beneath obligations to pay which none of them could meet — and still they bought."[41]

In Asheville while his father bought and sold, Johnny fed on a steady diet of music. Not only did he hear the latest tunes performed on boarding-house pianos by vacationers, but he hung around the resorts to listen as dance bands played the current Tin Pan Alley hits. On a visit in 1923, G. A. Mercer had noted "a convention of musical people from all over the U. S. in Asheville with headquarters in the [Battery Park] Hotel & the place is lively with concerts, etc." As a teenager spending part of his summer holiday away from Woodberry Forest School in the mountains, Johnny remembered going to performances of the Jan Garber Orchestra in nearby Hendersonville and dancing with older girls, while on other nights he might have heard the Blue Paradise Orchestra play at the Kenilworth Inn. Watching his parents dance to the sweet music might have inspired his "At the Jazz Band Ball" lyric: "In a cozy corner we can flip our wig / Like Mommy and Daddy did." In his autobiography he describes music as "omnipresent" in Asheville. An itinerate black piano player "ragging" a tune without the aid of sheet music made a strong impression on the boy. The styles he heard ran the gamut, from classical and Tin Pan Alley to ragtime, hot jazz, and hillbilly. During the 1920s , Asheville nurtured the careers of Jimmie Rodgers, the so-called father of country music, as well as the Carter Family and bluegrass pioneer Earl Scruggs, to name only the most famous of the hillbilly performers.[42]

Similarities abound between Rodgers and Mercer. While twelve years the senior, Rodgers found the same inspirations in the Mississippi of his youth as

Johnny experienced in Georgia. Jimmie listened to southern railroad men, black and white, sing blues that he interpreted into country, while Johnny turned the vernacular music he heard sung by black and white workers in town and along the coast into jazz. Suffering hardship as a motherless child in the sand-hills section of Mississippi, where his father occasionally cropped cotton, Rodgers moved to the thriving railroad junction of Meridian, where he met street toughs and visited black juke joints before being sent to live with a spinster aunt in the country. Like Mercer, Rodgers attended the Al G. Fields Minstrel Shows and imitated the blackfaced vaudevillians. He loved the new celluloid flickers at the picture shows. He enjoyed barbershop harmonizing and singing Tin Pan Alley hits around the piano with friends. His musically trained aunt, fiddle-playing kinsmen, and preacher uncle exposed him to a variety of musical styles, from the classics to hillbilly and sacred music. Like his father, Jimmie joined the railroad as a brakeman, a symbolic job for a restless soul, while Johnny rode the rails so frequently that the imagery fills his lyrics. Mercer mostly wrote the lyrics for Louis Armstrong to sing, while Rodgers actually provided the vocals to Armstrong's trumpet on the 1930 recording of "Blue Yodel No. 9," a landmark musical number that simply underscores the fluidity of blues, hillbilly, and jazz music in this transitional age. As Rodgers biographer Nolan Porterfield notes about the hybridity of southern music that derived from the region's multiracial culture, "The divisions, more imagined than real, existed largely in the minds of naïve fans and feckless scholar-critics more intent on writing about music than on listening to it." A potential job on the railroad — and a case of tuberculosis — cut Rodgers loose from Mississippi and brought him to Asheville in 1927 on the first of many stops as a rambler caught up in the southern diaspora.[43]

Although he did not know it, Johnny began severing his own ties to Georgia when as a boy he accompanied his family to North Carolina and then began school in Virginia. Like his father before him, widower G. A. concluded he could best benefit his boys by sending them off to boarding school. They joined a long line of kinfolk who attended Woodberry Forest School beginning back in 1903, when his brother-in-law's family had enrolled their boy, G. Hermann Lang, in the private academy. Located on rolling piedmont plantation land outside Orange, Virginia, Woodberry had attracted others connected to Savannah, such as distant Mercer cousin Jefferson Randolph Anderson. The school's origins dated to 1889, when Confederate Captain Robert S. Walker hired a tutor to educate his sons and neighboring boys on the grounds of the estate once owned by James Madison's brother William, which included a house designed by Thomas

Jefferson. The academy prospered, and Walker's son, J. Carter Walker, became headmaster in 1897. Under his direction over the next fifty years, the school institutionalized a policy of academic excellence and Christian duty steeped in the code of southern honor. Such a focus on gentlemanly character suited G. A. Mercer, who had sent George to the institution in 1904 with a note to the headmaster: "Here he is; keep him, *please*, and see what *you* can do with him." G. A. enrolled Walter in 1912 and Hugh in 1914; they joined their cousins, George Mercer Lang and Joseph Lang Mercer.[44]

The rigorous and cosmopolitan curriculum prepared students for a life in the professions. While nondenominational, Woodberry emphasized it wanted "no boy... whose parents do not sympathize with the Christian work in the School, or are unwilling to give to it their hearty support." Weekly "Sacred Study" and compulsory chapel reinforced this Protestant training. The school had six forms — comparable to grades seven through twelve — the boys passed through to graduate in order to enter college directly. In each form students took English and a foreign language — Spanish, French, or German — as well as mathematics. The curriculum recommended Latin for three years and offered general science courses, physics, chemistry, and history. Woodberry required a C grade in all classes to earn a diploma. The school's emphasis on academic integrity and sportsmanship required students to study and play hard. A contemporary of Johnny's at Woodberry corresponded with a friend: "I sure am sorry about not writing before, but they just keep you so busy up here that you don't get a chance to write. I like it up here though." The student explained the schedule: "They keep us in school until three o'clock and then keep you out for athletics until about five and then keep you in study hall from seven until a quarter to ten. Except for this I have the whole day to myself." Then he closed his letter with something Johnny might have added, "Must study French. Hard as hell." Having grown up with an accomplished baseball player for a father, the Mercer boys played the sport at Woodberry. The academic year began in September and ran into June, with a two-week break at Christmas and a weeklong break in March. Otherwise the boys remained on the campus, for the school rarely granted leaves of absence. Christmas, spring break, and during the summer, Walter and Hugh rejoined the family, filled with stories they shared with Johnny.[45]

Taking care to provide for his youngest son the same excellent education he had for the previous three, G. A. enrolled an excited twelve-year-old John Herndon Mercer at Woodberry Forest School in the fall of 1922. The anecdotes the boy had heard from his brothers and cousins, and his own memories of visiting them on campus, had built up an anticipation that nothing short of matriculation could satisfy. Thinking back on the occasion, he wrote for the school yearbook in 1934:

A callow youth I packed my trunks
And entered on five years of flunks
And if I'm better off today
Then this is all I have to say
The Good Lord must look after fools and drunks.

Johnny remembered that when he arrived, he and Malcolm Monroe "were the littlest boys in the school." In an early letter home Johnny wrote glowingly of his initial experiences. G. A. responded to the headmaster, J. Carter Walker: "John writes that he is very much carried away with Woodberry and is not homesick. He is a very independent boy, he has some individuality and I hope you will be proud of him." The men would live to see the boy become one of the institution's most illustrious alumni.[46]

Several incidents during Johnny's first years at school suggest he might have suffered from what today is called attention deficit hyperactivity disorder. Behavioral traits such as "eternal foot patting and drumming over his head" plagued Johnny and annoyed his classmates and teachers. Regular evaluations of Johnny's academic progress point to problems that characterize an inability to focus. In subjects that interested him, such as spelling and English literature, he made high scores, but the grades dropped in classes he disliked, such as foreign languages and mathematics. In one evaluation, Headmaster Walker noted, "I feel greatly discouraged about John. He is capable, but incorrigibly lazy." Certainly others believed he acted absentmindedly and overlooked his own health, conclusions reached by his father, a hypochondriac. Two months into Johnny's first term, G. A. Mercer informed the headmaster, "John writes me that he has poison ivy on his face. He had this in Asheville when he was there. Will you please see that he receives the proper medical attention, for if it is left to John himself, I'm afraid he will neglect it." A month later, the father wrote the headmaster: "John complained of his knee hurting him. Will you please see that he lets the Doctor look at it as John is liable to neglect it, and I know of several cases which led to very serious results through neglect." Aware of his tendency to suffer from injuries, Johnny later joked about it when proposing a song titled "Accident Prone, Leave Me Alone."[47]

Similar to Bethesda orphanage — being housed on an old plantation in Georgian red brick buildings — the prep school's main campus occupied a small portion of more than a thousand acres of Virginia piedmont land that made up the grounds of Woodberry Forest School. As Johnny remembered when writing his Latin teacher, Mr. R. W. D. Taylor, "I presume all Woodberry is still divided into three parts — the bulletin board, the study hall, and bounds." Playing games and doing other outdoor activities occupied the time of students when not in class. The patriarchal structure of the Old South persisted at Woodberry where, as one scholar concluded, "There was an emphasis on family, on hospitality, on honor, on the role of the gentleman, and of course, on conservatism." The school historian Elizabeth Norfleet recognized that "the Walkers wisely capitalized on the plantation family lifestyle they had grown up in themselves and became exemplars to the masters and their wives to look upon the students as their sons and themselves as in loco parentis. Eating three daily meals together and watching the young grow up can tie people very closely together; and even if the bonds are not made of filial or parental love, loyalty becomes a good and sturdy substitute."[48]

As on the old plantation, African Americans did the service work at Woodberry. The school employed a number of domestic workers who remained at the institution for so long that they became as much a part of the place as the faculty. Of course, the boys, many of whom formed bonds with the black workers, did so through the overall ideology of racial paternalism that permeated the place. An anecdote captures the deferential roles played on the campus: a boy might give the porter Champ Francis a tip and watch him imitate Headmaster J. Carter Walker, saying, "Dere goes Mr. Carter Walker stompin' de yearth wit' his haid in de elements." This racial exchange might be interpreted in a variety of ways. At its base level it revealed the acceptance of payment for a demeaning act not unlike handing a pet a treat for performing a trick. Yet it also showed the boys in league with the black man mildly mocking the white authority figure. Such a view connoted an almost carefree exchange between privileged white youth and black laborers that might also occur in the kitchen, in the garden, in the garage, on the train, or in any of the other hundreds of places where unequal acquaintances might meet on racially proscribed but friendly terms. In later life Johnny romanticized such deferential exchanges as the race relations he favored over the hostilities he witnessed on the nightly news. And just like the punch line of the porter, Mercer often closed his letters with snippets of dialogue written in the low-country Geechee that he had learned to speak growing up with the black domestic workers and their children on the Georgia coast. Now at Woodberry he mastered mimicry too.[49]

Johnny shared a similar background with his classmates. Woodberry drew its overwhelmingly southern student body — 165 boys in 1923 — from the same handful of states, led by Virginia and North Carolina. A sizeable number of "old boys" hailed from Atlanta, Tampa, Nashville, Little Rock, Charleston, Washington, D.C., and other southern metropolitan areas. Several Savannahians attended with Johnny. The boys had nicknames, and Mercer claimed several, from "Johnnie," as he first signed it, rather than the "Johnny" that later became the fashion, to "Doo" and "Colonel." Years later, Mercer regretted the "diminutive" by telling a writer: "That Johnny-bit. It makes me perpetually young." While he first published under the name "John Mercer," he returned to "Johnny" as a professional name, although his friends and associates called him "John." In his first year at Woodberry, Johnny had bunked like the other boys, each in a small cubicle with a single bed in the Walker Building. Later he shared with Frederick "Hamlin" Hobbs Jr. a double sleeping room with adjacent study space. Although friendly with these fellows and others during his five years in Virginia, Johnny apparently never developed a close association that produced among his classmates a lifelong confidant.[50]

The year Johnny arrived at Woodberry, his cousin Joe Mercer played tight end on the football team, as he had done in the 1921 championship year. As a "new boy," Johnny joined the "old boys" in singing the school fight songs, such as "Smarty":

Cheering, cheering, cheering,
Woodberry is winning —
Victory is our cry today.
Nothing can our boys dismay.

Football season gave all the boys a rush. One of Johnny's classmates described in a letter to a friend the late return to Orange of the football team an hour after midnight following a Saturday victory on the gridiron: "Everybody got up at 1 o'clock and welcomed them with a large bonfire and torches. It was freezing cold and I surely did hate to get up but I wouldn't have missed it for anything." Fifth- and sixth-form boys might receive permission to attend college football games in Charlottesville or Richmond.[51] The intense rivalry between Woodberry Forest School and Episcopal High School in Alexandria, Virginia, fueled the students' enthusiasm for football that stayed with Johnny throughout his life. These southerners saw sporting competitions as figurative displays of honor. As a second-form student the year cousin Joe Mercer captained the team, Johnny wrote in the yearbook the score for that fall's game: WFS — 14 EHS — 0. And as an alumnus with a couple of hit lyrics, Johnny composed a new fight song for the school that went in part, "Fight for the Orange and Black! / Keep that tiger roaring."[52]

Once enrolled, Johnny followed family custom at Christ Episcopal Church in Savannah and joined the choir. It performed in the red brick chapel built by the Virginia diocese of the Protestant Episcopal Church while Hugh and Walter had attended the school. Opened in 1913 and named after Scotland's patron saint, St. Andrew's Chapel contained a beautifully carved Carrara marble altar with a choir stall in the chancel. The headmaster's wife played the organ, and various students led the choir. Later in life Mercer joked about "never having made the choir except as organ pumper." An explanation of this remark may be found in his letter to Headmaster Walker: "I was a pretty good organ pumper though — albeit rather small. This distinction is somewhat dimmed by the fact that it took off five demerits." As organist Mrs. J. Carter Walker cared for neither Johnny's rhythmic singing nor his behavior. His classmates recalled that she "threw him out of the choir!" While he dropped it from his list of activities in 1925 and 1926, Mercer returned to the choir his last year in school when directed by his classmate and friend, Peter Ruffin of Virginia. Later, as a nationally successful singer, Johnny teased in "A Study Hall Sonnet," written for the 1934 edition of *The Fir Tree*: "And Mrs. Carter dies, I know, / To find I'm on the radio. / I couldn't sing so la ti do / For her. / I started off with great 'eclat'— / A pity that my voice went flat; / I pumped the organ after that, / As 'twere." A devout Christian, Johnny actively participated in religious services as a chapel assistant in the Wednesday night weekly prayer meetings led by the St. Andrew's Chapel Council.[53]

Demonstrating the longstanding familial ties to the ancestral homeland, G. A. Mercer arranged with J. Carter Walker for Johnny to come home at Easter in 1924 so that he might meet a kinswoman visiting from Scotland. The headmaster permitted Johnny to travel to Savannah, where the family hosted Nell Blackie, the old maid daughter of the now-deceased Lucy Herndon and Robert Blackie. Her father had been a partner in the prosperous Blackie Publishing Company with offices in Glasgow and Edinburgh, so she had inherited a share of the publishing firm's fortune. Every Christmas she sent her Mercer cousins the *Blackie's Children's Annual* that beginning in 1904 appeared for sale during the holidays, as well as other Blackie titles, often lavishly illustrated in the art nouveau style for which the firm had garnered a fine reputation. As a child Johnny allowed these books to feed his flights of fancy. Johnny called the older woman, a first cousin to G. A., his aunt Nell. A decade later, when songwriting took him to London, he made arrangements to visit her in Edinburgh.[54]

In the fall of 1926, Johnny returned to Woodberry Forest to complete the sixth form, expecting to graduate in the spring of 1927. The academic year proved to be the last of his formal education. For months the headmaster had sent G. A. Mercer such remarks as "I have John a good deal on my mind. He is continuing to do poorly in his Latin, a subject in which he has had chronic trouble and is not making the effort he ought to make." Johnny's participation — along with a handful of other boys — in several demanding extracurricular activities contributed to his poor academic showing.

With perhaps his first friend at the school, Malcolm "Henine" Monroe, and Peter Ruffin, Johnny joined the German Club and the Madison Literary Society. He also supported the football squad, though he played no sports himself. Neither did he engage the Woodberry Forest Dramatic Club. In his senior year *The Fir Tree* noted Johnny's helpfulness and innate optimism: "His willingness and desire to work in the interest of others and his unfailing brightness of personality and humor have made him one of the most outstandingly popular boys in the school." Yet, perhaps as a way to deal with his own internal struggles, Johnny also picked fights; reflecting back on their Woodberry days, a friend later reminded Mercer about fellow classmate "John Hamp who, as I recall, you used to enjoy beating the Hell out of every once in a while."[55]

Taking advantage of the opportunities to write and publish at Woodberry, Mercer volunteered for the staffs of *The Fir Tree*, editing in 1926 and 1927 its humorous subsection called *The Daily Dope*, and of the newspaper, called *The Oracle*, which he oversaw as managing editor his last year at the school. On the *Fir Tree*, Johnny worked under editor in chief Malcolm Monroe, and the two friends used *The Daily Dope* columns to rib their other friends, such as Peter Ruffin. Like his artistic cousin Joe Mercer, who had held editorial positions on *The Fir Tree* during Johnny's early years at the school, the boys found they enjoyed working with words. Johnny's associates recognized this trait by noting about him on his senior page in the yearbook, "Wit is thy attribute."[56]

Being in the environment of an elite boys' school during the jazz age created a laboratory for studying popular culture. Like Johnny, some of his classmates had older brothers, some of whom were Woodberry alumni. Many of these "old boys" attended college and shared with their younger siblings information on the latest fads. These younger brothers read publications that their older brothers also read. Beginning in 1921, students at the University of Virginia in Charlottesville produced a slick magazine called *The Virginia Reel*. It printed funny stories, cartoons, brief jokes, comical narrations, and poems. Both The Store on Woodberry's campus and Rickett's Drug Store in Orange carried the monthly publication that sold for a quarter a copy. The style of *The Daily Dope* drew inspiration from *The Virginia Reel*. Two topics dominated the original material and reflected the preoccupation of the students — dating and drinking during prohibition. Often the two themes appeared together as in a poem called "A Flapper's Christmas Song" with the lines, "Jingle, jingle, Santa Claus — With lots of rye and gin. / Oh do you wear that long white beard to hide the whiskey in?" Woodberry students found in the pages of *The Virginia Reel* other topics of interest such as smoking, fast cars, and fashionable clothing as well as the occasional off-color joke. On the cutting edge, *The Virginia Reel* provided a primer on national trends, and no doubt Johnny and his friends studied it as hard as they did their textbooks. The 1926–27 writings in *The Daily Dope* and in the annual spoof of *The Oracle* called *The Sorrycle* that appeared in *The Fir Tree* reflected copy that in substance might have appeared in *The Virginia Reel*.[57] Johnny and other "old boys" picked up tips on the latest music craze by reading *The Virginia Reel*. The magazine advertised the appearance of the nationally popular sweet jazz band Fred Waring and His Pennsylvanians at the University of Virginia. In *The Sorrycle* for 1927 there appeared a text probably written by Johnny and used as filler that singled out a number of jazz bandleaders: "Jean Goldkette, Jan Garber, Paul Whiteman, George Olsen, Tom Waring, Coon-Sanders, Fletcher Henderson, Robert Carmichael." The text revealed the "old boys'" favorites: the hottest jazz bands of the day. Suggesting his influence and musical talent, *The Fir Tree* recognized, "No orchestra or new production can be authoritatively termed as 'good' until Johnny's stamp of approval has been placed upon it. His ability to 'get hot' under all conditions and at all times is uncanny. The best explanation we can offer is that we do not properly appreciate melody at its best."[58]

Jazz bands regularly performed at Woodberry Forest dances. With his buddies Peter Ruffin and Malcolm Monroe, Johnny served on the hop committee, which planned the dances and selected the bands. The hops provided several opportunities each year for the young men to entertain young women at the school. A classmate of Mercer's wrote a friend, "We had our fall dances last Friday week and they were peachy. The girls were good looking as the mischief and the music was hot. The first one started at 10:30 Friday night and ended at 2:00 and the second started at 10:00 Saturday morning and lasted until dinner." In Johnny's last year at Woodberry, the committee hired the Lido Orchestra for the Mid-Winter Hop scheduled around Valentine's Day. Red lights and green cedar boughs decorated Assembly Hall. Johnny's date for the February 18, 1927, occasion, Miss Roberts, had a chaperone, as did the other girls who came for the banquet and dance.[59]

The culture of in loco parentis required arranged meetings of potential suitors. Thus Woodberry Forest School planned events for its boys with the area's academies for girls, such as St. Catherine's School in Richmond. An annual "Hallowe'en party for the boys" featuring "a treasure hunt perhaps with plenty of cider and doughnuts afterwards" provided the students something to anticipate. So too did the occasional dances that took place after the football games. Special excursions allowed the sexes to mingle in preparation for the dating that would follow in the summer and after graduation. Under the 1927 "Lover's Club" in *The Fir Tree*, which had as its members a number of sixth-form boys listed as if on a racing program, appeared "'Get Hot' Mercer" riding on "Red Hot." Although there is no evidence to suggest he engaged in "wenching" while at Woodberry — unlike his older brother George, who got caught in the act — Johnny's behavior made it clear he loved both the dances and the girls. In the 1940s, Mercer dismissed Mrs. R. W. D. Taylor's playful charge that he had forgotten Woodberry with a reference to a nearby girls' school: "Your letter was as welcome as a special delivery from Sweetbriar used to be, and I hasten to set you right."[60]

Johnny entertained fellow students with ditties and knock-offs of recordings. In the 1927 issue of *The Sorrycle* there appeared a reference perhaps to one of Mercer's creations: "Get that new song by Mr. John entitled 'Mighty Good Men.'" By mimicking the modern music he listened to, he mastered harmonic construction and jazz riffs he loved so much. At age fifteen in 1924, Johnny composed his first song and sang it to his classmates. It began, "Sister Susie, strut your stuff, show those babies you're no bluff." Years later, when interviewed on the BBC, Johnny remembered the song as part of the "Charleston age" and explained, "I think I borrowed a little from every song that was popular at that time like 'If You Knew Susie' and 'Sweet Georgia Brown' and 'Red Hot Mama.' These were the big songs and my song sounded a little bit like all of them." Mercer admitted the blatant rip-off from blues singers but observed "all creative artists begin by 'stealing' from others . . . But, it's how fast you develop, how high your standards are and how quickly you find your OWN style that sets you above and apart from your contemporaries."[61]

Among his schoolmates at Woodberry Forest and with Savannah friends, Johnny became "notorious as a fellow who would try anything." Having learned to play the trumpet — though not well — the teenager often stood near the stage during concerts watching jazz solos and pretending to play an "imaginary trumpet" in an expression of youthful "extreme enthusiasm." The editors of *The Fir Tree* wrote a senior prophecy about Mercer dated 1952 — some twenty-five years into the future — that read: "Well, well, here is 'Colonel' John Mercer, the Jazz Record king, who used to mimic several of the teachers in the old days, and one in particular." No doubt the reference is to the Latin professor R. W. D. Taylor, whom Johnny enjoyed imitating: "You can't improve on Shakespeare. Tempus fugit, tempus fugit!" Mimicry seemed to be commonplace at Woodberry, and Mercer mastered the art. The fortune-teller continued: "He was obsessed with jazz even then, and preferred writing words and melodies to following the campaigns of one Julius Caesar through the mazes of the Commentaries," a truth borne out by his grades in Latin. Then, in a description that captured Mercer's charisma and quoted a popular song of the day, the prophecy concluded: "How he used to carry on at the dances! A shrill whistle, a rolling wink of the eye, and 'Shake that thing!'"[62]

In love with music, Johnny had collected records for years. As a youth in Savannah he eagerly anticipated every other Friday because on those days local businesses received the latest record releases. With cousin Walter and other friends Johnny went down to the shops that carried new pressings and listened for hours. No doubt they stopped by Lindsay and Morgan Furniture Store on the corner of Whitaker and President streets, which advertised "talking machines" and carried records. Johnny remembered buying "every record I could get my hands on — that I could possibly afford," preferring the hottest blues and jazz recordings. Since record companies marketed music as segregated commodities, Johnny and his friends also went to the West Broad Street businesses — such as Mary's Records, which catered to a black clientele — to play "race records" by Bessie Smith or Louis Armstrong. They purchased the recordings because, as Johnny recalled, "The white owners had signs up for the colored people to read that said 'No Free Riders'—'Buy or Don't Listen.'" Not content with simply hearing the music, Johnny — like other jazz musicians such as Hoagy Carmichael and Lester Young — studied the performances that interested him the most and then imitated the sounds of the performers, in the process developing his own style, something Billie Holiday did too.[63]

Throughout his carefree teenage years Johnny could consume these products because his father had achieved great financial success through real-estate speculation. G. A. Mercer had started the enterprise with the assistance of one clerk more than thirty years before, but opportunities in rental, insurance, and development had expanded the operations. Mercer stood as president with C. S. Lebey as general manager while Otto Seiler expanded into insurance. Sons Walter and Hugh did a variety of jobs, while nearly twenty other employees showed the properties, managed the books, and kept the records. In addition to its success selling real estate, the company gained distinction for its willingness to insure properties owned by African Americans. Recognizing his financial prominence in 1924, the Savannah Board of Trade chose G. A. Mercer as its chairman and had him write the introduction to the board's *Red Book* for that year. As one of Savannah's leading businessmen, G. A. Mercer did a bustling trade taking in capital from all manner of small investors. He convinced more than three thousand people to join him in the gamble on real estate by buying certificates in the G. A. Mercer Company, then used their money to buy properties that, once developed or sold, returned to the certificate holders quarterly dividends at a rate more than double that offered by savings accounts. He retained his position as director of the Savannah Bank and Trust Company that by 1926, thanks in part to his real-estate speculations, listed $9.35 million in assets. Indeed, that year the G. A. Mercer Company had reached its pinnacle in an overheated real-estate market.[64]

During the heady 1920s, G. A. expanded along Florida's Gold Coast by opening the Mercer-Lebey Realty Company in West Palm Beach. Son Walter helped C. S. Lebey with the new development near the Atlantic Ocean. Frenzied land deals and profits had attracted all types of investors to Florida. As land speculators sold mangrove swampland along the inland peninsula to Yankee snowbirds headed South, and as new money joined gangsters in jazz-filled hot Miami, old money concentrated itself in high society's fashionable enclaves in Palm Beach for the winter hegira. Between 1924 and 1925, shortly after Mercer entered the real-estate market in the more middling West Palm Beach, the area enjoyed a 163 percent increase in building starts. So successful had been G. A. Mercer's investment banking business that he regularly advertised, "Twenty years in business without the loss of a dollar to our clients." Whereas banks paid only 2.5 percent on deposits, Mercer promoted his company as "the safe investment of money. 6 per cent, quarterly, net to you" paid "on sums of $500 or over."[65]

When the Florida land boom went bust, it took the air out of the G. A. Mercer Company. In late 1925, trouble appeared in paper claims to marginal properties in Florida that lost value and that by early 1926 had slowed the region's real-estate market to a crawl. By the summer of 1926, the bubble had burst, and the *Nation* commented: "The world's greatest poker game, played with building lots instead of chips, is over. And the players are now . . . paying up." The arrival of a devastating hurricane on September 18, 1926, which hit land between Miami and Fort Lauderdale with its counterclockwise winds whipping West Palm Beach, dealt the fatal blow. [66]

Despite what the company defended as relatively sound purchases in Asheville and West Palm Beach as well as solid real-estate investments in Savannah, once the downturn in the market started, the value of nearly all these properties declined. As the buyers trickled off and the income diminished, the G. A. Mercer Company scrambled to pay its quarterly dividends and other obligations. With the bubble deflated, the company's capital evaporated. The collapsed real-estate market forced the directors of the G. A. Mercer Company and its investors to realize they had gambled and lost.[67]

Away at Woodberry Forest when the crisis occurred in the spring of 1927, Johnny failed to comprehend the enormity of the financial difficulties because, in typical Victorian fashion, his family had not revealed the extent of the problems to him. Courtesy required one to look away from unpleasantries. Polite parents rarely discussed conflicts openly and never in public, just as they expected children to be seen and not heard.[68] He left Virginia for Georgia and the long Easter weekend in Savannah. Dropping by the office of the G. A. Mercer Company to ask for money to go to a movie later that Good Friday, April 15, 1927, Johnny accompanied his father to Chatham Savings and Loan on Bryant Street, the agent G. A. Mercer had chosen to handle the company's liquidation. The son listened as his father discussed his financial troubles with the bank's president, his friend and business associate, George W. Hunt. Only then did Johnny learn the extent of the damage. According to family lore, Johnny asked Hunt how much money it would take to pay off the certificates "without the loss of a dollar to our clients" and thereby save the business. "Can you raise me a quick one-and-a-half million dollars, Johnny?" came Hunt's answer. Johnny replied, "Not today, Mr. Hunt, but some day, if I make it big I'll see that anyone who bet on my father will not lose a dime." It turned out not to be an idle boast. Johnny recognized the loss as a gambling debt and swore in front of others to pay it out of family honor.[69]

Having Chatham Savings and Loan take over the G. A. Mercer Company enabled G. A. Mercer to avoid bankruptcy, a condition that southern gentlemen viewed as dishonorable. Others confronting such business troubles might have bankrupted and then written off the debt by paying back to investors pennies on the original dollar invested in certificates and thereby forcing the investors to take the loss. Instead, a proud G. A. Mercer determined to pay back every dollar the company had ever received by refunding the certificates at face value. He saw this strategy of debt relief as the only honorable thing to do. The arrangement placed the company's land holdings in receivership with the Chatham Savings Bank, which, under George Hunt, slowly liquidated the properties once the market revived. Waiting for buyers of houses and house lots took years as the Great Depression settled in, but the orderly process allowed Chatham Savings and Loan Company to return two-thirds of the money originally invested in certificates by the nearly three thousand fellow gamblers, dollar for dollar but without accrued interest.[70]

The collapse of the G. A. Mercer Company necessitated a restructuring of the family business. First G. A. Mercer turned over to George Hunt his personal fortune, some $200,000, as well as the remaining company-held properties in Savannah, Asheville, and West Palm Beach, for the bank to use in the liquidation. A $15,000 line of credit from the bank enabled Mercer to reorganize his old realty business into the new Mercer Realty Company, so that the fifty-nine-year-old man could make a living by managing rental properties and potentially developing land holdings owned by others. G. A. Mercer stood as president and son Hugh managed the effort as secretary. The insurance wing of the old company was reorganized as the Mercer-Seiler Insurance Agency, managed by son Walter and Otto Seiler, and soon joined by a Greek immigrant processed through Ellis Island named Nick Mamalakis. The agency became one of Savannah's leading actuaries and for many years fronted Bay Street in the Central Railroad and Banking Company building next to the U.S. Customs House.[71]

Because of his business losses, G. A. resigned his leadership positions. After he stepped down as a director of the Savannah Bank and Trust Company, its resources fell from a high in 1928 of $9.35 million to $3.81 million in 1932. The collapse of real-estate values in 1927 had preceded the stock market crash of 1929, and the slowdown affected all of Savannah by 1933. Bethesda also suffered, and as a result G. A. Mercer resigned as president of the Union Society in 1933. He also surrendered his post as a trustee of Chatham Academy. The business failure and subsequent loss of public stature and honor broke G. A. Mercer as a man.[72]

After Easter, Johnny returned to Woodberry Forest burdened by the family's financial crisis. In May, G. A. Mercer sent his son ten dollars to cover some obligations at the school, but comprehending the financial calamity, Johnny paid the bills and returned the balance to help out with the situation at home. Instead of using the money, Lillian placed the two crisp one-dollar bills printed in dark blues and greens in a separate envelope that recorded in her cursive script "Personal — $2 John sent back after failure in business."[73]

Certainly the financial difficulties burdened the boy, as his final grades at Woodberry revealed, with both reversals preventing him from continuing his education. Worried about his family, Johnny fritted away his last few weeks at school earning demerits and falling in class rank down to 61 out of 65. The monthly cards foretold of his impending academic failure. J. Carter Walker wrote G. A. Mercer on April 23, 1927: "this report holds not little prospect of John's graduating in June." Low marks in trigonometry and solid geometry proved his undoing, for failing grades in these subjects in April and May prevented him from earning the C he needed to graduate. At Woodberry Forest only those students with passing grades of seventy or above on final exams in the sixth form received a diploma, which represented a certificate of recommendation to college. Having failed to earn his diploma, Johnny figured he would not pass the entrance exams for college, where he had decided to follow his grandfather by attending Princeton. Family finances made taking any test a moot point. Whether he left at the end of May or stayed at Woodberry Forest School to participate in the end-of-the-year festivities is not clear. A telegram he sent late in the afternoon on June 14, 1927, from South Carolina announced: "Ford broke. Am stranded in Columbia. Send ten dollars immediately by Postal Telegraph." Johnny had hit rock bottom.[74]

By age seventeen, the boy had experienced a world of extremes. Only months before Johnny had enjoyed life with no worries or cares as a privileged child of wealth descended from a venerable family of great honor. Now he confronted an economic calamity that disgraced the Mercer name. His own shameful failure to graduate from Woodberry Forest diminished the value of his years away at school. Instead of heading to college, where he might have further postponed maturity, he found himself living at home and trying to earn his keep. He witnessed his Victorian father hold on to religion as everything else he believed in shifted like the sands on Savannah's beach. He saw his mother suffer the embarrassment of the arrest of her brother, Eddie Ciucevich, for bootlegging, when federal revenue agents seized his sloop packed with smuggled whiskies and choice liquors as it reached the inlet at Tybee. Unmoored by the forces of modernism, Johnny responded with ambivalence. While he favored the traditions of his forebears and remained grounded in their examples and teachings, Johnny watched as the ideology of his parents failed them, further pushing him to take a different route.

At the same time he embraced the rebelliousness of jazz as a cultural expression of his own reality. Defenders of virtue recognized the threat the music posed to the old social order. Just five years before, the Savannah City Council had banned "all forms of jazz dancing, as well as all forms of dancing to jazz music or syncopated music" in the city. Impossible to enforce, the action simply made the musical revolution all the more attractive to young men like Mercer.[75]

At first Johnny joined his two brothers in the reorganized Mercer Realty Company, where for the rest of 1927 and into 1928 he worked as an office boy, taking typing lessons, collecting the rents, and running errands. As brother Walter recalled, "We'd give him things to deliver, letters, checks, deeds and things like that and learn days later that he'd absent-mindedly stuffed them in his pocket. There they stayed." Walter added that it took the company months to recover from the effects of Johnny's "help." When not working for the family business, the teenager bonded with his buddies, dating, drinking, and hanging around with other social swells in Savannah, still relishing every new jazz release. So hip to the national popular culture, Johnny wanted nothing more than to experience the music at its commercial source — America's capital of modernism, New York City.[76]

3 New York City

· ·

Way up in New York City
They talk a different language,
They talk a different style —
So busy makin' money
They ain't got time to smile.

DURING THE SUMMER of 1927, seventeen-year-old Johnny concocted a scheme to visit New York City. His friend Dick Hancock played guitar in a band that performed on one of the Savannah Steamship Line's New York cruisers, the *City of Chattanooga*. Returning from a trip, Hancock reported back to an envious Johnny that he had heard in person at the Paramount Theater Paul Whiteman's band featuring a host of jazz greats, including trumpeter Bix Beiderbecke and the singing trio the Rhythm Boys, Harry Lillis "Bing" Crosby, Al Rinker, and Harry Barris. The metropolis represented modernism in America, and Mercer wanted to see this worldly capital and hear the jazz musicians who performed there. Family finances prohibited his purchase of anything as frivolous as a steamship ticket, so Johnny conspired with Hancock to stow away on the *City of Chattanooga* on its next trip north. Johnny informed his mother, who gave her consent, even arranging for him to stay with his Aunt Katherine and Uncle Robbie Mercer, who were housesitting that summer for Katherine's sister and husband in a townhouse near Park Avenue. Their son, Joe, held an apprenticeship with the great sculptor Daniel Chester French at the New York School of Design, so he lived there, too. Lillian convinced Katherine to allow Johnny to come visit Joe. Lillian contacted her sister Anne Ciucevich Rivers's former husband, Morgan Pritchard, who worked as a purser on the steamship line plying the waters between Savannah and New York City. The two contrived an alternative travel plan for the boy.[1]

Years later, Johnny remembered the day of departure. After boarding the boat in Savannah and ignoring the calls to "go ashore," he waited until the steamer had passed the city's famous "waving girl" and entered the open sea before walking out on deck to smoke a cigarette. Shortly thereafter a ship's officer accosted him and, finding that he had no ticket, pressed him to join the cleaning crew to pay off the passage, which turned out to be the solution that Lillian and Pritchard had worked out to prevent potential family embarrassment and legal troubles. Nevertheless the subterfuge resulted in Johnny reaching his destination on board the *City of Chattanooga*. In his autobiography, Mercer recalled, "What a way to first see the skyline of Manhattan! It was about five in the morning, the sun coming up behind the skyscrapers and a cold wind whipping my gray flannel shirt as I stood at the railing taking it all in. (Ready or not, New York, here I come!)." During the Roaring Twenties, a building boom had filled out the island's tip with office towers crowding around the earlier Woolworth and Singer buildings as New York celebrated its international role as headquarters for America's corporations.[2]

For a fortnight Johnny wandered around the metropolis. Lillian Mercer later confessed to a reporter, "I really wanted him to be an actor," although she added, "I don't recall now why I was set on a stage career for Johnny. There was nothing in the family background to incline him that way although his father and grandfather were powerful and dramatic speakers." To that end she had slipped him spending money. Johnny headed straight to the Paramount only to discover Whiteman's run had ended. National chains like Loews had built majestic palaces to showcase the latest motion picture releases, so Johnny went to the movies. The teenager spent his time walking around Tin Pan Alley, buying sheet music, and taking in the cultural opportunities New York offered, including two Broadway shows. Johnny saw Louis Groody sing "Sometimes I'm Happy" and other songs from Vincent Youmans's *Hit the Deck*, which played at the Belasco Theatre. He also attended *Rio Rita*, the musical sensation by Harry Tierney and Joe McCarthy that William Randolph Hearst bankrolled to open his brand-new art deco Ziegfeld Theatre. After attending top-of-the-line performances in the best venues, the young man became addicted to musical theater. Mercer left in love with New York City and show business.[3]

Johnny Mercer began his career in entertainment acting in Savannah's amateur productions. When home from Woodberry Forest School, he attended the Town Theatre performances staged in the Bijou Theatre, the old vaudeville playhouse on Broughton Street. Organized in 1925 as a civic enterprise to stage amateur performances for the community, the Town Theatre turned to Annot Willingham, the senior high school drama teacher, as its first director, a position she held until 1929. As a professional actress, Mrs. Willingham related the Savannah effort to the international little-theater movement then prevalent throughout the United States. She recruited noted director Daniel Reed of New York's Columbia Stage Society to offer suggestions and to read from Edgar Lee Masters's *Spoon River Anthology*. Wanting the theater to touch "the general life of the community," Mrs. Willingham believed it could "give to as many individuals as possible an opportunity for self-expression in the dramatic arts," a function as important to her "as that it should present good plays for the entertainment of its members." To get the group going, some 376 people bought ten-dollar annual subscriptions that contributed to a five-thousand-dollar budget used to finance the initial performances. Several of Savannah's elite families such as the Barrows, Cohens, Hugers, Hulls, Langs, Lynahs, McIntires, and Morrisons supported the effort, which later attracted Johnny, his cousin, Walter Rivers, and Walter's future wife, Cornelia McIntire, as well as the superintendent of the Bethesda Home for Boys, Ole Burroughs.[4]

Persuaded by a pretty face to try out for a Town Theatre production in late 1927 after his return from New York, Johnny received positive recognition for his debut role, foreshadowing his promising future in show business. Family friend Peggy Stoddard convinced him to join her in the community theater production of *Mary the Third*. The three-act play told the story of rebellious daughters in three generations of the same family at twenty-year intervals, revealing gender and generational clashes over the recurrent issue of love. It featured Stoddard playing the three Marys from the 1870s, 1890s, and 1910s in what amounted to a celebration of modernism trumping Victorian custom. Johnny played Mary's younger brother, a character pulled by the tradition of the past and the liberation of the future. The Savannah paper announced, "Johnny Mercer . . . is going to register one of the hits of the evening. He makes of the rather slight part one of the outstanding roles of the play." The reviewer noted that Mercer "has the very rare faculty of being able to stay in character while he is not talking — an art as we all know which many professionals have never mastered. He is a new find and promises to make his debut with great éclat." The favorable review, the positive experience he had acting, and the fun he had entertaining others boosted the confidence of the nearly eighteen-year-old.[5]

To expand the regional self-expression component of its mission, the Town Theatre opened its 1927–28 season by sponsoring a national contest for the best new one-act play on a southern subject, with the intent of entering the work in a New York competition. Annot Willingham, Daniel Reed, and Charles

Coburn — the nationally successful character actor from Savannah best known for his later 1953 film role in *Gentlemen Prefer Blondes* — judged the submissions, which numbered more than sixty. The Town Theatre staged the three finalists in spring 1928 but gave top honor to the comedy *The Hero*, by Frances "Fanny" Hargis, a student at Agnes Scott College who hailed from Savannah. Set in present-day Georgia outside Atlanta, the play confronts the past through the interaction of a Civil War veteran played by Ole Burroughs, his widowed daughter played by Mrs. Frank P. (Lucy Barrow) McIntire, and her fatherless son played by Johnny Mercer. The thespian troupe won the regional competition and then traveled to New York to compete against one-acts from across the United States and Great Britain in the sixth annual Belasco Tournament. Mercer relished the opportunity to return to New York City.[6]

In the spring of 1928, Johnny Mercer made his Broadway debut. The Savannah cast performed *The Hero* in the Frolic Theatre on May 11 and made it into the final round to be staged the next day in the old New Amsterdam Theatre on Forty-second Street. Bested by a Scottish troupe, the Savannah play won second place in the finals. Years later, Ole Burroughs wrote Johnny recalling, "The trip you and I made to New York in the promotion of culture and the arts, you as Sam Robbins and I as your grandpere Robbie. Ralph Bellamy [a famous actor] gave you a plug for being a good Sam. It was doubtless your work that got us second prize of cash, Edinburgh, practically professionals, running away with the Belasco cup." The *New York Times* also singled out "John Mercer" for praise. Leaving the dressing room with that post-performance applause-driven rush of adrenaline, Johnny met the actor Tony Brown, who offered positive words and a willingness to help him get started in acting. Mercer needed nothing else to convince him of his future course in entertainment.[7]

Back in Savannah that summer, Johnny got a job with a brokerage firm and started planning his next trip to New York. He marked the prices of sugar futures for Hentz and Company during the last of the stock market pre-crash craze, enabling him to learn the ropes of the commodities business, which came in handy later when he punched certificates on Wall Street to earn extra money. He remembered reading the tape and recording as a "chalk boy" the fluctuating prices of stocks on a big chalkboard in the days before the "electric 'tote' board" broadcast the figures. When an associate at the firm challenged the youth's Broadway aspirations, Mercer took such "umbrage" at the remark that he determined to return to New York, try his luck, and prove the naysayer wrong. As Johnny recalled about Savannah, "no girls, no music, no acting, no future that I could see, and no fun."[8]

Recognizing his son's unhappiness and willing to help him accomplish his dreams as long as they were honest, G. A. Mercer agreed to finance a three-month trial run for Johnny to break into show business. The youth had been encouraged by his co-star from *The Hero*, Lucy Barrow McIntire, who "advised Johnny to give songwriting and acting a try." Her son, P. B. McIntire, thought Johnny's "parents were very much against it," and he remembered that his mother encouraged Mercer, telling the youth, "Johnny, you want to do it so badly. You ought to just go ahead and try it. You are young enough to start over again if it doesn't work out." Years later, Johnny wrote Cornelia McIntire Rivers to thank her for a portrait she had painted of him and to suggest she inherited the spirit of her "indomitable mother." Both Johnny and his father realized that the fragile family business could not sustain another son trying to make a living selling real estate during the Depression. "I left the South because economically I could have never made a living in the South. I was the fourth son in a small business that couldn't have absorbed me and I had to go to find something to do," Mercer explained to jazz critic Willis Conover. "And I left and I came to the right place because I wound up in New York and Hollywood where my little talent was salable." Yet the diaspora entertainer confessed, "But I never forgot the South. I never forgot the friends I made there, the things I learned there, the way of life that I like."[9]

An invitation to stay with friends at Lake Mahopac during the late summer of 1928 took Johnny back to the Empire State. After two weeks at the resort, he traveled with his friends into the city to see the musical hit *Rain or Shine*, featuring jazz violinist Joe Venuti and guitarist Eddie Lang. While in line to buy tickets, Mercer saw Tony Brown and took the opportunity to tell him about his intention to become an actor; Brown reiterated his offer of help. Typical of people caught up in the southern diaspora, Johnny received support from family members already in New York, who eased the transition to metropolis. Both the broker Uncle Lewis and the evangelist Uncle Ed lived in the area, and one of them recommended a boarding house in midtown owned by a widow, where Johnny found temporary digs as he looked for acting jobs. Mercer applied at a number of theatrical firms and landed a part through the assistance of "a team of old lady agents" suggested by Tony Brown.[10]

From what Johnny later described as their "sleazy" office over the National Theatre, the agents recommended Johnny to Cheryl A. Crawford, a casting director of the Theatre Guild, who picked him to play extras for traveling shows scheduled for a six-month run. Back in 1914 to improve Broadway's intellectual climate, a group of producers had organized the Theatre Guild to stage works by George Bernard Shaw and Eugene O'Neill, among other dramatists. The modern designer Norman Bel Geddes decorated the Fifty-second Street playhouse that developed performances during the regular season for the New York audience and then sent them out on a national circuit. Having main-staged Eugene O'Neill's *Marco Millions* in 1927, the Theatre Guild prepared a traveling version that Crawford cast in the fall of 1928, picking Johnny to play a Chinese coolie. The Theatre Guild paired the O'Neill show with a revival of Ben Jonson's *Volpone*, for which Mercer won the bit part of a slave. These plays served to break Johnny into the professional world of the theater. Several times over the span of his career he revisited the positive experiences he had in these traveling shows for inspiration, as if trying to recapture an earlier excitement.[11]

Mercer eked out a living as an actor over the six-month run. In a revealing letter to his father sent before departing on the subscription tour, Johnny confessed to feeling "rather lonesome" but added, "I expect that all *great* men have to put up with those little things, eh kid?" He acknowledged money enclosed in a recent mailing: "Consider this check for $25 your last (I hope). I'm not making any rash promises but I hope to lighten your burden by taking care of myself from now on. And thanks a whole lot for the check Pop." Needing an overcoat, he later recalled the cold of Chicago that winter of 1929 as the Theatre Guild's traveling show made stops there and Cleveland, Baltimore, Philadelphia, and Boston after having opened in Pittsburgh. Once the Theatre Guild tour ended, Johnny returned to Savannah and visited with his parents in the spring of 1929. The local paper interviewed him at the time, noting that Johnny "is extremely enthusiastic over his new vocation and has optimistic things to say about the theater world." Shortly thereafter Mercer moved back to New York and hustled with agents for acting parts while working part-time in the stock market. With fits and starts and fateful meetings with helpful people, Mercer managed to make it in a profession known for destroying dreams.[12]

Twenty-year-old Johnny lived as a virtual transient in metropolis. He moved into a basement apartment on the West Side with fellow extra Sidney Mansfield, but left after being robbed and then discovering the homosexuality of his roommate. Reflecting on the matter in his autobiography, Mercer noted, "I'm not a prude and I wasn't a prude then, but I couldn't see living in a ménage a trois unless the third member were a girl, so as pleasantly as I could, I packed up." Other actor friends allowed him to join them in an apartment on Seventy-second Street located behind a red neon Coca-Cola sign. Mercer's prior experience in Savannah working with sugar futures enabled him to get a job on Wall Street as a runner, so he had some income while auditioning. At the same time Mercer's future collaborator Hoagy Carmichael made extra money running stock on Wall Street too. Johnny wrote his Woodberry friend, Fred Hobbs, about looking for acting work but assured him "am still the same no-account youngster myself — living for love & hot music." Several weeks of searching landed Johnny a bit part in a revival of a melodrama called *Stepping Out* being staged in Hoboken, New Jersey. Mercer rode the ferry from Manhattan for rehearsals. The show opened on May 29, 1929, and bombed after two weeks, closing without Johnny having earned a cent but making a friend in older actor Charles "Buddy" Dill, who taught him how to get by between acting gigs. Out of work again and needing to move, Johnny found his new friend willing to help.[13]

Established in the profession, Buddy Dill mentored the green Mercer. The men roomed in the Whitby Hotel to maintain a "good address," although a lack of funds restricted their diet to oatmeal. Johnny recalled these difficult days with fondness, commending Dill on his frugality while recognizing they still went to the Palace to see the show. Having been a fan of vaudeville since childhood in Savannah, Mercer studied the art form anew, drawing inspiration from it for the rest of his career. Johnny mastered the roles played by the actors and the variety of sketches they performed. No doubt he saw the routine of "Mr. Gallagher and Mr. Shean," in which Ed Gallagher played the straight man to the comic Al Shean, an uncle of the four Marx brothers. Recalling the weekly shows he witnessed in 1929 as the art form ended, Mercer compared them to a brilliant fireworks finale. Buddy encouraged Johnny's lyric writing and supported Mercer's brazen idea to share his songs with Broadway legend Eddie Cantor. One night Johnny went backstage of the Walter Donaldson musical *Whoopee* and gained entrance to Cantor's dressing room. The star offered encouragement but failed to place "Every Time I Shave I Cut My Adam's Apple" in a show. Producer George C. Tyler and the Theatre Guild Workshop cast both Mercer and Dill in *Houseparty*, a college-themed murder mystery that opened two weeks before the stock market crash of October 1929 but traveled for six months and kept them employed. In a letter home to Ole Burroughs, Johnny related how difficult it was to get a part and what life was like on the road, affirming that his love for show business kept him going.[14]

Throughout life, Johnny referred to "fate," the "wheel of fortune," and "lady luck" intervening at opportune moments. Indeed, chance meetings with key individuals pushed his career along. Had he not met Tony Brown, he might not have landed his first acting job. Had he not befriended Buddy Dill, he might not have worked in *Houseparty*. The show had as its stage manager a young man named Everett Miller whose friendship with Mercer proved decisive. Both Johnny and Everett liked jazz music. For years Mercer had toyed with lyrics while Miller had tinkered with tunes. The two decided to collaborate in what became a fateful transition in Mercer's life.[15]

Back in New York in March 1930 and looking for work along with the thousands of other unemployed, Johnny learned of a casting call by the Theatre Guild for the perennial revue, *The Garrick Gaieties*. Like the original *Garrick Gaieties* staged in 1925 and 1926 under the direction of the young songwriters Richard Rodgers and Lorenz Hart as a way to introduce fresh talent to audiences, the revived show promised to showcase the best new faces on Broadway. Although Mercer failed to get an acting part, he jumped at the chance to write songs for the sophisticated revue. Overnight he drafted the lyric "Out of Breath (and Scared to Death of You)" to a tune by Everett Miller that became Mercer's first published song and somewhat of a sensation when sung by fellow Georgian Sterling Holloway. As it turned out, Everett's father, Charlie Miller, worked for the T. B. Harms Music Company, which had published the works of the great songwriters Jerome Kern and Sigmund Romberg, among others, and it printed the sheet music from the show, which opened on June 4, 1930, and ran for the rest of the year. Drama critic J. Brooks Atkinson offered a positive review of the musical and, as the *New York Times* theater reviewer who could make or break a show, just about every other production on which Mercer collaborated over the next thirty years. The 1930 *Garrick Gaieties* also included music by lyricists Ira Gershwin and E. Y. "Yip" Harburg and composers Vernon Duke and Aaron Copland. Assisted by Charlie Miller, Johnny worked his way into the songwriting profession.[16]

The one-room apartment came to symbolize Mercer's early days in New York City. Johnny referred to it as an indicator of the lowest point in his budding career, suggesting he "had nothing to show for my two years there but a three-story walk-up on Jones Street in the Village, with clothes piled in the corner — all dirty — and a stove which let down from a hinge over the bathtub." On nearby Barrow Street resided his old theater coach, the actress Annot Willingham who, with her older children, had moved to New York for work and who provided Johnny with encouragement, the occasional meal, or a drink of bathtub gin. Like high school theater coaches everywhere, she sustained her prize pupil with love and support as he struggled to break into show business.[17] Years later, Lillian recalled visiting her son in what she described as "a terrible one-room apartment" that "had no sink or washbasin, only a bathtub." To her horror, but not unusual for a son wanting to demonstrate his independence, "Johnny insisted on cooking a chicken dinner in my honor — he's always been a good cook — and I'll never forget him cleaning the chicken in the tub." Like other creative people, Mercer loved preparing food and garnered a reputation for his spaghetti and bouillabaisse. He loved to eat, too, and often helped in the kitchen when at the houses of friends, going so far as to fix a dish or clean out the ice box.[18]

During the summer of 1930, Walter Rivers joined Johnny in the Greenwich Village apartment, which they rented for seven dollars a week. Johnny's "success" had convinced his cousin to join the southern diaspora and try his luck in New York. While stage-managing a production in Jackson Heights, Walter struggled as a writer, working alternately on a novel, a play, and poetry, for which he found an interested publisher. To help him get established, and no doubt to keep him in the city where he could watch over Johnny, G. A. Mercer financed Walter's effort to enter show business. In a letter Walter had asked for help, explaining, "You know, I rather hesitate to ask you for money because as long as I can remember you have been helping someone in the family along, and I had hoped that I would not become another drag. I have a terrible yearning for absolute independence and I never seem to be able to get along toward it."[19]

Wanting that same independence and finding good fortune in songwriting, Johnny cast his lot with the music industry. Lyrics had been his true love all along, and the scraps of verse and books of prose he had composed over his early years marked him as a writer despite his talents as a performer. Now in New York he observed the latest trends in a dynamic landscape marked by the modernism of art deco as expressed in the new Chrysler Building and the world's tallest structure, the Empire State Building. Johnny visited Broadway regularly to study the current shows. Despite the onset of the Great Depression, these years inaugurated the golden age in American musical theater, with ample hits for Mercer to enjoy. Writing both words and music, Cole Porter opened *Fifty Million Frenchmen* in November 1929 and then *The New Yorkers* in December 1930. Following the same general trajectory, George Gard "Buddy" DeSylva and Lew Brown wrote lyrics to Ray Henderson's music in *Follow Thru* and then *Flying High*. Likewise, Howard Dietz wrote the words to Arthur Schwartz's scores for *The Little Show* and then *Three's a Crowd*. The Gershwin brothers — George writing music and Ira writing words — opened 1930 with *Strike Up the Band* and closed it with *Girl Crazy*. Also playing that year was Jerome Kern's music for *Sweet Adeline* with lyrics by Oscar Hammerstein II. On stage, performers such as Kate Smith, Ethel Merman, Eddie Cantor, Bert Lahr, Fred Astaire, and Ginger Rogers appeared, and in the pit performed jazz greats such as the Fred Waring Orchestra and the Red Nichols Orchestra. No seminar could have better prepared a future songwriter for a career in popular music than Broadway in 1930, but the tutorial Johnny undertook limited his vision of what a musical could and should be as evidenced by his own labors for the stage. Remaining true to the modern form of musical demonstrated by Kern and Hammerstein's 1927 *Show Boat*, Mercer favored that "make-believe" world espoused by the romantic musical comedy.[20]

With prohibition still in effect, Johnny visited speakeasies to listen to jazz with friends such as Everett Miller. They might go to Fifty-second Street, where Jack and Charlie's sold liquor in teacups, or they might visit one of the many other gin joints down this stretch of road that offered live music played by white musicians. Some nights found them taking the A train to Harlem, where fellow white southern expatriates gathered on Lenox Avenue and 142nd Street at the Cotton Club to hear black jazz musicians such as Duke Ellington — Mercer's favorite — or Cab Calloway doing Lew Leslie revues, with lyrics by Dorothy Fields and music by a young pianist named Harold Arlen. Nearby at 2221 Seventh Avenue, Connie's Inn premiered Fats Waller's *Keep Shufflin'* and *Hot Chocolates*, with lyrics by Andrea Paul "Andy Razaf" Razafkeriefo. Jazz musicians performed in the basement of 2294 Seventh Avenue at Smalls Paradise or the nearby Barron Wilkins Exclusive Club or the Lenox Club. Bessie Smith sang her blues at the Alhambra Grill, and Louis Armstrong performed his at the Savoy Ballroom. Mercer took music lessons in these different classrooms, too, where he confronted the New Negro and absorbed the Harlem Renaissance.[21]

Determined to become a lyricist, Johnny hung around the watering holes frequented by the songwriters and music publishers of Tin Pan Alley, in particular, the English Tea Room in the Sherman Square Hotel on Broadway and the Walgreen's on Times Square. Alluding to the cacophony of sound created by songwriters pounding away on pianos in the office buildings along Twenty-eighth Street between Broadway and Sixth Avenue, the name "Tin Pan Alley" came to refer to all the publishing houses in New York City that dominated American popular music from the 1880s to the 1950s. Johnny frequently dropped by the offices of Harms Music, which published his "Out of Breath (and Scared to Death of You)." With Max Dreyfus as president, his brother, Louis Dreyfus, as vice president, and Rudolf Friml as secretary, the Harms-Friml Corporation captured a large share of the music-publishing business as the most prestigious firm on Tin Pan Alley. As an employee, Charlie Miller could introduce Johnny to the various songwriters who came by the office, such as the Gershwins, Kern and Hammerstein, Sigmund Romberg, and Vincent Youmans.[22]

Recalling his early days visiting "the alley," Mercer explained his behavior to music critic Willis Conover: "I have always been absolutely in love with songs. I knew them all, I sang them all. By the time I was ten or eleven, I knew every writer who was writing songs." He then named them: "I knew all [Walter] Donaldson's songs, Percy Wenrich, you name them, [Harry] Von Tilzer, Lew Brown, and when I got to be a songwriter, I met all these fellows and was so thrilled to meet them, and when I'd meet them I'd sing some obscure song that they'd written." Recognizing such behavior might be seen as ingratiating himself to them, Johnny admitted, "I'd sing them verses that they had forgotten. And I wasn't trying to play up to them or anything, I just sincerely loved songs." He recognized the advantage of this self-education: "So that may give me an edge about fitting words to music because I have this musical sense anyway. I have a pretty good ear." Mercer aspired to write what has come to be called the Great American Song, that is, a "short and compact" song that consists of an introduction called the verse that sets up what follows as the usual thirty-two bars of the refrain or chorus. Such songs are often broken down into four parts, represented as aaba: the opening, a variation of the opening, a departure or "bridge," and the return to the opening theme as a closing. Many of Mercer's songs followed this model of verse and aaba refrain with great success. The format proved quite versatile, being used by songwriters for ballads but also novelty, rhythm, and love songs. The best examples successfully married beautiful melodies with poetic lyrics to become classics in the Great American Songbook.[23]

Placing a work in a Broadway show offered the best outlet for a songwriter in this early age of radio and recordings, for it increased name exposure through sheet music sales. Being at the publishing houses provided Johnny the chance to write with a variety of composers. In addition to the book shows that followed a romantic storyline or some other plot, Broadway continued to be populated by revues similar to Ziegfeld's *Follies*, where scantily clad chorus girls served up the main feature, around which stars sang the latest sensation, with other song-and-dance numbers cobbled together to create the show. The need for filler provided opportunities to write music. Mercer joined Richard Myers in creating his second published song, "Another Case of Blues," for a show called *Tattle Tales* in 1930. Likewise, he joined Myers and Philip Charig on a show called *Pajama Lady* that included Johnny's lyrics for "Down through the Ages," "One, Two, Three," and "Three Guesses." Fate intervened when one day a couple returning from Europe with the rights to produce an operetta stopped by Harms in need of a lyricist willing to work on the West Coast. Mercer applied for and got the job.[24]

Starting in September 1930, Mercer spent three months in Los Angeles helping Lillian Albertson transform the Emmerich Kálmán operetta *Das Veilchen vom Montmartre*, "The Violet of Montmartre," into the San Francisco production *Paris in Spring*. Suggesting the global reach of popular music, the contract work involved translating a German score into English for American consumption. In New York composers Sigmund Romberg and Rudolf Friml had dominated the writing of operettas, but in Austria the big three remained Johann Strauss, Franz Lehár, and Kálmán. Already Broadway had enjoyed runs of Kálmán's *The Circus Princess* and *Golden Dawn*, so *Paris in Spring* suggested great potential had not an American style of musical comedy begun to displace what seemed to many as overwrought romantic operetta. At first Johnny found the work engaging, but grew frustrated by the challenge of compiling so many quality lyrics for a single production. Some of the songs, though, stood alone, such as "Don't Ask Too Much of Love" and "The Moon Shines Down." The exercise exposed Johnny to the wealth of music worldwide available for adaptation and occasionally when looking for inspiration, he found it abroad by creating transnational music. In the end, Mercer recognized his accomplishment with *Paris in Spring* and appreciated the experience.[25]

The California contract introduced Johnny to the charms of the West Coast. He loved the climate and admitted feeling entranced by "the smell of the bougainvillea and the red roofed cottages of Beverly Hills." He dined at the Brown Derby, played putt-putt golf, and toured Hollywood. He visited such hot spots as the Cotton Club, where he heard Louis Armstrong, and the Coconut Grove, where he met Bing Crosby. In an era when bungalows abutted orange groves and car traffic hardly existed, sunny California appeared a paradise. Back in New York, however, Walter Rivers received a letter from Johnny that suggested he was "a trifle disappointed in his California trip." In writing about the letter to G. A. Mercer, Walter explained, "I can't make out what the trouble can be, but I suppose it is just the 'creative artist' is always doubtful about his own work." To his girlfriend, Ginger Meltzer, Johnny bemoaned California: "The land of sunshine! Praise God! I'll soon be leaving it. I've never seen a bigger hick town than this one. And the blondes — I've never seen as many. And I hope I never see another one. It would be all right if they were naturals but they haven't even that excuse."[26]

The beginning of 1931 found Johnny back in New York trying to write lyrics for a living. Chance meetings with composers resulted in several songs; Mercer collaborated with Ralph Bolton on "Just Like a Falling Star" and with Gay Stephens on "Beyond the Moon." When Charlie Miller left Harms Music to form Miller Music Company, he hired Mercer as a songwriter for twenty-five dollars a week. As Johnny explained in a letter home, "As soon as I get even one song in a show, that will be doubled. If I get a successful one, I will probably have an income of several hundred dollars a week." He added with great faith that his penurious situation "won't go on forever." Johnny still received a monthly stipend from G. A. Mercer that helped him make ends meet. In a letter to his father Johnny optimistically noted, "Things are dull — but looking up, as they say, in my business life," and added, "I know I'll get there, pop — and I am considered good by contemporarys [sic] — which is something — although I haven't definitely come through." Then, as he did in other letters, Johnny reflected on the code of honor: "You've set me a wonderful example to follow and your character is a goal for me to aim at — if I half succeed — I'll be happy."[27]

With Alfred Opler, Mercer wrote "While We Danced at the Mardi Gras," which he considered his "first big popular hit." Miller Music published the sheet music with "words by John Mercer" in 1931. The song proved one of the few successes enjoyed by Opler, who, according to Mercer, "did most of the promotion work to get it started." The tenor Nick Lucas introduced the song. Musical journals listed "While We Danced at the Mardi Gras" as one of the top ten performed songs in 1931. The lyric points to the promise of the young songwriter. After setting the mood, Mercer lays out the story: "I begged for just one dance with you, / Instead I found romance with you." He then asks a series of questions: "Was the love that we made / Just a brief masquerade? / Was it gone with the song / that the orchestra played?" The second refrain speculates on love. "With a sigh, / With a glance / At the moon above, / Was it just by chance / We spoke of love? / Or did you somehow feel / That the wonder was real / While we danced / At the Mardi Gras?" For the rest of his career, Mercer revisited these themes of chance encounters, romantic interludes, and unresolved endings.[28]

Another break came through his friend, Everett Miller, who offered a tune that composer Henry Souvaine improved and that Johnny set with words. Harms Music published the result, "Would'ja for a Big Red Apple," in 1931. Playing on the theme of conquest in love, the verse opens with the recognition that "Greater men than I have sought your favor, / But you merely glance at them and grin; / You spurn the vermin, / Who offer ermine and just a bit of sin." The verse continues, "Even though these propositions bore you, / Even though you're weary of the chase, / Let me put a plan before you — / Maybe it will help my case." Then in the refrain, Mercer lays out the question: "Would'ja do it just for instance, / Would'ja for my fam'ly tree — / If I had a big red apple, / Would'ja fall in love with me?" The lyric demonstrates the influence of Cole Porter on the budding songwriter. Mercer identified Porter as his favorite songwriter when later interviewed on the BBC: "I just love the first things he wrote. They were so clever, they were so sophisticated, and then as he got older, his tunes got stronger and stronger." While Johnny's lyric reveals his admiration for Porter's wordplay, he also expresses a plea to his girlfriend for her undying affection.[29]

Not only had *The Garrick Gaieties* resulted in Mercer's first published song, but it also introduced him to the woman who would become his wife. In the chorus line danced a girl who struck Johnny's fancy, the attractive Elizabeth "Ginger" Meltzer. She had taken the stage name of Meehan and sought fame under the bright lights. They met at a 1930 cast party her mother hosted in their Brooklyn home. Sharing a love for musical theater and hot jazz, Johnny and Ginger hit it off. Both continued with their careers while dating as Ginger lived with her mother and sisters on Sterling Place and Johnny lived in Greenwich Village.[30]

While dating Ginger, Johnny looked for acting work. Apparently he held a few bit parts, including a role in Karel Capek's play *R.U.R.*, a nightmarishly modern drama about robots replacing humans. As Mercer explained years later, "I came to New York to be an actor when I was about 19 years old and I tried it for a couple of years, but I ate a lot of oatmeal and pressed a lot of my own shirts. I couldn't get any jobs so I began to write and I sang a little bit and I got with a couple of bands." Meanwhile, Meehan performed in *The Garrick Gaieties* and then accompanied a version of the musical revue on the road. Johnny described Ginger as attractive, with ample "charms" and brown "eyes that crinkled up when she smiled." She would have found him to be "cute," an inch shy of six feet, weighing around 170 pounds with blue eyes and a smile he flashed to reveal a lusty gap between his teeth. His boyish brown hair had yet to recede beyond his broad forehead. A series of telegrams Johnny sent her shows his determination to win her heart. As letters, narratives, and photographs revealed, he continued to love her throughout his life, and they remained devoted to each other. In praising her virtues, Johnny said Ginger "never had any false pride or false values, thank God, and she knew what it was to work for a living."[31]

Creating the persona Ginger Meehan allowed Rose Elizabeth Meltzer to escape her unhappy childhood. Born a middle child in New York City on June 25, 1909, to Russian Jewish immigrants, Elizabeth had two sisters, Claire and Debbie. At first her parents, Joseph and Anna Meltzer, lived with his extended family in a crowded tenement house before moving to Brooklyn. A great-uncle taught music, and the Meltzers arranged piano lessons for Elizabeth and dance lessons for her and Claire. After Joseph killed himself in 1926, Anna supported her daughters by sewing fashionable children's clothing. Elizabeth tried to fill the void left by the absences, but arguments with her mother strained their relationship. The difficulties generated in Elizabeth lifelong anxiety over money and stability, emotional distance from those she loved, and dependence on alcohol for refuge. In late 1927, at age eighteen, Elizabeth joined the chorus line as a dancer. She put behind her the dysfunction of her home life by appearing on stage as Ginger Meehan, a name she borrowed from another young woman. She befriended fellow dancer Dolores Reade, who later married Bob Hope, and Dixie Carroll, who later married Bing Crosby, but not before Ginger had dated the popular singer herself: in 1928, Ginger had a brief affair with Bing that ended abruptly when Crosby turned his affections to another. Smarting from that experience, Ginger recognized the Catholic Crosby would have never married a Jewish girl, and she must have found in the southern Mercer and his courtly ways a charming security. Henceforth she compared Johnny to these associates in the entertainment industry, often placing Mercer in an unflattering light by contrasting his wealth with that of Crosby and Hope.[32]

For the rest of his life, as his career took him on the road, Johnny corresponded with Ginger, and while she saved the letters he wrote, he complained that he never received letters from her. Whatever she sent appears not to have survived. While courting Ginger, Johnny corresponded, "Ah, little flower, if you but knew the misery this humble personage went through until he finally heard from his lotus blossom." In an attempt to explain himself, he informed her in one letter that "out of the South came a son of the brave," and signed off on another as a "warm blooded Colonel from Savannah — Gawgia!" From California he wrote her of Bing's secret marriage to her chorus girlfriend, Dixie Carroll, now using the name Dixie Lee. On the road with *The Garrick Gaieties*, Ginger received these letters and telegrams from her suitor with growing interest.[33]

After dating for nearly a year, Johnny proposed to Ginger and she accepted in the spring of 1931. Mrs. Joseph Meltzer announced the engagement and the *Savannah Evening Press* published the story under the headline "Popular Savannahian To Marry Northern Girl." Johnny's shocked parents — who had not yet met Ginger — learned of the engagement from the newspaper. They suspected the worst: that a fast chorus girl had stolen their innocent son. Modernist Johnny tried to assure them otherwise, writing, "Above all, it is not just sex. Don't think for a moment that it is." His protestations about his love for Ginger fell on deaf ears, even though he closed one letter to his mother with the line, "My mind is made up," signed "Bubba," and one to his father signed "your black sheep." Clearly he understood his bid for independence had violated the obligations of honor and custom by not involving his parents in the decision-making process as tradition required. His action betrayed the spoiled behavior of his youth and pointed to bigger problems ahead. Recognizing that they might never approve of the match, he nonetheless embraced the liberating approach of the modern age to sex and marriage.[34]

The Mercers' initial response to news of the engagement was to ask the lovers to come to Savannah. To apologize, Johnny readily agreed and requested travel money, adding, "I have promised not to get married without seeing you, and I keep my promises." Then his parents balked and suggested they travel to New York to meet Ginger there. Johnny rejected this proposal and told them to stay home. This dithering set Ginger and Lillian Mercer at odds, and the two never settled into a comfortable relationship. Given Johnny's overweening devotion to them both and their competition for his favor, perhaps closeness could not have been expected. Johnny tried to arrange a trip south, but Charlie Miller intervened, recommending he stay in New York while waiting to hear about lyric-writing opportunities. Mercer then wrote home, "We have pretty definitely decided to get married, probably in the next week or two," and after the event, he mailed home a photograph of Ginger for the wedding announcement in the *Savannah Morning News*.[35]

The betrothed united on the strength of a show that failed to get produced, in the glorious surroundings of Manhattan's St. Thomas Church. Too nervous to do his best work, Mercer had composed lyrics with Harold Adamson to Vincent Youmans's tune for "How Happy Is the Bride," a song dropped from the musical *Through the Years*. He had better luck arranging through family members with connections to the parish to have the religious ceremony in this prestigious church, perhaps to appease his incensed parents. Noted composer Dr. T. Tertius Noble directed the men's and boys' choirs at St. Thomas and from this post wrote some of the most significant Anglican Church music of the day. The former choirboy Johnny heard this sacred song during divine services on Sunday mornings. In a private ceremony in the chantry of St. Thomas conducted by the Reverend Harold L. Gibbs on June 8, 1931, the couple exchanged vows, and while Ginger put on the marriage band, Johnny declined to wear the wedding ring. Walter Rivers stood as best man for his cousin and witnessed the event, while Lillian Mercer and Charlie Miller attended, along with several other friends. At first the newlyweds lived in Brooklyn with the Meltzers. To help make ends meet, Ginger assisted her mother — called Nana by family members — sewing clothes while Johnny hustled lyrics, but six months passed with little to show for his efforts.[36]

Over the Christmas holidays the newlyweds traveled to Georgia so Johnny's family, friends, and Savannah society could meet his bride. The attractive couple attended the debutante ball held in the DeSoto Hotel, where the young songwriter, dressed in white tie and tails, escorted around the lobby and grand ballroom his lovely wife, whose large orchid corsage emphasized the full bosom in her low-cut satin gown. Ever gracious, Aunt Katharine invited Ginger to a ladies' luncheon she hosted for her new daughter-in-law, Virginia Winn Boxley, who had married Johnny's cousin Joe Mercer the previous spring but lived in her natal Orange, Virginia, where he taught on the Woodberry Forest faculty. Held at the Colonial Kitchens tearoom, the affair included as guests one of Johnny's former girlfriends, Anne Lawrence, and several other debutantes, as well as brother Walter's new wife, Dorothy Brown Mercer. Ginger survived the scrutiny of the society mavens but made it clear to Johnny that she disliked Savannah's social set. He also took her to Vernon View, where they posed for a picture under the Spanish moss of a large live oak tree near the river with Ginger's right hand in the crook of Johnny's arm and her left holding a "big red apple."[37]

Years later, family friends from Savannah commented about the newlyweds. Jimmie McIntire observed about Ginger that "she was so obviously in love with him and he with her, nobody thought there was anything funny about" a young man from Savannah marrying a young woman from New York. His younger brother, P. B. McIntire, acknowledged that Ginger "was a very very sweet person," but also that "some people didn't like Ginger too much." He explained, "Some of the snobbish folks thought that Johnny had married beneath himself or something like that," but he quickly added, "she was popular in my family." Jimmie found Ginger to be "an attractive person, and she didn't mind being second fiddle to him either." He elaborated, "She'd sit back" so "he could grandstand all he wanted to." Their behavior suggested to Jimmie McIntire that "they really were very compatible."[38]

Just as he criticized Los Angeles, Johnny had harsh things to say about New York City. On returning north, Johnny wrote his mother: "The trip back was swell but how I hate this place. So dirty and noisy and whatnot. I can hardly wait until I make enough dough to leave it all and come back to Savannah for good. It's hardest thing getting adjusted, especially if getting adjusted is unpleasant. Ain't it the truth now? Enty?" Later Mercer explained to the jazz critic Willis Conover his attraction to New York: "The glamorous thing of New York is the city itself. The size of it, the amount of people in it and the hustle and bustle of it, and the opportunity not only to meet thousands of people, but to be lost, to be anonymous. It's a great thing." But then he added, "Most of the people in New York are awful people. You know, they push and they have no manners and they're out to survive. That's not what I like about New York." Instead, he confessed to writer Henry Kane: "I love New York. It's alive. It's where things happen." Daughter Mandy Mercer Neder remembered her father "loved to be where the work was" and since he "worked all the time," he was in and out of New York. Back on Tin Pan Alley, Mercer wrote his mother, "I have started right to work again, not with what you could call a bang, but I have started and everything seems to be going smoothly." He then concluded, "I just wanted to write and tell you that I love you dearly and miss you like the devil. My precious sweetheart — Ginger sends love" and signed it "Mistuh Jawnny, 'Tide high, Eli,'" referring to the old days at Vernon View.[39]

After New Year 1932, G. A. Mercer corresponded with Charlie Miller about Johnny's chances of success as a lyricist. Having financed his son for four years now, the father questioned his potential. No doubt he also feared the couple he had supported since the previous summer might start a family and increase their demands on his still-meager resources. Charlie Miller responded to each point in G. A. Mercer's letter, first assuring him that "John is a literary genius and will some day hit his stride" and then explaining: "This work, such as John does, is rather spasmodic. He must be financed and encouraged so that when the time comes he will be ready to use his talents." Miller justified Johnny's low wages by suggesting he had been "unproductive," but that "he has a lot of material ready and with the publication of his two recent songs we hope his income will be

increased the coming year." Miller confided in G. A., father to father, in a frank-
ness that resembled Woodberry Forest headmaster J. Carter Walker's letters to
the concerned parent. Describing his problems with his own son, who wanted to
be a composer, Miller confessed, "Everett's mind is not an artistic one but rather
mathamatical [sic] with a tendency towards mechanics and invention," hence the
father's determination to make his son an engineer. Yet as if blind to his own son's
ambitions, Miller emphasized, "I don't think John is building up an unhappy
and dissatisfied life. A man is only happy when he does the work he likes and
from observations I don't think John would be happy in any commercial pursuits." The letter convinced G. A. Mercer to continue supporting Johnny for the
time being.[40]

Bankrolling Miller Music was a wealthy engineer named William Hartman
Woodin. A contemporary of G. A. Mercer, Woodin had chaired the American
Locomotive Company but on the side composed tunes for popular songs. Charlie Miller paired him with Johnny. The result, "Spring Is in My Heart Again,"
played on lost and regained love, a theme that Mercer mastered over the course of
his career. Following Franklin D. Roosevelt's election in November 1932, Woodin
became the New Deal's secretary of the treasury, cutting short the potential of
future collaborations with Mercer. Johnny partnered with other composers, in
particular, Peter Tinturin, with whom he wrote "Little Old Crossroad Store" and
"Music from Across the Sea." He added lyrics to music by Richard Himber on
"Life's So Complete" and Joseph Meyer on "In a Café in Montmartre." Mercer's
output in these early years revealed a talented writer capable of producing polished, if not inspired, lyrics.[41]

In 1932, Johnny had another fateful pairing, this time with the composer
Lewis Gensler, who recruited Mercer to assist one of the few female lyricists with
whom he worked over his long career, Hilda Gottlieb. The two wrote words for
several of Gensler's melodies, including "Seven Little Steps to Heaven" and "The
Alphabet of Love Begins and Ends with You." Mercer collaborated with Gottlieb
on the words to a tune by Gensler for the first song he ever wrote for the movies, "What Will I Do without You? (What Will You Do without Me?)," which
Warner Bros. planned to use in its 1932 picture *College Coach* although producers
cut it from the film. Nevertheless, the chance collaboration with Gensler later
opened the studio doors in Hollywood for Johnny Mercer.[42]

Fellow lyricist E. Y. "Yip" Harburg tipped Johnny off to the need for additional lyrics for a Broadway revue being developed in 1932. Harburg's former wife lived in the same Brooklyn apartment building as the Mercers. Like

Ginger, Yip was born a native New Yorker in 1896 to Russian Jewish immigrant parents, who named him Irwin Hochberg. He had attended City College and gone into business, but the stock market crash had freed him to pursue his first love: writing lyrics. Having met during *The Garrick Gaieties*, Mercer considered Harburg a mentor as he explained in his autobiography: "I must say a word or two here in gratitude to Yip who gave me work and encouragement when it was sorely needed." Johnny assisted Yip in writing words to music by Lewis Gensler for the show *Ballyhoo of 1932*. The cute "Falling Off the Wagon" transformed a confession about a nascent drinking problem into a love song: "Bacardi, martini, / We're over and finis and through! / I swore off, I laid off — / I paid off my bootlegger, too. / I said, 'Not another,' / I promised my mother and dad. You came along, / And now it's just too bad." Addressing the love interest, the song continues: "John Barleycorn can't compare with you. / I see the ceiling reeling, / I see two moons above." Mercer resolved the lyric with "I'm falling off the wagon, / And I don't need a shove; / I'm staggerin', / Boy, I'm drunk with love!" While Johnny playfully joked about drinking too much, the problem later plagued his life.[43]

The Messers. Shubert provided another opportunity that resulted in Harburg's great protest song, a style of writing anathema to Mercer. Notorious for their brutal treatment of writers, composers, and actors, J. J. "Jake" and Lee Shubert produced the perennial revue *Americana* that opened in October 1932 and ran until the end of the year. For the show Harburg contributed the lyric "Brother, Can You Spare a Dime?" to music by Jay Gorney, and the song became an anthem for the Great Depression. Mercer disliked politicizing music. Years later, after complimenting his "good friend" as "a sensational writer," Johnny complained about Yip: "He's always had a little protest in almost all of his songs. You look through the lyrics in *Finian's Rainbow* and you'll see a lot of protest in there, and he's always that way." Mercer referred to the show's overt critique of southern race relations, but its character of the leprechaun also reflected Harburg's wily demeanor. Johnny resisted radical social commentary in song lyrics: "I've always avoided, I steer away from it, I hate it. I don't want to complain. I feel songs are to be sung and to be entertaining. I don't see them as a weapon."[44]

Yip needed other songwriters, so Mercer recommended to him Harold Arlen, the pianist at the Cotton Club who had composed the hit "Get Happy," and the two of them collaborated. Born Hyman Arluck in 1905 to Russian Jewish immigrants, Arlen grew up in Buffalo, New York, where his father served the synagogue as cantor, and introduced his son to Tin Pan Alley songwriter Jack Yellen. The boy learned the piano but wanted a stage career and appeared in Vincent Youmans's 1929 fiasco *Great Day!* Composing music for and playing piano in Harlem musical revues, Arlen studied jazz, making him an ideal partner for Johnny. Harburg paired them up as all three men — Mercer, Harburg, and Arlen — began to establish reputations in the songwriting profession.[45]

For *Americana*, Mercer and Arlen produced "Satan's Li'l Lamb," the first of several significant collaborations. Harold wrote pulsating music that began with a slow blues beat. At first Mercer had trouble finding a lyric. Talking over the difficulties with fellow lyricist Harburg helped. Johnny said that Yip "is a terrific writer . . . God, he'll sit in a room all day and he'll dig and he'll dig and he'll dig. And it shows . . . Yip was a big influence in teaching me how hard to work. Sometimes we'd get a rhyming dictionary and a *Roget's* [thesaurus] and we'd *sweat*." Johnny's lyrics to "Satan's Li'l Lamb" reflect his personal experiences, suggesting his sore relations with his parents over his marriage to Ginger. "Give me gin to forget the sin-sin-sinner that I am, / 'Cause I'm only Satan's li'l lamb." The last line recalled the way Johnny signed letters to his father: "'Cause it's heads he wins / And it's tails you lose / When you're Satan's little coal-black lamb!" In the show Francetta Malloy sang the number, while three dancers performed modern choreography. Hearing the piece, Ethel Merman recorded "Satan's Li'l Lamb" backed by Nat Shilkret and His Orchestra. The subject matter kept the song off the radio, and the show ran for only seventy-seven performances, so it did not become a hit, but it displayed Mercer's potential as a lyricist.[46]

Despite the somewhat successful initial collaboration, Mercer and Arlen went their separate ways. Yip Harburg convinced Harold Arlen to join him and Ira Gershwin on the musical revue *Life Begins at 8:40* starring Bert Lahr. The Jewish presence on Broadway and Tin Pan Alley made for a tight-knit community among co-religionists that could make Gentiles such as Johnny feel left out. Nevertheless, Mercer embraced their cosmopolitan worldview and remained a close associate. Meanwhile Arlen and Harburg collaborated on "Over the Rainbow" and other songs for Metro-Goldwyn-Mayer's *Wizard of Oz* co-starring Lahr. Years passed before Arlen and Mercer worked together again. Once they did, they discovered they had a lot in common. The Jewish Harold had fallen in love and married against his father's wishes a Russian Orthodox woman named Anya, just as the Episcopalian Johnny, disobeying his parents, had married the Jewish Ginger. In addition to their private lives, the two men shared a love for jazz that they later incorporated into popular song in a fashion that brought out the best of their talents. In the interim, cut loose from Arlen, Johnny looked for a composer with whom to collaborate.[47]

After an arranged meeting between Johnny Mercer and Hoagy Carmichael, the two jazz artists began working in earnest. Thinking that a "song plugger" had introduced them, perhaps at the Onyx Club on Fifty-second Street or at the Spirits of Rhythm in Harlem, Carmichael remembered Johnny as a "young, bouncy butterball of a man from Georgia." Mercer recalled specifically that the introduction came through Eddie Woods, who worked in the stock room at Ralph Peer's Southern Music, the company that published Carmichael's songs. Johnny also said he "leapt at the opportunity to write with Hoagy."[48]

Born in 1899, Hoagland Howard Carmichael came of age during ragtime in the Indiana college town of Bloomington, where he learned to play the piano from his mother and, after a move to Indianapolis, from a local black musician who gave him lessons on how to make hot music. A Protestant like Johnny, Hoagy attended the public schools, where he booked the bands for high school dances and consumed the new jazz style. While studying at Indiana University, he met the great white jazz cornetist Bix Beiderbecke, whose Wolverine Orchestra played Hoagy's first song, "Riverboat Shuffle," which was recorded in 1925, followed by "Washboard Blues" and then "Stardust" in 1927. At first a sensation as an instrumental, "Stardust" with lyrics by Mitchell Parish and published by Mills Music in 1929 became a standard in the catalogue of Great American Song. In tune with the jazz age, Carmichael moved to New York, where, like Johnny, he worked part-time in the stock market as he plugged his songs. In short order he published three hits, "Rockin' Chair," "Georgia on My Mind," and "Lazy River," all initially recorded by top jazz artists, including Louis Armstrong, Benny Goodman, Joe Venuti, Mildred Bailey, Frank Trumbauer, Gene Krupa, and Beiderbecke. In some ways Carmichael had reached a plateau in his career, for with the death of Beiderbecke from pneumonia worsened by alcoholism in 1931, something in Carmichael died too. Thus the collaboration with Mercer rekindled a passion to compose jazz music.[49]

At first the two hit it off. In notes to his publisher, Carmichael recalled about Mercer: "Impressed with personality. Put him to work. He wrote good lyric to 'Old Man Harlem.' Not very big song tho." Rather than credit the words to Mercer, however, Carmichael convinced the novice songwriter to allow Rudy Vallee to claim credit as lyricist. This old practice of giving a popular performer rights to a song he did not write in order to help get it plugged grated on Mercer's nerves, and "Old Man Harlem" seems to be the only such example in his career. Their next two songs, "After Twelve O'Clock" and "Thanksgivin'," both love themes, received little notice despite the latter being recorded by the Casa Loma Orchestra. Then one day Mercer knocked at the door of Carmichael's new digs, a spacious apartment on Fifty-second Street near Park Avenue. Welcomed inside, Johnny told Hoagy he wanted to write a song called "Lazybones," taking the title from Carmichael's lullaby "Snowball." Interested, Hoagy sat down at the keyboard and later recalled he "accidently hit piano solo from Washboard and in 20 minutes we had the complete song." Mercer remembered he spent days agonizing over words for the verse. After yet another read-through of the lyric, Hoagy suggested the surprise last line, "You never heard a word I say." The end result sounded unlike any of the previous Tin Pan Alley "Back to Dixie" southern songs, for here a native son had combined rhythmic jazz with the region's vernacular to create a genuine image of the South.[50]

Ralph Peer — the great scout of jazz, blues, and hillbilly music — had recognized the quality of Carmichael's compositions and signed him to a contract with the Southern Music Publishing Company, so Hoagy and Johnny placed "Lazybones" with him. Once recorded by the "Songbird of the South," Virginian Kate Smith, and the Casa Loma Orchestra, and given frequent airplay over the radio, "Lazybones" became a hit within six weeks, selling 15,000 copies a day, requiring the company to hire additional staff to handle the volume. Released in 1933 at the rock bottom of the Great Depression, "Lazybones," with its audacious theme of idly wasting the day by a fishing stream rather than working at a job, resonated with Americans in an age of uncontrollable, massive unemployment. Carmichael claimed that prior to the song's appearance Tin Pan Alley sat virtually empty of people, but shortly thereafter, "the success of 'Lazybones' seemed to generate new confidence in the music business and within a year Times Square started to look itself again." In recognition of this accomplishment, and sales of 350,000 copies of the song in three months, the American Society of Composers, Authors and Publishers (ASCAP) recognized Carmichael and Mercer with a special award of $2,500 that the men split evenly. "My first real hit," Carmichael said of "Lazybones," measuring success in financial terms.[51]

The lyric of "Lazybones" combines images, customs, and sounds of a hybrid southern culture to create a sense of place that some critics have mistaken as being representative of African Americans only. Instead, Mercer's imagery in the lyric reflects the shared experiences of black and white people in his native South. "Lazybones, sleepin' in the sun, / How you 'spec' to get your day's work done? / Never get your day's work done, / Sleepin' in the noonday sun." References to having "your corn meal made," eating "chicken gravy on your rice," and finding "watermelon on the vine" complete the visuals of the region's multiracial food-ways just as the reference to fishing points to a favorite southern pastime. Carmichael's biographer, Richard M. Sudhalter, believed that "the dialect used in 'Lazybones' makes clear that the boy they depict is black," but there is nothing in the wording to suggest the race of the "lazybones" as much as the region he comes from. A stronger claim suggesting a racial link to the lyric may be made of "Old Man Harlem" because of the reference to the famed black section of New York City. Yet Johnny's words suggest not an old black man but rather the jazz-based, alcohol-induced nightlife that personified Harlem: "Old Man Harlem / Gives me Sunday headache / I've got Harlem in my bones." Revealing his familiarity with the Harlem jazz scene, Mercer continues: "He takes all your dough and keeps you skimpin' / Makes you old and gray before you're limpin'"; nevertheless, "Always finds me / Dancin' when the day breaks / But ol' Harlem keeps me rollin' on." While Rudy Vallee made a recording of "Old Man Harlem" and got credit for the lyric, Ethel Waters left the definitive version on wax.[52]

At its release, people interpreted "Lazybones" in different ways. United Press International reported from Germany that the white supremacist regime of Adolf Hitler — having just come to power in Germany — banned the "Nigger song" because it "encourages idleness and does not conform to Nazi ideals." The black newspaper columnist Carl Rowan, in a syndicated memorial to Mercer published in 1976, fondly remembered that "as a boy of 8 in Tennessee, wading barefoot in a creek looking under rocks for crawfish, I learned about 'the work ethic' from Johnny Mercer." As a catchphrase promoted by *New York Mirror* entertainment columnist Walter Winchell, "Lazybones" soon found itself attached to recreational products to promote sales as consumers responded to President Franklin D. Roosevelt's "Happy Days Are Here Again" and bought merchandise.[53]

The popularity of "Lazybones" derived in part from Johnny's ability to speak for the thirty million migrants caught up in the southern diaspora. Scattered across the country, these black, white, and Latino southerners took their hybrid culture with them into the manufacturing and service jobs of America. As wage earners, these southern consumers bought back their multiracial culture as a commodified product in the new recordings.[54]

After writing with Mercer, Carmichael spent six weeks traveling in Europe, finding there the widespread popularity of jazz, and then, upon his return to the United States, the phenomenal success of "Lazybones," which convinced him to renew the collaboration with Johnny. One effort, "Down T'Uncle Bill's," placed with Southern Music, with its rustic vision of a Thanksgiving holiday at home, fit that party standard so popular with people singing around the piano, whereas "Old Skipper," placed with Miller Publishing, proved largely forgettable. With "Moon Country (Is Home to Me)," however, the "partnership enjoyed its first full flowering and showed the breadth of its potential," according to Carmichael biographer Sudhalter. Hoagy's music captures the nostalgic tone that Johnny's lyric evokes with references to the rural ideal in America, which was vanishing in the modern industrial age. Mercer recalls his native region in glowing terms in "Moon Country," describing the "peach trees" and "sycamore heaven back South," where "folks . . . just live off the land" and food "melts in your mouth." The image of the "good for the soul country" captured in the song played well among people suffering from economic dislocation or displaced by the Great Depression. These songs by Carmichael and Mercer harken back to the stability of the turn-of-the-century twilight years described in the poetry by James Whitcomb Riley that both men had heard as children.[55]

Yet conflicts exacerbated by "Moon Country" fractured the friendship of Hoagy and Johnny and hindered future collaborations. In recalling Mercer, Carmichael said in his autobiography, "With proper guidance and diligent work, Johnny and I could have flooded the market with hit songs. We were attuned and I knew he 'knew' and he knew I 'knew.' But the chips didn't fall right. Probably my fault because I didn't handle them gently." This passage reveals several key observations, the first and foremost being that Mercer and Carmichael could write jazz-infused popular song and not simply Tin Pan Alley schlock. But more to the point here, Carmichael admitted he mishandled the relationship. "We didn't get along so well, like most teams. I guess main trouble was I considered him my helper. I got most credit because of established name." Ten years Johnny's senior, Carmichael carried this attitude into the collaboration. "My thinking [was] that I was more informed and more worldly wise than Johnny (being older). Don't think he liked or took it in [the] right spirit. Am sure now that my conception of property rights and values was unfortunate." An early manuscript of Carmichael's autobiography includes his account of writing "Moon Country" in which he explains to Ralph Peer of Southern Music Publishing: "I think this is the way it should be divided up, I should get so much for what I did and Johnny should get so much for what he did. This wasn't Johnny's feeling and it wasn't Peer's feeling either. They thought it was wrong . . . The contract was made up my way and I think Johnny resented it." Carmichael knew Ginger disapproved. When the song was published in 1934, the credits listed "Words and Music by Hoagy Carmichael and Johnny Mercer," no doubt with Hoagy getting a greater percentage of the take. The disagreement cooled the friendship. "We drifted and it was another case of where starting someone didn't pay dividends," concluded Carmichael. He soon left Southern Music although Mercer remained with Peer long enough to publish several other hits. Years later, Johnny confessed to André Previn that Hoagy was "a bastard" to work with.[56]

Instead of a steady stream of songs written with one composer, Johnny embarked on a career in which he collaborated with a handful of core colleagues and then nearly a hundred other composers through whom he produced only the occasional hit. Mercer failed to form a lasting partnership with either Carmichael or Arlen such as that of the Gershwin brothers, Rodgers and Hart, Rodgers and Hammerstein, or Lerner and Loewe. Indeed, Mercer's short-term collaborations with both Arlen and Carmichael reflected a pattern of temporary associations with composers that the songwriter repeated time and again throughout his professional life. Whether or not he ever looked for one, Johnny never found a partner with whom to build a large body of work. Speculation might lead one to conclude that Mercer proved difficult to work with, but little testimony from his collaborators suggests this to be true. Instead, it appears his musical interests varied so greatly that he could not commit to any songwriter. While shifting from one composer to another kept his songs fresh and timely, the absence of a long-term partner prevented him from developing that intimate relationship that builds to strengths. Nevertheless, Mercer wrote his better music with fellow jazz arranger-composers such as Arlen and Carmichael as demonstrated by the hits they created when working together again at various stages of their careers. Given the sporadic nature of the work, such impermanence in partnerships proved typical for many lyricists such as Yip Harburg, who had almost as many collaborators as Mercer and called the practice "composer hopping."[57]

Paul Whiteman managed the most successful jazz band of the 1920s and early 1930s, and many of the era's greatest jazz musicians apprenticed with him, including Johnny Mercer. By 1932, Whiteman's orchestra had begun what became a long engagement of regular performances at New York's Biltmore Hotel, performing in the Bowman Room in the winter and the rooftop Cascades Room in the summer. With Mildred Bailey on vocals and her husband, Red Norvo, on xylophone, the band created a syncopation that dancers relished. GM sponsored NBC Radio broadcasts of many of these concerts, and Whiteman billed his band, the Chieftains, as a nod to GM's Pontiac Division. Pontiac sponsored a Youth of America competition managed by Whiteman and held in the NBC studios as an *American Idol*–type contest during March 1932. Ginger, who recognized Johnny's talents as a jazz singer, convinced him to audition. The jazz arranger Archie Bleyer accompanied Mercer as he performed a fast number to land a spot in the sing-offs. Fifty finalists appeared before Whiteman and the band in the last competition, but among the "crooners, warblers, torch singers, and mammy wanters," Johnny recalled he stood out by singing "heart-rending ballads with the pathos of one who has loved and lost innumerable times." Whiteman declared Mercer the winner of the competition, an outcome that enabled Johnny to participate in the band's broadcast from the old vaudeville Palace Theater on March 25, 1932. Initially nothing came further of what Johnny had hoped would prove a big break.[58]

Yet the song "Lazybones" drew the attention of "Pops" Whiteman, who remembered Johnny from the Pontiac Youth of America competition the previous year. In 1933, he asked Mercer to audition with his organization. Retooling his outfit, Whiteman had in mind letting Johnny create a new Rhythm Boys to replace Bing Crosby's trio, which had left the band. Mercer got two friends to perform with him and, although the group did not click with Whiteman, Johnny did, for the jazz leader hired him to both sing and write songs. Sensing a shared southern sensibility he could exploit through duets, Whiteman paired Johnny with another recent hire, the Texan trombonist Jack Teagarden.[59]

A fellow southern diaspora entertainer, Teagarden journeyed from his Panhandle hometown of Vernon to New York City by way of numerous stops that introduced him to many styles of jazz. Born in 1905 to a descendant of pioneer settlers who had supported the Confederacy, Weldon "Jack" Teagarden grew up in a musical family that eked out a living running a cotton gin. Given his first trombone at age eight, the boy accompanied his piano-playing mother on Tin Pan Alley tunes and later assisted her in providing music for the silent movies shown in the town theater. In an orchestra that performed classical compositions by Giuseppe Verdi and others, the youth often embellished the written notes, revealing his penchant for improvisation. An annual tent revival staged near his house attracted him to the gospel sounds and syncopation of black worshipers. When his father died in the great flu epidemic, Jack left home to join the first of several bands, including Peck Kelley's Bad Boys that later featured Charles

"Pee Wee" Russell, a clarinet player from St. Louis. In the mid-1920s, Jack toured Mexico with the Original Southern Trumpeters, being billed as "The South's Greatest Trombone Wonder." As a member of the Peacocks, he played at the opening of the new Peabody Hotel in Memphis in 1925. Touring the Southwest in pickup groups, Jack met Wingy Manone, a trumpet player from New Orleans. By 1927, the Texas trombonist had arrived in New York, first performing with the white house band at the Roseland ballroom that alternated sets with the black house band under the baton of Fletcher Henderson. Here Jack befriended the black trombonist James Henry "Jimmy" Harrison as the two jazz artists shared their innate talent to make the instrument sing. A fellow southerner — Harrison hailed from Louisville, Kentucky — the two became inseparable, according to Coleman Hawkins, himself a native of Missouri who likewise worked as a diaspora entertainer. Months later, Jack was in league with jazz musicians from the Chicago school in Ben Pollack's band, including Jimmy McPartland on trumpet, Joe Sullivan on piano, Eddie Condon on guitar, and Benny Goodman on clarinet. In March 1929, Jack recorded at Okeh studios with an integrated ensemble featuring Louis Armstrong, on what became a seminal release called "Knockin' a Jug." From the Pollack band, Teagarden played with the Dorseys before joining the Whiteman outfit.[60]

In addition to being the greatest jazz trombonist of the age, capable of making the instrument sound as lyrical as a trumpet, Teagarden sang with a deep bass voice that complemented Johnny Mercer's baritone and tenor range. Working for Whiteman, the two developed an Amos and Andy–like routine. The duo sang "Ain't Misbehavin'," the Thomas "Fats" Waller song with lyrics by Andy Razaf that Jack had earlier recorded with his friend, Fats, as well as "Christmas Night in Harlem" and other pieces reflective of Harlemania as the "black metropolis" of the southern diaspora registered with the American public. With Jack in mind Johnny specifically wrote the lyric "Fare-Thee-Well to Harlem" to a tune by Bernie Hanighen that they placed with Ralph Peer's Southern Music Publishing Company in 1934. The duet included such lines as "Fare-thee-well to nightlife! / Goin' back where I can lead the right life" and "Things is tight in Harlem; / I know how to fix it: / Step aside, I'm gonna Mason-Dix it." The lead character then sings a syncopated series of jazz notes that develops the religious theme and concludes with a call for reverse migration: "All this sin is frighteous; / Goin' back where ev'rybody's righteous." In December 1933, the two gave a memorable performance of the duet and exchanged comic banter on the stage of the Metropolitan Opera House. Whiteman had also hired the exotic dancer Sally Rand to gyrate on certain numbers, and so Jack was able to appreciate Johnny's marksmanship as he flicked cigarette butts at the woman's balloons.[61]

The association with Teagarden might have preceded the Whiteman contract and resulted from evenings spent in nightclubs and at rent parties, where Johnny studied the hot music and met the black and white jazz musicians. A veteran of the Jean Goldkette Orchestra and Andrian Rolini's band, the St. Louis saxophonist Frankie Trumbauer performed with the Whiteman organization until the spring of 1932, when he left to form his own group. Johnny joined Trumbauer's band to make his first singing recording, "My Honey's Lovin' Arms," on April 5, 1932. The single captured Johnny's jazz inflection with a strong scat that revealed a debt to Louis Armstrong. Throughout 1932 and 1933, Johnny hung around the premier jazz musicians who congregated in New York at such speakeasies as Joe Helbock's Onyx Club on Fifty-second Street, uptown in Harlem at Pod's and Jerry's Log Cabin, or at Connie's Inn. He met his contemporary, the jazz fanatic John Hammond who, born into the Vanderbilt family and wealth in 1910, had attended prep school at Hotchkiss and college at Yale followed by a stint as a radical reporter for *The Nation* covering the Scottsboro Boys before promoting New York's jazz scene by arranging recording sessions for integrated ensembles. In November 1933, Hammond summoned a group of musicians to the studios of Columbia Records at 55 Fifth Avenue to back a young singer he had discovered months before performing her signature piece — Johnny Mercer's "Would'ja for a Big Red Apple?"— at Monette Moore's speakeasy on 133rd Street in Harlem. On clarinet, Benny Goodman headed the band, which included Joe Sullivan on piano, Dick McDonough on guitar, Gene Krupa on drums, Jack Teagarden on trombone, with his brother, Charlie, on trumpet, as well as the black trumpeter Shirley Clay, and the heretofore-unknown fourteen-year-old black singer Billie Holiday.[62]

When the group gathered on December 4, 1933, Johnny Mercer contributed a lyric to a tune guitarist McDonough toyed with called "Riffin' the Scotch." Captured on wax on December 18, the song was Billie Holiday's first record release. Somehow in the words Johnny anticipated the hapless fate surrounding the blues singer. Mercer recalled, "When I met Billie in 1933 . . . there was something about . . . the torchy quality of her voice." He added, "She was quite a pretty girl, but there was something about her — not just the torchy quality of her voice — that made you want to try to help her." Almost prescient, his lines in "Riffin' the Scotch" went, "I jumped out of the frying pan / Right into the fire, / When I lost me a cheatin' man / And got a no-count liar. / Swipe the old one for the new one, / Now the new one's breaking my heart."

The subject of being unlucky in love proved a regular theme in Lady Day's repertoire. Born in 1915 as Eleanora Gough, the young black girl discovered jazz while cleaning a Baltimore brothel that had a Victrola, "West End Blues," and other recordings by Louis Armstrong. Imitating the records, she began singing in area clubs. In 1929, she joined the southern diaspora, following her mother on the Great Migration to New York City, where she took the name Billie Holiday and looked for gigs. Like Johnny Mercer during these years, Billie hung around nightclubs listening to jazz musicians and perfecting an original style marked by clear enunciation. Mercer tailored several lyrics to fit Holiday, and she cut a number of wonderful recordings of his songs.[63]

When paired again with Bernie Hanighen, Johnny wrote hits for both Holiday and Whiteman. The two songwriters shared a similar childhood and love of jazz. Like Johnny from a privileged background in the American hinterlands, Hanighen grew up in Omaha, Nebraska, but attended Harvard College, where his love of jazz led him to writing music for the Hasty Pudding. He met Johnny in New York's bar scene listening to the bands perform on Fifty-second Street and in Harlem. For Billie Holiday Mercer wrote lyrics to a tune by Hanighen and Gordon Jenkins called "When a Woman Loves a Man," which she later recorded with friend and fellow diaspora entertainer from Woodville, Mississippi, the great Lester Young on tenor saxophone. After the Whiteman success of "Fare-Thee-Well to Harlem," Mercer and Hanighen wrote for Pops "Here Come the British," published by Irving Berlin in 1934. Designed as a novelty piece for the band, the song played on the theme of a history lesson, with a "Bang! Bang!" that thrilled audiences. Like so many of Mercer's collaborations, his partnership with Hanighen faded when a new composer attracted Johnny's attention, with sporadic reprises over the years.[64]

As part of the Whiteman organization Mercer worked with a variety of sidemen, including Matt "Matty" Malneck, a talented jazz arranger in Pops's orchestra who played violin and wrote tunes. Although he had grown up in Newark, New Jersey, Matty partnered with Johnny on a song for the Savannahian to sing with Whiteman called "Pardon My Southern Accent," published in 1934. Following a Cole Porter formula, Mercer framed his story with classical references but punctuated the chorus with "If you don't like my accent, / If you don't like my drawl, / Then just don't listen, / Let's start kissin' / Bet you'll fall!" The subject revealed his sensitivity at being southern in a national entertainment industry. The printing of the lyrics in such publications as *Song Hit Folio* helped popularize the words in an effort to sell more sheet music. Features on recording artists and photographs from movies further plugged the songs. Complimenting Mercer's talent, Matty Malneck told the agent Jack Robbins, Johnny "is the greatest lyric writer in the world, better than Hammerstein and Berlin."[65]

The fluid nature of working with Whiteman, traveling with the band, and picking up opportunities to draft lyrics for a variety of composers suited Mercer's style. Two of the songs from this period remained his personal favorites. Johnny explained that the idea for the first, "P.S. I Love You," came to him after reading the *New Yorker*'s regular feature, "Talk of the Town," which had one week labeled a subsection "P.S." to which Mercer appended the catchphrase "I love you." Recognizing a great song title, he then realized, "Well naturally it's got to be in the form of a letter." Later he claimed to have written it as an actual letter to Ginger that then struck his fancy as a potential lyric. As the refrain suggests with its opening, "Dear, I thought I'd drop a line," the song contains mundane references to daily affairs that reveal the longing of the writer for the missing lover. In an unusual turnabout, Mercer crafted his words first around the title and a dummy tune he composed, then shared the draft song with Gordon Jenkins, who set the lyrics to music with the resulting "P.S. I Love You" topping the charts in 1934. With Charles Bates, Mercer wrote his other personal favorite, "On the Nodaway Road." With its bucolic imagery of rural America, the lyric recognized the dignity of work by rewarding labor at the end of the day. Yet the public cared little for the romantic look at the drudgery of farm life. Mercer and Michael H. Cleary wrote the novelty song "The Bathtub Ran Over Again," which Jack Teagarden recorded with Sterling Bose for Decca. Whiteman produced a radio program called *Kraft Music Hall*, and in addition to singing, Mercer wrote situation comedies and parodies — they called them clambakes — for the NBC broadcasts sponsored by Miracle Whip Salad Dressing, which featured such stars as Al Jolson. Whiteman referred to Mercer's singing as "recitation in rhythm." Wearing a variety of hats, Johnny honed his skills as a songwriter and a performer.[66]

In February 1934, Mercer returned to Savannah for the first time in two years. Touting his success in entertainment, the *Savannah Evening Press* ran an interview with the lyricist, noting, "He is still the likable, modest chap that he was when he left Savannah in 1928." The interviewer rhapsodized that "he is not likely to be called 'Mr. Mercer' more than once by anyone, for his charming manner soon prompts even a stranger to call him 'Johnny.'" Describing his output, the interviewer reported that Mercer "works with several composers because so far he hasn't found a single person who writes tunes fast enough for the number of lyrics he turns out." Johnny elaborated on what prompted songs: "You see a word somewhere which suggests a title, or you just think it up." He later explained about collaboration that he liked to settle on the idea or title of the song with the composer, who then wrote the music for Mercer to set with words. Yet in his house Johnny kept a drawer filled with scraps of draft tunes sent to him by composers wanting to collaborate. When needed, Mercer took one out to ponder words that might fit the music, mulling it over until he settled on the right lyric. Johnny told the interviewer that he published one of the four songs he finished on average each month. If the product turned into a hit, then "the best writers can hope for is approximately $5,000 or $6,000," which was half the take when split with a composer. The paper also reported Mercer's declaration that "he loved Savannah and wanted to return here when he made enough money." In the most perceptive passage, the article concluded, "Johnny probably revealed the secret of his success when he admitted he had 'loved jazz' almost from its beginning in America. His spirit is in his work."[67]

The income Mercer earned from Whiteman enabled the young couple to move to Manhattan from Brooklyn, which allowed Johnny to really enjoy the fast-paced cosmopolitan life of the New York jazz scene: "It's all such a montage of work and drinking and nightclubbing, and publishing rooms writing all day and calling Ginger I'd be home late; or meeting her at some new little pad where a few of our old friends were waiting to introduce us to new ones, that I can't get the sequences of events straight." The pace never let up as he met new lyricists, composers, and musicians and wrote songs recorded by Benny Goodman or the Dorsey Brothers Orchestra. Johnny joined the New York jazz in-crowd, occasionally grabbing a drink at Jimmy Plunkett's bar on West Fifty-third Street, where musicians hung out between gigs. Radio carried live shows that required studio orchestras and provided regular work for songwriters like Johnny and musicians like Jimmy and Tommy Dorsey, with whom Mercer occasionally performed. These two brothers from Pennsylvania had started playing Dixieland music with Red Nichols and Adrian Rollini in the seminal California Ramblers and then joined the Goldkette Band out of Detroit, which included Frank Trumbauer, before forming the famed Dorsey Brothers Orchestra from 1928 to 1935. At Plunketts, the Dorseys mixed with Benny Goodman and other Chicago jazzmen, southerners such as Jack Teagarden, and midwesterners like fellow trombone player Glenn Miller. Red McKenzie, an older jazz vocalist from St. Louis, recalled the young Johnny "nervous at finding himself in the fast company of the Whiteman organization." Teagarden took the lead in easing Johnny's "stage fright" with rounds of alcohol.[68]

For jazz musicians, drinking proved as much a part of the profession as playing a horn. The friendships Johnny formed among these jazzmen lasted for life, as did the substance abuse. Drinking with Teagarden was nothing new to Mercer. Throughout his teens, Johnny had a ready supply of quality liquors thanks to his wealthy friends and bootlegging Ciucevich uncles, marking the beginning of his lifelong affair with alcohol, which deepened during his New York years. Usually booze made everything grand, but on occasion when he drank too much, the alcohol loosened the leash that kept his tongue in check. Unrestrained, Mercer made offensive remarks to friends and strangers alike. He felt ashamed once he sobered up and thought about his behavior. Yet at this stage in his life, alcohol simply added to the glamour and excitement of performing with the nation's leading jazz band.[69]

To learn the songwriting trade, Mercer observed the song pluggers who placed the products of Tin Pan Alley with jazz bands and in Broadway shows. Johnny visited the restaurants on the edge of the theater district like the original Lindy's on Fiftieth Street and its Fifty-first Street venue, getting to know several of the veteran hustlers. As a journeyman songwriter, he provided material for Broadway revues, nightclub acts, and jazz ensembles. By hanging out with Frankie Trumbauer, Benny Goodman, and the Dorsey Brothers, Mercer learned the latest jazz licks. Others tapped his talents to help them with songs, as when publisher Jack Robbins convinced Johnny to clean up a lyric by Macy O. Teetor to fit a tune by Phil Ohman for "Lost," which both the Jan Garber and Guy Lombardo orchestras recorded. "When I worked in bands, I'd sit with them between sets . . . in a small way I too, was a plug, and might make a record or sing their songs on a guest shot." With the growth of radio and the movie musicals, Johnny witnessed the evolution of the industry and saw the song pluggers relocate to Hollywood to take up shop at the Brown Derby restaurant. He would soon follow.[70]

When not booked at the Biltmore, Whiteman often took his band on the road, where by chance Johnny Mercer attended an early performance by Judy Garland. On May 27, 1933, the Whiteman organization played at the opening of the Chicago World's Fair of 1933–34, and returned in August for a two-week gig at the Oriental Theatre. Johnny caught an act by the Gumm Sisters, who also performed in the city. The sketch featured the precocious twelve-year-old Frances singing, in the words of vaudeville star George Jessel, "like a woman with a heart that had been hurt" the song "Bill" from *Show Boat*. Not long after, Frances Gumm took the stage name Judy Garland. A native of Grand Rapids, Minnesota, Judy was a child of the southern diaspora, for her father, the Tennessee native Frank Gumm, had attended the Sewanee Military Academy and the University of the South before vaudeville lured him out of the region. He married a piano player, Ethel Milne from Michigan, and the couple toured the Midwest as the singing duo Jack and Virginia Lee: Sweet Southern Singers. The arrival of children necessitated regular income, so Frank invested in a Grand Rapids theater. Baby Frances Ethel Gumm was born into show business in 1922. Her domineering stage mother created the act as the Gumdrops, although the innate vocal talent of Baby Frances made her stand out from her two older sisters. Mesmerized by her singing, little did Johnny know the impact Judy would have on his later life.[71]

The holidays of 1934 found the Whiteman Orchestra playing in the top of the Mount Royal Hotel in Montreal, Canada. Sold-out concerts every night to the appreciative locals made Mercer muse, "It takes me back to what it must have been like years ago, the glory that was Whiteman." Pops cultivated that image, arriving at the resort in a horse-drawn sleigh. While on the road, the twenty-five-year-old Mercer bonded with Charlie and Jack Teagarden, Frankie Trumbauer, and other musicians as they went skiing, drinking, and "wenching" in exercises of male friendship. Also he valued meeting the variety of performers associated with the Whiteman organization, including the pianists Ramona and Dana Suesse. From Montreal, Johnny wrote Ginger a love letter, noting, "Three years should have dampened our ardor somewhat, but they haven't, and the more I know you, the surer I feel that time never will. I know I'm not much of a bargain as a husband, but I'm what I am, and being that way, there'll never be anyone else for me but you." Weeks on the road made married life difficult for the young couple, so Johnny constantly searched for employment that might provide financial stability and allow for the start of a family.[72]

Mercer's success with the Whiteman organization landed him an RKO Radio Pictures movie contract in 1935 to write, act, and sing in Hollywood, for which Pops granted him a leave of absence. Still sporting a sickly yellow pallor from a bout of jaundice, Johnny took off with Ginger for the West Coast. The agent Zion Myers cast him in B films, however. He appeared in and wrote songs for two pictures, *Old Man Rhythm* and *To Beat the Band*, neither of which did well at the box office. Nevertheless, the time in California convinced the couple of its charms. It also introduced Johnny to individuals who later played key roles in the movie industry.[73]

Cast as a college student in *Old Man Rhythm*, Johnny also contributed the lyrics to music by Lewis E. Gensler for what became his first film score. Having previously worked with Mercer, Gensler recruited him for RKO. The two wrote several songs, including "Boys Will Be Boys, Girls Will Be Girls" and "Comes the Revolution, Baby," a number that featured Mercer in the singing. The film starred Buddy Rogers and George Barbier, while Johnny shared the screen with newcomers Lucille Ball and Betty Grable in bit parts. The pantomime Dave Chasen also appeared in the cast, but he soon quit acting to run what became one of Hollywood's most famous restaurants, Chasen's. In his most memorable scene, Mercer joins the chorus of students traveling on a train as they perform "There's Nothing Like a College Education." He sings from the luggage rack being used as a berth: "Oh, I left my old plantation in the South-a / With my southern accent drippin' from my mouth-a / Just to hear you Yankees talk to one a-nouth-a, / But I can't understand a word." After confessing his troubles in his German class, Johnny admits his success in the "lovemaking course," where "Every day my mark is an A; / I'll tell you why: I satisfy!" Then he clarifies, "Any time those coeds wanna pet, I pets 'em; / If they want to cuddle in my arms, I lets 'em; / It's my southern hospitality that gets 'em." In Savannah the film's showing at the Lucas Theatre won rave reviews from family and friends. Mercer performed well enough that RKO Studios picked up his option for the second film.[74] Although *To Beat the Band* showcased the jazz ensemble the Original California Collegians, the movie fared no better at the box office than *Old Man Rhythm*. Yet it did result in several quality songs. Johnny's friend from Whiteman's band, Matty Malneck, collaborated with him on the music for the score. The two wrote several numbers, including "Meet Miss America," "Eeny Meeny Miney Mo," and "If You Were Mine." The latter two songs provided the music for Billie Holiday to perform on her seventh recording session, captured in the studio in October 1935 with accompaniment by Teddy Wilson and His Orchestra.[75]

During the filming of *To Beat the Band*, Mercer met a young dancer and sometime composer who later became one of Hollywood's greatest stars. Fred Astaire and Ginger Rogers had been filming *Flying Down to Rio* on nearby studio lots. In addition to singing and dancing, Astaire composed music, and he gave Johnny a tune with the request that Mercer write words to fit the melody. The collaboration resulted in "I'm Building Up to an Awful Letdown." Its sophisticated wording provided light phrasing for Astaire: "My castles in the air, / My smile so debonair, / My one big love affair, / Is it just a flash? / Will it all go smash, / Like the nineteen twenty-nine market crash?" Over the course of their careers Mercer and Astaire crossed paths several times on Hollywood musicals, always to the benefit of each other's talents.[76]

Another independent success with Malneck demonstrated Mercer's abilities as a songwriter. The two wrote "Goody Goody," which became a big hit. Mercer later explained to Willis Conover, "It's just a phrase that everybody said but I just, I don't know why I got that particular approach to it. You know, the 'ha, ha, ha, goody, goody to me.'" Although over the span of his career Mercer did not often suggest alterations to his published songs, he wanted to revise this one. "Recently I changed one word which I think makes it a much better song... Instead of saying 'you rascal you,' I now sing it 'and I hope you're satisfied you baddy you,'" he told Conover in 1970, adding, "I think that it's one of my best songs." The reception of "Goody Goody" helped polish Johnny's reputation as a lyric writer in Tinsel Town, especially after Benny Goodman's recording of it topped the pop charts. The enthusiastic young lyricist on the West Coast with several successful songs attracted the attention of the studios just as the contract at RKO expired.[77]

When Johnny was offered a job as songwriter for a proposed musical revue to open in London, in 1936 he and Ginger took their first of many trips to Great Britain, not only to see the sights but also to revel in the British culture celebrated by his ancestors. The song publisher Jack Robbins, of Robbins Music Corporation, had recognized Mercer's talent and latched on to the budding songwriter, getting him to help Ohman and Teetor with "Lost" and pitch-hitting for others. Assuming the role of agent, Robbins arranged for Johnny to join producer Lew Leslie on another *Blackbirds* revue that used an old racial formula but needed new songs. Leslie had discovered the original "blackbird," the great singer Florence Mills. The first of the series, *Blackbirds of 1928*, featured music by the white songwriting team of lyricist Dorothy Fields and composer Jimmy McHugh, written for an all-black cast and including the hit "I Can't Give You Anything but Love." Two years later, Leslie returned with the black songwriter Eubie Blake, whose earlier *Shuffle Along* with lyrics by Noble Sissle had set the standard for all-black revues and who with lyricist Andy Razaf scored *Blackbirds of 1930*. When in 1933 Leslie tried again, the show closed after three weeks at the Apollo Theater.[78]

Despite his spotty track record, the veteran theater hustler convinced Mercer to write lyrics for Lew Leslie's *Blackbirds of 1936*. Leslie partnered the lyricist with Rube Bloom, a veteran jazz arranger-composer who had crafted revues during Harlem's golden age. Johnny knew Bloom from his earlier days hanging out with jazz musicians such as the Dorsey brothers. Bloom had cut records with Bix Beiderbecke, Frankie Trumbauer, and Miff Mole. In keeping with the previous shows, *Blackbirds of 1936* featured an all-black cast, including the tap dancers the Nicholas brothers and Tim Moore, who later played the Kingfish on the television version of *Amos and Andy*. Ginger joined Johnny on the Cunard crossing of the Atlantic but toured London alone.[79]

Johnny holed up with Bloom in the Savoy Hotel to write songs for Leslie's cast. Typical of Mercer's outlook, the lyric for "Keep a Twinkle in Your Eye" concluded with optimistic lines: "Thanks to the twinkle in your eye / And the twinkle in your toe, / You'll find that life is just like pie, / Wherever you go." As performed by the Nicholas brothers in the show, the words underscored the jazzy zest for living that Mercer routinely conveyed through his upbeat songs. The lyric for "Dixie Isn't Dixie Anymore" demonstrated Mercer's rejection of the old Tin Pan Alley trope of southern song that had perpetuated the moonlight and magnolias mythology, instead boldly showing how the South had integrated into the modern nation and thereby lost its distinctiveness. The lyric begins: "I just paid a visit to the sunny South, / Looking for the sights I used to see. / But I didn't recognize the sunny South. / Nothing there is what it used to be." Instead, the old landmarks of the Back-to-Dixie songs are turned upside down. Echoing Stephen Foster, the narrator notes that steamers not steamboats ply the Suwannee River, trolleys not hard times go by the cabin door. To service cars, "Highway 97" put blacktop on the old "bridle path" and stagecoach route, and that "famous old plantation has become a filling station." Indeed, "you won't hear those darkies in the fields as white as snow, / 'Cause they're all too busy singing on the radio." Woolworth's had replaced the old cotton exchange building and "where aunty had a shanty / There's a poster of Durante / Dixie isn't Dixie anymore." Mercer's clever lyric lines out his epitaph for the South. The show ran in London but did not make the initial transition to New York City.[80]

After *Blackbirds of 1936* opened in London, the Mercers traveled to Scotland and spent two weeks with Johnny's elderly "Aunt" Nell Blackie in Edinburgh. Nell had inherited the family home located on a southwesterly crest above the city in the leafy Braid Hills section of town along the road Bonnie Prince Charlie had followed when he returned to reclaim the British throne for the Stuarts. It had been a decade since Nell visited Savannah in 1924 and Johnny had traveled home from Woodberry Forest to meet her. In July 1926, just before the business failure, G. A. Mercer and Lillian had taken their twelve-year-old daughter, Juliana, on a trip to Great Britain to visit the first cousin in the ancestral homeland. Now Johnny got the invitation to stay with Nell Blackie and tour Scotland. While there he hoped to shed a sinus infection that had started in London, a recurrent problem throughout his life. He also wanted to play golf, a game he had picked up as a youth. "For two or three weeks I sopped up my Scotch and Scottish forebears, dug the moors, lochs and the castles, the heather and the grouse," he wrote in an early draft of his autobiography, describing the leisurely visit as "a sweet, peaceful interlude."[81]

While in Great Britain, Mercer exchanged with Jack Robbins a series of letters and telegrams about various opportunities in Hollywood. Other songwriters working with Robbins included Jimmy McHugh and Gus Kahn, and Jack held out the possibility of Johnny's partnering with Richard Whiting. Still working under a contract with Paul Whiteman, Mercer allowed Whiteman's manager, Jack Lavin, to rebuff Robbins's efforts to force him into an exclusive contract. Indeed, Mercer retained some flexibility and negotiated with others through his attorney, Arthur Fishbein. A strained relationship had developed between Mercer and Robbins that resulted from Johnny's resentment at being used to improve the songs by others that Robbins published. Hearing that Johnny would be offered a contract with Warner Bros. Inc., the celebrated composer of musicals Harry Warren, who worked for Warners, telegrammed Mercer, "If you let Robbins talk you out of this deal I think it would be a rotten trick." Changing agents, moving to different publishing houses, and breaking contracts with studios were commonplace occurrences in the entertainment industry, and the series of letters describing the split reflected Robbins's soreness at losing the talented songwriter. They severed the association in August 1936, but later patched up their friendship. At Mercer's request Robbins released back to him several of his as-yet-unpublished lyrics, including the Bernie Hanighen collaboration, "The Weekend of a Private Secretary." Yet Robbins Music Corporation retained the publication rights to several songs such as "Jamboree Jones" and a "western" number that Johnny's friend from the Whiteman organization, Fud Livingston, helped him place with Bing Crosby.[82]

Just before returning to the United States on the *Queen Mary*, Johnny received a telegram from Buddy Morris, the head of the music department at Warner Bros. Inc., officially inviting him to write lyrics for the studio. While negotiating Johnny's options in California, the Mercers stayed in the St. Moritz Hotel in New York. Hoagy Carmichael had visions of working for the studios, too, and after disengaging from Ralph Peer and Southern Music, he signed with the New York office of Warner Bros., hoping to be sent to the West Coast. But, as Carmichael resentfully noted, "When an opening to write songs in Hollywood came up, they sent Johnny Mercer and left me at home to tend the store." Harry Warren recalled that Hal Wallis, the Warner Bros. producer of *Casablanca* fame, "had asked me if I knew of a good team of songwriters and I'd suggested Richard Whiting and Johnny." The industry scuttlebutt recognized that the studios had recruited Mercer because in him they saw a talent that could combine jazz music with popular song for the new movie musicals. And in Mercer they found a man eager to return to the most salubrious climate he had ever known.[83]

Because Mercer had been seduced by the musical theater on his first visit to Broadway, his move to Hollywood evolved out of his desire to write for the stage; yet jazz remained the potent addiction in the songwriter's life and New York stayed in his blood. Rather than acting, he had made a living by merging the "hot" music with syncopated lyrics to craft popular songs that mined the multiracial South. A habitué of the city's jazz scene, Johnny apprenticed on Tin Pan Alley by day but accompanied jazzmen at night to Harlem and Fifty-second Street, performing with other diaspora entertainers who pushed the region's distinctive sounds to the center of American popular culture. The Savannah newspaper had observed that the songwriter "loved jazz," and despite the move to California, his association with jazz musicians continued unabated. When in New York, Johnny and Ginger dropped by to hear Tommy Dorsey's band playing the Pennsylvania Roof in the old Statler-Hilton Hotel or Jimmy Dorsey's band at the Onyx. As Johnny proudly noted in later life, he not only knew the Dorsey brothers but he considered them friends. Mercer denied having created the counter remarks sung by band members in the background of such songs as "Marie" while expressing his delight at the effect. "And it was a marvelous thing because the tempo was going just right for dancing and yet it was all this entertainment going on too," he recalled about the music — and his friend, "wonderful, I thought, an outstanding man." On one occasion, Tommy discovered the Mercers had arrived in New York to celebrate the songwriter's birthday, so he arranged a surprise. Johnny remembered a huge cake wheeled up to the table that "turned out to be full of lead sheets of my flop songs, which amused Tommy greatly and also pleased Ginger and me." An equal among jazz greats, Mercer continued to influence the musical genre from his new home on the West Coast.[84]

4 Hollywood

It makes your dreams come true
Just like the movies do,
Hooray for Hollywood.

WHEN JOHNNY MERCER arrived in Hollywood in 1936, the decade-old movie musical had achieved perfection. Since the addition of sound to film in *The Jazz Singer* in 1927, a specific genre of celluloid talkies concentrated on capturing the expanse of song. Such musical performances formerly had been limited to elaborately staged Broadway productions that became traveling shows in the nation's bigger theaters. Now as movie musicals the entertainment took place wherever a screen and a projector allowed. The visual demands of film required a transformation of the staged musical. During the next ten years advances in cinematography and technical investments by movie moguls enabled the production numbers to evolve as an art form that featured the stars and chorus singing and dancing on mechanical stages designed to appeal to the camera rather than the stationary audience. Musicals followed four distinct models: the revue that assembled various musical numbers; the "show within a show," or backstage musical; the classic operetta that followed a romance; and the youthful campus musical. All relied on dancing to activate the plot and string together the songs. At Warner Bros. Inc., director Busby Berkeley used fantastic sets, hundreds of extras, and overhead camera shots to make spectacular films that by the mid-1930s had launched the golden age of Hollywood musicals.[1]

The success of movie musicals at Warner Bros. created the demand for a new team of songwriters. To assist production, the studio hired Mercer to join Richard "Dick" Whiting to complement its Harry Warren–Al Dubin team. Having written such hits as "Japanese Sandman," "Miss Brown to You," and "On the Good Ship Lollipop," Whiting had an exceptional reputation. Born in Peoria, Illinois, in 1891, Whiting had worked vaudeville, plugged songs in Detroit, and gotten his break with "When It's Tulip Time in Holland," which led him to Hollywood and the movie studios. Whiting wanted to collaborate with Mercer, so a variety of players negotiated in order to pair the two. Yet unlike when writing for Broadway, where the composer and lyricist have a hand in the construction of the plot, the placement of the song, and the actors chosen for the performance — an involvement recognized by top listing on the playbill and marquee — movie studios limited the participation of songwriters to simply contributing the music. Directors and studio executives decided whether or not to use the songs, where in the plot to fit them, and who would be best to sing them, thereby giving the songwriters little more than notice in the credits. In return, the studios offered composers and lyricists steady contract work at substantial wages.[2]

The Whitings assisted the Mercers in their transition to Hollywood, as Johnny and Ginger settled into life under the orange trees among the elite of the entertainment industry. They purchased a Cape Cod–style house at 8218 De Longpre Avenue in Hollywood just off of Sunset Boulevard, where they lived for fifteen years. Johnny's friend, Bill Harbach, described the Mercer house as "cozy, understated, nothing pretentious, absolutely nothing pretentious." They attended St. Stephen's Episcopal Church on nearby Yucca Street, where other Hollywood Anglicans worshiped, including Cecil B. DeMille. Johnny played the golf courses in the area and, through the invitation of Whiting, received a guest card that allowed him to tee off at the Bel Air Country Club. Ginger participated in various ladies' social activities. Thinking back on his early days in Hollywood, Mercer remembered in particular the beautiful climate in Los Angeles: "On some sunny days when the wind is right it sparkles and it just looks like a dreamy city. And it's great because it hardly ever rains and . . . you can go to the ocean, snow, and the desert and the mountains all within an hour or two. I love California." He recalled two kinds of people on the West Coast in the 1930s: the "Mexican-Indian Californian" living in "certain neighborhoods" and "the tall, blonde, sunlit tennis-playing Californian." Many of the latter worked in the entertainment industry.[3]

The Whiting household in Beverly Hills served as a center of popular music in Hollywood, providing "exits and entrances" for major composers and lyricists. Whiting's daughter, Margaret, recalled a house full of the famous, whom she regarded as family, such as "uncles" Jerome Kern, Leo Robin, Gus Kahn, and Harry Warren. Others who frequented the Whiting household included George

Gershwin, Sigmund Romberg, and Arthur Schwartz. In recalling the atmosphere in Hollywood of the 1930s, Margaret said of entertainers, "We danced through the Depression. We made people happy. We gave them songs."[4]

Working with Dick Whiting, Mercer renewed friendships with fellow songwriters who migrated from New York as well as made friends among the players already established in the music industry and with newcomers seeking their fortune in the movies. As the dean of West Coast songwriters, Whiting knew everyone. Among the many lyricists with whom he worked, such as Gus Kahn, Ray Egan, and Buddy DeSylva, Whiting favored Johnny, having recognized Mercer's talents and happily acted as his tutor. Johnny met and wrote with such new songwriters as Edward Chester Babcock, who used the professional name of Jimmy Van Heusen and later partnered with Sammy Cahn.[5]

In Hollywood, Johnny renewed his association with Harold Arlen, E. Y. "Yip" Harburg, and George and Ira Gershwin. Indeed, Johnny donned his tennis whites to play the brothers, Harburg, and Arlen on the court at the Gershwin house on Roxbury Drive in Beverly Hills. George captured the day in photographs that display the brilliant men laughing at each other's jokes. Ginger grew close to Ira's wife, Leonore or "Lee," and the Mercers annually attended her New Year's Eve party. Other good friends Ginger made included Rosie Gilbert, the wife of L. Wolfe "Wolfey" Gilbert, who wrote "Waiting for the Robert E. Lee." The Gershwins regularly hosted other guests, including the composer Arnold Schoenberg. Under the sun in Hollywood, Mercer gained that feeling of professional success from among his peers that marked him as an emerging force in the industry.[6]

For the rest of 1936 and into 1937, Mercer worked with Whiting at Warner Bros. on the score for *Ready, Willing and Able*. The collaborators wrote several songs, the most famous of which, "Too Marvelous for Words," became Mercer's first hit in Hollywood. In discussing the song with jazz critic Willis Conover, Mercer recalled about the title, "That was just a phrase that was around, you know, and it fit his melody." Conover countered, "You know it's been said, Johnny, that you are the prime rater of a song lyric in the American language. And you say the expression 'too marvelous for words' has 'just been around.' Well, that's the whole point of that particular compliment." Indeed, many of Mercer's top songs took a catchphrase or slang of the day and made the commonplace spectacular, set to music. The movie featured Ruby Keeler and Lee Dixon dancing on a gigantic typewriter as they pecked out the words to the song. Packed with four production numbers, the complicated plot made the movie cumbersome, although the music pointed to the promise of the Whiting-Mercer collaboration.[7]

During the summer of 1937, Mercer negotiated with Buddy Morris his contract renewal with Warner Bros. Inc. Proud of his former protégé, Pops Whiteman sent his congratulations: "You will have the wonderful success which you deserve. Ours has been a very happy association and I want you to know that while you are not with my organization any longer if there is anything I can ever do for you do not fail to ask me." Mercer replied, "It is useless for me to try and tell you how grateful I am for the help and encouragement you have given me." Johnny stayed in touch with his former colleague at Robbins Music, the lyricist Gus Kahn, who had written scores for *Flying Down to Rio* and *Whoopee* as well as important songs from Johnny's youth, such as "Coquette," "No, No, Nora," and "Yes Sir, That's My Baby." In late 1937, Mercer received a gracious letter from Kahn: "I would gladly trade my catalog for your talent and the years you have ahead of you. I feel sure that it is not going to take you thirty years to catch up with me and pass me, but I am happy about this because you are my kind of a songwriter and, as I said long before you arrived, I consider you the best of all the young writers." Over the course of his career, Mercer validated the faith expressed in him by so many of these veterans of the entertainment industry.[8]

With the renewed contract, Mercer and Whiting continued their collaboration. In 1937, they began writing songs for *Hollywood Hotel*, which turned out to be Busby Berkeley's last musical spectacular for Warner Bros. The director pulled out all the stops on this show about a saxophonist wannabe actor played by Dick Powell paired with a wannabe starlet played by Rosemary Lane, with both getting their big break in the movies. The cast included several of Johnny's jazz buddies performing with Benny Goodman and His Orchestra. Whiting and Mercer produced all the new songs, including "I'm Like a Fish Out of Water" and "I've Hitched My Wagon to a Star." Played by a jazz band in the movie that featured on vocals Johnny "Scat" Davis backed up by Harry James on the trumpet and Gene Krupa on drums, the satirical "Hooray for Hollywood" became an instant hit and the overnight theme song for Tinsel Town. Margaret Whiting noted, "I think that's how they all felt about that town. I know I still feel that way with every lovely royalty check that comes in four times a year from ASCAP [American Society of Composers, Authors and Publishers]."[9]

The movie industry offered itself as a target to Johnny, as he explained years later about the song: "Hollywood seemed like a big put-on to me and I just tried to make a little fun of it." Lyrics such as "Where any office boy or young mechanic / Can be a panic" and "any bar maid can be a star made" suggest that success depends on the spin of Fortune's mighty wheel. With "Hooray for Hollywood," Mercer wrote one of his rare lyrics that regularly saw revision with updated lines such as these from the 1950s: "Where anyone at all from TV's Lassie / To Monroe's chassis / Is equally understood," or these from the 1970s: "But if your wardrobe is a little tacky / Go see Bob Mackie; / He'd make a monkey look good — / He'd give you styles to wear / That make you look like Cher!" Such original lines as "where you're terrific if you're even good" and "that phony super Coney Hollywood" reveal the cynicism that occasionally popped out of a typically positive Mercer song. An optimist, Johnny seemed generally cheerful and upbeat, but underneath that sunny disposition a fatalism lurked that occasionally sparked negative thoughts or realistic remarks. Raised in a household steeped in the Victorian culture of ignoring unpleasantries, Mercer disliked acknowledging the difficulties of life, preferring to avoid them whenever possible. Johnny's personal outlook provided a perfect fit with the land of dreams, for he favored the happy Hollywood ending that appeared in the movies and — more often than not — his lyrics, which often accentuated the positive.[10]

Within weeks of *Hollywood Hotel*'s January 1938 opening, Dick Whiting died, having long suffered from heart disease but growing severely ill during the filming. His death in February cut short the promising partnership for the studios. It was a terrible loss to Johnny, who valued immensely the experience gained from this master of popular music. With her father's death, Margaret Whiting also lost a mentor and teacher: "Daddy would take me into his confidence and play me his songs. Daddy would play for *me* to sing, and give me advice and encourage me." She recalled that Johnny attempted to fill the void: "He really took my father's place — as much as one could. Johnny had always been around the house when he was collaborating with my father. To him, I was always The Kid. Now he took The Kid under his protective wing." This informal guardianship meant that Mercer shaped Margaret Whiting's musical career. She noted: "He listened to me sing. Screwed up his forehead. Gave me his advice." Asking her what singers she liked, Mercer told her to "study them, their style, the way they phrase. Don't worry about copying them. You'll get your own style. Just listen. And learn." Then he told her to "grow up." Returning the favor of the father, Johnny served as her mentor, teaching her how to sing a lyric. Several years later, through his role as A&R man and president of Capitol Records, Mercer planned and launched Margaret Whiting's successful recording career by selecting the songs for her to sing. Her music hit the public at the very moment jazz evolved into the Age of the Singer, which lasted until the advent of rock 'n' roll. For his dedication to her, Margaret Whiting remained devoted to the memory of Johnny Mercer, for many years heading the foundation named in his honor.[11]

Richard Whiting's death left Mercer adrift but still tied to the studio through his contract, so he partnered with Harry Warren on several movies for Warner Bros., most of which starred Dick Powell and Pat O'Brien. Mercer and Whiting had started work on the 1938 *Cowboy from Brooklyn*, with "Ride, Tenderfoot, Ride," the best known of its songs but also including "I've Got a Heart Full of Music" and "I'll Dream Tonight" as the last of their collaborations. After Dick's death Johnny partnered with Harry Warren to finish the score and write its title song. Al Dubin, who had drafted most of the lyrics with Warren for the 1938 *Gold Diggers in Paris*, disliked Warner Bros. and Hollywood and soon returned to New York. Consequently Johnny helped Harry write supplemental songs for the film featuring the radio star Rudy Vallee, including "Day Dreaming All Night Long" and "My Adventure." With Dubin, Mercer had written lyrics for Warren's music to the 1938 *Garden of the Moon*. In addition to the title song, the movie included "Confidentially" and "Love Is Where You Find It." Johnny wrote all the words to the novelty number "The Girlfriend of the Whirling Dervish" that the bug-eyed comic and trombone player Jerry Colonna introduced in a scene featuring a jazz band. Mercer tried to explain the writing of such silly songs to Willis Conover: "When the tune comes along the subconscious does its work and finds the phrase to fit the tune. And I don't know where they come from at all times. Sometimes you invent them like 'The Girlfriend of the Whirling Dervish' or 'The Lady on the Two-cent Stamp' or 'The Weekend of the Private Secretary.' These songs are absolutely pure invention but they're hardly ever hits. But they're fun to do." Throughout his career, Mercer enjoyed writing and singing clever novelty songs. Warner Bros. just barely beat MGM and its epic *Gone with the Wind* into the cinema with its riposte *Jezebel* starring Bette Davis, for which Warren and Mercer wrote the title song used to promote the picture.[12]

From the score for *Going Places*, the song "Jeepers Creepers" won for Johnny his first of eighteen Academy Award nominations for Best Song. In a reversal of the usual practice, the song lyric preceded the movie. In Hollywood musicals the songs had little to do with advancing the plot or developing characters, as would later be demanded on Broadway. Mercer explained to Conover: "In a movie you just work up to that and you cue a song in . . . [that] doesn't have anything to do with the plot. You want a hit song, that's the point, especially if it's the title of the picture. That's great advertising." When considering music for the movie,

the songwriters Mercer and Warren played "Jeepers Creepers" for the producers, who liked the song, as did Louis Armstrong, who "sang it, he loved it too,
so he just named the horse Jeepers Creepers. That's what they did, that's how
they got around that," Mercer recalled. "The song was written before the horse
was named." The idea of the phrase "Jeepers Creepers" came from a comment
made by Henry Fonda in a picture that Johnny saw with Ginger at Grauman's
Chinese Theater. Mercer knew the phrase as a minced oath for "Jesus Christ."
Armstrong introduced "Jeepers Creepers" in the film, both singing and playing
to the racehorse as well as to fellow jazz singer Maxine Sullivan, and it became a
runaway hit and one of Armstrong's signature songs. Johnny valued his contact
with Louis and developed a friendly association with the jazz legend.[13]

When his contract expired at Warner Bros., Mercer began to freelance, which
allowed him greater freedom in choosing assignments that often paired him
with leading composers to write songs independently or for various studios. The
last of Mercer's collaborations with Harry Warren for Warner Bros., the 1939
Naughty but Nice, appeared with several undistinguished songs, except perhaps
for the funny "Hooray for Spinach." Mercer maintained contact with the studio's
music director, Buddy Morris, and later that year the two started M&M Publishing Company to keep in print many of the old songs Mercer loved from earlier
movie musicals and Broadway shows. Johnny renewed his partnership with Rube
Bloom, and the two men wrote two successful songs together in 1939. While
"Day In — Day Out" used themes and phrasing Mercer later repeated with great
effect in other songs, the passion the lyric expresses stirred the hearts of singers
and audiences alike. With such lines as "Then I kiss your lips / And the pounding becomes / The ocean's roar / A thousand drums," Lena Horne made it one
of her stock numbers. Also with Bloom, Mercer wrote "Fools Rush In," a ballad
of remarkable beauty. Taking the title from a quote by Alexander Pope, Mercer
explained that the phrase "fit that tune perfectly, I think that's one of my better
lyrics. A simple way to a very big, almost an operatic kind of tune. A great tune."
As typical of Mercer's best efforts, the words convey a complete story: "Fools rush
in / Where wise men never go, / But wise men never fall in love, / So how are they
to know? / When we met, / I felt my life begin; / So open up your heart / And let
this fool rush in."[14]

Mercer's brief collaboration with the composer Jimmy Van Heusen resulted
in several beautiful songs also published in 1939. Born Edward Chester Babcock,
the composer took the professional name Van Heusen (from the brand of dress
shirt) when he went to work in entertainment. Like Mercer and fellow lyricist

Sammy Cahn, Van Heusen received four Oscars for Best Song. He mainly collaborated with lyricists Cahn and Johnny Burke on songs sung by Bing Crosby and Frank Sinatra. With Mercer, Van Heusen wrote the cute "Make with the Kisses" and two other songs of note, "Blue Rain," which failed to make a splash, and "I Thought about You," which became a great hit. These last two play on lost love. The first begins, "Clouds cover up my horizon with blankets as dark as night; / Skies haven't cleared since you disappeared from sight," suggesting "Blue rain, / Falling down on my windowpane, / But when you return / There'll be a rainbow / After the blue, blue, rain." In thinking back on the song, Mercer remarked, "I don't think it ever 'happened' but I wish it had. Nice tune." In contrast, "I Thought about You" did happen, as it became one of the top songs written by the songwriters. The evocative lyric fits the mood of the tune so well that the musicologist Alec Wilder identified it as one of the gems of Great American Song: "I took a trip on a train / And I thought about you; / I passed a shadowy lane / And I thought about you." Mercer's familiarity with transcontinental train travel makes the lyrics feel natural as the song builds to the climax: "I peeked through the crack / And looked at the track, / The one going back to you, / And what did I do? / I thought about you."[15]

With "I Thought about You," Mercer wrote the lyric first, so that the composer had to set music to fit the words instead of the other way around. Typically, however, Mercer and the composer would agree on an idea for a song, captured in a title phrase that would trigger their imaginations. The idea for the title took weeks to develop, coming out of lengthy discussions involving storyline and time signature. As Mercer explained to writer Henry Kane: "First — the title. That encompasses the grand idea, the crux of the obsession, the thought; it all goes into that; that is, somehow, the bringing together of all of it; that's what hits first, that's what's way back in your mind brought together in sharp focus; the title hits like a bullet, and if it's right, there you have it, all of it, ready to go, in a succinct package — all the crazy, unconscious groping has merged into something real." Then the composer would create a tune that he offered to Mercer to set with words. When Willis Conover asked Mercer in 1970 how songwriting starts, Mercer plainly answered, "It starts with the title first." Having the complete lyric to "I Thought about You," Van Heusen took as the opening phrase music that had been used by other composers in two earlier songs, "I Had the Craziest Dream" and "Jersey Bounce." Talking about this unusual coincidence, Johnny explained, "Well, I think sometimes composers and lyric writers or whoever writes the tune is inclined to use pickups sort of like you use articles, *the*, and *an*, and *of*, you know . . . [then] you're into your melody and then it changes. I think 'Jersey Bounce' is probably the first one of those three songs so Van Heusen and [Harry] Warren [the composer of "I Had the Craziest Dream"] would have to be guilty subconsciously of taking those pickup notes [from "Jersey Bounce" by Edward Johnson and Tiny Bradshaw]. But I don't think that's unusual in the beginning of a song." Despite the success of "I Thought about You," Mercer and Van Heusen ended their initial collaboration.[16]

The studios kept Johnny busy with lyrics for Hollywood musicals, some good and others not so good. For Paramount Studios, Mercer joined several composers to create music for the film *Second Chorus*. With jazz clarinetist Artie Shaw, Johnny wrote "The Love of My Life," which in 1940 resulted in his second Academy Award nomination for Best Song. With Hal Borne, Johnny revealed his jazz abilities in the syncopated lyrics to "(I Ain't Hep to That Step but I'll) Dig It." For RKO Studios and Kay Kyser and his Kollege of Knowledge, Mercer joined Jimmy McHugh on the score for *You'll Find Out*. Despite receiving an Academy Award nomination for "I'd Know You Anywhere," and writing "The Bad Humor Man" and other pieces tailored for the trio of scary stars who appeared in the movie — Boris Karloff, Bela Lugosi, and Peter Lorre — the musical proved "a wholesale stinker," according to movie critic Clive Hirschhorn. For Paramount, Mercer and McHugh teamed up to write songs for *You're the One*, among them, "I Could Kiss You for That" and "My Resistance Is Low." Even working with a great composer like Arthur Schwartz could still result in some mediocre filler songs such as those in *Navy Blues* for Warner Bros.[17]

Johnny liked to write in silence. He would hear the composer play the music through a few times and with instant recall ponder the melody until he found his poetry. As a crutch he would refer to the composer's lead sheets and later used tape recordings of the tune when contemplating words. Once Mercer had three sets of lyrics for a tune he rejoined the composer to hash out the final song. Harry Warren disliked Mercer's preference for working in silence, and Jimmy McHugh's constant tinkering on the piano annoyed Johnny, so Mercer looked for other collaborators. He found great success with Harold Arlen, who years later recalled, "Johnny would sit there very quietly, listening while I played a few 'jots,' that is, possible themes for songs." Arlen remembered Mercer "wouldn't ever say very much" and "he was always a very quiet man, but I was secure in the knowledge that he would be back in a couple of weeks with something finished."

As a professional songwriter, Johnny created a particularly large body of work over the course of his career. His better songs revealed a jazz aesthetic and vernacular expression of life and locale derived from the multiracial culture of his southern heritage. Yet often he completed work-for-hire jobs in order to make a living. Frequently such film and stage assignments produced songs that lacked profound meaning and instead emphasized the type of movie, the plot, the singing abilities of actors and the characters they played, or most likely the potential commercial use of the music as records and sheet music, in short, a host of concerns. The licensing agency for songwriters and publishers, ASCAP, protected copyright by collecting royalties from users of the music such as radio stations and record companies and dividing the proceeds among its members according to a sliding scale that allowed for a secure distribution of funds to the creator and his or her heirs as long as the music remained protected by copyright and not in the public domain. Since the most popular songwriters brought in the most money in royalties, they stood at the top of the ASCAP ratings and reaped the rewards while newcomers admitted to the association received the lowest class rating as a base starting point. Because of the volume and quality of Mercer's published lyrics by the late 1930s, ASCAP advanced his rating from the middling Class CC to the upper middle Class B, hence significantly increasing his quarterly checks. By not having to deal directly with royalty issues, Mercer and other members in ASCAP enjoyed a freedom from financial matters that allowed for more creative activities. Not surprisingly, ASCAP members treated the organization as an elite fraternity, like an old guild in medieval Europe that jealously guarded the quality of the craft through selective membership.[18]

When not constrained by the requirements of studio work, Mercer wrote lyrics in a jazz idiom that often played on modernist themes such as sexual freedom. Often the words encouraged women to break free of the residual Victorian conventions of the day and rejected the double standard that held some women up as ladies while denouncing other women as whores. Johnny's spicy words fit well with the jazzy tunes composed by Bernie Hanighen, whom he had met up in Harlem at the end of the flapper era and partnered with on several songs while still living in New York. His lyric to their 1939 hit "Show Your Linen, Miss Richardson" dismisses traditional gender roles. Johnny suggests a woman can "dance in a gay, lady-like way," but she can also reveal the "lace on your petticoat, / Kick your heels at the proper note, / Show ev'rybody that you're really hep, / Give 'em that revolving step! / This is your innin', / Show your linen, / Dear Miss Richardson!" In support he brings the young men into the picture drawing on their multiracial southern culture as "Ev'rybody's beau / Formin' in a row / Strut along the aisle / Kitchen-style." Mercer recognizes the clash of standards: "The elder ladies / With their noses kinda turned up, / Burned up," while the "Elder gentry . . . is plumb struck / Dumbstruck." But Johnny presses on, advising the liberated woman to "Look all the elder ladies in the eye / And let your hair down, / Bear down" and "Pay no attention to the chaperone." Throughout his career, Mercer repeated in his lyrics the theme of sexual freedom first expressed a decade earlier during the Charleston craze.[19]

Mercer laced his lyrics with innuendo, stopping short of vulgarity but often using sexual relations as the basis of a song. Returning to the theme of the liberated woman, Mercer became more explicit in the 1938 hit "The Weekend of a Private Secretary," popularized by the Native American jazz singer Mildred Bailey, who sang with Paul Whiteman's orchestra. Reflecting the Latin influence on jazz music then in vogue, Bernie Hanighen provided a rumba sound, to which Johnny recounted the story of a single woman traveling to Havana, meeting "a Cuban gent" she describes as "a big sensation" who proves to be "quite a success." Johnny came back to the idea of casual sex in other songs. The theme of arousal figured into the titles and lyrics of "You've Got Me This Way (Whatta-Ya-Gonna Do about It)" and "I've Got a One Track Mind," written with Jimmy McHugh for the 1940 movie *You'll Find Out*. More often than not, however, Johnny's lyrics came off playful, as in "Make with the Kisses," written with Van Heusen, which has the lines, "Make with the sighs, / Make with the baby talk, / Give with the eyes!" Attractive women might appear as stereotypes in Mercer's lyrics, such as the secretary who marries her boss in "The Air-Minded Executive," written with Hanighen in 1940. The verse opens referencing the picture magazines that "Always print a beautiful calf," as well as portraits of the "Man of the Year," such as the song's subject, who "was an up-to-date go-getter." Flying his own plane to business deals, the boss took along his secretary, "And oh, the things he used to tell her / Above the roar of his propeller / Somewhere in the sky!" Overall, however, Johnny refrained from overly sexist imagery and explicit language, thereby usually avoiding the censors. Two notable exceptions are songs written by Mercer for the 1941 film *Navy Blues*, "Strip Polka," about the stripper Queenie, who "stops — / And always just in time!" which the censors ruled "unacceptable" because of the "low moral tone" of the lyric, and "Turn Out the Lights (and Call the Law)," a song dropped from the film because of the line "Here comes the man from Omaha! / He's in the groove and won't withdraw." Even the popular songs Mercer recorded that pandered to contemporary views of women as sexual objects contained layered meanings, as in Van Heusen and Burke's "Personality." Featuring famous lovers such as Romeo and Juliet, the lyric begs the question what did the men see in the women, and answers tongue-in-cheek that the female's personality (and not her beauty) created the sexual attraction. Bing Crosby's recording of "Personality" contains an ad-lib by Mercer.[20]

Out on the West Coast, Johnny proved of use to Bing Crosby. Their mutual friend Fud Livingston — a fellow Whiteman alumnus who had arranged jazz charts for Ben Pollack's band — encouraged Bing to add Johnny's "I'm an Old Cowhand" to Paramount's 1936 *Rhythm on the Range*. The crooner enjoyed Mercer's parody of western songs sung by a city slicker and made it the theme song for the movie. He liked the lines: "I know all the songs that the cowboys know, / 'Bout the big corral where the doagies go, / 'Cause I learned them all on the radio. / Yippy I O ki ay." Johnny came up with both music and words in 1936 while he and Ginger drove across Texas in a Ford convertible so that he might stand in Savannah as best man in Walter Rivers's wedding to Cornelia McIntire. In the film, Louis Prima performed the song with Bing and Bob Nolan's band, the Sons of the Pioneers. A white jazz trumpet player from New Orleans, Prima had a longstanding gig at the Famous Door on Fifty-second Street in New York before opening his own establishment on Vine Street in Los Angeles, which allowed him to appear in movies, most notably as King Louie in Walt Disney's *The Jungle Book*. Like Crosby, Prima made several recordings of Mercer's music.[21]

Settling into Hollywood, the Mercers kindled a friendship with Bing and Dixie Lee Crosby that lasted throughout their lifetimes. The typically modest Mercer thanked Crosby for putting "I'm an Old Cowhand" in *Rhythm on the Range*, suggesting, "I really think he saved my Hollywood career, because I began to get more offers after that," but in reality Johnny already had another number one hit with "Goody Goody," so attributing his employment to Crosby is a bit disingenuous. Bing recorded with great success the Mercer-Hanighen collaboration from 1937, "Bob White," with its hip expressions and jazzy kicker, "Whatcha gonna swing tonight," one of the first lyrics featuring warblers that the dedicated birdwatcher wrote. Stories abound of a whistling Johnny engaging mockingbirds in conversation. Of the South's fauna, songbirds proved the most popular in Mercer lyrics, being tailor-made for a crooner's whistle and voice. Johnny fondly recalled his friendship with fellow displaced southerner Dixie Lee Crosby, who hailed from Tennessee and with whom he shared a fondness for alcohol. Ginger enjoyed renewing her friendship with her former colleague from the chorus line. They became so close that their children played together, often attending each other's birthday parties, while in later years Dixie sometimes fled to the Mercer household to escape Bing's abuse. Thinking back Mercer acknowledged that "the unspoken sponsorship of Bing in those days, played no little part, I'm sure, in getting us off on the right foot. As another Paul Whiteman alumnus, no doubt he felt kindly disposed towards me."[22]

When Bing Crosby organized a benefit to raise money for jazz pianist Joe Sullivan, Johnny Mercer helped pull together the performance that two radio stations broadcast live. Sullivan had been a key figure from the Chicago school who played with Louis Armstrong and on Fifty-second Street around the time Mercer arrived in New York. Sullivan had accompanied Bing in films but upon contracting tuberculosis withdrew to a sanatorium. Crosby coordinated a five-hour concert on May 23, 1937, staged at the Pan-Pacific Auditorium before a crowd of six thousand that raised three thousand dollars to defray Sullivan's medical bills. The entertainment featured the orchestras of Jimmy Dorsey, Earl Hines, and Louis Prima, Fred Waring and his Pennsylvanians, Harry Owens's Royal Hawaiians, and others. Jimmy Grier led his band in playing Mercer's "Night over Shanghai" with vocals by Dick Webster. Also on the roster appeared such jazz greats as Woody Herman on clarinet, Red Norvo on vibes, and Ella Logan, who sang "Bonnie Banks of Loch Lomond." Johnny opened the second set with fifteen-year-old Judy Garland and pianist Art Tatum under the baton of Georgie Stoll and the Warner Bros. studio orchestra. They performed the new song "Swing High, Sing Low" by Burton Lane and Ralph Freed from Paramount's film of the same name, as well as the Warren-Dubin "September in the Rain" and other tunes. The year before Garland had made her feature film debut singing "Balboa" in *Pigskin Parade* and at the time of the benefit filmed *Broadway Melody of 1938*. Stardom awaited with *The Wizard of Oz* in 1939. Judy Garland wowed audiences with her glorious voice, a natural talent that attracted Mercer. To close out the show, Victor Young conducted his orchestra in Sullivan's "Just Strollin'" and songs sung by Crosby, Dorothy Lamour, and Martha Raye.[23]

As one of Hollywood's hottest properties, Johnny participated in a series of private performances by the industry's leading stars under the sponsorship of a mummers society called the Westwood Marching and Chowder Club (North Hollywood Branch). The charismatic Crosbys, assisted by a small nucleus of other performers associated with "Bing and Company," put together the entertainment for his private parties in 1938. Johnny and Ginger especially enjoyed the risqué events that paid tribute to vaudeville and featured the best talent in Hollywood. The group included Bing's lyric writer, Johnny Burke, and his wife, Bessie; Bing's orchestra leader, John Scott Trotter; the great jazz violinist Joe Venuti, whom Mercer credited with proposing the mummers society; and fellow actors Pat O'Brien, Jerry Colonna, and Bob and Dolores Hope. The invited entertainers prepared their routines in secret so as to surprise their fellow guests on the night of the performance. They held *The Midgie Minstrels* at Crosby's new house at 10500 Camarillo Street on April 16, 1938. Dressed in outlandishly tailored costumes in bright plaids reflecting colorful turn-of-the-century styles, the ensemble opened and closed the two acts, with sketches and performances in their best imitation of vaudeville filling the middle. Johnny and Ginger as the Merry Mercers performed his new song, "I Did It for the Red, White and Blue," written with Rube Bloom for Lew Leslie's *Blackbirds of 1936*. Mercer joined Venuti in blackface as End Men, while radio producer Herb Polesie played the role of Interlocutor. Although the memorable evening quickly spawned another mummery by Bing's friends, this performance apparently marked the only time Mercer donned the cork to entertain his colleagues.[24]

The next meeting of the Westwood Marching and Chowder Club resulted in Mercer joining Bing on a successful recording of their first duet. Gathered under a huge tent erected over the Crosbys' tennis court on June 25, 1938, the *Second Breakaway Minstrel Show* took place. On the guest list appeared such stars as Bette Davis and Fred MacMurray with Spike Jones's jazz band that included Johnny's old friend Tommy Dorsey. Johnny joined Bing in a makeover of a classic vaudeville routine, "Mr. Gallagher and Mr. Shean." Billed as "'Lasses Mercer and Chitlins Crosby," the two performed an "erudite analyseration of swing" that sketched out the history of jazz. As straight man, Bing hummed and scatted in the background. Johnny opens with "Oh, Mr. Crosby," then asks, "I've been reading in the latest magazine / That a jivin' jitterbug / Blew his top and cut a rug — / Will you tell me what that language really means?" Crosby answers back, "As a student of the slang they use pro tem, / That just means a solid gait — / Cut a murderistic pate." Back and forth the two go and then riff about jazz, concluding with Mercer joking, "I'm afraid that type of rhythm's not for me." The audience response convinced them to record the rhythmic duet with Victor Young's band on Bing's Decca label a week later, July 1, 1938, as "Mr. Crosby and Mr. Mercer," and it became "the summer's most amusing ditty," according to *Time*. On the flip side of the record they sang as a duet the recent Hoagy Carmichael and Frank Loesser collaboration, "Small Fry," which Bing had just filmed in his new movie *Sing You Sinners*. The amount of labor required to stage the vaudeville-styled events convinced the mummers to put on hold future performances.[25]

The obvious delight Mercer and Crosby experienced performing together led to guest appearances of Johnny on *Kraft Music Hall*. Back in 1934, Bing had hosted for CBS the Woodberry Soap radio program, but after several visits to *Kraft Music Hall* under his old boss, Pops Whiteman, Bing received an invitation from NBC to host the country's most popular variety program, which he did starting in December 1935 for the next eleven years. When the new season began on October 20, 1938, Johnny joined Bing for the hour-long program. Coverage in *Variety* complimented their duets:

> The program produced Johnny Mercer and a finely, diverting paraphrase of one of his latest tunes, "There's Mutiny in the Nursery." Everybody in the cast . . . participated and the upshot was as healthy a "plug" as any film release would want. The number is in Warner Bros.' *Going Places*. Mercer and Crosby preceded this item with a banter of special material on the theme of "Small Fry" and a bit of lively minstrel crossfire that had [Bob] Burns as interlocutor and a soft spot for the specimen of fine "needling" that accompanied the routine.

It was just one of several appearances Mercer made on Crosby's *Kraft Music Hall*.[26]

During these years before World War II, the Mercers regularly socialized with the Crosbys. A wide variety of musicians orbited in Bing's universe, such as Wingy Manone, a one-armed white trumpet player from New Orleans caught up in the southern diaspora who for years had entertained at Crosby's functions. That June, Johnny watched as Bing won the Lakeside golf championship. In February 1938, the Mercers enjoyed a dinner buffet at the Crosby house. No doubt in July they attended opening day at Crosby's Del Mar Race Track, and in August returned to see the horses run and watch the premier at the track of Bing's new film, *Sing You Sinners*. "It was my good fortune to know him when he was married to Dixie and his boys were small. They often rode on my back and I enjoyed the happy days around the track and poolside with this most attractive couple," Johnny wrote a mutual friend. Referring to Dixie, he noted, "She was very kind to me, as I was in such awe of him and she knew it. Also, I was a Southerner, and she made me feel at home. I shall never forget their kindness to a very young writer and performer." In recalling Crosby, Johnny wrote: "The interesting part of Bing to me is that he likes to be with jockeys, with millionaires, with beach boys and with caddies. He likes colorful people, he likes people who are amusing and aren't phonies. He's an unphony man. He's so distant, but he's a very genuine man." Crosby included Mercer in his list of favorite singers: "He sings fine blues, just about as well as anybody. A lot of people don't like the quality of his voice," (laughing), "but I like it." According to Rosemary Clooney, a diaspora entertainer from Kentucky, Crosby "loved Johnny Mercer" and "got along with him brilliantly. He liked Johnny's patterns of speech." When in 1939 Johnny began appearing regularly on radio broadcasts from New York, Crosby wrote regarding his absences from California: "We all miss your Saturday nite insouciance, but of course you should strike while the iron is hot — and you've got it good and hot right now." Once Bing Crosby and Bob Hope began their highly successful series of "road pictures" featuring beautiful women in exotic locales and Mercer started Capitol Records, the closeness faded, but the friendship endured.[27]

Mercer's lyrics suited Crosby's crooning. Bing recorded several of Johnny's songs, including "You Must Have Been a Beautiful Baby" with his brother Bob Crosby's orchestra, "Too Marvelous for Words" with Jimmy Dorsey's orchestra, and "Mister Meadowlark" with Victor Young's orchestra. James Cagney recalled a wartime Hollywood Victory Caravan performance on May 5, 1942, before nearly twenty thousand people packed into the Chicago Stadium; Bing walked onto the stage asking, "'Whadda yez wanna hear?'" to thunderous applause.

> "Ya wanna leave it to me?" and they exploded again, until the walls of the stadium nearly buckled. Finally he said, "Hit me Al" and our orchestra leader, Al Newman started his boys off on "Blues in the Night." They had only played the first two bars when the audience went into rapturous applause once again. Bing finished that song, and never in my life have I heard anything like it.

Cagney's comments underscore the successful marriage of Johnny's jazzy imagery to Crosby's swinging style. An observation Cagney made regarding Crosby applied to Mercer too: "When Bing came offstage, the perspiration on him was an absolute revelation to me. Here he had been to all appearances perfectly loose and relaxed, but not at all. He was giving everything he had in every note he sang, and the apparent effortlessness was a part of his very hard work." Others have criticized in Mercer a disdain for hard work that was in fact a deliberate display of ease by which he approached his labors. As jazz singers, both men demonstrated what Ralph Gleason — a critic for *Down Beat* and *Metronome* — said about Bing, that he represented "the personification of the whole jazz movement — the relaxed, casual, natural and uninhibited approach to art." Bing helped further Mercer's career, and in turn Johnny's lyrics contributed to Crosby's reputation as one of twentieth-century America's greatest male singers. As president of Capitol Records, Johnny mentored another one, Nat "King" Cole, while his label and his music helped repackage a third, Frank Sinatra.[28]

When in California to get away from the studios, Johnny and Ginger visited the hotels and dude ranches in Palm Springs. In 1938, rather than travel to Georgia for Christmas, Johnny invited his parents and sister to spend the holiday season with them in California. Since they would not be visiting Savannah, Johnny and Ginger altered the "clever verses" they had started sending out as yuletide greetings. The local paper reported "Savannahians were delighted this year to be included along with celebrities in the long list of persons extended greetings by Johnny Mercer in his novel Christmas card." It then published a portion of the holiday rhyme using proper names and seasonal references that every year family, friends, and business associates looked forward to receiving. With Savannah society suitably notified of the trip, G. A., Lillian, and Juliana joined Johnny and Ginger in the resort town. Located 125 miles east of the famous Paramount Gates, Palm Springs, with its Racquet Club and El Mirador Hotel, had by the 1930s become the weekend playground for the studio set. With tennis after dawn and golf before dusk, the Hollywood colony released the stress of Los Angeles. These actors, musicians, and executives avoided the direct sun with naps in the midday in order to enjoy the cool of the evening at parties in a libertine atmosphere marked by drunken licentiousness, the privacy of which the stars scrupulously protected. In addition to the old performers such as Greta Garbo and Rudy Vallee and hot performers such as Bing Crosby and Fred Astaire, the major songwriters took up weekend shop in Palm Springs. When on the West Coast, Johnny cavorted with his colleagues in the desert resort town.[29]

With the expiration of his studio contract in 1938, Johnny henceforth freelanced, which made his successful career bicoastal. Job opportunities kept him traveling between the movie studios in Los Angeles and the recording interests, radio shows, and theaters in New York. Mercer's daughter, Mandy, remarked, "He loved to be where the work was," that "he worked all the time," only taking "a busman's holiday to a club to hear the music." Ginger remained in the West Hollywood house at 8218 De Longpre, while Johnny took an apartment in the Sixties on Manhattan's upper east side. For the rest of his life, when not staying at the Plaza, Ambassador, or the Tuscany Hotel in Greenwich Village, Johnny kept a flat in New York. The freedom to be in metropolis at will enabled him to seek the excitement of an earlier jazz era while escaping a less than ideal domestic life.[30]

In 1939, Jake and Lee Shubert paired Johnny Mercer with Hoagy Carmichael to write a complete Broadway score. The collaboration held great promise for a Broadway that had lost its jazz-based edge, symbolized in the death of George Gershwin in 1937. Contributing two shows during this transitional moment in musical theater, Mercer looked to jazz. The earlier collaboration in London with Rube Bloom on Lew Leslie's *Blackbirds of 1936* had been revised for New York as *Blackbirds of 1939*, opening February 11 in the Hudson Theater. For inspiration it harkened back to the *Shuffle Along* knock-offs of the 1920s' Harlemania, with an echo of Dixieland jazz orchestrated by Whiteman's arranger Ferde Grofé. Despite the talents of the Nicholas brothers and Lena Horne — who as a newcomer to Broadway won praise from the *New York Times*, which called her "a radiantly beautiful sepia girl who will be a winner when she has proper direction"— *Blackbirds* lasted just nine performances, bringing down the curtain on the last of the all-black revues. With the jazz-based reputations of Mercer and Carmichael, the Shuberts hoped to catch the excitement of the swing era, but as a developed style of jazz, the big-band sound proved less suited to the stage than to the movies.[31]

Having moved his family to Hollywood in 1937 to work in the studios, Hoagy accepted the offer to collaborate again with Johnny when the opportunity arose. Since "Lazybones," which still remained popular, Carmichael had had his share of hits, including "Small Fry" and perhaps most notably "I Get Along without You Very Well." Yet his studio career had not taken off like that of Mercer, who was already firmly part of the Hollywood establishment. Now together again in the relaxed atmosphere of sun-washed California, Johnny noted Hoagy had changed over the seven years since their last partnership, as had he: "I had learned a lot, but he had softened up some, too." No doubt the idea of a Broadway musical appealed to Mercer, who had started his career with the goal of succeeding on the Great White Way. Having his name in lights remained a life ambition, for as Johnny told a reporter, "All Hollywood can give you is money. In New York, a man can gain prestige by working a musical show." To Carmichael, who had watched Indiana's other great composer of popular song, Cole Porter, have his string of show stoppers, the musical theater symbolized the height of success for the songwriter. He called Porter, Kern, Hammerstein, Rodgers, and Hart the "big boys" of songwriting and aspired to their league. Putting the past aside, the two men embarked on their second period of collaboration, again with mixed results.[32]

The Shubert Theatre syndicate dominated much of Broadway, and it hired Carmichael and Mercer to write the songs and lyrics for a London play it wanted turned into a musical. Originally called "Three Blind Mice" and written by playwright Guy Bolton of *Lady Be Good* and *Rio Rita* fame, the show briefly held the name "Three after Three" before finally being titled *Walk with Music*. The romantic comedy followed three single farmwomen from New Hampshire seeking wealthy men to marry in Palm Beach. One pretends to be an heiress accompanied by her maid and chaperone. The plan runs afoul when the heiress falls for a poor man, but the maid wins a wealthy suitor and the chaperone catches a Cuban nightclub owner. The scene shifts to Havana, in an attempt to hide the show's dull plot behind scantily clad showgirls. With the movement of the New York stage away from the old revues and operettas, plot had become an increasingly important component of a Broadway musical, and songs had to both develop characters and move the story along.[33]

For the creation of ten songs, the Shuberts paid Mercer and Carmichael each $500 in advance, promising 1.25 percent of box-office receipts plus 25 percent of any proceeds derived from movies or future performances. The cast featured established artists such as Mitzi Green, Stepin Fetchit, and Simone Simon, a French actress later replaced by Kitty Carlisle. For a year Hoagy and Johnny struggled with the show in rehearsal off Broadway and then as it toured regional theaters trying to work out its problems, the foremost of which was the lack of a strong plot to carry the music. The Shubert brothers interfered by repeatedly altering the script. Several songs submitted by the duo failed to resolve the difficulties in Bolton's book. The problems built up to one particularly tense rehearsal. After watching the cast perform the latest take, Jake Shubert yelled out, "Write another song!" Carmichael snapped. He raced up the aisle, grabbed Shubert's coat, and, taking him by the lapels, shook him, saying, "Don't ever talk to me that way again." While *Walk with Music* would be Carmichael's only Broadway show, for Mercer, it marked his first complete score.[34]

The reception of the show foreshadowed much of Mercer's fate on Broadway. This and nearly every other musical he participated in suffered from problems such as a weak book or generally lackluster music. Oddly enough, in the scores of almost all his Broadway shows there failed to appear that stand-alone hit song that made the musical. The Broadway stage seemed also to have moved on from Mercer's style of jazz-based music to a fuller symphonic sound, which Richard Rodgers excelled at writing. Since Rodgers and his collaborators Hart and then Hammerstein often wrote the book, too, they were able to integrate the music into their shows more fully so that the songs carried the plot forward rather than simply serving as a pleasant interlude as had traditionally been the case. Consequently, Rodgers gained a reputation for being ruthless in his control over a production and nasty in his treatment of others.

On June 4, 1940, Larry Hart telegrammed Mercer, "Good Luck," as *Walk with Music* opened on Broadway in the Ethel Barrymore Theatre to run for fifty-five performances. In addition to "I Walk with Music," the show featured "Ooh! What You Said" and "Way Back in 1939 A.D." The songwriters put a Latin spin on swing in "The Rumba Jumps!" an inventive effort to take the musical in an international direction that failed to catch on. *New York Times* theater critic Brooks Atkinson believed the "music would seem gay and tingling" if the plot did not hang on the show like a "stricken albatross." Mercer later ruminated: "It was a nice, ineffectual show, out of date and just not vital enough to stand up to *Pal Joey* and the music that was being written then. 'Corny' is the word we would have used then — but not [for] Hoagy's tunes. They were ahead of their time, as usual."[35]

The lack of success might have soured permanently the friendship had not Mercer and Carmichael collaborated on other songs during the year they worked on *Walk with Music*. In 1939, Carmichael had composed a four-bar theme to introduce a character based on cornetist Bix Beiderbecke for a proposed show called *Young Man with a Horn*. To be used as a leitmotif in the show, the Beiderbecke-like line, which Hoagy called the "Bix Lix," found immortality in a song composed with Johnny that became "Skylark." Carmichael expanded the initial notes into a thirty-two-bar aaba format and presented the music to Mercer. For months Johnny pondered the Bix Lix, searching for an image to spark the words. He told writer Henry Kane, "I remember once I had a tune inside of me, a lovely tune, but nothing wanted to happen with it. It was there inside of me for almost a year; and then the title happened; and the rest was easy. 'Skylark.'" On another occasion Mercer remarked, "I couldn't write it and I couldn't write it, and finally I saw the word 'skylark' somewhere on a billboard or in a book . . . It wasn't from the poem. It just associated itself with that tune. And I wrote that very fast. I don't think it took me half an hour." Mercer's lyrics turned Percy Bysshe Shelley's famous poem, "To a Skylark," inside out by focusing on the unhappiness of man rather than man's delight in the bird's song. Excited, Mercer called Carmichael to say he had a lyric, but when the composer responded, "What song?" Johnny had to explain which tune he was talking about, for Hoagy had long forgotten sharing the Bix Lix with Johnny. As Mercer sang the words over the telephone, the composer jotted the lines down on the score. Then the two went over the lyric: "Skylark, / Have you anything to say to me? / Won't you tell me where my love can be? / Is there a meadow in the mist / Where someone's waiting to be kissed?" Reflecting on Mercer's line "And in your lonely flight," Carmichael's biographer, Richard Sudhalter, noted, "Perhaps its most memorable feature is the bridge, or middle section, which casually changes key to the dominant, then works its way logically back around to the tonic, or 'home' key. There is not a phrase, not a moment, in which it resembles the bridge of any other popular song." Within minutes the songwriters had the final result that became their greatest collaboration. Popularized by fellow southern diaspora entertainer Dinah Shore, "Skylark" topped *Your Hit Parade* for three months in 1942.[36]

After "Skylark," Mercer and Carmichael resumed their respective jobs as musicians for hire by the studios while occasionally collaborating on a particular song. Whereas in New York the composer and lyricist were the celebrated authors of the Broadway show, in Hollywood top billing went to the producing studios and to the key actors. Not unlike the old Broadway revues in which song pluggers had placed their music, the movies wove odd pieces into the plots of musicals. Sometimes a director did little more than stick a song into a movie as when in 1943 Paramount Pictures inserted "The Old Music Master" in *True to Life*. Reflecting Johnny and Hoagy's shared love of jazz, the song, marked "Hot" on Carmichael's original sheet music, deserves closer attention, for Mercer used it as a history lesson to teach songwriters about rhythm. Set in the past, the verse opens on a musician composing in the classical style of Beethoven and Reginald De Koven soaring melodies when suddenly there appears "A little colored boy," who symbolizes syncopation. The youth tells the old man: "You gotta jump it, music master, / You gotta play that rhythm faster, / You're never gonna get it played / On the Happy Cat Hit Parade." Lining out the history of jazz, the boy warns that failure to heed his advice will render the composer "corny," but by adding syncopation to song he will "achieve posterity." The "amazed" music master, all "wide-eyed and open-mouthed," said: "How can you be certain, little boy? Tell me how." "Because I was born," the youth responds, "A hundred years from now!" He then "hit a chord that rocked the spinet / And disappeared into the infinite." Then the narrator returns to say, "Ev'rything has happened thataway!" Music critic Will Friedwald thought "The Old Music Master" "brilliantly encapsulates the cultural conflict — and resolution — that occupied deep thinkers for much of the 20th century" because it advocates integration. The song recognizes "rhythm, more than harmony, melody, form, texture or any other musical virtue, that later generations will want to hear. Wise words indeed." Friedwald also commends Mercer's references to Reginald De Koven, the American composer of light opera and the wedding standard "Oh Promise Me," as well as the famous lost "chord" of Sir Arthur Sullivan's song. In 1943, the Famous Music Company published this slang-filled jazz number that showed Mercer and Carmichael in command of cultural trends. The best recording ever made of the song remains the 1942 duet featuring Jack Teagarden as the Old Music Master and Johnny as the boy backed up by Paul Whiteman and His Orchestra on Capitol Records.[37]

Mercer's music had become ubiquitous, appearing in venues disconnected from him and from their original source. In a January 1945 *Newsweek* feature headlined "Mercerizing Johnny," the weekly magazine explained the technique of mercerizing fabric and then suggested: "Musical mercerizing is essentially the same process: Take a good tune and get Johnny Mercer to write the lyrics. Permanent high luster is almost always the result." As proof it then recounted his catalogue. While acknowledging Johnny's ear for talent and business acumen, *Newsweek* added, "Preeminently, he is a song mercerizer. His trade recognizes that he is unique among them. The recipe? 'Take a current situation,' he explains, 'and write a few catchy lyrics about it, and then set those to a fast swinging tune. Pick a subject that everybody's talking about . . . you can use love — but that's tougher.'" Mercer and his music resonated with the public by making current trends transcendent. A jazz musician in his own right, Johnny enjoyed celebrity status as a performer just as his music demonstrated the successful melding of jazz and popular song. As Peter Townsend has argued, "jazz was more than in contact with popular music — it was implicated in popular music, it could hardly be distinguished from it."[38]

What Mercer wrote for a singer or a movie became fodder for magazine cartoons, animated short films, and radio parodies. On the NBC Radio comedy *Alec Templeton Time* in 1940, the British host built a narrative around a fictional performance of a new piece of music at the Metropolitan Opera House in New York. After describing the excitement among the privileged few seated in the golden horseshoe and then panning over to the vast golden proscenium, Templeton announced that the velvet curtains had parted, cuing the music, whereby the strains of "And the Angels Sing" and not some new aria could be heard on the broadcast. Syndicated cartoons in the newspapers such as "Harold Teen" made references to Mercer's lyrics. Warner Bros.' *Merrie Melodies* animated shorts regularly used Mercer's music to underscore the actions of cartoon characters. Animators built a whole sketch around songs Mercer and Whiting composed for *Varsity Show* in 1937, including "Have You Got Any Castles, Baby" and "Old King Cole." In another cartoon, after natives captured a missionary in the jungle and placed him in a cauldron to cook for their queen, the victim began singing to the royal, "You're just too marvelous, too marvelous for words." Similarly, Daffy Duck fended off hungry cavemen to the tune of "You Must Have Been a Beautiful Baby." The same song is played by the band at Rick's in the movie *Casablanca* as background music behind the action. Mercer and his songs saturated an entertainment industry that after the Depression and war years generated — and recycled — products for consumption by a hungry world market as the popular culture of the United States began its ascent to global hegemony in the second half of the twentieth century.[39]

During the jazz age after World War I, shifting racial attitudes resulted in a weakening of white supremacy so that many musicians increasingly ignored the color line. As the larger society's racism abated, some nightclubs relaxed the practice of segregation. In the era between the wars, jazz became popular music. The genre provided the sounds for dancing and enjoyed mass appeal among black and white people alike. Desegregated bands led by Benny Goodman and Duke Ellington and others topped the charts during the Great Depression and remained popular throughout World War II. In the thick of it all, Johnny Mercer enjoyed his greatest success both as a songwriter and as a jazz entertainer. Revisionist scholars analyzing the era's song emphasize how swing music promoted interracial democracy and a new ideology of Americanism.[40]

While working on the Broadway show *Walk with Music*, Johnny reunited with the King of Swing, Benny Goodman, on *The Camel Caravan* radio program beginning in early 1939. Born in the tenements of Chicago the same year as Mercer, Goodman learned the clarinet in synagogue but gravitated toward jazz music played by both black and white musicians. Encouraged by the recording agent John Hammond, Goodman regularly desegregated his band, often playing music arranged by Fletcher Henderson that involved performances by African Americans. Goodman assembled some of the greatest musicians of the day, who hit their stride by interpreting swing music for a predominantly white, younger audience who enjoyed dancing to the hot sounds. Duke Ellington's 1931 hit "It Don't Mean a Thing If It Ain't Got That Swing" coined the name for the big-band style that became the most popular of all incarnations of jazz music, enjoyed by blacks and whites alike from the 1930s into the 1940s and the onset of the Age of the Singer. Goodman and others took the sounds of swing to a white supremacist America to promote desegregation in the decades before the civil rights movement. The themes of national unity that President Franklin D.

Roosevelt encouraged in response to the Great Depression and World War II found cultural expression through swing music.[41]

Since Mercer's days in New York freelancing with these jazz musicians in the early 1930s, Goodman's band had become a sensation. He went from pulling together small groups for gigs and recordings to forming his own band that played at Billy Rose's Music Hall in 1934 and then provided the hot music for Nabisco's popular *Let's Dance* radio program, which won for Goodman a national audience. The bandleader and his jazz musicians traveled cross-country on a tour that stumbled along until a fateful performance in the Palomar Ballroom of Los Angeles on August 21, 1935. The group had been playing sweet music — a milder version of jazz found to be commercially successful by established orchestras such as the Guy Lombardo Band — but the lack of audience response led Goodman and his musicians in the second set to cut loose with Fletcher Henderson's arrangement of "King Porter Stomp," to the delight of a new generation that coalesced around the swing music. Johnny heard his old friends there and experienced the sensation. Later Mercer said he witnessed the jazz musicians generate excitement by compiling the signature piece "Sing, Sing, Sing." For two months Goodman's band held forth from the Palomar in what had been the old Rainbow Gardens dance hall near Hollywood. Critical acclaim steadily built as the band moved to Chicago; a series of performances culminating in a March 1937 gig at the Paramount Theater in New York demonstrated the popularity of swing music among teenagers.[42]

In addition to Mercer's old friends, Jack Teagarden on trombone and Gene Krupa on drums, Goodman had added a great trumpet section with Harry James and Ziggy Elman and the African American vibraphonist Lionel Hampton. A diaspora entertainer, Hampton had left his Birmingham home for Chicago prior to his 1927 West Coast move to Los Angeles, where he played on recordings made by Louis Armstrong and in the studio band of Nat Shilkret. Similarly, James, a native of Albany, Georgia, had moved with his family to Beaumont, Texas, where he grew up playing the trumpet in Gulf Coast groups before being recruited by the Ben Pollack Band. These musicians typified the new jazz style of swing that Goodman and other white big bands (led by the Dorsey brothers, Glenn Miller, and Artie Shaw) and black big bands (led by Duke Ellington, Cab Calloway, Count Basie, and Jimmie Lunceford) made popular.[43]

Collaborating on *The Camel Caravan* formalized the decade-long relationship between Goodman and Mercer. For years Johnny had provided the clarinet player with songs that helped build his popularity. After moving from the Palomar to the Congress Hotel in Chicago in 1936, Benny Goodman introduced Mercer and Matt Malneck's "Goody Goody." The song featured the band's girl singer, a commercial component that kept the swing revolt against sweet music viable. In contrast to the 1940s Age of the Singer, in which the individual stood apart from the band, the girl singer of the 1930s swing era served as a key instrument in the overall orchestra. At the time Helen Ward held the job with Goodman, but she resisted singing "Goody Goody," later explaining, "I thought it was silly. I hated it so much that the first time I heard it I almost cried." Yet the singer's "wonderfully sprightly and spring-like" take on the tune topped the charts as one of her greatest hits. David Lehman observed that the 1930s era revenge song "could make you chuckle" as Johnny rhymed "hooray and hallelujah" with "you had it comin' to ya." Twenty-five years after its release, Richard Rodgers listened to Diahann Carroll sing the "old Johnny Mercer number, 'Goody Goody,' with such distinctiveness that it sounded like a brand-new song written expressly for her," a backhanded compliment to the quality of the songwriting. With Goodman in mind, in 1935 Mercer wrote lyrics to Bernie Hanighen's "The Dixieland Band," which with vocals by Ward sold well on the West Coast as a Columbia recording and then nationally on the Victor label remake that featured a swing sound. In a charming recording of "Cuckoo in the Clock," which Mercer wrote with veteran composer Walter Donaldson in 1939, Goodman imitated the chirps of the bird on his clarinet. Noting the "great affection" the bandleader held for Mercer, Goodman's biographer, Stanley Baron, suggested Benny found Johnny "a delight to work with, delivering his own best material with a gusto such as only a slightly mad creative talent could summon."[44]

By the time Johnny became a regular on *The Camel Caravan*, Goodman—who had a reputation for being difficult—had replaced Ward with the Texan Martha Tilton as his girl singer. Camel Cigarettes sponsored the show, which had been airing since 1934, playing the most popular dance music on radio. At the height of the swing era in 1937, Goodman and his orchestra took over the program for CBS and for two years broadcast on Tuesday nights *The Camel Caravan: Benny Goodman's Swing School*. As part of his performance Mercer announced the show and wrote weekly rhymes based on current events set to music from the top forty. These "newsie bluesies" became a popular staple of the broadcast and underscored his talents as an entertainer while reinforcing his celebrity. Mercer had begun performing such lyrical improvisations as "clambakes" for Whiteman's broadcasts. Against a jazz riff, Johnny improvised songs on such subjects as the races at the Indianapolis speedway or other innocuous events then in the headlines. He took Dana Suesse and Edward Heyman's "You Oughta Be in Pictures" and, accompanied by Goodman's band, turned the standard into "You Oughta Be in Pittsburgh," with rhythmic references to George Washington's surveying the steel city overlooking the Allegheny and Monongahela Rivers. Quoting a newspaper about a recent proclamation by President Franklin D. Roosevelt regarding a new national holiday in November, Mercer began, "We've come to a new way of living. / The twenty-third, they say, / Was Thanksgiving Day. / Well, I'd rather call it 'Franksgiving.'"[45]

Goodman's on-air challenge during an episode of *The Camel Caravan* to get Mercer to draft a lyric to a tune resulted in pure poetry set to beautiful music. Drawing on his Jewish roots, Goodman selected the Yiddish folk music of Eastern Europe as inspiration for two of his popular songs. Normally played on the klezmer accompanied by horns and drums, such shrill fraelichs provided wild dance music associated with traditional Hebrew celebrations. One night Ziggy Elman struck out with a fraelich on the trumpet. During the broadcast, Goodman challenged Mercer to provide words to the tune by the next week. The resulting lyric, "And the Angels Sing," became a hit that the King of Swing used as a theme song. With lightning flashes of the trumpet, Ziggy punctuated the lilting lyric of Martha Tilton in what biographer Baron described as "a triumph, small in scope yet genuine; words and music had been brought to dovetail perfectly." Mercer's words paint pictures: "Suddenly / The setting is strange: / I can see water and moonlight beaming, / Silver waves / That break on some undiscovered shore; / Then suddenly / I see it all change — / Long winter nights with the candles gleaming. / Through it all your face that I adore." Bing Crosby wrote Mercer, "'Angels,' to my way of thinking, is your best lyric to date. You're getting practically poetic. It's a hunk of a song."[46]

Goodman's stint with *The Camel Caravan* — and Mercer's — ended in 1939, but in 1940, Johnny took a seat on the board of directors of ASCAP to represent the "popular writer group." In notifying Mercer, the president of ASCAP wrote,

I have always considered you a young man of exceptional ability and unusual gifts and it is my genuine wish that you will assist us for many years to come in attempting to find the solution to the problems that confront us and to perpetuate the ideals of the Founders whose vision and understanding have brought into existence the greatest Society of its kind in the civilized world for the protection of those who create and publish the music and songs of the nation.

Little did Mercer anticipate during his year on the board that Congress would investigate ASCAP to determine whether or not it functioned as a monopoly and that a bitter fight would break out between ASCAP and the radio stations over licensing fees. Lyricists, composers, and publishers in ASCAP received royalties each time a radio station broadcast a song, and the amount charged became the basis of the conflict. The money once earned through the publication of songs and their performance in Broadway shows or movies paled in comparison to the potential profits derived from broadcast fees. To undercut ASCAP, the National Association of Broadcasters created a competitor, Broadcast Music Incorporated (BMI), in October 1939, and began to sign up independent songwriters, some long ignored by ASCAP. The five-year contract with ASCAP that required annual licensing fees of $4.5 million expired at the end of 1940, but instead of paying the higher fees ASCAP demanded, the broadcasters pulled all ASCAP-licensed songs from the air, substituting music in the public domain or licensed by BMI beginning on New Year's Day and running until October 1941, when the networks and ASCAP agreed to a lesser annual licensing fee of $3 million. As a result, ASCAP lost its control over the popular music industry and confronted a competitor in BMI that soon displaced it as the lead agency for songwriters.[47]

Defending his fellow songwriters in the established industry, Mercer found himself in the thick of the struggle against the radio stations. He wrote his mother:

> This fight between ASCAP and the net-works has taken up every spare min-
> ute that I've had. First in New York and now out here. We just had a meet-
> ing of the radio committee this afternoon and tonight Hoagy and I have
> to go and address the Young Democrats about the situation. It's a tough
> struggle but worth it if we can get the public to understand what those
> damn broadcasters are doing to the songwriters.

To generate public support for its position, the songwriters produced *ASCAP on Parade*, a regular radio program over 1940–41 that in one broadcast featured Mercer with Al Jolson, Cole Porter, and Ethel Merman. By demonstrating the quality of their craft, ASCAP members struggled to explain the difficulties of songwriting and what they saw as the threat of unfettered access to the market-place by music unlicensed by them. Yet the continual playing of a song over the radio shortened its air life considerably as the public developed an appetite for new hits. As a result, the quantity of songs increased while — critics argued — the quality decreased. During the feud, ASCAP represented the interests of the establishment and protected the Tin Pan Alley and Hollywood producers of American popular song, while BMI made recordings of old standards by Stephen Foster and others in the public domain, signed many country music performers for new material, and later captured rock 'n' roll bands. The conflict broke the hold on the industry by the ASCAP fraternity to which Mercer belonged and resulted in a democratization of popular music but also led Johnny to believe that the songwriting craft he admired so much had been irreparably cheapened.[48]

The independence Johnny enjoyed freelancing that allowed him to move with ease between Hollywood and New York also enabled illicit behavior. He relished the company of attractive women, objectifying them as "pretty," describing them almost as candy, dressed in "gossamer and spun sugar," and considering them designed for pleasure — targets for flirtation and seduction. Some women appreciated the sexist attention from Johnny and played to the hilt the role society cast for them, while others spurned his advances. The elite culture Mercer experienced growing up in Savannah promoted such gender relations and tolerated sexual indiscretions as long as they remained private affairs. Married Hollywood contemporaries and friends such as Bing Crosby and Bob Hope committed dalliances and fornicated with chorus girls and other women, and Mercer often betrayed similar behaviors. Johnny once confessed to Robert Rush, who worked for the Mercers, "You know, I've had the opportunity to go with all sorts of different women when I've been doing movies," adding, "Do you think I'm making a mistake by just sticking with Ginger?" Rush answered, "You have to live with yourself," to which Johnny replied, "Yeah, you're right."[49]

Ascribing to the Victorian moral code impressed on him by his forebears, Johnny separated extramarital sex from marital commitment. He adhered to the southern code of honor that valued "wenching" and other displays of virility. Throughout numerous brief affairs, Johnny remained committed to Ginger and even defended matrimony, for like other adulterers in his class he accepted marriage as a sacrament and institution of permanence, while paradoxically thinking little of sex outside its parameters. Neither did the damage done to his wife by his infidelity seem to bother him. Savannah's upper class discouraged divorce, with prominent individuals permanently separated from their spouses often finding themselves ostracized by polite society. The Protestant Episcopal Church, to which Johnny belonged, also frowned on the practice of divorce, for within the Anglican Communion the issue had brought down the king of England in 1936. For Mercer then, secretly running around with other women while married seemed the norm.[50]

Yet nothing prevented Johnny and Ginger from divorcing had they wanted to do so. Since several of his kinsmen — especially among the Roman Catholic Ciucevich clan — had ended failed marriages, there probably would have been little family uproar if Johnny and Ginger did likewise. In 1940, Johnny wrote to his mother about the recent divorce of his first cousin, Mercer Lang, from his wife, Adeline McCraney: "I can understand the sensation that Mercer's and Adeline's parting of the ways must have caused. I personally think it's a wonderful thing for both of them if it hasn't come too late. You know —'I hate to lose you — I'm so used to you now'— sort of thing." Johnny went on to defend his cousin, saying, "I always thought he got a terrific run-around, although I don't know what he was doing about it." Johnny expressed his true sorrow for the effect of the divorce on his Uncle Joe Lang, but added, "He's got too wonderful a sense of humor to let a little thing like a divorce in the house upset him." Within months, Lillian Mercer oversaw the divorce of her daughter, Juliana, from Gil Keith, and she might have welcomed Johnny's separation from Ginger, a wife she never really liked. Regardless of whether Johnny worried about another scandal on the Mercer family name, or he could not face the reality that his parents had been right to oppose his choice of a bride, or he figured he had become "too used to" Ginger to call it off, or the two shared an alcoholic dependency that kept them together, or he still loved the chorus girl who had first struck his fancy in 1930 — the fact remains that Johnny and Ginger stayed married. Although family and friends reported that the Mercers shared an unhappy relationship and appeared to cheat on each other, and while the two occasionally discussed divorce, they never followed through on the plan.[51]

Just months before writing his mother sympathetically about the dissolution of his cousin's marriage, Johnny began his ill-fated love affair with Judy Garland. He had seen her perform as Baby Frances in Chicago six years before and joined her three years later in the Joe Sullivan benefit. By 1940, the ingénue of *The Wizard of Oz* had matured into a voluptuous nearly eighteen-year-old. Like her friends, Margaret Whiting, Mickey Rooney, Mel Tormé, and Martha Raye, and other Hollywood teens, Judy had grown up fast. A regular on Bob Hope's *Pepsodent Show*, Garland attended a soiree the comedian hosted in Hollywood. For his guests at the party Hope had intended to perform with Garland the new hit "Friendship" from Cole Porter's current Broadway show, *Du Barry Was a*

Lady. Yet after introducing his old buddy Johnny — whom he had known since the early 1930s — to Judy, Bob must have noted the chemistry between the two, so he suggested they sing the song instead. They did, and a love affair ensued that would last off and on for thirty years. Long a fan of Johnny's music, Judy had learned to sing "Jamboree Jones" and "Bob White" and stood in awe of the likeable lyricist. Age proved an attraction as Garland had already been in intimate relationships with older men such as Oscar Levant and most recently clarinetist Artie Shaw, with whom Mercer had just written "The Love of My Life." Twelve years her senior and a charming man of music, Mercer had the right attributes to strike her fancy. Utterly enamored by Judy's innate singing ability and charisma, Johnny fell hard. In April 1940, they recorded "Friendship" for Decca. With its chorus, "It's friendship, friendship, / Just a perfect blendship. / When other friendships have been forgot, / Ours will still be hot," the song captured their on-again, off-again affair. Garland biographer Gerold Clarke understood "their relationship had become considerably more than friendly" by the recording date. "As besotted with Judy as Judy had been with Shaw, Mercer wandered around in such a lovesick daze that a friend of the family finally pleaded with her to let him go." Johnny later admitted, "I loved Judy Garland." He never lost his feelings for the exceptionally talented singer notorious for her sexual escapades, substance abuse, and lack of commitment, and despite it all, her behavior affirmed an abiding affection for him.[52]

Although the two kept their relationship secret, Mickey Rooney recognized that his childhood friend had fallen for an older man who was not her new betrothed, David Rose. As her childhood chum and co-star put it in the spring of 1941, "She was at last in love with someone who loved her." To protect the reputation of their hot property, MGM announced the engagement and pending marriage of Garland and Rose by hosting a party for the young couple at Judy's Stone Canyon Road mansion on June 15, 1941. Ginger and Johnny joined six hundred other guests at the lavish affair. After Judy and David eloped six weeks later to cheat MGM out of a publicity wedding, the studio then hosted a party at the Coconut Grove, where — according to Mercer friend Jean Bach — in front of Ginger, David, and the others, the indiscreet dancing between Johnny and Judy revealed their illicit romance. Soon everyone in the small town atmosphere of the movie industry seemed to know about the adulterous relationship. The lovers' rendezvous on the studio back-lot in Garland's private trailer strengthened the lifelong bonds of affection between the two. Although friends intervened to prevent the affair from becoming a public scandal, Johnny and Judy continued to cross paths: professionally on shows, at formal parties, and at informal gatherings with colleagues.[53]

Ever acting the Don Juan, Mercer made overtures to other women that if well received led to a dalliance, but he also accepted rejection with an ease that reflected the flirtatious nature of what he took to be a private game between adults. Some women responded similarly, while others did not find his behavior so harmless. After Johnny visited Savannah in 1935 without his wife of four years, cousin Walter wrote his fiancée, Cornelia McIntire: "I saw John last night for a few minutes and he told me about an amorous escapade with some little 'number' he picked up. It wasn't very interesting. The same old thing and I might add the same old John." Thirty-five years later, Walter received a letter from Dot Wolf, a recent divorcée and mutual friend in Savannah, who wrote in 1970 that "Johnny came by again the other nite and spent a couple of hours" with her. She explained to the widowed Walter — with whom she really wanted to start a romance — that they drank Scotch and reminisced about their youth in Savannah. Around this time the middle-aged songwriter maintained an active relationship with a much younger woman in Savannah who described their association as platonic and kept his letters to her. In an interview with his half-brother's daughter, the niece recalled with shock and disgust unwanted overtures made by her drunken uncle. Johnny remarked to Cornelia McIntire Rivers in a letter from the mid-1960s, "It's always fun around the McIntires, because they have — not only joi de vivre — but 'that Grade A Milk of Human Kindness — *Deep* in their hearts.' And do you know the reason? It is because they 'Gather Liprouge while They May!'" He might as well have described himself. For some paramours, Johnny painted watercolors, a hobby he had developed in the 1940s. For others he wrote songs, as women consistently provided inspiration for his music. Obviously Johnny enjoyed playing the field in an attempt to woo women for lovemaking. One might question his success, for as a gentleman he rarely revealed such matters, but as his lyrics make apparent, he enjoyed sex and engaged in it whenever he wanted a willing female. Daughter Mandy suggested her father found no shortage of partners either, by asking, "How do you say no when they stick it in your face?" And as the Kinsey Institute made clear in its reports a decade later, a significant minority of Americans behaved like Mercer.[54]

A child at heart who loved children, Johnny convinced Ginger to adopt with him a baby girl in the summer of 1940. For several years it had been his desire to start a family, but Ginger had not gotten pregnant, perhaps suggesting the couple had difficulties conceiving. Several of Johnny's Ciucevich kinsmen apparently suffered from infertility and turned to adoption, as did a rash of Hollywood stars, including Johnny's close friends, Paul and Margaret Whiteman, Bob and Dolores Hope, and Jerry and Flo Colonna, who named their son Robert John Colonna after their friends Bob Hope and Johnny Mercer. Whiteman recommended an adoption agency in Augusta, Georgia, that located the girl for the couple, who named the child Georgia Amanda Mercer. Soon Johnny wrote his mother, "Amanda is a great joy to us and has made a great difference in our lives already. We both have been going to bed earlier, drinking less, and consequently, have been less irritable." Shifting into the old Geechee dialect he enjoyed speaking as a youth, Johnny added, "The change in Ginger is remarkable. I guess 'e do tek a baby fuh mek um duh bud an' blawssum, yunty? Anyhoo, I am wearing out the knees of my trousers running after her and chasing her around the floor."[55]

Taken by this blue-eyed darling, the doting and proud father wrote a song for his daughter in 1942 with Fulton McGrath titled "Mandy Is Two." Billie Holiday's version of the song about the toddler who already acts like a big girl demonstrated the singer's understated elegance and the power of the lyric: "Mandy is two. / You ought to see her eyes of cornflower blue — / They really look as if they actually knew / That she's a big girl now." Holiday conveyed the idea "so straightforwardly and warmly!" noted one critic of the recording, adding, "How simple and unpretentious it is! Nothing rings false, as is the rule with commercial ditties attempting childlike naivete. It is almost inconceivable that something seemingly destined by every known law to become kitsch could be transformed into art." Thinking back on Billie Holiday's recording, Mandy Mercer remembered that "my mother would cry every time she heard it."[56]

The granddaughter pleased the family back in Georgia that had also grown with the marriage of Johnny's sister and the birth of her daughter, Nancy. Having graduated from the Pape School in Savannah, attended classes in Virginia, and studied voice at the Juilliard School of Music in New York, Juliana Mercer courted Henry Gilbert Keith, a banker studying finance. In the spring of 1939, Johnny visited the Keiths in Michigan and reported back to his mother that he "saw Gil in Detroit and I must admit he is one of the nicest young men I have ever met. If you ask me, Julie is lucky to have such a beau. He seems genuinely crazy about her and has loads of ambition — something which she seems to be lacking in." The Savannah papers announced the engagement of the couple in October 1939, an event that pleased G. A. Mercer, who liked his future son-in-law and wrote him that "Julie is becoming with joy and happiness." After the wedding the Keiths settled in Savannah, where Gil joined the Mercer firm. He soon discovered his new wife had mental issues that made managing domestic affairs difficult for her. And then she got pregnant. G. A. Mercer died the month before Julie gave birth to a baby girl in December 1940. The Keiths named their daughter Nancy after Juliana's sister who had died in 1914. The difficulty of the delivery encouraged Lillian to intervene in the couple's life, raising the newborn girl as her own. The mother-in-law's interference ultimately resulted in Gil's return to Detroit as the separation culminated in divorce.[57]

Religious to the end, G. A. Mercer died at the age of seventy-two on November 14, 1940, just hours before Johnny's arrival home by plane from California. His son had agreed to fly despite the sinus pain traveling in the unpressurized cabins caused him because he thought it would be faster than riding the train. He took his father's death hard, breaking down at the funeral held at Christ Church, followed by burial in the family plot at Bonaventure Cemetery. The local paper eulogized G. A. Mercer: "A man of gentle and friendly nature, he held a warm place in the hearts of many Savannahians and the community which he so greatly loved loses in his passing a man who contributed of his business ability and experience to the city's advancement and of his spiritual wealth to those about him." Quoting Ecclesiastes, G. A. often attributed his successes in life to following King Solomon's advice by "casting bread upon the water," and in memory of his father, Johnny later composed a song of that title, adding "from the most unexpected quarter / It comes back to you a thousandfold," so "Give your love to everybody." On several occasions Johnny had written his father expressing deep respect and admiration for the virtuous example he set in life, but now in death Johnny felt his expressions inadequate.[58]

Returning to California, Mercer threw himself into the music that provided him solace by pursuing opportunities in Hollywood. The studios often competed to see who could produce a film first on a particular theme in order to capitalize on a popular trend, an example being the background history of jazz. In the *Birth of the Blues*, Paramount placed its film in exotic New Orleans surrounded by great music from the period by the Original Dixieland Jazz Band and W. C. Handy. Johnny Mercer contributed both the words and music to an original song for the movie, "The Waiter and the Porter and the Upstairs Maid," sung by Bing Crosby, Jack Teagarden, and Mary Martin. With syncopation, the lyric spells out the rhythmic nature of jazz: "I went and got a dish-pan / to use as a cym-bal. / The por-ter found a reg-u-lar / Glass that he played. / The fin-gers of the wait-er / Were each in a thim-ble. / You should of heard the mu-sic / That the com-bi-na-tion made." At other points in the song, Mercer identifies dances associated with the multiracial South: "It's pretty hard to cakewalk / Or tickle a toe to / The ordinary music you always hear played," but upon adding syncopation to the old melodies, suddenly "We were ballin' the jack." The film opened in October 1941, two months before Warner Bros. released its take on a similar topic with a similar title.[59]

Several years had passed since Harold Arlen and Johnny Mercer had worked together, but now reunited by Warner Bros. on *Blues in the Night*, they began a series of collaborations that resulted in some of the best music of their respective careers. After Arlen wrote with Yip Harburg *The Wizard of Oz* score, including the 1939 Oscar-winning "Over the Rainbow," the songwriters had split up. Mutual friend Buddy Morris linked Harold with Johnny again, and in the late spring of 1941 they set to work. Based on Edwin Gilbert's play *Hot Nocturne*, the storyline concerned the artist's universal struggle with originality over commercialism as told through a jazz pianist and his love for a girl singer. The score adhered to the standard format for musicals, which called for four types of songs: a ballad, a commercial novelty song, a rhythm or riff number, and a blues song. The middle two, the novelty "Says Who? Says You, Says I!" and the riff "Hang on to Your Lids, Kids," serviced the story. The ballad, "This Time the Dream's on Me," and the blues that became the title song, "Blues in the Night," joined the catalogue of Great American Songs.[60]

With "This Time the Dream's on Me," Mercer revealed his abiding affection for Judy Garland. The lyric expressed an unusual display of pathos: "Somewhere, someday / We'll be close together, / Wait and see. / Oh, by the way, / This time the dream's on me." Raising doubts at the bridge, the refrain continues: "It would be fun / To be certain that I'm the one, / To know that I at least supply / The shoulder you cry upon." The song ends on a pathetically hopeful note: "To see you through / Till you're everything you want to be. / It can't be true, but / This time the dream's on me." The song captured the pitiful situation of the lovers. In later years, when Judy made "This Time the Dream's on Me" one of her polished gems, all the baggage she carried, the emotional scars so well-known to the public, made the eternally false optimism of the song all the more poignant. Yip Harburg once noted, "Honesty, not phoniness, moves people. Judy Garland was to singing what Gershwin's music was to music. They brought a quality and vitality that was typically and uniquely American." Harburg found the same America in Mercer's songs, acknowledging they had "the descriptive flair of a Mark Twain, and the melodies of Stephen Foster."[61]

No other partner suited Mercer as well as the simpatico Arlen, for the two men perfectly complemented each other's talents writing jazz-oriented popular song. Personally they shared similarities, too, as both men had unhappy marriages to women of religions not their own, turned to alcohol for escape as did their wives, enjoyed the company of other pretty females, and suffered the consequences of their abusive behaviors. Just as Johnny found Hoagy Carmichael too domineering, Arlen thought Yip Harburg mixed politics with entertainment too fervently. And both men loved to perform. As Mercer recalled, "We [didn't] come from the same neck of the woods or anything, but we really [had] a thing about jazz and blues, and creativity and originality, and structure." Four years Johnny's senior, Harold stood of average build with blue eyes and black wavy hair he kept slicked back. A sensitive man, he also befriended Judy Garland. Perhaps when discussing the process of collaboration with writer Henry Kane, Mercer thought of Arlen: "He's got some tunes. I've got some titles. Pretty soon they begin to blend; we keep batting the heck out of it. Little by little, it begins to come; songs come, nice ones, real sweet ones, words and music. We keep fixing, polishing, working. Pretty soon, we've rapped out some beauties — we hope! That's collaboration, working together, under pressure — on assignment." Having partnered with many composers, Mercer understood that "collaboration, sometimes, can be tough, depending upon the personalities of the two individuals — and, on assignment, you're just *thrust* together. Sometimes it's a natural team — no scuffing around, no rubbing the wrong way. Sometimes, it's the other way, but if you're a pro, you make the best of it, and produce your songs."[62]

For *Blues in the Night*, Mercer and Arlen made their music fit the story of the movie. The plot had a white piano player — not unlike Arlen — locked in jail, where he hears a black man singing a blues song that provides the inspiration for a new hit song for his jazz band. Arlen wanted to write music true to the blues, so he studied W. C. Handy's *A Treasury of the Blues* and set about composing his own version of the form. Arlen's original fifty-eight bars took the standard aaba song structure and incorporated into it two different twelve-bar melodies. Arlen referred to the involved leads — longer than the thirty-two bars of most songs — as his "tapeworms." Pleased with the result, the composer shared the music with the lyricist. Recalling years later how he could read Mercer's body language, Arlen described the "wink" Johnny would give when a hangover prevented him from getting much accomplished. With no such signal, Arlen played the music and left Mercer to ponder the words. Johnny always drafted several potential lyrics for a song, and later he shared the results with Harold. A line toward the bottom struck Arlen's eye, and although he had never revised a

Mercer lyric before, he suggested it become the opening stanza, and Johnny agreed, striking out the original line and substituting the syncopated, "My mama done tol' me / When I was in kneepants / My mama done tol' me, son!" Within a week the two men had their song.[63]

Recalling the creation of "Blues in the Night" three decades later, Mercer explained that when he and Arlen "sat down and tried to write a real first class blues," just as Arlen studied Handy, Mercer remembered his youth in Savannah: "I heard a lot of that down South and it's become quite fashionable now to sing those old 12 bar blues, 8 bar blues from the field." Although many people associate such singers with Mississippi, "We had a lot of them in Georgia, too," Mercer observed. Discussing the song with Willis Conover, Johnny said, "Well, 'Blues in the Night' is right out of Savannah, my background and all the things I heard when I was a boy and experienced." Once Mercer had a lyric to go with Arlen's music, the pair then worked on a title: Harold wanted "My Mama Done Told Me," while Johnny held out for "Blues in the Night." Unable to resolve their impasse, the two men agreed to "ask Irving and do what he says," and when they presented the two titles to Berlin, he sided with Mercer, "two against one. So we called it that."[64]

Even after Dick Whiting's death, his widow and daughters opened their house for informal parties at which Hollywood songwriters and performers entertained one another. Mercer and Arlen arrived late one night that summer of 1941 to try out "Blues in the Night" on the guests. Margaret Whiting recalled, "Harold sat down at the piano and played a few blues chords and Johnny began to imitate a train whistle." A crowd gathered as they performed their new creation, and Whiting observed, "The room grew very still. I looked around. Mel Tormé's mouth was hanging open. Judy [Garland] had her head down and just her eyes were peering up at Arlen. Everyone in the room knew something great was happening. Just to watch Arlen and Mercer perform was a treat. They 'wailed' before the term came into fashion." One wonders what Judy thought of the line: "A woman's a two-face / A worrisome thing / Who'll leave ya t' sing / The blues in the night." After the assembly made them play it nine times, according to Whiting, "We couldn't get Mel Tormé up off the floor, and for the first time Martha Raye didn't have anything funny to say. Everyone wanted to sing it. Judy and I rushed to the piano to see who could learn it first. I remember the excitement of that night — and most remarkably, there was not an ounce of envy. People were genuinely pleased for everybody else's success."[65]

Reflecting the hybridity of southern culture, "Blues in the Night" became a standard of the genre, ultimately headlining a London West End show that featured the music of Bessie Smith and other blues greats. In the movie the Jimmie Lunceford Orchestra, an African American jazz band from Memphis, performed the music with words sung by the black vocalist William Gillespie. Yet Lunceford resisted making his own recording until pressured to do so by Decca Records, which prepared a rare double-sided version of the song that went on to become one of his orchestra's best-selling releases. The black Lunceford never explained his resistance to the blues number created by white men. Dozens of other performers eagerly recorded "Blues in the Night," and its widespread popularity demonstrated the merger of musical genres, with southern music at the center of American popular culture.[66]

The reach of "Blues in the Night" raises questions about "authenticity" and the blues. Some purists believe blues singers can only sing blues, being protected from the corrupting influences of other musical styles. The chronicler of the blues, Alan Lomax — who began his book of folklore, *The Land Where the Blues Began*, with the observation, "A hundred years ago only blacks in the Deep South were seized by the blues," in a bid to authenticate through racial essentialism the style — toured the Mississippi Delta looking for "genuine" blues performers. In July 1942, Lomax discovered McKinley Morganfield, whom he declared the greatest of blues singers. Better known as Muddy Waters, the performer sang for Lomax his repertoire that day, including a variety of blues classics and the six-month-old Arlen-Mercer hit, "Blues in the Night." Like Ralph Peer of Southern Music and other recorders of the "pure" folk song, Lomax discounted the hit tune and concentrated on the blues numbers. Yet as the music critic Peter Townsend observes, "The history of 'Blues in the Night' and its popular reception in 1941–1942 suggests some further reconsiderations of the narrative of jazz," and blues. For Lomax, Waters sang thirty-four songs, nearly half of which would be considered country, jazz, or popular songs and not the blues of so-called roots music. The Mississippian had either seen the film or heard some of the thirteen versions of "Blues in the Night" then being broadcast over the radio and played on jukeboxes and had learned it to entertain his customers. As Townsend argues, "Jazz players were making pop records. Blues players were singing pop tunes." And popular music songwriters were creating blues and jazz numbers, for the genres had completely interpenetrated each other.[67]

War clouds blocked "Blues in the Night," the favorite nomination of many in Hollywood, from winning an Academy Award for Best Song. Mercer and Arlen watched as a majority in the Academy cast sentimental ballots for "The Last

Time I Saw Paris." Composed by Jerome Kern with lyrics by Oscar Hammerstein II, the song had appeared independently in 1940 before being interpolated into the movie *Lady Be Good*, an outcome that led some to argue — including Kern, who voted for "Blues in the Night" — that it should have been disqualified. The following year the Academy clarified its rules to require all nominated songs to have been written specifically for the movie in which they appeared. Yet by the time of the Academy Awards, Nazi Germany had occupied Paris and the United States had declared war against the Axis powers. The sentiment in the country changed as Americans geared up for fighting. Entering his most productive period as the war got underway, Mercer enjoyed sustained success as a songwriter and jazz performer who would soon add the title "record producer" to his list of accomplishments, but several more years would pass before he won that first Oscar.[68]

5 War Years

. . . .

Don't be hurt,
Don't be sore —
I'm a pal,
Nothing more.
This ain't love,
This is war.
I'm doin' it for defense!

FOR MONTHS, news of war spreading across Europe and Asia had
steadily increased in the United States. In September 1940, Johnny had written
his mother about the "frightening" Battle of Britain: "Doesn't seem possible that
all those places that I saw when we were in London are being bombed and torn
up." His concern turned to his aged cousin: "I was worried about Aunt Nell at
first — but now, I know that if she's safe at all she's probably having a hell of a time
and enjoying every Jerry that is being shot down." Turning on the radio to catch
the *I Will Arise* church program one Sunday morning, Johnny and Ginger heard
instead a bulletin announcing the Japanese surprise attack in Hawaii. They listened to the "marvelous, paternal delivery" of President Franklin D. Roosevelt's
"day that will live in infamy" speech before the U.S. Congress. A week later while
at dinner with friends, they confronted the first of many California blackouts.
The war had reached America.[1]

With the attack on Pearl Harbor and the entry of the United States into the
global conflict in December 1941, Mercer debated his options. A celebrity in his
own right on the eve of World War II, Johnny stood at the top of his profession
as both a songwriter and an entertainer. The thirty-two-year-old came from a
long line of military men and wanted to assist the war effort, but he wanted to
avoid the draft. He sought advice from the director of *Blues in the Night*, Anatole
Litvak, who after volunteering for the army received a commission as a major and
a Washington desk job. The army had other plans for Johnny, however, send-

ing him back to Hollywood to generate morale-building entertainment for the troops and the home front. Army colonel Thomas "Tom" H. A. Lewis called Mercer to discuss how the songwriter might assist the country in prosecuting the war through music. In peacetime Lewis ran an important advertising agency and moved among the Hollywood set as the husband of actress Loretta Young, so he understood the propaganda potential of the studio stars. At first Johnny resumed his work on pictures, but within a year he assisted Lewis by performing before the troops at military bases in California and creating broadcast material for the colonel's pet project, the Armed Forces Radio Service (AFRS).[2]

Other family members fought on the front lines, and Mercer followed their plight. One distant relative, "blood-and-guts" General George Patton, led the Third Army as it joined the Russians and other Allied forces in liberating Europe from the Nazis. Johnny knew of the shared kinship ties through their common ancestor, Revolutionary War hero General Hugh Mercer. Johnny held much closer to his heart cousin Walter Rivers, who in the 1930s had enlisted in the marines. Throughout the war in the Pacific, Walter kept with him the Confederate battle flag carried by his grandfather, G. W. O. Rivers of Walterboro, South Carolina, and the talisman generated media coverage that enabled his wife, Cornelia, and the McIntires, the Mercers, and the Ciuceviches to follow his general movements. Camp commander of a marine bombing squadron, Major Rivers oversaw its management on Okinawa during a campaign against the Japanese that attracted kamikaze raids. Hearing of these dangerous exploits, Johnny determined to do something for Walter once he returned home.[3]

With World War II, the Hollywood studios shifted the focus of the movie musicals to military themes, with Mercer generating patriotic material for public consumption. The excitement of mobilization inspired Johnny to interpolate jazz into popular song that captured the fancy of Americans in wartime. Paramount's contribution to the 1942 propaganda effort, *Star Spangled Rhythm*, set a formula the industry followed whereby a contrived plot strung together song and dance numbers that enabled the big stars under contract with the studio to appear in the movie, among them, Betty Hutton, Dick Powell, Alan Ladd, Fred MacMurray, Bob Hope, Jerry Colonna, and Bing Crosby. Johnny's contemporary and future collaborator Robert Emmett Dolan scored the film. Again Mercer teamed up with Arlen to produce "I'm Doin' It for Defense" and "On the Swing Shift," examples of jazz interpenetrating popular song for a Hollywood production. Three of the studio's beauties — Paulette Goddard, Dorothy Lamour, and Veronica Lake — presented cameos in "A Sweater, a Sarong and a

Peek-a-Boo Bang," a lyric that showed Mercer up on the latest fashion trends. With Mount Rushmore as the backdrop, Bing Crosby and ensemble belted out the blockbuster patriotic finale, "Old Glory." In his history of the Hollywood musical, Clive Hirschhorn called *Star Spangled Rhythm* "a bumper bonanza of unlimited talent," noting that "its chief purpose was to unleash on servicemen everywhere an hour and a half of unbridled entertainment as a 'thank you' for the good work they were doing at the Front."[4]

Given the need for everyone to pull together for the war effort, Paramount Studios showcased both black and white stars in the movie. Their interaction did not involve demeaning circumstances, nor did it suggest inferiority as the African Americans appeared in integrated settings as well as separately with jazz-infused popular song, underscoring the multiracial hybridity of the music. The African American Edmund Lincoln "Eddie" Anderson, better known by his stage persona Rochester, the butler on radio's *Jack Benny Show*, danced in the picture. A child of the southern diaspora born in Oakland, California, in 1905, Anderson had trained in vaudeville and appeared on stage and in movies, including *Birth of the Blues*. In *Star Spangled Rhythm* he performed "Sharp as a Tack," a number that had him begin the routine wearing a zoot suit that during the syncopation changed into a military uniform. Mercer's lyric rhythmically lines out, "Sharp as a tack, / With a belt in the back," and "Draped to the bricks / — Muggin' lightly, killin' the chicks." The not so subtle message transformed the symbolic rebelliousness of a street costume into the ultimate signal of submission to authority and social assimilation, thereby conveying a strong message of national unity behind the war effort. The jazzy lullaby "Hit the Road to Dreamland" tapped the popular quartet music then all the rage by having background vocals sung by the black gospel group the Golden Gate Four. The black and white stars of Paramount Studios joined together in the finale, singing Mercer's patriotic verse about settlers on the frontier who "started a song, / Someone added a note, / Someone added a word, / And soon the wide world heard, / Old Glory." These desegregated performances pointed to the incremental changes taking place in a Hollywood notorious for its racism.[5]

The collaborators struck gold with the song "That Old Black Magic," which Johnnie Johnston sang as the ballerina Vera Zorina danced to choreography by George Balanchine. Again Arlen and Mercer used a sustained rhythm that softly repeats to set the scene. With lines such as "I should stay away, / But what can I do? / I hear your name / And I'm aflame," the lyric points to the passion of falling in love while warning of the "tyrannical nature of Eros," as noted by

David Lehman, the editor of the *Oxford Book of American Poetry*. He commends Mercer for the construction of a couplet that a groom might say to his bride on their honeymoon: "For you're the lover I have waited for, / The mate that fate had me created for." Lehman observes, "The exquisite multisyllabic end-rhymes ('waited for / created for') reinforce the internal rhyme of 'mate' and 'fate' and lead to the kiss that captures the lover's heart." Indeed, the song climaxes with: "And ev'ry time your lips meet mine, / — Darling," then resolves into "Down and down I go, / Round and round I go," ending with "Under that old black magic called love!" The overtly sexual energy of the song no doubt contributed to its mass appeal. Mercer explained in an interview years later on BBC: "I never thought of it particularly as being sexy although you do try to have images that are different, that are new. You know, when the elevator goes down and your stomach sinks." To Johnny, "black magic" suggested that "he was really stuck on this girl."[6]

With "That Old Black Magic," Mercer confessed his passion for his lover, Judy Garland. Friends quoted Johnny telling Judy that the lyric expressed "the way he felt about her." Around the time Mercer and Arlen collaborated on the song, Garland got pregnant. She had failed to find happiness in her marriage with David Rose in part because the studio had kept her addicted to caffeine, nicotine, and pills in order to meet a grueling schedule. While she saw a child fulfilling a need for love in her life, her husband rejected the baby. Rose joined mother Ethel and MGM executives in arranging an abortion. Giving in to their demands, Garland never forgave them. The damage made Judy seem all the more vulnerable to Johnny.[7]

A week after turning eighteen in 1942, Margaret Whiting recorded "That Old Black Magic," which became her first hit song. Johnny had deemed her voice ready for the studio, comparing it to the silky sounds of Billy Butterfield's trumpet. Whiting's initial recording had paired her with Paul Weston's orchestra singing her father's song "My Ideal." But Johnny wanted her to perform "That Old Black Magic" with Freddie Slack's orchestra. They cut the wax and, once released by Capitol Records, it climbed the charts. Margaret admitted she "had no firsthand knowledge" of such passion as expressed in the lyric "where 'that elevator starts its ride / And down and down I go, / Round and round I go.' But I was nothing if not game." She received coaching from the songwriters. Margaret remembered Arlen had a "fabulous style of singing," and she recalled his lesson: "'Pulsate it,' he would say, and show me how. 'that old . . . black . . . ma-a-a-gic.' Not too smooth. Pulsate it." Margaret recalled Mercer giving her more general advice: "A song was like a one-act play. Exposition, development, then the big crisis and the denouement." She first heard the recording broadcast over the radio, with clarinetist Artie Shaw offering a critique, "An instant standard — a great record." Then Peter Potter's *Juke Box Jury* gave it a 100 percent approval rating. The public concurred; a million copies of her version sold, and then an additional half-million of the Glenn Miller Orchestra's version sold the first week of its release. A decade later in *Bus Stop*, oversexed Marilyn Monroe offered a campy rendition of "That Old Black Magic," while Frank Sinatra performed it in *Meet Danny Wilson*, and fellow Rat Packer Sammy Davis Jr. recorded the classic Vegas rendition. A popular film of the Louis Prima Orchestra performing "That Old Black Magic" with the conductor singing an animated duet with his girl singer and wife, Keely Smith, appeared in theaters across the country as a short prior to the main feature. Arlen's biographer, Edward Jablonski, noted with this song that henceforth the composer "insisted that the lyric was essential to the song's popularity."[8]

Despite the war, Hollywood continued to produce standard movie musicals that offered a few hours of escape for the general public. Mercer generated lyrics for these projects, too. The director and producer Victor Schertzinger oversaw such a film with *The Fleet's In* for Paramount. Now head of the studio, Buddy DeSylva arranged for Betty Hutton, the Broadway star of his production of Cole Porter's *Panama Hattie*, to make her Hollywood debut in the picture, appearing alongside William Holden and Dorothy Lamour. Schertzinger also composed the music, and he tapped Mercer to write the lyrics for what became a Hollywood musical simply packed with gems of songs. Hutton sang two numbers, "Build a Better Mousetrap" and "Arthur Murray Taught Me Dancing in a Hurry." The ballad in the movie, "I Remember You," provided hauntingly beautiful lines such as "Stars that fell / Like rain out of the blue." The lyric acknowledges "You're the one / Who made my dreams come true / A few kisses ago" and promises "When my life is through / And the angels ask me / To recall / The thrill of them all, / Then I shall tell them / I remember you." Another plaintive song from the film, "Not Mine," underscores the bittersweet nature of love: "Let somebody else's tears be shed, / Not mine. / Let somebody else's nose get red, / Not mine. / I like playing solitaire, / But until I draw a pair, / It's somebody else's moon up there, / Not mine."[9]

Cole Porter loved Johnny's rhythm number "Arthur Murray Taught Me Dancing in a Hurry," for which Betty Hutton delivered a spirited performance that demonstrated various dances. The lyric went, "I had a week to spare. / He showed me the ground work. / The walkin' around work, / And told me to take it from there." Porter telegrammed Johnny, "Your lyric about Arthur Murray is a joy. Please write much more and much oftener." Understandably, Arthur and Kathryn Murray remained among the song's ardent fans, sending Johnny a voucher for "sixty free dancing lessons. The only thing is, if you ever dance with Mrs. Murray, boy, she leads. She was teaching me but she was ... I said 'please,' you know. I was saying to myself, 'please let me lead.' She was pushing me around."[10]

The best-known song from *The Fleet's In* emerged a runaway hit for big bands, as "Tangerine" became a new jazz standard. The movie featured the Latin number about an Argentine femme fatale named Tangerine who keeps the men at bay. The lyric announces, "She is all they claim, / With her eyes of night / And lips as bright as flame," and then suggests, "Yes, she has them all on the run, / But her heart belongs to just one, / Her heart belongs to / Tangerine." Mercer recalled, "Victor Schertzinger played me the tune note for note just the way it is. We had to write it for a movie and I don't know why I called it 'Tangerine' except that it had a kind of a Latin flavor, the melody. And once I fell in, you know in the Argentine, and oh, I love it right now. Crazy about it." In the film the Jimmy Dorsey Orchestra introduces the piece using a modern alto sax style to set off the bridge and the band's shift to double time. The vocals reflect the transition as Bob Eberly begins the number slowly, but later Helen O'Connell kicks in up-tempo. In a very uncharacteristic manner, Mercer discussed "Tangerine" with music critic Willis Conover: "But I just love the song. It's a kind of a tune that I never tire of the melody. And I like the lyric enough so I'm always kind of proud of it every time I hear it. So it's one of my favorites." The untimely death of Schertzinger ended the promising collaboration.[11]

The 1942 musical *You Were Never Lovelier* enabled Mercer to write more poetry set to the music of one of his idols, Jerome Kern. The composer of *Show Boat* with lyrics by Oscar Hammerstein II had redirected American theater when that musical opened in December 1927. Shortly thereafter Mercer moved to New York and saw the show. He met Kern while sitting around the lobby at Harms. Johnny felt "awestruck but honored" to collaborate with the Broadway master. The film featured Mercer's old friend Fred Astaire — for whom Kern also enjoyed writing music — dancing with Rita Hayworth, the beautiful pinup who had taken Hollywood by storm. After summoning Mercer to his Whittier Drive house, the composer handed the lyricist "a bundle of manuscripts and virtually instructed him to come back with some suitable verses." A few weeks later, Johnny returned, and as Kern leafed through the lyrics, his eyes hit upon "I'm Old Fashioned," and "a smile creased his face." The composer called his wife into the room. "'Eva,' he said, 'just wait till you hear this lyric.' He then croaked it in his high voice, jumped up from the piano stool and kissed Mercer's cheek. Eva beamed as Jerry hugged him as though he were a long-lost son." In the lyric, Johnny sets up the simple pleasures of life such as "The sound of rain / Upon a windowpane, / The starry song that April sings," then the poetry expresses a simplicity in romance that captures its timelessness: "This year's fancies / Are passing fancies, / But sighing sighs, / Holding hands, / These my heart / Understands." Kern appreciated the other lyrics, too. In the film Xavier Cugat and His Orchestra played the music, including the title song, "You Were Never Lovelier." Conrad Salinger arranged "I'm Old Fashioned" as a duet sung and danced by Astaire and Hayworth as the highlight of the film. Movie critic Clive Hirschhorn found the sequence "one of the really great numbers in the history of the film musical."[12]

The ballad "Dearly Beloved" won an Oscar nomination for Kern and Mercer in 1942. Discussing the song with Willis Conover in 1970, Mercer explained how he got the title and hence the idea for the lyrics. While in Palm Springs waiting for his wife, he looked through some women's fashion magazines she had purchased. In one his eye alighted on an advertisement featuring a bride with her trousseau under a heading that read "Dearly Beloved," the opening salutation from the *Book of Common Prayer* used by the priest performing the wedding ceremony. As Mercer explained, "Of course I'd heard it all my life in church when I was a choir boy but it never occurred to me that it would be a song title." Yet on the day he saw the slick ad, Jerome Kern's lovely melody floated in his head, fitting itself around the title. Like so many of Mercer's songs, the opening verse expresses falling in love: "Tell me that it's true / Tell me you agree; / I was meant for you, / You were meant for me." The refrain captures commitment: "Nothing could save me; / Fate gave me a sign; / I know that I'll be yours / Come shower or shine." Mercer said, "So I called it 'Dearly Beloved' and he was very pleased," referring to Kern. "I think he made one change to the lyric."[13]

The rewarding experience working with Kern at the end of the great composer's career signified a watershed moment in Mercer's life, just as the minor lyric change suggests the respect Kern held for Mercer, a testament borne out by others. Kern's daughter, Betty, remembered that her father had a "tremendous respect for Johnny Mercer — because he would always have half-a-dozen lyrics ready on time." Margaret Whiting also remembered her "Uncle Jerry" telling her of his admiration for Mercer: "I respect him so much. I give him a melody and he comes back with a wonderful lyric. He has such fresh imagery. It's a pleasure to write with him." As examples of Mercer's work, Kern then played for Margaret "I'm Old Fashioned" and other songs from the Columbia Pictures musical.[14]

Although cut from *You Were Never Lovelier*, the beautiful song "Windmill under the Stars" allowed Kern and Mercer to capture the heartfelt desire of the wartime public for the restoration of peace to the world. The lyric harkens back to an earlier conflict: "There are poppies / And fleur de lis / That wait to blossom / In Brittany; / They raise their faces, / Hoping to see / And breathe the sweet air / Of liberty." The reference to the red flower, popularized in poetry and by such women as the Poppy Lady of Georgia, Miona Michael, symbolized the sacrifice made by Allied servicemen in the bloody victory over the Germans in World War I, warning Americans to brace themselves for a second global conflict with the former enemy.[15]

Between the wars the studios' experimentation with color production made the use of Technicolor commonplace by the 1940s. Mercer joined Arlen in writing the music for several films that featured the technological advance. James Cagney, who had just starred as George M. Cohan in the patriotic *Yankee Doodle Dandy* for Warner Bros., appeared in the 1943 *Captains of the Clouds*, with the songwriters providing the title music. With lines such as "We fly with the angels tonight; / You'll find us wing to wing. / We're angels of hell and we fight / For country and for king," the song proved so popular that the Royal Canadian Air Force adopted "Captains of the Clouds" as its official anthem of World War II. The songwriters also wrote "Palsy-Walsy" for *They Got Me Covered*. Paramount Studios boasted one of the servicemen's favorite pinups, Dorothy Lamour, who starred in *Riding High*, for which Mercer wrote with Arlen the song "He Loved Me Till the All-Clear Came." With Joseph Lilley, Mercer wrote the song "Willie the Wolf of the West." Also for Paramount Mercer wrote lyrics for tunes by Hoagy Carmichael for inclusion in the Dick Powell–Mary Martin film, *True to Life*.[16]

One of Mercer's better lyrics of the war years appeared as the title song for *Out of This World*, which he composed with Arlen for Paramount. They earned sixty thousand dollars for their efforts. Frequently Mercer got lucky with songs that used a trendy phrase of the day, as he did with "Out of This World." He explained to Willis Conover, "That was a popular expression at the time, kind of a musician's expression. And I think I was the only one to write it except Porter. Sometimes Porter and I wrote the same titles, never the same way, but I think he was also aware of what was being said, you know, popular expression." The lyric ends with "I'd cry out of this world / If you said we were through, / So, let me fly out of this world / And spend the next eternity or two / With you." Arlen thought it an exceptional "wedding" wherein the song represented a masterful fusing of lyric with melody, an assessment echoed by the music critic Alec Wilder. About "Out of This World," Johnny simply said, "I love that song. I think that's a special kind of a tune. And I think that's a good lyric too."[17]

The lyrics Johnny crafted often expressed themes related to wartime that betrayed a weakening of traditional constraints on societal norms. With Harold Arlen on the 1942 *Star Spangled Rhythm*, Mercer wrote "On the Swing Shift," one of the first songs to recognize the new role of women laboring in the factories. As observed by historian John Bush Jones, Mercer and his fellow songwriters relished writing lines with double entendres, often about casual sex. In *Star Spangled Rhythm*, Johnny played up the patriotic angle of a civilian going out with a serviceman in "I'm Doin' It for Defense." The opening has the girl tell the guy, "If this is gonna be romance, / I'm gonna wear the pants," and then, "If you kiss my lips and you feel me respond, / It's because I just can't afford a bond." She ends with the warning, "I'm a pal, / Nothing more. / This ain't love, / This is war." Warnings of a different sort announce "The Fleet's In," with its opening line, "Hey there, Mister, / — You'd better hide your sister, / 'Cause the fleet's in, / The fleet's in!" Two civilians caught in an air-raid warning find themselves alone in a blackout shelter, providing the one-night stand for "He Loved Me Till the All-Clear Came," written with Arlen initially for *Star Spangled Rhythm* but not used in that film, instead interpolated into *Riding High*. The song begins: "He had the strongest yen / In the dark and then / Suddenly the all-clear came." With the return of light the man disappears, leaving the woman to reflect: "Isn't that an awful shame? / And I think he really loved me, / He really, *really* loved me, / Till the all-clear came." For Capitol, Johnny recorded Donald Kahn's song "Sam's Got Him," which describes a geek drafted by Uncle Sam and turned into a hunk by the army: "In his khaki suit he looks so cute that the chicks all yell with delight / 'Mister Sam release that man for active duty tonight.'"[18]

Living on the home front provided Mercer with material that made light of shortages brought on by the war effort. His "Duration Blues" puts a clever spin on frustrations born of government regulations. "For anything and everything / There's stamps you got to use; / The D's and G's are groceries, / And I think the T's are shoes, / You have to be an FBI man / To figure out all the clues." Another verse notes that "Food will win the war, they say, / And that's okay with me, / But when I go to the corner store, / What do I see?" He answers: "There's Spam and Wham and Deviled Ham / And something new called Zoom — / Just take it home and heat it / To the temp'rature of the room. / And you can bake it, flake it, / Cake it, make it, take it anyway you choose." As for the fate of men, "You is in if you is 1-A , but / If you ain't then 'Who are you?'" The refrain responds: "The 3-A's is essential / And the 4-F's all have asthma, / 2-B gents are in defense, / Or else they're givin' plasma." Otherwise, "You ain't got nothin' / That the armed forces can use"; hence, "The unfortunate situation / When you get the Duration Blues." Listeners could easily relate to all the government red tape and hope for a quick end to the conflict.[19]

The war colored everything, even such dark films as RKO's 1943 *The Sky's the Limit*, which proved neither a propaganda piece nor a typical Hollywood musical, although it followed a war theme and included some of the greatest songs written by Mercer and Arlen. The story concerns a Flying Tiger mercenary home from China's war with Japan, played by Fred Astaire, who in this picture never dons his trademark white tie and tails. In New York City he pursues a photographer, played by Joan Leslie, who at first misdirects his attentions by encouraging him to enlist in the navy but then capitulates to his love as he departs for the Pacific. The songwriters prepared a home front number that joked about rationing and celebrated urban food plots. The song "Harvey, the Victory Garden Man" features Mercer's typical treatment of the man left at home. The army ranks Harvey 4-F, so he battles weeds in the garden and wins the girls. The diaspora entertainer Ella Mae Morse and the Freddie Slack Orchestra introduce the enthusiastic lyrics: "Come on you cats, / Aristocrats, / And dig, dig, dig" so that you can "Forget your troubles / Among the 'vegetubbles.'" In addition to the title song, "The Sky's the Limit," and the rhythm number, "A Lot in Common with You," Mercer and Arlen wrote a ballad, "My Shining Hour," and a blues, "One for My Baby (and One More for the Road)."[20]

"My Shining Hour" received an Academy Award nomination in 1943 for Best Song. The lyric, "Like the lights of home before me / Or an angel watching o'er me, / This will be my shining hour / Till I'm with you again," applies to everyone touched by the conflict. Mercer remembered that the words "shining hour" derived from earlier songs associated with World War I such as "Look for the Silver Lining" and "Keep the Home Fires Burning," which "connected it in my mind with the other World War." As Arlen's biographer, Edward Jablonski, notes, "Imbued with a direct melodic simplicity and a lyric to match of pure, simple poetry, 'My Shining Hour' is the film's thematic expression of wartime's uncertain hope." The music critic Alec Wilder believed the music and lyrics made for "the greatest American song ever written." Sharing that sentiment, Barbra Streisand used it to close out her live concerts. Yet the unsettling plot of *The Sky's the Limit* left audiences less than effusive about the movie, and "My Shining Hour" failed to win the Oscar that year.[21]

At one point in the film, Fred Astaire is drunk and angry while singing and dancing a dramatic solo routine to "One for My Baby (and One More for the Road)." Johnny thought of the assignment as a way to write a new, realistic kind of torch song, a loser's lament that bemoans the loss of a lover to hide failure in life. Referencing Mercer's lines "I've got the routine, / So drop another nickel in the machine," David Lehman notes that it "even refers artfully to itself." The lyrics express a complete story that satisfies the listener on several levels. Many singers made hits out of the song, with Frank Sinatra perhaps providing the definitive performance. In the movie Astaire gives the bartender Joe an earful of his troubles, with lines that sound like a Mercer confessional: "You'd never know it, / But, buddy, I'm kind of poet, / And I've gotta lotta things to say, / And when I'm gloomy, / You simply gotta listen to me / Until it's talked away." The more Astaire relates — which is little because "that's not in a gentleman's code"— the angrier he gets until in a violent bacchanalia the dancer busts up the lounge by breaking the glasses and mirrors over the bar in a fit of frustration that men and women across the country might relate to in a wartime era of pent-up emotions.[22]

For many entertainers — especially jazz musicians — drinking had become a way of life. Johnny embraced the cocktail culture despite his awareness of the dangers because of his alcoholic Uncle Ed and other family members. Johnny's father had begged his sons not to imbibe but, Johnny admitted later, "promises to my Dad with all the attendant rewards chug-alugged away with that [first] drink." He recalled, "I was in for a lot of unsteady legs, getting sick in the bushes, and reeling beds and ceilings before I was ever to truly enjoy alcohol." Mercer sought out social occasions at which to consume liquor, including binge drinking with friends. As he grew older, he sent associates cases of Scotch in advance of his visits.[23]

Drinking often appeared in Mercer's lyrics, and when choosing songs to sing, Johnny often selected party favorites written by others. One of his earliest lyrics, "Falling Off the Wagon," made light of trying to quit: "You came along, / — And now it's just too bad. / I'm falling off the wagon / And falling into love." Toward the end of his career, Mercer wrote words and music for an undated song he called "I Think We Need a Drink." Johnny enjoyed singing party favorites with the rowdies gathered around the piano, such as the ones he recorded, "Margie," "Louisville Lou," and "(Back Home Again in) Indiana." One such fun number that Mercer wrote with the Tin Pan Alley composer Walter Donaldson, whom he greatly admired, "On Behalf of the Visiting Firemen," had as its chorus "have a 'smile' on me," which encouraged drinking. The board of directors overseeing the 1940 World's Fair in New York City called "On Behalf of the Visiting Firemen" a "typical American theme song" and made the good-natured number the official anthem of the fair. The G. F. Heublein and Brothers company picked up on the line "For the Visiting Firemen!" to advertise its ready-made — just add ice — manhattans, martinis, and old-fashioneds. By the time Mercer recorded the song as a duet with Crosby in 1940, Bing had just about sworn off the hard stuff while watching his wife, Dixie, slowly succumb to the alcoholism that finally killed her in 1952. Johnny drew on his own well of experience to write sad testimonials to the tragedies of alcoholism such as the 1962 song "Drinking Again," written with Doris Tauber.[24]

In the darkest hours of the war Mercer wrote some of his brightest music, as his contributions with Arlen made clear in *Here Come the Waves*. While the Allies struggled to retake Italy from the Nazis and halt their advance on Moscow, at the same time pushing the Japanese out of the Marshall Islands and New Guinea, the Hollywood studios cranked out patriotic entertainments to build public morale for a war whose costs in lives and materiel steadily increased. Paramount's 1944 film stars Bing Crosby and Betty Hutton in a plot that turns on a benefit show staged by the women's unit of the U.S. Naval Reserve, better known as WAVES — Women Accepted for Voluntary Emergency Service. The show-within-a-show musical parodies the bobby-soxer female fans who swoon at the concerts of the new singing sensation Frank Sinatra. For the war effort Arlen and Mercer wrote a stirring title song as well as a propaganda piece called "Join the Navy." The film features one of Mercer's geographic wonders derived from his southern sensitivity to place, "There's a Fella Waiting in Poughkeepsie." The lyric plays on the names of towns noted for naval installations, including Hackensack, Pontiac, Daytona, and Pomona. The cute song as sung by Hutton offers the WAVES' response to the sailor's boast of a girl in every port with the sexually liberating line, "I'm strictly on my own tonight." Two love songs, "I Promise You" and "Let's Take the Long Way Home," found lives outside the film.[25]

The movie's big hit, "Ac-Cent-Tchu-Ate the Positive," grew out of the need for a production number to showcase the principals and cast in a song and dance routine. Having written everything else for the film, the pair struggled over this last assignment. After several days of effort, they quit work to drive around the hills of Hollywood. Mercer rode as Arlen leisurely headed home. Then the idea struck. "How does that little thing go? . . . I've heard you humming it — the spiritual?" Mercer asked Arlen. The tune the composer had subconsciously sung came forth, and from that rhythmic snatch of melody Johnny offered, "You've got to accentuate the positive?" Arlen added more syncopation, while Mercer responded with more rhythmic lines. They completed a draft of the song as they finished the drive to Arlen's house. Harold remembered, "It was the final one we needed for Bing Crosby . . . It must have pleased John — it was the first time I ever saw him smile." If true, Arlen's comment reveals how seriously Mercer approached his art. Margaret Whiting understood, for she recalled Johnny "flashed that adorable, almost elfin grin that he smiled when he was secretly very pleased." With lines like, "You've got to / Ac-cent-tchu-ate the positive, / E-lim-mi-nate the negative, / Latch on to the affirmative — / Don't mess with Mister In-Between!" and "You've got to spread joy / Up to the maximum, / Bring gloom down to the minimum, / Have faith, or pandemonium / Li'ble to walk upon the scene!" Mercer offered his philosophy on life as a palliative to the harsh news of the day. At the time a reporter suggested that Johnny, "who enjoys a series of worries and aches, went to see a psychologist. 'You've got to accentuate the positive,' advised the doctor." The phrase had stuck in his head, claimed the reporter. In an interview Mercer said a publicist sent him a Father Divine sermon with that title. Johnny thought, "What a colorful, wonderful phrase. And it kind of sings too. It's melodious. So I tucked that away in my mind." Often the writer collected his material in notebooks that he referred to when he needed ideas. "When Harold came up with this little tune, this offbeat little rhythm tune, it just popped into my mind." Sung in blackface in the movie, the song fared better when recorded separately by Crosby, and then by Mercer, which as a release for Capitol Records reached No. 1 and sat in the top ten on the Billboard charts for sixteen weeks. In 1945, "Ac-Cent-Tchu-Ate the Positive" received for the collaborators another Academy nomination for Best Song.[26]

While Johnny never wore a uniform he regularly assisted the war effort by joining Hollywood's mobilization to promote positive morale among the public and to entertain the troops stationed in bases and in hospitals on the West Coast. As Mercer explained, "I think music is pretty vital right now. The soldiers need it and want it, whether they're in training camps in this country or at the battlefronts overseas. Singing, whenever and wherever you do it, is great for morale. Of course, the same holds true for folks back home. When their morale needs a boost, the best way to give it to them is with good music." He performed for the Navy Relief Society at the Hollywood Casino on Sunset Boulevard, the Field

Artillery Replacement Training Center in Camp Roberts, the Air Transport Command at the Long Beach Army Air Field, and the U.S. Naval Hospital in San Diego, among other military installations. After his Hollywood Canteen performance in January 1943, its president, the actress Bette Davis, wrote to Mercer, "We will be more than happy to have you, whenever you feel you can spend some time with us again," and he continued his support of the canteen. He allowed performers to adapt his lyrics to suit their needs when singing them at USO camp shows.[27]

In addition to having his music played, Mercer appeared personally on numerous shows broadcast over the Armed Forces Radio Service (AFRS). His Hollywood acquaintance Colonel Tom Lewis assembled a variety of independent efforts into the military's morale-building entertainment system. In March 1941, the U.S. Army Bureau of Public Relations had appointed a Nashville broadcasting executive to run a military radio section that at first broadcast sports events but, at the recommendation of the Hollywood scriptwriter Glenn Wheaton, quickly expanded to spin popular records for the enjoyment of troops stationed abroad. By February 1942, on military outposts from Alaska to the Philippines to Panama, soldiers had set up independent, military-sanctioned radio stations and began broadcasting the special programming arranged by Lewis. On May 26, 1942, the War Department authorized AFRS to provide "a touch of home" to military personnel stationed abroad. The colonel wanted to create a signature variety show for AFRS programming that would request the involvement of top Hollywood stars. Wheaton responded to the idea by saying, "Request, hell! Command them to appear!" Thus began *Command Performance, USA!*, a show broadcast on military stations throughout the war and well after its end, often featuring Mercer as part of its retinue of entertainers who delighted the troops stationed in Europe, Africa, Asia, and South America and on the seven seas.[28]

Following the pattern of peacetime variety shows, *Command Performance, USA!* packaged the era's most popular performers into a positive weekly program written specifically for the nation's military. A stirring rendition of George M. Cohan's "Over There" kicked off the broadcast with a voiceover by Ken Carpenter, who announced the show through 1946, saying, *"Command Performance, USA! Coming to you this week and every week, until it's over, over there!"* Plugging the stars, Carpenter added, "The greatest entertainers in America as requested by YOU, the men and women in the United States Armed Forces throughout the world!" The first show, taped on March 1, 1942, featured Dinah Shore singing Johnny Mercer's "Blues in the Night." Usually the forty-five-

minute show played before a live studio audience in Los Angeles, although editing reduced the program to a thirty-minute broadcast. The military transcribed
the show on sixteen-inch vinylite disks called Victory-disks, or V-disks, which
ran at 33⅓ speed, and shipped them off to stations around the globe. The first
show broadcast on March 8, 1942, across shortwave radio from eleven stations in
such places as Australia, the Philippines, Ireland, and Iceland. As the war pro-
gressed, the listening audience expanded. By 1943, the U.S. Army Special Services
Division sent the V-disks to the front, where portable equipment called B kits, or
Buddy kits, allowed the disks to be played to the troops on the move. Field units
kept the shipment for a week before sending it to the next outfit. By the end of
1942, Ken Carpenter announced that the show reached a billion people in thirty
countries, making it probably the first truly global broadcast.[29]

Many of Mercer's friends appeared on *Command Performance, USA!*, as did
the songwriter himself on numerous occasions. The format combined music
with patriotic testimony and comedy sketches. Often Bob Hope co-hosted with
Bing Crosby crooning some particular favorite such as Frank Loesser's "Praise the
Lord and Pass the Ammunition." The stars appealed directly to their listeners,
as demonstrated by Dinah Shore on the Christmas Eve broadcast in 1942 when,
with her soft and sexy southern accent, she said, "As long as you're not in love with
anyone else, why don't you fall in love with me." That night the African American quartet the Charioteers joined Bing to perform "Basin St. Blues," while Ethel
Waters sang her signature "Dinah." On another occasion the Alabama actress
Tallulah Bankhead delivered a monologue on "What Is America." The comedy
team of Abbott and Costello performed their "Who's on First" baseball routine
one week, while on other occasions Red Skelton, Eddie "Rochester" Anderson, or
Jerry Colonna provided humor. An orchestra led by Fred Waring, Al Newman,
Stan Kenton, or Harry James played background music. A native of Nashville,
the diaspora entertainer Shore appeared on the show more than anyone else at
thirty-five times, followed by Crosby with twenty-nine visits and Hope with
twenty-six. Mercer appeared nearly two dozen times and often joined the all-star
lineup for special broadcasts such as the *Command Performance Victory Extra* on
August 14, 1945.[30]

Johnny's obvious delight in singing came across clearly in his appearances
on *Command Performance, USA!* He cut up with the young Texas jazz singer
Ella Mae Morse on the September 9, 1943, show. With great admiration, Mercer
joined Louis Armstrong on the May 20, 1944, program, where the jazz legend
performed "Lazy River" and Johnny sang his new hit, "G.I. Jive." A cowboy theme

unified the June 24, 1944, program, which featured Mercer with Frank Sinatra, the Andrews Sisters, Roy Rogers, and the Riders of the Purple Sage. Many of the country's greatest songwriters appeared on the November 25, 1944, show, including Jerome Kern, Jimmy McHugh, Johnny Burke, and Jimmy Van Heusen. For the special songwriters' program, Mercer sang his "Blues in the Night," and then with fellow collaborator Hoagy Carmichael, the latter's "Small Fry," written with lyricist Frank Loesser. Bing Crosby hosted the April 5, 1945, show, getting Johnny to perform with him their remake of a vaudeville routine called "Mr. Crosby and Mr. Mercer." Capitol's singing success, Jo Stafford and the Pied Pipers, with Mercer in tow, performed on the August 12, 1944, program. Old friends Hope and Colonna carried the comedy for the September 13, 1944, show, on which Johnny revived the popular song standard, "The Wreck of the Old '97." As was the custom on the program where "your request is our command," Mercer read out several names of military men and their units before launching into what he called "a shock of corn still standing in the field of American folk music." With a country twang in his voice, he sang "The Wreck of the Old '97," emphasizing the poignant last lines of the old song that warn wives, "Never speak harsh words to your true loving husband, / He may leave and never return."[31]

In addition to *Command Performance, USA!* Mercer regularly performed on other AFRS shows. The demand for original programming had grown to the point that AFRS was generating more than twenty hours of weekly broadcast material by the war's height in 1945. On one such AFRS program, *Mail Call,* Johnny sang his new Capitol Records hit "Strip Polka," and Dinah Shore sang Mercer's "Blues in the Night"; on another *Mail Call,* Mercer joined Bing Crosby in duets of "Small Fry" and "Mr. Crosby and Mr. Mercer." On the AFRS record request show *Sound Off,* Johnny played favorite records requested by the servicemen. A week after D-Day, Mercer joined Shirley Temple on the June 15, 1944, AFRS show, *To the Rear March.* He assisted in the creation of and performed on the AFRS program, *G.I. Journal.* In response to many of these performances, Mercer received letters of appreciation. Following Johnny's *Mail Call* appearance in November 1944, Colonel Tom Lewis wrote to convey his thanks to the songwriter and to relate that a Major Hayes, who ran the American Forces Network, had telegrammed his compliments on Johnny's work: "This is just by way of letting you know that the show was warmly received," Lewis noted.[32]

Not only did Johnny appear on the AFRS *G.I. Jive,* his song appeared as a catchy title song for the program. Now frequently wearing three hats, Mercer acted as songwriter, performer, and producer of "G.I. Jive" that, once released by

Capitol, became a hit in 1944. Exploiting the hybridity of southern culture, Mercer tapped the dynamic mobilization of black and white men in uniform to create a jazzy novelty number overflowing with slang and military jargon. The song describes the enlisted man's day in basic training with such lines as "Jack, that's the G.I. Jive! / Root-tee-tee-toot, / Jump in your suit, / Make a salute — voot!" Capitol Records' press agent Dave Dexter later suggested that Johnny got the idea while watching servicemen cross the streets as he waited for the light to change at Sunset and Vine in Hollywood. In a manner of minutes Johnny had jotted down the lyrics and thought up a tune. One of the nascent label's earliest hits, "G.I. Jive" received frequent airplay on the radio and grabbed the nickels of servicemen and women at the jukeboxes on military bases. It spawned a response in "Jill and her G.I. Jive" produced by the *Army-Navy Screen Magazine*. The AFRS programs required original variety material to stay fresh and attractive to the troops. Yet in its campaign against emotional "slush" on the air, the Office of War Information found Mercer's "Mandy Is Two" too sentimental, banning its broadcast on military stations.[33]

The AFRS created *Jubilee* as a black variety show to appeal to an African American audience in uniform. While leading black performers such as Lena Horne and Eddie "Rochester" Anderson occasionally appeared on *Command Performance, USA!* and other programs, the racism of the larger society limited these opportunities. Hence the effort of the AFRS to create such targeted programming. On *Jubilee* the gregarious Ernie "Bubbles" Whitman served as a master of ceremonies for programs that featured such hot groups as the Delta Rhythm Boys, the King Cole Trio, and the Count Basie Orchestra. Ever loquacious, Whitman provided rapid patter between pieces, making jokes about his large size and calling the show "Eelibuj... that's 'jubilee' spelled backwards!" He often prefaced performances with comments such as "before we distribute the honey from this hive of jive" or followed the bands with remarks such as "I must be jelly 'cause jam don't shake like I do!" The pinup beauty Lena Horne often performed. Like other guests she read out the names of servicemen and their African American units. On some shows an all-female big band called the Sweethearts of Rhythm played such jazz numbers as "Sweet Georgia Brown," while at other times Erskine Hawkins led his band in arrangements of his own "Tuxedo Junction" or other popular dance tunes. Black comics such as Rochester and Nicodemus Stewart performed monologues, while soloists such as Ida James sang "Is You Is or Is You Ain't My Baby" and Leadbelly sang "Rock Island Line."[34]

Often artists performed Mercer's music on *Jubilee* and, on rare occasions, white stars made guest appearances. Indeed, Lena Horne gave the radio broadcast premier of Mercer's "One for My Baby (and One More for the Road)" on *Jubilee*. On another week the Charioteers performed "G.I. Jive." Crosby appeared on the show to warm applause from the studio audience, as did Mercer. Johnny joined Ernie Whitman on a June 1944 *Jubilee* broadcast, and after some comic banter about the overweight announcer, Johnny sang "Waiting for the Evening Mail." On the same program Ethel Waters performed "Stormy Weather." Never strictly segregated, for both black and white performers appeared on both programs, the military tried to target racially distinctive audiences with the parallel shows but to no avail as anyone regardless of race could tune in to the AFRS broadcasts. Unfortunately, *Jubilee* — like *Command Performance, USA!* — never appeared on commercial radio in the United States, so the home front missed out on these marvelous programs.[35]

Throughout 1942 Johnny recorded for the War Department's radio program, *Song Sheet*. By the end of the year he had produced thirty-five programs, which featured popular songs such as "Margie," "Strawberry Blonde," and "Summertime." A band backed the singers in the recordings captured at MacGregor studio, where Mercer also made masters for Capitol Records. Once readied, the War Department reproduced the *Song Sheet* programs on V-disk transcriptions and arranged for them to be played to the troops at the front. The military brass thanked Johnny for his patriotic efforts. Brigadier General F. H. Osborn complimented Mercer's "American spirit," praise that another officer echoed: "You have certainly been co-operative, John, and the success of *Song Sheet* as a troop morale-builder is due, in most part, to your work." Colonel Livingston Watrous of the War Department's Special Service Division informed Mercer, "The reports received from the men overseas in all branches of the armed services prove how much they enjoy the entertainment people like you are giving to them."[36]

The AFRS made special transcriptions of popular programs from commercial radio that stripped out advertisements of such sponsors as Pepsodent and Chesterfield Cigarettes and added introductions tailored for its military audience. When Bob Hope embarked on his tour of the front lines, he arranged for Johnny Mercer to replace him on his *Pepsodent Show* broadcast in the summer of 1943 over both commercial and military radio stations. Although Mercer never traveled to war zones like Hope, his voice traveled to the service personnel on the front via AFRS V-disks and radio broadcasts.[37]

After the broadcast of Mercer's first hosting of the *Pepsodent Show* on June 22,

1943, he received a flurry of telegrams praising his performance. For the program Johnny had encouraged Hope to hire the still-unknown Stan Kenton Band for the summer. Also he wrote his only blatant commercial for a product. Referring to the "magic" ingredient in the toothpaste, Mercer's situation jingle begins, "Poor Miriam, / Neglected using Irium," then the phone rings and Miriam answers, "Hello" only to hear a male voice reply, "Sorry, wrong number!" followed by the chorus singing, "It's the saddest thing! / Don't be like Miriam — / Use Irium." When the *Pepsodent Show* gig ended that September, the program had featured the singing of top hits by Mercer, Ella Mae Morse, and the Pied Pipers — one of whom was Jo Stafford — backed by Paul Weston's orchestra. Reviewing the show, *Metronome* magazine observed that "using little but the materials of popular music," Mercer created a program that proved "a joy and a revelation to the music starved ears of the editors." For 1943, *Metronome* recognized Mercer's management of the *Pepsodent Show* as "the outstanding musical program of the year on the air."[38]

Some radio listeners thought Johnny might be African American. Mercer had gained fame for his jazz style that reflected the hybridity of his native southern culture. A fan writing to a Hollywood gossip columnist asked point-blank, "Is Johnny Mercer, the song writer, white or Negro?" A *Cosmopolitan* article tried to dispel "the two leading misconceptions about Mercer — that he is a Negro, and that he is a composer." After suggesting that he did not play piano although he occasionally wrote music, the ladies' magazine explained that Johnny "sounds like a gatey, groovy Harlem hep-cat." While running the *Pepsodent Show*, Mercer received a letter from an agent representing the black singer and saxophone player Louis Jordan soliciting a spot for his client on the program. He wrote the songwriter, "It might be a good publicity stunt — the greatest White blues singer, Johnny Mercer, and one of the greatest Colored blues singers on the summer show." In 1944, Mercer received a postcard from the Abraham Lincoln Junior Club of Chicago that announced it had "voted you the most popular young colored singer on the radio." The honest misconception derived from a failure to recognize the shared multiracial culture of southern black and white people that Mercer represented in his regional accent and rhythmic style of singing two decades before Elvis.[39]

At the critical moment in the war when defeat remained possible for the Allies, Johnny Mercer starred on his own radio program broadcast at home and abroad. Since 1939, Fred Waring and the Pennsylvanians had hosted the daily fifteen-minute *Chesterfield Time* radio show, but in mid-1944 the Liggett and

Myers Tobacco Company gave the job to Johnny Mercer. The company recognized Mercer's success with Hope's *Pepsodent Show* and wanted to capitalize on the talented songwriter's ear for popular music in order to increase its listening audience and thereby expand the potential market for its cigarettes. Every weekday evening from June to December 1944 the American public — and through rebroadcast over the AFRS military stations around the world a global listening audience — could hear *The Johnny Mercer Chesterfield Music Shop*. First airing just days after General Dwight Eisenhower initiated the Normandy Invasion and General Douglas MacArthur leapfrogged across the Pacific to the Mariana Islands, the program countered the harsh news of hard-fought struggles in the two major theaters of war. When Mercer went off the air at the end of the year the conflict seemed inconclusive as the Japanese had just initiated kamikaze attacks in a desperate and unsuccessful effort to win the Battle of Leyte Gulf and thereby hold on to the Philippines, while the Germans had counterattacked to stop General George Patton's tank force in the Battle of the Bulge. The year's slow gains seemed stymied by the determined resistance of enemies as the American casualties mounted. Through it all, Mercer and his *Music Shop* remained upbeat.[40]

Like bookends, Johnny selected opening and closing music that set the positive tone of the daily program. A rollicking stride piano played by Stan Wrightsman started the proceedings. On commercial U.S. stations Chesterfield Cigarettes pitched its product, while for military listeners Mercer chimed in with "Hey there fellas hope you feel tip top, this is Johnny Mercer in his Music Shop. All you soldiers, sailors and marines out there, all you gals in the service, we're on the air!" Every program ended with Mercer's "Dream," a new song for which he wrote both the lyric and music. Later Johnny explained the origin of the song to friends: "I was fooling around at the piano and I got a series of chords that attracted me. I played it for Paul Weston and he said, 'Why don't we use it for the theme song on the show?'" As Weston worked up an arrangement for the *Music Shop*, Mercer crafted the lyric. With a subtle plug for the cigarette sponsor, Mercer wrote, "Dream / When you're feelin' blue, / Dream, / That's the thing to do. / Just watch the smoke rings / Rise in the air; / You'll find your share / Of memories there." In an age of troubles beyond anyone's control, Mercer's lyric ended on a typically optimistic note: "Things never are as bad as they seem, / So / Dream, / Dream, / Dream."[41]

The scenario of the show had Mercer managing a record store. As the host, Johnny engaged in comic chatter with the announcer Wendell Niles and whichever special guest "stopped by" for the evening. Popular music played throughout, with Paul Weston and His Orchestra providing the accompaniment for Johnny's vocals and those of the bell-toned Jo Stafford, who now appeared solo, often backed by the male Pied Pipers harmonizing quartet, reflecting the shift into the Age of the Singer. A child of the diaspora whose parents had left Tennessee, Stafford had once sung with Tommy Dorsey's band and would soon marry Weston, a Phi Beta Kappa graduate of Dartmouth College. Mercer encouraged Stafford to seek a solo career and arranged for her debut on the *Music Shop*, and with the wide exposure she received through her recordings for Capitol Records, Jo Stafford became one of the war's top female singers. On some occasions Mercer showcased the new releases from Capitol, although generally a judicious selection of old standards and novelty numbers dominated the playlist, which also featured his own music. Three times each week the cast met to record, with two shows captured in the studio back-to-back on two days while the final session took place before a live audience of service personnel at a different military installation on Fridays. Mercer followed a format that featured guest stars on the Tuesday and Thursday programs and a "Memory Melody Spot" each Wednesday, with Stafford singing a favorite from the Great American Songbook. While NBC ran the fifteen-minute show every weekday at 7:00 p.m., the AFRS broadcast its transcriptions only on Mondays through Thursdays.[42]

To be his special guests, Johnny called on old friends, some from jazz days, the Broadway stage, and Hollywood movies. Trumpeters Wingy Manone and Billy Butterfield, clarinetist Matty Matlock, and a half-dozen pianists performed. Trombonist Jack Teagarden joined Johnny in singing their old Whiteman hit, "Fare-Thee-Well to Harlem," while the Latin bandleader Xavier Cugat played "Tico Tico" on violin. Child star Shirley Temple joined Johnny on the first broadcast of the *Music Shop*, and Lucille Ball — who had appeared with Johnny in *Old Man Rhythm* — sang with him on another show the duet "By the Beautiful Sea." Dick Powell, the male lead in many of the Warner Bros. musicals Mercer wrote lyrics for in the 1930s, also dropped by, as did the female lead of contemporary movie musicals, June Allyson. Stars of radio made special appearances such as Harold "The Great Gildersleeve" Peary, who sang "In the Gloaming." Some offbeat comics such as Vera Vague and Doodles Weaver did their routines, while Phil Silvers parodied Johnny with "I Lost My Sugar at a Hollywood Racetrack." The former crooner Rudy Vallee sang with Mercer "Recognize the Tune," while the former vaudevillian William Frawley joined Johnny on "Carolina in the Morning." Of course, Mercer's close colleagues and longtime friends — AFRS regulars Bing Crosby, Bob Hope, and Jerry Colonna — served as guests stars, too.[43]

Often Johnny used the *Music Shop* to reunite with former colleagues from his early days in entertainment. The character actor Sterling Holloway—who had introduced Mercer's first song, "Out of Breath (and Scared to Death of You)," in *The Garrick Gaieties* in 1930—made such an appearance on the October 3, 1944, show. For the occasion Mercer wrote a special new lyric. After Holloway sang the correct lyric, Johnny offered a reprise with "When I hear you quote / Those poor words that I wrote / As a lad of twenty-and-two, / I'm out of breath and scared to death of you," adding, "And here's the reason, for without a doubt / If you spread them about / Then my reputation is through, / I'm out of breath and scared to death of you." While stuck in character roles for the studio movies, Holloway ultimately gained fame by providing voiceovers for Walt Disney's cartoon characters in animated feature films.[44]

Beautiful Hollywood starlets, classical musicians, and newly discovered talent received invitations to appear on the show. Reflecting the sexist culture of the era, occasionally Mercer made offhand remarks regarding the appearance of some of his attractive female guest stars. When the actress Janet Blair complimented Mercer's performance of a number by saying, "I think you displayed rare form," he responded, "Well uh, you don't do so badly on that score yourself!" Blair countered, "Well now look uh, I was talking about music." When she moved on to recall the songs she once performed with a band, observing, "Isn't it funny how a tune keeps coming back to you?" a chastened Mercer cracked, "Yea, one of mine came back fourteen times!" Trying to broaden his audience, Johnny appealed to the classical arts with actress Diana Lynn performing on the piano a dramatic interpretation of "Pearls on Velvet" by Victor Young, while the Tin Man from *The Wizard of Oz*, Jack Haley, sang an operatic version of "G.I. Jive." To promote Jay Livingston and Ray Evans, a pair of songwriters trying to break into the profession, Mercer sang their new number, "The Cat and the Canary." Indeed, Mercer used the program to plug a variety of talent.[45]

In many of the *Music Shop* broadcasts Mercer demonstrated a self-deprecating humor that played down his success. After being introduced by Johnny, Warner Bros. actress Janis Page explained that folks in her hometown encouraged her to move to Hollywood to advance her career. Johnny quipped, "Isn't that funny? When folks in Savannah heard me sing they suggested I leave town too!" On another show, the King of the Cowboys Roy Rogers announced he intended to perform a number from his new movie. When Johnny asked about its quality, Rogers responded, "I guess it's as good as the songs you write." Mercer fired back, "Oh no, Roy! It can't be that bad!" After Rogers performed "Cow Poke Polka,"

Johnny asked him why in the movies he always sang while mounted on his horse, Trigger. The Hollywood cowboy answered, "With a voice like mine I find it safe to keep moving." Johnny retorted, "In that case I ought to do all my warbling in a P-38." The two then joined in on an exceptional duet of "I'm an Old Cowhand," with Roy contributing a trademark yodel. The modesty in Mercer's back and forth banter with his guests provided a lighthearted context for the music.[46]

Two programs featured popular stars of radio placed incongruously in Mercer's shop. In one sketch the snobby British actor Arthur Treacher appeared at the door looking for a butler. He ended up by demonstrating to the Pied Pipers the proper English diction to use when performing Ella Fitzgerald's hit, "A Tisket a Tasket." Another episode featured the fictional radio character of the black maid Beulah, played by the white man Marlin Hurt on the cast of NBC's *Fibber McGee and Molly* radio show. Created by former vaudevillians Jim and Marian Jordan, the program aired from 1935 to 1959 and pioneered situation comedy, leading to a number of spin-off programs, including *The Great Gildersleeve*, which starred Harold Peary, and *Beulah*, starring Hurt and, later in a nightly serial on CBS, Hattie McDaniel. Over the course of his appearance on the *Music Shop*, Hurt delivers the catchphrases his character had popularized, coming in on "Somebody bawl for Beulah?" and later saying about Johnny, "Love that man!" The situation has Beulah applying for the job of domestic worker for the Mercer household. Beulah explains her qualifications to Johnny by saying she's "the tidy little pixy that made the hall closet what it is today," referring to the running gag of the McGees opening the closet door and having the contents spill out. When asked by Johnny how much she charged per week, Beulah explained she had two prices, twenty dollars or thirty dollars. Then the maid asked Mercer, "What doos ya do when ya doos it?" After Johnny announced he was a songwriter, Beulah answered, "Well in that case I'll work for twenty a week until you get a steady job." Responding to Beulah's plans to sing around the house, Mercer asked her to demonstrate, so the maid cuts in with a mock blues: "It's a low down dog — a dirty groundhog been rooting 'round under my backdoor." Feigning shock, Mercer responds "Oh no, no Beulah we can't sing that kinda stuff around here." "What's the matter?" Beulah asks. "Don't you like pretty music?" Mercer requests something "high class." The maid breaks into a piece by Mozart. "Don't you know anything in between?" Mercer asks. The maid retorts in disgust, "You mean that jukebox stuff?" Johnny then convinces Beulah to join him in singing "Is You Is or Is You Ain't My Baby." The duet over, actor Marlin Hurt reveals himself as Beulah, while the studio audience bursts into applause. As insensitive as the concept of Hurt playing Beulah might be, the sketch contains several funny lines while revealing the "ambivalence of mimicry." The duet at the end points to the popularity of what later will be called "racial" crossover music, for Ida James had sung "Is You Is" on *Jubilee* the previous October.[47]

Especially for the *Music Shop* as a weekly bonus, Mercer wrote a new song and premiered it on air. One day he explained to his studio audience: "Having committed myself to come up with a tune of my own every week, I guess there's nothing for us to do but get on with it." He usually said a few words about the origin of the song. Johnny described one such weekly contribution as "a dreamy ballad sort of thing I wrote with Harold Arlen for Paramount Pictures." He then turned to Jo Stafford, who introduced the hauntingly beautiful "Out of This World." Such an exceptional song proved atypical of Mercer's weekly compositions, as more often than not he produced a novelty number featuring the latest slang. In explaining "Conversation While Dancing," Johnny noted that he and Paul Weston had "dropped into that emporium of jive the Palladium. Believe me, the cats were really jumping. We got to wondering what kind of talk if any goes on while these capers are being cut, and finally got into a huddle to come up with a brand new offering." Mercer and Stafford then sang the duet: "Do ya know what's groovy? / Have ya seen the latest movie? / Should I try and tip ya? / May I hip ya? / Yes, I know." With "Conversation While Dancing," for the first time Mercer joined Stafford on a Capitol recording without the Pied Pipers. On another broadcast of the *Music Shop*, Mercer explained, "I hope you'll over look the notes I contribute in this first little opus called 'Minding My Business.'" With a jaunty tune, Mercer sang out the lines: "I know it's nobody's business, no how, whatever I do, somehow, it's none of my business what happened to you." The lyric then sums up his attitude toward interference in the lives of others: "For instance Rockefeller never tried to make a car, still he's doing fine. Henry never fooled around with Standard Oil, it ain't in his line." The song ends with the admonition "They're minding their business. I know they never go wrong. And so I'm minding my business, just going along." These three examples demonstrated Mercer to be what he would describe as a "dependable" songwriter, one who could "produce" and deliver the "assignments" when required. He saw songwriting "as a job, like any other job, and with a job, one must compromise." He went on to note, "Working alone is one thing. Working in collaboration is another. And working on assignment is still another. A pro — a real pro — should be able to do all three."[48]

Occasionally Mercer picked a war theme for his weekly contribution, as demonstrated in "Birmingham Bertha," a reference to the Bechtel-McCone Airplane Modification Plant in Birmingham, Alabama, which would ultimately produce half of the B-29 bombers that helped the Allies win the war. He introduced the song with typically self-deprecating humor: "Well, having billed myself as a songwriter around town, sometimes I have a hard time living up to it. Just how hard is evidenced by this new thing I wrote for you customers today." The novelty lyric opens as a love song to the airplane sung by a member of her crew. "She's the one who puts on the finest show, from Pearl Harbor to Tokyo. Big, fat, beautiful Bertha—from Birmingham." The rhymes weaken as the song progresses: "When she parades down the landing field, everybody scrams—because who makes all of the di-rect hits, on those Zeros and Messerschmidts? Its big, fat, beautiful Bertha—from Birmingham." Even though the lyric to "Birmingham Bertha" lacks polish, the sentiment is clear.[49]

The military made its presence known in the *Music Shop* in other ways too. Another number performed on the program, "There'll Be a Hot Time in Berlin" had a problematic second line, "when the Yanks go marching in." Although Chesterfield Cigarettes let the song air over domestic radio, the AFRS cut it out for military broadcast. The compiler of AFRS records, Harry Mackenzie, speculates the deletion occurred in deference to the British, who had been fighting the Nazis since 1939. On another show Johnny sang Donald Kahn's new hit, "Sam's Got Him." No doubt these songs proved especially popular among the military service personnel who attended the Friday shows, which the *Music Shop* staged at the Long Beach Naval Hospital, the Birmingham General Hospital in Resedo, and the Santa Monica Army Air Forces Redistribution Station. The September 21, 1944, edition of a local newspaper proudly announced that "national prominence, via coast-to-coast radio broadcast, comes to Frobase Base. For tomorrow, the riotous *Chesterfield Music Shop* program will broadcast right here from our own gym, now being wired and set up for Johnny Mercer, head man of the show." The article identified the different times for units and crews of the company to arrive for seating. "The Chaplain says the doors will be battened down, no one to leave or enter after the show starts, so early is the word." Chesterfield donated a free package of cigarettes to everyone who attended.[50]

Military personnel conveyed their opinions of the show directly to Mercer. He received from Sergeant H. Brewer a detailed critique signed by twenty-three men in his unit: "Each evening, we lie down with the thought of relaxation, but your program comes on. Then, it's every man for himself—or Jo Stafford." About Mercer's self-deprecation, Brewer protested, "In spite of the way you tear your voice down, we like it." The V-mail letter got to its point: "We all feel yours is the best 15 minute program on the radio, but the fifteen minutes goes much too fast. How about making it half an hour? Then we could enjoy it twice as much!" Requests of particular songs followed for Mercer, Stafford, and the Pied Pipers to sing, including a complete rendition of "Dream," which once released on Capitol Records by the Pied Pipers became their number one hit recording.[51] The exposure from the *Music Shop* generated letters to Johnny from Woodberry Forest School "old boys." Edward S. "Eddy" Northrop, a lieutenant commander in the U.S. Navy, invited Johnny in February 1945 to an alumni dinner in Washington. He then described a recent tour of duty that took him across the Mediterranean Sea and through the Suez Canal to the India-Burma front. "I mention this because I was haunted by your golden (?) voice during my entire tour. The GI's say that it prepares them for battle like nothing else." Johnny wrote back, addressing his response to "Eddie": "It sounds pretty undignified for me to be addressing a Lt. Commander in such a familiar fashion, but I can remember when I used to send you to get my laundry." Unable to attend the Woodberry event, Johnny instructed, "Would hesitate to give more of my best wishes to any one person so tell them all hello for me and when you drink a toast to the school rest assured that I will be drinking with you in spirit (and probably in reality) although I am way out here in California." Peter Ruffin wrote, too, and Johnny responded: "Have seen quite a lot of boys from Woodberry in the service since the war started and, of course, it affords me great pleasure to be able to give them a drink or show them the town while they are here." Old friends and acquaintances from Savannah stationed on the West Coast also dropped by, such as Pope Barrow McIntire, who enjoyed his visit with the Mercers while stationed as an aviator cadet in Santa Anna.[52]

In 1944, the trade newspaper *Variety* published an extensive critique of *The Johnny Mercer Chesterfield Music Shop*. The editors noted, "What promises to be one of the most interesting experiments in the past several years along programming lines got away from the barriers Monday from Hollywood when Johnny Mercer stepped into the early evening NBC slot held down for the last five years by Fred Waring with excellent results both for him and the sponsor." Recognizing the cigarette company's effort to expand its market share, the review noted that the "new offering, judging from teeoff is slanted towards a younger audience and this, according to many astute observers, will make it tougher for Mercer to approach the heights attained by Waring." Targeting a diverse fan base, Mercer selected hokey novelty numbers that he enjoyed singing, such as "Pigeon-toed

Joe" and "Steamboat Bill." He also tried to retain the older Waring audience by performing such Tin Pan Alley favorites as "Sweet Lorraine," "Margie," "Sugar," "When the Bloom Is on the Sage," and "By the River Sainte Marie," songs he later released on an album with Capitol.[53]

The Johnny Mercer Chesterfield Music Shop cost the Liggett and Myers Tobacco Company around $14,000 a week to produce. Mercer earned the top salary at $2,000, with the best-known guest stars such as Lucille Ball receiving $1,000 for each appearance and lesser-known stars, such as Sterling Holloway, earning $500. As the music arranger and band conductor for the program, Paul Weston made $1,640, while the Pied Pipers pulled in $1,000, and Jo Stafford got $500. The band members split the $5,410 among them, and announcer Wendell Niles earned $400. When at the end of 1944 the company replaced Mercer with Perry Como, Johnny quit smoking Chesterfields.[54]

Although she never appeared on the *Music Shop*, on several occasions Judy Garland joined Johnny Mercer on programs for the AFRS, and their interaction suggested an ongoing romance. Ken Carpenter announced the show that had the two entertainers talking informally and singing to minimal piano accompaniment by Ivan Ditmars. As befitting two occasional lovers rekindling the flame, their first duet featured the Duke Ellington and Bob Russell song, "Don't Get Around Much Anymore." Three years had passed since their affair began, and although Garland had separated from first husband David Rose, initiated a fling with Tyrone Power, and would soon marry Vincente Minnelli, she made room for Johnny. Judy selected from her current film project, George and Ira Gershwin's *Girl Crazy*, for the second number on the program as she sang "They're writing songs of love, but not for me; / A lucky star's above, but not for me." Rather than respond with one of his own lyrics about a failed romance, Johnny performed "I Lost My Sugar in Salt Lake City (Salt Lake City Blues)," by Leon René and Johnny Lange from the movie *Stormy Weather*. The performance, later released on V-disk, ends with the two singing the wishful "Taking a Chance on Love," by John Latouche, Ted Fetter, and Vernon Duke from the film version of *Cabin in the Sky*. The tone of their voices during the May 1943 performance on *Personal Album* suggests intimacy in their relationship.[55]

Garland and Mercer also appeared together on several broadcasts of *Command Performance, USA!* For the 1945 Christmas show, AFRS brought the brightest stars of the previous programs together for a special *Command Performance, USA!* celebrating the Allies' victory in World War II. Bing Crosby opened by singing "On the Atchison, Topeka, and the Santa Fe." Jimmy Durante provided comic relief; the Harry James Orchestra played "Two O'Clock Jump." Mercer offered a spirited rendition of Stephen Foster's "De Camptown Races," beginning with, "Grandstand's filled with a happy crowd." He then called the race: "Eee. Bobtail leading at the quarter mile, / But look at the bay, got a lot of style. / Yes, now they're startin' on the homeward trek, / Looks like everybody's gonna collect, / It's a photograph finish — neck and neck." Capturing the postwar glee, Mercer sang, "Oh, those Camptown Races! / Oh, those happy faces! / Sure had a wonderful time." Bob Hope cracked, "Johnny, you sound more like Crosby every minute." Johnny joined Bob, Bing, and Judy Garland in a comedy sketch over the titling of "On the Atchison, Topeka, and the Santa Fe." Mercer attributed the title to a fight between two families in Kansas. Then a skit began with Johnny and Bob Hope cast as feuding patriarchs, with Garland having to side with one of them. She picked Hope, leaving the rejected Johnny to listen as Judy sang "Long Ago (and Far Away)." Other performers in the special show included Frank Sinatra, Dinah Shore, and Jerry Colonna. The program ended with the cast singing a Christmas medley and the Ken Carpenter voiceover: "Christmas 1945 and the bright melodies of the carols go swinging down the streets of Berlin and Tokyo too."[56]

The Overseas Radio Division of AFRS interviewed Mercer for its biographical segment, *Ten Minutes of Your Time*, for broadcast in 1944. The interview demonstrated that Johnny Mercer dominated his profession and completely understood the popular music industry. During the program a candid Mercer described the way he approached songwriting: "When I write a song I like to get the title idea first. Then if someone else is going to do the music, I want him to fit the melody to the title and complete the music for the song. After that I tackle the rest of the lyrics." Mercer said he had written about 500 songs and published half of them. Asked about the remaining 250, Mercer explained: "Lots of my songs have been written for pictures and generally the whole score of a picture isn't published. They usually only take the best two or three out of a total of maybe six or seven." On a similar note, Mercer had explained in Kenneth E. Palmer's "Musical Moments" column for a Savannah paper in 1940 that "if you want to write popular songs, you've got to make up your mind to one thing. The first hundred or so have to be written exclusively for the wastebasket. After that — maybe you've got a chance." In another interview, Mercer elaborated, "Only a small percentage of the songs written are ever published — remember there are many tastes to be pleased; and only a tiny percentage of those published ever really make it. So simple arithmetic has it that a guy has to write a lot of songs." He continued,

"When one is finished, and fixed, and ready, and he's happy with it — then on to the next. A song writer is *always* writing." Then Mercer explained success: "Let him listen to all the stuff, let him hear all the stuff, let him pay attention to all the stuff — but he must not try to copy any of it. He must be himself. He must be original," noting, "If copying would do it — everybody would do it; yet, maybe one in a hundred thousand actually make it as a songwriter. That one must have the zing, the feel, and the strength to be original; to do it his very own way."[57]

Foreshadowing the domination of American popular culture in the world, Mercer recognized the role of radio in "populariz[ing] a song overseas." He noted that "the sale of recordings has had quite a bit to do with it too." Indeed, the AFRS broadcasts from military stations on outposts in all four corners of the globe had enabled everyone within earshot of a radio to listen to the popular culture produced in the United States. Mercer saw the marketing as a double-edged sword: "In the pre-radio days, sales of a song were spread out over a long period of time because people wouldn't grow tired of hearing it played so much, whereas today, with radio shows using popular songs over and over again they don't last so long. Of course with songs passing out of the picture quicker, that makes room for new songs. I guess it's as good as it is bad." Mercer estimated the average song would play about six months, but that "one with a little more merit will continue to be used for maybe two years, while the really great ones, such as 'Stardust,' 'I've Got Rhythm' and a few others in that class never seem to die out." Johnny aspired to that catalogue of Great American Song.[58]

With *Time* magazine and others calling for a patriotic song that could unify the nation behind the war, Mercer commented in the *Ten Minutes of Your Time* interview on which current songs could fill the bill. He noted that during World War I songwriters had captured the era with the standards "Over There" as sung by George M. Cohan and the British "Pack Up Your Troubles in Your Old Kit Bag." In reflecting on the popular music of the current conflict, Mercer believed that Frank Loesser's "Praise the Lord and Pass the Ammunition" had about run its course, although the 1942 hit joined Irving Berlin's "White Christmas" as two of the war's most popular songs. (*Variety*, asking the same question about war songs early in the conflict, speculated that Johnny Mercer might write the hits of the age because of the success of his "You Grow Sweeter as the Years Go By" in England.) Mercer concluded the *Ten Minutes of Your Time* interview by singing one of his own contributions to the war's soundtrack, "Dream." He later joined Berlin, Loesser, and nine other bestselling songwriters in receiving recognition for their wartime music at the first Clef Award Presentation, held in Carnegie Hall September 28, 1945.[59]

While the military used the airwaves to broadcast popular songs as propaganda to the troops and a growing international audience, Johnny appeared frequently on commercial radio to build morale on the home front. During the 1940s, he made numerous special appearances as one of the hottest properties in Hollywood. For Lucky Strike Cigarettes, Mercer guest-hosted *Your Hit Parade*. He sang on *Request Performance*, sponsored by Campbell's Soups. On New Year's Eve 1942, Johnny and Betty Hutton joined Bing Crosby on his *Kraft Music Hall* broadcast over NBC. The network produced *Paul Whiteman Presents* during the summer of 1943, and on one program Pops and his former hostess and girl singer, Dinah Shore, welcomed Johnny. And when Mercer did not personally appear on such radio shows, the broadcasts often featured his music. Frequently, AFRS prepared transcriptions of these domestic programs for use by the military overseas.[60]

Certainly Mercer's songs appeared regularly on Lucky Strike's *Your Hit Parade* during its 1935 to 1959 run, first on radio and then for its last ten years also on television. Broadcast by NBC on Saturday nights, the program initially played the week's top fifteen songs — later the top ten songs — plus a few "Lucky Strike Extras." The American Tobacco Company's Lucky Strike cigarettes sponsored the show, and its advertising agency, Batten, Barton, Durstine and Osborn, used a secret process to select the winners. The accountants in the firm created a formula that added up the national sale of sheet music, tabulations from jukeboxes, and requests made to radio stations and live orchestras gathered from across the country. Using such a variety of indices to measure popularity prevented the music industry from rigging the contest through payola to disc jockeys at radio stations. Each program began with the announcement "Once again, the voice of the people has spoken," from there building suspense to the number one song aired in the few remaining minutes of the show. A young Frank Sinatra joined other soloists accompanied by band leader Lennie Hayton and his Lucky Strike Orchestra with its Hit Paraders chorus in performances of the selected top ten. The songs seemed randomly interspersed among cigarette ads, comedy sketches sometimes featuring W. C. Fields, and tobacco auction chatter until just enough time remained to play the top three songs.[61]

Before *Billboard* assumed the role, *Your Hit Parade* came close to providing a national gauge of a song's popularity. Mercer's music often appeared, as on May

12, 1945, when he held the top slots with "Dream" at three, "Laura" at two, and at number one, singing with Jo Stafford and the Pied Pipers, the duet "Candy," written by David Mack, Joan Whitney, and Alex Kramer. Four songs written by Mercer straddled the top ten on April 25, 1942, and May 2, 1942, "Skylark" and "Tangerine" and then "Blues in the Night," which fell out to be replaced by "I Remember You." Dave Dexter recalled that no one had ever accomplished that before. Mercer nearly repeated the feat in July 1945 with "Out of This World," "Dream," "Laura," and "Candy." With fourteen of his songs registering the number one spot, Johnny set that record for songwriters, while his standing of thirty-six songs reaching the top ten placed him third in the competition for writing the most songs to appear on *Your Hit Parade*. Typical of these hits, "And the Angels Sing" sat in the number one spot for four weeks in May and June 1939, while "Ac-Cent-Tchu-Ate the Positive" did the same during February and March 1945. Other top ten songs received favorable comment by *Your Hit Parade*'s Martin Block, who announced in October 1942 the number six hit, "Dearly Beloved," by saying, "It's that new Johnny Mercer–Jerome Kern song. And when those two get together on a ballad, it isn't long before all America is singing it!" Over the course of his career, Johnny sang thirteen songs (written by himself or by others) that made it to the top ten, with four of those reaching the number one spot: "G.I. Jive," "Ac-Cent-Tchu-Ate the Positive," "Candy," and "Personality." Other top songs included his duet with Margaret Whiting of "Baby, It's Cold Outside," the novelty number "Huggin' and a Chalkin'," and, with Benny Goodman, "Moon Faced, Starry Eyed." He later had success singing duets with Nat "King" Cole, including "Save the Bones for Henry Jones" and "Harmony." From *Your Hit Parade*'s outset on radio to its final broadcasts over television, Mercer's music appeared regularly, marking him as one of the nation's leading vocalists and songwriters.[62]

One of those number one songs, "Laura," came about in a backward fashion. The soundtrack to an unsettling movie called *Laura* that 20th Century Fox distributed in 1944 had no lyric. Directed by Otto Preminger, the murder mystery starred Gene Tierney, Vincent Price, and Clifton Webb. Mercer recalled, composer "[David] Raksin had a tune in it [the movie *Laura*] that was so big, and so beautiful, that people began to go to the music store and ask for, say 'I'd like the music from *Laura*.' And then they'd go in and say 'I want that music, '*Laura*.' Give me that *Laura* music.'" Mercer noted that because of the popularity of the film score, Abe Olman, the publisher at Robbins Music Company, asked "if I'd write a lyric, and I understand he had approached a couple of other people first,

I think Hammerstein, who was busy, and Irving Caesar, who wasn't interested or something." Gene Lees suggested that Oscar Hammerstein wanted to write a lyric for "Laura" but stipulated that his publishing company get the rights, something Olman refused to relinquish from Robbins. Philip Furia reports that Caesar — who had written such hits as "Tea for Two" decades before — contributed a terrible lyric that Raksin rejected, suggesting that Mercer be asked to write the words instead. Johnny continued, "Finally they asked me to do it and I was very interested the minute I heard the melody."[63]

Even before seeing the film, Mercer received from Olman a studio pressing of the underscore from *Laura*. Johnny fell in love with the music, which he described as "misterioso." Olman and Johnny agreed to title the song "Laura," since that's what customers called the tune. Commenting on the song title, Johnny explained, "Well, it didn't matter too much to me except that the mood of the song mattered. And the mood of the song is the face in the misty light, the voice, the eyes on the train, the face on the train, footsteps. You know, that to me, that's what the music said." With a title and the melody, Mercer began to compose and only then went to see the film, *Laura*, in a Beverly Hills cinema. He met Raksin and discussed the "mating" of the draft lyric to the refrain. Then the two collaborated on the words and music for the opening verse. Later Johnny explained the difficulty of the music: "because there are so few notes. And because the intervals are tough, the key changes are strange. And at the time it came out, it was most strange." From Mercer's perspective, his lyric reveals the feelings harbored within the music, but they also perfectly fit the storyline of the picture, becoming a postproduction movie theme song to which the fans could relate.[64]

From the outset, Johnny's lyric establishes the suspenseful mood reflected in the music. The verse sets up the uncertainty: "You know the feeling / Of something half remembered, / Of something that never happened, / Yet you recall it well." Then the subject of the mystery appears in the refrain set to the strains of Raksin's famous movie theme: "Laura / Is the face in the misty light, / Footsteps / That you hear down the hall, / The laugh / That floats on a summer night / That you can never quite / Recall." And as those enigmatic lines fail to clarify, Mercer adds, "And you see Laura / On the train that is passing through, / Those eyes, / How familiar they seem!" Then Mercer — the consummate storyteller who leaves this tale unresolved — concludes his evocation with the thrill of imagined romance: "She gave / Your very first kiss to you. That was Laura, / But she's only a dream." The lyric's evocation of time and memory tied to the senses of sight and sound and grounded in the reality of crowds and trains suited the era so completely that the song "Laura" reached the top of the charts after its release, Mercer's tenth song to hit number one on *Your Hit Parade*. Yet in 1947, when Mercer and Raksin tried to collaborate in the usual way on a similar theme for the movie *Forever Amber*, the result lacked the luster of "Laura."[65]

Both Irving Berlin and Cole Porter observed independently of each other that of all the songs they wished they had written, "Laura" topped the list. At a Hollywood party given by their mutual agent, Irving Lazar, Porter confessed to Mercer: "If there's one song I wish I'd written, it would be 'Laura,'" to which Johnny responded, "Hell, man, that would've been a hit if you called it 'Joe.'" Porter answered, "You couldn't call it 'Joe,' it's one syllable." Mercer retorted, "So call it 'Jo-oh.'" To trump the exchange, Porter announced, "Mr. Mercer, you don't always write the music," adding, "I do." Johnny queried the songwriter, "People are always asking me: What's more important, the lyric or the music?" Porter answered, "In this instance, it's the lyric." While accepting the compliment, the ever self-deprecating Mercer then turned to those standing around and said, "Tell him to hum the lyric." [66]

At the top of his craft, Mercer enjoyed the recognition of his fellow professional songwriters. In June 1942, the Writers' Classification Committee of ASCAP raised his status to Class AA. Since the licensing agency paid its members via a sliding scale derived from the number of songs in their published catalogue, ranking marked elite status and a sizeable increase in pay. Composers such as Carl Sigman, who wrote "Crazy She Calls Me" and "Dance Ballerina Dance," congratulated Mercer on his many new hits. Others, such as Harry Ruby, who wrote "I Wanna Be Loved by You," asked Mercer to collaborate. More often than not Johnny responded graciously to his colleagues. Always on the lookout for fresh talent, he also answered agents who solicited him for their clients, perhaps recalling his earlier eager days in the business. Even the producer Jack Robbins continued to request that Johnny record some of his songs on a new label he had started, trying to imitate the success of Capitol Records.[67]

Metro-Goldwyn-Mayer hired lyricist Johnny Mercer to collaborate with composer Harry Warren on its 1945 musical *The Harvey Girls*, starring Judy Garland. The fictional story featured attractive young eastern women seeking brighter futures in the West by waitressing in the Fred Harvey restaurant chain along the railroad. The plot resonated with Americans emerging from years of war, ready for a fresh start. Johnny's lines even fomented rebellion and sexual revolution: "In this day and age, girls don't leave home, / But if ya get a hankerin' you wanna roam, / Our advice to you is run away / On the Atchison, Topeka, and the Santa

Fe!" Visualizing the transcontinental ride, the lyric promotes migration: "Yes-sirree, here we are goin' all the way, / Mustn't quit till we hit Californ-i-a." For their part, Mercer and Warren hoped to redesign Hollywood musicals with *The Harvey Girls*, just as the 1943 *Oklahoma!* had revolutionized Broadway. Warren and Mercer wanted to kick-start a revival of movie musicals, which had declined in popularity since the 1930s. For the stage, Rodgers and Hammerstein had integrated the songs into the overall plot and distributed them to various performers rather than just to the leads. So too for the movie musical, Warren and Mercer wrote songs that advanced the plot and divided the singing roles among the entire cast.[68]

Rising to the challenge of writing a song that exploited the talents of his love interest, Judy, Johnny captured the pent-up energy — and passion — of the age in his lyric for "On the Atchison, Topeka, and the Santa Fe." While at first the words evoke the timelessness of the small-town life that everyone recognized the war had irrevocably changed, the music's imitation of a train engine racing down the track predicts a willingness to embark on an accelerating future. The pairing of Mercer with his old friend and former collaborator, Warren, proved perfect for the song: Johnny, still a dedicated rail traveler, captured the train image in his poetry, while Harry translated engine sounds and brake noises into compositions, having already written the music for both "Chattanooga Choo-Choo" and "Shuffle Off to Buffalo." The selection of Garland worked well too, as she joined the ensemble of *The Harvey Girls* to belt out the lyric of "On the Atchison, Topeka, and the Santa Fe."[69]

Years later, Mercer explained how the song came into being: "When most people ask me how did I write 'Atchison, Topeka, and the Santa Fe' I say I was riding on the Union Pacific at the time and I saw a boxcar which had those words." Johnny wrote them down in a little notebook he carried for the purpose. The title preceded the movie by several years: "I had thought that would be a great song, 'Atchison, Topeka, and the Santa Fe.' It sings, you know," Mercer explained to Willis Conover in 1970, "that combination of names just rolled." When the movie assignment came about, Mercer approached Warren with his idea, linking the railroad with the Harvey girls. "Fine," Harry responded, explaining he had "just the right tune for it." Contrary to what some believed, in return for writing the lyric that featured the Atchison, Topeka, and the Santa Fe Railroad Mercer did not receive free transit, despite his frequent travels on the *Super Chief* that coursed the line from Chicago to Los Angeles.[70]

The optimistic drive of "Atchison, Topeka, and the Santa Fe" helped make it the Academy Award winner for best song in 1946. The rules had changed since the 1945 Oscars had introduced as part of the event performances of the fourteen nominated songs. Members decided to limit the number of nominated songs to five beginning with the nineteenth Academy Awards for films produced in 1946. Both Mercer, with his "Blues in the Night," and Warren, with his "Chattanooga Choo-Choo," had been passed over for the 1941 Oscar. The 1946 nomination marked Mercer's eighth for Best Song, although he had yet to take home a gold statue. Winning this time elated both men. After Judy Garland bowed out of singing "On the Atchison, Topeka, and the Santa Fe" for the Academy Awards show, Dinah Shore performed the number. Hoagy Carmichael sang his own nominated hit, "Ole Buttermilk Sky," which he had also performed in the movie *Canyon Passage*. When Hoagy suffered the double humiliation of not winning the award and then being introduced by Sam Goldwyn as "Hugo Carmichael," Mercer promised his old collaborator that they would write another song that could win an Oscar.[71]

By the war's end Mercer stood in the forefront of the music business, not only as a songwriter for Hollywood movie musicals, swing era singers, and radio programs that often featured his own talents as an entertainer, but also through his management of Capitol Records. The synergy that resulted from his involvement in so many facets of popular culture kept his own creations on the cutting edge of national trends. Broadcast commercially and over military radio stations, and played on V-disks, Mercer's music became truly global as it reached markets heretofore untapped by the United States. In the postwar period the American entertainment industry built on these foundations to extend its bid for hegemony abroad. Yet at the same time, the number of movie musicals being filmed by the studios declined. The big-band sounds that had set Johnny's heart to soaring and feet to dancing gave way to the progressive jazz of a Stan Kenton or to the minimalist bebop of a Miles Davis. Capitol Records captured many of these sounds, too, as it emerged out of nowhere to become one of the top four record companies in the country.

6 Capitol Records

. . . .

You're clear out of this world.
When I'm looking at you,
I hear out of this world
The music that no mortal ever knew.

IN THE FIRST FEW MONTHS of World War II, Capitol Records organized as a challenge to the big three recording companies, and by the end of the conflict it had become so successful that it joined RCA Victor, Columbia, and Decca as one of the big four. Born in the weeks following the Japanese bombardment of Pearl Harbor, the upstart record company survived the restrictions of wartime through resourceful practices and careful management to emerge as one of the leading businesses in the music industry, often ahead of the others in both technological advances and marketing strategies. Being on the West Coast and tapping the multiracial culture that accompanied the southern diaspora, Capitol developed away from Tin Pan Alley to sell Americans a new sound reflective of the millions of people caught up in the migrations of the Great Depression and war years. Mercer molded the sound as both president and artists and repertoire (A&R) man at Capitol. He selected music — often jazz — that suited his style and that of the artists, many of whom also hailed from the South. While the meteoric rise of Capitol occurred against the backdrop of world war, in peacetime it rapidly developed global markets, ultimately being bought out by a European firm to become a truly transnational corporation.

The idea of an independent record label had occurred to Mercer on his return to California in early 1941 after two years of working in New York. Back in Los Angeles, he observed a wealth of idle talent — especially among singers and jazz musicians — available for hire on the West Coast. The instability of freelance work for the movie studios and the risks assumed when writing for the Broadway stage had convinced him to think of ways to supplement his own income. "I used to ask myself," Johnny explained to a reporter, "what talented people around

Hollywood did in between picture and radio jobs. I thought maybe I could organize them into some sort of co-operative and start a radio program." At first he
proposed a serial for broadcast called *The Angelinos* that would feature his Hollywood friends. Then he conceived of overseeing recordings by these musicians
that, with his direction, could surpass the quality of sound being produced in
New York by the big three labels.[1]

Mercer discussed the idea with Glenn Everett Wallichs, the owner of Music
City, an early superstore that sold records, sheet music, and radios at its emporium on Sunset Boulevard and Vine Street in Hollywood. Years later, telling the
story to jazz critic Willis Conover, Mercer remembered discussing *The Angelinos* with Wallichs: "I said 'why don't we start a record company.' I don't know
whether he said it or I said it, but we decided that we ought to start a record company, because there were a couple of little local independent records out at that
time. And he said, 'well, that's a good idea.' He said, 'do you think you could sell
them in the lobbies of the theatres, like the Paramount Theatre?'" The grandson
of a Methodist minister, Wallichs never drank, smoked, or cursed, habits that
placed him exactly opposite Mercer. Yet the record and radio salesman understood the distribution business and supported the idea. Johnny later said, "After
talking with Wallichs, however, I decided to go into the recording business and
use these people who weren't working steadily." Over lunch at Lucey's Restaurant with his old colleague, the songwriter and Broadway producer George G.
"Buddy" DeSylva, who recently had moved to California as head of Paramount
Pictures, Mercer outlined a proposal he felt the studio might like, only to discover an enthusiastic DeSylva willing to provide $10,000 of his own money for
startup capital. As Margaret Whiting recalled, "Both Wallichs and DeSylva,
businessmen, knew in whom they were investing." The three men incorporated
the partnership as Liberty Records on April 8, 1942, but because a British record
company had a similar name, they followed the suggestion of Ginger Mercer and
renamed it Capitol Records. DeSylva took an advisory role, Wallichs oversaw the
manufacture and distribution of the records, and Mercer controlled the creative
content of the music.[2]

Careful planning allowed the company to overcome potential setbacks in its
early months so that by the end of 1942 Capitol Records enjoyed steady sales of
new releases. As soon as the U.S. government instituted a quota system on shellac, a natural material secreted by beetles and used in the manufacture of disks
but made rare by the Japanese blockade of Malaysia, Capitol began stockpiling
old records to reclaim the shellac. In April 1942, the War Production Board fixed

the number of records permitted to be manufactured for domestic consumption and shifted industrial production away from personal radios and record players to products for military use, thereby curtailing the growing market for music by severely limiting availability of new records from the big three for preexisting turntables, radios, and jukeboxes. At the same time the War Department began a policy it would follow throughout the war of issuing phonographs, records of popular songs, and transcriptions of radio shows to deploying troops. To promote the label, Mercer provided the military with Capitol's latest records, and he regularly performed on Armed Forces Radio Service (AFRS) broadcasts the new Capitol releases.[3]

With the entertainment industry already suffering because of the war, the growing popularity of recorded music prompted a strike by professional musicians that threatened the fledgling company. Recognizing that radio stations increasingly broadcast prerecorded rather than live music, the head of the American Federation of Musicians, James Caesar Petrillo, in May 1942 warned that "records are killing off jobs for musicians." He ordered a strike against recording companies to begin in August, giving the industry only two more months to use his 140,000 union members. Capitol moved quickly: working long hours, Mercer oversaw the production of enough new masters to keep Capitol releasing singles well into the following year. Twenty-five years later, Johnny reflected, "The war and even the musicians' strike only made our little company better known and more quickly recognized." He attributed the popularity "to the shortage of other labels," which meant that "we got heard a lot. We could do nothing wrong." The inaugural year ended with Capitol having released 25 singles and earning sales of $195,000.[4]

The three founders intended Capitol Records to set higher standards for the industry. An optimistic Wallichs explained to *Down Beat* the label's objectives, leading off with jazz music: "We're going into the open market for the best songs and the best performers we can give the public. We plan a complete catalogue that will offer sweet music, swing music, Hawaiian, hill billy and race music." Unlike the big three, Capitol at first followed a strict policy of not making covers of songs already recorded by others so that each release featured new music. Mercer recognized the importance of artistic integrity. He also wanted to improve the quality of the sound recording. As the company newsletter stated, Johnny "assigns all tunes to artists and personally supervises every recording session." The exceptional quality of Capitol's recordings in its early years reflected the talents of Mercer as A&R man. By taking risks on relatively unknown performers, the company could pay a one-time recording fee of seventy-five dollars but no royalties to the artist, who then gained from any positive publicity just as the company plowed any profits back into production. Johnny and Glenn favored the acoustics found in the studio of the MacGregor Company located off Wilshire Boulevard. Capitol hired the Chinese American Victor Quan as its technician to oversee the sound equipment during recordings. Taking the masters made in the studio, the company hired out to independent producers the making of the 78-RPM shellac platters with up to three minutes of music on each side. Recalling the excitement of the early days, Margaret Whiting observed: "Capitol was revolutionary. Capitol was West Coast. The music sounded different, and it was fresh and breezy. The artists were new, and they were given greater freedom."[5]

From the outset Mercer used his leadership role with the company to involve his friends in the creation of new music that showcased the interpenetration of jazz and popular song. Johnny convinced Wallichs to pay Paul Whiteman's New Yorker Hotel Orchestra a substantial sum up front for the recordings, arguing that the prestige of the Whiteman name would enhance the reputation of the new label. In the company's first month of operation, "Pops" directed the band on four instrumentals that featured the trumpeter Billy Butterfield. Two months later, the Whiteman orchestra returned to record additional numbers with vocals, including Johnny singing with his former sidekick Jack Teagarden "The Old Music Master," a vocal appreciation of their mentor Pops — the old music master himself. In honor of Whiteman, Mercer made the orchestra's recordings of "I Found a New Baby" and, on the flip side, "The General Jumped at Dawn," the first release of the new label, Capitol 101, issued on a 78-RPM shellac platter.[6]

Yet Billie Holiday made the best Whiteman recording for the company performing as Lady Day on "Travelin' Light," Capitol 116. Mercer wrote the lyric to an instrumental by the fellow Savannahian and trombonist James Osborne "Trummy" Young, who had played with Earl Hines and His Orchestra. Living together but down on their luck and about to be evicted from their rental, Holiday and Young approached Mercer for help. Young offered the tune, which his friend Jimmy Mundy had arranged for Whiteman's band to play. Johnny heard it and knocked out the lyric, having Mundy write a new arrangement for Whiteman's band to record with Capitol. Trummy Young attributed the title "Travelin' Light" to Ginger Mercer. Again reflecting the hybridity of jazz, "Travelin' Light" featured a tune by a black man with a lyric by a white man sung to perfection by a black woman. The recording with Whiteman's band — historically made up of white players — included the African American Lester Young on tenor saxophone. Caught just before Holiday's descent into drug addiction, this particular blues song about a woman living without her man again seemed all the more poignant given the brutal abuse Billie suffered from a number of her lovers. The lyric captured the hopelessness of addiction: "Some lucky night / He may come back again, / But until then / I'm trav'lin' light." About "Travelin' Light," Mercer recalled, "She liked it a lot, Lady Day." She must have, as she made numerous recordings of the song. A biographer of Holiday, Stuart Nicholson, noted about this vocal that it "provides an intriguing miniature of her art." On the initial Capitol release, the record label incorrectly identified Jimmy Mundy as the composer, so Trummy Young complained: "I raised a little hell, and they gave me seventy-five dollars, and later, Johnny Mercer, who is from my home town Savannah, Georgia, got my name put on the tune."[7]

Around this time Mercer composed both the words and music for "Harlem Butterfly" as an obvious tribute to Billie Holiday. He had known her since the beginning of her recording career and had watched her emerge as one of the greatest jazz singers. Perhaps he also noted the beginnings of her slow and wanton self-destruction. The lyric speaks of some innate mark on the singer, like a child born with a caul: "The moon got in your eye / The night you were born. / Harlem butterfly, / You listened to the cry / Of some lonely horn." As if anticipating Lady Day's future, the song continues, "Oh, Harlem butterfly, / The writin's in the sky — / You'll come to no good. / But I'm not blamin' you. / I'm certain I would do / The same if I could." Then, as he occasionally did, Mercer paraphrased one of his favorite poets, this time Edna St. Vincent Millay and her poem "First Fig." His lyric went: "For even though a candle / Burn'd at both ends / Can never last out the night, / Harlem butterfly, / It really makes a lovely light." The jazz singer Maxine Sullivan made a popular contemporary recording of the song, as did Julie London two decades later.[8]

Scrambling to make more masters before the August 1942 strike set in, Mercer lined up his talent. He tapped a relatively unknown white eighteen-year-old jazz singer from Texas who had migrated to the West Coast named Ella Mae Morse. Mercer paired her with the Freddie Slack Orchestra, a group led by the veteran jazz pianist who had performed with the Ben Pollack Band and the Jimmy Dorsey Orchestra before moving to California. They recorded two novelty songs by composer Gene DePaul and lyricist Don Raye, "Mister Five by Five" and "Cow Cow Boogie." Both incongruously combined a cutting-edge urban beat with a western theme. After Ella Mae Morse performed the refrain of "Mister Five by Five,"

Johnny jumped in at the repeat to sing several lines before being cut off by her to finish the song. Released as Capitol 102, the record sold 250,000 copies its first week and topped a million by the end of the month. For Capitol's third record Mercer sang two of his own creations accompanied by Tommy Dorsey's earlier arranger Paul Weston and his orchestra with composer Jimmy Van Heusen playing piano. On one side Johnny sang "The Air-Minded Executive," which he had written in 1940 with Bernie Hanighen. On the flip side he sang "Strip Polka," for which he wrote both the words and music. With its background chatter by Mercer's friend vaudevillian Phil Silvers, a chorus that included Silvers, Van Heusen, Margaret Whiting, and others, and its good-hearted story of Queenie, the stripper who takes off her clothes but "stops — / And always just in time!" the young company achieved another phenomenal success. Although Hollywood censors had banned the song from the movie *Navy Blues*, once released as Capitol 103, "Strip Polka" sold more than a million copies. Margaret Whiting found the somewhat spontaneous and informal recording session uneventful. Upon reflection she thought the historic occasion "nothing important or epic-making" but rather "a lot of fun" and remembered that "at the end of the session, everybody emptied ashtrays, flipped off the lights and went home. And that was that." As the strike continued and the shellac shortage worsened, the combined sales of "Strip Polka" and "Cow Cow Boogie," along with Dennis Day singing "Johnny Doughboy Found a Rose in Ireland" and other Capitol releases that reached *Your Hit Parade,* made the nascent business viable, while the ranking at the top of the jukebox charts spoke to the music's popularity.[9]

Using unconventional methods, Wallichs and Mercer secured the independent Capitol's future. In an era when the big three — RCA Victor, Decca, and Columbia — dominated distribution through ready access to radio stations and music outlets, smaller labels had to develop their own networks. Initially Wallichs and Mercer acted like the song pluggers of old by contacting their associates in the California market and hustling their new releases, but then they began to simply mail out the records to the big stations across the nation. Capitol became the first company to regularly distribute to disk jockeys free copies of its new records — often as acetate or vinylite disks — thereby increasing airtime on the radio for its new pressings. In return for the free releases, radio executives gave Capitol old records to be scrapped as reclaimed shellac. Wallichs oversaw the acquisition of a half-million pounds of shellac in the first seventeen months in business, and by stockpiling the material necessary for the manufacture of the product the company made even more pressings. Setting up branch offices in Los

Angeles and Chicago, Capitol distributed its records to store owners for public sale. By 1943, the company had opened additional distribution centers in New York, Dallas, and Atlanta.[10]

To tap new markets the company hired Dave Dexter, a writer for the essential jazz magazine *Down Beat*, as its new press agent in 1943. Wallichs armed himself with free records and traveled to New York City, where Dexter introduced him to disc jockeys in that sprawling market. A natural promoter, the twenty-seven-year-old Dexter hailed from the Midwest, where he had listened to Kansas City jazz before moving to Chicago and then to New York. Dexter developed such strategies for Capitol as typing "exclusive" on the record labels given to two thousand disc jockeys across the country to generate excitement about and increase airtime for the music. From its modest rented space at 1483 Vine Street in "the heart of the world's entertainment capital" near the intersection with Sunset Boulevard in Hollywood, Capitol developed the most aggressive consumer-advertising program the industry had seen. In 1943, it began publishing its own magazine, the *Capitol News*, with an inaugural run of five thousand copies. From his days writing for *Down Beat* — which jazzmen had long preferred because of its critical reviews, sophomoric humor, and industry gossip — Dexter brought public-relations skills to *Capitol News*, publishing in sixteen pages short reports, feature stories, evaluations of releases, and a chatty column called "Dave Dexter's Surface Noise." By 1946, the company increased the run of the twice-monthly heavily illustrated magazine to 800,000 copies, which it distributed to radio stations and record outlets across the United States.[11]

In the early years Dave Dexter worked closely with Johnny Mercer. As Dexter recalled about his hiring, Wallichs told him he would "handle Capitol's publicity, our advertising, our public relations, and be a sort of assistant to Johnny Mercer in finding and recording talent when the union allows us to go back into the studios again." Dexter reported to a little partitioned office on Vine Street where an attractive blonde receptionist named Auriel MacFie operated the switchboard. Dexter worked six-day weeks with long hours as the company got off the ground, shipping orders from an old house behind the rear parking lot. He found Mercer "an unassuming, earthy, well-liked, light-hearted man who appreciated good jazz and who knew virtually everyone in the profession." He also discovered that Mercer maintained "erratic office hours," showing up around eleven in the morning to "poke around with his mail, inquire as to which records were selling best," and "then he would unfailingly amble out the front door and head for the Key Club in a block north to meet with musicians and songwriting pals over a noontime nip at the bar." Occasionally Dexter accompanied him, only to discover that "he told a limitless number of funny stories, his broad, soft Georgia accent making them all the more appealing." On other occasions Mercer engaged in competitions with the bar crowd to craft clever rhymes.[12]

In contrast to Mercer, Dexter recalled that consistency marked the behavior of Wallichs, who "functioned like he was programmed by a computer." Dexter remembered Wallichs's routine that had him behind his desk by eight every morning, "nattily attired in business suit, white shirt, conservative necktie, and shiny, laced shoes. He used the phone constantly and dictated dozens of letters, bouncing around the premises nervously, aware of the smallest details of Capitol's operations." As someone who frequented the hangouts of musicians, Dexter wore open-collared sports shirts and "scuffed loafers." One day Wallichs complained about Dexter's appearance and suddenly Mercer's voice could be heard from a back room: "Aw, hell," he said, "Not everyone dresses like a mortician. Who are we trying to impress?" Johnny appeared in front of Wallichs and Dexter wearing an open-collared sports shirt and scuffed loafers. "Let's not run Capitol like a factory, Glenn," Dexter recalled Mercer said softly. "Each of us is a little different from the others."[13]

Billboard explained Capitol's success by saying "the gents running it have the know-how." Jazz arranger-composer Paul Weston agreed: "It was just a very fortunate melding of executive personalities." The talents of opposites worked in tandem. Dexter described the three founders in an early newsletter: "Where Mercer moves easily, shuffling along in his Savannah style and talking calmly, Wallichs bustles about excitedly, attending to 16 matters at once and shouting orders. Mercer is a 'character,' but so is Wallichs. Together they form a knocked-out but highly potent team. Add DeSylva and it's plain nitro." A few years later, the business side crested over the creative impulse, and the company lost its attractiveness to Mercer.[14]

In March 1944, because of its phenomenal growth despite wartime shortages and musician strikes, Capitol signed an agreement with a two-year option to buy the Scranton Record Company, the world's largest manufacturer of records, to have it make the new pressings at its huge plants in Scranton, Pennsylvania, and Hollywood, California. Capitol's sales that year topped $2 million. Wartime taxes had hindered capital accumulation, so the company went public in 1946. The three founders retained 70 percent of the stock in the company. The sale raised $3.5 million, out of which the directors purchased the Scranton Record Company for $2 million, thereby acquiring the capacity to make 50 million pressings a year. Annual sales doubled from $6.5 million in 1945 to $13 million in 1946. That year the company released 120 single records and 19 albums, almost more than the total releases between 1942 and 1945, and half as many as expected to be released in 1947. Thus, four years after its start-up, Capitol had sold 40 million records, one-sixth of all discs produced in the United States. To expand its reach Capitol launched an international division in March 1947. As *Time* magazine noted that May, the figures did not satisfy "Mercer & Co," who expected to increase Capitol's sales to 60 million records, close to the 75 million produced by Columbia and the 100 million each that RCA Victor and Decca expected to sell in 1947. By this time nearly 15 million of the records in American households featured music by Johnny Mercer.[15]

Capitol's sales benefited from the southern diaspora as millions of black, white, and Latino laborers escaped the shackles of the region's cash-poor economy and moved to the Northeast, Midwest, and West Coast. In 1940, more than 400,000 southerners lived in the two major metropolitan centers of Los Angeles–Long Beach and San Francisco–Oakland. Metropolitan New York claimed 500,000 southern-born residents in 1940, while Chicago had more than 300,000. Overall, in 1940, some 4.5 million southern-born people lived outside the region, working as wage earners capable of consuming the South's multiracial culture now commodified in the new music produced by Capitol and other record companies. And as A&R man for Capitol, Johnny Mercer recruited southern diaspora entertainers for the new label.[16]

Outside the South, the ethnic neighborhoods of the North and West reinforced racial separation among southern migrants, who nonetheless found ways to express their regionalism in restaurants, nightclubs, and bars. Historian James N. Gregory evaluates southern music as performed by African Americans in the black urban centers of Harlem, Chicago's South Side, and Central Avenue in Los Angeles, while similarly looking at white musicians living in these metropolitan areas. Although he focuses on black blues and white hillbilly musicians, diaspora entertainers of all races created the new sounds of jazz. The black, white, and Latino musicians listened to each other's styles, picking up new techniques of playing, and following the same trends in the evolution of the genre as they shared the music they created. Capitol's best-sellers pointed to the company's successful marketing nationally of the region's hybrid sounds packaged as jazz-infused popular song.[17]

While RCA Victor, Decca, and Columbia continued to market the product of musicians as segregated commodities — racializing the music as suitable for "white" or "colored" consumption — Capitol recognized the irrationality of such racial segmentation. The company executives understood that good music appealed to people regardless of race, and consequently listed all artists alphabetically in marketing materials rather than separating black from white performers in an effort to segregate sound. Recalling buying "race records" as a youth at Lindsay and Morgan's in Savannah, Mercer realized the impracticality of labeling as "white" or "colored" the output of musicians when consumers could buy both, especially when considering jazz. At Capitol, Mercer personally oversaw the recording of black and white artists in an equitable fashion, focusing on the quality of the music. The records he produced made the company successful in its early years and account for its reputation for selling the fresh sounds of the southern diaspora.[18]

Under Mercer's leadership as president and A&R man, Capitol signed and recorded both black and white artists who reflected the shift of jazz into the Age of the Singer. During the swing era of the 1940s, vocalists had performed with jazz orchestras as another form of instrumentation, appearing as crooners or girl singers just as an instrumentalist might stand and improvise, but by the postwar period during the transition into jazz combos and progressive jazz, the singers emerged as headlined vocalists accompanied by their own jazz bands. Recognizing the trend, Mercer signed numerous singers to the Capitol label and encouraged them to record jazz-interpenetrated popular song. In addition to Ella Mae Morse and Jo Stafford, Capitol Records featured such diaspora entertainers as Julia Lee, Martha Tilton, Johnnie Johnston, Jesse Price, and the Dinning Sisters. New performers who epitomized the Age of the Singer such as Nat "King" Cole, Kay Starr, Margaret Whiting, and Peggy Lee established the company's reputation for outstanding vocalists years before Capitol signed Judy Garland and Frank Sinatra.[19]

The label approached song from a variety of perspectives. Folk music provided a product for Capitol to sell in the decade prior to the folk-song revival of the 1950s and 1960s. Having gotten his start entertaining the hands on western ranches and then touring the country as the Oklahoma Yodeling Cowboy, Jack Guthrie recorded western folk songs. The Knoxville, Tennessee, radio star Pappy Beaver performed Appalachian ballads. Another star of radio, Cliffie Stone, recorded folk songs, while Harry Owens — who wrote the Oscar-winning "Sweet Leilani"— interpreted Hawaiian music.

So many hillbilly diaspora entertainers lived in Los Angeles that Mercer quickly capitalized on their presence. Capitol expanded the market for regional music by making a more attractive product available nationally. Hillbilly performers such as Tex Ritter, Merle Travis, Wesley Tuttle, Jimmy Wakely, and Tex Williams combined the cowboy songs of folklore and Hollywood fame with the new western swing that developed as a response to the big-band sounds of jazz. Already a popular musician, Ritter grew up on the range in Texas and studied cowboy songs under folklorist John Lomax at the state university in Austin before migrating to New York City and Los Angeles to make a living as a performer of authentic cowboy folksongs. Among the first artists signed by Johnny Mercer in 1942, Tex Ritter joined an all-star group of musicians on several cuts that music historian Jeffrey J. Lange claims represents "the epitome of the western and country blend." As the label's A&R man, Mercer ran the studio, bringing in Capitol's Merle Travis, Wesley Tuttle, Johnny Bond, and Cliffie Stone to perform with Tex Ritter. The recordings favored Ritter's guitar and fiddle playing while featuring the "straightforwardness" of his "deep, weathered voice." Yet in places Mercer added strings to soften the sound, accordion music, or background vocals, as in the song, "Jingle, Jangle, Jingle." As with other Capitol recording stars, having completed the masters Tex Ritter took off on the road, traveling in the summer of 1943 across the South, with lengthy engagements in Spartanburg, Atlanta, and Montgomery. Capitol Records made Tex Ritter one of the stars of the new country western sound that southern diaspora consumers purchased across America.[20]

In addition to the white Georgian Mercer himself, no one reflected the hybridity of southern music on the Capitol recordings better than the black Alabamian Nat "King" Cole. Once signing the King Cole Trio to the label in 1943, Johnny helped make Cole the young company's best-seller. In 1923, the four-year-old Montgomery native had moved to Chicago with his family. While his Baptist father preached and his mother played the piano in the church, at home the radio broadcast jazz and nearby nightclubs headlined the arrival from New Orleans of trumpeter Louis Armstrong, who joined King Oliver, clarinetist Jimmie Noone, and pianist Jelly Roll Morton in making Dixieland jazz. Nat honed his piano skills by accompanying Earl Hines in a sizzling Chicago scene that regularly claimed visits by Fats Waller and Cab Calloway. At seventeen Cole joined the orchestra of a traveling revival of Noble Sissle and Eubie Blake's *Shuffle Along*, which had been the first all-black score to conquer Broadway. In 1937, the job landed Nat in Los Angeles, where he remained after the show folded, playing gigs on Central Avenue, the Harlem of the West Coast.[21]

In 1937, Nat Cole formed a trio with Wesley Prince on drums and Oscar Moore on acoustic guitar. For much of the year it played at the Sewanee Inn on La Brea, and it is probable that Johnny Mercer first heard the group there, where — given the omnipresence of movie music in Los Angeles — it might even have played his new song, "Old King Cole," written with Whiting in 1937 for *Varsity Show*. By 1938, the group called itself King Cole and His Sepia Swingsters and played at Jim Otto's Steak House, a venue on La Cienega frequented by Mercer. Early in Cole's career Johnny praised the talents of the jazz pianist and encouraged him to sing ballads. That September the newly renamed King Cole Trio made its first recording — a disk for radio broadcast — of Mercer's new song, "Mutiny in the Nursery," written with Harry Warren for the movie *Going Places*. By 1940, the trio had moved to the Radio Room, a club near the center of Hollywood, and Mercer heard them again, as did Paul Weston and Frank Sinatra. In July, Glenn Wallichs hired the King Cole Trio to entertain at the grand opening of his Music City superstore. As an example of the racist marketing of the big three, Decca recorded the King Cole Trio for its Sepia division of "race records" meant for African American consumers, releasing the singles in March 1941 but neglecting to market the group or keep up with the demand made by black and white consumers. The trio relocated to New York, playing East Coast clubs over the next two years with growing interest, especially when booked between Billie Holiday's sets at Kelly's Stables on Fifty-second Street, where a young Thelonious Monk listened intently to one of his favorite pianists. In June 1942, the King Cole Trio returned to California and the 331 Club, but with the drafting of Wesley Prince and the personal problems of Oscar Moore, the original trio broke up.[22]

Having just started Capitol Records, Johnny Mercer wanted to sign the King Cole Trio, but the group already had a contract with Decca, so happenstance led to Nat's first recordings on the Capitol label. Cole received an invitation to join Lester Young on tenor sax and Red Callender on bass for some masters made in Glenn Wallichs's studio on July 15, 1942, two weeks before the musicians' strike. The group recorded "Indiana" and "I Can't Get Started" as well as two songs that became standards in Cole's repertoire, "Tea for Two" and "Body and Soul." Popular music had never sounded this way before, according to Cole biographer Daniel Mark Epstein, who argues that the cuts "turned out to be a quintessential jazz statement." He added that it was "swing music on a jag, delirious with harmonic possibilities and testing the limits of form," which presaged the bebop yet to come. The pickup session over and the recordings in the can, the group separated, but in October Callender rejoined Cole in the black-owned Excelsior Studio to record "Vom, Vim, Veedle" and "All for You" with guitarist Moore. In Capitol's early months Wallichs bought up these and other masters for later release. The King Cole Trio felt it had bombed with Decca, so when its contract expired in September 1943, Capitol signed the combo, represented by Dave Dexter's friend, Carlos Gastel, with Nat on the piano, Johnny "Thrifty" Miller on bass fiddle, and Oscar Moore on guitar, to a generous seven-year contract with 5 percent royalties.[23]

With the strike over, Capitol brought the King Cole Trio into MacGregor Studios and made recording history with the jazz products of three sessions that Mercer mentored. The first recordings took place on November 30, 1943, under the watchful eye of Johnny, who sat on the piano bench next to Cole, while from the control booth Paul Weston balanced the bass and guitar of Miller and Moore with the piano and vocals. The trio made four cuts. The most significant, and the one Mercer most favored, "Straighten Up and Fly Right," was written by Cole and became his signature tune, while another, "Jumpin' at Capitol," provided an instrumental to promote the company. Two weeks later, the King Cole Trio returned to record four love ballads, including "Sweet Lorraine" and "Embraceable You." These songs as sold by Capitol epitomized music designed for everyone's consumption. Yet customary racial proscriptions forbade black men to sing love ballads to white women, so when Capitol Records marketed these recordings as products for everyone to purchase without warning labels marking them as "race records," it violated racist taboos that had segregated such sounds. Nothing in the recordings suggested Cole's "blackness" any more than previous Mercer recordings reflected his "whiteness," as if such ideas carried through song. Instead, the singing of the two men revealed the multiracial character of popular music interpenetrated by jazz. The last of these three sessions, captured on January 17, 1944, brought the trio back to MacGregor studio for an instrumental set with a resulting "Body and Soul" and "The Man I Love" expressed in a style later articulated to great acclaim by bebop artists. Cole biographer Epstein concluded that "although Weston and others insist that Nat always chose the material for his sessions, we must see in these the guiding hand of Mercer. During the same period the Trio was recording extensively for MacGregor Transcriptions and others, some fifty sides, yet the Mercer-produced titles are clearly superior in song selection, arrangements, and sound quality."[24]

As with other artists such as Margaret Whiting, Johnny Mercer mentored Nat "King" Cole. On numerous occasions Nat and Johnny rehearsed at the living room piano of the Mercers' De Longpre house in North Hollywood songs intended for recording by Capitol. The trio produced more than twenty-four sides released by Capitol in 1945, including the novelty number "Frim Fram Sauce," and then in March 1946, "Get Your Kicks on Route 66," which quickly topped the charts, followed by "I Love You for Sentimental Reasons." Johnny's daughter, Amanda, remembered hiding under the dining room table and listening to the men work. Thinking back on the sessions years later, she confessed that Cole "was my big crush of all time" and that "my heart still beats thinking about it. It was just the most thrilling thing in my life." Nat and Johnny practiced Mel Tormé and Robert Wells's new piece, "The Christmas Song," which the trio recorded in August 1946 at the YMCA studios in New York City. With its evocative "chestnuts roasting on an open fire" lyric, Mercer wanted the music to reflect the clean jazz combo sound. When Cole requested an orchestral accompaniment to make the sound more accessible to a general public, Johnny grew angry over what he saw as the "Trio's 'fluffing off' jazz." Cole and his manager, Carlos Gastel, insisted, so Mercer relented as Capitol added a harp and four violins. Released in December 1946, the record became one of the most popular of all holiday classics.[25]

As Nat's agent, Gastel succeeded in convincing NBC to create the *King Cole Trio Time*, one of the first weekly radio programs hosted by an African American on a major network scheduled during primetime. The Saturday night show first aired nationwide on October 19, 1946, and ran a year and a half, with Capitol Records providing many of the guest stars on the nearly eighty programs, including Johnny Mercer, Jo Stafford, Peggy Lee, and Pearl Bailey. At the same time Bing Crosby booked the trio on *Kraft Music Hall* not only to perform music but also to act in skits, something previously unheard of for black musicians. Because the "progressive" King Cole Trio broke through so many color barriers, *Metronome* named it "the major influence of music in 1946" and arranged for Johnny Mercer to deliver the award over the radio.[26]

Another of Nat "King" Cole's greatest hits came by way of Mercer. An enrobed mystic called Eden Ahbez had shown a song he had written to Mercer, who encouraged him to take it to Cole, then playing at the Lincoln Theater in Los Angeles that May 1947. This street-corner Yogi master, who lived under one of the *L*'s of the HOLLYWOOD sign, had written "Nature Boy" to a tune he plagiarized from a song by Herman Yablokoff. The ballad told a spiritual story expressing the universal truth of love. When Ahbez showed up at the stage door and succeeded in getting "Nature Boy" into Cole's hand, the singer found what he later characterized as a "Jewish song" that painted the horrors of the Holocaust and the hopes for the founding of Israel. On August 22, 1947, Capitol recorded Nat Cole performing the song and using spoken words "out of tempo," backed up by an orchestra of string and wind instruments. For a second time Petrillo led the American Federation of Musicians out on a strike scheduled to begin with the new year, so Capitol again stockpiled masters, and "Nature Boy" became one of the company's intended releases for the forced lull in recordings. With clear Hebraic overtones, "Nature Boy" soared to first place with its launch on March 29, 1948, during the struggle for Israeli independence. The African American *New York Age* editorialized about the reception given "Nature Boy": "We think it is an important artistic success and we couldn't help beaming with pride — inside — to hear some of the comments: 'That feller, King Cole, he's colored, isn't he?'"[27]

An anecdote about Nat Cole told by Dave Dexter underscores the concern of the executives to maintain positive race relations at Capitol Records. Early in his contract with the label, Cole took offense at artwork publicizing one of the trio's releases. A drawing that appeared in the advertising for a single upset Cole, who burst into Dexter's office yelling, "It's an insult, man. You ought to be as ashamed of it as I am." The image depicted a "black angel" on a poster for record shops to display. Cole thought it looked "like an old-fashioned picka-ninny." While not conceding that point, Dexter agreed it did not look like "a Titian." Dexter explained to Cole: "We employ an old lady up in the hills of Hollywood to illustrate our promotional and advertising material, some woman Wallichs has favored since he first opened a record shop. I agree it's lousy artwork but no racial slight is implied or intended. It won't happen again." After telling Wallichs and Mercer about the incident, "they discontinued Capitol's reliance on the little old lady up in the hills and contracted with a major California advertis-ing agency to handle our growing account on a permanent basis." Cole remained on the Capitol label from his initial contract in 1943 until his death in 1965, selling more singles and albums than any other artist. Dexter observed, "With-out him, I doubt that the company would have thrived and expanded as it did throughout the quarter-century that followed."[28]

With the war over, Johnny Mercer fulfilled his wish to do something for his cousin Walter Rivers by hiring the veteran as the press and public relations manager for Capitol's East Coast office. The returning war hero — a deco-rated marine major later promoted to lieutenant colonel for his role in help-ing to take Saipan, Iwo Jima, and Okinawa — moved with his wife, Cornelia

McIntire, back to New York in January 1946. Both had lived there in the early 1930s, when Walter struggled as a writer and actor and Cornelia studied at the Art Students League, so while he worked at Capitol Records, she opened a gallery on Park Avenue called Portraits Inc. to paint the famous, including Jo Stafford and Johnny Mercer. Johnny arranged for Walter to be Capitol's A&R producer for Cole's "The Christmas Song." In recognition of the title's success, the National Academy of Recording Arts and Sciences later awarded Rivers a Grammy in 1974 for his role as A&R man on Cole's recording. At first the Riverses enjoyed life in Manhattan, attending Broadway shows and museum exhibits. Then, in 1947, they adopted their first son, David. Henceforth being an entertainment executive did not sit well with the forty-one-year-old new father, who often attended recording sessions into the early morning. Criticism of Rivers's leadership at Capitol led him to quit the company and eventually return to Savannah, where Walter took a position with Southern States Container, a corporation co-owned by Cornelia's brother, Jimmie McIntire, that made steel cargo containers later used on George Mercer's Great Dane trailers. When Reynolds Metals purchased the company, the Rivers family — now including a second son, Paul, adopted in 1952 — moved to Birmingham.[29]

The Mercer family expanded in the postwar years, too. Johnny and Ginger adopted a son, John Jefferson Mercer, a few weeks after his birth on April 5, 1947. They used the same agency in Augusta, Georgia, they had contacted in 1940 when adopting their daughter, Georgia Amanda. Now eight, Mandy relished having a little brother. As a child she often accompanied her father to the studios, where he worked while she played around the sets. Amanda recalled, "I don't know what my mother was always doing, but he was always babysitting me." On some occasions he dropped her off at the *Bozo Show* or perhaps the stages at Disney Studios and then picked her up later. As Capitol began producing children's records, Mandy and Jeff grew up listening to the recordings, offering the company president firsthand evaluations by young, avid consumers.[30]

Recognizing an untapped children's market, Capitol hired Alan Livingston in 1946 to develop a line of products. A graduate of the Wharton School of Business and brother of songwriter Jay Livingston, Alan Livingston created a commodity called Bozo the Clown that integrated a picture book cued to a sound recording, with *Bozo at the Circus* the first release. Its success led to additional Bozo records and a television program. Capitol joined with Warner Bros. to produce records by Mel Blanc as Bugs Bunny and other cartoon characters. Livingston helped create Tweety Bird and brought Woody the Woodpecker to the label. Capitol produced popular recordings of fairy tales by child star Margaret O'Brien. It recorded storytelling by radio personalities "Smilin'" Ed McConnell of the *Buster Brown Show* and Harold Peary, better known to listeners as the Great Gildersleeve. Other stars of radio, such as Bob Hope and the characters Fibber McGee and Molly, also signed with Capitol. These recordings, combined with Livingston's marketing sense, soon helped the children's division account for 20 percent of the label's business.[31]

Capitol's release in November 1946 of a set of recordings featuring material from Walt Disney's movie *Song of the South* helped popularize the album format and demonstrated the company's successful marketing strategies. The record producers negotiated with the Disney Company to secure the rights for its original cast album of the animated full-length picture based on the retelling of African American folktales that Joel Chandler Harris attributed to his fictional character Uncle Remus. Advertising the records as consisting of "Original Walt Disney Music" and "Original Walt Disney Dialog" produced by the "Original Walt Disney Cast," Capitol Records compiled *Tales of Uncle Remus for Children*. James Baskett, the African American actor who had played Uncle Remus in the movie, as well as other cast members, including white child stars Bobby Driscol and Luana Patten, provided the narration. With musical accompaniment by Billy May and his orchestra, the original cast joined Johnny Mercer and the Pied Pipers on such vignettes as "Running Away" and "Brer Rabbit and the Tar Baby." Packaged as an attractive three-record album set and illustrated with Disney drawings of Brer Rabbit, Brer Bear, and Brer Fox, *Tales of Uncle Remus for Children* sold well. Capitol selected the album as the inaugural Specialized Promotion in 1946 that linked the company's release of the recordings with the release of the movie in theaters. Livingston arrived at Capitol in time to watch the marketing blitz unfold as the company provided dealers "with complete window displays, local advertising in newspapers and on the radio, give-aways for children, special preview showings of the picture," and other tie-ins that linked Disney, its distribution of the film through RKO, and Capitol in common cause.[32]

Johnny Mercer collaborated on a handful of projects with the Walt Disney Company. For *Tales of Uncle Remus for Children*, he recorded covers of "Zip-a-Dee-Doo-Dah" and "Ev'rybody Has a Laughing Place." Allie Wrubel had written the music and Ray Gilbert the lyrics for the movie, but Johnny liked the songs and made the recordings with Paul Weston, his orchestra, and the Pied Pipers as Capitol release 323 which sat in the top ten on the Billboard charts for eight weeks. When "Zip-a-Dee-Doo-Dah" won a nomination for best original song, Johnny and the Pipers performed the Oscar winner at the Academy Awards Ceremony. In 1947, Mercer recorded another Disney song, "Fun and Fancy Free," composed by Ben Benjamin with lyrics by George David Weiss, for the *Mickey and the Bean Stalk* cartoon. Disney compiled it with other shorts as the feature film animation *Fun and Fancy Free*. Soon Capitol released a dozen Disney products from *Lady and the Tramp* to *So Dear to My Heart* and *The Sorcerer's Apprentice* to the *Story of Robin Hood*. Livingston's success distributing the product line from 1947 to 1949 led to Capitol's proposal to market a subsidiary "Disneyland" label that it owned. Disney responded by ending the arrangement and launching its own subsidiary, the Walt Disney Music Company, with *Cinderella* as its first record release in 1950. After the initial splash, Mercer's involvement with Disney ended, and he only returned to the company on two other occasions for minor projects.[33]

During Capitol's early years Mercer recorded several hits on the label that underscored his infectious joy for life with all its pleasures and pains, which he expressed through music. The line, "My oh my, what a wonderful day!" from "Zip-a-Dee-Doo-Dah" reflected Johnny's attitude caught in the recording studio, a playfulness that can be heard in his voice on "Strip Polka" and "G.I. Jive." Whatever he committed to wax for Capitol, Johnny quickly plugged on the radio and other entertainment outlets as a way to build the company while promoting his career. In 1944, Capitol released its first full album, *Songs by Johnny Mercer*, featuring him singing with Jo Stafford and the Pied Pipers. For the label, Mercer also recorded some of his favorite songs written by others, such as Leon René and Johnny Lange's blues number with its lyrical twist, "I Lost My Sugar in Salt Lake City." Recalling his youth, Mercer made a recording of David G. George's once popular ballad, "Wreck of the Old '97." Johnny sang with Paul Weston and the Pied Pipers, "My Sugar Is So Refined," by Sidney Lippman and Sylvia Dee, and on the reverse the similarly tongue-in-cheek "Ugly Chile (You're Some Pretty Doll)," by Clarence Williams. Other songs he recorded with success for Capitol included "In a Lazy Mood," "Blues in the Night," "Bobwhite," and "The Dixieland Band." He also made an album featuring old standards he loved as a youth, such as "Sweet Georgia Brown," "Lulu's Back in Town," "Button Up Your Overcoat," and "Louisville Lou," which includes patter that sounded like the slang Mercer heard in Savannah. Similarly, on his recording of "The Most Surprised Party Is Me," his spoken dialogue resembled the narratives of the African American comic Nicodemus who appeared regularly on *Jubilee*.[34]

Self-conscious about his singing talent, Mercer carefully picked the songs he recorded, avoiding ballads and often selecting well-known numbers despite company policy that discouraged making covers. Years later, he explained: "Oh, I liked most songs. Because I'm a songwriter I picked a lot of great songs to sing like 'Personality,' which I didn't write"— his friends Jimmy Van Heusen and Johnny Burke had written the song for a Crosby-Hope road picture. Released by Capitol in 1946, Mercer's cover displayed the "pixy" attitude that journalists often ascribed to him, something the public liked as the record soared to number one on *Your Hit Parade*. About "Personality" and his other recordings, Johnny said, "These songs have enough entertainment value in the words so that they don't notice my voice. Or in the case of 'Candy' [also number one on *Your Hit Parade*], it lay just right for my voice. I could manage 'Candy.' The notes were not quite too long. They were just enough. You know?" Johnny admitted that he "must sound terribly introspective on my part. I don't know about the singing. I like to sing for fun. But I mostly like to hear other people sing, who *can* sing."[35]

Revealing his deep religious nature and roots in the Anglican tradition, Johnny arranged for a children's choir from Los Angeles to record Christmas music as the company's second album. The St. Luke's Choristers often performed on movie soundtracks, and the choir's recording of *Seasonal Hymns: Carols and Chorales* hit the top ten nationally. In addition to the sacred holiday music, the company produced singles of holiday novelty tunes by the singer Yogi Yorgesson with the Johnny Duffy Trio performing "I Yust Go Nuts at Christmas" and on the reverse "Yingle Bells."[36]

For Capitol's third album, *New American Jazz*, Johnny invited several of his favorite jazz musicians — some of whom had fallen on hard times — to record as a special studio band in 1944: trombonist Jack Teagarden; drummer Arthur James "Zutty" Singleton; guitarist David Michael "Dave" Barbour; and Barbour's wife, the girl singer Peggy Lee, under the leadership of trumpeter William E. "Billy" May. Having failed yet again at leading his own band, the Swingin' Gates, an unemployed and alcoholic Teagarden watched as his wife filed for divorce. The diaspora entertainer Singleton had grown up playing jazz in New Orleans with Papa Celestin and on Mississippi riverboats before winding up in Los Angeles, where in 1943 he led Dixieland bands and gigs on radio shows. Formerly with big bands, May had also moved to California but when not recording in the studios found himself working on the assembly line of a defense plant. Similarly, Barbour had apprenticed with Wingy Manone and Red Norvo before accompanying such jazz bands as Benny Goodman's, through which he met and married Lee, who then quit singing to be a stay-at-home wife and mother. Now Johnny, assisted by Dave Dexter, brought these and other jazz artists together on Capitol's *New American Jazz*, which created a stir among players and fans of the music.[37]

Just as Johnny had turned to Pops Whiteman to make the first record sold by Capitol, Mercer convinced other jazz band veterans to make pressings for the label. Remembering the joy he felt listening to the Jan Garber Orchestra as a youth, Johnny signed it to record an album called *College Medleys* that featured alma maters and fight songs, which hit the top ten in sales; a second album called *More College Medleys* did equally well. It was Johnny who suggested to the drummer Andy Russell that he make a recording of "Bésame Mucho," which sold half a million copies in 1944. From that year until 1947, Russell produced eight top ten singles for Capitol. Other best-sellers included Alvino Rey and His Orchestra, Billy Butterfield and His Orchestra, Sam Donohue and His Orchestra, and — in 1948 with "A Slow Boat to China" — the reorganized Benny Goodman and His Orchestra.[38]

Peggy Lee emerged as a Capitol star following her return to the studio under Mercer's watchful eye. Originally from North Dakota, she had sung her way to Chicago, where a chance performance before Goodman ignited her career. She had her first hit with his band, "Why Don't You Do Right?" in 1942. Lee had fixed opinions regarding the terms of her comeback, so Mercer accommodated her at Capitol. Few women wrote songs professionally, but having crafted lyrics to fit tunes by her husband, Dave Barbour, Lee wanted to record her own material. Gastel represented them at Capitol, sharing with Mercer two of their songs. Johnny approved, arranging for a session on December 27, 1944, where Peggy sang "What More Can a Woman Do?" and "You Was Right, Baby," backed up by Barbour on guitar and Billy May on trumpet. Neither song displayed "the slightest echo of a canary's big-band chirping," according to Lee's biographer, Peter Richmond, who instead points to Lee's "facility for translating jazz and blues for the masses." Capitol sold 750,000 copies of "You Was Right, Baby," thrusting Lee into the spotlight and making it impossible for her to return to a domestic life.[39]

Peggy Lee shared more of her lyrics with Mercer, who generously suggested criticism. Long a fan of Johnny's catalogue, Lee remembered, "He helped me. He said, 'You have a really good idea there, but I think you should rewrite this, and that.' I tore it up and rewrote it, and it made all the difference." One song she worked on with Mercer, "I Don't Know Enough about You," caught the cool jazz feel just emerging in December 1945 when she recorded it at MacGregor Studios. For nearly five months the song sat in the top ten on *Your Hit Parade*, selling a half million copies. Although privately Peggy struggled with her husband's alcoholism, together they wrote music about the experience that Capitol let them record, including "It's a Good Day" in 1946 and "Mañana (Is Soon Enough for Me)" in 1948, the latter backed up by Carmen Miranda's Brazilian chorus featuring stereotypical views of "lazy" Mexicans and selling 1.5 million copies. Also Johnny got Peggy to sing "Golden Earrings" in 1947, and it sold 2 million records. These last three songs, all written with Barbour, made Peggy Lee *Billboard*'s "Number One Vocalist" in 1948 and sold 4 million records by the end of 1949. From 1945 with "Waitin' for the Train to Come In" to 1949 with "Riders in the Sky," Peggy Lee scored a hit single in the top ten for Capitol every year.[40]

Margaret Whiting saw herself like Peggy Lee and Jo Stafford as "vocal pin-ups" for the servicemen abroad, the "recording equivalents of [Betty] Grable and [Rita] Hayworth," whose pictures adorned the walls of barracks just as these Capitol recordings spun on "phonographs all over the world" spread their messages of love and sounds of home. Also like Lee, Whiting received personal attention from Mercer, whose keen ear paired the artist with the perfect song. Having signed Margaret to the Capitol label in 1942, Johnny invited her to assist him and Paul Weston in searching through material as they waited for the musicians' strike to end. She recalled "a lot of pretty songs. Some wonderful ones." Then one day Johnny invited Margaret to hear Weston play a "flow of chord progressions . . . both sophisticated, and simple and direct. Then I began to listen to the words. They were all picture images. A kind of longing. A warmth." Whiting asked, "What is it" and Mercer replied, "It's your next record." Thus began their work on her best selling single, "Moonlight in Vermont."[41]

Ever the mentor, Mercer walked Whiting through the piece, helping her turn words and notes into magical music. At first Margaret protested, saying she did not understand what "Moonlight in Vermont" meant. "I've never even been there," she said about the state, to which Johnny replied, "Don't worry. I'll go through it with you. Now, what does Vermont mean to you?" She thought of the pictures on calendars: "Lots of snow. Waffles and maple syrup . . . Real villages, church steeples, leaves." Margaret remembered he said, "Now describe spring," as "Johnny led me through the four seasons," as an impressed Paul Weston "sat there and watched." Mercer worked with Whiting on the more difficult lines, "You've got 'pennies in the stream'— that's not literal — that's the wonderful glittering look of metal when sun hits water," but when they reached the line "Ski tows down a mountainside," both drew a blank. "What are ski tows?" Margaret asked, to which Johnny answered, "How do I know? I'm from Savannah." He then called up the songwriters, John M. "Johnny" Blackburn and Karl Suessdorf and asked if the word might be changed to "ski trails." The song took shape under Mercer's coaching: "Somehow . . . I want you to give me the four seasons. Crunchy cold. Then warm. The first smell of spring. Just hit the tone dead sometimes, the way you do, and then add the vibrato at the end. And just think of the images. I trust you, kid." When they went into the recording studio, Margaret remembered "breaking the song into sections, I could feel the sad warmth of fall, the smell of leaves. I began to sing. The band was wonderful. Then, when Billy Butterfield's trumpet came in, all silver and glittering, it changed my voice. We were like two instruments." When she described "Telegraph cables they sing / Down the highway / Travel each bend in the road," she imagined "the width of the entire country, the road going off into infinity." As they listened to the playback someone said, "Oh my God," while "Johnny just nodded his head up and down, up and down, as if to say he knew it all along." Released in 1944, "Moonlight in Vermont" sold 2 million records for Capitol its first year.[42]

In tune with the changes taking place in jazz, Johnny enabled older musicians to make records for Capitol featuring the earlier sounds that he loved. Out of respect and appreciation for their craft and regardless of the commercial potential of the product because of the postwar decline in jazz record sales, Mercer lined up several jazzmen who cut sides on the label. The trombonist Walter "Pee Wee" Hunt — an Ohio native who had played with Jean Goldkette before joining the Casa Loma Band under the director Glen Gray — found himself at the end of the big-band era spinning records as a disc jockey in Hollywood. He got a group together that enjoyed playing New Orleans–style jazz. Johnny heard its tongue-in-cheek send-up of the 1914 "Twelfth Street Rag" and recorded the single that, once released in 1948, helped spawn the Dixieland Band revival. The Chicago guitar and banjo player Albert Edwin "Eddie" Condon, who had performed with Bix Beiderbecke and a variety of bands until running his own club in Greenwich Village from 1945 to 1967, made a 1950 recording of "At the Jazz Band Ball," singing Johnny's lyrics set to the 1918 tune by Original Dixieland Jazz Band members D. J. La Rocca and Larry Shields. The one-armed New Orleans trumpeter Wingy Manone, who had performed with Goodman and Crosby, wrote with Mercer in 1952 "Hello, Out There, Hello," with its playful lyric addressing extraterrestrials: "Though you are a strange and foreign race, / If you are equipped to fly through space, / Pay a little visit to our place." Manone joined Mercer, the Pied Pipers, and Paul Weston and His Orchestra in a recording of his own song "Tuscaloosa

Bus," but it went nowhere. These and other veterans of the earlier Dixieland style enjoyed a brief revival of the hot jazz sound at a moment when the once-popular music evolved out of swing and into bebop.[43]

An anecdote regarding Capitol's recordings of the Coleman Hawkins Quartet on March 2, 1945, reveals both the pleasure Mercer derived from these recording sessions and the divisions tearing jazz apart. At three in the morning Johnny arrived at the studio with a large bottle of whiskey to watch the famed veteran black jazz bandleader, who in biographer John Chilton's words appeared "steady as a rock, bouncing through arrangements and solos with never the slightest suspicion of a falter." A witness noted, "At no time during the seven hours of the session did the Hawk remove the hat which was jammed precariously on the back of his head." A living legend, the Missouri native first performed in Kansas City but migrated to New York City, where he had played with Fletcher Henderson's orchestra from 1924 to 1934. The popular tenor saxophonist accompanied black and white jazzmen alike. For several years he performed in Europe but returned to New York in 1939, conducting an integrated band at Kelly's Stables and other venues. At the end of the war, Hawkins headed a sextet in California, where Capitol recruited him.[44]

While Johnny listened, the man at the controls in the Radio Recorders studio, Dave Dexter, argued with members of Hawkins's quartet over the modernist music. Several upcoming figures of the bebop movement played with Hawk that night: pianist Sir Charles Thompson, drummer Denzil Best, bassist Oscar Pettiford, and trumpeter Howard McGhee. After McGhee spoiled several takes of one number with wrong notes, or "clinkers," Hawkins made him sit out the session. Dexter recalled, "McGhee, I believe, was not drunk [but] was on some kind of narcotics. He was belligerent and uncooperative from the start of the session. He fluffed every bar, and Bean [Hawkins] was embarrassed." With Hawk's approval, Dexter telephoned the veteran white trumpet player Ernest Loring "Red" Nichols, who had played with the California Ramblers and the Five Pennies back in the 1920s, but upon sitting in with the Coleman Hawkins Quartet, proved too out-of-touch to handle the dissonant chords and charged tempos of the head charts. Dexter remembered, "But when we began to record semi-bebop charts Hawkins had made up for the album, Nichols stumbled around on his horn as ineptly as McGhee had earlier. It wasn't Red's kind of music and I should have known that." McGhee recalled, "Hawk had a tune that Red Nichols couldn't play in no kind of way," and so the trumpeter sat there "giggling" at his replacement while Oscar Pettiford laughed. McGhee said, "When we'd gone into the studio, we didn't go into there playing none of that old-time shit." Dexter remembered, "Poor Red couldn't cut that near boppish music, and after a couple of hopeless takes he went home." McGhee rejoined the group and finished the recording. Afterward he "said to Hawk, 'Man, you don't need Dave Dexter, you're Coleman Hawkins.'" The venerable jazzman replied, "'Maggie, you don't understand. This is business.'" In his history of West Coast Jazz, Ted Gioia described the "watered down recordings" for Capitol as a "strange mishmash: McGhee plays in a pure bop style, while Hawkins pursues his own hybrid style, one that revealed a rich harmonic sense, which even the most ardent modernist couldn't fault, but retained a rhythmic feel looking back to the 1930s."[45]

Johnny watched jazz evolve from the popular dance music he loved into an art form that polarized around race and politics. As swing declined in the postwar era, big bands expanded, building progressive music up by adding more and more, while jazz combos proliferated, pruning sound down to its barest essentials. Also Dixieland, or traditional jazz, enjoyed a brief comeback. Louis Armstrong participated in the revival of the old hot New Orleans style, having publicly scorned bebop, while younger musicians improvised along the lines of the modernist trends. In the wake of Glenn Miller's "Moonlight Serenade," jazz bandleaders rearranged the instrumentation to remove all traces of dance music. The larger bands played innovative jazz so complex — and often very fast and loud to showcase the talents of the musician — that it could be heard but not danced to, thereby losing mass appeal. The Harry James Orchestra hitched to this wagon with its recording of the Duke Ellington and Juan Tizol hit "Caravan." The musical culture lost the enjoyment of physical movement, as progressive jazz and bebop became art forms that attracted hipsters who listened intently. By the 1950s, the public turned elsewhere for dance music, ultimately discovering doo-wop and rock 'n' roll. The heightened racial climate of the postwar era contributed to divisions among jazzmen, as bebop became an expression of black cultural empowerment. Critics began rewriting the history of jazz to emphasize African American contributions at the expense of white musicians, who increasingly fell from favor.[46]

Hostility to a jazz culture of drug use and the Red Scare tactics of the Cold War further divided musicians, as reactionaries attacked the music as part of a larger postwar backlash against the New Deal. In the 1930s, jazz had celebrated the seemingly harmless and still legal smoking of marijuana "muggles," or "Mexican cigarettes," from Fats Waller's "Viper's Drag" to Benny Goodman's "Texas

Tea Party" that featured Jack Teagarden, but by the 1940s, heroin had become the drug of choice among jazz musicians, and its use risked addiction and stiff federal penalties. Postwar jazz played against a backdrop of drug busts with the arrests of Billie Holiday, Charlie Parker, and Stan Getz. Because jazz promoted integration and attracted radicals during the Great Depression, Cold Warriors leveled charges of communist sympathies against Artie Shaw, Lena Horne, and Yip Harburg. When the head of MGM Studios asked Johnny Mercer if he was a Communist, the songwriter fired back that the question was an insult to his heritage.[47]

At Capitol, Mercer responded to the postwar changes in a variety of ways. Through promotion of the Nat "King" Cole Trio, he pushed a vocal style of bebop through jazz-infused popular song: the singer accompanied by the spare sounds of the combo. Despite bebop's hostility to the voice, the idiom inspired several Mercer songs, including "My Baby Likes to Bebop," written with Walter Bishop Jr. Johnny joined Nat and the trio on Capitol recordings of this song paired with "You Can't Make Money Dreamin'," while also singing duets with Cole on "Save the Bones for Henry Jones" and "Harmony," all captured in the recording studio in 1947. The most successful bebop vocalist, Ella Fitzgerald, also recorded "My Baby Likes to Bebop." A frequent patron of Los Angeles night-spots, Johnny witnessed the creation of the so-called West Coast jazz by visiting the integrated club Billy Berg's, located near Mercer's office at Capitol Records on Vine Street, which hosted such greats as Billie Holiday, Louis Armstrong, Lester Young, and in December 1945 the New York City high priests of bebop, Charlie Parker and Dizzy Gillespie. Behind them stood Miles Davis, who in early 1949 made a series of landmark recordings for Capitol. Although Johnny preferred the transformation of the big-band sound into progressive jazz, he appreciated bebop too.[48]

Capitol captured on wax some of the most progressive jazz being recorded, such as that performed by Miles Dewey Davis III. A diaspora entertainer and trumpeter like the South Carolinian John Birks "Dizzy" Gillespie, Davis came from metropolitan St. Louis, where he also heard Charlie "Yardbird" Parker perform in 1944. After a stint at Juilliard in New York, Davis traveled with Bird, playing with him and Diz on the famous November 1945 recording of "KoKo." Then Davis joined the Billy Eckstine Orchestra and later the Claude Thornhill Band, but he returned to record with the Charlie Parker Quintet. By the summer of 1948, the black Miles Davis collaborated with the white composer Gil Evans and white baritone sax player Gerry Mulligan on his own experimental compositions, which he performed for two weeks in September 1948 at the Royal Roost Club on Times Square in New York City. Capitol A&R man Pete Rugolo sat in the audience one night with Johnny Mercer's cousin Walter Rivers, who Mercer had hired as an executive for Capitol. Once the musicians' strike ended after union leader Petrillo lifted his second ban against musicians recording in December, the company signed the group to the label. On January 21, 1949, Miles Davis and His Orchestra had the first of three recording sessions that resulted in the 1950 releases of a series of landmark 78s through which the musicians countered the hard bebop of Dizzy and Bird by appealing to the smoother sounds of Claude Thornhill and Duke Ellington. Capitol later combined most of these sides into a twelve-inch album, *Birth of the Cool*, in 1957. Considering the commercial potential of the records, Davis biographer Ian Carr asserts that "Capitol showed courage — even recklessness — in the people they signed. Miles Davis was a young trumpeter whose virtues were not at all easy to spot." In place of the roughly jagged and frenetic, confrontational and antilyrical bebop, came a delicate, introspective, and lighter sound inspired by Lester Young's readings of Bix Beiderbecke and Frankie Trumbauer that epitomized the cool West Coast sound. While Miles Davis and His Orchestra recorded only instrumentals, one selection, the 1944 "Moon Dreams," by composer Chummy MacGregor, originally had a lyric by Johnny Mercer that the songwriter had sung on a previous recording for Capitol. No doubt playing a role in the signing of Davis, Mercer favored this cool jazz as more accessible even if the critics dismissed it as a "watered-down" version.[49]

As bebop and cool jazz grew in popularity, the audience for swing declined, and the orchestras started to dissolve. Some broke up with the deaths of their leaders — Glenn Miller's in 1944 and Jimmie Lunceford's in 1947. The Dorsey brothers merged their outfits in a bid to keep playing but later disbanded, ending up in the same scrapheap as the Casa Loma Band, the Fletcher Henderson Orchestra, and the Bob Crosby Band. Other jazzmen, like Duke Ellington, "kept going in a strange new world of bop that frankly puzzled him," in the words of Dave Dexter. Likewise, Lionel Hampton kept a band together. For a while these groups played before aging audiences across America and Europe, then later toured the world for the U.S. Information Service as cultural ambassadors in the global fight against communism.[50] Still others followed the latest trends such as Count Basie, who broke up his big band and led a combo. Some found something else to do such as Cab Calloway, who acted. Many, like Noble Sissle, simply quit.

A dearth of African American songwriters made collaboration with black composers difficult, yet Mercer managed to write lyrics for several. The jazz vibraphonist Lionel Hampton, whom Johnny had signed with Capitol, provided an instrumental craving words in 1954. Having organized his own band in 1940 with the help of his former boss, Benny Goodman, Hampton toured for the next several decades. With composer Sonny Burke, Hampton fashioned a tune for which Mercer wrote sheer poetry. Johnny heard the instrumental "Midnight Sun" over the radio while driving from Palm Springs to Hollywood and began drafting lyrics in his head during the two-hour trip. To Johnny, the title suggested poetry that offered visuals of fire and ice as descriptions of a former lover. First the song recalls the passion: "Your lips were like a red and ruby chalice, / Warmer than the summer night; / The clouds were like an alabaster palace / Rising to a snowy height; / Each star its own aurora borealis — / Suddenly you held me tight, / I could see the midnight sun." Mulling the title over in his head as he listened to the music, Johnny first thought of "aurora borealis" and then words that rhymed with it, and as he said, "that kind of started the song." The bridge bothered Mercer because he felt the words did not quite fit the tune: "Was there such a night? / It's a thrill / I still don't quite believe, / But after you were gone, / There was still / Some stardust on my sleeve." The closing refrain recalls the spent love: "The flame of it may dwindle to an ember / And the stars forget to shine, / And we may see the meadow in December, / Icy white and crystalline, / But oh, my darling, always I'll remember / When your lips were close to mine / And I saw the midnight sun." Whether sung or played as an instrumental, "Midnight Sun" became one of the great jazz standards of the 1950s.[51]

Having long been a fan, Mercer encouraged Capitol in 1953 to contract with Duke Ellington and His Orchestra, which then included Billy Strayhorn. The first recording session resulted in the instrumental, "Satin Doll," a tune Johnny liked. Ellington had Mercer review three compositions, with the suggestion that he write the lyrics. Two had titles —"Blossom" and "Satin Doll"— while Mercer jokingly referred to the third, untitled song as "Taking the Dayplane" an homage to the composer's big hit "Take the A-Train." Johnny wrote words and published the first two. Ellington's appearance at the Newport Jazz Festival in 1956 ended a slump in the big-band leader's career. Around the same time Charlie Parker and Dizzy Gillespie began using the instrumental "Satin Doll" as a starting point for bebop riffs. Johnny added hip lyrics to the snappy tune, and "Satin Doll" as a vocal took off after its 1958 release. The imagery depicts the femme fatale: "Cigarette holder, / Which wigs me, / Over her shoulder, / She digs me — / Out cattin', / That satin doll." Mercer later modestly said of the lyric: "It might be alright. I think it held the tune back some but you couldn't really hold that tune back. It was what a lyric writer calls a rocking chair song. You just don't have to do any work." In his concerts Ellington introduced "Satin Doll" by saying, "The next song is dedicated to the most beautiful lady here. We will not point her out because we do not want her to feel conspicuous. We will just let her sit there and continue to feel guilty."[52]

During Capitol's early days Mercer signed the bandleader Stan Kenton for a series of recordings typical of the progressive jazz sound. For the rest of the decade Johnny watched the jazzmen follow this particular trajectory to the point of collapse. At first a straight-laced workaholic driven by ambition, Kenton led a band of young musicians like himself, all in their twenties and eager to take jazz to the next level. The big break came in the summer of 1941, when Kenton booked the Rendezvous Ballroom at Balboa in Newport Beach, south of Los Angeles. Teenagers flocked to the resort for the sun and sex and for the sounds coming from the massive auditorium, which could accommodate three thousand patrons on its dance floor and in its surrounding seats. All the big-band orchestras played there — Goodman, Ellington, Lunceford, Shaw, Dorsey, Basie, James — and there Mercer first heard Kenton's band. He watched the six-foot-four-inch bandleader "wildly flailing his long arms, pleading, cajoling, smiling, demanding, and holding the final fermatas for an eternity." Not unlike Savannah Beach at Tybee Island with its Tybrisa dance pavilion, Balboa attracted Johnny with its Rendezvous dance hall, hot music, and youthful audience. Soon the Mercers rented a house on nearby Lido Isle as a summer getaway.[53]

A visionary intent on expanding jazz into a more serious music that fans of classical recordings might like, Kenton clashed with Mercer and other Capitol executives over the progressive style. After the summer gig at the Rendezvous, Kenton's band made a series of recordings in the MacGregor Studios for the Armed Forces Radio Service (AFRS). They returned to MacGregor for the Capitol recordings made in November 1943. Of the four sides, "Do Nothin' Til You Hear from Me," "Harlem Folk Dance," "Production on Theme" (the band's theme song at the time, later retitled "Artistry in Rhythm"), and "Eager Beaver," Mercer favored the last as the most marketable. Kenton struggled against commercialization, running his organization on a shoestring, receiving loans from the likes of Dave Dexter — an early advocate of the group — and through his manager, the "Happy Honduran" Carlos Gastel, landing plum bookings at the Palladium. To resolve the conflict over artistic control, Capitol executives Mercer, Wallichs, and Dexter reached an agreement with Kenton: in return for autonomy during the recording sessions, Stan promised to plug the company and all its artists at every opportunity. True to his word, when interviewed he talked not only about the Stan Kenton Orchestra but also about the other bands and singers on the label. He carried the Capitol product into the towns and cities he played, leaving with the dealers and radio stations records that featured the Kenton band but also Margaret Whiting, Nat "King" Cole, Peggy Lee, Jo Stafford and the Pied Pipers, and Johnny Mercer. As Kenton's biographer, Carol Easton, noted: "Capitol's sales executives, unaware of the deal with Wallichs, marveled at his willingness to go miles out of his way to plug someone else's records and called him their ambassador. And disc jockeys, flattered by his availability (a welcome change from the self-important performers who condescendingly gave them little more than a hard time), knocked themselves out to play his records." Within a few months, Capitol assembled several of the sides in the album *Artistry in Rhythm*.[54]

The Capitol recordings increased the popularity of the Stan Kenton Orchestra. With Johnny briefly at the helm of the *Pepsodent Show* in the summer of 1943, the radio program signed the Stan Kenton Band to a ten-month contract to entertain the troops. By 1944, the white jazz singer Anita O'Day left Gene Krupa's band and through her manager, Gastel, associated with Kenton for a year. During that time the legendary jazz singer made a number of important recordings with the group, including a song favored by Mercer, "Her Tears Flowed Like Wine." O'Day brought one of the label's musicians, the black drummer Jesse Price, to the studio for the May 1944 Capitol recording. She convinced Kenton to allow Price to play on the cut. Later she explained, "I thought it might save the session," and "that was the first time the band ever swang." Kenton's first commercially successful single, "Her Tears Flowed Like Wine" hit fourth on the pop charts and sold more than a million records. Jack Teagarden's protégé Stan Getz, a young, white tenor saxophone player who later gained his own fame in jazz circles, joined the sax section. The growing popularity of Kenton's orchestra encouraged the bandleader to expand the progressive sounds by hiring the arranger Pete Rugolo, who shared his vision of a symphonic jazz called neophonic. Then Kenton's experimentation overreached as his numbers began to sound like movie scores, culminating in *City of Glass*, an ambitious work by composer Bob Graettinger that at its premier in 1948 left the Chicago audience stunned. Falling back on old jazz standards and letting Carlos Gastel book gigs that featured his band but also such clients as Nat "King" Cole, Anita O'Day, and June Christy, Kenton continued to make progressive recordings at Capitol for decades.[55]

As the ballrooms went dark after the war and the jazz bands shifted to playing concerts, Kenton's good friend, Woody Herman, won acclaim for the sound of his "Herd," the tag a journalist gave the musicians who followed the bandleader. At first playing with sweet bands led by Isham Jones and others, Herman had broken out to form his own group, which in 1939 recorded "Woodchopper's Ball" and thereby established its hot reputation. In 1941, he made covers of the Johnny Mercer and Harold Arlen songs, "This Time the Dream's on Me" and "Blues in the Night," for which Woody sang the lyrics. Beginning in 1945, Herman made a series of recordings for Columbia using his "First Herd" of musicians who favored the bebop sounds of Dizzy Gillespie. Then the musicians' strike hit and the Columbia contract expired. Under Mercer's influence as A&R man, Capitol offered Woody a lucrative deal, and the band began recording again in 1948. Reorganizing the band as the "Second Herd," Herman created a new sound using a powerful sax line called the Four Brothers that included the remarkable tenor saxophonist Stan Getz, who had left Kenton's outfit. Having fallen under the influence of Lester Young, Getz played cool jazz and during the group's Capitol recording sessions on December 29 and 30, 1948, demonstrated his talent on "Early Autumn." Getz's biographer, Donald L. Maggin, suggested: "The solo connected powerfully with the romantic fantasies of postwar America and started him on the road to stardom." The difficult composition of the instrumental "Early Autumn" as sketched out by Herman, developed by his arranger Ralph Burns, and given an inspired improvisation by Getz, became a runaway hit.[56]

As with a couple of Mercer's postwar successes, the jazz music stood as an instrumental before the songwriter added the popular lyric. Herman had left Capitol Records at the end of his two-year contract but then met difficulties recording; because sales of big-band sounds had declined, the big labels such as Columbia pushed a new pop sound. Woody joined with record producer Howie Richmond on an independent label. Richmond wanted the band to record "Early Autumn," but Herman said, "I'd like to get a lyric. Maybe Johnny Mercer might do it." Richmond asked the songwriter, who then explained he had loved the instrumental so much that he had already written a lyric. Burns polished the song to vocalize the melody to which Mercer set his poetry. In 1952, the Richmond Organization published the music that Woody sang on its initial recording. Later, Johnny remarked about the wistful imagery, "I think it's one of my best lyrics." He added, "Not a big hit, but you can't tell the public what they like — they usually pick the right ones." Biographer Gene Lees understood the song portrayed "the mood of men coming home from the war to find the world they knew all changed." That idea comes across at the bridge, when Mercer writes: "That spring of ours that started / So April-hearted / Seemed made for just a boy and girl. / I never dreamed, did you? / Any fall could come in view / So early, early." No doubt Johnny related the loss of the swing music he loved to the dilapidated image of a site he once enjoyed, for the sadness in the beautiful lines comes across clearly as they recall Tybrisa: "There's a dance pavilion in the rain, / All shuttered down." Mercer had provided the epitaph for the swing era.[57]

Just as jazz changed in the postwar era, so too did western swing. Having mastered the production of popular music infused with jazz, Capitol began making country and western music more accessible as pop song. As with Tex Ritter's blended sound on the label's 1942 recordings, performers Johnny had recruited during the company's early years now joined together as crossover artists. The southern diaspora entertainer Jimmy Wakely, a native of Arkansas and refugee of Oklahoma who had moved to California and starred in western movies, had signed with the label in 1946 to front a string band singing ballads. Wakely joined Mercer's protégée Margaret Whiting on a number of critically acclaimed and commercially successful singles in 1949. The duets, "Slipping Around" paired with "Wedding Bells" followed by "I'll Never Slip Around Again" and "Let's Go to Church Next Sunday Morning," played on the ever-popular country theme of marital fidelity. For a while Whiting and Wakely performed together at the Ryman Auditorium in Nashville and appeared on the cover of *Billboard*. To shed his hillbilly image and reach "the upper echelon," as he called it, Wakely also recorded for Capitol with the Nelson Riddle Orchestra.[58]

Ernest Jennings "Tennessee Ernie" Ford combined contemporary rhythm and blues with country and western to create a sound that portended the rock 'n' roll revolution. While training as a singer, the Bristol, Tennessee, native spun records at stations in his hometown, in Knoxville and Atlanta, and then in California, where he later joined the cast of Cliffie Stone's popular country music program. Like Stone he soon signed a contract with Capitol Records. His harder edge gained him fame, but he adopted a softer image and recorded the crossover hit "I'll Never Be Free" with Kay Starr in 1950. Like Wakely, Ford also performed with orchestras. For years he hosted a popular television variety program, *The Ford Show*, on which Johnny Mercer appeared. In Los Angeles, with its large, local audience of southern diaspora consumers, Capitol Records made the West Coast country scene a rival of Nashville's and demonstrated the success of the crossover music. As Jeffrey Lance, a scholar of the subject, notes, "California country recorded by Capitol often bore little resemblance to country music produced east of the continental divide; instead, it more readily bore the imprints of sophistication and musical experimentation and less emphasis on lyrical quality and evocative vocals." To emphasize the difference with the Nashville sound, Lance concludes, "Closer to mainstream pop and western swing than to honky-tonk or the music of the progressives, postwar California country was more light-hearted and spirited than heavy-handed and spiritual." As a consequence, the country and western music helped push Capitol's record sales to new heights. Considering the blended sound of pop and country, it is hard not to see Johnny Mercer's fingerprints on the crossover successes of such performers as Tennessee Ernie Ford and Jimmy Wakely.[59]

In some cases the artists placed Capitol Records on the cutting edge of technology. Experimenting with multiple tape recordings and electric instruments, guitarists — and Johnny's friends — Les Paul and Mary Ford made groundbreaking masters that once pressed into discs sold six million records for Capitol in 1951. As a result, Capitol became the first recording company to use magnetic tape. Les Paul's friend Leo Fender introduced him to inventor Paul Bigsby, and the two men discussed the electrification of the guitar. Les Paul suggested to Paul Bigsby that a telephone receiver might work to pick up the sounds. Paul Bigsby tinkered with the idea and later brought Les Paul the first solid-body electric guitar. Les Paul then shared the innovation with Capitol recording artist Merle Travis, who later made the instrument famous. Aware of the breakthrough, Johnny Mercer bought one of Paul Bigsby's prototype instruments to send to his boyhood friend (and stowaway coconspirator) Dick Hancock back in Savannah.[60]

The only one of the big four headquartered on the West Coast, Capitol Records not only tapped some of the best talent in America but also took advantage of technological advances in the entertainment industry. During the war, it had addressed the shortage of record players by producing its own line of turntables and needles, and it had pioneered in the use of magnetic tape. Initially caught behind in the "war of the speeds," Capitol overcame its shortcomings to emerge as the first company to issue records at all three speeds: the original 78 RPM, the single 45 RPM, and the long-playing 33 ⅓ RPM. Indeed, the upstart record company quickly took the lead on innovation in the industry.[61]

The unprecedented success at Capitol tarnished its luster for the creative Johnny Mercer, who disliked administrative duties and increasingly left the paperwork to others. He responded to the growing demands by deferring to the simpatico Wallichs, whose attention to detail better suited the running of a business. Indeed, the talents of both men had made the company a success. Like Johnny, Wallichs had recognized the potential of children's records and steered the company into those waters while also picking up a classical catalogue featuring the Hollywood String Quartet and the Pittsburgh Symphony Orchestra under conductor Fritz Reiner. After five years at the helm, Mercer recognized the business had expanded beyond his reach and stepped down as president on September 10, 1947, so that the board of directors could approve as the new president Glenn Wallichs, the man who had been doing the job while serving as vice president and general manager. At the same time because of his failing health, Buddy DeSylva resigned as chairman of the board. While no longer officers of the corporation both DeSylva and Mercer remained active board directors who, along with Wallichs, owned seventy percent of the company stock. Nevertheless it proved a bittersweet moment as Johnny privately resented his loss of control over something he had created that had simply grown too big for his inattention. Proud of his success and still a major shareholder in the enterprise, Mercer wanted Capitol Records to flourish. He explained the changes to the media: "Now that Capitol has grown so large, I found that the office of president requires more time than I am able to give it. I am working on a new musical among other things and must give more time to writing music. Wallichs has recently carried most of the duties of president and we all felt he deserved recognition for it." Johnny attributed much of the company's success to the man: "I don't know if anybody knows what a genius Glenn Wallichs is, not only at organization and hard work, but at picking and handling men."[62]

With Capitol Records' new management in place, Mercer dropped his regular routine of stopping by the corporate headquarters. Capitol moved into larger space with a sleek international design at 1507 Vine Street closer to the intersection with Sunset Boulevard. The ultramodern interior boasted a "stairway for the stars" lined with photographs of the company's leading black and white performers. On the second floor, Wallichs provided Mercer with an air-conditioned office paneled in bleached walnut and a staff to facilitate his A&R efforts. Yet with the reduction in administrative duties, Johnny kept irregular hours and pursued other interests. While he continued to promote artists for Capitol contracts and to suggest repertoire they might sing on the recordings, he did so with less frequency. Dave Dexter, then Capitol's public relations director, recalled about the songwriter's disengagement that after DeSylva's death from a heart attack in July 1950, "Johnny Mercer disappeared. There were no farewell parties, no ceremonies, no nothing. The founder and former president who had accomplished so much on Capitol's behalf in its early days simply walked away from our Sunset-and-Vine executive offices and never came back." An anecdote suggests that Mercer arrived one morning to be asked by a perky new receptionist if he had an appointment. Dexter reflected on Mercer: "He was an inspirational boss who never, to my knowledge, pulled rank with employees." As Johnny later told him, Capitol "suddenly got too big. It wasn't fun anymore." For a quarter century after Mercer's departure, Dexter continued working for Capitol, "all the time deploring Mercer's absence and watching a covey of lawyers and Ivy League business majors take over the company's direction."[63]

Everything seemed to change in postwar America for Johnny Mercer. As he approached middle age, the songwriter recognized that the transformation in society wrought by the global conflict played out in the entertainment world, too. The jazz that for twenty years had colored his life and inspired his music no longer resonated with the public. Still, he followed its trajectory out of swing and into progressive jazz and bebop, as evident in his songwriting. A decline in production of what critics call the classic Hollywood musical that had captivated audiences throughout the Great Depression and World War II had left Mercer at odds with the studios that needed less of his services. Sensing these shifts in popular culture, Johnny turned his attentions back to his earlier fascination with musical theater. By relinquishing the administrative demands at Capitol Records to Wallichs and eight years later selling his share in the company, he simply confirmed his determination to succeed on Broadway. As Mercer could not suppress his creative songwriting impulse, in place of the jazz he once harnessed for inspiration he turned outward, reinterpreting foreign music for American consumption as transnational song.

Against the fast-paced life of the record company executive, Mercer struggled to maintain his role as a family man by marking the milestones that passed. In 1951, he recognized twenty years of marriage to his wife by writing the lyric "Here's to My Lady" to a tune by Rube Bloom. Just as Wagner had surprised his wife, Cosima, with "Siegfried Idyll," Johnny surprised Ginger on the night of their twentieth wedding anniversary by arranging for a band to perform "Here's to My Lady" while they were out at a club dancing: "Though the years may grow colder / As people grow older, / It's shoulder to shoulder / We'll be," he admits, "But be it sunshine or shady, / Here's my love to my lady. / I pray, / May she always love me." He managed to top that gift by using money from the sale of Capitol Records to pay for their twenty-fifth wedding anniversary celebration in 1956. Johnny had intended to rent the ballroom of the Hotel Bel-Air, but afraid of how its staff might treat his black friends, he talked with restaurateur Mike Romanoff instead, who guaranteed him equal treatment for all his guests at Romanoff's. Assured there would be no problem, Mercer rented out the entire famous restaurant located on Rodeo Drive for the black-tie affair. His business associate, Barbara Robbins, described the twenty-fifth anniversary as a "sensational party. Everybody was there." The Mercers had invited their friends from the movie studios, such as Bob and Dolores Hope, and from the recording studios, such as Nat and Maria Cole. Referring to his African American guests, Robbins recognized Johnny's sensitivity to racism: "He went out of his way to make sure they were accepted." For entertainment, Mercer hired Nelson Riddle and His Orchestra to perform the music behind a progression of singers all performing the Mercer numbers they had made famous. Helen O'Connell sang "Tangerine" and Judy Garland performed "The Atchison, Topeka, and the Santa Fe." Calling it "the most spectacular party I've ever been to," family handyman Robert Rush remembered, "Everybody that was anybody was there, and with this orchestra and the entertainment, I mean you had a half million dollars' worth of entertainment, just coming from all of these people that loved Johnny and had done his songs."[64]

In January 1955, the multinational corporation Electric and Musical Industries Ltd. (EMI) of Great Britain bought Capitol Records. In addition to its highly lucrative domestic market, Capitol also claimed a successful international division. The purchase marked the first global consolidation in the U.S. record industry. The three founders of the company — Johnny Mercer, Glenn Wallichs, and the estate of George G. "Buddy" DeSylva — sold their original 248,435 shares of common stock to EMI for $17.50 each, some $4.50 above the market price per share. Also, EMI bought an additional two-thirds of the remaining 476,230 outstanding shares of Capitol stock. The total capitalization for the deal ran $8.5 million. The sale required the founders to relinquish all shares of stock and dissolve any affiliation with the company, although Wallichs remained as president and general manager of EMI's new Capitol subsidiary. The death of DeSylva had led to the decision to sell. DeSylva's widow wanted her inheritance in cash, and Wallichs agreed to the idea of consolidation with EMI.[65]

Only Mercer wanted to retain control of the company, but he capitulated to the wishes of the others. "I didn't want to sell," Mercer told a reporter. "I liked the idea of keeping the company for our children." Despite being largely absent from Capitol the previous few years as a result of his activities on Broadway, Mercer had retained a proprietary interest in the business. The year before, Capitol had begun constructing near the intersection of Sunset and Vine in Hollywood its iconic stacked-records tower. At the time, Johnny wrote his mother, "Capitol is building a great big office building out here, and they had a luncheon for Glenn Wallichs, who with the enthusiastic young men who work there is responsible primarily. Walter might be interested. He and I accounted for at least a few bricks, as it were." Years later, writing Cornelia McIntire Rivers, Johnny reflected on the sale: "I'se sorry, honey, I wasn't big enough to swing holding on to Capitol Records; once Buddy DeSylva died there just didn't seem to be anybody on my side, and the Europeans were drooling at the mouth to buy it. I did try not to sell — but was out-numbered, though not out-gamed. Who knows, life might have been different for us all." His share of the sale price totaled about $1.5 million. Now a wealthy man thanks to his brilliant success at picking talent as a record company executive, Mercer generously used some of the proceeds of the sale to benefit his family and friends while searching for opportunities to fulfill the remaining ambition that drove his life.[66]

7 Broadway

· ·

There's no business like show business
A Wise man was heard to say.

HAVING PROVEN HIMSELF as a jazz musician, in the recording industry, and in Tinsel Town, Johnny Mercer wanted validation on the Great White Way and spent much of his time after the war creating Broadway shows. The jazz scene in which he had consistently intersected with the leading performers had faded from view while the number of Hollywood musicals steadily declined, so he turned his attention to writing romantic comedies. The musical theater had seduced him on his first visit to New York City. He placed his first song in a revue initiated by Rodgers and Hart, and he wrote his first — and some of his last — lyrics for the stage. Tin Pan Alley considered the New York theater world the hallmark of success, so achieving a box-office smash secured one's reputation as an exceptional lyricist or composer. Mercer aspired to this fame. From his days as a child studying the *Student Prince* and other happy-ending operettas to his tutorial in the Depression-era song and dance numbers, he apprenticed in a make-believe world that offered its audience a pleasant escape from the problems of everyday life. Johnny never veered from the formula of positive entertainment that righted society's wrongs and found love along the way. Having taken that leap into the modern world, Mercer retained a Victorian faith in a natural order set in motion by a supreme being that held to a vision of the sinfulness of man made whole through redemption, beliefs that appeared in the lyrics of his Broadway songs.

Written with Harold Arlen and produced in 1946, *St. Louis Woman* became Mercer's first postwar effort and contained some of his best songs for the musical theater. The producer and head of MGM's musical division, Arthur Freed, persuaded Mercer and Arlen to join Ed Gross in a theatrical production by promising to sign up MGM artists Lena Horne and the Nicholas Brothers, with whom Mercer had collaborated on Lew Leslie's *Blackbirds*. Freed wanted a successful

Broadway show that he could then recycle into a Hollywood musical. He offered the Broadway play *God Sends Sunday*, which Harlem Renaissance writers Countee Cullen and Arna Bontemps had created from a book by Bontemps. Gross had retained the African American authors to revise the script for the musical, which would feature an all-black cast. In pairing the black authors up with the white songwriters, Freed arranged the first significant interracial collaboration on Broadway. Once Mercer and Arlen set to their task, they recognized the major problem with the book — a weak plot. Halfway through, the story falls apart, a shortcoming that existed in the original Bontemps manuscript. Previously on Broadway the music often allowed such weaknesses in a plot to be overlooked, but ever since 1943, when *Oklahoma!* fused song and dance with story, audiences demanded that book musicals be strong throughout, with lyrics advancing character development and storyline. The authors never resolved the problem with Bontemps's book, but other obstacles hurt the effort, too.[1]

The war years forever changed the musical theater, not only by redesigning the book, as evidenced by *Oklahoma!*, but also by altering the content. Where once all-black revues had been a staple of New York's entertainment industry with their stock characters depicting the gambler and the fast woman, the defeat of fascism abroad had emboldened a protest movement at home in opposition to stereotypical images of African Americans in popular culture. The National Association for the Advancement of Colored People (NAACP) had launched boycotts of shows it determined demeaning, and soon its executive director, Walter White, a native of Georgia, decried what he saw as negative stereotyping in the proposed musical, *St. Louis Woman*. He had not complained a decade before when the same script as the play *God Sends Sunday* ran on Broadway, but this time he denounced the Mercer-Arlen musical as "sordid" because it "pictured Negroes as pimps, prostitutes, and gamblers with no redeeming characteristics." White reacted in part to the protests of Savannah native Fredericka "Fredi" Washington, a modestly successful star of stage and screen who resented the lead role of Della Green going to Horne and not her. Set at a St. Louis racetrack and in a tavern managed by Biglow Brown, played by Rex Ingram, the story followed the fortunes of the principals as they worked out conflicting love interests, the foremost being Biglow's betrayal of two women, Della and Lila, played by June Hawkins. Harold Nicholas played the lead role of the jockey Augie, who was attracted to Della; his brother, Fayard Nicholas, played the jockey Barney, who was sweet on the comic character Butterfly, played by Pearl Bailey. Others in the cast included Juanita Hall, who later gained fame as *South Pacific*'s Bloody Mary.

Similar settings and characters had appeared in such movies as *Stormy Weather* and such shows as *Porgy and Bess*.[2]

From NAACP headquarters, an imperious White marshaled civil rights forces in the Urban League and Interracial Film and Radio Guild to join his campaign against *St. Louis Woman,* and soon Horne received hate mail calling her a "harlot" for taking on the role of Della. Enamored of White — whom she knew from family ties in Atlanta — and the NAACP, Horne withdrew from the cast and joined in the protest, claiming the show "sets the Negro back 100 years, is full of gamblers, no-goods, etc. — and I'd never play a part like that!" Of course, Horne had already played similar roles, such as Georgia Brown in Freed's 1943 film for MGM, *Cabin in the Sky*. In it a naked Lena had lounged in a bubble bath as the seductive mistress of Lucifer before being sent to tempt a gambler in a nightclub. Having long looked for the right vehicle to promote his star attraction, Freed found Della perfect for Horne because it featured great singing with little acting. In an attempt to prevent any criticism, Freed had sent the *St. Louis Woman* script to White, unintentionally fanning the flames. Actually Horne wanted to play the part specifically written for her by Mercer and Arlen and hoped that Freed would make it into a film. She enjoyed acting with her friends Ingram, who had played Lucifer against her Georgia Brown, and the Nicholas brothers, who had starred with her in *Blackbirds of 1939*, where she broke onto Broadway singing Mercer's music and receiving praise from critics. Since then she had performed many Mercer standards, even introducing on radio "One for My Baby (and One More for the Road)." Meeting privately with Freed, a crying Lena explained she'd "love to do the part" but that "it looks like I'll have to give it up." So, Ruby Hill played Della instead. In response to the boycott, *Variety* condemned Walter White, who "has set himself up as a czar of Negro entertainment who wants his imprimatur on every role assumed by a Negro actor." Likewise, Bailey defended the production and criticized those who objected to the characters. Noting that the plot "has nothing to do with the weightier problems of our day," its author, Bontemps, defended his representation of 1890s black life around a racetrack as historically accurate and implored, "It is a love story." Yet the problematic book, conflicts over which actress would play Della, and the controversy stirred up by White doomed the show.[3]

Despite the beautiful music and lyrics by Arlen and Mercer, *St. Louis Woman* remained cursed. Cullen's untimely death on January 9, 1946, left Bontemps struggling to revise the book on his own. To salvage the show the producers brought in the director Rouben Mamoulian, whose credits included *Oklahoma!*

and the successful revival of *Porgy and Bess*. He rearranged parts, dropped songs, and added new material in a long, three-act production that worked better than before but still failed to jell. On March 30, 1946, the show opened in Broadway's Martin Beck Theatre, competing with a revival of *Carmen Jones* — Oscar Hammerstein II's all-black treatment of Bizet's opera — and Irving Berlin's *Annie Get Your Gun*. The curtain rises on Della in a tavern confessing to Augie, "Any Place I Hang My Hat Is Home," while Butterfly sings to Barney the show-stopper, "Legalize My Name." Betrayed by Biglow, who has revealed his affections for her rival, Della, Lila sings "I Had Myself a True Love." The act closes on the rousing "Cakewalk Your Lady." In act 2 Della and Augie swear devotion in "Come Rain or Come Shine." Cursed by Biglow, Augie begins losing races and then loses Della while the barkeep's former lover, the jealous Lila, kills Biglow and sings "Sleep Peaceful, Mr. Used-to-Be," followed by the chorus performing the mournful "Leavin' Time." Act 3 opens at the racetrack with Butterfly explaining "A Woman's Prerogative." With his luck turned, Augie — now winning races — wins back Della and sings "Ridin' on the Moon." Although "Come Rain or Come Shine" reached *Your Hit Parade*, weak reviews greeted the show's opening, and after 113 performances *St. Louis Woman* closed.[4]

Proud of his accomplishment, Johnny arranged a cast recording for Capitol, one of the first full-length Broadway scores ever undertaken by a record company. As long-playing records remained two years in the future, the company released the recordings on shellac 78-RPM disks. From April 7 to 9, 1946, the original cast gathered for the recording of the show's music. With the dialogue and cumbersome plot removed, the songs stood out like gems. From Lila's heartfelt, "Now I ain't got no love / And once upon a time / I had a true love," to Butterfly's suggestive "Though his bank shows a big balance / And he seems heaven-designed, / If the boy's short on his talents, / It's a woman's prerogative to change her mind," to Augie's infectious "Old Jinx had me cornered, / But I found out when to shake it, / And my true love helped me break it — / Now I'm ridin' on the moon," Johnny's lyrics sparkled with originality while developing character and advancing plot. Arlen's compositions proved to be the best Mercer ever worked with for the musical stage, but unlike Augie, Johnny never shook off the bad luck that jinxed his Broadway efforts. Once released, the cast recording of *St. Louis Woman* gathered the respect of critics, who appreciated the quality of the music. Capitol's record set quickly became a collector's item and was reissued in 1993 on compact disc. After the curtain fell on the show, Arlen's orchestrations disappeared, and the various instrumental parts have never resurfaced. Attempted revivals either proved disastrous or simply failed to materialize. The director Robert Breen, who had great success with *Porgy and Bess*, took *St. Louis Woman* and by interpolating other songs into the score revised it for Paris as *Blues Opera* in 1955; that effort failed, so in 1959 Breen revisited *St. Louis Woman* and assisted by African American arranger and composer Quincy Jones staged *Free and Easy*, first in Amsterdam before abruptly folding in Paris in January 1960, leaving the cast and crew stranded. For years Freed tried unsuccessfully to arrange a filming of *St. Louis Woman* using such actors as Sammy Davis Jr. and Diahann Carroll. Describing the score as "glorious," Lena forever regretted her decision according to Horne biographer, James Gavin, who said she blamed the NAACP and the Urban League for blocking her from "doing an all black musical" that had been written for her. Nevertheless she made Della's "Come Rain or Come Shine" one of her signature pieces. With the show over, Mercer and Arlen departed as friends, both determined to strike Broadway gold with other collaborators.[5]

As the country demilitarized in the immediate postwar years, the Armed Forces Radio Service (AFRS) continued to broadcast shows that included the occasional performance by Mercer as entertainment for troops occupying Europe and Asia. Some wartime programs such as *Command Performance USA!*, *Personal Album*, *G.I. Journal*, and *G.I. Jive* persisted in peacetime. The AFRS picked up other programs produced by the networks and broadcast them to the troops. On April 27, 1946, Johnny joined Joan Edwards on *Your Hit Parade* to sing the new duet "Oh, What It Seemed to Be" by Bennie Benjamin, George Weiss, and Frankie Carle. Johnny appeared on the *Nat "King" Cole Trio* network show that the AFRS picked up and broadcast on August 30, 1947. Indeed, Mercer's music found a steady outlet via the radio on the networks and such AFRS originals as *Phonograph Album*, which featured his songs for the length of one day's fifteen-minute show, or on *Remember*, a program on which screen stars played the tunes of yesteryear, as when Robert Young spun platters of Johnny's music and reminisced. Mercer regularly appeared across the spectrum of the entertainment industry, from radio shows to Capitol releases to songs produced for the movie studios and musical theater, thereby remaining one of the country's leading entertainers.[6]

Having enjoyed hosting *The Johnny Mercer Chesterfield Music Shop* in 1944, the songwriter took a breather from Broadway to return to the airwaves in 1948 on *Call for Music*, sponsored by the Philip Morris Tobacco Company. As a thirty-minute weekly program, *Call for Music* featured other southern diaspora entertainers performing popular songs fused with jazz. Johnny co-hosted with fellow

Whiteman alumna Dinah Shore from Nashville, Tennessee, as Albany, Georgia, native Harry James and his orchestra provided the background music for their solos and duets. All three had regularly appeared on such World War II radio programs as *Command Performance USA!*[7]

Producers tweaked the show's format over its half-year existence to make the material more appealing. A typical program began with Shore, Mercer, and James playing an arrangement of a hit song, such as "Put 'em in a Box," "Mañana," or "Bride and Groom Polka." Then each artist individually sang a number. Philip Morris bracketed the show's opening and closing with its advertising image of the bellboy selling cigarettes in the lobby by having Johnny Roventini sing out in a high-pitched and perfect B flat with an annoying twang, "Call for Philip Moooooooorreeeeees." The announcer Jack Rourke read commercials at both ends and in the middle of the show that often extolled the brand as being recommended by "imminent nose and throat specialists" for fighting "cigarette hangover" and sore throats. At first Philip Morris mimicked competitor Lucky Strike's *Your Hit Parade* by using its own formula for picking the nation's most popular songs as the public's "call for music." The program tried Broadway medleys performed as solos, duets, and instrumentals by the trio of stars. By the end of its run, *Call for Music* simply presented the stars enjoying the popular songs of the day.[8]

During the war, recordings by the three performers had topped the charts. For her part, Shore delivered on ballads such as "I'll Be Seeing You," "Spring Is Here," and "Nature Boy," while also carrying fast-paced standards such as "Brazil," "Little White Lies," and "Hooray for Love." On various programs the Jewish Shore wished everyone a Happy Easter, broke out in a jazzy rendition of "Dixie," and appealed movingly for listeners to help flood victims by donating to the Red Cross. The breadth of her performance augured her future on television as a popular hostess of variety programs from *The Dinah Shore Chevy Show* (1950–54), to *The Dinah Shore Show* (1954–62), to *Dinah's Place* (1970–74), to *Dinah!* (1974–80) to cable prior to her death in 1994.[9]

Harry James used *Call for Music* to promote progressive jazz. Weekly he demonstrated the wall of sound produced by his powerful orchestra. James cranked out fast-paced and complex arrangements of such Duke Ellington tunes as "Take the A-Train" and "Cottontail," prompting Shore to quip, "Harry James, no fair, you've been practicing!" The band masterfully executed such high-octane pieces as "February Has 28," with its shrill trumpet solo by James and the equally aggressive improvisation by the Puerto Rican valve trombonist Juan Tizol. In introducing the piece James said, "I've got something here that's as modern as tomorrow." Dinah countered, "They tell me it's the new look in music," to which Harry responded, "We call it the new listen." The scripted dialogue suggested an awareness that progressive jazz was losing its mass audience because it demanded too much from the listener. About James's role on the show, the drummer Buddy Combine recalled, "It was amazing. Harry would read from his script since he had a running part in the show. Then he would conduct the band with one hand, and he would never miss a beat while playing the trumpet with the other hand."[10]

As co-host for *Call for Music*, Johnny Mercer performed a variety of songs. On most shows he sang one of the novelty numbers he enjoyed writing as "pure invention," such as "Veronica," about the harmonica-playing beauty on the pier at Santa Monica, or he sang one he favored such as Bob Hilliard and Carl Sigman's "Thousand Island Song," about the man who left his girl on an island but forgot which one, with Johnny weaving in references to Tybee. Although he rarely sang his own songs, Johnny performed an early favorite that he wrote with Charles Bates called "On the Nodaway Road," which reflected the influence of Hoagy Carmichael's "Washboard Blues." Occasionally Johnny sang a beautiful ballad, such as "My Gal Is Mine Once More," written by his friends, the lyricist Howard Dietz and the composer Arthur Schwartz, for the new Broadway show *Inside USA*. Johnny's pleasure at singing show tunes comes across clearly in his duets with Dinah on a medley of songs from Irving Berlin's *Annie Get Your Gun* on a March 1948 broadcast and in other segments on Broadway. On another occasion the entertainers performed old standards, with Shore singing Stephen Foster's "Oh, Susanna," James playing "Sleepy Time Down South," and Johnny cutting up with "Shortnin' Bread." After Shore delivered the first refrain of "Wait 'till the Sun Shines, Nellie" with its call for chastity, Johnny jumps in promoting promiscuity by telling Nellie not to wait but to enjoy life instead: "go and get a big umbrella then go out and catch a fella." Certainly the performers gave that impression week after week.[11]

Unkind critiques of *Call for Music* undercut the program's potential. In his syndicated review, music critic John Crosby castigated James who, as the husband of pinup Betty Grable, caught "tiresome jokes" about being the beauty queen's spouse. Reflecting on the shifting tides of musical tastes, Crosby criticized Shore's southern accent as being "as thick as magnolia." He saved his worst invective for Mercer; while recognizing that Johnny sang "second only to Bing Crosby as a master of rhythm," the critic ridiculed Mercer's voice, "if you can call it that," as "foggy, hollow, casual and extremely self-assured." Similar negative evaluations hurt the show. To be sure, the program could come off a bit hackneyed, and on occasion the music sounded uneven in its distribution among the three artists. First broadcast in the prime time CBS slot of 10:00 p.m. on Fridays, then moved by NBC to 8:00 p.m. on Tuesdays. *Call for Music* went off the air on August 10, 1948, after only a few months. Perhaps a fatigued public desired to move away from the sounds of progressive jazz and beyond such popular stars of wartime as Shore, Mercer, and James. For Johnny the cancellation convinced him to concentrate his efforts on Broadway.[12]

For his next attempt at a musical production, Johnny collaborated with a fellow songwriter from Hollywood, Robert Emmett Dolan. Born in Hartford, Connecticut, in 1906 of Irish ancestry, Dolan had worked on the West Coast about as long as Mercer. The men had met at Paramount while putting together *Star Spangled Rhythm*. Later Dolan headed the music department at MGM when the studio dominated the Hollywood musical, scoring such movies as *The Bells of St. Mary's*. The two had written songs together, including "Cinderella," in 1947, before embarking on a major Broadway undertaking. In his autobiography Johnny complimented Bobby's talents as a composer and suggested that the best of the three shows he wrote with him — *Messer Marco Polo* — had yet to be performed. Perhaps Johnny's early days in the theater acting in Eugene O'Neill's *Marco's Millions* with its similar setting inspired him to tackle the subject of the Venetian's visit to China as a love story between the trader Marco Polo and Tao-Tuen, or "Golden Bells," from the court of the great Kubla Khan. Songs from the score include "The Sad Little Rain of China," "Golden Bells," and "The Best Love of All." In "The Human Race Is Human after All" Mercer comically dismisses racism: "Almost every single fellow, / Be he brown or red or yellow, / Or as multicolored as a Spanish shawl, / When he's first put up for shipment, / Each receives the same equipment, / So the human race is human after all." While he favored the songs, the show never got staged. Yet a previous effort called *Texas, Li'l Darlin'* did make it to the Great White Way.[13]

Apparently audiences in the Truman era of Cold War politics found *Texas, Li'l Darlin'* "too conventional." The book, written by John Whedon and Sam Moore, radio scriptwriters known for the popular broadcast *The Great Gildersleeve*, follows an old-time Texas politician confronting the postwar "G.I. revolt." The actor cast in the lead role of Senator Hominy Smith, Kenny Delmar, had worked vaudeville and developed the character Senator Beauregard Claghorn on Fred Allen's radio show, a voice recalled today as copied by Mel Blanc for the rooster Foghorn Leghorn in Warner Bros. cartoons. Another veteran vaudevillian and well-known actor of the stage, Loring Smith, played the role of news magazine editor Harvey Small. Hominy's daughter, Dallas Smith, played by Mary Hatcher (and later Betty Jane Watson), provides the love interest in the story falling for the returning serviceman and political challenger Easy Jones, played by the young tenor Danny Scholl. Much of the humor derives from the age-old tensions between rural and urban folk, in this case southerners versus the northeastern establishment as represented by Boston publisher Brewster Ames II, played by Fredd Wayne. The producer Lawrence Langner picked newcomers despite a frustrated Johnny's desire for bigger names. Mercer later lamented: "I think it should have been called *Ride 'em Cowboy* and should have starred Jack Oakie and Dorothy Shay," the former a successful country tenor and the latter more popularly known as the Hillbilly of Fifth Avenue. The show opened on November 25, 1949, in the Mark Hellinger Theater against blockbusters *Kiss Me Kate* by Cole Porter and *South Pacific* by Rodgers and Hammerstein.[14]

The song that introduces Senator Hominy Smith suggests the localized nature of southern politics. In "Texas, Li'l Darlin'," Hominy sings the praises of the Lone Star State and the attitude of distinctiveness felt by its residents. When he asks in his political speech, "Where do you good folks expect to go / When this vale of tears is o'er?" the crowd chants back: "Texas!" The title song, performed by Hominy Smith and the ensemble, is a paean to the Lone Star State: "I gaze across the prairie / From under my sombrery / And I'm in love with everything I see. / Texas, li'l darlin', / I know y'boundaries by heart. / Like Messrs. Rand McNally / I know each hill and valley, / That is to say, / I know the ones they've had the time to chart." In explaining his love for this "State of States," Hominy solicits their votes. Just to be sure he wins, Hominy steals them too, thereby securing his "rule of the rustics." No doubt Mercer — who frequently visited family and friends in Savannah — marveled over Georgia Governor Gene Talmadge's ability to appear like a good-natured rube while stealing money and elections. Yet the racism that infected the campaigns of the demagogic Talmadge or that of the Dixiecrats in 1948 did not appear in Mercer's lyrics. Rather Johnny has Hominy Smith claim to be "the champion of the downtrodden, both rich and poor alike." Yet some of those "downtrodden" voiced their frustration with the senator — who had promised them houses he never built and now, having fought the enemies abroad, returned home to fight the enemies of honest government. Before the war, Easy had dated the senator's daughter Dallas, but as he explains in "The Big Movie Show in the Sky," service in the Pacific changed his life. Structured like a revival hymn, the song features an unusual sixteen-bar chorus with refrain sung by the ensemble that critics described as having an antiquated feel similar to

Depression-era musicals. "When your final chip is cashed / And the Pearly Gates swing wide, / And there is old Saint Peter / Askin' you to come inside," Easy sings, with the ensemble answering, "Bye and bye, bye and bye, / Can you look yourself in the eye, / When you come on the screen up yonder, / At the Big Movie Show in the Sky?" About Judgment Day, Easy warns: "So, pardner, better mend y' fence / And tend to your corral / And don't go trespassin' / With the other feller's gal. / Be sure you do some actin' / Of which later you'll be proud — / 'Cause that's one movin'-picture show / Where retakes ain't allowed!"

As the political campaign heats up, Hominy finds an ally in *Trend* magazine editor Small — a thinly veiled caricature of *Time* magazine's Henry R. Luce — who has descended on the Texas backwoods in search of a savior for the Republican Party. Realizing he could do business with the corrupt Hominy, Editor Small identifies Senator Smith as the perfect candidate to groom for president. The two express this cynical understanding in the show-stopping duet "Politics." The lyric reveals Mercer's talent for repartee as the two singers engage in witty retorts and quick responses. President Harry S. Truman gets razzed for his piano playing and gutting of the White House during its restoration while reference is made to administration scandals. Characterized by the line, "the people choose a man who's good at politics," Mercer's lyric offers a humorous and rather harmless putdown of postwar American government: "If you can raise the flag and wav'er, / Never grant a favor, / Smile and tell 'em maybe, / Always kiss the baby," Hominy sings, adding, "If you can please the big employers / And the workers' lawyers, / Keep 'em busy fightin' / While the fish are bitin', / Don't improve conditions, / 'cept for politicians, / Then demand a little fee — why You're in politics!"

The senator's daughter Dallas has gone east to try acting but returns back south, singing, "They Talk a Different Language," which she introduces in a duet with Hominy, backed up by the "Three Coyotes" sung by the Texas Rhythm Boys. Dallas observes about New York: "It was s'doggone crowded, / I felt s'hemmed in there, / I come back home to Texas / To get a breath of air." Once back home in Texas she renews her relationship with the returning veteran Easy in a duet called "A Month of Sundays," but the campaign creates distance between the lovers just as a rival appears in the form of the Boston Brahmin Brewster. With "Take a Crank Letter," Mercer develops the playboy character of the *Trend* owner by having his secretaries at the publishing house sing: "Oh, he makes you feel as cozy as he can — / 'Never mind the chair, just sit on that divan.' / A 'Please take a letter — no, take off that sweater — now isn't that better?' —

type man." A phrase in an article Johnny read in *Time* magazine suggested the title for "Affable Balding Me," a duet in which "Back Bay" Brewster hits on "hourglass-figured" Dallas. The show ends with Easy winning Dallas and the two joined by Hominy singing "It's Great to Be Alive." The idea for this song occurred to Johnny while writing a letter to his mother, for he thought of father-hood with the lines "It's great to be in love, / To have a roof above, / To watch the little ones arrive, / Your own descendants — / Deductible dependents, / — It's great to be alive." Although no single song stands out from the score, the lyrics for several are quite clever and point to an abiding sense of place. *Texas, Li'l Darlin'* had a respectable run of 221 performances, but Mercer maintained that bigger stars in the cast could have pushed it over the top.[15]

Creating a Broadway show kept Mercer in New York for weeks on end, and as fate had it on several occasions he renewed his relationship with Judy Garland. The happiness she had experienced when filming *The Harvey Girls* in 1946 had dissipated, with MGM firing her over conflicts with studio officials and fellow stars, followed by her first suicide attempt in 1950. Alienated from her mother, Ethel, and distanced from her homosexual husband, Vincente Minnelli, Garland reached out to male friends. Against the backdrop of MGM's *Summer Stock*, Garland evaluated her options, looking for performance opportunities in New York. One night Judy entered the Golden Key, a lounge in Manhattan, where by chance Johnny Mercer sat at the piano, singing. When he saw Garland, he began performing her hit recordings. She soon joined him and "sang her heart out" until dawn. She had been accompanied by Michael Sidney "Sid" Luft, a manager of minor movie stars, and although they left together, she failed to meet him the next day as promised.[16]

Attempting to rebuild her career, Garland appeared on Bing Crosby's and Bob Hope's radio and television variety shows, which kept her before the public. Un-fortunately, news in the spring of 1951 of her divorce proceedings from Minnelli also kept her name in the tabloids. Meanwhile, Luft (whom she would marry that June), as her manager, created a revival of vaudeville routines for her. He sold it to the Palladium in London, after which it traveled across Great Britain before returning to the United States. Booking her in New York's classic but rundown vaudeville theater, the Palace, Luft intended the show to be Garland's big comeback. Despite her innate talent, which garnered critical acclaim, Gar-land suffered from insecurity. Her accompanist, Hugh Martin, suggested to their mutual friend Jean Bach that "Judy is as nervous as a cat about this opening. And I thought if you would get together a few friends who were simpatico, and just have a relaxed evening and a little music, it'll get her grooving again and she can do a little singing and get back into the thing of live performing." Bach agreed to host the event, a cocktail party, at her Charles Street brownstone in Greenwich Village on October 16, 1951, the night before the opening at the Palace. The guest list of New York notables from the entertainment industry included Johnny Mercer. Judy arrived without Sid. Bach had invited pianist Stan Freeman to play, and when he began Cole Porter's obscure "I Happen to Like New York," Johnny and Judy gravitated to the piano to sing: "Every time I go away, off the beaten tracks, / I live only for the day when I know I'm back." According to Bach, after the party ended the two lovers spent the rest of that warm night together in each other's arms under the stars on the backyard terrace. The next morning the Bachs heard the front door slam as Johnny left with Judy in her waiting limousine. That opening night the little Gumm girl did not disappoint, and her "miracle" comeback performance at the Palace lasted into 1952.[17]

After Johnny's death, the discovery of his unpublished lyric for "When October Goes" offers a heartbreaking peek into his affair with Judy. The song opens with the contrast of the cold of winter against the warmth of fall, "And when October goes / the snow begins to fly," and moves to the view from the terrace, "Above the smokey roofs / I watch the planes go by." Then Johnny recalls the reverie: "The same old dream appears, / And you are in my arms / To share the happy years. / I turn my head away / To hide the helpless tears — / Oh, how I hate to see October go!" He ends with a pathetic confession: "I should be over it now, I know; / It doesn't matter much / How old I grow — / I hate to see October go!" To Jean Bach, who knew of Johnny's earlier relationship with Judy, the October night suggested "a remembrance of things past." Certainly this and similar meetings fed Johnny's and Judy's sexual appetites as they "gathered lip-rouge where they may," but it seems for Johnny there remained something much deeper at heart. Others dismiss such notions. Referring to Judy Garland, Johnny's daughter Mandy noted, "He'd forget about her when she wasn't around," and then said, "The song is about growing old. It is that simple."[18]

The former vaudevillian Phil Silvers shared a close friendship with both Johnny and Judy, having recently co-starred with Garland in *Summer Stock* and having cajoled Mercer into his next attempt for the Broadway stage. Two weeks after Garland had revived her fortunes and those of the Palace, Silvers headlined *Top Banana* as it opened on November 1, 1951, in the Winter Garden. Mercer wrote both the words and music of the score, and the plot centered on a television show, ironically the very medium that a changing Broadway competed against.

As the lead in the show exclaims, "Television is a wonderful invention. . . . You can reach millions of people — but they can't reach you." Increasingly, live theater struggled to survive in a feast or famine cycle whereby productions became either blockbusters — like the previous season's *The King and I* by Richard Rodgers and Oscar Hammerstein II and *Guys and Dolls* by Frank Loesser — or busts. Only nine new musicals opened the fall 1951 season, the lowest number in more than fifty years, and a fickle public cared for none of them.[19]

As a vehicle for the vaudeville antics of Phil Silvers, the burlesque plot of *Top Banana* existed to drive his humorous skits and to link them with Mercer's musical numbers. Indeed, over the previous few years Silvers had convinced everybody — Johnny, the producers, the financiers, the writers — to create the show specifically for him. Mercer had enough confidence in his own abilities as a composer — having had "Dream" as a number one song on *Your Hit Parade* — to accept the project. Developing a character modeled on Milton Berle and his televised *Texaco Star Theatre*, Silvers played the clown Jerry Biffle, while comedienne Rose Marie played his assistant, Betty Dillon. The action takes place on the set of Biffle's television show and in a department store. Told by the sponsor Blendo Soap to develop a love interest or be canceled, Biffle discovers that the girl introduced for the part, Sally, played by Judy Lynn, has fallen instead for the show's crooner, Cliff, played by Lindy Doherty. With a generous spirit, Biffle helps Sally win Cliff's heart. While Biffle and his ensemble of clowns sing a variety of numbers, including "The Man of the Year This Week," "O.K. for TV," and "A Dog Is a Man's Best Friend," the better songs feature Biffle in duets with Betty, such as "A Word a Day." Also titled "Ambiguous Means I Love You," the song, like so many others by Mercer, demonstrates his love of the English language. The lyric calls out a word then follows with an inaccurate definition, such as "emphasize," "When you try a suit to see if it fits"; then "homily," "in the South, they eat a lot of it — grits"; then "euphonious," "That's an instrument Hungarians pick"; then "anecdote"; "If you're poisoned, take it quick." In "I Fought Every Step of the Way," Betty sets up her solo as a boxing match in Madison Square Garden that describes a date: "While I played hard to make / For propriety's sake / He was makin' his play. / I won't say that his hands were busy — / Let's just use the word 'ricochet.'" After Cliff croons, "You're So Beautiful That," he joins Sally in the duet "Only If You're in Love." When they see the young lovers, the sponsors relent and Biffle stays on the air.[20]

Unlike the Rodgers and Hammerstein model of the modern musical, in which song and story blend into a majestic theatrical performance such as *The King and*

I, which enjoyed an initial run of 1,246 performances after its March 1951 opening, *Top Banana*, according to its critics, lacked integration between songs and skits, much like 1920s-era musical comedies. With Mercer's characteristic optimism, the number "Top Banana" presented a romantic view of the theater world. The title referred to achieving the lead comedian slot in a burlesque show with its vaudevillian chorus of "If you wanna be the top banana, / You gotta start at the bottom of the bunch." The book by Hy Kraft proved too weak to land a big success, although Silvers received a Tony for his efforts. The show ran for a year at the Winter Garden Theatre, but the 350 performances did not generate enough income to pay off the initial backers. Running contemporaneously with *Top Banana*, Alan Jay Lerner and Frederick Loewe's *Paint Your Wagon*, which had opened November 12, suffered a similar fate, lasting only 289 performances and losing money. Two months later, the revival of Rodgers and Hart's *Pal Joey* with its unredemptive storyline of a no-good scoundrel swept the box office as a postwar public registered its preference for cynicism. To be fair, *Top Banana*'s subject matter did not suit the symphonic sounds of *The King and I* with its numerous hits such as "Shall We Dance," but it also lacked a single outstanding song such as "They Call the Wind Maria" from *Paint Your Wagon*, a surprising outcome given Mercer's talents as a songwriter, and a problem that plagued his other musicals.[21]

Leaving the lukewarm reception of Broadway, Mercer returned to the Hollywood studios where he hit gold time and again. Already Warner Bros. had recycled his music, taking songs he wrote with Harry Warren for a 1934 film and interpolating them in the 1949 *My Dream Is Yours*. Ending his nearly three-year absence writing for the movies, Johnny freelanced, picking up opportunities as they presented themselves. He wrote with Leon René and Al Jarvis the title song for Columbia's *Make Believe Ballroom*. With Sammy Cahn, he wrote "Clink Your Glasses" for Milton Berle's movie *Always Leave Them Laughing*, which also featured Bert Lahr. For the comic actor Danny Kaye, Johnny wrote lyrics with Kaye's wife, Sylvia Fine, for *The Inspector General*, a Warner Bros. picture based on the 1834 Russian classic of bureaucratic ineptitude by Nikolay Gogol. In 1950 Johnny collaborated with Harold Arlen on Columbia's *The Pretty Girl*, writing "Ah Loves You," among other songs. That year Arlen and Mercer's "That Old Black Magic" reappeared in Columbia's *When You're Smiling*. Also in 1950, Mercer and Whiting's hit, "Too Marvelous for Words," appeared in *Young Man with a Horn*, the fictionalized biopic of Bix Beiderbecke starring Kirk Douglas, with trumpet solos dubbed by Harry James. Hoagy Carmichael narrated the soundtrack, which overviewed the Great American Songs written by Johnny's friends but not the ones made famous by the cornet player, for most of the songs in the film appeared after Beiderbecke's death in 1931. [22]

At the start of his career, Johnny had appeared on film, and while he regularly performed on radio and then television, he never returned to the medium of movies, but since then stuck to writing while his friend Hoagy Carmichael increasingly starred in Hollywood productions. During the war, Carmichael got cast as a piano player in the 1944 Warner Bros. picture *To Have and Have Not*, with storyline by Ernest Hemingway and script by William Faulkner. The movie introduced the actress Lauren Bacall and starred Humphrey Bogart. In one scene Hoagy plays the piano as Bacall sings to Bogart the Carmichael-Mercer collaboration "How Little We Know." While director Howard Hawks considered using a sixteen-year-old Andy Williams's dubbing as the vocals, he decided on Bacall's voice instead for the final cut: "Who knows why an April breeze / Never remains? / Why stars in the trees / Hide when it rains? / Love comes along / Casting a spell — / Will it sing you a song? / Will it say a farewell? / Who can tell!" In 1949, Paramount hired Mercer and Carmichael to write music for a Betty Hutton project called "The Keystone Girl" based on the heroine who starred in *The Perils of Pauline* and other silent films. Although the movie remained unmade, Johnny and Hoagy wrote several funny songs for it, including the absurd "He's Dead, but He Won't Lie Down," as well as two love ballads, "I Guess It Was You All the Time" and "Any Similarity (Is Just Coincidental)." Carmichael's biographer, the jazz trumpeter Richard Sudhalter, observes that the last title "is a song of considerable charm, which performers in search of overlooked Carmichael-Mercer gems might do well to explore." [23]

While working on the Hutton project, Carmichael drove down to Mercer's Palm Springs house, where upon his arrival, he told a dirty joke that ultimately provided the gist for their shared Oscar. In 1950, Johnny had purchased a southwestern-style house at 282 Camino Carmelita in the secluded Palm Canyon Mesa section tucked away among the rocky hillsides that stretched into the desert beside the San Jacinto Mountains. One of the earlier houses in the Hollywood colony, the stuccoed white modernist structure sat beside a pool enclosed within a low retaining wall that contoured into the landscape. Beneath a large Tomayo painting of a watermelon, the Mercers entertained the Crosbys, Hopes, Barrymores, Bushkins, and others when they participated in progressive suppers. The guests traveled from house to house to eat a variety of courses that made up a varied meal, perhaps the inspiration for the verse: "Sue wants a barbeque, / Sam wants to boil a ham, / Grace votes for bouillabaisse stew." Cast as a story,

Hoagy's joke begins with the king of the jungle throwing a party that everyone attends except the jackass. When the lion sends an emissary to inquire why, the jackass responds, "In the cool, cool, cool of the evening I'll be there." The theme fit the surroundings of Palm Springs, where Mercer turned the joke into a lyric that Carmichael set to music. The wordplay of the various verses revealed Mercer's debt not only to W. S. Gilbert but also to that other great Victorian master of the English language, Edward Lear: "'Whee!' said the bumblebee, / 'Let's have a jubilee!' / 'When?' said the prairie hen, 'Soon?' / 'Shore!' said the dinosaur. / 'Where?' said the grizzly bear, 'Under the light of the moon?' / 'How 'bout ya, Brother Jackass?' / Ev'ryone gaily cried, / 'You comin' to the fracas?' / Over his specs he sighed." Soon the two had a song but not a movie. A producer recalled the demo when assisting Frank Capra on a project and, once tweaked a bit, "In the Cool, Cool, Cool of the Evening" became the theme for Paramount's *Here Comes the Groom*. Bing Crosby and Jane Wyman's energetic performance helped the duet win the Academy Award for Best Song in 1951. With this, his second, Johnny delivered on his promise to Hoagy that the two could land the prize, and they walked up together to receive their Oscars.[24]

Back in Hollywood, MGM hired Mercer to help with the few musicals still being made. Arthur Freed chose as his subject *The Belle of New York*, a turn-of-the-century musical that after closing in 1897 on Broadway became the first American show to succeed on London's West End. In place of the Hugh Morton and Gustave Kerker score, Freed hired Johnny Mercer and Harry Warren to set to music the story of a committed playboy caught by a Salvation Army–like urban mission girl. Five years before, the songwriting team had broken up over a misunderstanding when Warren read a Capitol Records promotional poster announcing "Mercer's *Atchison, Topeka, and the Santa Fe*" to be a slight because it had not mentioned him as the composer, when in reality it advertised the release of Johnny singing what became his most popular single. A spiteful Warren refused to speak to Mercer until around the time they started work on this project. With its lush settings and special effects, the movie took a half-year to film. The show starred Fred Astaire dancing with Vera-Ellen on a skyline of clouds to "Seeing's Believing." In the choreographed number "Thank You Mr. Currier, Thank You Mr. Ives," changing background scenery evoked the famous etchings of the four seasons by the nineteenth-century artists. Anita Ellis dubbed Vera-Ellen singing "Baby Doll," which briefly broke out as a pop tune. Johnny handcrafted for Astaire the song "I Wanna Be a Dancing Man," which captured the essence of the entertainer: "Gonna leave my footsteps on the sands of time . . . Least until the tide comes in." Also for MGM, Mercer wrote with Johnny Green "Derry Down Dilly" for *Everything I Have Is Yours*, which starred the dance team Marge and Gower Champion. With composer Arthur Schwartz, Johnny scored the 1953 film *Dangerous when Wet* starring swimmer Esther Williams with guest "appearances" of the cartoon characters Tom and Jerry. Songs such as "I Got Out of Bed on the Right Side" and "In My Wildest Dreams" enlivened the plot: Williams's character swimming the English Channel.[25]

Other studios hired the freelancing Mercer, too. For Columbia Pictures, Johnny joined Harold Arlen in writing "Fancy Free" and other songs for *The Pretty Girl* in 1950. Paramount took "I Guess It Was You All the Time," one of the songs Johnny originally wrote with Hoagy Carmichael for the shelved Betty Hutton project, *The Perils of Pauline*, and incorporated it into *Those Redheads from Seattle*. The film critic Clive Hirschhorn described the movie as "a 3-D musical with 2-D characters and a 1-D plot." The film included music by Jay Livingston and Ray Evans, a songwriting team that Mercer had mentored and that won acclaim for "Mona Lisa," among other songs. Also for Paramount Pictures, Johnny wrote with Robert Emmett Dolan the songs for Bob Hope and Hedy Lamarr's *My Favorite Spy* in 1951. For Universal International, Mercer contributed a new version of "Glow Worm" to *Walking My Baby Back Home*. For United Artists, Mercer assisted in the adaptation of *Top Banana* when the studio captured on film a performance in New York's Winter Garden Theatre.[26]

The busy songwriter had long juggled his professional career with his personal life, remaining in the same modest residence in Hollywood until a proposed freeway convinced him to move in 1954. For nearly twenty years the Mercers had lived in the small Cape Cod–style house just off the strip at 8218 De Longpre Avenue, adjacent to Beverly Hills but distant enough from studio life. With each addition to the family Johnny had added on rooms, but state plans to build a connector through the neighborhood convinced the Mercers and their neighbor director Billy Wilder to sell their land. Mercer gave his house to his secretary, who had it cut in half and moved to Long Beach. California never built the freeway, so developers constructed multistory apartments on the site. Ginger wanted a house commensurate with Mercer's status as one of the country's foremost songwriters custom-built in the swanky neighborhood of Bel Air, but her desire would remain unfulfilled for the next five years. Instead, the family moved into a big summer home on Lido Isle in Newport Beach. The Mercers hired local decorator Robert "Bobby" Rush to renovate, and he remained the family handyman for the next forty years. A teenager at the time, Mandy remembered that 108 Via Karon sat three houses up from the pier that stretched out toward the Pacific Ocean. "Mother was just furious," she recalled about the move. "She couldn't believe it" and "was so mad." The house sat just across the bay from Balboa, where a decade before Johnny had heard Stan Kenton playing the new progressive jazz at the Rendezvous Ballroom. The Mercers remained on Lido Isle throughout the children's school years as Johnny, Mandy, and Jeff escaped the pressures of celebrity status by relaxing in the laid-back beach community.[27]

On Lido Isle the Mercers made friends with neighbors Polly and Matt Ober, who lived around the corner at 328 Via Piazza Lido. Ginger and Polly volunteered together at the local hospital and participated in various fund-raisers that often involved Johnny's contribution as a celebrity. Although he had little in common with the decorated Korean War marine, Johnny and Matt became friends too. Both families had sons about the same age, with Mike Ober and Jeff Mercer becoming "blood brothers" and best friends. Johnny took Jeff and Mike to scouting events and to watch football and baseball games, especially when the Dodgers played. "Uncle Johnny" enjoyed all the neighborhood kids, driving them down to the beach in his old car or around the island in a golf cart, taking them to games, the circus, or movies. Locals dubbed him the Pied Piper of Lido Isle. An avid swimmer and boater, Mercer particularly liked to float in the water using a big truck-tire inner tube and wearing a straw hat. The coastal atmosphere of Newport Beach reminded Johnny of Savannah Beach, as the California surf echoed the waves crashing on Tybee.[28]

Like his Savannah ancestors before him, Mercer turned to religion for help in living an honorable life as he struggled with alcohol addiction. St. James Episcopal Church occupied a corner near his house on Lido Isle, and Mercer regularly stepped in to attend services, often alone. On some occasions he stopped by to pray, even when walking home from a night out with the Obers. At other times when on the way home after attending a party and reaching St. James he would remark to Polly, "No, I don't think we ought to go in, Poll. I don't feel like I belong in a church." She understood his unrestrained drinking had provoked the sentiment.[29]

Alcohol addiction had long troubled the Mercers, a problem brought home by an accident that resulted from the new commute that the move to Newport Beach entailed. At 2:00 a.m. on September 23, 1954, while coming down the off-ramp from the freeway, Johnny crashed into two other cars at the intersection of Imperial Highway and Pioneer Boulevard in the Norwalk subdivision of Los Angeles. California highway patrolmen took the forty-four-year-old Mercer in for a blood test and then gave him a 502, the citation for driving under the influence of alcohol. At first unwilling to admit he was drunk, Mercer entered a plea of not guilty, which would then necessitate what would likely be a humiliating public trial. He had circumvented previous citations, but this time the publicity of the accident prevented such an outcome and eventually convinced him to admit his guilt at the hearing. Newspapers ran his arrest photo under the headline "Johnny Mercer is fined $200 for drunk driving." His reputation besmirched by the shame of the conviction, Mercer determined to regain the honor lost. Because his job still required his commute into the city several days a week, Johnny recruited others to chauffeur him to Hollywood during the six-month probation, including the handyman Bobby Rush and his neighbor, Matt Ober. When Ober died suddenly in 1965, Mercer stepped in as a surrogate father of sorts for his son, Mike. Later the Mercers rented a townhouse on Sixth Street near Fairfax in the Prudential Building so that they might entertain in Hollywood. The conviction for drunk driving had taught Johnny a lesson, as is apparent in his revised lyric for a *Bing Crosby Christmas Special*: "Glow, little glow worm, it's the season / for joy and love — and even reason. / So whether leaving or arriving, / Don't have a drink while you are driving. / Should you be forced to wet your whistle, / Be not an airborne flying missile, / Just nestle 'neath the mistletoe / 'N' glow, little glow worm, glow."[30]

Giving work a rest, Johnny arranged a major vacation for his family. In June 1954, he took his wife and children to Hawaii as a present to Mandy on her middle-school graduation. Like the other Americans who imagined the "isles of golden dreams," the Mercers experienced the beauty of the atolls firsthand. They stayed at the Halekulani Hotel on Waikiki Beach. As a youth in the 1920s, Johnny loved the "Hawaiian" music then popular and played a ukulele, causing one to wonder why he did not return from Hawaii filled with musical ideas that found fruition in song. Similarly, Mercer sent his sister, Juliana Keith, a check so that she could "get away" from Savannah, and he mailed money to cover the expense of his niece Nancy's fees for summer camp, noting, "It's one of the few things I always wanted to do but never got a chance to, but then Vernon View more than made up for it. There was always so much doing there with the boys and all the kids my age." Shortly thereafter his mother, Julie, and Nancy moved out of the house at 226 East Gwinnett Street that had been their home for thirty years and into a smaller house at 110 East Forty-ninth Street. Two years passed before Johnny took his family to visit these relatives and other friends in Savannah.[31]

In one of the last great original Hollywood musicals, Mercer wrote the lyrics for MGM's *Seven Brides for Seven Brothers*, which won the 1954 Oscar for Best Picture. The studio paired him with jazz arranger-composer Gene De Paul, a native New Yorker who had written for Johnny and Capitol Records the hits "Cow Cow Boogie" and "Mister Five by Five" and who later wrote the theme music for *Sesame Street*. *Seven Brides for Seven Brothers* follows Stephen Vincent Benet's short story, "The Sobbin' Women," which relocates the Roman myth of "The Rape of the Sabine Women" to the Oregon frontier. Backwoodsman Adam Pontipee, played by Howard Keel, takes a wife, Milly, played by Jane Powell, and encourages his six brothers to do likewise. After hearing the ancient story, the brothers start singing "Sobbin' Women," with its lines: "Seems they cried and kissed, and kissed and cried, all over that Roman countryside." Having met nice girls from town, the boys decide to kidnap their brides-to-be, barely making it back before an avalanche blocks the passage to their isolated cabin, leaving them snowed in for the winter. One wag described the movie as "man tames woman." Indeed, Michael Kidd's testosterone-charged choreography in the riotous barn-raising scene provided for "the most vigorously acrobatic dance routine ever filmed," according to Clive Hirschhorn. Rather than the violence of the Roman myth, the brothers woo their conquests into subjection. Sexual energy provides a tautness to "Lonesome Polecat," with its bebop sound, beat-like poetry, and stylized ballet. From the outset with Adam's masculine "Bless Yore Beautiful Hide" to Milly's exuberant "Wonderful, Wonderful Day" and the brothers' and brides' exhilarating "Spring, Spring, Spring," Johnny integrates the characters into the storyline. Critics described the music as "happy" and the lyrics as "sassy." Had it been written for Broadway with the dancing constrained for the musical stage, perhaps Johnny would have won his coveted Tony, for thirty years later when revised and mounted at the Alvin Theater, *Seven Brides for Seven Brothers* received a nomination for Outstanding Original Score in 1982–83.[32]

Mercer enjoyed another Hollywood success with *Daddy Long Legs* in 1955. When Fred Astaire signed with 20th Century Fox to do the picture for Darryl Zanuck, he requested Johnny Mercer to write the score. The original 1912 novel by Jean Webster had already been made into a play and two films telling the story of a wealthy American patron, played by Astaire, who anonymously sponsors a beautiful French orphan, played by the waiflike Leslie Caron, only to fall in love with her. Mercer composed both the music and the lyrics with the most celebrated contribution being "Something's Gotta Give," which earned an Oscar nomination for Best Song in 1955. The lines fit the mature dancer and helped rationalize the differences in ages between the co-stars: "When an irresistible force / Such as you, / Meets an old immovable object / Like me, / You can bet as sure as you live, / Something's gotta give." Other numbers include "C-A-T Spells Cat" and "Sluefoot," which Astaire uses to introduce a new dance routine that moviegoers can try at home. Interpolated into the film is the Pied Piper's recording of Johnny's "Dream." One scene has Astaire, ever the playboy, banging away on a drum set explaining "The History of the Beat," which allows Mercer to recount the story of jazz: "And scholars professorial / Began to dig the beat. / They dug back in the archives / To when ragtime had its fling, / Through Sugarfoot and Dixieland, / When people shook that thing. / They tried to trace its progress / From the cotton fields away; / They analyzed it, / Categorized it / To the present day." Between cymbal crashes and drum rolls, Astaire works through jitterbug to swing, bounce to bop. Perhaps not the greatest of lyrics, nevertheless the rhythm singer had provided the rhythm dancer with melodies he could literally perform, and in return Astaire once again demonstrated what Mercer called "hit insurance."[33]

With fewer full Hollywood musicals to write, Mercer provided occasional songs — some old, some new — for studio productions that included musical numbers. Warner Bros. reused Mercer and Arlen's "One for My Baby" in its 1955 *Young at Heart*, a remake of its 1938 *Four Daughters*. When Universal-International decided to make *The Benny Goodman Story*, it signed on Mercer and Matty Malneck's "Goody Goody," which the clarinetist had made famous. Columbia paired Johnny Mercer with Gene De Paul to provide songs for a 1956 remake of the 1934 comedy *It Happened One Night* called *You Can't Run Away from It*, starring June Allyson and Jack Lemmon. In addition to the title song and "Temporarily," the collaborators wrote "Howdy Friends and Neighbors" and "Thumbing a Ride." Yet the weak musicals reflected the changing times, as did the 1956 Hollywood debut of the recording phenomenon Elvis Presley in *Love Me Tender*.[34]

Again Broadway beckoned. Tapping the formula used successfully in *Seven Brides for Seven Brothers*, the producers of *Li'l Abner* hired the still-hot team of Johnny Mercer and Gene De Paul to write the score and choreographer Michael Kidd to create the dances for the book musical by Norman Panama and Mel Frank. The story derived from a newspaper comic strip drawn by Al Capp that featured hillbilly characters in outrageous situations reflecting stereotypical views of southern mountain folk. For nearly a decade various collaborators — such as Alan Jay Lerner and Joshua Logan — had attempted to shape a Broadway show out of the concept. Mercer found that with this production, unlike many of his theater experiences, he had "a lot of fun getting it together." He complimented Capp, who had "a great gift for puncturing the foibles of everyday life" and told the *New York Times* that he "enjoyed knowing him and working with him." Revisiting *Li'l Abner* years later, Johnny recalled about Panama and Frank that "for a lyric writer it was the happiest kind of experience, as they handed me a list of 'suggestions' for song titles and ideas that was voluminous. They must have been voracious followers of the comic strip, and phrases, expressions and 'Capp-isms' were sprinkled throughout their list, plus many original ideas."[35]

The storyline follows Dogpatch, the fictional settlement in the southern mountains, and a subplot follows the town's relationship with the federal government. The two acts trace Li'l Abner, played by Peter Palmer, as he attempts to remain single despite the efforts of three women, his local sweetheart Daisy Mae, played by Edith Adams, the beautiful Stupefyin' Jones, played by Julie Newmar, and the minx Appassionata Von Climax, played by Tina Louise. While the carefree occupants of Dogpatch speculate over which woman will catch Abner on Sadie Hawkins Day — the annual opportunity every November 15 when the tables turn and women propose to men — federal officials select Dogpatch as "the most useless community in America" and therefore an ideal target on which to test an A-bomb. (The plot of *The Simpsons Movie* turned on a notion similar to Capp's, that the government might condemn a community such as Springfield as "the most unnecessary place in the whole U.S.A." and therefore worthy of destruction.) No doubt the plot struck at Mercer's heart, for just up river from his hometown, the federal government had removed an entire community called Ellington, South Carolina, to make way for the atomic–weapons producing Savannah River Site. Yet once the military realizes the potential value of the Kickapoo Joy Juice that turns Li'l Abner into a super hunk is made from yokumberries found only in Dogpatch, the village is spared annihilation.[36]

Critics praised the lyrics. The duet between Abner and his sweetheart, Daisy, "Namely You," had already begun plying the airwaves as a single, but their other duet, the gem "(You Can Tell when There's) Love in a Home," and most of the other songs remained wedded to the show. With the exception of "If I Had My Druthers," which Abner sings as a paean to laziness, the best lyrics derive from Mercer's satirical treatment of politics.

Four pieces garnered acclaim for their cutting wit that lacerated government, capitalism, the military, and science. The opening chorus features the characters of Dogpatch joining Marryin' Sam, played by Stubby Kay, in saluting the local hero, the cowardly Confederate general Jubilation T. Cornpone, who from his statue presides over the town square. Having grown up around politicians who praised the Confederacy as a unifying strategy for the one party Democratic Solid South, Mercer parodied the traditional storyline of honor associated with stone soldiers on county seat monuments. With "Jubilation T. Cornpone," Johnny deflates America's bombastic militarism: "When we almost had 'em but / The issue still was in doubt, / Who suggested the retreat / That turned it into a rout?" As he later explained, "I kidded the South in kind of an affectionate way because I'm very strong about the South. I still like Robert E. Lee better than Ulysses S. Grant." Written at the height of the Eisenhower Consensus, Mercer had the temerity to question Congress with his "The Country's in the Very Best of Hands." Cast as a duet between beefcake Abner and shyster Marryin' Sam, with the Dogpatch ensemble joining in, the lyric offers a satirical send-up of political impasse. It cleverly uses the traditional song, "Dem Dry Bones," as a bridge that connects the voter to representative democracy only to twist the idea into explaining inaction on the part of congressmen. Underscoring the criticism are comments about the ballooning federal budget and growing national debt. The men sing: "Don't you believe them congressmen / And senators are dumb — / When they run into problems / That is tough to overcome — / They just declares a thing / They call a moratorium — / The Upper and the Lower House disbands!" Capp had chastised the corporate takeover of society with his character General Bullmoose who provides an acerbic critique of the military-industrial complex. Mercer builds on the idea, for in one musical number the chorus exclaims, "What's good for General Bullmoose / Is good for the U. S. A." and in a vaudevillian vamp called "Progress Is the Root of All Evil," Johnny has the elitist Bullmoose bemoan business regulations with the lines "Billionaires are getting old-fashioned. Labor is the new-fangled craze." In "Oh, Happy Day" Johnny decries scientific discoveries that presaged cloning and with comic relief frets over the creation of human beings in laboratories with a lyric reminiscent of Aldous Huxley's *Brave New World*: "Oh, happy day, when we can choose their looks / From formulae in scientific books / And add their personalities from psychiatric tomes / And assembly-line husbands, / Conveyor-belt wives / Settle down in push-button homes!"[37]

In his analysis of Broadway musicals titled *Show Tunes*, Steven Suskin notes about *Li'l Abner* that Mercer provides "one of Broadway's best sets of comedy lyrics ever." Through songs about Dogpatch, Mercer revealed his own philosophy of life, as *Theatre Arts* recognized in its January 1957 review, complimenting Johnny's "knockabout satire and whimsy." Mercer published the sheet music for *Li'l Abner* through his company Commander Publications, located at 1610 North Argyle Avenue in Hollywood. Mercer's old agent Jack Robbins had a son named Marshall Robbins, whom Johnny had hired in 1951 to help with *Top Banana*. For the next twenty-five years, Marshall and his wife Barbara Robbins assisted Mercer with various musical enterprises, including Commander Publications, and in the process grew close to the family.[38]

During rehearsals, Johnny complained to his wife and children of the loneliness he felt being away from home and staying in hotels. Writing to Ginger one Sunday morning before church, he confessed, "The show looks pretty good, but could be improved, if we've enough sense between us to do it. I pray we have. You pray too, and maybe we'll get lucky for a big hit." The show opened in Washington, D.C., on September 17, 1956, in the historic 1835 National Theatre. A letter home begins "mighty lonesome here in this old hotel room," but Mercer quickly cuts to his prognosis: "the show looks great." Referring to the warm reception received from the audience, which included the Democratic Party presidential candidate, Johnny wrote, "Ging, you will be interested to know — as will you, Mandy — that Adlai [Stevenson] was in to catch it the other night and dug it the most." In another letter, Johnny addressed Jeff as the "man of the house" in his absence, and wrote: "Hi Sport. Hope you're taking care of the family for me." He added the note, "Kiss Mommy for me and be good to Sister. Dad."[39]

With *Li'l Abner*, Mercer landed his greatest Broadway success. After several weeks in the capital the show moved to Boston and Philadelphia before opening at the St. James Theater on West Forty-fourth Street on November 15, 1956, beginning a two-year run on Broadway. Cole Porter telegrammed: "Johnny I wish you everything good tonight. I have been a fan of yours for many years. All my best." Johnny sent leading lady Edie Adams red roses on opening night. But thinking back, Mercer figured "some alchemy must have disappeared because the show that came into New York was not as well received as the one that played Washington," which he attributed to the provincialism of the political town that the metropolis lacked. Given the fate of the show as a perennial high-school musical that has not yet been revived on Broadway, perhaps he was right. In his November 16 evaluation for the *New York Times* Brooks Atkinson observed "on the whole, the composer and the writer of the lyrics have been luckier than the librettists." He concluded "*Li'l Abner* is a genial, busy, good-looking show with a number of excellent songs and jovial performers." *Li'l Abner* ran for 693 performances on Broadway, suggesting the successful integration of song and plot for an entertaining show that nevertheless lacked a stellar, timeless song set to the kind of beautiful melody that might sustain a symphonic treatment like those of Richard Rodgers and Frederick Loewe. The musical and subsequent film reinforced the popularity of the Sadie Hawkins Day fad whereby school girls asked boys to dances. Overall, the positive press regarding *Li'l Abner* demonstrated that for the musical theater Mercer had hit his mark with biting sarcasm and comic irony.

Confronting new media and new sounds during the 1950s, Mercer strove to adapt without sacrificing his principles. He participated in a variety of programs broadcast over radio. In June 1953, CBS began a fifteen-minute evening program called *The Johnny Mercer Show*, featuring the songwriter spinning disks and singing songs while exchanging banter with announcer John Jacobs. The first show aired on his twenty-second wedding anniversary in 1953 and after philosophizing about the institution of marriage, he played Perry Como's recording of "Here's to My Lady," Johnny's twentieth anniversary present to Ginger written to music by Rube Bloom. In 1954, Mercer moved to NBC Radio and a new show, where one broadcast had him praising a recent recording by his old friend, Bing Crosby. The AFRS picked up these and other programs featuring Johnny for its broadcasts. During the summer of 1955, Mercer joined Fred Astaire on a program called *On a Sunday Afternoon* that featured singers performing light music accompanied by the Alfredo Antonini Orchestra. Yet the public was turning from radio to a new medium.[40]

Although still in its infancy in the early 1950s, television quickly emerged as America's favorite form of entertainment, and Johnny began making regular guest appearances on variety programs, a practice he continued for the rest of his life. In 1950, Mercer appeared on a televised "dance party" hosted by the Arthur Murray School of Dancing. In 1951, Johnny joined a young boy also named "Johnny Mercer" on ABC's *The Name's the Same*. On another game show, rather than have the panelists guess his name, they had to figure out what person he most wanted to be, and Johnny chose Marilyn Monroe. In 1952, he helped *This Is Your Life* celebrate the career of collaborator Harry Warren. In 1953, Johnny performed on the *Twenty-fifth Annual Academy Awards*, the first to be broadcast over television, singing with Peggy Lee the Harry Warren and Robin Leo song, "Zing a Little Zong," from Paramount's *Just for You*. In 1955, Father James Keller interviewed Mercer on the half-hour ABC television program, *The Christophers*, broadcast from Union Theological Seminary in New York. The program promoted religious tolerance with the motto: "It's better to light one candle than to curse the darkness." During the spring of 1955, Mercer performed on *The Bob*

Crosby Show, receiving from the sponsor a Broilquik Rotisserie as a gift. Johnny appeared in the fall of 1955 on the nationally syndicated *"Tennessee" Ernie Ford Show*, for which he arose early to make the dawn broadcast. Mercer's association with the popular country singer and television personality stemmed from their work together the decade before at Capitol Records.[41]

During the first years of the original *Tonight Show* with Steve Allen on NBC television, Johnny appeared several times in 1953–54. His friend, producer William "Bill" Harbach, made the connection: "Every time Johnny was in town, I would book him on the show because Steve Allen was mad about him, being a songwriter himself, and here was this giant, you know, who was going to come on our little television show late at night at one in the morning." Harbach remembered, "Johnny would do marvelous duets we'd work out with Steve." Then the modest Mercer stepped forward, telling Harbach, "You know, Bill, I just don't want to keep doing my songs all the time. Let me do other people's songs for a change." Harbach agreed, "So what we rigged up — Steve Allen would say, sitting at the piano, 'Johnny, you know you've written about almost every subject in the world.'" Mercer responded, "Well, I've written about a lot of them." Allen continued, "Let me see if I can catch you up. I'll sing a song of Cole Porter's or something like that, or I'll sing one of your songs, and you see if you can get anybody to match it." Harbach recalled that Johnny "would do this duet with Steve, and it goes about seven minutes, and it's brilliant." On another occasion Harbach arranged an entire hundred-minute show of Mercer songs with Allen playing the piano while surrounded by Johnny, Steve Lawrence, Eydie Gorme, Andy Williams, and Pat Kirby, and all backed up by Skitch Henderson and His Orchestra.[42]

Briefly Mercer had his own short-lived television program too. From July to September 1955, Johnny developed a half-hour CBS television game show called *Musical Chairs*. In addition to a weekly female guest soloist, other panelists included the pianist, songwriter, and occasional actor Bobby Troup, who also led the studio orchestra, and Mel Blanc, the voice of several Warner Bros. cartoon characters, including Bugs Bunny. The vocal group the Cheerleaders provided backup for the visiting singers Margaret Whiting, Peggy Lee, Denise Darcel, and Rose Marie. The show featured musical questions to be answered by panelists impersonating the recording artists. Other rounds required improvised lyrics. Correct answers won points for the panelists, who played for home viewers, with the winner receiving a cash prize. The brief run enjoyed by the program demonstrated the total interpenetration of jazz and popular song but also signaled the slow decline in popularity of the Age of the Singer.[43]

Variety shows that featured such stars as Johnny Mercer demonstrated the successful transference of the old radio format to the new medium of television, now presented in an even more entertaining fashion. On such programs, Mercer often introduced songs he had written for the movies or the stage, as when on *The Bob Crosby Show* in 1955 dancers demonstrated the routine in Johnny's "Slue-foot" for *Daddy Long Legs*. Later that year Mercer appeared on television with Hoagy Carmichael singing "Lazybones." *The Steve Allen Show* had him on in 1957 with Capitol recording stars Tennessee Ernie Ford and Peggy Lee. They all sang a parody of "Ac-Cent-Tchu-Ate the Positive," with Tennessee "accentuating the countrified," Peggy the cool jazz of the "citified," and Johnny "the southern-ness" of life. For *The Rosemary Clooney Show* that MCA-TV Revue syndicated in 1956, Johnny made a running joke of a new song he had written with Harry Warren to a tune borrowed from Franz Schubert's "Unfinished" Symphony No. 8 called "Remember Dad on Mother's Day" in a comic plea for recognition in the era before Father's Day. A diaspora entertainer from Kentucky, Clooney sang several Mercer standards and joined the songwriter in a duet of his new collaboration with Gene De Paul titled "What-Cha-Ma-Call-It." The regulars on the show, Nelson Riddle and His Orchestra and the male quartet the Hi-Los, performed "One for My Baby" set in an ice-cream parlor. On the program, Johnny had fun singing his 1936 "Jamboree Jones" with the quartet's Clark Bur-roughs, as well as his 1937 "We're Working Our Way through College." As with other variety shows in the early years of prime-time television, the quality of the performances remained remarkably high and the content squeaky clean. Audi-ences viewed these southerners as national celebrities. Talking with writer Henry Kane about his appearances on television, Mercer said: "It's not the money, of course. I admit I get a kick out of it. Maybe I'm a hambone at heart. Sometimes I may sing, sometimes we sit around and chat, sometimes I hang around and listen while a real singer sings some of my songs." He acknowledged, "Since television, yes, people have gotten to know me; I mean, my personality."[44]

Mercer's performance on the short-lived but critically acclaimed *Nat "King" Cole Show* in 1957 proved particularly significant among his television appear-ances during these years as he showed support for the pioneer program. A few months before, Ku Klux Klansmen had picketed Cole's concert in Birmingham's Municipal Auditorium carrying signs that read "Down with Jungle Music."

During the black superstar's singing of "Autumn Leaves," white vigilantes stormed the stage and attacked Cole, stopping the song. They saw in the singer's art a challenge to racist concepts of black masculinity and white supremacy. The all-white audience gasped in horror at the Klansmen's actions and applauded when a bloodied Cole graciously returned to the stage. Yet civil rights activists such as Walter White criticized the native Alabamian for playing segregated concerts. Cole responded: "I had hoped that through the medium of my music I had made many new friends and changed many opinions regarding racial equality." Cole's television show was the first variety program hosted by a black man on a national network. Despite a lack of support from corporate sponsors who feared losing white customers, the program limped along because of the willingness of white guest artists, including Capitol Records' stable of singers Margaret Whiting, Peggy Lee, and Johnny Mercer, to forgo their usual fees. On the program Cole introduced Mercer, who came on the stage, shook his hand, and said, "I'm ready if you'll give up that tenor spot." Nat asked Johnny what he wanted to sing and the old mentor responded, "Send for Me," a rock 'n' roll tune and Cole's latest hit. Motioning to the sheet music arrayed on the set behind them showing Johnny's many contributions to popular music, Nat asked, "Why aren't you doing something from your own closet here?" adding, "You know that's my song." But an undeterred Mercer eager to cover his colleague's number launched into the top forty hit. Afterward Johnny joined Nat in singing the spirited duet they first recorded in 1947: "Save the bones for Henry Jones, / 'cause Henry don't eat no meat!" Obviously enjoying the fellowship, the two old associates ended their song with another hearty handshake. Such public acts between a black man and a white man at the height of massive resistance in defense of white supremacy in the South — indeed, broadcast between the Montgomery Bus Boycott and the desegregation of Little Rock's Central High School — broke racial taboos and demonstrated their disregard for the racist etiquette of their native South.[45]

As a master wordsmith, Mercer claimed a thousand songs by the time of his appearance in 1962 on NBC's old *Kraft Music Hall*, now called *The Perry Como Show* after its host. Yet the modest Mercer tried not to sing any of them. At the outset of the program, Como observed, "If it weren't for guys like Johnny, characters like me would be out of business." Then he added, "Johnny didn't want to sing any of his songs tonight." A medley followed called "Tonight I'll Sing the Songs of Somebody Else," using snatches of songs that alternated between Mercer's lyrics and those of his fellow songwriters in a friendly back and forth between Johnny as the conductor of the show's vocal group, the Ray Charles Singers, and the vocal group itself, arranged as a symphonic choir. After the singers performed a few bars of "Dream," Mercer interrupted with a few lines from "Stardust," having identified Hoagy Carmichael and Mitchell Parish as the songwriters, only to have the singers cut him off with "Tangerine" as the exchange continued for several minutes. It was Johnny's way of plugging the music of his friends, which he also did on other television programs. A similar exchange took place on *The Andy Williams Show* in 1963: to demonstrate the wealth of material written by Mercer, Andy challenged him to walk through the alphabet, stopping to sing the title of one of his songs that began with that letter, which Johnny promptly did twenty-six times. On both programs the modest Mercer — who scrupulously credited the composers — acquitted himself as a masterful entertainer. When the rhythm and blues star Ray Charles appeared on the *Dinah Shore Show*, Johnny Mercer stepped out of the wings to join him on the set. After exchanging compliments — Mercer telling Charles what a fan of his he had been for years — Charles suggested they sing Johnny's "Georgia on My Mind," and Mercer — after clarifying the popular misconception by explaining that his friends Hoagy Carmichael and Stuart Gorrell actually wrote the song — then performed the number as a duet, offering one of his most soulful performances caught on film.[46]

Already wealthy from songwriting, Mercer resolved to use some of his proceeds from the sale of Capitol Records to restore the family's honor by repaying his father's debts. In January 1955, the multinational corporation Electric and Musical Industries of Great Britain bought the ownership shares in Capitol held by Mercer, Glenn Wallichs, and G. G. "Buddy" DeSylva, with Johnny netting more than $1.5 million. An excited Mercer dropped by the apartment of his Commander Publications employees, Barbara and Marshall Robbins, to show them the check from the sale. She recalled Johnny turned to Ginger and asked about his plans: "'Do you want to do this?' She said, 'It's your money.'" To which he replied, "My father's name will be clear." In March 1955, Johnny wrote confidentially to George W. Hunt of the Chatham Savings Bank (formerly the Chatham Savings and Loan Company) in Savannah, "Can you give me the figures of the indebtedness still outstanding to the investors of the old G. A. Mercer Co.? I know this occurred a long time ago, but as a matter of personal curiosity I would like to know what is owed, and if you have a record of the investors, their heirs or assigns?" Hunt, whose office on Bryan Street lay across the alley from the Mercer Insurance Agency on Bay Street, conferred with Walter Mercer about how to respond. Johnny's brother, who was meeting with his vice president, Nick Mamalakis, at the time, said, "Give him the information." Hunt's response to Johnny explained that of the $1,070,807 loss in 1927, the Chatham Savings and Loan Company had liquidated most Mercer properties and paid off 72 percent of the debt, leaving an unpaid balance of roughly $295,000 to redeem the remaining certificates at 100 percent. In addition, the G. A. Mercer Company retained real estate on Burnside Island, which included part of the old undeveloped Vernon View subdivision on the coast and the newer Rio Vista subdivision with its marketable residential lots on the back island. Johnny learned that no action had been taken and that no payment had been made to the certificate holders since shortly after G. A. Mercer's death in 1940.[47]

Responding to Hunt's answer, Mercer revealed a sensitivity to public opinion in the reply he dropped in the mail in Chicago while riding the rails on the *Chief* en route to the Ambassador Hotel on Park Avenue in New York City. "George, if there is to be any criticism of this move, I would rather not do it at all. It has been my ambition since boyhood to pay off my father's debts in this venture, and I had thought this would be appreciated by the stockholders (?) and would, in effect, 'clear the name' of the company. If this is not the case, forget it. If, however, it is the case, let's proceed to go through with it." The envelope contained a check for $300,000 — which Johnny had forgotten to sign. Having undertaken the effort in the strictest of confidence, Mercer intended to repay the debt in secret. Opening Johnny's reply, Hunt's jaw dropped when he saw the check. He rushed across the alley to tell Walter, "That crazy Johnny mailed me a check!" The brother replied, "I thought he would." Mamalakis suggested, and Walter and Hunt agreed, to recommend to Johnny that, rather than pay off the certificate holders at a loss — which afforded him no tax advantage, as he was not responsible for the debt — he establish instead scholarships in his parents' names so he could claim a deduction. The men returned the unsigned check with their proposal. Promptly Johnny answered: "Nick, you are talking with your head — I'm speaking with my heart!" and signed it with a big "J." Hunt received another $300,000 check — this time signed by Mercer — which he deposited in the Citizens and Southern National Bank. On April 7, Hunt returned a "memorandum of agreement" that covered "the handling of the funds you are donating toward the complete liquidation of the G. A. Mercer Company." With rumors flying around the city, the *Savannah Evening Press* broke the story about the pending payment on the outstanding certificates, identifying the source only as "a most generous gesture on the part of an interested individual." In financial and social circles everyone knew the money came from Johnny but kept his identity secret because "they did not know the wishes of the individual." The buzz attracted the national news services, and stringers from the AP and UP caught up with Mercer at 20th Century Fox on the set of *Daddy Long Legs*, interviewing him there and publishing his identity in stories wired on April 15, 1955.[48]

Having been compelled to act by his sense of southern honor, Mercer observed repeatedly that the publicity was unwelcome. In explanation, Johnny told the UP reporter: "It's been a boyhood ambition to pay these debts so there will be no slur on the family name." He explained, "It was supposed to be kept a secret." After clarifying, "Everyone will be paid every dime they thought they might [have] lost in the company," he ended, "But I won't say any more. It's strictly a family affair. It concerns only my mother, my brothers and myself." To George Hunt, Mercer wrote,

> I'm sorry about the publicity. My idea would be to take a small dignified advertisement, explaining that the bankrupt company has now paid it[s] debts in full, as per the wishes of my father. Also an explanation of it's [sic] failure being due to the failure of larger companies in which it had invested, might be advisable. Then a word of thanks for your long, loyal, unswerving devotion in accomplishing the liquidation after all — and during all — these years. This would be signed by his four sons and perhaps my mother if it is agreeable to them.

Announcing the deposit of the $300,000 check, the *Savannah Morning News* of April 19, 1955, said, "Johnny Mercer, with modesty that had been undiminished by his great success, had hoped to keep the whole transaction a secret." Like his grandfather, Colonel George Anderson Mercer, who, when confronted by the gambling debts of his wayward son Ed, quietly paid them to restore the family honor, Johnny acted similarly regarding his father's business debts. In the process he restored his own tarnished reputation, removing the stain caused by his shameful conviction for drunk driving the previous November. He later confessed that he hoped his action would enable his mother to hold her head up higher around certain people who over the years had blamed his father for all their troubles.[49]

The family expressed its appreciation for Johnny's generous gesture. His mother wrote, "Oh darling, I am so proud of my son I could die!" She speculated he had "holed up somewhere until all this public acclaim will have died down." Brother Walter fired off a telegram to Johnny in New York at the Ambassador

Hotel: "My congratulations and heartfelt thanks in which I know all the family join for the wonderful thing that you are doing." A similar message came from other Mercers such as Uncle Robbie, who said,

> I just have to tell you, as so many others have done, that I think what you are doing in memory of your Father, is a very wonderful and beautiful thing. I don't believe there are many (if any) who would give up what you are doing to pay off debts that were not of your own.... I think this act of yours is "Your Finest Hour," as it also shows greatness of character, which would not be done without a deep love for one who certainly loved you.

The Ciuceviches joined in. "Practically everyone I meet tells me how wonderful it is," Aunt Kate confessed. "Your father left you with fine memories of honor and truth, and you are carrying on." She added, "Your mother is very proud and happy. You have really brought sunshine into her life." Then Aunt Kate observed, "And as my Jewish neighbor next door said, 'He must have a wonderful wife for them to discharge a moral obligation [from] such a long time ago.'" Johnny's mother, Lillian, closed her letter with, "my love to Ginger," and quoted her brother-in-law, "As Joe O'Leary said, few wives would see eye to eye with their husbands in such an issue." Lillian then added about her daughter-in-law, "but she has always been so understanding, and I think loved and admired Pop too." The remark by the mother-in-law suggested a sympathetic view of Ginger, who often seems the shrill wife who criticized Johnny's gifts of money to family members and his failure to buy fashionable consumer goods. Ginger understood this was his money and his family, and she stood by him as he garnered national acclaim for his act.[50]

Befuddled by the unusual story of family honor in the modern day, the print media from coast to coast made of it a morality tale. The Birmingham *News* editorialized: "Mr. Mercer says he didn't want any publicity. We believe him. Publicity can be had for cheaper tabs than that." In October 1955, a racy tabloid called the *Lowdown* featured a smiling Mercer on its cover with the headline "Most Stories about Hollywood People Are Sordid and Unsavory. THE LOW-DOWN Is Proud to Tell a Story Which Might Have Come Out of the Bible Itself." Recounting the payment of his father's debt, the paper omitted reference to Johnny's drunk-driving conviction of the year before. In New England the Hartford, Connecticut, newspaper took the opportunity to decry current business standards: "The Mercers felt a moral obligation that is all too often lacking in business transactions. And in a world where many persons do not have a responsibility for their own debts, to say nothing of the debts of their parents, Johnny Mercer stands as a man apart." Likewise, in the South, a Memphis newspaper lamented that "we could use more men with Mercer's integrity." Shifting focus to music, it added, "and come to think of it in light of the current *Hit Parade*, we could use some more song-writers with his talent," a sentiment repeated in a West Coast paper.[51]

Everyday citizens as well as well-known people who did not personally benefit from the act responded to the media coverage with compliments in personal letters to Johnny. One man from Arkansas, having read a feature in *Reader's Digest* about the repaid debt, said it all in a letter to Johnny: "Thank you for restoring my sadly wavering faith in people by your wonderful deed." Mercer's peers such as band leader Fred Waring and Bill Dozier of CBS Television said things similar to what Leo Talent of the Jackie Gleason organization expressed, "There should be more Johnny Mercers in the world." A judge in Alabama observed, "I have no knowledge of your history or your abilities, but this I am positive of — your mother and father, or one of them, were strong useful people — you come from good stock — you were reared in a wholesome home." An advertising executive in Wisconsin noted, "I've never met you, except over radio and TV . . . [and] . . . through one of the three greatest newspaper stories that ever hit the headlines in the 57 years that I've been around: Salk — Einstein — and YOU." The owner of a Fifth Avenue store with branches in Paris and London wrote, "The laurel wreath of greatness is yours to wear. Few people in my book have earned the right to hold their heads quite so high. G. A. Mercer had to be a great guy to have sired so great a son."[52]

Pointing to his father, Johnny responded to the public outpouring with characteristic modesty. Mercer said, "But I'm glad about the many wonderful letters I've received about my father . . . and vindicating us in what we've always believed — that he was truly a wonderful man with an impeccable sense of honor." Nick Mamalakis wrote Johnny, "It is a real wonderful feeling to be associated with an organization with the character and integrity possessed by Walter and Pop, and we assure you that the announcement gave [all] of us a real exhilarating feeling." G. A. Mercer's personal secretary, Veda Royall, wrote Johnny, "I know what he went through with trying to 'pay off' and how hard he tried, and I know it must give you a very warm feeling inside to know that you did something that would have made him so happy." Johnny had said similar things to the AP reporter about his father's effort to pay off the debt: "He felt pretty bad about it when it happened. He wished he could do it. . . . He made good all he could. I just tried to finish it up."[53]

Others recognized the act derived from a culture of honor honed in the boy. R. W. D. Taylor, Mercer's Latin teacher at Woodberry Forest School, wrote: "Mrs. Taylor and I think that your decision to pay the unfortunate and long-standing indebtedness of your Father is one of the finest things I have ever known of in my long life." Other "old boys" likewise chimed in as a testament to the school's mission. Back in Savannah, Johnny's childhood friend and classmate Malcolm "Mac" Bell wrote as treasurer of the Bethesda Home for Boys, which, as a beneficiary of more than a thousand dollars, had used the money to subsidize its eighty charges. The bounty had derived from wills written by G. A. Mercer for free because of the bequest in certificates to Bethesda.[54] A year after Johnny sent the check, claims had been made on all but twenty-five certificates, totaling a value of roughly $13,000 still to be paid out. By the end of 1957, the Chatham Savings Bank board of directors closed the books on the liquidation of the G. A. Mercer Company, having refunded at face value almost all the certificate holders. Of Johnny's $300,000 donation, $291,964.92 had been paid to creditors. The balance and the capital gained from selling Burnside Island property amounted to roughly $45,000, what Hunt described as the "residual," a word Johnny found of interest, using "residues" in his lyrics for Li'l Abner. The Chatham Savings Bank sent Mercer a check for $45,000, but Johnny mailed it back with instructions to donate one-third each to the Episcopal Bishop of Georgia's Fund, the Elks Children's Hospital in Atlanta, and the Victor B. Jenkins Jr. Memorial Boys' Club — which later named its new gym after G. A. Mercer — donations that strengthened Johnny's ties to his home state.[55]

In the fall of 1956, Johnny and Ginger traveled by train to Savannah, their first trip there in several years. He visited with his mother and sister in their new house at 110 East Forty-ninth Street. Brother Walter accompanied Johnny and Ginger to a meeting of the Savannah Chamber of Commerce that recognized his reimbursement of the certificate holders. Regretting the shortness of the visit, Johnny promised to return for a longer stay the following year.[56]

From California, Mercer made a generous donation to Christ Church Episcopal in March 1957, the check being presented to the entire congregation by Uncle Robbie Mercer, who was a longstanding member of the vestry. The church used the donation to construct a classically framed doorway on East St. Julian Street for the new chapel. Johnny sent a similar check to Woodberry Forest School that elicited the following response: "It is well that the Old Taylors have stout hearts! I am sure neither of us ever endorsed a check so large or one received with deeper gratitude." Fittingly, the money paid for a new chapel organ. As headmaster, Johnny's cousin and Uncle Robbie's son, Joe Mercer, received the gifts for Woodberry. When he had taken the post, Johnny had joked with the Taylors, "In case cousin Joe gives you any trouble, remind him of his low breeding . . . not family of course." When asked in 1956 how best to approach Johnny for a donation to Woodberry, Joe had advised the fund-raisers: "Although he is thoroughly generous by nature, he has led Virginia and me to the conclusion that he is a bit bitter and resentful about this business of 'everybody always trying to dig you for money' as he phrases it." His cousin thought the songwriter had "become somewhat cynical." Also he thought that in time Johnny might support music scholarships for the school.[57]

Johnny made good on his promise to return to Savannah in July 1957, when he took his ten-year-old son, Jeff, to spend several weeks visiting family and friends. For part of the vacation they stayed on Tybee Island, where Ciucevich cousins who had married into the Collins and O'Leary families lived and where the Hammonds kept a beach house. During the visit Johnny participated in community life, including crowning the winner of a baby contest, having won one himself in Savannah nearly fifty years before. When father and son returned to California, they brought home turtles they had caught in the salt marsh.[58]

While in Savannah that July, Johnny had offhandedly remarked that he would not mind owning a place at which to entertain family and friends on future trips to Georgia. Brother Hugh Mercer, still running the real estate arm of the family business, looked for an appropriate residence, eventually suggesting the Thomas W. Gamble home, called Back River Pines, on Burnside Island. The Dutch-gambrel-roofed, eight-room house had been built in 1938 by the former mayor of the city and—with its seven-hundred-foot frontage along the Back River and eighteen acres of woodlands and gardens—offered a secluded setting for escapes to Savannah. Just downstream from Bethesda and back-island of Vernon View and the ocean, the site reminded the songwriter of his youth. Back in 1943, older brother George A. Mercer Jr. had purchased the Grove Point Plantation on the Ogeechee River not far from the Gamble home. By the end of 1957, Johnny had authorized Hugh to broker a deal with attorney Alex A. Lawrence—the brother of Johnny's former debutante girlfriend, Ann—and widow Gamble for the property.[59]

In the summer of 1958, Johnny returned to Savannah and moved into the house on Burnside Island that he called Vernon View. He set about redecorating the 4,200 square foot structure that, despite its impressive setting, came off as a rather unimposing suburban residence. Later described as "functional and unpretentious" by a journalist, the house had a large dining room with adjacent living room. An enclosed sun porch off the kitchen featured a built-in bar and wrap-around windows with stunning views of the river. Mercer installed a large walk-in cupboard off the kitchen with floor-to-ceiling shelves, no doubt to keep stocked with food for his guests. During his trips he often phoned in orders to Johnny Harris's Restaurant for fried chicken and barbecue with which to feed his poker buddies, fellows such as Jack Cay and Curtis Lewis. He offered the place for use by his mother and sister as well as his brothers, Hugh and his wife, Louise, and Walter and his wife, Dorothy. Walter especially enjoyed "fishing, crabbing, shrimping, and rowing and casting" on the Back River. "Mom says you use the house occasionally," Johnny wrote Dorothy, "I'm sure glad someone is making some use of it, especially as you seem to love and enjoy it. I wish I could get back more often." He added in a letter to Walter, "Hugh must understand money is only a means to an end — but it's nice to have the comfort of it — materially and mentally." During the winter months Lillian, joined by her granddaughter Nancy, often picked a box full of Empress, Debutante, Professor Sargent, and other camellia blossoms from the bushes on the property to ship to the Mercers. Johnny wanted the land divided around the house into lots he set aside in his will for his children, Amanda and Jeff, as well as for his nieces, Ann, Louise, and Nancy. In return Johnny asked for assistance with general upkeep of the place through minor repairs and the paying of utility bills. Mercer employed a grounds-keeper to watch the house when vacant, and he gave plenty of warning when he might arrive for visits.[60]

While staying in his new Savannah house in 1958, Johnny attempted to address the problem weak books caused in his previous Broadway attempts by writing his own musical, titled "Beauty from Ashes." The script began with the concept that "heaven is each person's idea of heaven." Set in the afterlife, different people from different times — a philosopher, a businessman, and a southern lady — interact in heaven. Into this mix appear the male and female principals, two young people whose lives are cut short. Through divine intervention they ultimately return to earth with knowledge of what might have been, going back with powers to alter circumstances for the better. Mercer mailed the script to his friend Dick Myers, who noted the absence of a sustained storyline, a problem seconded by

Ginger's friend, Peggy, an editor at Bantam Books. Both readers complimented the vignettes and strong characters created by Johnny. Peggy described it as "the kind of show that will make anyone come out of the theatre thinking a little more than they did when they went in, and with a warm, kindly feeling, and a sense of delight and nostalgia." Over the winter of 1959, producer Stanley Gilkey considered the script for a theatrical run, but it never materialized.[61]

Still seeking the box-office success that had eluded them over their careers, Harold Arlen and Johnny Mercer partnered for one last collaboration, a new musical called *Saratoga*. Since *St. Louis Woman*, Arlen had mixed luck on Broadway, most notably with Truman Capote in 1954 on *House of Flowers* and with E. Y. "Yip" Harburg in 1957 on *Jamaica*. Harold convinced Johnny to join him on a new project derived from the novel *Saratoga Trunk* by Edna Ferber, who thirty years before had given Kern and Hammerstein the story for *Show Boat*. The director Morton "Teak" DaCosta, who claimed as prior successes *The Music Man* and *Auntie Mame*, took on the jobs of both writing the book and directing the show. The female lead, Carol Lawrence, had just completed a run on Broadway as Maria in *West Side Story*. From *Seven Brides for Seven Brothers* came Howard Keel as the male lead. Working with what seemed to be an unlimited budget, Cecil Beaton created sets and scenes with matching costumes so elaborate that they wowed the audience. As investors — production costs topped a whopping $480,000 — Arlen and Mercer joined others in sparing no expense as the best Broadway had to offer contributed to the show including Jean Rosenthal, who designed the lighting; Ralph Beaumont, who choreographed the dances; and Harold's brother Jerry Arlen who oversaw musical direction.[62]

Early on, Johnny recognized problems with *Saratoga*. While in Savannah that spring of 1959, he wrote to his family back on Lido Isle, "I'm a little brought down about the show since I read the novel, but am hoping for the best because of the people involved." He spent the summer in California working with Arlen on the score, traveling to Beverly Hills with song lyrics, and returning to Newport Beach with reel-to-reel tapes of music. Cast in August, rehearsals began in September, with an opening in Philadelphia scheduled for late October. Again Mercer wrote home of his loneliness, wishing he "were several people so [he] could be many places at once." About *Saratoga* he added, "Things progressing slowly. Don't know if we'll ever get that 'smash'— too many cooks — in love with their own cooking." The tryout opening in Philadelphia's Sam S. Shubert Theatre on October 26, 1959, resulted in more changes. Over the next five weeks, trying to revise the book musical while also directing the show, DaCosta moved sketches around, dropped songs, and added others in a fashion that confused the cast and songwriters.[63]

In many ways *Saratoga* resembled the old romantic operettas. Lawrence, playing Clio Dulaine, an illegitimate Creole woman returning to New Orleans from Paris to claim her rightful place in elite society, dances a charged cakewalk-like number called "Petticoat High" with African Americans in the French Market. Her maid, Kakou, played by the Juilliard-trained contralto Carol Brice, sang what some critics considered the best song in the show, "Goose Never Be a Peacock," with its lines: "So don't walk around all biggety-like / Or squinchify up too small, / 'cause maybe you is / The very best you of all!" Setting her sites on a wealthy man, Clio heads to Saratoga Springs, where she finds another adventurer, the vengeful Montana frontiersman Clint Maroon, played by Keel. Intending to right a wrong done his family by Robber Barons, Clint leads an all-male ballet in "The Railroad Fight." In the Darwinian "Dog Eat Dog" Clint swears: "Ain't about to fall in line. / No, I ain't gonna rob 'em / And I ain't gonna steal, / But I aims to try and get what's mine!" He joins an all-male chorus in singing: "'cause the slow lose the money to the swift, / And the swift lose the money to the shrewd." Having identified the Robber Barons as the beneficiaries of government policies — indeed owning the politicians — Mercer has them derisively mock the gullible public as they perform the barbershop quartet: "The Men Who Run the Country." The Robber Barons reintroduce the anticorporate capitalist theme by singing, "Oh, we're the men who run the country / For a little private gain / As we desecrate the woodland / And we inundate the plain!" Gleefully the captains of industry explain: "We keep things humming, humming, / Tellin' folks prosperity is coming, / And while they're saving, and slaving, / We make a million dollars on the side." Set as a barbershop quartet, they harmonize: "Oh, we devastate the prairies / And we decimate the flocks / And we saturate the market / With some questionable stocks," but if scandal erupts, then "We erect a large museum or a public edifice / And the people think we're very, very nice!" In a casino Clio and Clint perform "Game of Poker," a duet about love with the lyric: "You've won, / But oh, / You've lost your heart / Along the way!" Having fallen in love, they sing "You or No One," and the show ends on the "fabulous" porch of the re-created old United States Hotel and Spa in Saratoga, where Mercer's own forebears had once played cards.[64]

With *Saratoga*, Johnny gambled and lost on one of Broadway's biggest white elephants. Beaton's over-the-top designs — complicated sets of moving scenery

Well known today for its gushing fountain, Savannah's Forsyth Park in Johnny's youth appeared overgrown with the water shut off to the cast iron figures, as demonstrated by this contemporary photograph that shows two boys standing beside the iron railing and a woman off to the right. Courtesy of the Georgia Historical Society, Savannah, Georgia.

A family portrait features G. A. Mercer with his second wife, Lillian Ciucevich, holding her newborn daughter Nancy. John Herndon Mercer looks on, while his three half-brothers, George (with wife Bessie Wheless), Hugh, and Walter stand in back. Courtesy of Pearce W. Hammond, Bluffton, South Carolina.

LEFT: West Point graduate and Planter's Bank cashier Hugh Weedon Mercer hired architect John Norris to design his trophy house in Monterey Square. With defeat in war the Confederate general lost his fortune and Mercer House, dying an expatriate in Baden-Baden, Germany. Courtesy of the Prints and Photographs Division, Library of Congress, Washington, D.C.

RIGHT: Johnny favored his grandfather George Anderson Mercer, who, after fighting for the Confederacy and sitting two terms in the Georgia General Assembly, ruled the family as an honor-bound patriarch while practicing law in Savannah until his death in 1907, two years before Johnny's birth. Johnny Mercer Collection, Popular Music Archives, Georgia State University Library, Atlanta, Georgia.

Johnny's mother, Lillian Barbara Ciucevich, held here in the lap of her mother, Julia Merritt Ciucevich, named her son after her father, the Croatian immigrant John Ciucevich, who is holding son Eddie while siblings Mary and Frank look on in this typical portrait of a late nineteenth-century immigrant family in America. Johnny Mercer Collection, Popular Music Archives, Georgia State University Library, Atlanta, Georgia.

« FACING PAGE, BOTTOM: Scions of Savannah's elite, Johnny Mercer's uncles pal around with friends in 1890. From the left stand Robert Lee Mercer, friends Ferris Cacer and Arthur Whitehead, Edward C. A. Mercer (in back), G. A. Mercer (Johnny's father, dressed in white tie), Lewis Mercer (in mackintosh), and first cousin Savage Clay. Johnny Mercer Collection, Popular Music Archives, Georgia State University Library, Atlanta, Georgia.

RIGHT: Land speculation led G. A. Mercer to buy Burnside Island in 1909 with this house overlooking the bluff at Vernon View, where the Burnside and Vernon rivers merge and flow into the Atlantic Ocean. Pictured here are G. A. and Lillian Mercer in the months before Johnny's birth; the woman standing with them is probably one of the Ciucevich sisters. Mercer Family Collection, Lane Library, Armstrong Atlantic State University, Savannah, Georgia.

BELOW: Johnny Mercer poses with the young guests at his fifth-birthday party, 1914. From the left stand the birthday boy, Bobby Young, Ann Laurence, Virginia Laurence, Jimmie McIntire, Cornelia McIntire, Grace Lovel, and Babbie McIntire. In the middle row stand Juliette Frank, Walter Jordon, David Wright, Walter Rivers, Frank Ciucevich, and Babo Hull. At the back are butler Dan, holding Bob Serevan, and mother Lillian. Johnny Mercer Collection, Popular Music Archives, Georgia State University Library, Atlanta, Georgia.

Three-year-old Johnny stands with eleven-year-old Hugh beside the front stairs to 118 East Hall Street, where the Mercers lived during the formative years of Johnny's childhood. Of his three half-brothers, Johnny grew closest to Hugh, who occasionally accompanied him on trips to New York City. Johnny Mercer Collection, Popular Music Archives, Georgia State University Library, Atlanta, Georgia.

The Ciucevich family contributed greatly to Johnny Mercer's formative years, as evidenced by the photograph of the "musketeers" playing in the courtyard of grandmother Julia's house at 301 East Charlton Street with Johnny in the front center, Frank Ciucevich on the left, Johnnie Ciucevich in glasses on the right, and Walter Rivers standing behind with his arms around them all. Courtesy of Julia Paige and Robert "Bob" Ciucevich, Savannah, Georgia.

ABOVE: Scouting took deep root in Savannah, where troops for boys organized in the same parish — Christ Church (Episcopal) — that supported Juliette Gordon Low as she founded the Girl Guides. In the photograph, members of Savannah's Girl Scouts of America perform first aid on a young Johnny, who, in his Boy Scout Troop 11 uniform, patiently awaits his promised reward of a cold "co-cola" for playing victim. From the Collection of the Juliette Gordon Low Birthplace, Girl Scout National Center, Savannah, Georgia.

RIGHT: Home from Woodberry Forest, sixteen-year-old Johnny Mercer stands on the front porch of the house on Gwinnett Street in Savannah shortly after New Year's Day, 1926. In the years his parents lived here, Johnny stayed infrequently, instead spending most of his time at school in Orange, Virginia; in Asheville, North Carolina; or at Vernon View on the Georgia coast. Mercer Family Collection, Lane Library, Armstrong Atlantic State University, Savannah, Georgia.

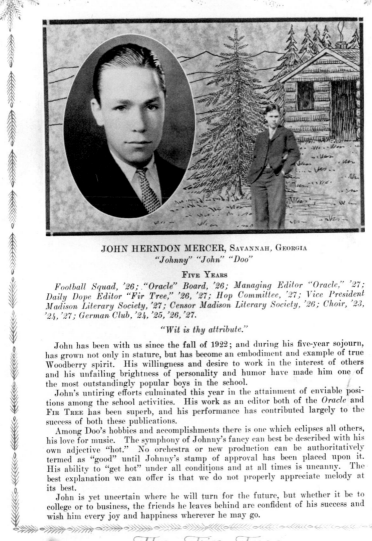

JOHN HERNDON MERCER, Savannah, Georgia
"Johnny" "John" "Doo"

Five Years

Football Squad, '26; "Oracle" Board, '26; Managing Editor "Oracle," '27; Daily Dope Editor "Fir Tree," '26, '27; Hop Committee, '27; Vice President Madison Literary Society, '27; Censor Madison Literary Society, '26; Choir, '23, '24, '27; German Club, '24, '25, '26, '27.

"Wit is thy attribute."

John has been with us since the fall of 1922; and during his five-year sojourn, has grown not only in stature, but has become an embodiment and example of true Woodberry spirit. His willingness and desire to work in the interest of others and his unfailing brightness of personality and humor have made him one of the most outstandingly popular boys in the school.

John's untiring efforts culminated this year in the attainment of enviable positions among the school activities. His work as an editor both of the *Oracle* and Fir Tree has been superb, and his performance has contributed largely to the success of both these publications.

Among Doo's hobbies and accomplishments there is one which eclipses all others, his love for music. The symphony of Johnny's fancy can best be described with his own adjective "hot." No orchestra or new production can be authoritatively termed as "good" until Johnny's stamp of approval has been placed upon it. His ability to "get hot" under all conditions and at all times is uncanny. The best explanation we can offer is that we do not properly appreciate melody at its best.

John is yet uncertain where he will turn for the future, but whether it be to college or to business, the friends he leaves behind are confident of his success and wish him every joy and happiness wherever he may go.

The Woodberry Forest School annual, *The Fir Tree*, of 1926–27 includes senior pages with Johnny Mercer's providing a biographical sketch, listing his numerous activities — singing in the choir, participating in the literary society, and writing for student publications — and suggesting, "Wit is thy attribute." Johnny Mercer Collection, Popular Music Archives, Georgia State University Library, Atlanta, Georgia.

Six months after his marriage to Ginger Metzler in New York, Johnny brought her home to Georgia to meet his parents and to introduce her to Savannah society at the annual Debutante Ball of 1931 held at the old DeSoto Hotel, where this photo was taken in the ornate lobby. Johnny Mercer Collection, Popular Music Archives, Georgia State University Library, Atlanta, Georgia.

In the 1930s, Johnny began composing Christmas cards with original verses for friends and associates. He mailed out this picture in 1939 just as CBS cancelled *The Camel Caravan: Benny Goodman's Swing School*, for which he provided songs and regularly performed the improvisational "Newsie Bluesies," which had rhymes similar to the one that accompanied this card: "Mrs. Mercer cannot swing it — She is corny, she is square / Mr. Mercer cannot sing it as he's going off the air. / So together they both say: 'Swing and sway with Santa K.'" Mercer Family Collection, Lane Library, Armstrong Atlantic State University, Savannah, Georgia.

Merry Christmas

In 1935, Johnny signed a contract with RKO Studios to act in and write for movies such as *Old Man Rhythm*, for which this promotional still shows him swinging a golf club. Mercer had learned to play in Savannah, which had the first golf course in the United States, and he remained an avid fan of this and other sports. Johnny Mercer Collection, Popular Music Archives, Georgia State University Library, Atlanta, Georgia.

A member of the colony of established songwriters who moved to the West Coast after having met and worked together on the East Coast, Johnny joined his collaborator Harold Arlen on the tennis courts of the Gershwin compound in Beverly Hills. George Gershwin snapped this photograph there around 1936. Courtesy of the Ira and Leonore Gershwin Trusts.

As a teenager Mercer studied the art of the great jazz musician Louis Armstrong, later having the good fortune to work with him personally, writing the song "Jeepers Creepers," which the trumpeter introduced in the 1938 film *Going Places*. Photograph ca. 1940s. Johnny Mercer Collection, Popular Music Archives, Georgia State University Library, Atlanta, Georgia.

In 1938, Bing Crosby's friends informally organized as the Westwood Marching and Chowder Club to put on private entertainments for Hollywood's leading stars. Here Johnny, having just removed the burnt cork following his minstrel routine, informally delivers his characteristic rhyme to a group of fellow mummers, with Bing Crosby and Herb Polesie standing in back and, left to right, an unidentified woman seated next to Mercer, Dixie Lee Crosby, David Butler, and Bessie Burke. Johnny Mercer Collection, Popular Music Archives, Georgia State University Library, Atlanta, Georgia.

The wives of the Westwood Marching and Chowder Club members performed as dancing girls. The three women visible in this photograph are, from left, Ginger Mercer, Bessie Burke (wife of Crosby's principal songwriter Johnny Burke), and Dixie Lee (wife of Bing). Not shown is Flo Colona, wife of trombonist and comedian Jerry Colona. Former chorus girl Dolores Reade Hope (wife of the comedian Bob Hope), who had once performed with Ginger and Dixie, did not attend that evening. Johnny Mercer Collection, Popular Music Archives, Georgia State University Library, Atlanta, Georgia.

The board of the American Society of Composers, Authors and Publishers (ASCAP) held its anniversary dinner in the Ambassador Hotel in Los Angeles in 1940, the year Mercer sat on the board. A loyal member of ASCAP, he attended the gatherings regularly and won awards for having his music played so frequently. Mercer is sitting just below center in the photograph. Johnny Mercer Collection, Popular Music Archives, Georgia State University Library, Atlanta, Georgia.

Documenting the upstart record company's amazing success, a photojournalist snapped "The Capitol Gang" showing the founders of Capitol Records in their Sunset Boulevard offices in July 1943. The idea for a West Coast record company occurred to Johnny in 1941, and he convinced entertainment mogul George G. "Buddy" DeSylva, right, and music entrepreneur Glenn Wallichs, with telephone, to invest. Courtesy of Gettyimages.

LEFT: Quick to link up with the Hollywood entertainment industry, nascent Capitol Records negotiated a deal with Walt Disney to produce soundtracks of his films beginning with the 1946 record *Tales of Uncle Remus* from the featured animation *Song of the South*. Mercer took his cover of Ray Gilbert's "Zip-a-Dee-Doo-Dah" to the top of *Your Hit Parade*. Courtesy of V & J Duncan, Antique Maps, Prints & Books, Savannah, Georgia.

RIGHT: After hearing Nat Cole and his trio perform jazz, Johnny encouraged the piano player to also sing and then mentored his career at Capitol Records. Cole subsequently had numerous top sellers as one of America's favorite singers. Mercer appeared on both the radio and television versions of *The Nat "King" Cole Show*. Johnny Mercer Collection, Popular Music Archives, Georgia State University Library, Atlanta, Georgia.

The Mercers adopted Amanda Georgia Mercer in 1941 and John Jefferson Mercer in 1947. The photo of them playing the piano suggests the happiness they brought to the songwriter as they completed his vision of a family by providing him with children to love and spoil. Special Collections and Archives, Georgia State University Library, Atlanta, Georgia.

This 1945 photo of Johnny singing with his daughter Mandy (left), with a matching gap in her teeth, and her cousin Nancy (right), the daughter of Johnny's sister Juliana Keith, reflects his joy in both family and music. Mercer Family Collection, Lane Library, Armstrong Atlantic State University, Savannah, Georgia.

In the darkest months of World War II from June through December 1944, the Savannah songwriter played upbeat music as host of *The Johnny Mercer Chesterfield Music Shop* broadcast domestically over NBC Radio and internationally over the Armed Forces Radio Service, which reached a global audience estimated at a billion people. This photograph shows one of the Friday performances recorded at a military base, with sponsor Chesterfield Cigarette's "They Satisfy" banner in the background. Johnny Mercer Collection, Popular Music Archives, Georgia State University Library, Atlanta, Georgia.

Reflecting his interaction with America's greatest jazz musicians, Mercer appeared in this late 1940s photograph with his friends, from left, fellow songwriter and pianist Hoagy Carmichael of Indiana, Texas trombonist Jack Teagarden, and New Orleans trumpeter Wingy Manone. Johnny Mercer Collection, Popular Music Archives, Georgia State University Library, Atlanta, Georgia.

« FACING PAGE, BOTTOM: After World War II, Mercer arranged for his cousin Marine colonel Walter Rivers to join Capitol Records as an executive and enabled him to produce Nat "King" Cole's recording of "The Christmas Song," which won an early Grammy. Johnny Mercer Collection, Popular Music Archives, Georgia State University Library, Atlanta, Georgia.

Al Hirschfeld's drawing of popular songwriters places Johnny Mercer in the company of his peers. The individuals who created the Great American Songbook depicted here are, counterclockwise from the lower right, Irving Berlin, Ira Gershwin, and Johnny Mercer, with Jerome Kern in glasses standing next to a smiling Dorothy Fields. Continuing behind Johnny to the left — with crazy eyes — Harold Arlen, Cole Porter, Larry Hart, and Richard Rodgers. Hirschfeld has playing the piano Duke Ellington, George Gershwin and — with stars for eyes — Hoagy Carmichael. Al Hirschfeld. Reproduced by arrangement with Hirschfeld's exclusive representative, the Margo Feiden Galleries Ltd., New York, www.alhirschfeld.com.

In 1948, NBC Radio hired Johnny Mercer to cohost the *Call for Music* program, which for several months featured fellow southerners Harry James, a trumpeter from the Benny Goodman Orchestra who had formed his own band, and the popular girl singer and fellow Whiteman alumna Dinah Shore. Johnny Mercer Collection, Popular Music Archives, Georgia State University Library, Atlanta, Georgia.

Jazz vibraphonist Lionel Hampton, who had played with a number of bands in the 1930s, including Benny Goodman's, before heading his own orchestra, composed an instrumental called "Midnight Sun," to which Mercer crafted poetic lyrics. Photograph 1954. Johnny Mercer Collection, Popular Music Archives, Georgia State University Library, Atlanta, Georgia.

TOP: Taken near their house on Lido Isle in Newport Beach, the Mercer family portrait shows a proud father Johnny with son, Jeff, holding the dog Tippy-Canoe; wife, Ginger; and daughter, Mandy, in the 1957 Ranchero convertible, a picture of happiness from sunny California. Bud Selzer, photographer. Johnny Mercer Collection, Popular Music Archives, Georgia State University Library, Atlanta, Georgia.

MIDDLE: For several months in 1955 Johnny Mercer appeared on and helped produce the television program *Musical Chairs*, which featured a panel of experts entertaining questions about lyrics and music related to popular song. Johnny Mercer Collection, Popular Music Archives, Georgia State University Library, Atlanta, Georgia.

BOTTOM: Duke Ellington asked Johnny Mercer to set lyrics to several of his and arranger Billy Strayhorn's compositions, with one result being the jazz standard "Satin Doll." Around the time of the photograph, Johnny had convinced Capitol Records to sign a contract with the Duke and his orchestra. Pictured here with Mercer listening to Ellington are pianist Billy Kyle on the left and trombonist Trummy Young, with whom Mercer wrote "Trav'lin' Light." Courtesy of Frank Driggs.

For three decades Johnny Mercer and Judy Garland carried on a love affair. Here Judy joins Johnny at a party with singer Pat Boone on the far left, singer Freddy Martin in the middle, and singer Tony Bennett on the far right. Johnny Mercer Collection, Popular Music Archives, Georgia State University Library, Atlanta, Georgia.

The trombonist and comedian Jerry Colonna helped introduce "The Girlfriend of the Whirling Dervish" and remained a good friend of the Mercers, while the popular singer Lena Horne made hits out of "Day In — Day Out" and other Mercer songs. Johnny Mercer Collection, Popular Music Archives, Georgia State University Library, Atlanta, Georgia.

LEFT: For the 1961 movie *Breakfast at Tiffany's*, Johnny Mercer won his third Academy Award for Best Song with "Moon River," composed by Henry Mancini (left) and announced by actress Debbie Reynolds at the awards ceremony. It remains the fourth most popular movie theme song in the world. Johnny Mercer Collection, Popular Music Archives, Georgia State University Library, Atlanta, Georgia.

RIGHT: In a performance in Philharmonic Hall in New York for ASCAP in 1967, Mercer joined Broadway composer Richard Rodgers at the piano, with jazz great Ella Fitzgerald on the left and singer Patricia Marand on the right. Fitzgerald selected a baker's dozen of Mercer's best for an album in her Songbook series, making him the only lyricist selected for the honor. Johnny Mercer Collection, Popular Music Archives, Georgia State University Library, Atlanta, Georgia.

During a visit to Savannah in 1967, Johnny joined Mercer family associate and friend Nick Mamalakis on the left and half-brother Walter Mercer in the middle at the pool of the Jenkins Boys Club, to which Johnny had made a generous donation in memory of his father, G. A. Mercer. Johnny Mercer Collection, Popular Music Archives, Georgia State University Library, Atlanta, Georgia.

TOP: Mercer performed several times on *The Mike Douglas Show*, a popular daytime program that often featured variety bits. Broadcast in 1968, this number ended with Margaret Whiting ducking behind the episode's cohosts, the singing duo Tony Sandler and Ralph Young. Johnny Mercer Collection, Popular Music Archives, Georgia State University Library, Atlanta, Georgia.

MIDDLE: Seated on the ground with children in Forsyth Park at the 1969 Savannah Arts Festival, Johnny had traveled home to visit with family and old friends, later making a new friend in lounge pianist Emma Kelly. Johnny Mercer Collection, Popular Music Archives, Georgia State University Library, Atlanta, Georgia.

BOTTOM: In the late 1960s, Johnny Mercer helped organize the Songwriters Hall of Fame as a way to celebrate the lyricists and composers of the great American songbook by recalling their contributions through the placement of historical markers. Here Irving Caesar, Johnny, and Dore Schary stand with the marker commemorating Broadway legend Vincent Youmans. Johnny Mercer Collection, Popular Music Archives, Georgia State University Library, Atlanta, Georgia.

TOP: First Lady Pat Nixon invited Johnny and Ginger Mercer to Washington, D.C., in January 1970 as part of the White House Record Library Commission appointed by President Richard M. Nixon to create a stellar collection of sound recordings for the enjoyment of the occupants and their guests in the nation's first residence. Under the leadership of the commission's chair, Willis Conover, seated in this photograph to the far right rear in the Music Room, Johnny, talking with the First Lady, joined others in compiling a list of popular albums. Johnny Mercer Collection, Popular Music Archives, Georgia State University Library, Atlanta, Georgia.

MIDDLE: Having met Johnny Mercer on his arrival in Hollywood and maintaining a close relationship with him as both friend and singer on the Capitol label, Margaret Whiting remained devoted to the songwriter after his death, assisting his widow, Ginger Mercer, in creating the Johnny Mercer Foundation in 1982 and then running the organization for much of the next thirty years. Courtesy of Margaret Whiting.

BOTTOM: Lionized as a living legend, Johnny Mercer headlined the Lyrics and Lyricists series of the Young Men's and Young Women's Hebrew Association hosted by Maurice Levine. By the time of the March 1971 performance, Mercer had begun to reflect on his career in popular entertainment. Johnny Mercer Collection, Popular Music Archives, Georgia State University Library, Atlanta, Georgia.

During the 1970s, Johnny and Ginger Mercer spent months out of the country every year, often in London or Paris. In addition to seeking opportunities to write with international composers, Johnny took in the sights, including Notre Dame Cathedral. Johnny Mercer Collection, Popular Music Archives, Georgia State University Library, Atlanta, Georgia.

Throughout their respective careers, Bing Crosby regularly performed Johnny's songs, and Johnny regularly appeared on Crosby's radio and television variety shows, where the two gained fame for their fun-loving duets. The old friends joined in what would be Johnny's last recording session, captured by Ken Barnes (left) for United Artists Records on October 17, 1974, in the Burbank, California, Heritage Studios. The former partners performed two duets to the accompaniment of pianist Jimmy Rowles (center): "The Pleasure of Your Company" and "Good Companions." Johnny Mercer Collection, Popular Music Archives, Georgia State University Library, Atlanta, Georgia.

To dedicate the Johnny Mercer Theatre in Savannah, civic leaders booked the touring revue *4 Girls 4* and adapted it to suit the May 28, 1978, occasion. Having performed Mercer's music throughout their careers, the girl singers in the show selected songs they had helped make famous, with Rosemary Clooney singing "Come Rain or Come Shine," Helen O'Connell singing "Tangerine," Rose Marie singing "I Fought Every Step of the Way," and Margaret Whiting singing "That Old Black Magic"; then they all appeared on stage for the grand finale as captured in this picture. Johnny Mercer Collection, Popular Music Archives, Georgia State University Library, Atlanta, Georgia.

Throughout his life the global southerner returned to coastal Georgia to find solace and renewal along the salt marsh. This 1975 shot of Johnny Mercer was probably taken near Highway 80 on the way to Tybee Island. Johnny Mercer Collection, Popular Music Archives, Georgia State University Library, Atlanta, Georgia.

with elaborate costumes — trapped the show in the 1880s and made Mercer fume. Barbara Robbins recalled, "It was all for the gays, which made Johnny crazy." The old joke about not being able to hum the scenery applied to this period piece that won Beaton a Tony but never came to life. The musical lacked the magic Arlen-Mercer touch that might have resulted in a jazzy song whistled by the audience as it left the theater. The love interests Carol Lawrence and How-ard Keel "never looked at each other," according to Robbins, who blamed their lack of chemistry as failing to spark interest in the story. Physically and mentally ill, Arlen suffered a breakdown, leaving his brother Jerry to resolve any musical problems as the orchestra's conductor. Mercer stepped in to compose both music and lyrics such as "Gettin' a Man" and "Why Fight This?"— the latter summing up his attitude about the show: "This may be the chance of a lifetime / No one wants to miss. / Yes, I can fight the devil's own luck / But why fight this?"[65]

In the midst of the turmoil surrounding the final weeks of rehearsal, an old Savannah friend arrived in New York City and called on Johnny. Mercer had a flat on Eighty-sixth Street, and Nick Mamalakis met him there, but as it was midday, the two rode back downtown to the Plaza to eat. Afterward Mercer in-vited Mamalakis to accompany him to the *Saratoga* rehearsal. As they walked down Fifth Avenue, suddenly Johnny pulled away and said, "Nick, wait here a second. I want to go in and say a little prayer." They had arrived near the gothic Little Church around the Corner, the Episcopal Church of the Transfiguration on Twenty-ninth Street. Taken aback, Mamalakis said, "Well, Johnny, you blue-blooded Episcopalians don't let any other Christians go into your church?" He recalled Mercer spun around and apologized, "Please forgive me. I shouldn't have said it that way," and then they both went in to pray. Back on the street, Mamalakis asked, "Well, I guess you prayed for a little help on *Saratoga*." Mercer responded, "Nick, I have never asked the good Lord for anything. I just thanked him for all of the blessings that he has bestowed on me. I've never said, 'Lord, please do this.' I always said, 'Thank you, Lord.'" Mamalakis ended the anecdote, suggesting Johnny's religious belief derived from the deep faith instilled in him by his father.[66]

Saratoga needed a miracle, for harsh criticism followed the Broadway premiere on December 7, 1959, in the Winter Garden Theatre. What should have been a smash, given the talent involved, received lame reviews. Everyone identified the weak book as the prime culprit, but several critics pointed to the lackluster song-writing. The *New York Mirror* summed it up: "The score is bouncy but undis-tinguished, not off Harold Arlen's top shelf. And Johnny Mercer's lyrics are not up to his usual standard, even those he pens for Tin Pan Alley or Hollywood." And although Mercer had "strewn the American landscape with phrases that are now part of the vernacular," Brooks Atkinson of the *New York Times* lamented that "in one degree or another, all the old pros are off their form in *Saratoga*." In his lead having called the "lavish musical ... dull," Atkinson blamed the director's lack of focus: "Give Mr. DaCosta a script or a scenario by someone else and he can invest with excitement on the stage. But he has not been able to sail his own scenario out of the doldrums. *Saratoga* is an uninteresting show." *Women's Wear Daily* headlined "Pretty as a Picture but Old Fashioned." The *Mirror* said likewise, "They've come up with an old-fashioned song-and-dancer, reminiscent of the moderate successes we used to get 30 or 35 years ago." A more biting critic noted it was as if *Oklahoma!* and *Pal Joey* had never occurred. Haunted by his youthful attraction to the uplifting, escapist musical comedy of Broadway, Mercer seemed mired in the *Show Boat* era, a shortcoming that handicapped his contributions to musical theater. Unlike lyricist Stephen Sondheim, whose *Gypsy*, written with composer Jule Styne, had opened just months before, Johnny disliked the troubling side of life, the ambiguities and lack of a positive resolution. Barbara Robbins accompanied the Mercer family that attended the opening night, and before the curtain rose on *Saratoga*, Styne walked down the aisle loudly telling his companion, "Saw it in previews. Really bad. Really bad!" Years later, Mercer explained the failure: "I'm always doing jobs I don't want. I thought my work the poorest I have ever done—even ruining one of Harold's tunes with a mediocre and unimaginative lyric." Arlen's melodies failed to inspire and are unperformed today. Although *Saratoga* presold more than a million tickets and cost nearly a half a million dollars to produce, it closed after only eighty performances.[67]

Another friend from Savannah witnessed the disappointment Mercer experienced with the failure of *Saratoga*. A frequent traveler to New York City on business for his Atlanta law firm, Pope Barrow McIntire—the younger brother of Jimmie McIntire and of Walter River's wife, Cornelia—had been encouraged by Johnny to attend the opening but declined, instead accepting an invitation to join him for lunch the following day, figuring "We could have a kind of a celebration or a wake." McIntire recalled, "I turned on the television in my hotel room that morning, and a drama critic described *Saratoga* as being the biggest bomb to hit Broadway in many years. I said, 'Oh my, this is going to be some lunch.'" They gathered at the "21," that famous former speakeasy on Fifty-second Street that Johnny had visited in the age of prohibition when Jack and Charlie ran the joint and that now served as the city's most distinguished restaurant. McIntire met the Mercers for a lunch that "lasted about two and a half hours as Johnny drowned his sorrows." Judy Garland accompanied by her former husband, Vincente Minnelli, sat at an adjacent table but quickly joined the Mercer party. A chronic liver condition that had her in and out of the hospital, a troubled marriage with Sid Luft that bordered on divorce, and financial problems that kept her desperate for money, had again reduced Garland's fortunes. Yet Capitol Records, with whom she had signed a contract shortly before Mercer sold the company in 1955, had planned a promotional tour for 1960 to sell her albums in Great Britain, an event that heralded another comeback. At low points in their careers and sharing their bouts with insecurity and in need of emotional support, the two musical geniuses remained true to that Cole Porter song they had recorded decades earlier, "When you're ever in a jam, here I am!"[68]

Coming off his success with *Gypsy*, the composer Jule Styne wanted to turn a Tennessee Williams play into a musical. Having optioned *The Rose Tattoo*, the English-born Styne determined he needed to collaborate with a native southerner, so he contacted Johnny Mercer about writing lyrics. Inveterate theatergoers, the Mercers had seen many of Williams's plays on Broadway and internalized the not-so-subtle message of southern decadence. Johnny joked about it in private letters to Cornelia McIntire Rivers, referring to *Cat on a Hot Tin Roof* when writing: "'Thank you Daddy'— or maybe Big Daddy, depending on what Tennessee Williams play I have most recently seen." Initially entertaining the idea, Mercer invited Styne over to discuss the possibilities regarding *The Rose Tattoo*. In the interim, he read the script about the lonely Sicilian widow's passionate love affair with a virile Italian truck driver on the Gulf Coast. Apart from its sultry setting, the 1951 Tony Winner had little to do with the region, while undermining traditional morals. On the appointed day Styne arrived at Mercer's house to evaluate the proposal, and he recalled a dramatic confrontation in which Johnny flung down the script, declaring, "That goddamned Tennessee Williams doesn't know anything about the South." Mercer certainly rejected the idea, and while he disagreed with the Mississippian's presentation of their shared homeland, given the subject matter of this particular play, it might also be that Johnny felt he had nothing to offer a story about working-class Italian immigrants. As Johnny's friend Jean Bach recalled, "He was very annoyed with Tennessee Williams and Tennessee Williams' take on the South. He said, 'He hasn't got it right,' you know, the depravity and all that stuff. He said, 'He's never been to any lovely country clubs,' and he really was kind of defending the 'Old South.'"[69]

Actually Williams claimed a similar heritage among the southern elite and his plays portrayed an individual's failure to uphold honor, thereby offending Mercer who preferred such matters remain private and who saw such performances as stereotyping the southern gentry as degenerate. Friend William "Bill" Harbach described Johnny as "gently southern, I mean not that heavy southern." In an interview, Johnny linked his own identity to southern nationalism: "Southern means that the South should have won the war. That we haven't forgot it." Mercer went on to suggest, "Being a gentleman is also a good thing. That's what the Southerner prizes. The Southerner prizes his lady. He prizes the manners. He likes to sit around and drink in a polite way. He doesn't push his personality into your life." These points laid out the code of honor that Mercer subscribed to with its patrician, patriarchal, and paternalistic characteristics. He recognized that "if you're a thinking man and you do believe the South is wrong, those Southerners probably leave," but Johnny, having joined that southern diaspora, quickly added that he did so only to make a living. Southerners lived the way they did, Mercer asserted, because they were "brought up, I think, in the plantation days and it's very hard to change four or five generations of a way of life." Mercer believed northerners will "say more what they think to you than the Southerner will. He won't say it. He'll hide it, you know? It's a question of being polite really. It's a question of respecting your individual privacy." Johnny added, "I think that's why Southerners resent having other people tell them what to do." Mercer believed that being southern "doesn't mean anything about race." He understood that for much of the South's history African Americans suffered as "a menial class," while the white elite held power as "the monied class," which provided the "reason the Negro left the South . . . because they didn't have any money down there," to which Johnny added, "I don't blame them." But to him black and white southerners shared the same culture rooted in interpersonal relations bred on the plantation whereby "a gentle person or a gentleman or a lady could be black or white."[70]

To counter the image Tennessee Williams presented on the Broadway stage, Mercer invited three couples from among his New York friends to spend the holidays in the South. He approached a trio of pals about the idea: Jimmy Downey, whom Johnny had known growing up in Savannah, and two producers from New York's entertainment industry, Bob Bach and Bill Harbach, the son of lyricist Otto Harbach who had written "Smoke Gets in Your Eyes" with Jerome Kern. Over the 1957 Christmas and New Year's holiday, Johnny and Ginger entertained Jean and Bob Bach, Jimmy and Marge Downey, and Bill and Faye

Harbach in Savannah. The guests departed from Manhattan's Penn Station, and on their arrival at Savannah's Union Station Mercer met them in a stretch limousine to take them to the DeSoto Hotel. Bill Harbach recalled "all of us were wined and dined and taken in that car around all of Savannah, and he was showing us all the sights, all the histories of the Civil War and his family and where he went to school." It being the festive time of year as the elite celebrated the Christmas cotillion, the Mercers took their guests to parties at the Oglethorpe Club, where they met Johnny's old friends and family members. They visited his house on the Back River and attended the quintessential southern coastal cookout, the oyster roast. Johnny enjoyed sharing with his guests other regional fare too. As Jean Bach recalled, "We'd go to different people's houses, and they lived very grandly, which is a neat contrast to the kind of crazy Fifty-Second Street life that we were all used to here in New York." Rather than the debilitated southern aristocracy weakened by inbreeding or gone to seed like the characters on Broadway, the New York visitors met the old-monied local gentry. "Everybody had Aubusson rugs and Baccarat chandeliers, and they were charming and gracious," Bach remembered. At the New Year, the guests dropped by with Johnny to visit the homes of his childhood friends, where they ate the traditional holiday dish of black-eyed peas and rice. "And we had to have a spoonful of 'hoppin' John' at every house we went to. I didn't quite understand that; the first time I went, I filled my plate up and of course it's only symbolic, to give you good luck for the rest of the year." Harbach remembered that Johnny "paid for the whole bill. He was just sensational. We had a great time." Suitably impressed, Jean Bach, who later made an important documentary about jazz in Harlem, returned to New York City with Mercer having complicated her vision of the South.[71]

Although he later regretted the decision, Mercer agreed to write another musical for Broadway called *Foxy*. The producers took Ben Jonson's *Volpone* — the 1606 Jacobean play subtitled "The Fox" that as a revival some thirty-five years before had given Johnny his break into the New York theater world — and as *Foxy* moved the story from Venice to the Yukon region of Canada during the 1896 Klondike Gold Rush. The settings suggest corruption by wealth where people worship gold and act as animals. The comedy featured Foxy, a deceitful old man who convinces others of his imminent death in order to extract gifts on the pretense of leaving the giver an inheritance. The story pits greed against greed. Bert Lahr signed on to play Foxy, and the role suited the vaudevillian talents of the Cowardly Lion from *The Wizard of Oz*, who had since starred in *Waiting for Godot* and other plays. Stanley Gilkey and Robert Whitehead produced the show, while Johnny joined his old collaborator Robert Emmett Dolan in putting together a score. A weak book written by the comic writer Ring Lardner Jr. and Ian McLellan Hunter and a weak director, Robert Lewis, whose previous credits included *Brigadoon* but who could not rein in Lahr, doomed the production. Using theater tricks he had practiced fifty years before, the aging star shamelessly stole every scene, treating them as vaudeville skits in a vicious exercise in self-absorption.[72]

Like the original *Volpone*, the show opens with a prologue that implies a literate performance featuring a handful of actors singing in an intimate setting, but the cast quickly expands to include an ensemble with song and dance routines typical of Broadway musicals. The role of Doc, played by Larry Blyden, carries the plot, often explaining the thoughts behind the actions of Lahr's character, Foxy. In the prologue, Doc announces: "Gold! / Women! / I have the honor to say / Our play, / Risque and rowdy, concerns the problem of greed / And where its practice can lead." It is Doc who conspires with Foxy to feign a fatal illness and thereby win favors as detailed in "Many, Many Ways to Skin a Cat." In addition to a host of prospectors, a group of prostitutes forms the ensemble, with Madam Brandy, played by Cathryn Damon, leading "Rollin' in Gold" to justify their lives. The female romantic lead, Celia, played by Julienne Marie, sings "Celia's Dilemma" with its rationale: "What a blessing to be told / That I'm worth my weight in gold! / Seen in that light, / It's really quite / An honor to be sold!" But her true heart's desire is to marry and settle down, so she struggles against the dehumanization of prostitution, "May I point with pride / That the spiritual side / Cost him practically nothing at all," to which the female chorus responds, "She's built for work or play — / She's a bargain either way." The more cynical characters join Foxy in singing "Money Isn't Everything" with its lines, "He trusted you, / But you welshed on him — / Friends, it's then you grow wise." Then Doc joins Brandy in extolling "Larceny and Love" with the lyric: "Maybe that is why we get along — / Just a pair of bunco artists / Born to deceive, / Adam and Eve / With an ace up our sleeve." The prospector Ben, the male romantic lead played by John Davidson, abandons the gold fields for excitement in town, performing "This Is My Night to Howl," but then he meets Celia. In the duet, "Talk to Me, Baby," they sing "If you cannot toss your heart gaily in the ring, / Love me while the moment lingers. / If you cannot cross your heart that I'm ev'rything, / Try at least to cross your fingers." Afraid of her feelings for Ben, Celia sings "Run, Run, Run, Cinderella," with its lines: "He said, 'Talk to me, baby, / And tell me lies.' / But all I told was the truth." The wiser heads Doc and Brandy take their leave with "I'm Way Ahead of the Game," while Foxy sketches out his life story with "Bon Vivant." He joins his deceived followers with "In Loving Memory," as they sing, "Money isn't everything / Once the spirit has fled. / Can it bring back anything / Once you're — shall we say — dead?" Foxy eludes their capture by climbing the golden proscenium of the Ziegfeld The-atre. In the "Finale," the ensemble reprises the moral of the story: "Money isn't everything, / Die just once and you'll see," when suddenly news arrives of the gold discovered in Alaska, and the lesson is lost.[73]

The Canadian government capitalized on the setting of the musical to inaugu-rate a festival that it hoped would attract tourists by providing the Palace Grand Theater in Dawson City, Yukon, for rehearsal space and initial performances. On July 2, 1962, *Foxy* opened its six-week Canadian run as the star attraction for the first Dawson City Gold Rush Festival; yet despite being subsidized by the Yukon Territorial Council, few theatergoers attended the show that closed with the tourist season in late August. While complimenting the "ripsnorter that romped through the legendary and romantic past of Canada's gold rush days," the *Vancouver Sun* also evaluated *Foxy*: "It will have to be drastically overhauled before they can show it to a Broadway audience." The songwriters revised *Foxy* before holding new tryouts in Cleveland, Ohio, where it opened on January 6, 1964, in the Hanna Theatre for a week before traveling to the Fisher Theater in Detroit for a month-long run. Mercer recognized problems and hoped that more rehearsals might salvage the show. He wrote Lahr, "This is the first time I've ever seen a performer do my material better than I meant it. Usually we're happy with 75% or 80% of what we would like — but you find laughs where the laughs aren't even there! You're just marvelous and I love you."[74]

Once *Foxy* arrived in the Ziegfeld Theatre on February 15, 1964, the crit-ics loved Lahr too, gushing about the bad puns and old antics, though reviews proved less warm about the show itself. Staying at the Savoy Hilton Hotel on opening night, Mercer received telegrams wishing the show success from fellow songwriters, the lyricist Dorothy Fields, and composers Alan and Marilyn Keith Bergman. Ginger telegrammed, "Your son and I are cheering rooting and send-ing all our love and wishes for you and Foxy," signed with that old Broadway joke, "The little old investor lady." The most positive review appeared in the *New York Times*: "The lyrics of Johnny Mercer are often bright, and Robert Emmett Dolan's tunes are bouncing and graceful in a way reminiscent of the self-assured twenties." The producer of the show, David Merrick, had a bigger box office with *Hello, Dolly!* so he simply struck the sets on *Foxy* after eighty-five performances despite full houses. The crusty legend in entertainment, Lahr, received a Tony for his role. The Ziegfeld had opened with a show that was the first musical Johnny ever saw on Broadway, and *Foxy* turned out to be one of the last staged in the theater, for three years after it closed the house fell to the wrecking ball. The old vaudevillian Lahr watched the demolition of the Ziegfeld in disbelief and then died himself several weeks later, marking for Mercer the end of another era in American show business.[75]

8 Movie Theme Songs

The world that we really should chart
Isn't mountains or rivers,
It's the world of the heart.
We'd all see our own counterpart
In the faces of others
In the world of the heart.

AS THE MOVIE MUSICAL declined in popularity, Hollywood studios employed songwriters to write theme songs for films, figuring that a catchy tune and snappy lyric could advertise the picture. Used as a motif, the music appeared not only at the opening and closing credits as a song, but throughout the movie's soundtrack as atmosphere underpinning key moments in the film. Thus the music and the movie became inseparable. Given the value of such theme songs, the studios hired the top talent to compose them. As an entertainer and celebrity, Johnny Mercer had made the transition from radio to television, appearing on the occasional variety show as a popular guest star. Yet the antivocal attitude of bebop and the end of the Age of the Singer diminished opportunities to write the kind of art songs that had filled the Great American Songbook. Instead, songwriters watched untrained doo-wop and rock 'n' roll musicians performing their own material take over the popular market, too. Collaborating on movie theme songs provided one of the few avenues for getting music played before a larger audience. For years Mercer had partnered with jazz composer-arrangers, men whom music critic Henry Pleasants identified as "jazz-oriented" to emphasize the melding of jazz with popular song.[1] Mercer continued the practice of collaborating with these jazz composers while writing lyrics for movie theme songs that proved quite successful.

Of course Mercer's music had provided a unifying theme in movies for decades, beginning with "I'm an Old Cowhand (from the Rio Grande)," which Paramount interpolated into the 1936 picture *Rhythm on the Range* and then played at the opening and closing credits. Often using the same title as the name of the film, a theme song had to develop character and plot even if the movie included a couple of other songs like a musical. Johnny joined composer Gene De Paul on the theme song "You Can't Run Away from It" for a 1956 Columbia picture about a fiancée who flees an arranged marriage only to fall for someone else. Showing his willingness to approach rock 'n' roll, Mercer wrote both the words and music for "Bernardine," a 1957 college caper, for 20th Century Fox. The lyric speaks of teenage love: "You're a little bit like ev'ry girl I've ever seen. / All your separate parts are not unknown / But the way you assemble 'em's all your own — / All yours and mine, dear Bernardine!" On his recording, Pat Boone croons above the chords of an electric guitar: "Say you'll wait for me out by the rocket base, / And we'll both blast off into outer space / At oh-oh-oh-oh Bernardine!" Johnny collaborated with his old friend Matt Malneck on "Love in the Afternoon" for an Allied Artists picture produced by Billy Wilder that starred Audrey Hepburn and Gary Cooper. The lyric referred to an affair, a subject that Mercer came back to frequently in his midlife: "To think that love nearly passed us by! / Then I happened to be / Where you happened to catch my eye, / And now / Both our hearts are filled with June / Because of love in the afternoon." Ginger found the lyric second rate.[2]

For an increasingly rare movie musical, Mercer collaborated with composer Saul Chaplin on *Merry Andrew*, released by MGM in 1958. The score, arranged by Nelson Riddle, included quintessential Mercer songs such as "The Square of the Hypotenuse," "Everything Is Tickety Boo," and "You Can't Always Have What You Want." In "The Pipes of Pan," Johnny recalls Greco-Roman mythology with a nod to the recent Broadway sensation *Peter Pan*: "I mean the astral alien, / The creature bacchanalian / No good Episcopalian / Believes in." As a teacher in a circus, Danny Kaye competed with a chimpanzee to be the film's star. In 1959, *Li'l Abner* made it to celluloid in Technicolor and Vistavision. While Johnny's lyrics occasionally appeared in the odd film or as a theme song, a decade passed before he participated in writing another movie musical for Hollywood.[3]

Instead, Johnny explored opportunities to write for television. On April 10, 1959, CBS broadcast *Swing into Spring* with Johnny providing the lyrics to the theme song composed by Bob Swanson. The Benny Goodman Orchestra played the number sung as a duet by Ella Fitzgerald and Peggy Lee with the Hi-Los providing the background chorus. The peppy lyric of the four refrains plays on the names of months: "Let's leap into May, / Knee deep into May" and "Let's hop into June, / Kerplop into June." Mercer partnered with his old friend Fred Astaire on the words and music of a television special called *Another Evening with Fred Astaire* that NBC broadcast on November 4, 1959. The masters of rhythm designed a danceable lyric in the song "The Afterbeat." The verse explains that everybody knows the downbeat but that "another beat has always been there, too!" From that Astaire develops his jazz-infused dance routine with the lines: "But the offbeat, / Like a backbeat, / Or an echo beat, / That's the afterbeat." Calling the rhythm "infectious indeed, built as it is around the pause between the accentuated beats," the *New York Times* believed "Mr. Astaire very probably has launched a new song-and-dance hit." Mercer saw these as serviceable songs that lived the duration of the broadcast, and therefore at first dismissed the long-term potential of television. According to Johnny's daughter, Mandy, when family friend and composer Vic Mizzy contacted Mercer about writing a lyric for a new sitcom being produced by ABC, the lyricist tossed off a few lines about the oddball characters that populated the cartoons by Charles Addams that he had read for years in the *New Yorker*. "They're creepy and they're kooky, / Mysterious and spooky, / They're all together ooky, / The Addams Family / Their house is a museum / Where people come to see 'em / They really are a scream / The Addams Family." When Mizzy asked Mercer if he wanted credit for the lyric, Johnny declined, saying, "Naaaa, don't bother," figuring thirty minutes of Gomez, Morticia, and the assortment of outlandish relatives would never last on air. Of course, Johnny later realized his mistake as Mizzy copyrighted the lyric, for *The Addams Family* remains in syndication on cable television with people everywhere chiming in to snap their fingers and sing the theme song.[4]

With the changing times and tastes of the public, Mercer found lyrics he wrote with notable composers being unperformed as he experienced increased difficulty placing music with singers. In 1957, he collaborated with Vernon Duke on "Yours for Keeps" and Matt Malneck on "Rainy Night," but no performers picked up these songs, which consequently went unpublished. A similar fate awaited collaborations with former partners Lewis E. Gensler in 1958 on "Sleepyhead" and with Gordon Jenkins in 1959 on "Lovers in the Dark." Mercer joined with celebrity composers such as Steve Allen on "Baby" in 1959 and Percy Faith on "Bouquet" in 1961 but with similar results. Even when working in 1962 with masters of melody such as Hoagy Carmichael on "Jack-O'-Lantern" and Rube Bloom on "If You Come Through," Johnny had little luck. Without a vehicle like a movie to promote the song, it became harder and harder to get the music played.[5]

An active correspondent, Mercer often wrote notes to friends and colleagues. He received a spirited response from Yip Harburg in the spring of 1959. His fellow lyricist thanked Johnny for a compliment and went on to explain the nature of their shared craft. "Actually, *Hit Parade* or no *Hit Parade*, it is for the handful of Inner-sanctum-nicks that we really write. The Johnnies, the Iras, the Coles, who however far flung the archipelagos they live in, are always looking over our shoulder at each singable syllable, double entendre and triple rhyme... And so Johnnie-O, your note was better than benzedrene, more nourishing than fillet [sic] mignon. There is a special halo about the WRITTEN word. I find it more persuasive, more real than phone calls, wires, or any of the celebrated emanations of the coaxial cables. That someone moves to a desk, takes up a pen in love and amity, never ceases to thrill me." In many ways Johnny simply continued a practice he had seen his father exercise for years, writing letters of condolence, encouragement, and praise out of a desire to "cast bread upon the waters."[6]

Mercer's experience writing a song with a grandmother from Ohio reflected this generous nature. In February 1957, Sadie Vimmerstedt had scribbled on a daily calendar page the note, "Dear Johnnie: I want you to write a song for me." The cosmetic saleslady who managed a perfume counter in Youngstown offered the line, "I want to be around to pick up the pieces when somebody breaks your heart." Then she explained that turnabout seemed fair play: "I felt that is the way Nancy Sinatra feels about Frankie boy." Vimmerstedt had overheard a news story on the radio concerning how Ava Gardner had abandoned Frank Sinatra a few years after Sinatra had left his first wife, Nancy Barbato, for the Hollywood beauty. Afterward Sinatra had hit rock bottom until, in 1953, he signed with Capitol Records, which paired him up with the Nelson Riddle Orchestra. Thereafter, the singer turned around his faltering career with "concept" long-playing albums. Sadie Vimmerstedt stuck her note in an envelope addressed to "Johnny Mercer, Songwriter, New York, N.Y." Somehow it reached Johnny, who, taking the idea to heart, crafted a tune and a lyric titled "I Wanna Be Around." Registered for a copyright as an unpublished song in 1959, it sat around for several years until picked up by a singer and then published, with Johnny splitting the royalty fifty-fifty with Vimmerstedt, despite his having composed the music and contributed most of the words. She wrote him, "The song is way beyond my expectations." He responded, "Don't you know there wouldn't BE a song — if it hadn't been for you???" A note from Johnny in October 1962 reported, "I heard that Tony Bennett is singing the song in Las Vegas and it is a big hit. Also that he might record it. Keep your fingers crossed." That month Bennett recorded the song in an arrangement by Marty Manning. The release of the single on February 18, 1963, and then its inclusion in a March album of the same name rocketed

Bennett to the top of the charts, marking another number one *Your Hit Parade* single for which Mercer contributed both words and music.[7]

As the successful songwriter turned fifty, Johnny sought refuge in Savannah's traditions as a way to ground his global life in the legacy of his southern past. He made arrangements for his daughter to join her cousins as a debutante in 1959. For decades, every Christmas the city's elite presented the young ladies to society through a series of parties centered around an opening cotillion and, a few days later, a debutante ball. As a youth Johnny had regularly escorted teenage women to the events. A private social group of white men that represented the city's old aristocracy, and in some ways its persistent power structure, selected the girls. Made up of family friends, the group invited the Mercer daughters to debut. Johnny joined his brother Walter as sponsors for the three girls, all around age eighteen: Walter's daughter, Louise Mercer; Juliana's daughter, Nancy Keith; and Johnny's daughter, Mandy Mercer. The children of family friends were among the nineteen girls chosen that year, including Jimmie McIntire's daughter, Connie. Friends in Savannah hosted various events for the debs, such as a milk punch party, a tea dance, and a buffet supper given by Mr. and Mrs. Robert Thomson for the Mercers. For more than a week the Oglethorpe Club buzzed with cocktail parties associated with the debutantes. At the annual ball held in a festive DeSoto Hotel outlined in sparkling lights, the young women wore white dresses and received their guests, holding delicate bouquets of pink flowers. After marching in the processional that inaugurated the dance, they waltzed with their fathers and escorts, all the men dressed in white ties and tails. A ball hosted by the Mercers on Christmas Day put the 1959 social season over the top. Johnny rented the main ballroom of the DeSoto Hotel and hired two big bands — one from Savannah and the other from New York — so that when one completed a set the other could begin without a lull in the music. The dazzling decorations under the crystal chandeliers included life-size Christmas trees encased in ice. The newspaper reported, "Guests danced to special arrangements of nostalgic tunes prepared by John Mercer, comprised of his favorite songs and those of daughter Amanda." It added, "This is the gayest season ever seen in Savannah!" It proved one of the grandest parties ever held in the terra cotta–trimmed landmark as well as one of the last, for within a decade developers had demolished the old DeSoto Hotel.[8]

The holidays at home offered Johnny an opportunity for self-reflection on his career and family life. Against the festivities of the debutante ball stood the lackluster response to his latest Broadway attempt, *Saratoga*, and the equally troubled revival of *St. Louis Woman* in Amsterdam called *Free and Easy*. Interviewed by a reporter in Savannah, Johnny explained, "No other show is in the offing at the moment," although he had accepted invitations to appear on both the Dinah Shore and the Perry Como television programs that winter of 1960. As his career evolved, he also watched his family life change: Mandy moved to New York to study acting, while Jeff, now twelve, had entered puberty. As an often-absent father, Johnny had tried to make amends by spoiling his children. On previous trips to Georgia, he had allowed Mandy to stay with her cousins, Ann and Louise, at the Barbizon Boarding House for Ladies and Jeff to smuggle home to California a diamondback terrapin and two alligators. During this visit, Johnny supported the Savannah Occupational Training Center for the handicapped by appearing on local television to raise money for the charity. He caught performances by the local jazz pianist Kenneth Palmer Jr., as well as the black folksinger Tedd Browne. While talking with the *Savannah Evening Press* reporter, Johnny became nostalgic, suggesting he had often wanted to write a song about Savannah that might capture "the smell of marsh grass, the slow tempo, the sort of Old World flavor, the nice manners." He mused about his earlier songs, observing "Lazybones," his first success, "doesn't wear well," and that he had no favorite other than "whichever is a hit is it." He even confessed he no longer painted watercolors. Despite his success, the perennially optimistic middle-aged Mercer appeared wistful and restless during the interview.[9]

Johnny recognized in the contributions of his ancestors a stability that seemed lacking in the larger world. The songwriter returned to his hometown in the spring of 1961 to celebrate the 175th anniversary of the Chatham Artillery, an organization once headed by his great-grandfather, Civil War general Hugh W. Mercer. For two nights that May, the Tommy Dorsey Orchestra entertained in Savannah, often playing arrangements of Mercer's tunes. The songwriter himself performed alongside the swing band once led by his old friend who had died in 1956. Johnny especially enjoyed belting out "Hard Hearted Hannah (the Vamp of Savannah)!," a song often attributed to him but written by Milton Ager, Jack Yellen, Bob Bigelow, and Charles Bates.[10]

In October 1962, an observance in recognition of his grandfather's contributions to Savannah's board of education brought Johnny back to the port city. He had been invited to speak at the dedication of the George Anderson Mercer Junior High School — the first air-conditioned school in the state of Georgia — in suburban Garden City, not far from the Five Mile Bend truck farm of the Ciucevich clan. Johnny opened by saying, "I wish grandfather were here to see this, and to give this speech." Echoing his ancestor's attitudes, the grandson proposed that education should "advance the 'thought and wisdom of mankind.'" He added "that he was happy that 'controlled environment' only referred to the building facility because thinking and learning should be 'free as the air we breathe.'" Two months later, he attended the unveiling of a portrait of Revolutionary War general Hugh Mercer by the Daughters of the American Revolution at the Mercer Hospital in Trenton, New Jersey. Comparing himself to the hero of the Battle of Princeton as depicted in the painting, the balding Johnny joked that his great-great-great-grandfather had more hair.[11]

Proud of its native son, the Georgia General Assembly passed a resolution in the winter of 1965 authored by Representative Dan Sewell of Savannah asking Mercer to "prepare an official State song for the Assembly's consideration." Johnny had misgivings, no doubt thinking that the 1930 "Georgia on My Mind" by his old friend and former collaborator Hoagy Carmichael, with lyrics by Stuart Gorrell, could suffice for a more popular interpretation, but the lawmakers assured him they wanted something by a native Georgian. A hymn-like official state song written by Lily S. Wheaton called "Georgia" existed, as did Tin Pan Alley takes such as "Georgia, a Song of a Sunny Southern State" by Mercer's old friend and collaborator Walter Donaldson, with lyrics by Howard Johnson. When the state of West Virginia had asked Johnny to write for it "a contagious sort of a singable song" in time for its 1963 centennial, the songwriter had declined, but when his home state came calling, the songwriter felt obligated to say yes.[12]

As occasionally happened in his career, despite reservations he accepted the challenge, only to be disappointed by the outcome. In writing the state song, Mercer turned to the poetry of another descendant of Georgians for inspiration: "Feeling I could do no better, nor write more sincerely, than Stephen Vincent Benét, I used a few of his couplets from *John Brown's Body* for the basis of my song." The magisterial epic had been published in 1927, and Mercer arranged attribution for Benét as he incorporated a stanza of the poem into the chorus of his state song, "Georgia, Georgia." By Georgia Day, February 13, 1966, Governor Carl Sanders had received the submission for the General Assembly to review. Back in Savannah the marching band of the Benedictine Military School prepared it for the annual St. Patrick's Day Parade. The Leopold Adler Company had printed the lyric for free distribution. The song began: "Georgia, Georgia, / Where do I start? / Words can sing, / But not like the heart — / There's no land in all this earth / Like the land of my birth!" Yet the eight verses, each with a different chorus, proved unwieldy. Tabling the motion to adopt, the General Assembly sent the matter back to committee, where it died at the end of the 1966 session under the gold dome. Nonetheless, feeling the lyric captured the lost Georgia of his youth, a proud Mercer included the poetry in his autobiography, along with the speculation that the legislators feared the song favored Savannah over other regions of the state. Ironically friends in his hometown had long criticized the songwriter for not featuring the city's name in lyrics, to which Mercer replied that when writing words he often thought about "Savannah; Orange, Virginia, where I went to school; Atlanta that I visited a lot; and other nearby towns. They made a composite city to model a lyric by." Yet he also confessed, "Although I have never written a song directly about Savannah, so many of my lyrics are filled with boyhood images that you might almost say they all sprang from there." Two years later, as a consolation prize, the new governor, Lester Maddox, commissioned Mercer an "Admiral in the Georgia Navy."[13]

The television journalist Charles Collingwood interviewed the Mercer family for *Person to Person*, a program earlier hosted by Edward R. Murrow. The format took the cameras into the home to capture the domestic life of the celebrity by wandering from room to room. Filmed at the Via Koron address in Newport Beach, the segment aired on June 28, 1961. Johnny talked about songwriting and Ginger, and the children politely responded to questions, with only the mynah bird refusing to cooperate. The picture of familial bliss offered at the end of the show, with the Mercers happily gathered on the patio, belied the troubles beneath the surface: teenage rebellion, adult alcoholism, and marital unhappiness. Like most American families in the Age of Consensus, these issues remained personal problems. Johnny wrote his friend Murray Baker, "I managed to avoid Ed Murrow for years, but Charles Collingwood finally caught up with me."[14]

Around the time of the *Person to Person* interview, Johnny played a round of golf at the Bel Air Country Club, and coming around the green, he spied a for-sale sign on a house at the thirteenth hole. He called up his handyman, Robert "Bobby" Rush: "I've got a surprise for Ginger for Christmas," intending for the decorator to redo the house. Knowing Ginger too well, Rush responded, "You're going to have a surprise, because I'm not doing anything for your wife without her knowing about it." Johnny bought the house, but did not join the club because it discriminated against Jews. Ginger oversaw the renovations, taking one bedroom for herself and turning another into a walk-in closet to house her clothes, with a separate room for her shoes, which she segregated between summer and winter, with space for matching purses. Johnny had his room "clear at the other end of the house," according to Rush, "because they would sleep and wake up at all different hours all night long, and if they were in the same room, they drove each other crazy." Mercer also turned the garage into a studio where he could work writing songs. The family moved into the house high up in the Bel Air section of Beverly Hills at 10972 Chalon Road in the late fall of 1961. From his patio, Johnny watched golfers putting on the same greens he had played with Dick Whiting thirty years before. The move delighted Ginger because again she lived near her close friends Lee Gershwin, the wife of lyricist Ira Gershwin, and Rosie Gilbert, the wife of publisher L. Wolfe Gilbert, and together they volunteered for women's groups, engaged in liberal politics, and supported charitable organizations.[15]

Even with a house in Bel Air, the Mercers appeared modest, avoiding ostentatious display. Bill Harbach recalled the interior of the house that Ginger had decorated with French furniture and other European antiques: "Marvelous things all around, awards and things like that, and memorabilia of his career, but very — no chi-chi — just very simple, straight away unpretentious. No glitz." Henry Mancini remembered it as a "lovely home in Bel Air, not really very large in view of Johnny's incredible catalog of songs and his ASCAP [American Society of Composers, Authors and Publishers] rating, but beautifully decorated and charming." Henry and his wife, Ginny, had become close friends with Johnny and Ginger, and he remembered the lot "seemed to be snuggled in a hollow of trees next to the golf course, and at the back of the property Johnny had a studio where he wrote." Having kept the Newport Beach house as a coastal retreat after moving to Bel Air, Ginger later explained to a reporter they used all four residences: "We use our ranch-style house at Palm Springs for vacations and always spend Christmas in our old colonial home in Georgia." The reporter noted the Mercers believed "it is better to buy a home than stay in hotels if they like a place enough to visit more than once." Johnny appreciated the value of real estate as an investment, an attitude he shared with his father.[16]

With the move to Bel Air, the Mercers enrolled Jeff as a freshman in nearby Brentwood Academy. Johnny had wanted his son to attend his alma mater, Woodberry Forest, but the boys' boarding school in Orange, Virginia, had rejected Jeff's application, to the great disappointment of his father, who thought of the institution as the family school. During the 1950s, two of Johnny's brother George Mercer's grandsons — Christopher F. and Pearce W. Hammond — had attended Woodberry when cousin Joe Mercer still served as headmaster. Apparently Johnny had appealed to Joe on Jeff's behalf, but to no avail. The alumni director of Woodberry, Gerald L. Cooper, wrote the songwriter in 1967, "Knowing nothing about the details surrounding your son's application to Woodberry, I nonetheless can appreciate your changed feelings about the school and think it is particularly good of you to have consented to serve as class agent." Mercer agreed to solicit donations to the Amici Fund, which financed the foundation. For years Johnny had contributed regularly, and despite the denial of his son's admission, he continued to encourage others to donate money to Woodberry.[17]

Johnny and Ginger indulged their children and suffered the consequences. In a letter to the Taylors at Woodberry written in the 1950s, Mercer admitted to "doing our best to see that the children grow up into good people, and profit by our mistakes — or accomplishments — as the case may be." Amanda preferred Newport Beach to the superficial Beverly Hills world created by Hollywood. As a rebellious teenager, Mandy smoked and once ran away, staying at a neighbor's house. When she had not returned home for the evening, Bobby Rush recalled: "God, you would've thought that she'd been captured by white slavery. Johnny went crazy. So did Ginger." After Mandy's graduation from Newport Harbor High School, Johnny arranged for her to study acting in New York, where instead she fell in love with the jazz musician Robert "Bob" Corwin and married him in 1960. The Mercers held the wedding at the Hotel Bel-Air because the Bel Air Country Club refused to accommodate African Americans and the wedding guests included Nat and Maria Cole. The Corwins returned to California and moved to nearby Brentwood, where Mandy, pregnant and with a stepson Jonathan, could visit her parents and Bob could assist Johnny with transcriptions. Mercer delighted in the birth of his grandson, James "Jamie" Corwin, and the two shared Johnny's November 18 birthday. Mercer tried to help Bob with his career although the son-in-law wanted to make it on his own. Despite the tensions in the household, the Corwins remained close to the Mercers. When Johnny traveled to Canada in the summer of 1962 for the early rehearsals of *Foxy* in Dawson City, Jeff — who would transfer to Newport Harbor High School that fall — traveled with him. The fifty-two-year-old father and his fifteen-year-old son enjoyed the outdoor beauty of the Yukon. The two had always gotten along, partly because of Mercer's overly indulgent manner, but also because of Jeff's relaxed attitude. After high school, Jeff continued to live at home, where his parents fretted over his apparent lack of interest in anything except girls and cars. He joined his father in a music-publishing venture as a way to make a living.[18]

As adults, Mandy and Jeff remembered a family life made as normal as possible given Mercer's constant absences, celebrity status, and access to vast wealth.

In later years the two recalled as teenagers overhearing snippets of arguments between their parents as well as tender moments. Mandy noted about Johnny's love for Ginger, "He bought her flowers every single day." Yet their parents' complicated relationship played out against the cocktail culture. Other people who knew the Mercers presented less charitable views, repeating third-party rumors about difficulties in the marriage that almost led to divorce. In preparation for his biography of the songwriter, Gene Lees interviewed the siblings together, quoting Mandy discussing Johnny and Ginger's relationship: "He was mad at her. Always. I thought she was just aloof. And then my brother told me how angry she was. I'd hear the fighting and thought it was both of them." But Jeff corrected her again, "No, it's Mom. She's just got a burr up her ass all the time." The unhappiness in the household and disagreements with the children left lasting scars.[19]

Deep-seated feelings of insecurity and jealousy provoked fights. As a songwriter who relied on the public's consumption of his music, Johnny remained at the mercies of the marketplace as the measure of his success. No doubt occasional bouts of insecurity made him irritable, and alterations in the entertainment industry made Mercer especially nervous. Because of his celebrity, strangers often asked Johnny for autographs. Tired of the hounding, daughter Mandy remembered pleading, "Daddy, let's go! I want to go home now!" Mercer responded, "Sit down! If it wasn't for them, you wouldn't have any food in your mouth so you sit down . . . and you wait for me," adding, "You owe it to the people . . . You owe the clothes on your back to these people, so you sit down and shut up, and I'll keep signing them." In his autobiography, Johnny admitted "how annoying it can become when a stretched out hand, holding an autograph pad or a camera is always stuck in your kisser." He found most autograph seekers believed "they own the celebrities" and he understood why "celebs spend so much time hiding away and avoiding public gatherings." Mercer recognized people just wanted the contact with the celebrity "and that nine times out of ten the little piece of paper will be tossed carelessly aside and they'll probably tell their girl friend: 'Oh, him, he's nothing. He wears a toupee and his teeth are capped!'"[20]

Being Jewish, Ginger feared anti-Semitism, although she "never admitted" her heritage, claiming to descend from Austrian Christians. As an agnostic, she had insisted on raising the children without religion, something that bothered the religious Mercer. As Ginger aged, she fretted about changes in her appearance. Polly Ober, who described her friendship with Ginger as being as "close as two coats of paint," recalled that Ginger said that "there were problems, constantly, of women coming on to Johnny, you know, he is a cute, attractive, fun guy." Having proven himself unfaithful, Mercer hit on the women too. Ginger never forgave Johnny for the adultery that served as an open sore in their relationship. Yet Bobby Rush believes Ginger "never knew what impact she had on her husband — I don't think. She really didn't know how much he loved her." Rush recalled driving the two from Lido Isle to the train station, listening as they argued the whole way. At the platform, Johnny turned to Ginger and said, "Well, give me a kiss," which she did, then he boarded and disappeared, leaving her in tears. Rush said, "I don't believe you! I mean, here you are arguing with him all the way into town. And I turn around, and you're crying!" Ginger responded, "You want to know something? Tomorrow, I'm going to miss him."[21]

Money made matters worse. Growing up in Savannah, Johnny had enjoyed the life of the spoiled elite. Even with his father's loss of a fortune, Johnny never truly suffered from want, surviving his lean years in New York with an adventurer's spirit and with financial help from his parents. Ginger experienced the opposite; her father's suicide made her family's situation ever more precarious, teaching her the hard lesson of material need. Writing a colleague in 1956, cousin Joe recognized: "Johnny's wife Ginger is tight-fisted and apparently keeps a weather eye on all of his spending. It was she who first got him to settle down and make sound investments, and I believe she still influences him strongly in all his financial affairs." Mandy remembered the fights. Learning of some extravagance, Ginger would scold Johnny, "You should save more money and do this and do that and nah-nah-nah-nah." Johnny would shout back, "It's my money. I spend it the way I want." Mandy said, "He wanted to spend it on his family, you know. He was ridiculous. He spoiled us all to death. His children, his grandchildren, his mom, his nieces, his nephews . . . He'd spoil her family, and she'd get mad at him for spending." Johnny loved to surprise relatives with trips, arranging for Ginger's mother and sister to travel from Florida through the Panama Canal to California or sending Ginger and her sister to Asia. Ginger would point out to Johnny that "she wasn't as rich as Dolores Hope," Mandy recalled, noting, "Of course Bob was very stingy."[22]

As a consumer, Johnny enjoyed buying clothes and looking fashionable. When walking New York's streets with writer Henry Kane one September day in the late 1950s, he stopped to window-shop at a haberdasher's. Kane described Mercer's outfit as a blue-gray lightweight suit with leather belt, "button-down, button-cuffed, Brooks'-type, white shirt, collar slightly flared," boasting "a gay regimental tie with red, white, and gray stripes." Mercer limited his wardrobe to a few Brooks Brothers suits and ties and a handful of casual shirts and trousers, but for Ginger he bought several mink coats, including one dyed red to wear at Christmas. Joe Mercer mentioned the cars: "A Cadillac for Ginger and an old jalopy for Johnny." Indeed, in the 1940s they owned a Cadillac convertible. When in 1953 to celebrate its fiftieth anniversary in business Buick issued the Skylark convertible, Johnny bought one for Ginger because it had the same name as the song he and Carmichael had written a decade earlier. Near the end of his life, as Ginger traded her Jaguar in every year for the latest model, Johnny tooled around in a beige Ford Pinto hatchback. Having achieved great wealth, Mercer shunned the materialism his wife embraced.[23]

Drinking proved a nemesis for both Johnny and Ginger, as stories abound regarding their problems with alcohol. Polly Ober recalled about Johnny, "When he belted that grape too totally, bingo!" She added, "Ginger belted the grape too. But she was always a lady." Johnny's business associate Barbara Robbins remembered, "They fed off each other. If he was drinking, she wouldn't drink. If she was drinking, he wouldn't drink." Thinking about it, Robbins added, "It was very strange . . . there was a period of time when they were really mad at each other, and they both drank. And they fought quite a bit." She saw them both as alcoholics and believed that if someone had spoken with them about their problem, neither would have "stopped drinking" and Johnny would have said "not to bother him." One must wonder if in the autobiography Johnny is talking about his own family life when describing neighbors who drank too much, cursed each other, and fought all the time. Jean Bach remembered a night out with the Mercers at the Copacabana nightclub in New York watching chorus girls dancing in the revue from their seats at a ringside table. Typically, they had been drinking, and "the emcee came out and said, 'Ladies and gentlemen, we're honored tonight to have with us that distinguished songwriter, Johnny Mercer,' and they'd put the spotlight on him, and he's sound asleep." Bach added, "You know, having had a drink, he was out of it. He did a lot of sleeping." Similarly his collaborator Harold Arlen, when out on a binge, might wake up on the neighbor's lawn in Beverly Hills. When *Newsweek* published its feature "Mercerizing Johnny," it noted Mercer's behavior at parties: "At the end of the evening he sometimes curls up and goes to sleep under the piano." The same fate occasionally happened to Ginger. Her son, Jeff, remembered coming home from school one day to find his mother passed out and sprawled upside down on the stairs.[24]

For Johnny, drinking went hand-in-glove with the entertainment industry. Hired by Glenn Wallichs to assist Mercer with recordings, Dave Dexter discovered Johnny "liked to gather his thoughts and bend elbows at the bar with his cronies." Over the course of Henry Kane's noon hour interview with Mercer at the Harwyn bar in New York, the songwriter never ate but drank "Scotch on the rocks, in an old fashioned glass, a twist of lemon peel," and smoked Oasis cigarettes. When the writer asked Mercer if he drank while he worked, Johnny replied, "Never . . . I drink moderately. I drink when I'm relaxing. Work? That's serious. Drink, to me, that's not serious, that's part of relaxation. Work is work; work is not part of relaxation; so I do not drink when I work." As an afterthought, Mercer added, "I'm a great man for moderation, in all things, even work. I believe in moderation. Me? I'm moderate in so many things, in all things." Waxing philosophical, Mercer suggested, "I suppose that's part of my deep-down philosophy — there is always another day," adding, "Please have another drink." Kane then noted, "His glass was empty. He is a quick drinker." Johnny knew the Harwyn bartender who sent a fresh round, the second of four. The writer commented on Mercer's manners too, observing that when Johnny bought from the cigarette girl a package of Oasis, he ordered an extra pack of Kane's brand too, then proceeded to whip out a lighter whenever Kane withdrew a cigarette.[25]

The years of emotional abuse left the Mercers devoted to each other and to alcohol in a co-dependency neither could shake. In the 1940s after adopting the children, they had tried to cut back, but by the 1950s Johnny struggled as he climbed on and fell off the wagon time and again. He controlled the alcohol by only drinking beer during Lent. When dry, Mandy remembered him being "so proud of himself." From 1964, Ginger's health required that she limit her alcohol intake to wine, though hard liquor proved irresistible. Several times Johnny reported to his mother, Lillian, lines like the following from 1963: "You will be happy to know I haven't had a drink for over a month and a half, and expect to continue that course as long as I can — which may be from now on — I feel so much better — and from all indications, am so much nicer and easier to live with — not just my family think so — but all my friends and acquaintances too." And a few years later, "I'm wagon-ing it again."[26]

Like other creative people, Mercer sought release, using alcohol as his drug of preference, and like many inebriated people, Mercer could be rude to others. Friends such as Hoagy Carmichael did likewise, earning a reputation as a mean drunk. When in his cups, Johnny could retort with expletives to requests made or questions asked by friends, fans, or strangers. People close to him remembered that three stiff drinks of scotch often relaxed his code of conduct enough to release his inhibitions that enabled him to say things he never would have said if sober. As Mercer warned his collaborator, André Previn, "I get nasty when I get drunk." Gene Lees reported on this facet of Johnny's life in his *Jazzletter* under the headline, "Roses in the Morning," when, after having hurled a hurtful comment at some celebrity, Mercer sent flowers as penance. The practice played out in Hollywood style in the movie *You Were Never Lovelier* with the song "These Orchids" by Mercer and Jerome Kern: the Bell Boys Quartet brings in dozens of cellophane-wrapped flowers to an offended woman while singing take "these orchids please, with apologies, and another note." Johnny joined Harry Warren at the Playboy Club to hear Margaret Whiting perform, but after drinking too much he shocked her by saying, "You sing too goddamn loud. You're like Streisand. Why don't you sing the way you used to sing?" The "kid" never forgot the criticism. Lees recalled an anecdote from a Capitol Records Christmas party at which Johnny began to insult Jo Stafford, who stopped him with the comment, "Please John, I don't want any of your roses in the morning." Similarly, the manager Carlos Gastel turned the tables on an inebriated Johnny, saying, "Talent gives you no excuse to insult people." Yet it helps explain his behavior, for when drinking in public and listening to mediocre musicians, Mercer often cut loose with caustic remarks about their performances. Polly Ober recalled incidents in which Mercer offended women who were not celebrities, "but he would always send them beautiful flowers the next day" as a sign of his contrition. "And it worked, though. I mean, the women would, you know, just calm down. Everything was fine again. Because you know, Johnny was such a sweetheart, and such a likeable guy, my God, how could you stay mad at him?"[27]

He often hurt the people closest to him. Once when at a dinner party with Capitol Records executive Alan Livingston and others, Johnny got mad at Ginger and emptied his drink glass on her head. On another occasion, Alan's older brother, the songwriter Jay Livingston, observed Johnny in a nightclub beside the pianist Jimmy Rowles, singing a mean-spirited blues about his wife, who was sitting at the nearby table. Ginger suffered his public attacks in silence. Other verbal assaults resulted in near calamity. In 1953, Mercer attended a party given by his agent, Irving "Swifty" Lazar, to celebrate the imminent filming of *A Star Is Born*, starring Judy Garland. A few months before, Garland's estranged mother, Ethel, had dropped dead alongside her car outside the factory where she worked making airplanes. When Judy arrived at Lazar's party, a drunken Johnny accosted her, "Why did you let your mother die in a parking lot?" The comment drove her to hysterics. When the host suggested she retire to the ladies' room to collect herself, Garland locked the bathroom door and slit her wrists in a suicide attempt.[28]

Mercer understood how drinking damaged his relationships with people. In his 1970 interview with Willis Conover, he observed, "I find that most people who drink, it eventually affects something, probably the liver, or the bile or something, because most steady drinkers as they get older tend to get less and less friendly and more and more vitriolic." Johnny rationalized, "When you're young you're happy longer and nobody gets mad, and you laugh, and you get sick. But when you get old and you've been drinking a lot, you don't get sick, it just sits there and you get mean and sallow and . . ."; then he cut off. Conover had commented on Mercer's reputation: "He can turn into something pretty salty when he's had a few drinks and tell people off." Johnny responded, "I can say mean things but I don't mean them. I really don't. It's just the whiskey talking." He protested, "I really like people. I harbor no grudges. I don't like to be taken advantage of, I don't think anybody does. But I essentially am an optimist and a very friendly man. I like almost everybody I meet." Most people knew the cordial Johnny and thought highly of his reputation, never suspecting that beneath the sunny Dr. Jekyll exterior lurked a drunken Mr. Hyde symbolic of that universal warring between good and evil that every individual faces. It could be a jarring experience for an autograph seeker wanting to meet the famous Mercer to instead be cursed by an inebriated Johnny who turned and walked away.[29]

Johnny Mercer and Bobby Darin each had an overall charming demeanor occasionally marred by bad-boy behavior. Born Robert Walden Cassotto to a poor Italian family in the Bronx, he adopted the stage name Bobby Darin after graduating from high school, also taking a songwriting job with Don Kirshner in the Brill Building on Broadway. Like Johnny, Bobby loved jazz and blues. He attended concerts by Ray Charles and made as his first record a cover of Huddie "Leadbelly" Ledbetter's "Rock Island Line." Darin wrote and recorded his first hit, "Splish Splash," in 1958. He landed another best-seller the next year with "Dream Lover." Success allowed Darin to choose music selectively, and he turned to art song in 1960, recording a jazzed-up version of "Mack the Knife" from Bertolt Brecht and Kurt Weill's musical, *The Threepenny Opera*. An English version of the French song "La Mer" by Charles Trenet called "Beyond the Sea" topped the charts as Darin won Grammys for his efforts. Hollywood cast him in movies, where he met Sandra Dee, marrying her in 1960. His career had sky-rocketed by the time he met Mercer.[30]

As both men liked the novelty songs of yore, in 1961 they decided to record an album singing old favorites as duets, accompanied by Billy May and His Orchestra. In selecting the retro songs for *Two of a Kind*, the men picked numbers fun to sing though not well-known, such as "Mississippi Mud" and "East of the Rockies"; old favorites such as "Indiana" and "Ace in the Hole" also appear. Inventive songs such as "Who Takes Care of the Caretaker's Daughter," "I Ain't Gonna Give Nobody None of My Jellyroll," and "My Cutey's Due at Two-to-Two Today" allow the ladies' men to play cavalier. Then a medley of "Paddlin' Madelin' Home" and "Row Row Row" revisits vaudeville. Mercer contributed the lyrics for the last three numbers, "Bob White," "If I Had My Druthers," and the title song, "Two of a Kind." Commenting on the Mercer-Darin collaboration, Stanley Green remarked in the liner notes,

> you are not likely to mistake the voice or the style of one for the other, but they both possess such a compelling rhythmic drive, combined with a casualness of approach and an unerring sense of timing and projection, that their joint vocalizing turns out to be the most welcome musical treat since — well, since Johnny and Bing Crosby used to get together on radio and on records.

Quoting a line from the title song, "Like peas in a pod and birds of a feather," Green concluded, "Unquestionably these 'two of a kind' performers were having a ball when they cut this one." Music critic Willis Conover interviewed Darin at the crest of the singer's meteoric rise, and Bobby noted his affinity for the songs of Mercer and Mancini: "Yeah, I tell you they could write songs for me every day of the week and twice on Sunday. I've never heard anything that falls short of sensational that they've done."[31]

An insatiable love of music and inability to turn off the creative impulse brought Johnny Mercer and Henry Mancini together in a partnership that produced the most commercially popular music either ever made. Born in Cleveland, Ohio, to Italian immigrants in 1924, Enrico Nicola "Henry" or "Hank" Mancini attended Juilliard School of Music before playing as the pianist and arranger for the Tex Beneke and then the Glenn Miller orchestras. With the collapse of the big-band era, Mancini moved to Hollywood in 1952 and started writing for Universal Studios, becoming a successful composer and arranger for film scores, including *The Benny Goodman Story*. Music critic Henry Pleasants identified Mancini as one of the leading "jazz composer-arrangers" keeping alive the interpenetration of jazz and popular song through the writing of scores for Hollywood movies and television. In California, Mancini met and married

Virginia "Ginny" O'Connor, who sang as one of Mel Torme's "Mel-Tones," and had even performed with Johnny Mercer on the 1940s radio show *Swing Time*. Henry Mancini's big break came when movie producer Blake Edwards hired him as his music director, enabling the composer to create the atmospheric soundtrack for such television series as *Mr. Lucky* and then for the influential *Peter Gunn*, which won a Grammy in 1958. When putting together *Peter Gunn* as a television pilot, Mancini had featured Mercer's "Day In — Day Out" in a bebop style, using the agitated beat of a bongo to generate excitement. During the second season of the program, an instrumental by Mancini had struck Johnny's fancy, and he asked Henry if he could contribute words to the song, called "Joanna." Delighted by the connection with Mercer, Mancini agreed, for he had marveled over Johnny's prodigious output for years.[32]

Johnny wanted to work with Henry because they shared a background in jazz. Yet a comment by Mancini has led to an exaggerated belief in an inaccurate decline in Mercer's status as a songwriter. From the vantage point of the late 1980s Mancini suggested, "This was the low point of Johnny's artistic life. Illiterate songs were high on the charts, and doo-wop groups were thriving." Certainly, the popular music of the 1950s did not inspire Mercer. The resurgence of New York songwriting from the Brill Building filled the airwaves with what he saw as mindless pabulum reminiscent of the silly ditties of Tin Pan Alley. With "Do Wah Diddy Diddy" and "Yakety Yak" topping the charts, almost everyone in show business predicted the imminent death of the Great American Song. Johnny wrote a friend in late 1961: "I have trouble enough getting my own tunes recorded today unless they are in a movie or a show. The A&R men seem to have forgotten my name." His complaint continued, referring to his last success sung by Frank Sinatra, on his all-time best seller, *Come Dance with Me!*, in 1959. "I can't even get my own placed. 'Something's Got to Give' I think, was the last active song I've had in some time. I think you do better these days with songs like 'Fido Knows Best,' 'Chung King Chicken Cacciatore,' etc."[33]

No matter how pitiful the popular music scene, the image of a played-out Mercer before the Mancini collaboration is simply inaccurate. Around the time Johnny contributed lyrics to Henry's "Joanna," he wrote the words and music for "The Facts of Life," a theme song that netted Mercer his twelfth Academy Award nomination. Although it did not win an Oscar for the Best Song of 1960, it pointed to his continued success as both a composer and a lyricist. The Norman Panama and Melvin Frank production starred Johnny's old friends Lucille Ball and Bob Hope. The title song played on procreation: "Now, concerning the birds and bees / Inhabiting all those trees, / Establishing all those families, / Up with each daisy, / Singin' like crazy, / Storin' up honey, / Savin' their money — / Those are the facts of life." The song received airplay once recorded by the hot duet Eydie Gorme and Steve Lawrence. Similarly Johnny's duets with Bobby Darin underscored his continued marketability. Mercer remained in demand, with appearances on television and on radio. Guest shots on variety programs kept him in a favorable light before the public. He might bemoan his lackluster career on Broadway, but another musical with its chance of success always beckoned. Now no longer involved in Capitol Records, he had started Commander Publications, which enabled him to print sheet music. Thus his complaining about rock 'n' roll did not signify the end of his career any more than accepting an invitation to work with the relatively unknown Mancini marked the return of success. Rather, it demonstrated Johnny's longstanding custom of following the example set by his father to "cast bread upon the water" and respond positively to the opportunities that returned.[34]

The two men soon got their chance to write a movie theme song for Hollywood. When Paramount hired Edwards to direct *Breakfast at Tiffany's*, based on the novella by Truman Capote about southerners trying to make it in New York City, Edwards turned to Mancini to score the film. The studios wanted someone else to write the theme song, especially as the picture starred Audrey Hepburn, who did not sing well enough to satisfy the movie moguls, but Mancini — who had scored many pictures but had never been given the chance to write a theme song — convinced Edwards to let him try. Limiting himself to Hepburn's octave-and-a-half range, Mancini built a melody around C and other white keys. He played it for Edwards, who loved the tune and asked for the name of a potential lyricist. As he recalled later, Mancini "went for the best," suggesting Mercer.[35]

Hearing Mancini's theme song in the happy key of C, the usually optimistic Mercer responded, "Hank, who's going to record a waltz? We'll do it for the movie, but after that it hasn't any future commercially." Johnny left with a tape recording of the music and started casting about for images. Mercer later explained to jazz critic Willis Conover: "It was kind of fashionable in those days to get a song that was tied into the picture. Once you heard the song, you'd immediately think of the picture." Mancini learned what Jerome Kern and Harold Arlen had understood from their collaborations with Mercer: when ready — and on time — Mercer would appear with the lyrics. "I made the mistake of calling him once and he let me know he wasn't ready," Hank confessed. Unaware of Mercer's kinship to the general, Mancini reflected, "Had Johnny been a military man, he would have been another Patton. He used to attack a song three ways. He could hear a melody and see different angles from which to approach it and then write three different lyrics, each one valid, each one fully worked out, and each one different from the others."[36]

When ready, Mercer met Mancini in the ballroom of the Beverly Wilshire Hotel with separate lyrics in hand. Hank played the song, and Johnny sang his first offering called "I'm Holly," about the Hepburn lead. Mercer sang: "I'm Holly, / Like I want to be, / Like holly on a tree back home. / Just plain Holly, / With no dolly, / No mama, no papa / Wherever I roam." Johnny had figured the producers might like it "because it's right out of the picture, maybe Capote would like it, I don't know." After singing it for Mancini, Johnny confessed, "I don't know about that one," speculating that his other option "might be a bigger hit." The music had a "Mississippi feeling" to it, so Johnny had thought in terms of "summery" images of the South. With the lead character from Texas, he thought of a muddy river, a "Red River," and used that as a working title for a while but decided it was too close to "Red River Valley," so he shifted to the idea of "June River" or "Blue River" and presented that image to Mancini with the caveat the title might change because several songs had similar names and Mercer disliked reusing song titles. "Anyway we hit on 'Moon River' finally," he noted. "When it occurred to me to say huckleberry friend, I said, ooh that's good, and I left it in." Then he sang the lyric: "Moon River, / Wider than a mile, / I'm crossin' you in style / Someday."[37]

Thinking back on the music as it filled the ballroom, empty except for Mercer and himself, Mancini contemplated the creative act:

> Every once in a while you hear something so right that it gives you chills, and when he sang that "huckleberry friend" line, I got them. I don't know whether he knew what effect those words had or if it was just something that came to him, but it was thrilling. It made you think of Mark Twain and Huckleberry Finn's trip down the Mississippi. It had such echoes of America. It was one of those remarkable lines that gives you a rush. It was a clincher.

Talking to an interviewer later, Mercer recognized the comparison to the great writer by suggesting that his childhood at Vernon View had been as idyllic as Tom Sawyer's, hunting blackberries and huckleberries in the pastoral South. He knew the line "My huckleberry friend" captured that feeling of innocence:

"We're after the same Rainbow's end, / Waitin' round the bend, / My huckle-berry friend, / Moon River / And me." When Margaret Whiting balked at the words when he tried them out on her, Mercer reassured her that they fit. The theme song joined the score of the picture, and with rushes completed, Edwards prepared a version to show the producers. As theme music and picture, "Moon River" and *Breakfast at Tiffany's* work perfectly together; a choral group sings it during the opening and closing credits, Hepburn performs it as a solo while play-ing a guitar on the fire escape, and the music swells beneath the movie's action. As Edwards noted, "I think they'll always be tied together for me. I can't think of one without the other." As Mancini recalled later, after the producers determined that the film needed to be shortened, the head of Paramount, Martin Rackin, declared upon seeing a preview of the final cut, "Well, the fucking song has to go." Director Edwards kept it in, and the rest is history.[38]

On one level *Breakfast at Tiffany's* is a movie about the southern diaspora, starting with the displacement of the novella's Alabama author, Capote, to Man-hattan. The narrative concerns Holly Golightly, played by Hepburn, a refugee from the failed sharecropping South who has created an attractive persona that she intends to use to get rich. The global southerner is seen through her interac-tions with cosmopolitan New York, represented by the perpetually upset "Japa-nese" neighbor, offensively played by Mickey Rooney, and the wealthy Argentine Golightly aims to marry. The ivy league male protagonist, a writer like Capote but a heterosexual who services a wealthy woman to supplement his income until he gets published, played by George Peppard, symbolizes the corrupt northeast-ern establishment, while Golightly's estranged husband, played by Buddy Ebsen, haunts the picture like an inescapable southern past. "Old dream maker, / You heart breaker, / Wherever you're goin', / I'm goin' your way," Golightly sings, add-ing, "Two drifters / Off to see the world — / There's such a lot of world / to see." Mercer's lyric points to the plight of many caught up in the diaspora, for whom the "rainbow's end" remains "just around the bend." Written at the height of U.S. global dominance as a hegemonic power, Mercer's song exposed the restless spirit of the national character. He expressed the country's quintessential faith at a moment when the consensus still held and the public still believed in the American Dream. The message was not lost on filmmaker Oliver Stone who rec-ognized the ideological power of "Moon River" by using it to underscore the dra-matic shift from belief as seen in the suburbs of America to action in the jungles of Vietnam in his 1989 Oscar-winning movie, *Born on the Fourth of July*.[39]

An eager world wanted to believe in America, too, as it consumed *Breakfast at Tiffany's* through Paramount's international distribution, fueled in part by Hepburn's global star power. Within a month of the film's October 1961 U.S. release, the studio rolled out *Breakfast at Tiffany's* in the Asian and South American markets. By the holidays, the picture had premiered across Western Europe. Having cost $2.5 million to make, the film grossed $8 million in the United States and nearly double that through worldwide distribution. The American Film Institute continues to rank *Breakfast at Tiffany's* as one of the most popular films of all time, with "Moon River" holding the number four spot of the top hundred most popular movie theme songs. This song and Mercer's other collaborations with Mancini made him the fifth highest moneymaker for ASCAP in the early 1960s, just behind Irving Berlin, Richard Rodgers, Cole Porter, and Harold Arlen.[40]

Although the Academy passed over *Breakfast at Tiffany's* for a nomination as Best Picture in 1961, "Moon River" received the honor as Best Original Song. To celebrate, Hank and Ginny Mancini rented a limousine and picked up Johnny and Ginger on the big night. The Academy Awards ceremony took place on April 9, 1962, in the Santa Monica Civic Auditorium, and many of Mercer's friends attended. Bob Hope emceed, and Newport Beach singer and newcomer to Hollywood Ann-Margret performed Mancini's other nominated theme song, "Bachelor in Paradise." Andy Williams sang "Moon River," which he had already recorded for an album, as the song began on its way to becoming his signature piece. For the first time in Academy history the camera zoomed in on the nominees at the crucial moment of the announcement to personalize the televised event. With envelope in hand, Debbie Reynolds read out the names of Mercer and Mancini as Johnny exclaimed, "Martinis for everybody!" Hank remembered, "Johnny grinned that impish smile of his and we went up and picked up two Oscars." The award — his first in a decade — reaffirmed Mercer's status as one of America's greatest songwriters.[41]

Andy Williams turned "Moon River" into his personal trademark. Like many in the Hollywood community, Williams recognized the song would win the Oscar. He happily performed it on the Academy Awards ceremony before an international television audience of nearly ninety million. Williams recalled: "Many people just assumed that I won. You know my mother called me on the phone and she said, you won!" He had already planned to capitalize on the song's success, guaranteed to increase after the Oscar broadcast, by releasing the LP *"Moon River" and Other Great Movie Themes*; "My album came out the next day which was good timing on the part of Columbia Records and it sold about 400,000 in two weeks." Recognizing that he had become as linked to the song as its creators, Mercer and Mancini, Williams "started to do it as the theme of my television show and then that's how the identification just grew and grew." Johnny Mercer later said he "wrote 'Moon River' for a film where it became the signature tune for one man." The BBC identified that man as "arguably the most popular international singing star" of the 1960s. Between his recordings and his television shows, Andy Williams became "immensely popular" in England, Japan, Malaysia, Somalia, indeed, around the globe. Johnny Mercer's lyrics fueled that popularity. Williams recalled about the song in his 2009 memoir, *Moon River and Me*, "When I hear anybody else sing it, it's all I can do to stop myself from shouting at the television screen, 'No! That's my song!'"[42]

Accolades came from everywhere for Mercer's third Academy Award. Friends in Hollywood such as Ray Gilbert, a fellow songwriter who composed music for Disney, including "The Three Caballeros" and "Zip-a-Dee-Doo-Dah," telegrammed Mercer: "I hate you because you are so good but I love you because you are so great. Congratulations." The *Savannah Evening Press* editorialized, "We don't want to seem immodest in boasting about the accomplishments of our Mr. Mercer, and since the Academy has seen fit to give him an Oscar, we think the hometown folks should add an affectionate pat on the back." In response, the Chatham County Board of Commissioners renamed the Back River that ran behind Burnside Island the Moon River on April 27, 1962. Speaking on "behalf of all the county's citizens," the commissioners "hereby congratulate Johnny Mercer on the merited recognition accorded 'Moon River' and that he hereby be invited to spend more time at his Burnside Island home enjoying the view of 'Moon River.'" The commissioners recognized "the inspiration that enabled Johnny Mercer to write this notable song undoubtedly came in part from his observance of the moon rising from behind Skidaway Island and the silver reflection thereof in the placid waters of Back River adjoining his home." Johnny — who returned to Savannah to celebrate around that time — then started calling his Dutch colonial that sat beside the waterway the Moon River house. Later that summer, Johnny slipped away with Ginger for a return voyage to Hawaii, where they privately celebrated his success.[43]

The next film with Mancini and Edwards that Mercer would collaborate on concerned the plight of a pair of hopeless alcoholics. The movie title, *The Days of Wine and Roses*, came from a line by the English Victorian poet Ernest Dowson. Again Mancini started on middle C, and this time jumped up to A but kept the song in a major chord. He played it for Johnny, who made a tape recording of the music. As Hank recalled, Johnny's way of working was to "hear the tune over and over again." Mercer worked from a portion of the poem:

They are not long, the weeping and the laughter,
Love and desire and hate;
I think they have no portion in us after
We pass the gate.
They are not long, the days of wine and roses;
Out of a misty dream
Our path emerges for a while, then closes
Within a dream.

As Mancini recalled, before long Mercer telephoned: "Hank, I've got it, I've got the lyric." Mancini traveled with his wife on their boat down to Lido Isle to hear Johnny sing his words. "I was a little envious of Ginger because her ears were always the first to hear all that wonderful poetry that Johnny wrote." The surreal lyric consisted of just two sentences. The first recalls Dowson's poem with a nod to Edgar Allen Poe: "The days of wine and roses / Laugh and run away / Like a child at play / Through the meadowland / Toward a closing door, / A door marked 'Nevermore' / That wasn't there before." The next lines are pure Mercer: "The lonely night discloses / Just a passing breeze / Filled with memories / Of the golden smile that introduced me to / The days of wine and roses / And you." Mancini liked what he heard.[44]

The lyric for "Days of Wine and Roses" came to Johnny quickly, taking him only "ten to fifteen minutes" to write, as he recalled. "I didn't have much to do because the title was by Ernest Dowson and I had this great tune and it just seemed as if maybe Ernest Dowson was up there guiding my hand. But I couldn't get it down on the paper fast enough." While ever modest by suggesting Dowson and Mancini had done all the work and handed him a "rocking chair song," Mercer did confess, "It's a nice lyric I think, but I don't know, you can get some arguments on it." To Willis Conover Mercer explained,

I don't know if it makes sense to some people. Like Andy Williams says he doesn't understand the word "nevermore" but allegorically I understand it. On a door that you don't see, it's like a Dali painting, you know. You're walking through a meadow and suddenly there's a door and there's a word on it. You see past that, and past that you can't go. At least if you go through you can't come back. Anyway those were the feelings that I had when I wrote the lyric. I couldn't write it down . . . I think I wrote it in five minutes. I couldn't write it down fast enough.[45]

Mercer and Mancini auditioned the song on an old barnlike soundstage at Warner Bros. before Blake Edwards and the movie's male star, Jack Lemmon, himself a jazz pianist. A single bulb illuminated the cavernous space. Mercer sang "in his best bullfrog voice with a crack in it and the jazz inflection that was always there somewhere." Mancini remembered: "When we were through, there was a long, long, heavy, terrible silence. It probably lasted ten seconds, but it seemed like ten minutes. I kept staring into the keyboard. Finally I couldn't stand it, and I shifted myself around to look at Blake and Jack. And there was Jack with a tear rolling down his cheek, and Blake was misty-eyed. We didn't have to ask them if they liked the song." Whenever he recalled the anecdote, Lemmon choked up with emotion again. The "Days of Wine and Roses" won for Mercer and Mancini another Oscar, Best Original Song for 1962. As with "Moon River," they also picked up Grammys from the National Academy of Recording Arts and Sciences. The American Film Institute ranks "Days of Wine and Roses" thirty-ninth of the hundred most popular movie theme songs. In a radical departure, the Academy of Motion Picture Arts and Sciences excluded individual performances of the 1962 nominations for Best Original Song from the April 8, 1963, broadcast of the Academy Awards being staged by Arthur Freed, to the consternation of the songwriters. While Robert Goulet performed a medley of the five nominees, the complaint of the composers and lyricists against Freed's action resulted in the Academy returning to complete performances of the nominees in 1964.[46]

Elated by consecutive Oscars, Mercer celebrated with family and friends. From Savannah, Nick Mamalakis wired Johnny: "Hop the 'Atchinson, Topeka, and the Santa Fe,' come to 'Moon River,' and let's have some 'Days of Wine and Roses' 'In the Cool, Cool, Cool of the Evening.'" Delighted by the suggestion Mercer wired back, directing Nick to a favorite bar on Habersham Street. "Take the whole gang to Johnny Ganem's and tell them the drinks are on me."[47]

Johnny and Hank collaborated on yet another successful movie theme song, this time "Charade," for a 1963 Audrey Hepburn–Cary Grant film. Again as movie theme music, the song with and without lyrics filtered throughout the film. The producers gave the songwriters the title and espionage plot of adventure and romance set in Europe. Mancini composed dramatic underscoring with a haunting melody for Mercer's lyric. While somewhat abstract, the words reference scenes such as a puppet show and an empty stage: "Fate seemed to pull the strings; / I turned and you were gone. / While from the darkened wings / The music box played on." As Mercer biographer Philip Furia recognized, the song pays homage to Johnny's love of vaudeville with its lines: "Oh, what a hit we made! / We came on next to closing, / Best on the bill, / Lovers until / Love left the masquerade." The song won Mercer and Mancini another Academy Award nomination for Best Original Song of 1963, but this time no statue. Yet the run of Mercer-Mancini songs became standard fare for singers such as Andy Williams and Johnny Mathis, who sold millions of records featuring these titles.[48]

Two of the movie themes that received nominations for Best Original Song by the Academy in 1965 engaged Johnny, although only one contained a lyric by him. Mercer had collaborated with Mancini on the music for another Blake Edwards film, *The Great Race*, which starred Tony Curtis, Natalie Wood, and Jack Lemmon and included the numbers "He Shouldn't-a, Hadn't-a, Oughtn't-a Swang on Me!" and "Get a Horse." Jackie Ward dubbed the nominee song for Wood, "The Sweetheart Tree." It lost to "The Shadow of Your Smile," from *The Sandpiper*, a film starring Richard Burton as a straying minister attracted to the free thinker Elizabeth Taylor. The trumpet player and jazz arranger Johnny Mandel had first approached Johnny Mercer about writing lyrics for a tune he had composed for the movie. Mercer complied with another of his abstract efforts. Johnny's words went: "Today I'm in a mood I can't explain. / It might be just a sudden summer rain. / Today I saw a bird that broke its wing, / Which isn't in itself a tragic thing." The bridge continues: "Yet I had the feeling start / I had seen my counterpart, / And love would come and break my heart / Once again in spring." Upon hearing the draft lyric, Mandel told Mercer "It's not exactly what I'm looking for." So they followed custom, "a silent agreement with most collaborators that if the song doesn't make it, they have their tune back, we have our lyrics back and we forget it. It was a nice try and that's all." Mercer suggested to Mandel that he ask Paul Francis Webster, whose lyric for "The Shadow of Your Smile" won over the producers as well as the Academy. Mercer admitted that he had failed to write an acceptable lyric, but revealed a touch of envy with his comment: "I figured with 'the shadow of your smile' maybe that he was in love with a lady with a mustache."[49]

Mercer had better luck writing with Mandel the title song of *The Americanization of Emily*. The film starred one of the hottest properties in Hollywood in her second film role. Julie Andrews had won acclaim on stage for *My Fair Lady* and in 1964 racked up an Oscar for *Mary Poppins*. Although "Emily" did not receive a nomination that year for Best Song, it showcased Mercer's talent for manipulating language. As biographer Furia noted, the title had no true rhyme, but rather than hide the fact, Johnny "instead brought it to the forefront and wrote about its sound in images that create a visual rhyme." The lyric went: "As my eyes visualize a family, / They see dreamily / Emily too." Warner Bros. disliked the ending and altered it in the movie and sheet music: "They see Emily, / Emily too." The change annoyed Johnny, who nonetheless admitted about the lyric, "I don't think the words are as good as the music. The music is lovely."[50]

Numerous times over the course of the decade, Mancini turned to Mercer for help on songs, often for movies that he scored, many of them for Edwards. In 1962, Johnny joined Hank on the title song for *Mr. Hobbs Takes a Vacation*. When Mancini partnered with Italian lyricist Franco Migliacci to write a song for Fran Jeffries to introduce in *The Pink Panther* in 1964, he recruited Mercer to craft English lyrics for "It Had Better Be Tonight" (Meglio Stasera), which a variety of artists have since recorded, including Mancini's daughter, Monica. For *Man's Favorite Sport?* released in 1964 and starring Rock Hudson and Paula Prentiss, Johnny conjured up masculine images, noting that "Since the world began — / The fav'rite sport of man is girls!" In 1966, Mercer assisted Mancini with the title song to *Moment to Moment*. On one occasion, when too busy to collaborate with Mancini, Mercer recommended the songwriting team of Jay Livingston and Ray Evans, who crafted the lyric for the 1965 theme song "Dear Heart." Similarly, in 1966, while Mancini scored *Not with My Wife, You Don't!* he turned to a young composer named John Williams to write the music with Mercer, so the two collaborated on a theme song as well as "A Big Beautiful Ball" and "My Inamorata."[51]

In 1970, Mercer and Mancini scored the unusual *Darling Lili*, an attempt to revive the Hollywood musical that featured Blake Edwards's wife, Julie Andrews. The film about a World War I German spy failed to live up to expectations. In addition to the title song and several others from *Darling Lili*, Mercer and Mancini contributed "Whistling Away the Dark," which Andrews retained in her concert repertoire, telling an interviewer that she liked the evocative nature of the lyric: "So walk me back home, my darling, / Tell me dreams really come true. / Whistling, / Whistling, / Here in the dark with you." Despite the nomination for an Academy Award for Best Original Song in 1970, the seventeenth received by Johnny, "Whistling Away the Dark" lost the Oscar to "For All We Know" by the Carpenters. The 1970s had arrived.[52]

While collaborating with Mancini, Mercer worked with a variety of other composers too. He contributed a song to the patriotic blockbuster *How the West Was Won*. Produced by MGM in 1962, the saga starred John Wayne, Henry Fonda, George Peppard, Gregory Peck, Karl Malden, Richard Widmark, James Stewart, Debbie Reynolds, and Agnes Moorehead. Music advanced the storyline, and Johnny Mercer worked with Robert Emmett Dolan and others in assembling a variety of American folk tunes and new songs for Alfred Newman to use in the score. For the film Mercer and Dolan contributed "What Was Your Name in the States?" His interest piqued, Johnny started exploring the history of traditional music in America, a subject that would appear in his autobiography. With composer Alex North, Mercer wrote the theme song for *Cleopatra*, an overwrought Oscar-winning extravaganza starring Elizabeth Taylor and Richard Burton. Although 20th Century Fox cut "The Nile" from the film, the lyric about the timelessness of the river suggests human vanity. The studio again hired Mercer to write with Gerald Fried a theme song for *The Cabinet of Caligari*, released in 1965. In 1966, two films had theme songs by Mercer and his old friend Johnny Green, Universal Pictures' *Johnny Tiger* and Columbia Pictures' *Alvarez Kelly*. Warner Bros. hired Mercer to write with David Raksin a theme song for *A Big Hand for the Little Lady*, released in 1966. Paramount hired Mercer to write with composer Neal Hefti the theme for *Barefoot in the Park*, released in 1967.[53]

Unable to stop writing but having less success getting the songs performed professionally, Mercer continued to produce music. His list of collaborators expanded as he worked with almost everyone who asked. In 1964, he wrote "Tonight May Have to Last Me All My Life" with Don Borzage and "Single-O" with Donald Kahn. In 1965, he wrote "Beautiful Forever" with Frederic Spielman and "Have a Heart" with Gene DiNovi. In 1966, he wrote "Tender Loving Care" with Ronnell Bright and "Deirdre" with Michael Masser. In 1967, he wrote "Papa Good Times" with Les McCann and "Too Good to Be True" with George Shearing. In 1968, he wrote "Just across the Mountains" with Arthur Kent and "Lotus Land" with Ted Grouya. In 1969, he wrote "Wait No More" with Elizabeth Firestone and "I'll Never Forgive Myself" with Al Kaufman. In 1970, he wrote "Misguided Faith" with Brian Minard and "Little Acorns" with Arthur Kent. In 1971, he wrote "Twilight World" with Marian McPartland and "Shake It, but Don't Break It" with Erroll Garner. These were all relatively new partners and all published songs that went nowhere. Johnny even volunteered a fight song for the Chatsworth High School in Los Angeles and "We Are the Werewolf Den" for his grandson Jamie Corwin to sing with Cub Scouts. When he could,

Mercer recorded himself on his own numbers, such as "Shooby Doobin,'" a ditty he wrote with Jerry Gray in 1966. Despite all the effort, Mercer had his last major *Your Hit Parade* success with Frank Sinatra singing "Summer Wind" in 1965.[54]

On the rare occasions when the studios called, Johnny joined collaborators he had first worked with thirty years before to create theme songs. He partnered with veteran composer of Hollywood musicals Harry Warren on the title song for the 1967 movie *Rosie!*, which starred Rosalind Russell. He collaborated with his old jazz buddy Hoagy Carmichael on several projects during the decade, including the title song for *Hatari!*, a John Wayne movie directed by Howard Hawks in 1963 that included Mancini's "Baby Elephant Walk." France provided Hoagy and Johnny the inspiration for "A Perfect Paris Night" in 1963 and "Fleur de Lys" in 1971, but "The Song of Long Ago," which the two men published in 1969, spoke to the reality of being songwriters attracted to nostalgia. Johnny and Hoagy also produced such numbers as "Sudsy Suds" in 1968. Old friends with whom Mercer collaborated included Rube Bloom on "If You Come Through" (1962), David Raksin on "Mirror, Mirror, Mirror" (1966), and Harold Arlen on "Let's Go, Sailor" (1968).[55] Increasingly Johnny heard from these and other colleagues who felt dissatisfied by the changes in society and bothered by growing old.

A steady stream of letters came from Arlen, who liked to rib Mercer. Commenting on Johnny's loss of hair, Harold wrote: "As to the Executive Suite, as some members of my race might say, 'It looks good on you.' The Executive Mantle has cloaked your shoulders for many years, so Don't Change a Hair for Me." When Johnny admitted to Arlen he had quit drinking, Harold responds: "As for the Colonel — no more mint juleps — no more inhalers — has you been measured for a Chastity Belt?" Harry Ruby, the composer for the Marx Brothers' movies *Animal Crackers* and *Duck Soup*, started sending Johnny critical letters laced with an occasional anti-Semitic remark. Mercer's responses have apparently not survived and such racist comments are absent from his correspondence with others. No doubt Mercer and Ruby would agree with Arlen's nostalgic look back at Hollywood: "I have often remarked that the thirties and early forties gave all who had talent a major showcase for their songs. Those of us who loved writing for Brudvay, took our potshots, and whether we were successful or not, we soon returned to Chlorine Canyon and an assignment was happily waiting. What a productive period that was — plus the kind of living that only a fool would knock." Elsewhere Arlen recalled that "great life" enjoyed by the songwriters: "most of us played golf or tennis, or swam and did our writing at the same time.

I wrote at home. I could write at midnight, or five in the afternoon, at nine — it made no difference. As long as I came up with something that the so-called producers liked."[56]

Likewise, Mercer's old associates in show business Bob Hope and Bing Crosby refused to retire quietly and continued performing, searching for a receptive audience. A stream of wars, now including the quagmire of Vietnam, kept Bob Hope entertaining the troops. Hope's old sidekick, Jerry Colonna, however, no longer worked with him, instead playing gigs at a casino in Reno, Nevada, and a hotel in Puerto Rico. Bing Crosby had become a perennial favorite hosting Christmas season variety shows. He wrote Johnny about his new recording of "It's the Time to Be Jolly," by Sonny Burke and Les Brown, that despite its holiday theme drew little lasting attention.[57]

Life had been less kind to the old jazz performers with whom Johnny had enjoyed his early years in the entertainment industry. After suffering a stroke and being reduced to poverty, Fletcher Henderson died in New York City in 1952. Within six months of Tommy Dorsey's death, brother Jimmy died in 1957. Billie Holiday had been arrested on drug charges from her hospital bed prior to dying there in 1959. An alcoholic, Jack Teagarden died of pneumonia in 1964 the day after playing his last gig at the Dream Room in New Orleans. Nat "King" Cole spent much of 1965 dying of lung cancer. No wonder that when melancholy, a drunken Mercer might blurt out, "All my friends are dead," or, when in despair ask, "Why not me?" Friends such as Margaret Whiting understood, "There had always been a dark side to John." He admitted as much to the "gentle reader" of his autobiography, asking, "You notice I haven't mentioned malaise du Coeur, a wounded psyche nor any sadness of spirit, but I've had them. You may find traces of them in my songs, however, and I hope it's the only place you do." A good example of the melancholy may be found in the lyric of "I Wonder What Became of Me," a song dropped from *St. Louis Woman*: "Oh, I've had my fling; / I've been around and seen most everything. / But I can't be gay, / For along the way / Something went astray, / And I can't explain, / It's the same Champagne, / It's a sight to see, / But I wonder what became of me."[58]

The death of Judy Garland in 1969 at the age of forty-seven struck Johnny particularly hard. His on-again, off-again love affair with her had lasted thirty years. Just as the Cole Porter lyrics in "Friendship" promised, Johnny and Judy had often provided each other aid. When in 1963 Garland staged her final comeback with CBS's *The Judy Garland Show*, televised weekly, Mercer offered his support. Throughout the June 1963 to March 1964 videotaping of the variety show, Garland punctuated the program with Johnny's lyrics, from "Bob White (Whatcha Gonna Swing Tonight)" on episode 3, a duet of "Day In, Day Out," with Lena Horne on episode 4, a comic version of "One for My Baby (and One More for the Road)" with Jerry Van Dyke inserted into episode 5, to "On the Atchison, Topeka, and the Santa Fe" and "Jamboree Jones" on episode 13 and "I'm Old Fashioned" on episode 18. She sang five Mercer songs on episode 21: "That Old Black Magic," "Hit the Road to Dreamland," "Let's Take the Long Way Home," "Any Place I Hang My Hat Is Home," and "Come Rain or Come Shine." In a handwritten playlist titled "January Music/Garland Music" that included songs never used on the program, Judy listed "I Walk with Music," "How Little We Know," "Skylark," and "Travelin' Light." Judy asked Johnny to take the program's theme music, written by Mort Lindsey, and fit it with lyrics about her daughter, Lorna. For the February 9, 1964, broadcast of episode 20, Garland performed songs for her children. After Judy's singing of "Liza" and "Happiness Is Just a Thing Called Joe," standards in her repertoire, she announced a new song written especially for her youngest child by "one of America's greatest lyricists, Johnny Mercer." As the studio audience applauded the songwriter first and then Garland's daughter, who arrived on stage, Judy sang "Lorna." At the end of the taping, the cast and crew commended Garland's stellar performance with a standing ovation. Many critics praised the show, a compliment to her innate talent as one of the century's leading vocalists. Conflicts arising from disagreements with television executives and fellow performers, unfortunate Nielsen ratings, and a divorce from her third husband, Sid Luft, led CBS to drop the program. As alcohol and drug abuse undermined the quality of her performances and her debasement continued unchecked, a distraught Garland would call Mercer at home, begging for help. He occasionally answered her pleas but increasingly left her to her own devices. Judy's slow self-destruction reached its inevitable end with a drug overdose on June 21, 1969. Informed of the news, Johnny broke down crying over the loss of his sometime soul mate. With Harold Arlen at his side, Johnny joined the two hundred invited guests who attended Garland's funeral, an Episcopal service in the chapel of the Frank E. Campbell Funeral Home in Manhattan, while thousands of people watched from behind barricades.[59]

In a 1970 letter to his California friend and Newport Beach neighbor Polly Ober, whose husband, Matt, had died in 1965, Mercer ruminated over the death of Garland: "I was just too depressed to cope with the loss of my friends, beginning back with Matt and soaring to a crescendo last year." Confronting love — and death — Mercer quoted one of his own songs, "You Can't Run Away from It." He added, "Getting to be sixty (for a child at heart) is the roughest time, for people younger than you begin going, and you wonder why in hell and what in hell is still keeping you here?" He ended his letter with the modest observation, "Thank God for work."[60]

Many of Johnny's contemporaries in entertainment struggled to find employment, suffered from poor health or other problems. Several of the old bandleaders, such as Count Basie, Duke Ellington, and Benny Goodman, followed grueling schedules on the road to perform before aging fans. For months on end they traveled abroad at the behest of the U.S. State Department to promote good will by playing that currency of cultural hegemony, jazz. Lena Horne wandered the jazz clubs of London and Paris, too, until her U.S. comeback in a one-woman show in 1980. Scandals stalked Frank Sinatra as his mafia connections kept him ensconced in Las Vegas. As his father had done, so too Johnny recognized the lives of his associates. Mercer and bandleader Bob Crosby cohosted a concert featuring forty black and white jazz musicians at Carnegie Hall to raise money to pay guitarist Eddie Condon's hospital bills. When the young comedian Ernie Kovacs died in a tragic car accident, Johnny joined the celebrities at the funeral, and if he could not attend a memorial service for someone he worked with or admired, as when the obscure and alcoholic songwriter Willard Robinson died in 1968, Johnny sent his regrets over missing the funeral, in this case with a note that referred to the deceased's hit song, "Thanks for all the Deep Summer Music. Sweet Dreams." Mercer had lived long enough to watch several eras die out, but unlike the dazzling blaze of vaudeville's last days, his world of the Great American Song simply faded to black.[61]

Not only did Mercer dislike the transformation of the entertainment industry, he despised the changes occurring in California. Johnny concluded that nearly every GI ever stationed on the West Coast must have chosen to move there after the war, an ironic outcome for the man who once recorded that paean to California in-migration, "San Fernando Valley." Indeed, Johnny's own recording of "On the Atchison, Topeka, and the Santa Fe," which sold millions of copies for Capitol, featured a special lyric: "Yessirree, here we are goin' all the way, / Mustn't quit till we hit Californ-i-a." Yet two decades of unchecked growth had spoiled the state. Mercer still searched for beauty beneath the sprawl, as in his 1965 song "California's Melodyland," for which he wrote both the words and music: "Mountain peaks all covered with snow / Rise above the deserts below. / Sapphire pools neath shimmering stars, / Freeways jammed with millions of cars." By 1966, Johnny had rhymed in his Christmas card verse: "I love the modern gleaming cars / but miss the sight of frosty stars, / I like the freeways change of scene / but hate the distances between." A decade later humor hides the anger as Mercer mentions the victims of development in "(They're) Pavin' California," written with jazz pianist Jimmie Rowles. Johnny starts with people: "We're pilin' in the Pinto, Circumventin' San Jacinto — Pack the kids in, / 'Cause the bid's in — / Man, they're pavin' California!" Then he moves to the animals: "The lizards and coyotes / All are off to the Dakoties, / While the rattler's / A Seattler, / 'Cause they're pavin' California." And finally plants: "The orange is no safer; / It is flatter than a wafer. / Tang is better / And it's wetter — / Man, they're pavin' California!" Overbuilt neighborhoods in the hills surrounding Los Angeles contributed to the destructive mud slides and fires. Caught in the big Bel Air blaze of 1961, Johnny stood on the roof of his new house at 10972 Chalon Road, spraying it with a garden hose to prevent it from catching fire.[62]

The urban race riots and racial backlash fomented by politicians such as Alabama Governor George C. Wallace and Californian Richard M. Nixon encouraged a reactionary response toward race relations in America. The idea of race as a social construct changed over time and served as a modifier throughout Mercer's life. For his love of the music being made, Johnny overlooked the racism in the society around him. He had joined in New York's interracial jazz scene, which promoted a democratization of America during the Depression and war years, and then watched as Cold War liberalism confronted the emerging civil rights movement. Mercer's Capitol Records ended the racial segmentation used by the industry in marketing recordings, and Johnny advocated for his biggest seller by recording duets with Nat "King" Cole in 1947 and by performing with him on Cole's radio and television shows, the first ones hosted by a black entertainer. A renewed defense of white supremacy beginning with the Dixiecrat revolt of 1948, followed by the rise of massive resistance against the 1954 *Brown v. Board of Education* decision, clashed with demonstrations in the streets and black power protests, all heightening racial tensions among jazz musicians whose visions of integration faded. Johnny witnessed the Watts uprising in 1965 and wrote about it to his mother: "The riots have been so pathetic and sad it has us all depressed, but haven't touched any neighborhood outside of their own miserable environs." He noted, "It's kind of like having a little Vietnam right in your own backyard, with troops coming down from Camp Roberts." Describing his own vision of the beloved community, Johnny commented on being one of the thousands of fans, black and white, who attended a Dodgers game to see Jackie Robinson, the great black Georgian who had integrated professional baseball. Mercer concluded his letter home with a remark that pointed to his own understanding of racial hostility, directed to his mother's African American cook: "Tell Nancy if she can do something about the Black Muslims [sic], I'll try and do something about the White Trash!" Music had taken Mercer beyond race, and he never looked back, but he retained a patrician outlook that recognized class differences and blamed the racial troubles on the lower orders.[63]

The anger expressed by black nationalists and the use of direct action confrontation by civil rights leaders offended Mercer as affronts to polite society. While he rarely acknowledged the power relations that privileged white people, he supported the call for equal access. Although not identifying Mercer by name, jazz critic Gene Lees described an attitude expressed by "a white Southern friend" who "had many black friends and indeed had grown up close to blacks." Lees recounted an anecdote that came from a conversation with Mercer: "One night, after a few too many drinks, he said something with a sort of amiable irony that concealed, I realized, the fact that he meant it. We were talking about the progress in 'race relations' that seemed to have been achieved. And he said, 'I dunno, I think I liked it better the way things were in the old days. You know, when we kept them and took care of them — like pets.'" The shocking remark underscored deep-seated paternalism toward African Americans, perhaps reinforced by such comments as the widely quoted statement by Miles Davis, "I want to kill just one white man before I die." Lees took Davis's assertion as a joke, just as he dismissed the comment by the white southerner, but he also recognized that societal tensions had disrupted interracial friendships.[64]

Against the backdrop of the civil rights movement, an overt racial consciousness cultivated by black bebop artists and white jazz critics created the climate for a black music ideology marked by black separatism, free jazz, and the exclusion of white musicians. On the cusp of the Black Power movement, the African American intellectual LeRoi Jones (Amiri Baraka) published a racial essentialist claim to jazz.[65] He saw black musicians as the innovators and dismissed white musicians such as Mercer as simply imitators who appropriated the style of others, an argument that has persisted to the present and found widespread popularity.[66] The effort to canonize black jazz musicians at the expense of white ones culminated in the Jazz at Lincoln Center concert series developed by Wynton Marsalis in the 1990s. When Ken Burns scripted his nineteen-hour documentary *Jazz* for the Public Broadcasting System in 2001, he leaned heavily on Marsalis and his racially biased view.[67] By the millennium, popular histories had erased the roles played by white musicians so that common perception held that only black people played legitimate jazz. Such a conclusion unreasonably dismisses the likes of Johnny Mercer as pale imitations of "real" jazz musicians.

While some black jazz musicians accepted the argument for racial essentialism, others rejected the view as racist. One of Johnny's favorite performers, the black pianist Willie "the Lion" Smith, who spent his career playing with jazz musicians of both races, argued in his memoir that "although Negro musicians have always had a hard time getting jobs with radio and TV studio bands, they frequently want to use our styles of playing. To do this, they have to use us because we are the ones who not only originated it, but are the only musicians giving the music authenticity." By "they," Smith meant white producers, while the "us" referred to black musicians, whom he saw as the only legitimate creators of jazz. Now Smith knew Mercer, for Johnny had joined Duke Ellington as co-hosts of a seventieth birthday party for the Lion held November 21, 1967, at the Top of the Gate on 160 Bleecker Street that featured special performances by Count Basie, Eubie Blake, Nina Simone, Tal Farlow, and Billy Taylor. Strongly disagreeing with such racist assumptions as expressed by Smith, Louis Armstrong criticized the politicians who enacted segregation laws: "These people who make the restrictions, they don't know nothing about music. It's no crime for cats of any color to get together and blow." He then went on to scorn a black music ideology: "Race conscious jazz musicians? Nobody could be who really knew their horns and loved the music." Armstrong spoke for all the great jazz musicians — black and white — who like Mercer regularly played and recorded with each other, caring little for so-called racial differences.[68]

Revisionists have challenged the ahistorical arguments that underpin the black music ideology and the racial essentialism that surrounds many evaluations of jazz. These writers have returned to the historical record the roles played by white jazz musicians. Watching the divisions fester while editing *Down Beat* magazine in the 1960s, the white Gene Lees heard white jazz musicians call the reverse racism they experienced "Crow-Jim." Lees became one of the first and most eloquent voices to address what he recognized as an injustice to jazz musicians. He carefully traced the innovations of white musicians copied by their black associates.[69] Likewise, the jazz trumpeter Richard Sudhalter painstakingly identifies the hundreds of white jazz musicians who joined their black colleagues in creating the multiracial music. In the magisterial and encyclopedic study *Lost Chords*, Sudhalter argues that jazz provided a "picaresque tale of cooperation, mutual admiration, cross-fertilization; comings-together and driftings-apart — all *despite*, rather than because of, the segregation of the larger society."[70]

African American colleagues recognized Mercer's abilities as a jazz musician and valued his involvement in their lives. Black songwriter and southern diaspora entertainer Eubie Blake, who contributed such shows as *Shuffle Along* and Lew Leslie's *Blackbirds* to Broadway and such songs as "I'm Just Wild about Harry" and "Loving You the Way That I Do" to the Great American Songbook, complimented Mercer in 1953 after seeing him on *The Steve Allen Show*: "Well first I want to tell you I am an old timer, and I've seen them all. Ophays, I mean. You are in my estimation the greatest Rhythm Singer of all Ophays I've ever heard." Blake ended with the observation, "My wife and I got a great kick out of your work. Sounded just like 'the Brother' meaning one of my kind." While Blake used the slang "ophays" to describe white people, Louis Armstrong used the slang "spades" to describe black people, once signing a picture to Johnny with the observation, "Man, more *Spades* love you than you have *no idea. Yea.* Go on Boy." The references demonstrate the hold over society of constructed racial identities that likewise bound Mercer. Family assistant Bobby Rush describes being with the Mercers outside Sardi's and bumping into Bobby Short, the great African American jazz pianist and child of the diaspora, who had mastered the café society style of singing. "And Bobby Short had on a porkpie hat, a buttoned down collar shirt, a knit black tie, a suit from Brooks Brothers, and penny loafers on with white socks. And he hugged all of us and kissed Ginger on the cheek and Johnny, myself, gave us a hug." They talked for a while and after Short left, Mercer turned to Rush and offered a similar evaluation as he had received from Blake and Armstrong: "Man, how white can you get?" In a May 5, 1955, thank-you note, Short replied to an evening out with the Mercers, saying, "That was such a ball and I'm so grateful that you asked me," revealing a heartfelt appreciation is evident and underscores the interaction of black and white jazz musicians in an age of segregation.[71]

By the late 1960s, as the United States seemed to come unraveled, the songwriter, now nearing sixty and increasingly critical, looked with disgust at what he and other Americans saw as a society out of control. Yet unlike Hoagy Carmichael and other associates who wrapped themselves in patriotic Americana and defended the status quo, Johnny joined in the criticism of the establishment. Friends attested that Mercer generally kept his politics to himself. While Ginger advocated the liberal causes of the Democrats, Johnny, who once had supported Roosevelt's New Deal, now leaned toward the Republicans and their defense of traditional values. As foreshadowed in *Li'l Abner*, *Saratoga*, and *Foxy*, Mercer faulted capitalistic greed, science, and militarism as at the heart of society's ills. Writing his mother on election day, he described the campaign as "an event people are hoping will alleviate the miserable conditions which life seems to be falling into! Inflation, instant everything, plastics, and all the rest!" In response to a newspaper article about genetically modified aspens, Mercer wrote a poem called "Trees" that bemoaned a world in which corporate-funded technology had replaced the natural process of evolution. The first lines read in part, "A tree whose beauty life and soul / Starts in some laboratory bowl . . . While God, (if he's a live, of course) / Accepts retirement pay by force."[72]

Since the 1930s, the Mercers had mailed Christmas cards that each year contained a new verse written by Johnny, but during the 1960s the tenor of the yuletide greetings acquired an ominous tone. Mercer wrote "While seated 'round your Christmas tree, think of the trees that used to be . . . The old and new — a lovely sight, they made almost as bright a light, as that far tree in Viet Nam, whose one bright bauble is a bomb." Having a son eligible for the draft no doubt encouraged Mercer's opposition to the war. Yet propaganda he wrote for World War II came back to haunt him as David Halberstam reported that the United States Continental Army Command at Fort Monroe, Virginia, responded to the growing criticism of American foreign policy by issuing an official directive to be read to all servicemen headed to Southeast Asia: "As songwriter Johnny Mercer put it, you've got to accentuate the positive and eliminate the negative." Johnny's response could be found in an untitled poem with its sarcastic lines about the military-industrial complex: "I have children my wife adores / So I send 'em all off to wars / Where they shoot someone else's sons / Ain't that wonderful? — That sells guns." Mercer abhorred the wanton destruction of life, as evident in a poem he submitted to the Wilderness Society to publish in its magazine, *The Living Wilderness,* in 1972: "Ain't you proud of me? — I'm a man / I spoil everything that I can / And I'll never be satisfied / Till I've ruined the countryside / I catch all the fish in the seas / Burn up forests and chop down trees / Fill the rivers with sludge and oil / Wash the minerals from the soil / I kill tigers and leopards, too / I put everything in the zoo." In that classic southern conservative streak harkening back to Thomas Jefferson and the commonwealth, Johnny attributed the degradation of the planet to unbridled human interests trampling over the general welfare. Out of this existential chaos, Mercer grabbed at Søren Kierkegaard's faith by expressing his own belief in love and a natural order to life. Like a character in a Walker Percy novel, Mercer struggled to find his way out of the malaise.[73]

Determined to make peace with the changes in society, Mercer responded rather generously to the democratic age of rock 'n' roll. Johnny publicly recognized the cultural revolution as "here to stay" and as offering "the music of today's young people." Yet the eternal optimist believed the untrained singers needed to take more time writing their music: "They sort of have to learn that before they can go on to better-quality music, more abstruse music." He believed that with each album purchase "their taste improves." Similarly, he observed, "There's a lot of talent coming out of rock 'n' roll, both writers and performers. Some of these kids who made it big early will mature and do worthwhile things." In private, however, Mercer decried what he considered the deplorable condition of popular song. "I am so disgusted with what they are calling lyrics and how nasty they are," he said, complaining about the younger generation's music to Nick Mamalakis during a visit to Savannah. "There was only one tune on the radio. And it was ugly, nasty. And it was just going up and down the scale, up and down. And all it was saying, was 'I want it, I've gotta have it, I need it.'" The master wordsmith asked Nick rhetorically, "What kind of lyric is that? Why are they letting that go on the air?"[74]

Many of Johnny's colleagues offered less charitable evaluations regarding the state of the music industry. Equally appalled at what he heard coming out of the radio, Harry Warren pointed to a lack of musical training among the youthful songwriters. Warren said, "They use a major chord and a seventh and then go back to the major chord — and they repeat the same words over and over. There's hardly any form to it. They say people like this stuff. Well, I think it's because the record companies have forced them to like it. It's too much for me: I can't figure it out." Fellow songwriter Arthur Schwartz pointed to similar forces. "We feel that there has been a process of manipulation that the American public, and the rest of the world, has had imposed upon them by monetary influences, mainly in the broadcasting industry. In this period we have had music of admittedly inferior quality which has corrupted the taste of our youth." Trained as a lawyer and long associated with ASCAP, Schwartz referred to a rearguard response. "A great many of us composers are fighting hard to combat this monopoly. This worst music is a blight upon us and it would not have happened except for the commercial attitude of the broadcasting industry in America. It would not have been born and it would not have blossomed without a definite and continuous manipulation in the millions and millions of dollars." Back in 1940, the tight-knit ASCAP fraternity had lost its monopoly over popular song when bested by the broadcasters, Broadcast Music, Inc. (BMI), and other independent producers. The rock 'n' roll revolution simply reflected the democratic outcome that market forces exploited with payola and other tricks of the trade.[75]

In 1968, Mercer joined his friends from Palm Springs, the music publishers Howard S. "Howie" Richmond and Abe Olman, as the cofounders of the National Academy of Popular Music/Songwriters Hall of Fame in order to recognize and honor influential songwriters from the past as a way to encourage appreciation for the Great American Song and to promote public awareness of copyright protection. After Irving Berlin declined to stand as its figurative leader, Richmond convinced Mercer to head up the effort as its first president, while Olman agreed to serve as manager. They incorporated in 1969 and headquartered the National Academy of Popular Music at Ten Columbus Circle in New York while undertaking plans to establish a museum. Writing to the scholar David Ewen, author of biographies on George Gershwin and Richard Rodgers, Mercer explained he had "to get this started. I don't like to fail in any promised enterprise." The need to revise the nation's copyright laws to protect songs for more than the fifty-six years then in force had led the effort to educate the public about the authors of the music that they loved because most people never associated the song with the songwriter. The task suited Mercer, who excelled at promoting others and their music.[76]

As president Mercer presided over a board of directors that included many of his associates in show business. He also helped create a board of honorary trustees made up of old friends Bing Crosby, Duke Ellington, Richard Rodgers, and Frank Sinatra. An advisory council added the names Alec Wilder, Guy Lombardo, and Ervin Drake. Mercer hoped these powerful people could help the organization by electing fellow musicians to a list of great songwriters that the proposed museum would celebrate and use as advocates for copyright education. Johnny saw the chore as "placing into membership the deserving writers in the American scene over the past 200 years and those of the present day." Mercer also wanted to limit honorary membership to a minimum of "D.J.'s, record men, entertainers, and yes, even publishers" in order to keep the "non-profit, honorary organization" in the hands of songwriters. In 1970, Mercer oversaw the board of directors as it chose by acclamation to honor fifty of America's leading deceased songwriters, such as Katharine Lee Bates, who wrote "America the Beautiful," as well as the living legends Irving Berlin and Richard Rodgers. On March 8, 1971, the organizers hosted the first Songwriters Hall of Fame banquet at the New York Hilton, with more than six hundred lyricists and composers of the

Great American Songbook in attendance. The 1,600 dues-paying members had approved a list of thirty nominations from which to elect ten inductees into the Hall of Fame. Such singers as Margaret Whiting, Al Hibbler, Gordon MacRae, and Mercer himself performed the hits of the thirty nominees, along with Frank Sinatra, who said to the assembled songwriters, "Without you, I would have been selling ties in Hoboken." Johnny Mercer joined old collaborators Harold Arlen, Hoagy Carmichael, Duke Ellington, Harry Warren, and James Van Heusen, as well as Dorothy Fields, Alan Jay Lerner, Ira Gershwin, and Rudolf Friml as the first ten honorees elected into the Songwriters Hall of Fame. Representatives of the new generation of songwriters such as Hal David and Kris Kristofferson, handed out the miniature Pinolas to the winners with the exception of ninety-one-year-old Friml, who was handed his prize by eighty-eight-year-old Eubie Blake, who in turn received a standing ovation. Nearly every year since then at a formal banquet the Songwriters Hall of Fame has inducted its new members.[77]

The Songwriters Hall of Fame had wanted Irving Berlin — the grand old man of Tin Pan Alley — to participate. For years Johnny had corresponded with the songwriter of "Alexander's Ragtime Band," "What'll I Do," "Puttin' on the Ritz," and the musical *Annie Get Your Gun*. They routinely exchanged telegrams on opening nights of each other's Broadway shows, and Johnny kept "the Chief" on his Christmas card list. Complimenting a performance by Berlin on *The Ed Sullivan Show* in 1968, Johnny wrote, "I don't know if you realize the esteem you are held in by your contemporaries and 'students'—but I just wanted to add my two cents to the majority opinion." Mercer continued: "You are just too much! My favorite was watching you sing . . . anyone could see how you love songs . . . and I just want to thank you for the example you set and all your help along the way." Above his signature he wrote, "In true admiration." Jean Bach identified Johnny's heroes as "Cole Porter and Irving Berlin," and suggested that Mercer "admired Berlin so much" that he did an imitation of the songwriter: "It was so charming . . . he would be standing, and he'd bend over a little bit . . . put his hands behind his back . . . he just thought that was so amusing." But when the Songwriters Hall of Fame recognized the achievements of Berlin at its first banquet in 1971, the veteran declined to accept the award in person. Mercer shipped the prize to him and in a letter described the night as "warm and nostalgic, friendly and loving." He added, "We closed a happy evening by all singing 'Say It with Music,'" which Berlin had written fifty years before. When the Songwriters Hall of Fame inducted thirty-one new members including Jack Yellen, Andy Razaf, E. Y. "Yip" Harburg, and Pete Seeger at its May 1972 banquet in the

Americana Hotel before an audience of six hundred, Irving Berlin exploded with rage. He ranted at Abe Olman, "You've just destroyed the Songwriters' Hall of Fame. By opening it up to everybody, you have destroyed its exclusivity." Ending his support of the organization, he "lashed out at others . . . wounding and astonishing everyone with whom he spoke," according to Berlin's biographer, Laurence Bergreen, who attributed the outburst to insecurity aggravated by age. When Mercer stepped down as president of the Songwriters Hall of Fame in 1973, Berlin acknowledged, "If it hadn't been for my respect for you, not alone as a songwriter, but as a person, I would not have become a member." An ever gracious Mercer accepted the compliment, writing in 1974, "Thank you for all favors . . . seen and unseen. You are the champ in a great profession . . . and I guess the only thing I respect more . . . are songs themselves!"[78]

In turning the presidency over to fellow lyricist Sammy Cahn in 1973, Johnny praised the group as "an organization representing the profession and the men I have loved and admired all my life." Mercer tried to explain the relationship between lyricists and composers:

> Songs are made up of words and music, but which is the more important is still a moot question among those of us who write them. We authors feel the melody is comparatively unimportant until we attach our deathless words to it, but as my friend and collaborator, Harry Warren, says, "You can't hum a lyric." He has a point there, so to him and all the other composers I have had the pleasure and good fortune to work with . . . I extend my thanks and gratitude. Fellows, it's been grand.[79]

Some of Mercer's cohorts cared little for a trip down memory lane. Yip Harburg sent a note to Johnny's request that he submit a few remarks about his fellow collaborators with the observation, "This is too sensitive a task for me to tackle at this time." He added, "As soon as I get a couple of shows off my chest and my bones begin to feel the feebleness of age, I shall get down to the rump business of 'summing it all up.'" But others were more charitable. Jimmy McHugh wrote, "Truly, John, you are a true friend and a real 'follow through' person for which I thank you very much and the Lord for making it possible for me to know you." Still others such as the acerbic Richard Rodgers said to Mercer, "You and I belong to a mutual-admiration society. My regard for you and your work is surely no less than your feeling about mine." Some songwriters such as Cole Porter had already died. Others like Ira Gershwin, after donating memorabilia about himself and his brother George to the Library of Congress in 1967, quietly withdrew from public view. Through the Songwriters Hall of Fame, Johnny revisited his greatest love — music — by way of recognizing the lives of composers and lyricists. In other ways Mercer demonstrated his admiration for fellow songwriters, as when he joined admirers of Vincent Youmans at his birth site in unveiling a bronze marker attached to the marble side of Stampler's Restaurant on the corner of Sixty-first Street and Central Park West. Youmans, with whom a neophyte Mercer had tried to write lyrics for the 1931 musical *Through the Years*, had great success with "Tea for Two" and such other Broadway shows as *No! No! Nanette!* and *Flying Down to Rio* before alcoholism and tuberculosis tragically destroyed his life.[80]

In 1969, the Nixon administration appointed Johnny Mercer to a commission charged with creating a White House Record Library for the enjoyment of the president's family and guests. Representing popular music, Mercer joined a group of leading figures in the entertainment industry: *Billboard* editor Paul Ackerman for country, folk, and gospel; music critic Willis Conover for jazz; historian Irving Kolodin for classical music; and City College professor Helen Roach for the spoken word. On January 29, 1970, First Lady Patricia Nixon convened the commission in the music room of the White House, discussing with its members and special guest Irving Berlin the various albums of recorded sound being selected as "the finest representation of our varied American cultural interests." The recordings included both music and the spoken word for both "educational interest and lasting pleasure."[81]

For his portion of the project Mercer assembled an impressive list of popular music albums to add to the White House collection. As Johnny explained in a foreword that accompanied his recommendations, "We have tried to pick a representative cross-section of the songs and singers that America loved best." He noted, "They shine like stars in the night, like jewels in the red clay." Mercer took into account what "the man in the street sang, hummed, and danced to, what he whistled in the shower, paid his hard earned dollars for and looks back nostalgically upon as a high point of the good times in his life." Because of Mercer's dislike for rock 'n' roll, *Billboard* assigned an editor, Don Ovens, to recommend to him "outstanding recent releases." Mercer's selections included music by singers Tony Bennett, Billie Holiday, Peggy Lee, and Perry Como, but also Elvis Presley; Dionne Warwick; Peter, Paul, and Mary; Elton John; and John Denver, among others. Groups such as the Ray Conniff Singers joined the Rolling Stones, the Beatles, Creedence Clearwater Revival, and Jefferson Airplane. Although

Conover catalogued jazz for the collection, Mercer included under the popular music heading recordings by Louis Armstrong, Duke Ellington, Paul Whiteman, Lionel Hampton, and Herb Alpert. He also added the Latin sounds of Laurindo Almeida and Antonio Jobim and a Christmas album by Julie Andrews. While many of the selected performers such as Frank Sinatra, Ella Fitzgerald, and Andy Williams as represented by their greatest-hits albums included songs by Johnny, no individual recording by Mercer found its way into the catalogue.[82]

The chair of the White House Record Library Commission, Willis Conover, interviewed Mercer for a radio program during which the men discussed the experience. Johnny used the opportunity to endorse the nascent historic preservation movement. At the commission's initial meeting in the Music Room, Mercer had sat next to the first lady, but as he confessed to Conover, "I was inarticulate when I was with Mrs. Nixon, I really was. I couldn't say a word." He enjoyed the private tour of the White House: "I couldn't speak for looking. I was just looking at all those beautiful rooms, all the portraits of past presidents. All the history and the things that must have gone on under that roof and the dignitaries that must have visited. It's quite impressive and it's quite beautiful." Perhaps he reflected on his grandfather and other ancestors who had once visited as guests of presidents. Critical of how "progress" destroyed so much of America's built environment, Mercer mentioned the historic preservation effort in Savannah, where "they're just beginning" to restore old structures following the demolition of the City Market in 1954. "I don't mean rebuild it like Williamsburg. I mean shore it up. Keep the façade and put in great plumbing and air conditioning but keep the antiquity like Paris does." He noted, "If you go to Paris you'll see that they don't fool around with those artworks or those old buildings. They just bring them up to date on the inside. And that's what has been done to the White House and that's what should be done in every historic place in America." As a grounded southerner, he understood the importance of locale: "Keep the indigenous thing that the natives of that particular place are proud of . . . If you'll go to Richmond, Virginia, you'll see it's all fairly Jeffersonian in architecture. There's a similarity and it makes for a great attractiveness of the region. And I wish it were done more everywhere." Johnny concluded that historic preservation "ought to be done the best way we can do it without destroying the historic significance and the old historic beauty."[83]

Settling into late midlife, Mercer came to terms with the fleeting nature of celebrity. Still modest despite the self-absorption of the Me Decade, a reflective

Mercer began to allow a philosophical understanding to replace the cynicism that had clouded his outlook on the 1960s. Jack Lemmon directed his friend Walter Matthau in the 1971 picture *Kotch*, which featured a theme song written by Johnny with the composer Marvin Hamlisch, who within five years would write "The Way We Were" and *A Chorus Line*. The collaboration with Hamlisch resulted in "Life Is What You Make It." Lines such as "Smile, the world is sunny" reflect Johnny's optimistic attitude. Other lines capture his opinion of life: "Fame may run to catch you / Or look right at you / And pass you by," yet as always the hope remains that "Somewhere out there / Love waits to see you through." The inevitable ending, "Life is what you make it, / And what you make it / Is up to you," expressed a sentiment shared by many of Mercer's generation, who prospered in postwar America and failed to understand how people could blame the system for their own shortcomings. "Life Is What You Make It" received Mercer's eighteenth and last Academy Award nomination for Best Song, but it lost to Isaac Hayes's "Theme from Shaft."[84]

The changes in American musical tastes as evident in the two distinctively different Oscar nominations had left Mercer at odds with the entertainment industry. For nearly fifty years his music had enjoyed widespread acceptance among the general public, from ballads to rhythm and novelty songs to the great movie themes. Regularly his music had topped the *Billboard* charts and *Your Hit Parade* either as songs he wrote sung by others or as recordings of him singing his own songs or those of others. His peers in the Academy of Motion Picture Arts and Sciences had recognized his talents with eighteen nominations for Best Original Song and four Academy Awards. His colleagues had elected him to membership in the Songwriters Hall of Fame. Yet the divergence of jazz into bebop and popular music into rock 'n' roll and the subsequent decline of the Great American Song made Mercer's style of songwriting an anachronism. Rather than retire like his colleagues Harold Arlen and Ira Gershwin, Johnny had an innate creativity that refused to let up, encouraging him to look abroad for inspiration as he increasingly partnered with foreign composers to write transnational songs.

Now lionized as a legend, Mercer participated in an event that showcased his successful career writing jazz-interpenetrated popular song for the Great American Songbook. As a reflection of his first-rank status, Johnny received an invitation to kickoff the 1971 *Lyrics and Lyricists* series sponsored by the Ninety-second Street Young Men's and Young Women's Hebrew Association. On March 14, 1971, an appreciative audience packed into the hot auditorium at the Ninety-second Street Y to enjoy "An Evening with Johnny Mercer." Host Maurice Levine had inaugurated the series the year before with E. Y. "Yip" Harburg. To help celebrate Mercer's lengthy career, Levine recruited Margaret Whiting and Bob Sands, accompanied by Richard Leonard on the piano.[85]

For nearly two hours the entertainers performed an assortment of songs from Mercer's catalog of nearly fifteen hundred lyrics that included the lesser-known gems "My Shining Hour" and "Early Autumn." They rounded out the segment with a dizzying twenty-nine numbers from *Your Hit Parade* that Mercer called his "bread-and-butter songs" and that ranged from "Lazybones" to "Moon River." Also he sprinkled throughout unpublished pieces such as "Me and the Ghost Upstairs." Because he liked the four choruses from "Spring, Spring, Spring" that movie producers had cut from the film *Seven Brides for Seven Brothers*, Mercer sang them: "To itself each amoeba / Softly croons, 'Ach, du lieber,' / While the proud little termite / Feels as large as a worm might" and "See the gay little finches / In connubial clinches, / As each fleet little swallow / Finds a swallow to follow." Just as he recited lines deleted from films, Mercer performed lyrics for movie themes that composers rejected, offering his own words to Johnny Mandel's tune that Paul Francis Webster turned into "The Shadow of Your Smile." Sound engineers recorded the evening for release on an LP. Covering the event for the *New York Times*, John S. Wilson recognized Mercer "had to sing them in medleys to even scratch the surface of his remarkable output." But he also criticized Johnny for the "'and-then-I-wrote' approach, skimming the surface of his career but offering little insight about the craft of lyric writing or his methods of work." Throughout the evening, the modest Mercer shared the credit by telling anecdotes about his collaborators. He also offered a few words of advice to would-be songwriters, "You can't let a song hang around too long, some one else is going to write it," he said.[86]

The performance addressed questions about the changing quality of lyric writing over time. Host Levine concluded the program by asking Mercer to comment on Tom Wicker's criticism of the Depression- and war-era songwriters who appeared stuck in a "moon-June-spoon format." Pausing, Johnny responded, "Well, we were in more of a rut than these kids today are in, but it was a more attractive rut." About the evening *Variety* noted, "Mercer is somewhat bitter at the rush of the untrained and unscholarly who have emerged into writers of major hits." Yet the industry publication complimented the songwriter as "a man who loves language enough to treat it reverently and want to play with it and give it forms that are plastic, literate, and amusing at times. There are trick rhymes and subtle rhymes and frequently a delicacy of feeling." Pointing to the standing ovation the capacity crowd gave Mercer at the end of the "wonderful evening," the director of music at the Y complimented Johnny: "Thanks a million for putting such a bright spot on the lives of so many people — and I'm counting on you to keep on doing just that for a long, long time to come."[87]

9 Global Southerner

. . . .

Like painted kites,
The days and nights
Went flying by.
The world was new
Beneath a blue
Umbrella sky.

HAVING LONG KEPT a finger on the pulse of popular culture, Johnny Mercer turned outward in the postwar era as America embraced the world as a hegemonic power. The global southerner remained firmly grounded in his historical hometown of Savannah while spending months abroad working and touring as a citizen of the world. Already his music had found a receptive international audience. While the jazz-interpenetrated popular song declined in popularity and the movie musicals drew to a close, music coming from Europe and South America inspired Mercer to new heights of creativity. Johnny joined an international community of composers crafting transnational songs. Just as the sale of Capitol Records to EMI had demonstrated the emerging worldwide cultural hegemony of the American entertainment industry, so too Mercer's transformation of French and German songs into top forty hits in the United States and his attraction to bossa nova revealed the potential of transnational music. Having long been a cosmopolite in New York City and Los Angeles, Mercer spent nearly half of each of the last five active years of his life traveling abroad, often living in London or Paris, but wherever he hung his hat and called home, his compass pointed toward Savannah.

Growing up in a port city, Mercer understood that a larger world extended beyond Georgia's shores. No doubt as a boy he had puzzled like the pirates over Scotsman Robert Louis Stevenson's *Treasure Island* map that positioned the chest in proximity to Savannah. He read about Penrod's adventures in the French Foreign Legion. He learned the histories of the British royal families, perhaps as recorded by the ever-romantic southern favorite Sir Walter Scott, whose volumes lined the bookshelves in the Gwinnett Street parlor near the family portrait on the mahogany secretary of Mary, Queen of Scots. When playing Gilbert and Sullivan on the gramophone or piano, Johnny could sing along with the Japanese Lord High Executioner, the Pirate King on the seven seas, or the gondolier in Venice, depending on which operetta he chose. His Ciucevich kin connected him not only to Austria but also, through marriage, to Ireland, just as his black playmates represented to him Africa. With his buddies, Johnny sang popular folk songs such as "The Bastard King of England" from the days of Robin Hood and "The Ballad of Abdulla Bulbul Ameer" from the Crimean War. Groceries in the city's various ethnic communities displayed for sale exotic goods that Johnny and his friends enjoyed eating, such as Greek ice cream made by the Leopold brothers at their fruit stand. Indeed, Savannahians had long connected to the wider world.

Initially an exotic southerner in New York and Hollywood, where he stood out in his white linen suits and Panama hats, Johnny Mercer saw the world outside the South as exotic, too, freely commodifying stereotypes from other cultures. Various parts of the globe provided backgrounds for several of the early pieces he wrote for the studios. Typical of these kinds of songs, his "Night over Shanghai," written with Harry Warren for the 1937 film *The Singing Marine*, used Asian images such as "lighted lanterns in doorways" to create a mood that revealed longings of love. Again with Warren, Johnny assisted fellow lyricist Al Dubin in collapsing several "Oriental" cultures into "The Girl Friend of the Whirling Dervish," a comic piece in the 1938 film *Garden of the Moon* about a beauty from "old Bombay" who gives her boyfriend the runaround while he busily makes "an honest rupee" by "dervishing with all his might." Tapping his early experience in the Theatre Guild's traveling show as an extra in Eugene O'Neill's *Marco's Millions*, Mercer took the setting and with Robert Emmett Dolan scored a Broadway musical called *Messer Marco Polo* that, while never staged, told the love story of the Venetian explorer and a Chinese maiden using the splendor of Kubla Khan's court as a backdrop. Johnny had several *Your Hit Parade* songs that exploited the exotic. His 1938 "Weekend of a Private Secretary" made light of the sin awaiting the visitor to corrupt Cuba. The singer explains, "I went to Havana, / To look at the natives, / To study their customs, / Their picturesque ways." Likewise, a 1942 success played on the public's ever-popular fascination with Argentina: "South American stories / Tell of a girl who's quite a dream, / The beauty of her race." The woman, "Tangerine," is so gorgeous that "when she dances by, / Senoritas stare / And caballeros sigh."[1]

Similarly, at first Johnny packaged the South as an exotic export, as others had done in the fashion of Tin Pan Alley. Such early Mercer songs as the 1933 "Lazybones" with Hoagy Carmichael and the 1934 "Pardon My Southern Accent" with Matty Malnick had offered a twist on the typical back-to-Dixie lyrics by not using southern stereotypes and instead localizing the story in the region. Suited to the task of writing southern-themed songs, Mercer collaborated with Bernie Hanighen on several numbers, such as the 1934 tale of reverse migration called "Fare-Thee-Well to Harlem" and the 1935 "Dixieland Band," about a jazz combo scoring a trumpet player who turns out to be the Archangel Gabriel. As the years passed Mercer and Hanighen shifted the subject from the South to jazz itself, as in the 1937 "Bob White (Whatcha Gonna Swing Tonight?)" and the 1941 "I Boogied when I Should Have Woogied." By the end of the Great Depression, Dixie had lost its luster as a topic for the songwriter. Henceforth, rather than selling the South, the region provided a style of music — jazz — and an occasional landscape for other action.[2]

As Mercer began to travel outside the United States, his worldview as a global southerner expanded. His first opportunity to leave the country occurred in 1936, when he traveled to Great Britain ostensibly to write quintessential songs of the exotic South for an all-black musical revue. The Broadway producer Lew Leslie, who had championed the format in a series of productions, had hired Mercer to join the composer Rube Bloom in writing a score for a show that featured the tap-dancing Nicholas Brothers. The *Blackbirds* concept had run its course by the time Mercer and Bloom got involved, although the two contributed several great numbers, such as the optimistic "Keep a Twinkle in Your Eye." They also wrote the insensitive "Jo-Jo, the Cannibal Kid," who passed up eating "roots and berries" for "missionaries." Yet in packaging the South in such songs as "Dixie Isn't Dixie Anymore," the words pointed to modernism, for the region of Johnny's youth had given way to progress. Mercer too had given way by first joining the southern diaspora and now engaging in international travel that led to stints abroad writing music. Throughout his life he returned to Great Britain.[3]

Classical music with its timeless and universal appeal also inspired Mercer. Although he cared little for operas, Johnny favored the lyrical composers of the late nineteenth and early twentieth centuries. As he explained to writer Henry Kane, "I've moved a long way from the rhythm-beat of my youth. I've moved to stuff I didn't appreciate at all as a youngster. Nothing real heavy, mind you — but I find that I go more and more these days to Debussy, Puccini, Rachmaninoff, Tchaikovsky." He found these men "real melody-fellas," noting, "I'd have loved to have written some lyrics for those boys. They kind of reach me where it tickles soft; sweet stuff, romantic; to me, kind of nostalgic. Honestly, today we'd call it ballad stuff." Not surprisingly, Mercer turned to just such a classical piece for his own ballad. He followed the example of his mentor, Paul Whiteman, who had made a popular arrangement of Nikolai Rimsky-Korsakov's "Song of India" in the 1920s that Johnny's friend, Tommy Dorsey, turned into a swing tune in the 1930s. Recalling the majestic sounds of the original score, Johnny selected words that made a universal statement on the striving of humanity over the centuries. Opening the song with descriptions of India's beautiful landscape, Mercer's lyric steadily builds to a crescendo: "There's the maharajah's caravan, / Unfolding like a painted fan, / How small the little race of man!" Then at the song's bridge is the climax: "See them all parade across the ages, / Armies, kings and slaves from hist'ry's pages, / Played on one of Nature's vastest stages." In the resolution that follows in the refrain, Johnny brings his timeless story up to the present: "A lonely plane flies off to meet the dawn, / While down below the busy life goes on, / And women crowd the old bazaars." In June 1953, the popular Italian American tenor Mario Lanza recorded "Song of India" in what his biographer called "a masterful performance that ranks with the finest of his career." Hearing it on its release, the jazz singer Mel Tormé noted, "What came out of that speaker enthralled me, a lyric of such scope, such dimension that I thought to myself: I never have to go to India — Lanza just brought it to me." Tormé was shocked but not surprised to learn the masterful Mercer had crafted the lines. Often when given exceptional melodies or when striving to write transnational music, Mercer reached for the universal as if to speak for all humanity.[4]

By nature transnational, music has never known firm boundaries as the strains of a tune or the sentiments of a lyric make borders irrelevant. Certainly the music industry never recognized international borders, as it produced records for sale in every country possible. Standard practice had long been to take a popular song from elsewhere and give it localized lyrics that could then be sold in the global phonograph world.[5] One of Mercer's early assignments had been to translate into vernacular English the lyrics to Emmerich Kalman's *Paris in Spring*, following the typical process of American commodification of European popular song. At the same time, the reverse occurred as foreign composers such as Igor Stravinsky consumed that southern musical export, jazz. By the postwar era, a new kind of music appeared as songwriters from different countries and cultures actually collaborated on popular song designed for global distribution. Travel made such international partnerships easier as lyricists and composers worked together to create a hybrid transnational music that often had as its foundation the fashionable jazz-infused Great American Song then all the rage.

France provided Mercer with an exotic setting for several early songs. While the boy had once played as a musketeer, now as a man he imagined himself among the jazz expatriates improvising their own nightclub in a Parisian suburb. Written with Joseph Meyer, the 1933 "In a Café in Montmartre" used the international currency of jazz to recall lost love. In the 1955 musical *Daddy Long Legs*, Leslie Caron lives in a French orphanage teaching English as a second language, so Mercer composed "C-A-T Spells Cat" as a way to engage the linguistic divide. "*Maintenant ecoutez* / To speak, how you say? To *comprende le* speech *Anglaise* / We learn our A-B-C." The years of studying French at Woodberry Forest School had made Johnny comfortable enough with the language, and he enjoyed traveling in the country, visiting on several occasions.[6]

With "Autumn Leaves," Mercer fashioned a truly transnational song. The Hungarian composer Joseph Kosma wrote the music to "Les Feuilles Mortes" (The Dead Leaves), a haunting melody that reminisced of brighter days and things past in a postwar Europe littered with death. French surrealist poet Jacques Prévert contributed a lyric that conjured up sad images of lost love. Yves Montand — the protégée and lover of Édith Piaf — gave the song wide distribution when it appeared in the 1946 French film *Les Portes de la Nuit*. Capitol Records bought the rights to the song so that Mercer could fit English words to the poignant tune. Johnny let the option nearly expire before jotting down the lines to what he later called "the biggest-income song I ever had." Jo Stafford's 1950 recording for Capitol got "Autumn Leaves" on *Your Hit Parade*. Jazz singers and musicians made the song a regular of the repertoire with releases by Bing Crosby, Artie Shaw, Sarah Vaughan, Steve Allen, and others. Piaf performed both the French and English versions for broadcast Christmas Eve in 1950 on NBC's *The Big Show*, radio's last great variety program designed to halt television's advance. In addition to the French folksongs the "little sparrow" performed for the newly elected president Dwight Eisenhower during his visit to Paris prior to his inauguration, Piaf sang as requested, "his favorite, 'Autumn Leaves.'" Perhaps the great tenor saxophonist, Lester Young, spoke for all jazz musicians when explaining he had to visualize the lyric before improvising a solo on such a standard of the Great American Songbook. Certainly Johnny's words helped make "Autumn Leaves" a regular selection on recordings by such musicians as Cannonball Adderley, Dizzy Gillespie, Stan Getz, and Wynton Marsalis. The pianist Roger Williams's 1955 recording stayed on the charts for six months and held the number one spot for four weeks, marking the beginning of the song's life as a staple of lounge singers and piano players. In 1956, the director Robert Aldrich interpolated the song as sung by Nat "King" Cole into his film *Autumn Leaves*, which won an award at the Berlin International Film Festival.[7]

While the song reflects the potential of transnational music, the success of Mercer's lyric lies in its theme of lost love, a subject he had mastered. Prévert's words recall the happiness lovers once shared in the bright sunlight, but now a cold north wind carries away their memories and regrets like the dead leaves in the night. Johnny's version expresses that vision more economically: as "The falling leaves / Drift by the window / The autumn leaves / Of red and gold," the former lover recalls kissing the lips of the woman whose "sunburned hands I used to hold." But with the approach of "old winter's song," he pines for his lost love: "But I miss you most of all, my darling, / When autumn leaves start to fall." Mercer wrote his lyric in a half hour, the time it took him to ride from Hollywood to the Los Angeles terminal train station. Reflecting on the song, he thought the tune great, the title good, and the lyric, well, "it's all right. It fits the tune. I don't think it's very original," he confessed to jazz critic Willis Conover.[8]

Other French chansons attracted the attention of Mercer, who crafted thoughtful translations that made the songs popular, especially with jazz singers. In 1951, he undertook the composition of an English lyric for a song by M. Philippe-Gérard, the pseudonym of Philippe Gérard Bloch, a native of São Paulo, Brazil and son of French parents whose friend, Maurice Ravel, had recommended musical training for the boy. After study at the Paris Conservatoire, Philippe-Gerard lived and worked in France as a songwriter and composer for film and television. The French poet Angèle Vannier contributed a lyric that captures the postwar feeling of the aging coquette or boulevardier who recalls happier days before the war to a wistful waltz tune by Philippe-Gerard that became "Le Chevalier de Paris (les Pommiers Doux)." Édith Piaf introduced the song in 1950. Mercer turned the French into "When the World Was Young (Ah, the Apple Trees)" with its secondary title derived from the refrain.[9]

The song pleased Mercer. His lyric went: "Ah, the apple trees, / Sunlit memories, / Where the hammock swung! / On our backs we'd lie, / Looking at the sky / Till the stars were strung — / Only last July, / When the world was young." In talking about it with Conover, he said, "It seemed to me just my way of remembering how it was in the old days, because the song in French, as well as in English, talks about a man who has been to war, comes back disillusioned, or a girl who's been around the pool comes back disillusioned, and remembers

how it was when she was young. Before the world got to her, and disappointment and everything." When writing the words Mercer said he "remembered
all these things that I remembered as a boy, you know. Not necessarily me, just
things. Things that were . . . little labels of an age like jack o'lanterns and vests of
appliqué, you know." Peggy Lee made a popular recording of Mercer's lyric for
"When the World Was Young" on her 1956 album of smooth jazz titled *Black
Coffee*. Frank Sinatra had a success with Mercer's "When the World Was Young"
in 1962 on *Point of No Return*, the sixteenth and last of the conceptual albums
produced by Capitol Records. Marlene Dietrich released a German version titled
"Die Welt War Jung (Ja Der Apfelbaum)," although Hildegard Knef made a bigger German hit out of the song. The jazz singers Blossom Dearie, who recorded
it in 1966, and Nancy Wilson, who recorded it in 1967, also had the song in their
repertoires. When he met with Conover in 1970, Mercer confessed, "Now I've
just come back from Paris and the Frenchmen over there tell me that the English
lyric is far superior to the French lyric."[10]

Mercer found inspiration in another French chanson that led to a decade-
long collaboration with the composer Michel Legrand. A native Parisian, born
in 1932, Legrand studied at the Paris Conservatoire under the legendary Nadia
Boulanger, and while classically trained — winning top honors as both composer
and pianist — he loved jazz after hearing Dizzy Gillespie in concert. Columbia
recruited him to record French chason for American distribution resulting in
his 1954 album *I Love Paris,* which he followed with other releases including the
1958 *Legrand Jazz* that featured performances by John Coltrane, Miles Davis,
Bill Evans, and Ben Webster. Music by Legrand and music producer Eddie Barclay had been fitted with a French lyric by Eddie Marnay to become the song
"La Valse des Lilas." Mutual friends introduced Mercer to Legrand. On several
occasions Johnny had ridden with Bob and Jean Bach from New York to the
Newport Jazz Festival in Rhode Island, and one year the jazz singer Blossom
Dearie joined them. An eccentric with a pure, sweet, high voice, Dearie fascinated Mercer, and the two became friends. Jean Bach remembered that Dearie
exposed Mercer to Michel Legrand's music. Back in 1952, Blossom had moved to
France and formed the Blue Stars of Paris, a singing group, with Legrand's sister,
Christiane, and jazz writer Bob Dorough. While recording an album, Dearie
wanted to include a lyric by Mercer for a song by Legrand, but it took Johnny
an inordinate amount of time to finish his adaptation. "There was one word in
there that he wasn't pleased with. He was such a perfectionist and he was waiting for the mot juste," Jean Bach remembered, suggesting, "They finally speeded

him up and said, 'let's take it as it is' or something." Dearie made the recording in September 1958, and "Once upon a Summertime" appeared on her 1959 album of the same name.[11]

The lyric tells the story of a young girl trying to describe the feeling of being in love. One of the great performers of the piece, the jazz singer Mabel Mercer, whom Johnny had heard years before at the Onyx Club on Fifty-second Street, struggled with the words of the song until she got the sentiment of the lyric just right. She toyed with the line, "I felt as though the mayor had offered me the key to Paris." After shifting the emphasis from word to word, Mabel finally understood Johnny's intention. As she explained: "Oh, I think I have it. It's very preposterous that the mayor of Paris would ever give a young girl in love a key to the city. It's just so unlikely that it has to strike this girl as being very funny." Mabel added a giggle that perfectly conveyed that meaning to the audience: "You were sweeter than the blossoms on the tree. / I was as proud as any girl could be, / As if the mayor had offered me the key / To Paris!" Yet as with other wistful songs of lost love, Mercer uses the changing seasons to express regret: "Now, another wintertime has come and gone; / The pigeons feeding in the square have flown; / But I remember when the vespers chime / You loved me once upon a summertime." Mercer enjoyed the collaboration with the talented Legrand, suggesting to Willis Conover: "I'll tell you I'm so excited about Michel. He's such a first-class writer. He's younger than I and I don't think he's Kern yet, but he's awfully good." Upon considering "Autumn Leaves," "When the World Was Young," and "Once upon a Summertime," music critic Edward Habib noted, "Mercer wrote English passports for three of the most popular French songs ever to cross the Atlantic." The examples reveal the movement of music across international borders — here with Mercer's careful selection of English words to fit existing French lyrics and tunes — all being transformed in a "third space" of transnational exchange, in Johnny's case brought about by the hybridity of jazz.[12]

A regular at the Newport Jazz Festival, Mercer enjoyed the opportunity to see, hear, and associate with other jazz greats even as the genre splintered into factions. Jean Bach recalled Mercer's "feet were in both camps" because of the esteem in which he was held by such musicians as Duke Ellington, Charlie Mingus, and Gerry Mulligan. Not all jazzmen fared so well, as writers for *Down Beat*, fond of bebop, criticized Armstrong's handkerchief on the head and rolling of the eyes as just too old style. Because Armstrong chose the Fourth of July as his birthday, the Newport Jazz Festival annually celebrated "Louis Armstrong Night" with a "Happy Birthday Jam" led by Louis. As a special treat in 1957, organizers wanted a parade of jazz pioneers to play the jam session, including trombonists Kid Ory and Jack Teagarden, saxophonist Sidney Bechet, and others who had once appeared with the trumpeter in New Orleans and Chicago. Yet these arrangements had occurred without Armstrong's approval and without any opportunity to rehearse. When organizers tried to replace his singer, Velma Middleton, with Ella Fitzgerald, Armstrong had had enough. He insisted his band would perform as prepared but no more. At the end of his set, when Johnny Mercer and Ella Fitzgerald wheeled in a giant cake and led the thousands gathered at Newport in a rousing chorus of "Happy Birthday, Louis," the consummate professional backed them up on his cornet but declined the piece cut for him. He then dismissed the old musicians who waited in the wings for the signal to come on stage for the jam session with the comment, "No one hangs on my coattails," and he intoned the National Anthem to end the concert. While the audience knew nothing of the conflict, it reflected yet another aspect of the crisis confronting jazz and Mercer's association with the musicians who made the music.[13]

When Ella Fitzgerald recorded her 1960 concert in Berlin's Deutschlandhalle that became the Grammy Award–winning album *Ella in Berlin: Mack the Knife*, she opened the performance with Johnny Mercer's "That Old Black Magic." The crowd overflowing the twelve-thousand-seat arena — the same space that a few decades before had hosted Hitler rallies — roared its approval and swayed to the sounds of American jazz as Fitzgerald then revved up versions of Cole Porter's "Just One of Those Things" and the Gershwins' "The Man I Love." Many of these standards appeared in her Songbook series that helped make her one of the top female vocalists of the twentieth century. As another southern diaspora entertainer, Fitzgerald had moved with her family from her native Newport News, Virginia, to New York, where she fell for jazz after hearing recordings by Louis Armstrong. To develop her own style, Ella listened intently to the white female harmonizing group from New Orleans, the Boswell Sisters, in particular copying the intonation and clear articulation of Connee Boswell. With her distinctive scat, Ella Fitzgerald joined Chick Webb's orchestra as the girl singer, performing at the Savoy and Roseland ballrooms, and soon was singing Porter and Mercer standards for the sophisticated audiences at the Waldorf-Astoria. When bebop supplanted swing bands, Ella eased right in as the first — and greatest — vocalist to master the new approach to jazz. Johnny agreed with Duke Ellington that "about Ella, she's beyond category and that's the truth." In 1964, she recorded *Ella Fitzgerald: The Johnny Mercer Songbook*, a baker's dozen of his best songs backed by the Nelson Riddle Orchestra. It was the eighth and final new subject in her Songbook series — and the only one devoted to the works of a songwriter principally recognized as a lyricist, for the other seven featured the composers. She performed "in high spirits, singing somewhat more fancifully than was her custom for this series," according to her biographer. Music critic Will Friedwald recognized that Fitzgerald devoted an album to the songs of Mercer because for Ella, "the lyric is only something to swing on," and as "that most down-to-earth of wordsmiths," the jazz musician Johnny naturally provided words with rhythm.[14]

Previously Mercer had found inspiration in German operetta, lieder, and stories he read as a child in Savannah. His debt to romantic visions of medieval chivalry appeared in his references to the Rhineland, as evident in the lyric for "Out of This World," written in 1945 with Harold Arlen, which referred to a fairy tale princess so beautiful that "no armored knight out of a book was more enchanted by a Lorelei than I." For Universal International's 1953 film *Walking My Baby Back Home*, Mercer contributed a new version of "Glow Worm." It was originally composed as "Glühwürmchen" in 1902 by the German Paul Lincke for the operetta *Lysistrata*; Lilla Cayley Robinson gave it English words in 1907 as "Glow Worm" for Lew Fields's musical *The Girl behind the Counter*, at which time it became a hit in the United States, reappearing in the 1939 film *The Story of Vernon and Irene Castle*. When Johnny decided to write a new lyric in 1952, he drew on his southern heritage, contributing a rhythmic breakdown using the image of a regional pest: "Thou aer-o-nau-tic-al boll weevil, / Il-lu-mi-nate yon woods primeval." The Mills Brothers, a black jazz quartet that sang background for Bing Crosby and other performers, later made a recording of the song, which became their best-known hit.[15]

Thrilled by the challenge of transnational music, a middle-aged Mercer tackled German lieder for great American vocalists such as Andy Williams, Tony Bennett, and Frank Sinatra. Johnny freely translated Bertolt Brecht's "The Bilbao Song," originally written in 1929 with composer Kurt Weill for the 1929 show *Happy End*. Sharing the music's feeling of bittersweet loss, Johnny contributed an English lyric that went, "We'd sing a song the whole night long / And I can still recall, / Those were the greatest, / Those were the greatest, / Those were the greatest days of them all." Andy Williams recording of "The Bilbao Song," accompanied by the Archie Bleyer Orchestra, became the young tenor's first success singing a Mercer song.[16]

The transnational song, "Summer Wind," released by Frank Sinatra in 1966 proved to be Johnny Mercer's last top forty hit; it reached number one on the *Billboard* charts. In 1965, Mercer had heard Danish singer Grethe Ingmann perform the German song, "Der Sommerwind," with music by Heinz Meier and German lyrics by Hans Bradtke. One of Germany's most popular lyricists, Bradtke would have another hit with "Tammy (Can You Hear the Wind that Whispers to You)." Johnny crafted his own words to fit Meier's melody. The result, "Summer Wind," uses the seasons to capture the passing of life and love. After pairing "two sweethearts" who "strolled the golden sand," Mercer notes, "I lost you to the summer wind." He laments: "The autumn wind, / The winter winds, / Have come and gone, / And still the days, / The lonely days, / Go on and on." But to no avail as, "And guess who sighs / His lullabies / Through nights that never end? / My fickle friend / The summer wind." Sinatra's recording of the song, backed by Nelson Riddle's leitmotif of the breeze as expressed by the reeds, revealed a masculine perception of loss. Over the years Sinatra made hits out of many Mercer standards such as "One for My Baby (and One More for the Road)," but he also performed lesser-known songs, such as "Talk to Me, Baby," and closed his radio and television shows by singing "Dream." Daughter Nancy Sinatra identified Johnny as "Dad's favorite lyricist." Ol' Blue Eyes recognized that Mercer's lyrics had boosted his career, remarking that "there were so many times I depended on him to write something for me, and he never let me down."[17]

Just as Johnny looked to Europe for inspiration, he turned as well to Latin America for new sounds, especially in the postwar period. Fantastic images of Cuba in particular had colored Mercer's imagination in the past. In the 1930s, he collaborated with the Cuban composer and bandleader Alfredo Brito, writing an English lyric for the beautiful "Ninfa de Ojos Brujos," or "Beneath the Curtain of the Night," in 1934. Similarly, he partnered with another Cuban composer and bandleader, Xavier Cugat, to create "Loca Illusion" in 1940. By the 1950s, Johnny collaborated with Jose Antonio Mendez, writing the song "Quiereme y veras," or "Every Now and Then." Mendez helped popularize the Cuban ballad style of singing called *filin*. These songs tapped the rumbas, sambas, and tangos that gained in popularity during the period. Indeed, with Brito cofounding Havana's Tropicana, where Nat "King" Cole once performed, and Cugat headlining at the most famous nightclubs in North America, the men and their bands popularized a new Latin sound. Johnny and Hoagy Carmichael had played with Latin rhythms in their 1939 song, "The Rumba Jumps!" with its "Hep, hep!" linking the jazz with the Latin beat. Johnny's song lyric describes a San Domingo band that studied jazz in Harlem before returning to the Caribbean, where they "started in to play / The way they learned to play / Back in the U.S.A." As the words suggest, the period between the world wars encouraged a sharing of musical styles. During the 1940s, Mercer ordered several publications from the Music Division of the Pan American Union in Washington, D.C., to learn more about Latin American music.[18]

The development of international markets by Capitol Records and others under the U.S. Good Neighbor Policy made jazz omnipresent in Latin America as record companies flooded the Caribbean Basin, Central America, and South America with pressings by such big bands as those led by the Dorsey brothers and Duke Ellington. In 1948, Capitol Records targeted the Brazilian market, hiring the Rio de Janeiro broadcaster Luis Serrano, who had worked in New York, to develop the potential of Brazilian musicians for an affiliated record company while promoting Capitol's new releases. He created a nightly show on Rádio Globo that plugged U.S. jazz while advocating the formation of local fan clubs for the new sounds. Avid listeners of songs recorded by Frank Sinatra proved numerous among Brazilians, who organized the Sinatra-Farney Fan Club, named also for the popular Brazilian crooner and pianist Farnésio Dutra, who took the stage name Dick Farney. Other fans organized a club that celebrated Stan Kenton, whose progressive jazz drew upon Latin musicians, instrumentation, and compositions to make a Latin swing and jazz sound. Members of the fan clubs had to be able to sing or play instruments in the style of the jazz musicians they admired. Thanks to the availability of Capitol records, Johnny Mercer's music populated the airwaves and appeared on the record players of the clubs, where fans debated the merits of the different performers of various songs. Out of the hybrid environment of these clubs in the middle-class neighborhoods of Rio de Janeiro emerged the talents who created bossa nova.[19]

The trajectory of the bossa nova movement paralleled the fortunes of democracy in the country. For decades, Brazilians had suffered through a series of military coups and dictators until in 1956 the citizens democratically elected a president, Juscelino Kubitschek, who confidently predicted dramatic growth for the country and economic prosperity for its people. To promote development, he launched a five-year plan that included the building of a new capital — the futuristic Brasilia — in the interior of the vast country on the central plain high above the jungle. The optimistic era made all things possible, as concrete came to symbolize the nation's potential. Brazilian builders poured a new city into forms just as poets created a *poesia concreta* and musicians a modernistic bossa nova. Mercer found the ideas of creation awe inspiring and in 1961 took the song "Serenata Negra" by Vico Pagano, Carlos Loti, and Tito Madinez and wrote words for "Brasilia," an homage to the sparkling new capital city: "Have you seen Brasilia? / Skyline of tomorrow," the lyric begins, "in the midst of nowhere, / Shiny and bright / Like a jewel in the rain." Describing the construction of designer Oscar Niemeyer, Mercer notes, "Architects have utilized the moonlight / Like lattice work on the lawns." Then he invites in an interlude, "Come with me for a flight there; / Let me show you its charms. / Come with me for a night there; / Spend the night in my arms." The song resolves in the coda, "Once you leave Brasilia, / You will not forget it. / It will remain in your vision / Like a spell. / Brazil, Brazil, Brasilia — / Farewell!"[20]

The atmosphere of Latin America intrigued Johnny, who during the 1950s partnered with Brazilian composers he had met in Hollywood and who would later emerge as key figures in the bossa nova movement. For decades Carmen Miranda had symbolized Brazil in the United States, and in her movies Nestor Amaral performed in the Bando da Lua. As a composer, Amaral partnered with Ray Gilbert, who wrote the lyrics for *The Three Caballeros*, a Walt Disney combination of animation and travelogue that served as a tribute to Latin America. Released in 1944, the movie starred cartoon characters Donald Duck, a Brazilian parrot, and Mexican rooster; Carmen's sister Aurora Miranda; Amaral; and the Brazilian classical guitarist Laurindo Almeida. Having long held the odd studio assignment, Almeida joined Amaral in contributing scores for such films as the 1953 *Latin Lovers* that starred Lana Turner and Ricardo Montalban. Mercer probably met Almeida when he played guitar in the Stan Kenton Band. Johnny took music composed by Almeida and Amaral and wrote lyrics for "Sighs," which he published in 1953. A series of recordings in 1953–54 by Almeida and the American saxophonist Bud Shank displayed the sophisticated and understated cool jazz tones of the sambas that marked the hybridity of the transnational music. So, too, did the styling of the young Brazilian singer and guitarist João Gilberto, whose peculiar plucking of the strings set the rhythm of the incipient bossa nova. All these men recognized the influence of cool jazz recordings — many on the Capitol label — by Peggy Lee, Miles Davis, Gerry Mulligan, and Chet Baker, on what emerged as the Latin jazz-samba.[21]

By the end of the 1950s, the release of several key recordings launched the bossa nova movement in Brazil and abroad, starting with the 1958 song "Desafinado." The guitarist Gilberto sang in his intimate way the lyrics by Newton Mendonça that made an inside joke of off-key singers. The young composer of the new music, Antônio Carlos "Tom" Jobim, conducted the orchestra on the recording.

A self-reflective line in the lyrics refers to the jazz-samba sound: "This is Bossa Nova, this is very natural." Where once complex rhythms and elaborate harmonies had marked samba, now a tighter syncopation drove shifting harmonies to make a sophisticated "new fashion," or "bossa nova," of singing, ideally suited to the combo or individual with a guitar. The Brazilians transformed the cool jazz of the bebop age into a clean Latin sound. Released in 1958 by the Odeon label, the single "Desafinado," or "Off-Key," as well as the earlier "Chega de Saudade" (No More Blues), also written by Jobim and the Brazilian poet Vinicius de Moraes, raced to the top of the charts. The soundtrack from the award-winning film *Orfeu Negro*, or "Black Orpheus," shot in Rio de Janeiro by Marcel Camus, included music by Jobim, Moraes, and the Brazilian guitarist Luiz Bonfá, securing the popularity of the bossa nova and making it a worldwide phenomenon. By 1961, Capitol had released in the United States the album *Brazil's Brilliant João Gilberto*, featuring these and other songs sung in Portuguese. American jazz musicians, including Charlie Byrd and Stan Getz, visited Brazil, where they absorbed the new style heard in Rio's nightclubs along Copacabana Beach. Soon Getz had joined with Jobim and Gilberto on a record that included "The Girl from Ipanema," or "Garota de Ipanema," sung by Gilberto's wife, Astrud. Once released as a single in 1964, the song soared to number one, and Astrud's gentle singing style pushed her into the limelight as an international superstar.[22]

Liking the sounds he heard, Mercer joined in on the bossa nova craze. In 1961, the guitarist Laurindo Almeida and his Bossa Nova All Stars, a group that featured Jimmy Rowles on the electric organ, recorded an album on Brazilian instruments that put a Latin spin on several jazz standards. Called *Viva Bossa Nova!*, the album included not only "Desafinado" but also "Moon River." Finding the interpretation interesting, Mercer partnered with Laurindo Almeida, contributing lyrics for a song called "Old Guitaron" released in 1964. Written in the bossa nova style, the lyric captures the rhythm: "Show me how, Guitaron above, / How the angels would sing if they made love; / Or if you can only impart, / The music she puts in my heart, / She'll hear me sigh and fly — / To me like a dove." That same year Johnny collaborated with Luiz Bonfá on "Love Like Yours," with its lines: "Here in the drowsy delight / The storm's a million miles away." Not published until 1969, the song appeared in the television movie *River of Mystery* that NBC aired on October 1, 1971. Several of Bonfá's earlier songs written for Dick Farney or with Tom Jobim became hits in Brazil. As the guitarist for the film *Orfeu Negro*, Bonfá had gained international recognition for his composition of the movie's title song, "Manhã de Carnaval." Despite Johnny's efforts to create transnational music with the well-known Brazilian musicians Almeida and Bonfá, the collaborations failed to generate any lasting outcome of significance. Meanwhile, a military coup in 1964 had ended Brazil's optimistic era of democratic governments and ushered in a new authoritarian regime whose spirit signaled an end to the bossa nova boom, although the wave had just begun to crest in the United States.[23]

Independently recognizing their mutual sensibility toward music, Johnny Mercer and Tom Jobim shared a desire to work together. Not only did their compositions build upon a foundation of jazz, but the lyrical themes in bossa nova had much in common with the subject matter found in the Great American Songbook, especially those hits written or favored by Mercer. In describing jazz-samba Jobim once said, "Bossa nova is serene, it has love and romance, but it is restless." The Brazilian poet Vinicius de Moraes contributed many of the lyrics to Jobim's songs, using a personal approach to describe the subtlety of love against the salty reality of life. The same could be said for Mercer's music. In 1964, Johnny Mercer telephoned Tom Jobim to say "he would love to compose something with him." Mercer identified Jobim as his favorite composer: "He's so tender and melodious and writes beautifully," Johnny explained to Willis Conover. The idea of collaborating with the southerner made the Brazilian "sigh." Tom had long admired Johnny's lyrics to such songs as "Midnight Sun," "Too Marvelous for Words," and "Blues in the Night." Indeed, Jobim disliked some of the English translations for his Portuguese phrases and those of Moraes and Mendonça, which he thought bordered on stereotypes like the banana boat and coffee songs of the past. Jobim relished the idea of the sensitive Mercer writing thoughtful English lyrics to fit his music. Unfortunately for the two men, at that time Mercer's membership in the American Society of Composers, Authors and Publishers (ASCAP) and Jobim's membership in the competing Broadcasting Music, Inc. (BMI) forbade the collaboration. Had the organizations not prohibited the partnership, the United States might have received some truly great transnational music that potentially could have revived the era of jazz-infused popular song despite the success of rock 'n' roll.[24]

The Canadian songwriter Gene Lees, who had crafted English lyrics for some bossa nova music, once talked with Mercer about Tom Jobim. In the early 1960s, Lees had moved to Rio de Janeiro to work with Jobim on English translations for bossa nova songs. In 1962, he turned Jobim's "Corcovado" into "Quiet Nights of Quiet Stars." Four years later, Henry Mancini introduced Lees to Mercer at a birthday party in Los Angeles for composer John Williams. After that February

1966 meeting the two lyricists became friends. On one occasion Johnny mentioned to Gene his desire to collaborate with Tom Jobim. In his biography of Mercer, *Portrait of Johnny*, Lees remembered a conversation he had with Johnny's friend William "Bill" Harbach, the television producer who recounted a story regarding Mercer and Jobim. After the 1967 release of the Reprise album *Francis Albert Sinatra and Antônio Carlos Jobim*, which included Lees's lyrics for "Quiet Nights of Quiet Stars" and other English versions of the Brazilian songs, Harbach had played the album for Johnny, who listened intently. Recalling the occasion, Bill said, "It's beautiful, you know, with the new beat, and the whole thing. And I remember him sitting on the edge of the couch with his eyes shut, looking straight down and his eyes are shut listening to this music." At the end of a "beautiful bossa nova song," Mercer cried out in despair over the state of American popular music, "God, why didn't the kids go this way?"[25]

Savannah always raised Johnny's spirits, so when abroad or at work in New York or Los Angeles, he found solace in thinking about its familiar shaded squares and old landmarks. If he could not travel there but felt too strong the pull of home, he sent a letter to the editor of the local newspaper describing his feelings. Or he mailed a note to Lillian Mercer, as demonstrated one Mother's Day in the mid-1960s: "Wish I could be there to take you out to 'Moon River' and get you loaded while all the other sons were taking their mothers' to Williams' or Johnny Harris'." After referencing the popular restaurants on the road to Tybee, Johnny reminisced about former favorites: "Wouldn't it be nice if we could resurrect Bannon's with its river view and marvelous crab stew!!!" He added, "It's sure been a long time since the days of 'oyster buy,' enty?" referring to the call black hucksters once made when selling seafood in the streets of Savannah. Then he confessed, "Mom, I want you to know I've had a marvelous life so far, and will continue to have, no matter what happens, because of the things you gave me and instilled in me — kindness, humility, loyalty, a grand sense of humor and a love for music, and all the pretty things — as well as the underdog. I tank'ee ma'ma! — and I love you — Bubba." Whenever he could get to Savannah, he made sure to spend time with his mother, as he did while celebrating the New Year in 1967, taking her to lunch at the Pirates House and pausing to look at his framed picture hanging in the restaurant's Hall of Fame. A month later, Johnny appeared on television with Dionne Warwick, Simon and Garfunkel, the Mamas and the Papas, the Byrds, and Smokey Robinson and the Miracles on the special *The Songmakers*, which ABC broadcast coast to coast in color.[26] Recognizing his celebrity, the local community recruited Johnny to serve as master of ceremonies for the 1967 Savannah Arts Festival. From April 10 to 14, Mercer assisted in a variety of ways, from conducting "talent tests" to discover the star potential of area aspirants to performing in a pops concert with the Savannah Symphony Orchestra. Most of the events occurred in Forsyth Park, where artists displayed their paintings. The Savannah Madrigal Singers prepared versions of Mercer standards to sing for the occasion, and Johnny joined New Orleans jazz trumpeter Al Hirt and his band at the festival's climactic event.[27]

After the arts festival, Johnny spent some time on the Georgia coast, visiting Ossabaw Island. Just across the Burnside River from his old haunts at Vernon View, Johnny sought renewal along the salt marsh, starting a journal there on April 26, 1967, that culminated in his unfinished autobiography. Looking out from the shoreline of the Atlantic Ocean, Mercer compared his life to the "changing beach," where "the patterns of nature are immediate and eternal." He contrasted the existentialism of Jean-Paul Sartre with Albert Camus's absurdity but called out for "a higher existence . . . beyond our comprehension." Johnny admitted he sought "a strata of existence unlimited by the weather of the surface experience: transcending the spring rain of birth and the winter freeze of death." Now approaching sixty, Mercer confessed, "I'm no longer content to splash along the water's edge and play among the dunes."[28]

While enjoying the unspoiled beauty of the barrier island and working on a musical, Mercer probably engaged informally the artists' colony created by the island's owners, Eleanor "Sandy" Torrey West and her husband, Clifford. They began the Ossabaw Project in 1961 as a retreat where creative minds could pursue work uninterrupted by the outside world. The Torrey family's former winter haven served as a virtually uninhabited open space in which artists could roam, while the family's Pittsburgh Plate Glass fortune provided the funding necessary to support the venture. The Wests used the grand Spanish-style main house to host such guests as composer Aaron Copland, sculptor Harry Bertoia, painter June Ball, author Annie Dillard, scientist Eugene Odum, geographer Chester de Pratter, and other artists and scholars who spent time on Ossabaw chasing their muse. Years before, the Wests had purchased Uncle Robbie and Aunt Katharine Mercer's house at Vernon View in order to use the pier as a boat launch to Ossabaw. Having known Sandy since the 1930s when he danced with her at a debutante cotillion in Savannah where he offered up the memorable compliment, "Your hairline has rhythm," Johnny seemed a perfect fit for the Ossabaw Project.[29]

In 1967, Mercer tried again to write a book musical for Broadway. Calling the effort *Mike*, Johnny turned Mickey Spillane's stories about the detective Mike Hammer into a series of songs for a musical comedy. The screenwriter Charles Tannen conceived the project, writing a script with Tay Garnett for which Mercer composed nineteen songs. The show opens with "Ballad of a Private Eye," which gives a history of detective fiction from Sherlock Holmes to James Bond to set the story. With "Any Way the Wind Blows," Johnny introduces Mike: "I get my eggs at Toot's / Or at Dinty Moore's or Stark's; / Off to P. J. Clarke's / Droppin' bright remarks." The setting is New York: "Then I walk west of Broadway / Through the chaparral and sage / Where Jack E. Leonard's holding up the Stage." According-ing to Mike, street smarts are "The Equivalent of a Haa-vud Education," for "when you can figure who digs who / And where and how, it's equal to / A brain as wise as any in the nation." Mercer develops the violence behind Mike's charac-ter with "The Bully Boys" and "He Never Even Knew What Hit Him." Mike's love interests are introduced as Velda and Trudi in "Kiss and Tell," although as a "Cat With Nine Lives" it is clear he's a lady's man. His enemies, Jay, Chink, and Bubbles and Boys, are identified in "You Can't Lose." Through the life of the detective, Mercer explores the subconscious with an eye toward Freudian analy-sis, as explained in "Gerfrunkt!" and "My Crazy Old Subconscious Won't Leave You Alone." Of all the songs only one found play, "I Wanna Be in Love Again," which Velda introduces in the show: "I wanna know the thrills again, / The fever and the chills again; / The quiver of the lightning fork, / And the million porcu-pine quills again. / I long to feel my temples pound / And pulses race again, / As helpless as a fox / Caught in a chase again." Written in 1964 and interpolated into *Mike*, "I Wanna Be in Love Again" enjoyed distribution through recordings by Marlene VerPlanck, Jackie Cain, and Roy Kral. Even though Mercer hired a combo and sang the lyrics himself on a demo recording to shop to potential financial backers, *Mike* never got produced.[30]

In the summer of 1967, Johnny returned to his house facing the Moon River on Burnside Island to spend a few days visiting with family and friends in Savan-nah. The vacation provided an opportunity to see his charitable donations at work. Johnny had given the Victor B. Jenkins Jr. Memorial Boys' Club fifteen thousand dollars to pay off the debt on a gymnasium. "Just say that I wanted to commemorate the memory of my father," he explained when the Exchange Club placed a tablet on the building. Brother Walter, who had served as president of the civic organization, and Nick Mamalakis, who sat on the board, had encour-aged the donation. The gift strengthened Johnny's ties to his hometown as a grounded southerner.[31]

Similarly, a return to the Savannah Arts Festival in the spring of 1969 enabled Johnny to visit with family and friends, something he relished all the more as death began to claim those close to him, such as his eldest brother, George, who had died the previous September. Ginger accompanied Johnny, and the two spent much of their time with Walter and Cornelia McIntire Rivers, who came down from Birmingham, Alabama, where cousin Walter ran the branch office of the McIntire's old Southern States Container Company, now a subsidiary of Reynolds Metals, and Cornelia taught art classes. She also volunteered as chair of Birmingham's Festival of Arts and exhibited a painting in the Savannah show. The previous few years had been rough on the old friends. Back in 1964, Ginger had nearly died from hepatitis following a trip to Asia and later underwent an operation, while in 1968 Cornelia suffered from throat cancer, Walter had his prostate removed, and Johnny broke his foot. Mercer corresponded with the Riverses, "I know it's depressing, but everyone is getting so old!" After his return to California, Johnny wrote Cornelia to say what fun he had being "around the McIntires" at the festival and then complimented her painting. He went on to say, "It is not given to all of us to pick and choose what we can do, but God kind of lays a gift on us (some of us anyway) that is perhaps better than we deserve. At least, I feel that about what has been given me—and there isn't a day that goes by that I don't say, either silently or out loud, 'Thank you Daddy.'" Johnny understood that Cornelia had been diagnosed with terminal cancer and would undergo treatment in Birmingham. She died weeks later, while Walter lived for another decade, succumbing to cancer in 1982.[32]

With people he met and liked, Mercer's generosity knew no bounds, as demonstrated in his relationship with performer Emma Kelly, suggesting the truth behind Johnny's lyric "howdy stranger, so long friend" from the Mercer-Arlen song, "Any Place I Hang My Hat Is Home." A few months before the 1969 arts festival, Johnny's nephew Hugh Mercer, while attending a party, listened intently to a woman pianist. Trained as an architect, the younger Hugh, like his father and namesake, loved jazz, the Great American Songbook, and New York City, often visiting with his informed uncle and debating the merits of various singers such as Ella Fitzgerald, Eydie Gorme, and Mabel Mercer. That evening Hugh had asked pianist Emma Kelly to play "Moon River," following up with an all-Mercer request list that she fulfilled without difficulty. Impressed by the extent of her repertoire, Hugh concluded she "knew every song he ever wrote," and called his uncle in Bel Air so that Johnny might speak with her. Curiosity compelled Emma off the piano bench and over to the telephone just to hear Mercer's voice.

Instead, Hugh handed her the receiver and suddenly she stood talking to the famous songwriter. Johnny asked Emma to sing the first eight bars of "If You Were Mine"—the song he wrote with Matty Malneck in 1935 that Billie Holiday had recorded early in her career—which Kelly did easily. A conversation followed that ended with Mercer extracting a promise from Kelly to meet him during his next visit to Georgia, and that occurred during the arts festival.[33]

Well known across South Georgia for her piano playing, a shy Emma Kelly never sang the words of the many songs she knew until mentoring by Johnny Mercer provided the self-assurance she lacked. Arriving in Savannah that spring of 1969, Mercer telephoned Kelly, but at first she did not know who the John Mercer on the phone might be until he insisted that she join him for dinner, and then she suddenly realized "Johnny" had come to town. She begged off because of her job at the lounge, but Mercer had already called her boss at the Quality Inn to secure her night off. With no other excuse, Emma consented, and Johnny picked her up and drove her to the Moon River house, where his mother had prepared supper. A friendship developed between Emma and the Mercers after that first meeting. The fifty-one-year-old native of Statesboro, Georgia, who as a wife and mother of ten children started performing professionally to supplement the family income, had long played at weddings and civic clubs the popular songs of the day. As he had done with Margaret Whiting, Jo Stafford, and Nat "King" Cole decades before, Johnny began to coach Emma, teaching her phrasing and how to deliver the nuances in a line. He showed her how to mask difficulties hitting notes by changing keys rather than octaves and singing softly. Despite her husband's admonition that she should stick to piano playing as she had done since the age of four, Emma now began to sing. Mercer encouraged her to spend more time on her career, to which Kelly responded, "But John, I have a *family*." In response to his concern over her late-night driving home to Statesboro, she occasionally stayed with Lillian and Juliana in Savannah. By 1970, Johnny decided Kelly had trained enough, so unbeknownst to her he arranged for a sound system to be installed in the lounge at the Quality Inn. When Kelly arrived for work, next to the piano she found a microphone set up for her to sing into, with Johnny waiting to hear the first set. Recognizing her nervousness, he left shortly after she began but aware of their success, as Emma embarked on a new career as Savannah's most popular lounge singer.[34]

On return visits Mercer often stopped at the Quality Inn to hear Kelly perform. Since she had memorized "fake" songbooks and did not play with sheet music but nonetheless had a vast repertoire, Johnny wanted to catalogue the titles of all the songs she knew. Trying to "stump her," he would call out song titles, and if she could perform the song all the way through, he wrote the title in a notebook. Soon he dubbed Emma Kelly the Lady of 6,000 Songs. The counting did not end there, however, for the two had decided to register Emma with the *Guinness Book of World Records* as the person who knew more songs than anyone else on earth. Over the next three years, when in Savannah Johnny made a point of spending time with Emma on this project.[35]

Shifting his gaze back toward Europe, Mercer renewed his collaboration with the Frenchman Michel Legrand. The two had met earlier in the decade when Johnny created English lyrics for the French song "Once upon a Summertime." Since then Legrand had enjoyed success writing film scores for the studios. The jazz arranger-composer had gained recognition with his music for movies beginning with Agnes Varda's 1961 New Wave classic *Cleo from 5 to 7*, in which Legrand makes a cameo appearance, and the films directed by Jacques Demy that starred Catherine Deneuve, such as 20th Century Fox's *Umbrellas of Cherbourg* in 1964 and *The Young Girls of Rochefort* in 1967 for Warner Bros. He secured his reputation with lyricists Alan and Marilyn Bergman on the Oscar-winning "The Windmills of Your Mind" in 1969 and on "The Summer of '42" in 1971. While working with Mancini on the music for *Darling Lili*, Mercer again collaborated with Legrand, getting the young songwriter to assist the two veterans in arranging the music and drafting supplemental French lyrics for the Mancini-Mercer song "Les Petits Oiseaux," or "The Little Birds."[36]

In the fall of 1969, the Mercers boarded the *Queen Elizabeth 2* for the Atlantic crossing on the luxury ocean liner because of Johnny's refusal to fly. They enjoyed first-class accommodations with dining at the captain's table. One night during the voyage Mercer entertained his fellow travelers aboard the ship. Upon arrival in Paris, Johnny joined Ginger on tours of the city, sending California friend Polly Ober a postcard that November showing Georges Recipon's sculpture of a nymph on the Alexandre III bridge over the Seine River with the remark, "This is the only cat who has seen more of Paris than we have." The Mercers visited museums and galleries. As an admirer of art, having long studied it through magazines, Ginger persuaded Johnny — who likewise appreciated fine art and dabbled in watercolors — to buy a painting by the French impressionist Edgar Degas.[37]

While in Paris, Mercer and Legrand began a collaboration on a musical they hoped to stage on Broadway or perhaps turn into a Hollywood musical similar to *Seven Brides for Seven Brothers*. They attempted to adapt the ever-popular 1897 French drama by Edmond Rostand, *Cyrano de Bergerac*, for the musical stage.

The romantic story follows the plight of the long-nosed Cyrano, who writes love letters to Roxane but because of his shyness has the handsome Christian de Neuvillette stand beneath her balcony to deliver his poetic confessions, with the natural consequence that Roxane believes the words are Christian's and falls for him instead of for Cyrano. Mercer and Legrand completed the score for their show *Cyrano*, having written what Mercer called eleven "wonderful songs." He explained to Willis Conover his hopes for the musical: "Well, it's very ambitious. I kind of have my fingers crossed and hope that it'll see the light of day." Aware of the hazards of operetta in the modern musical theater, Mercer explained, "The reason I say I have my fingers crossed is that I feel that as great as it is with all the dueling and the old, the romantic flavor of dialogue and the way the play is constructed, it may be hard to 'get over' today as a very romantic musical. But if we get a great performance and a great singing performance from some actor and a good score I think we have a chance." Despite finding interest among backers, Mercer never saw the musical produced.[38]

The Mercers spent much of the late 1960s and early 1970s abroad. As the writer Hugh Fordin recognized about Johnny, "He loved to travel. Which is so unusual too, about a songwriter. Songwriters usually are deep anchored." Of course Johnny had always kept Savannah as his home port, but he explained in a letter, "I have been in Europe a lot lately, and enjoy it." The couple traveled around Great Britain, including a visit to Ireland, where the glib "newsie bluesies" author kissed the Blarney Stone. During these trips he always included at least a brief visit to his ancestral homeland of Scotland. In November 1969, he met with *Melody Maker* reporter John Gibson in the quiet corner of an Edinburgh hotel bar and expressed his pleasure at pursuing "an honest living" that allowed "Paris for a month to work on a musical." The Mercers returned to France several times, occasionally staying at La Residence Du Bois at 16 Rue Chalgrin. Writing to Polly, Johnny described the charming little inn, with its tranquil garden and rude concierge, as being "surrounded on all sides by hookers!" He observed, "to wake in the morning to the street cries of 'voulez vous poussez' (do you wish to push, I think?) and 'amour, monsieur?' is a little native touch that I find amusing." He then reflected that it was too bad that he had not arrived years before, "when I was foolhardy enough to do something about it." In August 1970, the Mercers sent Polly a photograph of a billboard showing a beautiful model in a brassiere with a grinning Johnny reaching out to cup her larger-than-life breast. That year they traveled down to Nice and stayed beside the Mediterranean in Antibes. In 1971, Johnny took Ginger to Canada rather than back to Europe.[39]

Interspersed with the international travel came trips to Savannah. Johnny regularly hopped the East Coast Seaboard Line's *Silver Meteor* down to Georgia, as in February 1972, when he performed at the opening of the new Savannah Civic Center. Also he stopped by the Bethesda Home for Boys to dedicate the board room in memory of his father. Back in Europe in 1972, the Mercers rode the trains from the Netherlands into France and Italy. Later that year, Johnny and Ginger went to Spain, where they spent most of their time that summer in Barcelona, not returning to America until September. During the winter months of 1973–74, Mercer came in contact with his Eastern European heritage by visiting the homeland of his immigrant grandfather. Johnny took Ginger; his sister, Julie; and her friend, Ida Thomas, with whom he had written "My Jekyll Island" in 1972, on a cruise of the Mediterranean. They traveled into the Adriatic and up the nearby Yugoslavian coast of Croatia to the Dalmatian island of La Gosta, the home of his Ciucevich forebears. In particular he wanted to see the birthplace of the patriarch whose name he shared, his grandfather, Captain John. For the native Savannahian grounded in the institutions of the port city on the Georgia coast, finding his maternal ancestry linked him as a citizen of the world to ancient civilizations.[40]

Hip to the new look, the global southerner grew a beard during his European travels in 1973. Responding to Johnny's hirsute appearance, Lillian Mercer said he "looked like hell." Johnny had always been fashionable. In place of the Brooks Brothers button downs with sporty rep ties, he boasted camel-colored turtlenecks and slacks. A Greek fisherman's hat became a favorite accessory. Since needing eyeglasses in the 1950s, Johnny began to sport a variety of frames that could make him appear either old-fashioned, learned, or stylishly modern.[41]

Ever responsive to international songs that struck his fancy, Mercer looked for potential collaborators on transnational music. While in Rome in 1972, he arranged for an introduction to the Italian composer Salve D'Esposito, whose "Anema e core" had gained global attention. The two men met and shared music. Johnny left with copies of sheet music of Italian songs that he hoped to craft with English lyrics. Already these songs had words by a variety of Italian lyricists. In his notes Mercer described as "pretty" the Salve D'Esposito song "Tutta N'Vita," with Italian lyrics by Armando Ciervo and Johnny's own attempts: "Am I surprised? Seeing your eyes . . ." With D'Esposito's "N'ora D'Ammore," which had a lyric by Enzo Bonagura, Mercer wrote "All men have a moment, a wonderful moment." Drafts of ideas accompanied other D'Esposito songs, such as one Johnny noted he "liked," "Nun me sceta," with its Italian lyric by A. Malmassari. Two lyrics by Carlo da Vinci accompanied tunes by D'Esposito, "Una casa in riva al mare" and "Fuoco a mare." Perhaps the latter song attracted the best lyric of this set: "When you kiss me / Comets in the night sky / Music in the trade winds / Fire in the sea." Similarly, in Milan, Johnny called on songwriter Giuseppe Gramitto Ricci, gaining permission to adapt his Italian lyrics of "Silezionso Slow" into English, with Mercer's Commander Publications controlling the American copyright. Ricci responded, "I too I hope that, thanks to your interest, this composition can become a hit in America." While the efforts did not lead to a published song — much less a successful recording — the attempts demonstrated Mercer's desire to write transnational music with international composers.[42]

Hungry for new songs with global appeal, Mercer even considered a partnership with Paul McCartney. In 1966, it appeared that the Beatles might break up for good. McCartney recalled, "Many years ago, through a friend, I had heard that Johnny was interested in writing the lyrics to a tune of mine called 'Love in the Open Air,' that was featured in a British film called *The Family Way*." Indeed, Mercer had long been in the practice of notifying a composer of his interest in writing lyrics for an instrumental he had heard. McCartney continued, "I said that that would be a nice idea but, to this day, I kick myself for not having followed it up more energetically because nothing ever came of the idea and suddenly it was too late." By 1967, the Beatles had regrouped and embarked on a new trajectory that became a statement of the counterculture, *Sgt. Pepper's Lonely Hearts Club Band*. Johnny told Willis Conover that he liked some of the Beatles' music: "'Here, There and Everywhere' is a wonderful song. 'Yesterday' is a lovely song. 'Rocky Raccoon' is a great song. Funny, you know, to me." To a Savannah reporter he explained: "The Beatles are all right. They have a cute sense of humor, but I don't particularly like their behavior. However I think the Rolling Stones' behavior is much worse." Years later, daughter Mandy observed that the pairing of Mercer with McCartney would have been incompatible because of the celebratory references to "dope" in Beatles' tunes, a form of lawbreaking that Johnny could not abide.[43]

Margaret Whiting remembers the story from another perspective. She claims that music publisher Marshall Robbins had overheard McCartney say that he would like to collaborate with Johnny Mercer. Sensing the potential of the partnership, Robbins convinced Margaret to make a pitch to Johnny. On a rainy day in Bel Air, Whiting visited with Mercer and later recalled his response to her query of what he thought of McCartney and the Beatles: "Well, you know, I'm tough on new writers. I don't think they dig deep enough. They don't take the time to get it right. They don't put it away and come back to it. They just pump it out and let it go." Then Mercer stopped and noted, "But the Beatles, they're an enigma. Just when I think I've got them down, they turn around and surprise me." Johnny added, "And Paul McCartney. He's got a fresh point of view. It must be that Liverpool thing." When Mercer asked Whiting what she thought about McCartney, she responded: "I think he's sensational. I think he's a genius. He's not brash. He writes the way you do. I think you'd be great together." To this, Mercer replied: "Well, Kid, I agree with you. If it's true that Paul really wants to work with me, I'm genuinely flattered. I'd love to lay a few lyrics on him. But you caught me at a bad time. Ginger hasn't been feeling well." With that, he cut off the discussion, leaving Whiting to speculate over what might have been.[44]

Younger colleagues John Williams and Blossom Dearie provided outlets for Mercer's creativity. A successful arranger, Williams had yet to break out with his own original compositions such as his Oscar-winning score for *Jaws* in 1975, which set him on course to write the music for other Academy Award–winning blockbusters: *Star Wars, E. T. The Extra-Terrestrial, Schindler's List, Saving Private Ryan*, and the *Indiana Jones* and *Harry Potter* series. With Williams, Johnny wrote the theme song to *The Long Goodbye*, a film noir set in 1970s Hollywood and based on a Raymond Chandler novel, with Elliott Gould playing Philip Marlowe. The movie begins and ends to the strains of the original 1937 recording of "Hooray for Hollywood." Then with background action taking place, the opening credits appear with the title song, "The Long Goodbye," performed in a most novel way by different artists, depending on the character and the setting. The Dave Grusin Trio starts with a vocal provided by jazz trumpeter Jack Sheldon that changes with the scene to rhythm and blues singer Clydie King. When the setting shifts to a grocery store, the sound comes out as a Muzak-like version by Morgan Ames' Aluminum Band and later can be heard played by the Tepoztlan Municipal Band. The lyric speaks of missed opportunities: "There's a long goodbye, / And it happens ev'ry day / When some passer-by / Invites your eye / To come his way. / Even as he smiles a quick hello, / You've let him go, / You've let the moment fly; / Too late you turn your head, / You know you've said / The long goodbye." Sheldon later gained popularity as the voice on several songs written for the children's educational series *Schoolhouse Rock!*, which appeared on ABC television beginning in 1973. Blossom Dearie also sang on the Saturday morning cartoon series because her old partner of the Blue Stars of Paris, Bob Dorough, wrote the songs for *Schoolhouse Rock!*[45]

With Johnny Mercer, Blossom Dearie collaborated on "I'm Shadowing You." She wrote the music for his lyric: "Everywhere you go / I think you ought to know / I'm shadowing you." With tricky rhymes the singer stalks her lover: "In Venice / I'll be a menace / In your Italian motel. / In Paris, / I shall embarrass / You on the rue de Chappelle." Also Johnny wrote both words and music for a song that Blossom recorded on her 1976 Daffodil album of the same name, "My New Celebrity Is You." The lyrics sketch out an impressive life with references that pay tribute to many important people in a fashion not unlike Johnny's Christmas cards: "I've sung with Ethel Merman, / Swung with Woody Herman, / Played a gig in Germany with Ogerman too. / I nodded at a sermon / Billy Graham barely got through. / But anyone can see / My new celebrity is you."[46]

Having "cast the bread upon the waters," Mercer watched as various opportunities returned to him. The luck he had adapting French songs into English convinced him to try the reverse, writing an English lyric to something he called "Passe" with the desire to see it translated into proper French as a transnational song. The lyric spoke of the ephemeral nature of life and love: "Our little song / That everybody sang all summer long / Passe." He debated publishing it under the name "Jean Mercier," but the French agent assigned to plugging the song recommended he keep his own "Johnny Mercer" while noting, "there is such a snobbism for anglo-saxon music here." Similarly, Mercer, having discussed collaboration with Antônio Carlos Jobim a decade before, received a telegram from Rio de Janeiro on April 5, 1972, that read "DEAR JOHNNY ALL MY SONGS ARE AVAILABLE FOR YOU LETTER FOLLOWS LOVE JOBIM." Yet no follow-up letter appears to exist and apparently nothing came of the proposed partnership.[47]

Growing nostalgic, Johnny wrote Dave Dexter of Capitol Records and asked about acquiring old albums and masters of old recordings. A delighted Dexter complimented Mercer: "Nice to know that your creative juices are still flowing." Then Dave admitted, "Along with several thousand other excellent packages, yours has long been deleted, I'm embarrassed to report." He went on to explain, "Our active catalog is comprised almost exclusively these days of rock combos and Ken Nelson's country artists." Then in frustration Dave added, "I'd obtain a quantity of them for you, Johnny, if any were available even in warehouses or branches, but in recent years deleted product — and I've never liked the term — has been destroyed. There just aren't any." Decrying the state of popular music, Dexter confessed, "I just can't listen to the radio any longer. Pop music is at its lowest level of my lifetime." Then he reminisced: "Capitol was never the same after you left. With Wallichs gone almost two years, it has changed even more. I'm elated if I recognize someone in the elevators once a week." Mercer typed on the bottom, "Boy, our efforts are really written in water — or wind — aren't they."[48]

In reviewing his accomplishments, Mercer fretted about the absence of a Broadway blockbuster. Tin Pan Alley tradition held to the belief that only the songwriter who landed the sold-out show had truly achieved great success. For the most part misfortune had plagued Mercer's previous Broadway attempts, and psychologically he remained trapped in the footlights. In 1972, the writer Hugh Fordin interviewed Johnny for a project on Broadway for producer Arthur Freed and detected Mercer feared being forgotten lest he write that immortal musical comedy. Fordin described a "failure sense I sensed about him. God, failure! I mean I can tell you about failure from some of the other writers that I've talked to. And understandably failure. But Johnny was certainly not a failure in anything." Indeed, his string of *Your Hit Parade* songs, his success as an entertainer, his management of Capitol Records, even his respectable contributions to Broadway all pointed to success.[49]

As if to verify his stellar reputation as a songwriter, Mercer received an invitation from New York University's Town Hall at 123 West Forty-third Street to appear as the opening act of its series of programs called *5:45 Interludes*. *The New York Times* music critic John S. Wilson called the January 10, 1973, concert "a casual low-keyed performance" and described the "husky-voiced, rhythmic way of punching at a tune and lifting climatic phrases with tantalizing twangy yells" that characterized Johnny's singing style late in life. Dressed in plaid pants, a navy sweater with striped shirt, and his Greek fisherman's hat, Mercer performed many of his own favorites rather than his *Hit Parade* catalog. He picked "Just a Little Old Tune," which made light of the difficulties of songwriting, and "Pineapple Pete," which recalled the silly ditties of an earlier era. Accompanied by Jimmy Rowles on the piano, the two performed their recent collaboration, "Frasier (The Sensuous Lion)," a novelty number published in 1973 that became a short-lived wonder. The lyric told the real-life story of King Frasier, an elderly circus lion retired to a California zoo who mates with several lionesses to the delight of his new keepers and Johnny, who related to the aged lover. To keep the attendees from leaving disappointed at not hearing their favorite Mercer song he sang a medley that featured his biggest hits reduced to eight-bars and a title. In reviewing the performance, Wilson appreciated the "unpublished, unrecorded, 'undiscovered'" music made obsolete by rock 'n' roll, but observed, "Johnny Mercer has a trunk filled with songs that nobody wants to hear." Wilson noted an exception in "Fleur de Lys," which Johnny had written with Hoagy Carmichael, for he characterized this "excellent ballad" that Tony Bennett later recorded as a "lovely, diaphanous piece." The composer's son, Randy Bob Carmichael, who attended the sold-out performance, reported back to his father that Johnny "mentioned you several times during the program." Having grown up visiting the Mercers, especially at the holidays when the families would gather to sing Christmas carols, Randy Bob watched with delight as Ginger entered the theater and sat in front of him. They renewed their friendship as she invited him backstage to visit with Johnny. Yet with little interest among record producers for this kind of popular song and with fewer opportunities to write for Hollywood, Mercer concentrated his efforts on the musical stage, supported by Ginger, who convinced Johnny he could shake that bad luck and still write a great show.[50]

Considering various options, Mercer shopped around for the appropriate project. For several years he had discussed ideas with friends, including Lawrence Kasha, of the Wilding communications agency, with whom he corresponded in 1965. Johnny shared with him the script *Three Arabian Nights*, which he had written years before with Franz Steininger. Kasha talked about several other possibilities, including one they referred to as "the Priestley play." Coming off his 1962 hit, *How to Succeed in Business without Really Trying*, Frank Loesser pitched ideas to Johnny for a collaboration, but Mercer declined. Likewise, the composer Vernon Duke, who had gotten his break on Broadway in the 1930 *Garrick Gaieties,* in which Mercer's first song appeared, had asked Johnny in 1966 to join him in transforming Esther Forbes's novel *Love and Obey* into a musical. Turning down the invitation, the lyricist noted, "If (George) Abbott, or somebody that good, undertook the adaptation, I'd think again, but I don't want to start on a whole score unless I think we have a fair shake. Such as *Mame* or *Fair Lady* where you have a strong book to give your score a chance!" Although Duke persisted, Johnny never changed his mind, finally writing Duke in 1968, "I still feel the book, while it has a certain old-fashioned charm, is not for me." Instead, Johnny read Booth Tarkington stories and considered another novel by Edna Ferber. In 1971 Mercer formed Vulnerable Productions with stage-and film writer and producer Henry Ephron to back Broadway shows. With Robert Emmett Dolan, Mercer pursued a revival of *Texas, Li'l Darlin'* in 1972 that proposed swapping the Henry Luce character for one based on Hugh Hefner and starring Bing

Crosby, but on the advice of John Whedon, who had written the original book for the musical comedy, they dropped the idea as too dated. With scriptwriter Don Devendorf, Johnny worked on lyrics and talked with Henry Mancini about scoring a musical comedy called *The Pig War*. The plot follows the 1859 conflict over the San Juan Islands in the Pacific Northwest that almost resulted in war between the United States and Great Britain. He continued to promote the show *Cyrano*, arranging for its score to be played before potential producers by the composer Michel Legrand during one of his visits to California.[51]

By November 1970, the composer and maestro André Previn solicited a possible collaboration with Mercer. A native of Germany, Previn had immigrated to America in 1939 and later moved to Hollywood, where as a jazz pianist he began arranging for MGM. Capitol's Dave Dexter had met the teenage André as he wrote out jazz arrangements, and Mercer probably met him at that time too. Between 1958 and 1964, Previn had won Oscars for four movie scores, including *Gigi* and *Irma la Douce*. With his second wife, the lyricist Dory Langdon, he wrote popular songs such as "Yes," recorded by Judy Garland, and "River Shallow," recorded by Nancy Wilson. Having spent four years constructing a score called *Coco* with lyricist Alan Jay Lerner, Previn wanted to work with someone like Johnny Mercer, a famous lyricist who could also accommodate his work schedule in England, where he had moved in 1968 to conduct the London Symphony Orchestra. Accepting the invitation, Johnny responded by referencing Langdon and Previn's song from the movie *Daisy Clover*, "You're Gonna Hear from Me," and explaining to the composer, "That first bar and the changes you use there made me want to write with you."[52]

Producers had approached Previn to score a film musical based on Louisa May Alcott's 1868 novel *Little Women* with the idea that his now third wife, Mia Farrow, could play the heroine, Jo March. Liking the proposal, Previn asked Mercer if he would write the lyrics. In making his pitch, the composer suggested that a counter to the sexual liberation being celebrated on stage and in film in such reigning hits as *Oh! Calcutta!* and *Myra Breckenridge* might make a smash, and he pointed to a *Time* magazine cover story on Ali MacGraw that featured "the return of romanticism in the movies." The idea proved attractive enough for Johnny to think of romantic themes for something he called "The Age of Innocence." Lyrics survive for the title song, and "Taste," with its lines: "Breeding is intuitively knowing / What a lady and a gentleman / Would never, ever do!" Mercer planned to use the slang of the day and incorporate Jo's sister Amy's stuttering into the lyrics using long words. Then the two would-be collaborators thought better of the subject and began considering alternatives over the winter and spring of 1971.[53]

Although the *Little Women* project failed to materialize, Mercer did collaborate with Previn on the nostalgic, and in many ways innocent and romantic, *The Good Companions*. Based on the novel of the same name by J. B. Priestly, the storyline follows a troupe of thespians called a "concert party" that performs a song and dance revue similar to a traveling musical as it tours England during the 1920s. Critics compared Priestly to Charles Dickens because of his successful characterization of place and class, while the public made him the most popular fiction writer in Great Britain between the wars. Traveling with the Theatre Guild the winter of the book's American release in 1929, Johnny took to the romantic view of life on the stage. He gave a copy to then-girlfriend Ginger, and they read it aloud to each other. It had remained one of Mercer's favorites, a touchstone of his career in entertainment with Ginger, for he referenced the title in the opening lines of the verse to his anniversary song for her, "Here's to My Lady." Also a fan of the novel, Previn endorsed the suggestion but warned Mercer that "it's a very English idea," to which Johnny responded by requesting "a gazetteer of all of the sensational names of small towns and villages" that dotted the countryside. The songwriter savored the notion of writing witty lyrics in the spirit of W. S. Gilbert.[54]

During 1972, Mercer and Previn carried on a transatlantic correspondence while working on *The Good Companions*. In agreement that successful collaboration rested on "absolute honesty, freedom (and tact)," the two artists reread the novel, sketched out ideas for songs, and developed a series of titles from which to work. They hired a young English writer, Ronald "Ronnie" Harwood, to turn the novel into a script, perhaps thinking his inexperience crafting for the stage would allow them more control. With ideas in hand, they met in a studio at the music publisher Chappell in London, where Previn recorded a ballad and several other melodies, and Mercer shared some sample lyrics derived from the characters. After drafting some songs from this initial collaboration, the two separated. In April 1972, Mercer mailed Previn titles for sixteen songs with accompanying lyrics in a separate envelope, explaining he also had dummy tunes for each one that clarified mood. Having internalized so much of the novel, Johnny apologized for getting "carried away like this" but explained, "The lyrics just kept coming and coming and I figured better to get them down than have them going to waste on the night air." Recognizing that the "titles, ideas and phrases in this letter have all come to me with some sort of tune attached," Mercer quickly added:

"I seldom pay attention to these little melodies, as my composer-collaborator is far more gifted than I in harmony, construction and all the techniques that make him what he is. *But* — if I feel deeply that the mood is wrong, or the concept is a mistaken one, I feel obliged to show you what prompted my original lyrical idea." He added, "I am not a 'glory grabber' and never say 'I wrote that melody' but, the song is the thing, and, if I have a worthwhile idea, please use it, as I intend to do, should you present me with a felicitous phrase — or even a complete canto!" In asking to work with Mercer, Previn had made clear: "I am not at all sensitive about my tunes; obviously I like some of them, but nevertheless, any time you dislike a phrase, a note, an ending or a whole tune, just tell me and I will instantly try to write you another one." Over the summer of 1972, Previn and Mercer met during the conductor's visit to the United States. That August, Johnny wrote an "unabashed fan letter" to "Mr. Priestley," expressing his appreciation for the opportunity to turn *The Good Companions* into a musical comedy, explaining: "I think it could be another *Fair Lady* or *Show Boat* and would proceed as though I were holding, not a mere diamond, but a small, precious baby in my hands."[55]

The collaborators met in England from the spring into the late summer of 1973. Mercer had invited Previn to join him in Palm Springs, where "we can play loud enough to plague Loewe and hopefully, Lerner, who live within earshot!" but instead they went to London, where Johnny and Ginger rented a flat at 46 Upper Grosvenor Street near the square for the year so they could stay in the city when not driving down to Previn's eighteenth-century country house, The Haven, Dawes Green, in Surrey. Referring to the visits with the Previns, Ginger suggested Johnny's interaction with Mia and their twin boys revealed that, "Despite his bon vivant tastes, Mercer always was a dedicated family man." Yet the limited amount of time actually spent working with Previn on the musical proved frustrating to Mercer, who often had to wait for the maestro to return from traveling. When Previn was not conducting, the two gathered in Previn's rural studio. Rather than peck out the tunes on the piano, Previn composed in his head and wrote the notes on staff paper, then passed it to Johnny, who read the music and set it with words. Years later, André recalled, "It must have been kind of funny, the two of us sitting on opposite sides of the room in dead silence and after a few hours we had a song." Yet it took the partners months to complete a draft of the score.[56]

When the curtain went up in Manchester on the tryouts for *The Good Companions* in the summer of 1974, it revealed the Dinky Doos, a group of theatrical performers who are stranded in the midlands after their manager runs off with the troupe's funds and pianist. To escape their dull lives, three strangers fall in with the actors. First is a Yorkshire carpenter named Jess Oakroyd, played by John Mills, who is popular with everyone except his wife, so he leaves home following the defeat of his favorite football team. Jess volunteers to build the sets and sings and tap-dances to "Ta, Luv." Next Miss Trant, a young spinster who had missed her chance at love played by Judi Dench, decides to invest her newly acquired inheritance in the troupe. She sings the most poignant numbers in the show, from "The Dance of Life" to "It's Always Darkest Just Before the Dawn," which displays the ubiquitous Mercer optimism: "So, when you've sunk so low / That even down resembles up, / The biscuit-tin itself is overdrawn, / Remember the prediction / Of the tea leaves in your cup: / It's always darkest just before the dawn." A harried schoolteacher who harbors the desire to write but gives piano lessons instead, Inigo Jollifant, played by Christopher Gable, offers fresh material to the company. Together the three newcomers perform the "Footloose Sequence" as they leave their past lives behind. Then joining with the actors led by Dinky Doo manager Mitcham, played by Malcolm Rennie, they become the Good Companions, singing "(May I Have the) Pleasure of Your Company." Act 2 opens with Mitcham and Inigo singing the duet "The Good Companions" as the reorganized "concert party" goes on tour. With "And Points Beyond," Mercer demonstrates his love of place names, having the cast touring England by singing: "Manchester 'n' Chinchester –n' Colchester –n' Winchester, Dorchester 'n' Rochester 'n' Leeds!" Priestley's sensitivity to locale and regional dialect had attracted Mercer to the novel, characteristics the songwriter tried to replicate in his lyrics. With the duet "Susie for Everybody," Inigo reveals his love for the cast's soubrette, Susie Dean, played by Marti Webb. Once the show reaches Sandybay Pavilion, Susie gets her big break. Then Inigo successfully publishes his first book, Jess departs for a new life in Canada, and Miss Trant is reunited with her long-lost Scottish lover as the Good Companions disband. Having gloried in the quaintness of rural England, the show ends happily. All the songs develop character and keep the action moving, while the plot relies on theater clichés such as "the show must go on," "a star is born," and "every big laugh hides a little tear." Unlike the interwar-era novel, which painted Great Britain in the grim gray of a Dickens landscape, the musical comes off saccharinely sweet and sunny.[57]

When *The Good Companions* reached Her Majesty's Theater in London's West End, members of the audience cried as the curtain fell on opening night, July 11, 1974. About the tears, the octogenarian Priestly maintained, "It's not for the characters. It is for an England they think they have lost." The first critics emphasized the "charm, warmth, and appealingly sentimental schmaltz" of the show. The *London Times* offered the highest praise: "Mercer can hardly help writing singable words (he even contrives — as no native writer has done — to fashion a lyric from English place-names) and André Previn's music, not quite in the first class, bubbles and surges beneath them." Another critic said, "Johnny Mercer's lyrics have, as you would expect, zip and dexterity. He manages English English at all levels well, and the rhymes chime away like bells."[58]

Cast members suggested they "had a happy time" both on and off stage during the run of the show as it nightly "filled the cavernous auditorium of Her Majesty's Theatre well into 1975." Two of England's greatest character actors of stage and screen, John Mills and Judi Dench, have since won Oscars for other performances. Mills eagerly took on the role of Jess because it offered him an opportunity to don tap shoes for the first time in forty years since his early days in productions by his friend Noel Coward. Mills recalled, "After the vocal of 'Ta Luv' I went into four choruses of a complicated tap routine (it nearly killed me during rehearsals, but it was worth it). On the first night it stopped the show. The fact that most of the audience probably had no idea that I had spent eight years in musicals must have had something to do with the really wonderful reception I was given." At first Mills and Dench found the director, Braham Murray, to be "a very intelligent, brilliant young man," but once rehearsals "started we looked at each other, and nothing seemed to be happening in the way that we thought it might happen. He was wonderful in talking about *Good Companions*, but that's about where it finished," Mills said. So the two "were forced largely to direct themselves, and did this so successfully that they stole most of the notices." In *Punch*, critic Jeremy Kingston recognized the character touch Dench employed as Miss Trant of "blurting out an inmost wish then covering her face with an outspread hand. But the strong foundation of her comic technique is her power to suggest, by voice, expression, gesture, that her hold on happiness is tenuous, that every happy moment, merry incident or kind word is the rarest treasure. Her quality is such that she can make us suspect our hold on happiness is no less fragile." Dench's biographer, John Miller, recognized that "*Good Companions* marked a milestone in Judi's career that has only become apparent in retrospect — this show was the last one for which she had to audition. Ever since, she has been offered her parts unconditionally." Speaking for the actors, Mills said *The Good Companions* "was one of the happiest companies I have ever worked with, and we were all sad when after nine months the show closed."[59]

Not everyone liked *The Good Companions*, for some papers published caustic reviews. These critics commented that the score approached the expansive sounds of the modern musicals, only to draw back to the 1920s-era comedy songs for the set pieces that never fully integrated with the plot. In short, from its design to its execution the musical came off as old-fashioned. The Fleet Street headlines assailed *The Good Companions* as "A Diet of Yorkshire Pudding" and "Corn on the Sob!" Many of these critics favored the "rock opera" sound of Andrew Lloyd Webber's *Jesus Christ Superstar*, which after its 1971 Broadway success in New York had opened in London's West End in 1972, beginning an eight-year run that served as a harbinger of musical theatre. Johnny sent his sister, Juliana, the clippings with the note, "Take these notices and read them to Mother (but don't tell anyone about the poor notices). Fortunately the show is a *hit* and audiences love it!!" Unfortunately, three days after the musical opened, the Irish Republican Army began its first ever series of terrorist attacks in England proper, with bombs exploding in Birmingham, in Manchester, and at the Tower of London, killing tourists. Fear gripped the nation as people stayed home. After 252 performances, *The Good Companions* closed its West End run with no plans to open on Broadway.[60]

While in England to collaborate with Previn on *The Good Companions*, Johnny recorded an album that would include some of his lesser-known songs that he particularly liked. The producer Ken Barnes persuaded Johnny to make the album and enlisted the arranger Pete Moore to orchestrate fourteen charts for the Harry Roche Constellation to play. Several of England's best jazz musicians—Steve Gray, Tony Fisher, Duggie Robinson, and Roy Willox—improvised solos. While Barnes and Mercer picked several standards such as "Moon River," "Satin Doll," "Days of Wine and Roses," and "Summer Wind," as well as the old favorites "You Must Have Been a Beautiful Baby," "Show Your Linen, Miss Richardson," "Goody Goody," and "Something's Gotta Give," the remaining six songs proved obscure: "Talk to Me, Baby," "Shooby Dooin'," "Little Ingenue," It's Great to Be Alive," "Little Ol' Tune," and "I Wanna Be in Love Again," the last two with words and music by Mercer. Recorded in London's Pye Studios in January and February 1974 and released in Britain later that year, *Johnny Mercer Sings the Songs of Johnny Mercer with the Harry Roche Constellation* marked the last full studio album Mercer would make.[61]

Jazz critic Benny Green provided opening remarks on the liner notes that summarized Mercer's innate talent. Green explained his association with the songwriter: "Ever since Johnny Mercer began spending time in London in 1970, one of the prime delights of life has been to sit and pass the time of day with him, for apart from being one of the most gifted light versifiers of the twentieth century, he is also a student of the craft, and knows down to the last syllable the manneristic devices by which a connoisseur may distinguish a Hart from a Porter, an Ira Gershwin from a [Noël] Coward." Having established Johnny's encyclopedic knowledge of popular song, Green detailed his training method: "Mercer frittered away his youth in the wisest possible way, by singing duets with Jack Teagarden, a stroke of genius which he followed up by recording duets with Crosby, and which he duplicated not so long ago by recording yet more duets with the late Bobby Darin." In talking about music with Mercer, Green quickly picked up on "his own undue modesty, which is the only excessive thing I have ever managed to discover about him." Green valued Mercer's majestic successes like "Moon River" but preferred the "sophisticated realism of the joke-songs," as well as the "lighthearted, worldly-wise wry philosopher of songs like 'Talk to Me, Baby.'" In Mercer's singing of the latter, Green found "all the wisdom in the world that exists on the subject of popular singing," for it displays "Mercer's instinctive rhythmic grasp, the relaxed nature of his vocal style, the indubitable rightness of his phrasing." While suggesting that Johnny was "the most gifted part-time composer that the popular field has so far produced," Green commented on the long list of Mercer's collaborators, concluding, "Grab his lapel and you are buttonholing the pantheon of American songwriting." Having started in the profession forty years before, Mercer had met just about everyone ever involved in the popular music business.[62]

Producer Ken Barnes also recorded Johnny singing with Bing Crosby selections from *The Good Companions*. While working for United Artist Records, Barnes played for Crosby several numbers from the show and Bing singled out "The Pleasure of Your Company" as something he wanted to record for the album in production, *That's What Life Is All About*. Yet as a duet, he needed the "other half," so Barnes suggested they get Johnny. Mercer agreed, and on October 17, 1974, the old friends gathered for another recording session. They met at Mercer's Heritage Studios on Oak Street in Burbank, where a rhythm section led by Pete Moore accompanied the former partners as time melted away. Over thirty-five years had passed since "Mr. Crosby and Mr. Mercer," but the men fell right in together. For the occasion, Johnny crafted special lyrics:

CROSBY: May I have the pleasure of your company —
MERCER: [spoken] Sure! Where we goin'?

CROSBY: As we trip the light fantastic we call life?

MERCER: If I can have the pleasure of your company, / I'll be a Robbie
                 Burns to your Will Fyffe.

CROSBY: [spoken] I want to be Harry Lauder.

MERCER: You got it.

CROSBY: Old boy, old bean, by which I mean / We'll find a bar on which
                 to lean.

MERCER: Becoming at increasing speed / Fast friends indeed.

Similarly, on their recording of "Good Companions," the fans of vaudeville ad-lib after Johnny's verse "Even when the raindrops tumble, / Good companions never grumble, / 'Them's the breaks,' / As Willie Shakespeare used to say." Crosby interjects, "Oh yes, he's widely quoted," with Mercer retorting, "He said it all!" Then to the tune from "And Points Beyond," Bing adds, "To Omaha / And Wichita, / We'll travel through the good old U.S.A.," with Johnny quipping "Like Lewis and Clark!" Together they resolve: "And points beyond. / This old life's a game of cricket / Each must play. / For we're the Good Companions / And we're on our way. / On our way." Once released, the album sold a quarter million copies. Asked for his fee, Mercer said, "You can pay me the same as I got for my first professional singing engagement — twenty dollars." It proved to be his last studio recording.[63]

While in London for *The Good Companions* in 1974, Johnny began noticing something wrong with his health. For months Mercer had experienced dizziness with an accompanying loss of balance that increased in frequency as he worked on the musical. After a night at The Haven with the Previns, André watched as Johnny "stumbled and held on to Ginger, then he had to sit down. He said to her, 'I don't know what's wrong with me.'" R. W. "Bob" Montgomery of the British music publishers Chappell & Co. wrote Johnny on June 5, 1974, "I am sorry you have not been well recently, and I hope you are now fully recovered." In a letter to a friend written with a shaky hand in early 1975, Johnny described "an accident I had in London last year in a fall from a bus. I have been undergoing tests ever since and have been too listless and dizzy to get my work properly done." Closing the note Mercer added, "I'm not sure I understand the music business any more. It has changed so, as have so many things, that both the songs seem different as well as the singers." When he fell off the bus in England an emergency crew took him to the hospital, but he remained unaccounted for to family and friends, who initially had no idea where he might be. British doctors assessed Johnny to determine the cause of his malady. They encouraged the songwriter to seek medical help back in the United States.[64]

Arriving in New York in August 1974 from Europe, Mercer stayed a few days, then traveled down the coast as per his custom to visit his mother in the Oceanside Nursing Home near Fort Screven on Tybee Island, where she had lived since 1970. Finding her Alzheimer's so advanced that she could barely recall his name, Johnny left distraught. Briefly he visited his sister, Juliana, and other family members and friends. Since his own health had by then deteriorated, he began to suspect what the future might hold. He returned to California in September 1974. At a meeting of the American Guild of Authors and Composers hosted by Johnny Green, Margaret Whiting saw Johnny, whom she had been close to since her father's death in 1938. His appearance frightened her: "He had lost a lot of weight. He looked awful. He was stumbling. I thought, Oh my God." Accompanied by Ginger, Johnny suggested Margaret and her mother, Eleanor Whiting, join them for dinner. Walking to the car Margaret remembered, "Johnny started to weave. I gave him my arm to steady him. He stopped and leaned on a tree. Then he put his arm around the tree and looked at me." Mercer said: "Isn't this awful, Mag? I'm scared." She told him to go to a doctor, but Johnny replied, "If there's something wrong, I don't want to be a vegetable. I want to die." The growing concern over his medical needs consumed the Mercers for the next calendar year.[65]

Johnny wrote to his Mercer niece Liz Hammond in early 1975, thanking her for her Christmas card and explaining, "We didn't send any this year. We have been busy trying to get well after some surgery and an accident in London." He referred to Ginger's "lady type" operation of February 1973 and added about his own incident with the bus, "Trying to recover our wits — and our balance." He closed, "Hope our paths meet again at Tybee!" Responding to a card from his Ciucevich cousin Frannie, Mercer said, "I'm glad you're so musical . . . we have a lot in common. I can't do without it!" Then offering sage advice just as his grandfather George Anderson Mercer liked to do, Johnny added, "I'm also glad you like to write . . . it is a lot of fun and you will like it even more as you get older and better at it. Have you tried any short stories yet?" The British journalist John Gibson responded to a note from Johnny, joking, "So I'm due you a Dewars," and then added that he looked forward to Mercer's return to Edinburgh "in the spring," a trip the Mercers failed to make.[66]

Ginger took Johnny to see specialist after specialist as his condition worsened over the course of 1975. According to Gene Lees, every neurosurgeon consulted declined to operate on what they diagnosed from X-rays and from Johnny's symptoms as a brain tumor. As Mercer's correspondence decreased after January 1975, the couple withdrew further from public view. Friends noticed their absence. Johnny continued to try to write songs and maintain a professional schedule, but his illness made that difficult. Doctors believed the tumor — perhaps growing and cancerous but unclear at the time — was pressing against his brainstem in a position that most felt made it inoperable. Wanting to avoid surgery, Johnny sought alternative treatments, eating almonds out of a belief in their curative powers. On rare occasions he met with associates or dined with friends at his favorite Hollywood restaurant, Chasen's. During the late summer of 1975, Mercer returned to the East Coast assisted by his son-in-law and arranger, Bob Corwin. Johnny wanted to visit family and friends. In New York he joined his niece Nancy for dinner at the Palms, where she noticed something terribly wrong as she watched her beloved "Uncle Bubba" pretend to eat a steak, hiding the food in his napkin. Although sober, the imbalance caused by the tumor made him appear drunk as he stumbled, incapable of walking unassisted. Another night Johnny met up with television producers and old friends Jean and Bob Bach and Bill Harbach. At supper they encouraged him to seek an operation, and upon pressing the matter, Harbach heard Johnny repeat his fears: "I don't want to be a vegetable." Despite the deterioration of his motor skills, Mercer retained the use of his mental faculties.[67]

An invitation to appear on *The Mike Douglas Show* brought Johnny Mercer home to Savannah for what would be his farewell visit. The Hollywood star Burt Reynolds provided the main attraction for Douglas's daily variety show, which taped three ninety-minute programs in Georgia that fall. Having ventured into directing, Reynolds was filming his movie, *Gator*, in coastal Georgia, and Douglas took the opportunity to interview the handsome former football player from Florida. Douglas also used sites around Savannah, such as the shrimp fleet at Thunderbolt Marina, Fort Pulaski, and Bailey's Forge on Bay Street, as settings for the popular midday television program. On Sunday morning, September 21, 1975, camera crews set up in Monterey Square for the filming of Johnny's segment, with of his great-grandfather General Hugh Weedon Mercer's trophy house as a backdrop. Next-door neighbor and noted historic preservationist Lee Adler recalled waking that morning to a piano playing outside his window. By the time he dressed and rushed out to greet Johnny, a crowd had gathered to watch. The set consisted of two peacock-feather wicker chairs in which a bouffanted and overweight Douglas and a gaunt and gum-chewing Mercer sat and talked. Time had not been kind to either man since their last show together seven years before. Yet as they sang duets, the music erased the years. The immortality of the lyrics came across clearly even when Johnny stumbled over words with uncharacteristic forgetfulness. He mentioned his intention to visit his mother on the morrow to celebrate her ninety-fourth birthday.[68]

Traveling around Savannah, Johnny made a point of telling his family and friends goodbye. In addition to his mother, Lillian, now trapped in dementia, and his sister Juliana also suffering with mental disorders, only his half-brother Hugh remained alive, although he would die the following February 1976. Johnny popped in the Mercer Insurance Agency on Bay Street to see Nick Mamalakis and the office staff even though Walter had died in January 1970. He visited his Ciucevich cousins on Tybee and recalled the old days playing around the Tybrisia Pavilion, which had burned down in 1967. In addition to the Collinses and O'Learys, Johnny stopped by to talk with his Ciucevich cousin Julie Paige, the daughter of his Uncle Eddie. He watched her husband as he built his family a new residence at 29 Meddin Drive that would be round like the nearby lighthouse. She remembered that though it was still early autumn, Johnny wore an overcoat with a hat pulled down, looking unwell and a shadow of his former self.[69]

Yet Johnny's performance on *The Mike Douglas Show* seemed to contradict the reported medical testimony that later appeared in *Variety*. The trade publication suggested that in the months before the fall 1975 operation, "Mercer showed the effects of the tumor afflicting his brain to such an extent that he needed support in any location, often fell down, was in need of constant medication for pain, and spoke only a few words at a time. His ability to care for himself was almost totally dissipated, and he was a person totally without understanding."[70]

Whatever his condition and despite his long-held fears of doctors, Johnny agreed to radical brain surgery on October 24, 1975, at Huntington Memorial Hospital in Pasadena. After others had declined, fearing the tumor inoperable, Ginger had found a neurosurgeon, Dr. Theodore Kurze, who believed the growth benign and agreed to operate. At the time a leading member of the University of Southern California's medical faculty, Kurze was credited with revolutionizing neurosurgery worldwide through the introduction in 1957 of the binocular-operating microscope and other specialized equipment. Johnny's staff at Commander Publications, Marshall and Barbara Robbins, sat with Ginger in the waiting room of the hospital during the surgery. Barbara remembered, "The doctor came down crying." A malignant glioma had spread to both lobes of the brain, pressuring the brainstem in an inoperable stranglehold. Kurze had no choice but to sew Johnny up. Forty years before, a similar situation had claimed the life of George Gershwin on the operating table. Johnny Mercer emerged from surgery alive but reliant on machines. No one watching *The Mike Douglas Show* would have suspected that by the time Johnny's segment aired on October 30, 1975, this man who for decades had entertained the world with such energetic verve and love of life would lie incapacitated in a hospital bed. Without the surgery, Mercer's quality of life would have undoubtedly continued to deteriorate, with more frequent brain seizures perhaps similar to those experienced by his grandfather shortly before his death. Yet drugs could have alleviated Johnny's pain and he would likely have retained consciousness for at least some period. Instead, the family attorney, Herbert Dodell, explained that after the surgery "Mercer was never ambulatory nor even in an upright position. He was for this entire period incapable of coherent speech or thought and was a person totally without understanding."[71]

Other testimony questions that of the lawyer, as family members and friends believed Mercer's mind still worked after the operation but that his condition changed with additional medical treatments. As Johnny lay in intensive care, Barbara Robbins sat with Ginger in the hospital room suite every day, needle-pointing and fielding calls. She remembers Mercer left the operating room in a coma but regained consciousness. Her husband, Marshall Robbins, printed up a list of Johnny's songs in the shape of a pyramid that they posted at the foot of his bed. Nurses referred to his standards when talking with him. One brought a guitar and began singing "Moon River" and Johnny spoke out, "I wrote that." Margaret Whiting understood, "The nurse who was with him would come in and listen to a song that was coming out of the TV set and ask who wrote it, and Johnny would say, 'I did.' And most of the time he was right." Barbara Robbins claimed he recognized and spoke with her "until he really got into the heavy chemo." She thought with the radiation treatments "he became quadriplegic." Protective of Mercer's pride, Ginger shielded him from the public and said nothing except to hint at the possibility of recovery, even to family members. Yet the occasional reports in *Variety* and the Mercers' holiday greeting in December 1975 suggested otherwise: "This Christmas card, I think, may be the last you people hear from me," signed, "from these old versers, the gift of love — from all the Mercers."[72]

Out of respect to Johnny, Ginger restricted visits to family members only, at times denying even them entrance. Barbara Robbins recalled, "Ginger would not permit anyone to see him. She protected his privacy and his dignity. He wouldn't have liked that." She added, "Even when I went in to say, 'Hello,' it would be on a pretext of bringing cranberry juice or something. I'd say, 'Hi, John!' and I'd barely look at him. And he'd, you know, nod." Friends "weren't allowed to come," Mandy said. "She didn't want them to see him the way he was." Instead, Barbara and Marshall Robbins created a barrier. "I was at the hospital for as long as he was there, every day with Ginger," Barbara recalled. "And we were with her every single night until he died." When not in the hospital, Ginger stayed at a hotel in Pasadena. "She closed herself off from everybody, to the extent that she wouldn't even talk to Irving Berlin when he called once a week." Instead, Barbara "talked to him. I took the call." Fans mailed get well cards. From Savannah came a volleyball and a poster signed by all the youth at the Jenkins Boys Club. Los Angeles schoolchildren stopped by the hospital to sing a bicentennial history lesson about the Revolutionary War that Johnny had written early in his career, "Here Come the British, Bang! Bang!" Hank Mancini wrote, "Being the 'music' half of the team, I'm not very good with 'words.' I can only say simply — Ginny and I love you and Ginger very much."[73]

In the months after the surgery Johnny lost dozens of pounds and then lay intubated in the hospital bed. He remained in Huntington Memorial Hospital for five months before Ginger — responding to changes in insurance coverage — arranged to have him discharged and installed in a makeshift hospital room in his studio behind their Bel Air home. For three more months Mercer received round-the-clock medical care while existing in what appeared to be a vegetative state. Yet one of the nurses told Barbara that during the televised broadcast of the Tony Awards she saw him watching the tube with tears rolling "down his face every time he recognized someone." Jim Corwin recalled his grandfather "would look right at you. He couldn't talk. He couldn't talk. But his eyes were open. He would look like he was alert, but he couldn't respond. He couldn't respond at all." Mandy added, "Except he'd cry." Bill Harbach believed Mercer responded when Ginger said, "Johnny, Bill's here. He's going to take me out to dinner." Harbach saw that "he smiled, which made me feel so marvelous. He just smiled. But his eyes were shut." At the age of sixty-six, Johnny Mercer died on Ginger's birthday, June 25, 1976.[74]

Tributes and memorials to Mercer proliferated following his death. In an obituary for the *Los Angeles Times*, Zan Thompson captured the quintessential Mercer: "He had a kind of hooting, unbelieving quality in his voice which laughed at himself and at the incredible goings-on of his fellow travelers on the midnight special. He saw the world squarely, but with his eyes squinted with laughter and he sang the same way." The *New York Times* observed: "Mr. Mercer was an unusually prolific and versatile songwriter, who was as successful in turning out breezy, vernacular lyrics for 'Jeepers Creepers,' 'Goody Goody' or 'G.I. Jive' as he was in the romantic vein of 'Dearly Beloved,' 'Skylark' and 'Moon River,' the mood-settings of 'Blues in the Night,' 'Laura' and 'That Old Black Magic,' or in modernizing an old song such as 'The Glow Worm.'" Bing Crosby wrote Ginger, "I appreciated him a great deal, too, and I was grateful to him for a lot of things he did for me and a lot of things that he did that he let me be a part of." Pearl Bailey telegrammed, "Johnny was not only beautiful to music, Johnny was beautiful to humanity. I shall miss him very much as a friend but as long as there is music there will be Johnny Mercer." From the White House, President Gerald R. Ford wrote: "His mellow voice revealed that he was a child of the South; but his phrases were full of affection for people everywhere.... Johnny Mercer had a gift all could enjoy." International newspapers such as the *London Times* carried obituaries of Mercer's death.[75]

The professional organizations that he had contributed to over the years hosted memorials on both coasts. The Academy of Motion Picture Arts and Sciences held a simple service in the Samuel Goldwyn Theater in Los Angeles on July 1 that featured no music or religious ceremony, just an urn and a eulogy by former collaborator and composer-conductor Johnny Green. A number of songwriters attended, including Henry Mancini, David Raksin, Alan Bergman, Jay Livingstone, Ray Evans, Sammy Cahn, and Hoagy Carmichael. The American Society of Composers, Authors and Publishers paid homage to Mercer in the Music Box Theatre in New York later that month, appropriately featuring performances by Harold Arlen, Margaret Whiting, Mel Tormé, and Al Hibbler, as well as recorded tributes by Bing Crosby, Dinah Shore, and Fred Astaire.

Savannah mourned the loss of its favorite son. The combined editions of the local papers ran a lengthy editorial praising the man. The editors recognized Mercer as a global southerner who had grounded himself in his native soil: "Oh, Johnny traveled a lot, writing songs for Hollywood musicals, or for Broadway productions, or for shows overseas. But no matter where he might be hanging his hat at a given moment, Johnny always regarded Savannah as home, and it was to Savannah that he would gravitate, time and again, for happy reunions with family and friends who were many." After describing his success as a songwriter, the paper acknowledged his generosity toward others in his repayment of his father's debts and in the large sums he donated to the Jenkins Boys Club and to the Bethesda Home for Boys, "with which his Savannah family had been intimately involved for several generations." Calling the entertainer "an extrovert of a sort," the editorial elaborated: "Mr. Mercer's endearing quality was a rather contradictory modesty and a strange shyness." In public he might sing a medley of Mercer hits upon request, but "he shunned rather than sought the limelight." Suggesting that "Savannah loved Johnny Mercer just as he loved Savannah," the local editorial concluded, "He is dead at a relatively young 66, but never dead in our hearts. Always Our Johnny." Years later, Savannahian Mary Harty echoed the obituary when discussing Mercer with writer John Berendt: "We all knew him . . . and loved him. We always thought we recognized something of Johnny in each of his songs. They had a buoyancy and a freshness, and that's the way he was. It was as if he'd never really left Savannah."[76]

Yet in Savannah, the Mercer family seemed in disarray, for at first no one stepped forward to take charge of funeral arrangements. The news of Johnny's death came to Lillian at the Tybee nursing home through a radio announcement that a nurse heard and repeated to the Alzheimer's victim. An unstable sister Juliana and a distraught Ginger complicated the matter. Finally, Johnny's nephew George Mercer, half-brother George's eldest son — called George the Third — stepped forward to express his views for the family. Despite the wishes of others, he declined any plans for a public funeral in Christ Church, suggesting that was "not the Mercer way" and that the matter would be handled privately. No doubt this reflected the wishes of Ginger. Ever loyal to the Mercers, Nick Mamalakis helped with local arrangements. Pierce Brothers Mortuary in Hollywood had cremated Johnny and coordinated through Irvine Henderson Funeral Home in Savannah interment in the family plot at Bonaventure Cemetery. Ginger sent Johnny's ashes by air to Georgia. She then followed on another plane, as did Mandy, but not Jeff.

In the days before the Fourth of July, Georgians began to celebrate two hundred years of the nation's independence as the Mercers prepared to bury their beloved Johnny. Savannah had been the site of one of the bloodiest battles in the American Revolution, where patriots joined by French marines had attempted to force the British from the city in the October 1779 Siege of Savannah. With the failure of the fighting, the French skirted Bonaventure Plantation on their flight to the coast. Seventy years later, a developer turned the landscaped grounds into a rural cemetery. On July 3, 1976, family members and friends gathered on the bluff above St. Augustine Creek and the Wilmington River to attend the brief ceremony and witness the interment of Johnny's ashes. An assistant Episcopal priest from Christ Church participated in the ancient ritual with Thomas Cranmer's immortal words from *The Book of Common Prayer*: "All we go down to the dust; yet even at the grave we make our song: Alleluia, alleluia, alleluia."[77]

Ginger had recruited Johnny's surrogate son, Mike Ober, now a nondenominational minister, to deliver the eulogy. His mother, Polly, had proclaimed his prepared remarks as "perfect — Johnny would love it." At the funeral, identifying the great commandment given by Christ to all Christians, Ober said of Mercer, "Johnny loved his fellowman, his neighbor, as himself." Rather than "deify Johnny," he suggested that Mercer "had flaws just like all of us have flaws by the mere virtue of being members of the human race." Yet Mercer "was a man after God's own heart," thereby exhibiting "a quality of Godliness." Mike told of bringing his fiancée to meet the Mercers: Johnny "greeted me as he would a son. I often related to Johnny in a paternal way, particularly after my own father died." On hearing the news of the pending nuptials, Mercer uncorked a bottle of wine and went to the kitchen to find some food, "a little cheese and crackers, some Jerusalem artichokes. (He usually had some funky pickled things lying around the kitchen.)" That day the Mercers dropped everything to celebrate with the betrothed. In concluding his remarks, the young minister and family friend recalled a framed quotation by Abraham Lincoln hanging in Mercer's study: "Show me a man, proud of the place in which he is from, and I'll show you a place proud of that man." Johnny had come home to Savannah, Ober said, but "our loss is heaven's gain."[78]

The family buried the songwriter's ashes in Bonaventure section H, lot 48, with his father, G. A. Mercer. Nearby remained a space for his beloved "darling" mother, Lillian, and next to Johnny a place for Ginger. In an adjacent plot are Uncle Joe and Aunt Nannie Lang and across the way Uncle Robbie and Aunt Katharine Mercer. A few plots over are the graves of his grandfather the colonel and the marker for his great-grandfather the Confederate general, as well as the Herndons and his half-brothers, Walter, Hugh, and George, and their descendants. Just as his grandfather George Anderson Mercer had envisioned, under the sprawling live oaks, palms, and evergreen azaleas the Mercers are assembled in death. On Johnny's large, plain marble slab, Ginger had the stonemason carve the lyric, "And the Angels Sing." On her own matching stone the sculptor chiseled, "You Must Have Been a Beautiful Baby."[79]

Generous in life, Johnny had planned to be generous in death. Having previously set up trust funds for his children, Jeff and Mandy, Johnny left the bulk of his estate to Ginger, also remembering in his will his mother, Lillian; his sister

Juliana Keith; and his mother-in-law, Ann Meltzer, with quarterly payments from ASCAP royalties. Living on Tybee Island, where Ciucevich kinfolk could visit, Lillian died a year after her beloved Bubba on September 9, 1977. Juliana soon replaced her mother in the Savannah Beach Convalescent Home and died there on October 8, 2000. Johnny had joined Jeff in operating Heritage Studios in Los Angeles, and he owned Commander Publications, Mercer Music, and Blabber Mouth Music, all of which he left to his children to share equally. He gave Jeff the Moon River house (which he promptly sold) and left Ginger the Bel Air and Newport Beach houses. Having waited to divorce her husband, Bob Corwin, until after her father's death, Mandy later remarried and remained in California, while Jeff moved up the West Coast to Oregon.[80]

The deaths of Johnny and his three half-brothers left only a handful of Mercer children and grandchildren in Savannah. By the end of the twentieth century, no males with the Mercer surname survived in the family line, although several nephews and nieces in the Hammond and Kline families continued to work in the city. Later, Johnny's favorite niece, Juliana's daughter Nancy Mercer Keith Gerard, moved back to her hometown. Yet while Ciuceviches abound, the Mercer name that had for 150 years been known through five generations of community presence and civic leadership no longer had living representatives in the port city. Nevertheless, thanks to memorials adopted in memory of Johnny, the name Mercer began to appear on roadways and buildings. At the same time, family and friends incorporated a foundation to perpetuate Mercer's life and career by promoting the Great American Songbook.[81]

Conclusion

· ·

Ev'rybody on yon twinkling star,
Doesn't matter on which one you are,
If you're diggin' me on your radar,
Hello out there, hello!

ALONG WITH THE NOTICES of Johnny Mercer's death that appeared in the Savannah papers in the summer of 1976 came calls for a suitable memorial for the favorite son. Historic preservationists used the songwriter's name in 1977 to gain support for their fight to prevent the demolition of the Lucas Theatre on Abercorn Street. An elaborate Adamesque-style movie palace with Italian marble, terra-cotta flourishes, and a domed interior, the Lucas had opened in 1921 for silent films but transitioned to talkies, requiring formal attire of coats and ties for men and dresses for women until it closed in 1976. By promising to open the Johnny Mercer Theatre-Restaurant in the space, the preservationists saved the historic structure that had shown *Old Man Rhythm* nearly fifty years before. Lending a hand in the campaign, Ginger and Jeff Mercer arrived in Savannah in the spring of 1977 to attend the seventeenth annual Savannah Arts Festival, which honored Johnny's memory with an all-Mercer theme. Indeed, just as the Abe Lincoln quote that Johnny displayed in his study exclaimed, Savannah remained proud of the famous songwriter who had so proudly called the port city home.[1]

By 1978, community leaders decided to rename the performing arts theater in the Savannah Civic Center in memory of Johnny Mercer. Back in February 1972, Mercer had coordinated with Hollywood scriptwriter and Savannah native Hal Kanter a memorable opening concert for the city's new state-of-the-art performance facility. Architects had designed the building to appease a variety of patrons, from fans of grand opera and jazz combos to those of rock concerts and trade shows. The inaugural event featured Johnny singing some of his own songs and the music of his friends, as well as performances by a variety of artists reflecting a smattering of musical styles. Banker Mills B. Lane, a native of Savannah who as head of the Citizens and Southern National Bank had moved to Atlanta, thanked Mercer for contributing to the show by writing, "You are one of Savannah's most valuable citizens and assets." He called the kickoff concert "just magnificent in every respect" but added, "I'm a little too old to be in sympathy with the music beat of the day." To plan an appropriate ceremony dedicating the theater space in Mercer's memory in 1978, the city again turned to Hal Kanter.[2]

Paying tribute to "Savannah's Ambassador to the World," the memorial concert topped all others ever held in memory of the songwriter with its combination of performances, testimonials, and participation by relatives and close associates. Ginger headed the list of family and friends attending the Memorial Day weekend event, which began at 8:30 p.m. on May 28, 1978. As entertainment, Kanter recruited *4 Girls 4*, a touring revue then making the rounds of major metropolitan centers, starring Rosemary Clooney, Helen O'Connell, Rose Marie, and Margaret Whiting singing hits from the Great American Songbook. The women structured the show around their personal interactions with Mercer. The program opened with a set by Helen O'Connell, who had sung "Tangerine" with Jimmy Dorsey's band for the film *The Fleet's In*, followed by Rose Marie, who had starred on Broadway in Mercer's *Top Banana*, singing "I Fought Every Step of the Way." After the intermission Rosemary Clooney performed a variety of Mercer's songs, having recorded many of them, including her hit "Come Rain or Come Shine." Margaret Whiting appeared last as she had known Mercer the longest, opening with her chart-topper "That Old Black Magic" and closing with "I Remember You." The songwriter Sammy Fain, who had written "Love Is a Many Splendored Thing" and "I'll Be Seeing You," also performed and spoke about Johnny, saying that "among his fellow songwriters, Mercer was the most respected of craftsmen."[3]

In addition to the stellar singing performance of Mercer material by the original artists, the American Society of Composers, Authors and Publishers (ASCAP) sent songwriter Gerald Marks to make a presentation on behalf of the music organization's twenty-five thousand members. The author of "All of Me," Marks said ASCAP could identify Mercer as "Savannah's ambassador to the world," because his songs "are known by all peoples in all regions of the world." Marks elaborated: "His 'Moon River' is sung up the Volga and down the Danube," and other lyrics "are sung in remote corners of the world by people who don't have the remotest idea of what an Academy Award is but they know his songs." The global reach of American popular culture accomplished through record sales, movie distribution, and radio and television broadcasts made this possible. "That's what I call an ambassador," Marks added, because "he got into corners of the world where no regular ambassador could hope to get."[4]

Aware of her husband's global significance and determined to perpetuate his memory, Ginger Mercer established the Johnny Mercer Foundation in 1982. She redirected a portion of her quarterly income from his ASCAP royalties that she had inherited at his death to fund the endeavor while promising to endow the foundation with the remaining ASCAP royalties once she died. Ginger recruited Margaret Whiting to represent the charity to the larger world as chair of the non-profit board on which several of Johnny's friends and associates served, including Mercer's old band arranger Paul Weston and television talk show host Steve Allen. Ginger also arranged for the Johnny Mercer Foundation to hire her lover, Marc Cramer, as director. The nonprofit corporation supported a variety of causes for children by donating large sums to charities that helped the hearing impaired and fought leukemia, as well as UNICEF and other groups the Mercers had supported for years, such as the Audubon Society. Later the mission expanded to include the promotion of the Great American Songbook, especially in educational resources for children. Using the image of the Pied Piper of Hamlin to refer to Johnny's "piper man" lyric for "Summer Wind" as a symbol of his charismatic attraction to youth — the kid-at-heart who carted the neighborhood children down to the beach on Lido Isle — the foundation set about raising money to increase its en-dowment, and thereby also its donations, to various causes.[5]

Recognizing the richness of Johnny Mercer's personal papers, Ginger decided to place these resources in an archive and searched for a suitable repository. In 1968, Johnny received the first of several solicitations from Gene M. Gressley, the director of special collections at the University of Wyoming, asking Mercer to contribute musical memorabilia to the school's primary resources on cinema. The arranger and composer Adolph Deutsch, who had worked with Mercer on *Seven Brides for Seven Brothers*, sent a follow-up letter, explaining he had placed his papers in the Laramie library and encouraged Johnny to do likewise. Other institutions, principally the University of Southern California; the University of California, Los Angeles; New York University; the Library of Congress; the Smithsonian Institution; and the Academy of Motion Picture Arts and Sciences busily collected the materials of Mercer's contemporaries. Yet family friend Nick Mamalakis suggested to Ginger that Johnny's memorabilia belonged in the South. She agreed. While searching for a suitable repository in Georgia, Gin-ger considered the Georgia Historical Society in Savannah, which specialized in eighteenth- and nineteenth-century coastal resources and already had an assortment of Mercer and related family papers, including items donated by Johnny himself. Just three months after the songwriter's death, the society's president, the Savannah banker and Johnny's old friend Malcolm "Mac" Bell, announced that banker Mills Lane had given the archives his collection of eighty shellac records of Mercer music, many of which featured the songwriter singing his own lyrics. Yet the staid institution once headed by Johnny's grandfather seemed incapable of managing the larger collection owned by Ginger. The society's new director explained in 1982: "We are still collecting materials, but we are faced with a critical problem of space."[6]

The efforts of the Mamalakis brothers Nick and George convinced Ginger in 1981 to donate to Georgia State University (GSU) in Atlanta Johnny's correspondence, draft lyrics, published sheet music, books, and photographs — in short, his private and professional papers — as well as his memorabilia and his unfinished autobiography. Nick's brother George, who had Americanized his last name to Manners, served as dean in the administration at GSU, and he convinced the school to create a new Popular Music Archives in its Special Collections Department to attract the Mercer papers. Later Ginger arranged financial assistance for the archives from the Johnny Mercer Foundation through an annual appropriation. After Ginger Mercer's death on October 21, 1994, a second donation of personal papers and artifacts arrived at GSU. Her will left the proceeds of her estate, including Mercer's intellectual property and the ASCAP royalties, to the Johnny Mercer Foundation, now headed by Margaret Whiting. By then, more than half of the revenues generated by his estate derived from foreign sales of his music.[7]

Several drafts of Johnny's unfinished autobiography arrived in the papers donated to GSU. When visiting Ossabaw Island in 1967, Mercer had begun a journal that offered an opportunity to reflect on his life and career. His friend Bob Bach and others had encouraged Johnny to write a memoir, and since such fellow songwriters as Irving Berlin, E. Y. "Yip" Harburg, Hoagy Carmichael, and Ira Gershwin and performers such as Fred Astaire and Bing Crosby had already done so, he thought the exercise might not appear a conceit. Writers had begun publishing analytical evaluations of the Great American Songbook, Hollywood, and Broadway, so by writing an autobiography, Johnny could present his story to the public. Working with Mercer in 1969, Bach compiled a list of songs and began contacting holders of copyrights about reprinting the lyrics in a proposed volume, "Where Ever the Four Winds Blow: The Wise and Witty Words of Johnny Mercer," that he pitched to friends at Viking Press.

Nothing came of the volume of lyrics, and the publishers wanted a memoir. By 1973, Johnny sent a working manuscript to Viking Press editor Merrill Pollack, who offered criticism, pointing out problems with the concluding chapters that failed to provide an adequate overview of his career. Pollack wanted Johnny to "give us your own voice that discusses more fully what the chapter title promises: 'Among My Souvenirs.'" But self-effacing Mercer refused to discuss his own achievements, turning instead to an article by Sidney Carroll published in *Esquire* magazine that he wanted to reprint. Then Mercer's health declined, so he ended the narrative quoting from *Foxy*, "As far as I'm concerned, 'Whatever happens from here on out, / I won't be sorry I came. / I've had the kind of adventure I read of — / I'm way ahead of the game!'"[8]

With the publication of the autobiography on hold, Ginger pursued other avenues to get something in print about Johnny. Working with a potential biographer, she notified Irving Berlin in 1981 that she had found someone to write "THE book that is long overdue." Ginger identified the British music critic and jazz radio host Benny Green and added that he would "work, in part, from Johnny's autobiography which, to say the least, is sparse and completely devoid of his numerous accomplishments, commendations and accolades." Unfortunately, Green never finished the project. No doubt frustrated over that failed effort, Ginger compiled — with the assistance of Cramer and Bach — a memorial volume titled *Our Huckleberry Friend: The Life, Times and Lyrics of Johnny Mercer*, published in 1982. Then she turned the autobiography over to jazz writer Gene Lees in the hopes that he might edit the manuscript into a publishable book.[9]

Mercer's autobiography functions largely as a memoir of things he had seen and heard but not a recitation of his many successes. He prefaced the chapter "Among My Souvenirs" by recounting his meeting with another famous Mercer during a trip to Scotland in 1973. Johnny visited the noted Edinburgh surgeon Sir Walter Mercer, whose shared ancestors had remained behind when Johnny's forebear Dr. Hugh Mercer fled to America in 1746. Personal physician to Winston Churchill, author of an important book on bone surgery, and professor at the Royal College of Surgeons, Sir Walter wanted Johnny to see the diplomas and awards displayed in his private study. The event prompted Johnny to reflect on what he might show a visitor, writing in his autobiography: "Besides my family, I have 4 Oscars, 2 Grammys and 1 Emmy." With great humility Mercer ends this review of his life story with the words, "While I have no accomplishments like Cole Porter or Irving Berlin to point to ... I point (with pardonable pride) to what I have." Even as he overcame his severe modesty, Mercer undercut his own achievements by comparing himself to the Broadway giants. As a fellow songwriter, Porter and Berlin considered Mercer first rate. Throughout Johnny's career Porter sent him personal compliments, having once remarked that he wished he had written "Laura," something Irving Berlin also confessed. Upon hearing the news of Mercer's death, Berlin telegraphed Ginger: "Johnny was not only a truly great songwriter but he had the deep respect and affection of all his friends." Several years later, when Bob Bach contacted the dean of songwriters for remarks to include in *Our Huckleberry Friend*, Berlin — echoing lyricist E. Y. "Yip" Harburg's comment sent to Johnny years before — called Mercer a "songwriter's songwriter" and then added, "Mercer is a great, great songwriter — and I use that word 'great' advisedly because it's thrown around so much."

Using the standards of the Oscar, Grammy, and Emmy, Johnny Mercer scores higher than Irving Berlin and Cole Porter. While Berlin won a Tony for his 1951 score *Call Me Madam*, of his six nominations for Best Original Song, only one received an Academy Award, the 1942 *Holiday Inn* theme "White Christmas," which remains the fifth most popular movie song of all time in the list maintained by the American Film Institute, following "Over the Rainbow" at No. 1, "As Time Goes By" at No. 2, "Singing in the Rain" at No. 3, and "Moon River" at No. 4. Porter never won an Oscar despite four nominations. He did receive the first Tony Award for his 1948 musical, *Kiss Me, Kate*, and a Grammy in 1961 for the original cast recording from *Can-Can*. Of course Johnny Mercer won four Academy Awards for Best Original Song and received Grammys for "Moon River" and "Days of Wine and Roses." He served as president of the Academy of Television Arts and Sciences, which distributes the Emmys, and the organization gave him one in recognition of his career in entertainment. He also received two Golden Globes for "Whistling Away the Dark" and "Life Is What You Make It." The only award Mercer failed to win was the Tony, although others working on his shows received them.[10]

If writing for the musical stage is the only measure of success considered, then Mercer remained in the second tier of American songwriters, something he understood only too well. When interviewing Mercer in 1974, writer Hugh Fordin "sensed" that Mercer "knew that he couldn't do a Broadway show and it would be a success, and that was a big hole, one of the many holes in his heart." Fordin discussed the matter with Margaret Whiting, who told him to "think about the books." Fordin realized "the book writer has a lot to do with it. And also the producer and putting all the magical things together, but the book writer does to a greater extent." Niece Nancy once asked her uncle about his lackluster experiences on Broadway, and Mercer responded: "We never could get the right actors, or the right book, or the right choreographer all together at the right time." Certainly Mercer tried, working with great producers, including the Shubert brothers, Rouben Mamoulian, Norman Panama and Mel Frank, Morton "Teak" DaCosta, and David Merrick; great actors such as the Nicholas brothers, Kitty Carlisle Hart, Pearl Bailey, Phil Silvers, Rose Marie, Carol Lawrence, Howard Keel, Bert Lahr, Judi Dench, and John Mills; and great designers and choreographers such as Cecil Beaton and Michael Kidd. Having written about good fortune and fate his entire career, Johnny understood the fickle nature of show business. The closest he came to writing what should have been a Broadway success according to most critics, *St. Louis Woman*, is at heart a story of overcoming superstitions and shaking bad luck. The score, by Harold Arlen, had the greatest melodies of any musical comedy on which Mercer worked, certainly when compared to some of the mediocre music he received for other shows, which explains why songs from it are still performed. Yet controversy swirled around *St. Louis Woman* like vultures waiting to descend, a bad omen foretelling the future. Old jinx seemed to dog Johnny on other projects too, from what he described as miscasting on *Texas Li'l Darlin'*, the overbearing Bert Lahr in *Foxy*, and finally the bomb blasts of the Irish Republican Army during *The Good Companions*. Unlike Little Augie, Johnny never broke the hex to win the race.[11]

If popularity among the public and peers is a measure of success, Mercer stands out among songwriters. His catalogue of Great American Songs topped *Your Hit Parade* in numbers unmatched by his contemporaries. During his lifetime he set the record, with fourteen of his songs reaching the number one spot, while he came in third for the total number of songs to make it to the weekly top ten by placing thirty-six on the list. Yet no songwriter found four of his creations cycling through *Your Hit Parade's Top 10* at the same time, as did Johnny, who watched "Tangerine," "Blues in the Night," "I Remember You," and "Skylark" move up and down the charts in the weeks of April and May 1942. Alone among the leading songwriters, Mercer also made recordings of his own and other people's music, and over the course of his career Johnny sang on thirteen records that reached the top ten, with four of his performances hitting the number one spot on *Your Hit Parade*. No other songwriter managed to do that, which is remarkable enough for a singer. Of Mercer's approximately 1,500 songs, at least 100 became hits. While Mercer placed second for the most Academy Award nominations for Best Original Song with eighteen, he won four Oscars, tying with three other songwriters, Sammy Cahn, Jimmy Van Heusen, and Alan Menken, for the most wins. These rankings alone placed Mercer at the forefront of his contemporaries.[12]

In the entertainment industry, Mercer remained a key player throughout his career, transitioning from the stage to radio to movies to television. While he went to New York to try his hand at acting, he turned to songwriting to make a living and moved to Hollywood for the steady work he found in the studios. At the time of Mercer's death, Los Angeles radio producer Warren Craig concluded Johnny had created eighty-seven hit songs introduced in sixty-five films. By 2008, others tabulated the total higher, suggesting Mercer music appeared in more than 385 movies, and with each passing year the figure grows, for many of his songs outlasted the films for which they were written. During his career, Johnny worked with all the major studios, from RKO, Warner Bros., and Paramount to Columbia, MGM, United Artists, and Universal; with most of the major directors, from Busby Berkeley and William Wyler to Elia Kazan, Billy Wilder, and Howard Hawks to Blake Edwards; and with many of the stars, including Dick Powell, Ruby Keeler, Bing Crosby, Bob Hope, Dorothy Lamour, Betty Hutton, Fred Astaire, Rita Hayworth, Judy Garland, Humphrey Bogart, Lauren Bacall, Esther Williams, Audrey Hepburn, and Julie Andrews. He partnered with all the great Hollywood composers, from Richard Whiting and Harry Warren to Henry Mancini and John Williams. His music appears in movie musicals from their heyday of the 1930s to their last gasps in the 1960s, while also playing as incidental music and great theme songs. At the same time Mercer appeared regularly on radio, from his first big break in the 1930s with Paul Whiteman to the final radio shows in the 1950s. His appearances on the *Kraft Music Hall*, *Camel Caravan*, *Command Performance USA!*, *Jubilee*, *Your Hit Parade*, the *Chesterfield Music Shop*, and *Call for Music* made him a celebrity in his own right. He easily transitioned into television, performing on almost all the major variety shows, from the early Rosemary Clooney and Nat "King" Cole programs, to those of Dinah Shore, Steve Allen, and Mike Douglas, to the holiday specials of Bing Crosby, Perry Como, and Andy Williams.

Expanding on his success as a songwriter and performer, Mercer ventured into the production realm of entertainment, cofounding Capitol Records in 1942. Already having followed Irving Berlin into the music publishing business, Johnny went beyond the paper boundaries of Tin Pan Alley by creating the actual music sold on discs and heard over the airwaves. Mercer's grasp of popular culture enabled Capitol to undercut the big three record labels as it rapidly seized market share and became a global competitor. By tapping the multiracial talents of diaspora entertainers and turning the hybrid musical heritage of the South into a commodity, Capitol packaged the jazz-infused popular song that consumers clamored for, selling millions of records during the Age of the Singer, as country-and-western swing, and West Coast cool jazz. Capitol marketed these sounds around the globe as American popular culture became hegemonic in the postwar world, prompting such responses as the Brazilian bossa nova. Ever attuned to trends, a discerning Johnny rejected the raw rock 'n' roll, and once he realized the dead end reached by his former collaborators, he turned outward, seeking international composers with whom to partner in a bid to write transnational song. When evaluating the totality of the man's contributions as a songwriter for Broadway, for radio, for Hollywood movies, for record sales, as a popular entertainer on radio and television, and as cofounder of Capitol Records, no other songwriter appears as successfully involved in so many facets of America's entertainment industry in the twentieth century as Johnny Mercer.

The testimony of his colleagues and friends remains another way to measure success. Professionally, fellow lyricists and composers honored Johnny by naming their top award — given annually by the Songwriters Hall of Fame — the "Johnny Mercer." People who suffered one of Johnny's drunken darts might harbor the mean things he said in their hearts, but others accepted the apology and forgave the man. Certainly most of Mercer's close associates had nothing but praise for their friend. Barbara Robbins said of Johnny, "He was loving, talented, always there for you — a real southern gentleman, always. I can't say a bad word about John," adding for her husband, Marshall, "he was our family." As the handyman for the Mercers, Robert "Bobby" Rush saw the personal side of the household, suggesting Johnny tried to prove to his adopted children "all the time that they were, indeed wanted." If on the street someone made a passing remark, Mercer often stopped to engage the person in conversation. If a friend suggested they do lunch, Johnny got out his calendar to set a date. Mercer never gave advice but used "for instances" to teach by example. Rush recognized: "There were lots of different sides to Mr. Mercer. But I think his friendship and his love for just anything and everything came through." Henry Kane closed his interview with an accusation: "You're a hell of a nice man, Mr. Mercer," adding, "It comes through like there's a leak." A blushing Johnny replied "nonsense" as the two men shook on it. Kane concluded, "He has a strong warm firm hand."[13]

Jazz provided the thread that runs throughout Mercer's career, for his best music reflects the breadth of that musical tradition. As Dave Dexter recognized in his 1946 history of the genre, *Jazz Cavalcade*, "jazz has been sung since there was jazz to be heard." Many of the key artists of the 1930s and 1940s recognized Mercer as an exemplary rhythm singer and jazz musician. When asked by Dexter to list their twelve favorite jazz records, Bing Crosby, Wingy Manone, Jimmie Noone, and Jo Stafford listed performances by Johnny. As a talented jazz musician he worked with Paul Whiteman, Louis Armstrong, Jack Teagarden, Mildred Bailey, Jimmy and Tommy Dorsey, Billie Holiday, Benny Goodman, Jimmie Lundsford, Lionel Hampton, Ella Mae Morse, Lena Horne, Jo Stafford, Kay Starr, Stan Kenton, Anita O'Day, Peggy Lee, Ella Fitzgerald, Dinah Shore, Harry James, Duke Ellington, Blossom Dearie, Julie London, and other jazz greats. From the outset, such songs as "Skylark," "Travelin' Light," "Early Autumn," and "Blues in the Night" became standard jazz charts. Even those instrumentals for which he crafted lyrics — especially "Laura," "Midnight Sun," "Satin Doll," and "Autumn Leaves"— gained popularity among jazz artists in part because of the contribution of his words. He sought out jazz arranger-composers to work with and had his greatest successes collaborating with fellow jazz musicians who had previously written jazz charts. From his earliest hits with Hoagy Carmichael and Bernie Hanighen, to his golden era with Harold Arlen and Rube Bloom, to his last years with Duke Ellington and Henry Mancini, Johnny's careful collaborations resulted in numerous jazz standards. Today, Mercer's music remains in the repertoire of all serious jazz performers.[14]

By Mercer's death in 1976, the southern diaspora that had expelled him from the South as an entertainer had drawn to a close. A curious shift had occurred as native southerners and their children began to return to the region then promoted as the Sunbelt. At the same time, scholars began questioning the very existence of southern distinctiveness. Just as the multiracial southern diaspora had altered the nation's population, so too the region's multiracial music forever changed America's popular culture. In 1974, the journalist John Egerton, himself a native Georgian, captured the essence of the transformation in his study *The Americanization of Dixie*. Egerton worried that the "amalgamation" of the regions would destroy the good in the South and leave the reunited country with a "homogenized puree" of a popular culture. Thirty years later, in *Dixie Rising*, journalist Peter Applebome described as mainstream a music whose antecedents once appeared to be distinctively southern. Mercer had lived through the changes. He began life in the waning days of Tin Pan Alley's peculiar South that northern songwriters from Stephen Foster to Jack Yellen packaged as exotic "Back to Dixie" tunes for American consumption. Mercer and other diaspora entertainers took their hybrid culture represented by jazz, blues, and hillbilly and blended the sounds with the popular song format to create something original. The new music — be it the jazz-infused Great American Song, country-and-western swing, or rhythm and blues and rock 'n' roll — entertained America and the world.[15]

People looking for the South in Mercer's music find it in his sensitivity to locale, from the use of place names and dialect to references from the natural environment. In 2006, the New Orleans performer Dr. John (Malcolm John Rebennack Jr.) released his album *Mercernary*, which relished Johnny's ability to capture the region's multiracial culture in song. Referring to Mercer's "down-home lyrics" in an interview on National Public Radio's *All Things Considered*, Dr. John explained, "I felt more connected with him than I knew. I knew the guy was from somewhere in the South. Little things he said . . . [and] the way he thought of those lines, the one in 'Moon River,' 'huckleberry friend,' no body but some body from the South would say something like that." On the album Dr. John included a new song he wrote for fun called, "I Ain't No Johnny Mercer." When producers for Oprah Winfrey decided to make a musical of native Georgian Alice Walker's novel *The Color Purple*, they hired songwriters Brenda Russell, Allee Willis, and Stephen Bray to write the music and lyrics. The resulting songs echoed that other famous Georgian, Johnny Mercer. The show opens on a playful scene of little sisters Celie and Nettie singing "Huckleberry Pie." Later the character Shug Avery sings to an adult Celie "Too Beautiful for Words," with its lyric "Don't you know you're beautiful, / Too beautiful for words." Whether intentional or not, the similarities to Mercer's "Too Marvelous for Words" underscore contemporary songwriters' inability to escape the master wordsmith.[16]

Having found scraps of paper with lyrics that Johnny had jotted down for later consideration and development among his personal effects, Ginger Mercer determined to find a composer who could turn them into songs. After discussing the matter in 1983 with Margaret Whiting and with friends at Chappell Publishing in London — the senior director Teddy Holmes and the standard department manager Mark Rowles — Ginger agreed that the popular singer and American songwriter Barry Manilow could undertake the project. Ginger recalled that Johnny had remarked positively on Manilow's hit "Mandy," while Margaret had known Barry since his New York days accompanying Bette Midler in a gay bathhouse. Long a fan of the Great American Songbook, Manilow expressed delight at the quality of the words, thrilled by the opportunity to write music for lyrics penned by the great songwriter. He recorded perhaps his best effort, "When October Goes," for his 1984 Arista release *2 A.M. Paradise Café*. The album went platinum, with "When October Goes" its lead hit. In 1990, Manilow recorded Mercer's "When the Meadow Was Bloomin'" and "I Guess There Ain't No Santa Clause" on his *Because It's Christmas* album, which also went platinum. All told, Manilow created about eighteen songs from the scrap lyrics he received from Ginger. "The tunes came like that," Manilow said, snapping his fingers and adding, "I struggle with the pop stuff till I bleed." He mailed the finished lyrics off to Columbia Records, which placed them with Nancy Wilson, who released the album *With My Lover beside Me* in 1991, which contains eleven of the songs and a medley of the lyrics sung as a duet with Manilow. Henry Mancini's daughter, Monica Mancini, recorded her 2000 album, *Dreams of Johnny Mercer*, which listed seven of the new Manilow-Mercer songs, including "Something Tells Me" and "Love Is Where You Find It." From Manilow's recordings to those of Wilson, Mancini, and others, Johnny's residual lyrics continued to top the charts.[17]

Other lyrics Mercer completed before the tumor prevented him from working found posthumous release. In 1974, Johnny had written with Jimmy Van Heusen the song "Empty Tables" for Frank Sinatra. With its lines, "And I'm doing the same old numbers, / Yes, and I'm telling the same stale jokes; / But there's nothing out front but memories / And a lot of transparent folks," followed by the kicker, "'Cause I'm singing to empty tables / Without you," Mercer captured the "saloon-torch-suicide" feeling Sinatra and Van Heusen wanted. Arranger Gordon Jenkins paired it with Stephen Sondheim's "Send in the Clowns" as a set but then dropped "Empty Tables" from the initial recording. Instead, Sinatra reworked this "underrated" song into a spare background piano accompaniment by old friend Bill Miller that resulted in "some of his finest moments," according to biographer Will Friedwald. Another treasure hidden until after Mercer's death turned out to be his only collaboration with the jazzman Benny Carter. A contemporary of Johnny's, Carter had played with all the greats, from Fletcher Henderson to Duke Ellington. After the war he moved to Los Angeles and worked as an arranger, partnering with Mercer on "A Kiss from You." The nearly eighty-year-old Carter accompanied jazz vocalist Billy Eckstine, himself seventy-four years old, on a 1986 recording of the song.[18]

Because of the immortality of music — every day new people hear Mercer's songs — his catalog continues to regenerate. To be sure, the style of popular song Johnny wrote has waned in popularity, but the quality of his better work assures regular play. Every kind of musician imaginable has been attracted to Mercer's music, resulting in his songs being continually recorded. The practice of making covers had fallen out of favor among rock 'n' roll bands that preferred to perform their own songs; nevertheless, the custom continued as artists as diverse as Aretha Franklin recorded "Ac-Cent-Tchu-Ate the Positive," Ringo Starr recorded "Dream," Carly Simon recorded "Laura," and Elvis Presley recorded "Fools Rush In." The 1980s punk rocker Billy Idol covered the 1965 hit "Summer Wind," an odd pairing perhaps, but not unusual. A more common practice proved that of maturing rock star Linda Ronstadt, who recorded "Skylark" and other standards accompanied by the Nelson Riddle Orchestra for an album that introduced a new generation of listeners to the music of the Great American Songbook. American artists as diverse as the jazz pianist Diana Krall, the rapper Queen Latifa, the country singer k. d. lang, the male chorus Chanticleer, and the female trio Bodacious Ladyhood have recorded Mercer's songs. The Swedish sensation Bjork covered "I Remember You," punker Iggy Pop made a video of "One for My Baby (and One More for the Road)," Don Henley released "Come Rain or Come Shine," Leon Redbone claimed "Lazybones," and Bono joined Tony Bennett in a duet of "I Wanna Be Around." The Athens, Georgia, band R.E.M. included its version of "Moon River" on the extended album *Reckoning* released in Europe and added the song to its concert repertoire, while Widespread Panic used "Travelin' Light" as inspiration for its own song. (Indeed Dave Schools, the bassist for the popular jam band Widespread Panic, is Johnny's great-nephew, being the son of Mercer's niece, Nancy Mercer Keith Gerard.) Consequently, Johnny's work lives on in a fashion unmatched by that of his friends Bing Crosby, Bob Hope, and Judy Garland, who with each passing year fade a bit more into memory. Their life's work remains trapped in celluloid or on vinyl even as their now historic film footage and classic recordings pop up on the Internet. These icons of entertainment all received their images on U.S. postage stamps, as did Mercer in the American songwriters series of 1996. And while the stage shows of Andy Williams in Branson, Missouri, and the tours of Tony Bennett will end one day, Mercer's music will continue to be recorded by artists who discover him anew.

Mercer's music has regularly appeared on television in a variety of contexts. For years network programs such as *Entertainment Tonight* introduced segments with "Hooray for Hollywood." Tire commercials used "You Must Have Been a Beautiful Baby" to sell car safety. The ultimate bellwether of cultural relevance in the decades around the millennium, Matt Groening's animated weekly program *The Simpsons* has featured Mercer's music prominently on several occasions. One episode has Bart in Branson, where viewers discover the show's bully Nelson loves the singing of Andy Williams as he exclaims, "I didn't think he'd do 'Moon

River,' but then—bam!—second encore!" Homer retorts, "The song I wrote you is so schmaltzy it'll make 'Moon River' sound like a farting orangutan." In the parody "Days of Wine and D'oh'ses," the resident alcoholic Barney swears off Duff beer and takes up piloting a helicopter, leaving codependent Homer without a drinking buddy. Another episode has the antihero Bart walking away from a failed romance to Sinatra singing "Summer Wind." Other cartoon artists mined Mercer's work for ideas. Johnny's lyric "One for My Baby (and One More for the Road)" provided Jack Davis a theme for a cartoon that appeared in *Playboy* magazine. For *The Far Side*, Gary Larson titled a panel "The curse of songwriter's block," which showed the sun rising over a tired lyricist with sheet music on a piano scribbled with "Jeepers Creepers, where'd you get those" and the words "eyeballs," "retinas," "tear ducts" crossed out.[19]

Movie soundtracks continue to feature Mercer's songs, a sure sign of their longevity and universality. *The Pope of Greenwich Village* (1984) incorporates "Summer Wind" in various guises throughout the picture. *L.A. Confidential* (1997) uses "Ac-Cen-Tchu-Ate the Positive" and "Hit the Road to Dream Land," while *You've Got Mail* (1998) uses "Dream." *Ocean's Eleven* (2001) features "Blues in the Night" and "Moon River," while the horror film *Jeepers Creepers* (2001) plays on the title song. Similarly, *P.S. I Love You* (2007) includes the hit of that name. More obscure songs, such as "Love Is on the Air Tonight," which Mercer wrote with Richard Whiting, is heard in *Radioland Murders* (1993), while "If I Had a Million Dollars," which Mercer wrote with Matty Malneck, is performed in *Seabiscuit* (2003). Many films continue to rely on Johnny's standards such as "Tangerine," "That Old Black Magic," "Autumn Leaves," and "Goody Goody." Every year since 1933 the movie industry has released at least one major film featuring a Mercer song.[20]

Likewise, on Broadway, Mercer's music has peppered numerous shows. Perhaps a sick Johnny attended a performance in 1975 of Bette Midler's *Clams on the Half Shell Revue* that incorporates "Drinking Again," written by Mercer to music by Doris Tauber. Johnny had died by 1978 when "Satin Doll" appeared in *The American Dance Machine* and "I Wanna Be a Dancin' Man" in *Dancin'*. An effort to bring a staged version of the film *Seven Brides for Seven Brothers* to Broadway in 1982 lost something in the translation, although an earlier song written with Harry Warren, "Sunny Side to Every Situation," found reuse in the 1980 staged version of the Hollywood movie musical, *42nd Street*, which enjoyed a revival in 2001. Similarly, "Satin Doll" reappeared in the Billy Strayhorn and Duke Ellington retrospective *Sophisticated Ladies* in 1981. A revue launched in

1982 and still enjoying tours that celebrates the lives of such singers as Ma Rainey and Bessie Smith called *Blues in the Night* uses the title song as well as "When a Woman Loves a Man." Other Mercer standards continue to surface in shows, some of which have failed to click with audiences. By 1997, an ambitious production of all Mercer music, titled *Dream*, opened on Broadway. Despite featuring his better hits — some three dozen standards — the retrospective had no lasting impact. Instead, Mercer's songs appear in random shows that often concern dancers, such as the 1999 production *Fosse*, about the choreographer Bob Fosse, which uses "Hooray for Hollywood" and "I Wanna Be a Dancin' Man"; or the big-band tribute *Swing!*, which uses "Blues in the Night" and "G.I. Jive"; or the 2003 production *Never Gonna Dance*, about Fred Astaire, which uses "Dearly Beloved" and "I'm Old Fashioned." Perhaps one day, investors will remake one of Mercer's Hollywood musicals into a Broadway show, or producers will turn to the musical comedies Johnny scripted but never saw staged and find there a gem waiting to be polished into a blockbuster. Certainly Mercer considered *Messer. Marco Polo*, written with Robert Emmett Dolan, one of his best works, and he tried to update with Dolan *Texas Li'l Darlin'* for a revival, and had great hopes for his collaboration with Michel Legrand called *Cyrano*.[21]

In Savannah, Emma Kelly kept Mercer's memory alive by playing his music nightly in bars. After years at the Quality Inn, she opened Emma's Piano Lounge on Bay Street in September 1985. Throwing herself a seventieth birthday party at the lounge three years later, Kelly struck on the idea of recognizing Mercer's eightieth birthday on November 18, 1989, in the same way. For some Savannahians and certainly for tourists, Emma Kelly became a public representation of the famous songwriter. After closing Emma's Piano Lounge in 1991, she began playing various nightclubs, most notably Hannah's East, near the Pirate's House Restaurant, which had been one of Johnny's favorite stops on his return visits home. At Hannah's, the eighty-three-year-old Emma Kelly hosted Mercer's ninetieth birthday celebration in November 1999. By that point she had gained a national following through her appearance playing herself in the movie adaptation of *Midnight in the Garden of Good and Evil*.[22]

What started out as a nonfictional account of a murder in Savannah became a phenomenon as the 1994 *New York Times* best-seller kick-started a tourism craze and subsequent Hollywood production. A travel writer who used the port city as a respite from the bustle of New York, John Berendt capitalized on the trial of Jim Williams as a sustained narrative to support a series of vignettes assembled together as *Midnight in the Garden of Good and Evil*. The book uses

Mercer's music to generate atmosphere. Authorities had accused Williams — a gay antiques dealer and historic preservationist who owned Mercer House — of shooting his lover in the parlor of the restored mansion once owned by Johnny's great-grandfather. Having arrived in Savannah after the fact, Berendt befriended Williams and negotiated a contract to tell his story. In the process Berendt crafted a well-written saga rooted in a factual style of first-person fiction. Berendt's talent for the short piece proved exceptionally well-suited to capturing the various characters who populate his narrative chapter by chapter. Despite the lovely setting of Savannah, the plot proved less sustaining for the movie directed by Clint Eastwood, who contributed to the soundtrack by performing "Ac-Cen-Tchu-Ate the Positive."[23]

While it may seem incongruous for "Dirty Harry" to sing such an optimistic song, Eastwood's longstanding appreciation for jazz attracted him to Johnny Mercer. In undertaking a biopic about the songwriter, the Johnny Mercer Foundation first hired Georgia documentary producer Becky Marshall and then Eastwood and his film-making partner, Bruce Ricker. Marshall knew Savannah, while Eastwood and Ricker had made several documentaries, including films on Thelonious Monk, Tony Bennett, Count Basie, Ray Charles, Fats Domino, and Dr. John. Because of their personal contacts, Eastwood and Ricker gained rare film clips and interviews with key individuals who had worked with Johnny, including Julie Andrews, Blake Edwards, André Previn, Alan Bergman, and John Williams. The filmmakers assembled hundreds of interviews, recordings, and footage from movies and television to compile *Johnny Mercer: "The Dream's on Me,"* which offers viewers the first complete overview on film of the songwriter's life. The documentary aired as the centerpiece of a Mercer retrospective on Turner Classic Movies that broadcast over several days a number of his Hollywood musicals during the November 2009 centennial of Mercer's birth. Also, *Johnny Mercer: "The Dream's on Me"* saw release as a Warner Bros. Home Video, replay in Britain on the BBC, and nomination for an Emmy for Best Documentary.[24]

There had been an earlier effort in 1973 to produce a retrospective of Mercer's career, but Johnny declined the request, saying, "I think there has to be a reason for a special about me." Death offered that opportunity when in 1976, Bing Crosby included a memorial to Mercer in his Christmas special by singing a medley of Johnny's hits with guest star Bernadette Peters. Other musicians, such as the jazz pianist Marian McPartland with vocalist Teddi King, staged concerts devoted to Mercer's music. Legendary oral historian Studs Terkel broadcast a program on Mercer on WFMT in Chicago. Los Angeles radio personality Warren Craig produced the first complete overview of Mercer's music on his weekly program for KXLU called *The Broadway Songbook*, which he described as offering "the work of America's top composers and lyricists — songs, famous or obscure, featured in stage and screen attractions from the turn of the century to the present." Craig put together ten hour-long programs that charted the progression of Johnny's career through his music. Each program queued a few bars from "On the Atchison, Topeka, and the Santa Fe" to begin and end the hour, then chronologically aired the rich variety of Mercer's songs performed by a host of entertainers. While other radio and film programs followed, none recounted Mercer's life as well as Craig's radio series until Eastwood and Ricker's *Johnny Mercer: "The Dream's on Me."*[25]

In addition to the release of the documentary, a host of celebrations marked the 2009 centennial of Johnny Mercer's birth. Savannah took the lead with a year-long calendar of events that featured concerts, book fairs, school programs, and the dedication of a bronze statue. Mayor Otis S. Johnson appointed former Savannah schoolteacher Dianne S. Thurman to head up the city's steering committee, and with the assistance of public relations expert Sandy Traub and Johnny Mercer's niece Nancy Mercer Keith Gerard the Johnny Mercer Centennial Committee coordinated events. They made education a key focus of their efforts, reaching thirty-five thousand school children by selecting Johnny as the subject of the Georgia Historical Society and Historic Savannah Foundation's annual Georgia Day parade. The arts education organization Camp Broadway brought its resources into the Chatham County Schools, training music educators and assisting students in writing lyrics. Johnny's songs entertained ten thousand Savannahians who gathered for "Picnic in the Park with Mercer," filling the space around the Forsyth Park fountain where he had played as a boy and sang as a star at the annual arts festival. Joined by a variety of performers, including the "Johnny Mercer Puppet" created by Andrea Beasley, vocalist Marlene VerPlanck headlined the centennial concert held in the Johnny Mercer Theatre of the Savannah Civic Center. The Friends of Johnny Mercer, led by its president, David Oppenheim, had promoted the man and his music for years, raising the funds to erect a statue by sculptor Susie Chisholm in the just restored Ellis Square. Based on the famous photograph from the 1930s showing Mercer in hat and trench coat leaning against a fireplug on a New York sidewalk, the street-level, life-size figure smiles at pedestrians on the site of Savannah's old City Market, just feet from where his grandfather and namesake, John Ciucevich, once operated a grocery store on Bryan Street. On what would have been his hundredth birthday, November 18, 2009, the Centennial Committee, assisted by family members, unveiled the bronze and then played "You're in Savannah," a new song it commissioned using a poem by Johnny set to music by longtime Disney songwriter Richard Sherman and performed by Michael Feinstein.[26]

While the city of Savannah recognized Mercer as its Man of the Year, the state legislature adopted a resolution declaring his birthday of November 18 Mercer Day throughout Georgia. To coincide with the centennial and in recognition of the Mercer holdings in its Popular Music Archives, Georgia State University held the first scholarly conference to analyze the man and the music of his day. From New York, Margaret Whiting continued to oversee efforts by the Johnny Mercer Foundation to support these and other activities that celebrated the life of the lyricist. Over the past quarter century, the foundation's board of directors had changed as Johnny's close friends retired, being replaced by such songwriters as Ray Evans, Alan Bergman, and Ervin Drake, and such recording executives as Al Kohn of Warner Bros. and Michael Kerker of ASCAP. From the office of legal affairs at GSU came John Marshall, who served as treasurer. In offering a portal to all things Mercer, the foundation's website suggests, "It is almost impossible to get through an entire day without hearing at least one Mercer song."[27]

Centennial observances occurred elsewhere in America and abroad, too. In Hollywood, the Academy Awards ceremony on November 5, 2009, recognized Mercer's contributions to the industry with a retrospective that the 1,400 in attendance, including Mercer's grandson Jim Corwin, his niece Nancy, and Stratton Leopold, a film producer from Savannah, received with an extended standing ovation. In Palm Beach, Michael Feinstein joined David Hyde Pierce in a special observance at the McCallum Theater, for which Johnny's daughter, Mandy, sat on the board. At Carnegie Hall, the New York Pops under director Steven Reineke played a centennial concert, while the Oak Room of the Algonquin Hotel hosted Daryl Sherman, Maude Maggart, and Andrea Marcovicci in Mercer retrospectives. On the centennial itself, Robert Kimball and Deborah Grace Winer led an all-star cast at the Ninety-second Street Y in "I Remember You: A Lyricists Centennial Tribute to Johnny Mercer." Special Mercer-themed programs aired from Minneapolis/St. Paul on KFAI Radio, from Austin on KOOP Radio, and from Atlanta on WRFG Radio. Likewise radio and television stations across the United Kingdom broadcast programming about Mercer from the BBC while special shows aired in Australia. Johnny's music highlighted the London Jazz Festival and provided the program for a tribute at the Cork Opera House in Ireland. The

Glasgow International Jazz Festival identified Mercer as the greatest Scottish jazz musician and lyricist of popular song and defended the claim with concerts of his music. Jazz performances in Canada, Germany, and France rounded out the centennial observances. In honor of the anniversary, YouTube mounted a "Johnny Mercer 100s Channel," featuring a hundred videos of popular artists performing Mercer's music. The "Black Magic" dark red hybrid tea joined other roses named after Mercer songs, such as the "Shining Hour" deep yellow grandiflora, "Summer Wind" orange-pink shrub, and "Moon River" mauve miniature, while Jackson & Perkins and Wayside Nurseries listed the "Wine and Roses" weigela and "Tangerine" azalea for sale. And at the *New York Times*, puzzle master Elizabeth C. Gorski used Mercer clues to construct the Sunday crossword puzzle "Man of Many Words" for November 15, 2009.[28]

Fifty years before, at the height of Johnny's career, the *New York Times* had recognized a transformation in popular culture that suggested Mercer's contributions had transcended time and space to become part of the vernacular landscape. Similarly, *Newsweek* had touted the Mercerized language of the day.[29] Music that had once seemed regional and outside the mainstream had moved to the center of the nation's popular culture. So indelibly southern, Johnny's lyrics provided reference points for others engaged in creating culture in America. At the same time, the global reach of U.S. popular culture made Mercer's impact international, while the subject matter of his music — so often a story of love and loss — made it universal. Ever so grounded, be it "From Natchez to Mobile / From Memphis to Saint Joe," the global southerner's songs can be heard "wherever the four winds blow," for just as the region's multiracial jazz that inspired him influenced transnational music, so too Johnny Mercer's immortal songs are part of the world's popular culture.

NOTES

Abbreviations

JM Papers, GSU   Johnny Mercer Papers, Popular Music Archives,
                              Georgia State University, Atlanta, Ga.

JM & GM Papers, GSU   Johnny Mercer and Ginger Mercer Papers, Popular Music
                              Archives, Georgia State University, Atlanta, Ga.

Mercer Family   Mercer Family Collection, Lane Library, Special Collections,
Collection, AASU   Armstrong Atlantic State University, Savannah, Ga.

Mercer Family Papers,   Mercer Family Papers, Georgia Historical Society,
GHS   Savannah, Ga.

Introduction

The epigraph is from "Moon River" (1961), with music by Henry Mancini from the movie *Breakfast at Tiffany's*. See Robert Kimball, Barry Day, Miles Kreuger, and Eric Davis, eds., *The Complete Lyrics of Johnny Mercer* (New York: Alfred A. Knopf, 2009), 293.

1. Defining the region that makes up the South has long kept historians busy. This book defers to such standards as W. J. Cash, *The Mind of the South* (New York: Vintage Books, 1941, 1991); Gavin Wright, *Old South, New South* (New York: Basic Books, 1986); C. Vann Woodward, *The Burden of Southern History* (Baton Rouge: Louisiana State University Press, ca. 1960, 1986); and Numan V. Bartley, *The New South* (Baton Rouge: Louisiana State University Press, 1995). At the same time, I recognize the influence of sociologist Immanuel Wallerstein and his three-volume *The Modern World-System* (New York: Academic Press, 1974–89) on providing a framework by which to situate the subject as a southerner. The work here has also benefited from the scholarship being assembled under the rubric of the Global South, which recasts the region's past by asking a host of questions set against the backdrop of a changing world. Rather than focus inward and find arguments rooted in an exceptional history, this book looks outward and finds a distinctive locale interacting with international forces. Literature professor Kathryn McKee, anthropologist James L. Peacock, and historians Charles Reagan Wilson, James C. Cobb, Harry L. Watson, and Edward L. Ayers are among the scholars at the forefront of the new interpretations evident in such special publications as "Global Contexts, Local Literatures: The New Southern Studies," *American Literature* 17, no. 4 (December 2006), and "The Global South," *Southern Cultures* (Winter 2007). On the construction of southern culture, see Immanuel Wallerstein, "What Can One Mean by Southern Culture?" in *The Evolution of Southern Culture*, ed. Numan V. Bartley (Athens: University of Georgia Press, 1988), 1–13.

2. Bertram Wyatt-Brown, *Southern Honor: Ethics and Behavior in the Old South* (New York: Oxford University Press, 1982). According to Wyatt-Brown, in contrast to the North, "honor, not conscience, shame, not guilt, were the psychological and social underpinnings of Southern culture" (22). In *The House of Percy: Honor, Melancholy, and Imagination in a Southern Family* (New

York: Oxford University Press, 1994), Wyatt-Brown traces the ethic over generations, recognizing that "honor is that which is contained in another, no man grants honor to himself; rather, he receives it from others" (9). Hence, families like the Mercers guarded their hard-won reputations.

3. Gene Handsaker, AP Newsfeatures, "Hollywood II," April 30, 1948; *Newsweek*, January 29, 1945; Henry Kane, *How to Write a Song (as Told to Henry Kane)* (New York: Macmillan, 1962), 71; Max Wilk, *They're Playing Our Song* (New York: Atheneum, 1973). Kimball, et al., *Complete Lyrics*, 27, 176; Fred Hobson, *Tell About the South: The Southern Rage to Explain* (Baton Rouge: Louisiana State University Press, 1983); Brian Ward, "By Elvis and All the Saints," in Joseph P. Ward, ed., *Britain and the American South* (Jackson: University of Mississippi Press, 2003), 189. For decades, scholars explained southern history only in contrast to the North. Perhaps with *Origins of the New South* (Baton Rouge: Louisiana State University Press, 1951), C. Vann Woodward has written the most influential book following this trope. In recent years the scholarship of James C. Cobb has chipped away at such a confining analysis. See Cobb, "An Epitaph for the North: Reflections on the Politics of Regional and National Identity at the Millennium," *Journal of Southern History* (February 2000), and also "From 'New South' to 'No South': The Southern Renaissance and the Struggle with Southern Identity," in his *Redefining Southern Culture: Mind and Identity in the Modern South* (Athens: University of Georgia Press, 1999). See also James C. Cobb and William Stueck, eds., *Globalization and the American South* (Athens: University of Georgia Press, 2005). As Peter A. Coclanis demonstrates with his contribution to this latter book, "Globalization before Globalization: The South and the World to 1950," the process has been ongoing since the beginning of colonization. Coclanis and David L. Carlton explore this reality in *The South, the Nation, and the World: Perspectives on Southern Economic Development* (Charlottesville: University of Virginia Press, 2003). The Global South suggests that rather than perpetuate old northern/southern binaries, the South should be evaluated as a distinct region integrated into the world. See also James L. Peacock, *Grounded Globalism: How the U.S. South Embraces the World* (Athens: University of Georgia Press, 2007).

4. Johnny Mercer joined the likes of Howard Odum, William Faulkner, and the Vanderbilt Agrarians as "Modernists by the Skin of Their Teeth," to use the words of Daniel Joseph Singal who, in *The War Within: From Victorian to Modernist Thought in the South, 1919–1945* (Chapel Hill: University of North Carolina Press, 1982), argued that between the world wars "an immense cultural change . . . had taken place in the region" (xi). Singal contrasts a Victorian ideology that before World War I had defined southern culture in terms of Christian morality, white supremacy, and a code of honor derived from Western civilization with a postwar modernist ideology that leveled hierarchies — be they of race, class, or gender — and promoted moral relativism and an accommodation to the irrational forces of the universe. An ambivalent Mercer advanced into the modern era, trying to retain aspects of a code of honor he admired, while paradoxically promoting the integration of the region into the rest of the nation and the world. See also 3–33, 111–13, 197, 261–63.

5. Bob Bach and Ginger Mercer, eds., *Our Huckleberry Friend: The Life, Times, and Lyrics of Johnny Mercer* (Secaucus, N.J.: Lyle Stuart, 1982); Philip Furia, *Skylark: The Life and Times of Johnny Mercer* (New York: St. Martin's Press, 2003); Gene Lees, *Portrait of Johnny: The Life of John Herndon Mercer* (New York: Pantheon Books, 2004); Kimball et al., eds., *Complete Lyrics*. The coeditors had produced other edited collections of lyrics of Cole Porter, Frank Loesser, Ira Gershwin, Noel Coward, P. G. Wodehouse, and Kurt Weill, among other books. Sammy Cahn and the Songwriters Hall of Fame published a collection of Mercer sheet music as *Too Marvelous for Words: The Magic of Johnny Mercer* (New York: Alfred Publishing, 1985). See also Leonora Gidlund, "Johnny Mercer: Resources for the Study of an American Lyricist," M.A. thesis, Georgia

State University, 1984. Stanley Booth, "Johnny Mercer: Music Master," *Georgia Music Magazine*, Fall 2009.

6. James N. Gregory, *The Southern Diaspora: How the Great Migrations of Black and White Southerners Transformed America* (Chapel Hill: University of North Carolina Press, 2005). Gregory defines diaspora as "historically consequential population dispersions of various descriptions, those inspired by opportunity as well as by oppression." He notes that in 1920 some 2.7 million southerners lived outside their native region and that the number steadily increased until it peaked in 1980. The shift in populations altered U.S. race relations and further integrated the once-separate region into the nation. For the figures, see 11–19. Gregory recognizes that diaspora southerners interacted in what he calls a "third dimension," but the analysis here builds on the ideas of Homi K. Bhabha, *The Location of Culture* (London: Routledge, 1994). Themes articulated by Bhabha, such as interdependence and mimicry, dismiss essentialist assumptions and support the argument being made here for hybridity in southern culture.

7. Drawing on recent developments and frequently filled with anecdotal evidence, the scholarship of James L. Peacock proposes a way to think of southerners in the larger world that this book develops in its analysis of Johnny Mercer as a "global southerner" who remained "grounded" in his native Savannah while becoming a world citizen. See Peacock, *Grounded Globalism*; and also James L. Peacock, Harry L. Watson, and Carrie R. Matthews, eds., *The American South in a Global World* (Chapel Hill: University of North Carolina Press, 2005).

8. Viewing race as an ideological construct and race relations as changing over time, this analysis supports the interpretation set forth by Barbara J. Fields, "Ideology and Race in American History," in *Region, Race, and Reconstruction: Essays in Honor of C. Vann Woodward*, ed. J. Morgan Kousser and James M. McPherson (New York: Oxford University Press, 1982). Building on the idea of race and the scholarship of the Global South, the argument here proposes breaking down the old binary of black and white that has long been used to define southern culture and instead considering the hybridity of the region's heritage. Such an analysis requires a defamiliarization of old racial narratives in order to consider the border crossings that continually occurred among Native American, black, white, Latino, and other ethnicities in the South. George Brown Tindall, *Natives and Newcomers: Ethnic Southerners and Southern Ethnics* (Athens: University of Georgia Press, 1995), 24. See also Tindall's *The Ethnic Southerners* (Baton Rouge: Louisiana State University Press, 1976); Cash, *The Mind of the South*, 51; B. A. Botkin, "Folk and Folklore," in *Culture in the South*, ed. W. T. Couch (Chapel Hill: University of North Carolina Press, 1934), 570. Botkin adds, "If the present survey has unavoidably given an impression of over-simplification and false unity, then in their more detailed portraiture black and white folk groups would show a mingling of Creole, Cajun, Indian, West Indian, and Mexican elements (not to speak of other European nationalities transplanted but not quite naturalized in the South)" (578). See also Lawrence W. Levine, *Black Culture and Black Consciousness: Afro-American Folk Thought from Slavery to Freedom* (New York: Oxford University Press, 1977); David Hackett Fischer, *Albion's Seed: Four British Folkways in America* (New York: Oxford University Press, 1980); Grady McWhiney, *Cracker Culture: Celtic Ways in the Old South* (Tuscaloosa: University of Alabama Press, 1988).

9. Malone quoted in Ted Owenby, ed., *Black and White Cultural Interaction in the Antebellum South* (Jackson: University Press of Mississippi, 1993), 151; on the multiracial origins of southern music, see, for example, David Carlton, "To the Land I Am Bound: A Journey into Sacred Harp," *Southern Cultures* 10, no. 3 (Summer 2003): 49–66; Shane K. Bernard, "Twistin' at the Fais Do-Do: South Louisiana's Swamp Pop Music," *Southern Cultures* 2, nos. 3–4 (1996): 315–28. Out of Louisiana's "rhythm and blues, country and western, and Cajun and black Creole music" tradition comes Mac Rebennack, who performs as Dr. John (315–16). William Ferris, *Give My Poor Heart*

Ease: Voices of the Mississippi Blues (Chapel Hill: University of North Carolina Press, 2009). On African Americans and the country music mainstay in Nashville, see Louis M. Kyriakoudes, "The Grand Ole Opry and the Urban South," *Southern Cultures* 11, no. 2 (Spring 2004): 67–84; Lomax quoted in Gavin James Campbell, "'Music with the Bark On': The Southern Journeys of John and Alan Lomax," *Southern Cultures* 4, no. 3 (1998): 118. For many years Campbell edited the "Up Beat Down South" section of *Southern Cultures*, and it contains other examples of multiracialism in southern music. Charles Joyner, *Shared Traditions: Southern History and Folk Culture* (Urbana: University of Illinois Press, 1999). See also Joyner, "Top Ten Southern Folk Singers" (73–78) and the rest of the special issue, "Roots Music," *Southern Cultures* 17, no. 4 (Fall 2010).

10. W. T. Lhamon Jr., *Jump Jim Crow: Lost Plays, Lyrics, and Street Prose of the First Atlantic Popular Culture* (Cambridge, Mass.: Harvard University Press, 2003). See also Bhabha's chapter, "On Mimicry and Man," in *The Location of Culture*, 85–92, in which he recognizes "mimicry is at once resemblance and menace" (86) and argues "the *menace* of mimicry is its double vision which in disclosing the ambivalence of colonial discourse also disrupts its authority" (88). Deems Taylor et al., eds., *A Treasury of Stephen Foster* (New York: Random House, 1946); Ken Emerson, ed., *Stephen Foster and Co.: Lyrics of America's First Great Popular Songs* (New York: Library of America, 2010). On Foster, see also Ken Emerson, *Doo Dah!: Stephen Foster and the Rise of American Popular Culture* (New York: Simon and Schuster, 1997); William W. Austin, *"Susanna," "Jeanie," and "The Old Folks at Home": The Songs of Stephen C. Foster from His Time to Ours* (New York: Macmillan, 1975).

11. The adoption of the International Copyright Law of 1891 provided protection for American songs worldwide for the first time and helped consolidate the industry. See David A. Jasen, *Tin Pan Alley: The Composers, the Songs, the Performers and Their Times* (New York: Donald I. Fine, 1988); Nicholas E. Tawa, *The Way to Tin Pan Alley: American Popular Song, 1866–1910* (New York: Schirmer, 1990), 44–45; and Hazel Meyer, *The Gold in Tin Pan Alley* (Westport, Conn.: Greenwood Press, 1958); Rayford W. Logan, *The Negro in the United States: A Brief History* (Princeton, N.J.: D. Van Nostrand, 1957). Mercer, quoted in Wilk, *They're Playing Our Song*. Through the Tin Pan Alley publisher Henry Waterson and personal meetings with the composer, Berlin had access to the scores for Joplin's "A Real Slow Drag" from his opera *Treemonisha* and the "Mayflower Rag," both of which are said to have inspired "Alexander's Ragtime Band." See Charles Hamm, *Irving Berlin: Songs from the Melting Pot; The Formative Years, 1907–1914* (New York: Oxford University Press, 1997), 107–8. While others disagree with him, Hamm argues that "even if a phrase or a melodic fragment of one of Joplin's pieces did find its way into 'Alexander,' it still doesn't follow that Berlin 'stole' the song from Joplin."

12. Henry Pleasants, *Serious Music — and All That Jazz: An Adventure in Music Criticism* (New York: Simon and Schuster, 1969), 192; Dave Dexter Jr., *The Jazz Story: From the '90s to the '60s* (Englewood Cliffs, N.J.: Prentice Hall, 1964); Marshall W. Stearns, *The Story of Jazz* (New York: Oxford University Press, 1956); James Lincoln Collier, *The Making of Jazz: A Comprehensive History* (New York: Delta, 1978); Grover Sales, *Jazz: America's Classical Music* (New York: Prentice Hall, 1984). Revealing the hybridity articulated by Bhabha, jazz artists often mimic European and African musical traditions.

13. Pleasants, *Serious Music — and All That Jazz*, 33; Alec Wilder, *American Popular Song: The Great Innovators, 1900–1950* (New York: Oxford University Press, 1990); André Previn, interview with Clint Eastwood and Bruce Ricker, Popular Music Archives, Georgia State University, Atlanta, Ga.

14. Charles Reagan Wilson and William Ferris, eds., *Encyclopedia of Southern Culture* (Chapel Hill: University of North Carolina Press, 1989); Charles Reagan Wilson, gen. ed., *The New Encyclopedia of Southern Culture*, vol. 12, *Music* (Chapel Hill: University of North Carolina Press,

2008), 290–91. Both the original encyclopedia and the subsequent series of volumes represent milestones in southern scholarship that deserve praise for documenting the region's distinctive heritage.

15. Gavin James Campbell, *Music and the Making of a New South* (Chapel Hill: University of North Carolina Press, 2004); Steve Goodson, *Highbrows, Hillbillies and Hellfire: Public Entertainment in Atlanta, 1880–1930* (Athens: University of Georgia Press, 2002).

16. Patrick Huber, *Linthead Stomp: The Creation of Country Music in the Piedmont South* (Chapel Hill: University of North Carolina Press, 2008), 91; Jeffrey J. Lange, *Smile when You Call Me a Hillbilly: Country Music's Struggle for Respectability, 1939–1954* (Athens: University of Georgia Press, 2004).

17. Elijah Wald, *Escaping the Delta: Robert Johnson and the Invention of the Blues* (New York: HarperCollins, 2004); see also the fresh analysis in R. A. Lawson, *Jim Crow's Counterculture: The Blues and Black Southerners 1890–1945* (Baton Rouge: Louisiana State University Press, 2010); Peter Townsend, *Pearl Harbor Jazz: Change in Popular Music in the Early 1940s* (Jackson: University Press of Mississippi, 2007). The scholarship of William Ferris explores folk traditions of African Americans that emphasize the links between the sacred and secular worlds. The evidence he assembles in *Give My Poor Heart Ease* documents the South's hybrid culture. Not surprisingly, given the segregation he experienced growing up in Mississippi, Ferris finds the materials reflect a separate black culture. Yet one can read the interviews and see a multiracial southern culture reflective of shared traditions that belie racial distinctiveness. By breaking down the old binaries of black and white, a hybrid heritage emerges as evidenced through religion, diet, leisure activities, and even music. Pete Daniel, *Lost Revolutions: The South in the 1950s* (Chapel Hill: University of North Carolina Press, 2000); Michael T. Bertrand, *Race, Rock, and Elvis* (Urbana: University of Illinois Press, 2000).

18. In addition to jazz musicians, hillbilly, country, bluegrass, blues, and gospel performers moved away from their home region in order to work professionally; see Nolan Porterfield, *Jimmie Rodgers: The Life and Times of America's Blue Yodeler* (Urbana: University of Illinois Press, 1979); Jay Caress, *Hank Williams: Country Music's Tragic King* (New York: Stein & Day, 1979); Thomas Goldsmith, ed., *The Bluegrass Reader* (Urbana: University of Illinois Press, 2004); Michael W. Harris, *The Rise of Gospel Blues: The Music of Thomas Andrew Dorsey in the Urban Church* (New York: Oxford University Press, 1992); Wald, *Escaping the Delta*.

19. Kimball et al., eds., *Complete Lyrics*, 116, 140, 142, 188; see also the Mercer-Manone duet, "The Tailgate Ramble," from the original Capitol recording rereleased on *Mercer Sings Mercer* (Los Angeles: EMI Music Special Markets, 2009).

20. Kimball et al., eds., *Complete Lyrics*, 140. Whiteman quoted in *The Jazz Age*, 42.

21. See the exciting study, Karl Hagstrom Miller, *Segregating Sound: Inventing Folk and Pop Music in the Age of Jim Crow* (Durham, N.C.: Duke University Press, 2010), for a groundbreaking analysis of the recording industry's role in racializing southern music. Arguing against ethnocentrism and the racist binary of power and identity in his essay, "'Race,' Time and the Revision of Modernity," in *The Location of Culture*, 236–56, Bhabha emphasizes liminality through which people interact regardless of race and class. Citing Franz Fanon, Bhabha "rejects the 'belatedness' of the black man because it is only the opposite of the framing of the white man as universal, normative" (237).

22. Samuel Charters, *A Trumpet around the Corner: The Story of New Orleans Jazz* (Jackson: University Press of Mississippi, 2008), 68, 76, 77, 6. Ever conscious of racial and ethnic divisions, Charters identifies in New Orleans three groups responsible for jazz: "the Uptown African Americans, the Downtown Creoles, and the different national groups who were lumped together as 'white,' and who included the children of recent Italian and Sicilian immigrants. Living in in-

tegrated neighborhoods, these black and white musicians listened to and occasionally played with each other even as enforced segregation tried to separate their communities and their jazz styles" (68). He also counters the myths that surround early jazz figures such as the black Buddy Bolden and the white Jack Laine. For an original analysis that takes the regional music to America, see Court Carney, *Cuttin' Up: How Early Jazz Got America's Ear* (Lawrence: University Press of Kansas, 2009).

23. On Turpin, see Charles J. Elmore, *All That Savannah Jazz* (Savannah, Ga.: Savannah State University, 1998). For a creative analysis that considers the lives of these two jazz greats, see Joshua Berrett, *Louis Armstrong and Paul Whiteman: Two Kings of Jazz* (New Haven, Conn.: Yale University Press, 2004).

24. Berrett, *Louis Armstrong and Paul Whiteman*, 1–18; Thomas A. DeLong, *Pops: Paul Whiteman, King of Jazz* (Piscataway, N.J.: New Century, 1983); Jasen, *Tin Pan Alley*, 91–93, 156–58.

25. Max Jones and John Chilton, *Louis: The Louis Armstrong Story* (Boston: Little, Brown, 1971); Berrett, *Louis Armstrong and Paul Whiteman*, 20–36. Oliver died in a row house at Gaston and Montgomery streets according to Julius Hornstein, *Sites and Sounds of Savannah Jazz* (Savannah, Ga.: The Gaston Street Press, 1994), 23.

26. Jeffrey Magee, *The Uncrowned King of Swing: Fletcher Henderson and Big Band Jazz* (New York: Oxford University Press, 2005).

27. Beiderbecke and Trumbauer came from Adrian Rollini's band, while Venuti and Lang came from the Five Pennies, as did fellow Redheads who also joined Whiteman's band, Loring "Red" Nichols on cornet and Irving Milfred "Miff" Mole on trombone. Armstrong's wife, Lillian Hardin — a native of Memphis — on piano, Johnny St. Cyr on banjo, Johnny Dodds on saxophone, and Kid Ory on trombone comprised Louis Armstrong and His Hot Five.

Chapter One. Grounded Southerner

The epigraph is from "Georgia, Georgia" (1966), with words and music by Mercer, having taken inspiration from Stephen Vincent Benet's *John Brown's Body*. See Robert Kimball, Barry Day, Miles Kreuger, and Eric Davis, eds., *The Complete Lyrics of Johnny Mercer* (New York: Alfred A. Knopf, 2009), 332.

1. "Hugh Mercer," in *Dictionary of National Biography*, ed. Sidney Lee (New York: Macmillan, 1909), 13:264–65; See Mary Stuart Mercer Walker, "General Hugh Mercer" (sketch), 1910, box 4, folder 16, and Mercer genealogy in collection 553, Mercer Family Papers, GHS), Savannah, Georgia. The reformer John Row ranked among Mercer's forebears in seventeenth-century Scotland. It appears that a family member, perhaps G. A. Mercer, donated the letters of Hugh Weedon Mercer and George Anderson Mercer to the GHS in 1928; probably Hugh Mercer donated more materials in 1952; and Johnny Mercer added copies of his grandfather's diaries between 1961 and 1965.

2. The several biographies include Frederick English, *General Hugh Mercer, Forgotten Hero of the American Revolution* (Lawrenceville, N.J.: Princeton Academic Press, 1975); John T. Goolrick, *The Life of General Hugh Mercer* (New York: Neale Publishing, 1906); and Joseph M. Waterman, *With Sword and Lancet* (Richmond, Va.: Garrett & Massie, 1941). The motto on the family crest reads "crux Christi nostra corona" (Christ's cross is our crown). Military correspondence regarding Hugh Mercer's role in the French and Indian War can be found in the J. A. Maxwell and Hugh Mercer Collections, Chicago Historical Society, and at the Library of Congress, Washington, D.C. On the Scottish diaspora, see Celeste Ray, *Highland Heritage: Scottish Americans in the American South* (Chapel Hill: University of North Carolina Press, 2001).

3. David Hackett Fischer, *Washington's Crossing* (New York: Oxford University Press, 2004),

recounts General Mercer's role in the Revolutionary War and quotes him responding to the British demand "Call for Quarters, you damned rebel" with "I am no rebel" and attacking the redcoats with his sword (332–33). A popular hit in 1934, the song includes the lines: "All at once his horse got skittish; / Here come the British / Bang! Bang!" See Robert Kimball, Barry Day, Miles Kreuger, and Eric Davis, eds., *The Complete Lyrics of Johnny Mercer* (New York: Alfred A. Knopf, 2009), 26. The June 1958 *Metropolitan Museum of Art Bulletin* argues that son John stood as John Trumbull's study for the general in his famous painting, *Battle of Princeton*. On the Daughters of the American Revolution, see *Trenton (N.J.) Sunday Times-Advertiser*, December 2, 1962; see the November 9, 1964, schedule of the service in Christ Church, Philadelphia, box 4, folder 17, and in folder 16, the letters of John Herndon Mercer (hereafter JHM) to John Melville Jennings, president of the Virginia Historical Society, January 23, 1958, and John F. Barrett to JHM, January 31, 1958, all in collection 553, Mercer Family Papers, GHS.

4. See *Journal of the House of Representatives of the United States at the Second Session*. The portrait of Mary Queen of Scots is in the possession of Johnny's niece, Nancy Mercer Keith Gerard, in Savannah. Lady Christina Stuart, the daughter of John Stuart, Earl of Traquair, Scotland, is buried in Burton Parish Churchyard, Williamsburg. See John Insley Coddington, "Ancestors and Descendants of Lady Christina Stuart," *National Genealogical Society Quarterly*, as well as materials on Cyrus Griffin in box 4, folder 12, collection 553, Mercer Family Papers, GHS. Colonel Hugh Tenant Weedon Mercer and Louisa Griffin had five children (Hugh Weedon Mercer, George Weedon Mercer, Julia Weedon Mercer, John Cyrus Mercer, and Louisa Mercer). Benson J. Lossing, ed., *American Historical Record* 3, no. 35 (November 1874): 483–85. "Christmas Day in '76," *Richmond (Va.) Standard*, April 17, 1880, reports the Mercer family tradition of modesty by including the comment by H. T. W. Mercer that "I dislike everything savoring of any display or ostentation on any occasion, especially in matters relating to my own family." He contributed to the founding of the Virginia Theological Seminary of the Protestant Episcopal Church in Alexandria.

5. See the seminal study by Bertram Wyatt-Brown, *Southern Honor: Ethics and Behavior in the Old South*, 25th ann. ed. (New York: Oxford University Press, 2007), which draws distinctions between "primal honor" and "gentility" while explaining how the two coexisted in the South. Bound by the concepts of primal honor, the Mercers also displayed the characteristics of gentility. In Stephen W. Berry II, *All That Makes a Man: Love and Ambition in the Civil War South* (New York: Oxford University Press, 2003), a critique is offered, for he suggests that rather than a code, honor should be seen as a "spirit of éclat" because "all Southerners had to determine what the word meant to them, and they did so with considerable variety and finesse" (20–22). Generations of Mercers followed a similar code of honor as expressed by the Percys and documented in Bertram Wyatt-Brown, *The House of Percy: Honor, Melancholy, and Imagination in a Southern Family* (New York: Oxford University Press, 1994). George W. Cullum, *Biographical Register of the Officers and Graduates of the U.S. Military Academy at West Point, N.Y., from Its Establishment, March 16, 1802 to the Army Re-Organization of 1866–67* (New York: D. Van Nostrand, 1868), 325–38; Hugh Mercer to Sir (Secretary of War John C. Calhoun), December 14, 1821, Mercer to Dear Sir (President James Monroe), June 21, 1822, with the notation "it being amongst my first wishes, to give my sons the best education in my power & to rear them before the altar of their country," Mercer to Calhoun, December 13, 1822, all in the National Archives of the United States. *Register of the Officers and Cadets of the U.S. Military Academy*, June 1827, 8.

6. Mary took a fancy to Robert E. Lee and the two remained friends, with Lee writing Hugh a touching note of condolence after Mary died. The Mercers named a son after him, Robert Lee Mercer, who never married. Mary Stuart Mercer married Henry Harrison Walker of Virginia and Georgia Anderson Mercer married Robert Apthorp Boit of Boston; on Mercer's friendship

with "Bob Lee," the "colonel," and the namesake of their son, see Hugh Weedon Mercer (hereafter HWM) to Mary Stites Anderson Mercer (hereafter MSAM), March 20, 1849, box 3, folder 1, collection 553, Mercer Family Papers, GHS; on Mary Stites Anderson and the kinship ties to the Gordons, Andersons, Steenbergens, and Cuylers, see the Hartridge collection 1349, GHS. Justice Wayne built the house later owned by the Gordon family and today operated as a house museum by the Girl Scouts of America. Juliette Gordon Low lived there as a child and then as an adult after she returned to Savannah, again living in the city of her birth from 1912 to 1927. Genealogical Committee, Marriages of Chatham County, Georgia, vol. 1, 1748–1852 (Savannah: Georgia Historical Society, 1993), 161; State of Georgia Military Records, 1829–1841, 88, microfilm, Georgia Department of Archives and History, Morrow, Ga. The Old Castle just off Bull Street on the third lot of Tyrconnel Tything in Derby Ward had a series of house numbers over the century, beginning with 93 Congress Street, then 113 Congress Street when Kaufmen's Restaurant stood next to it, and finally 107 East Congress Street before it was bulldozed. The 1866 *City Directory* listed it as the third house west of Drayton. The Savannah Cadastral Survey of 1937 showed a four-story brick structure with a hip roof stretching 121 feet across the front and 40 feet deep with a back porch; by that time the slave and carriage houses and other outbuildings had been removed. A photograph located in Scrapbook 1, collection VM2126, GHS, shows Christ Church in the foreground and the house in the background. For years there has been nothing on the site but a parking lot. See also the invaluable Mary L. Morrison, ed., *Historic Savannah* (Savannah, Ga.: Historic Savannah Foundation 1979), 27–31. The family retained ownership of the property until 1892.

7. On the Herndon genealogy, see John M. Herndon to Hugh Mercer, January 27, 1949, and related materials in box 4, folder 10, collection 553, Mercer Family Papers, GHS, and in box 127, folder 2318, Hartridge collection 1349, GHS; Lucy Lee Pierson Welsh and Pattie Cooke, *The Gordons of Scotland and Kenmore* (n.p., 2004), 15, 51–57; John T. Goolrick, *Old Homes and History around Fredericksburg* (Richmond, Va.: Garrett & Massie, 1929).

8. A landmark study of the city that exposes the divisions of class, race, and gender in a detailed narrative that demonstrates how the elite tenaciously held on to power is Jacqueline Jones, *Saving Savannah: The City and the Civil War* (New York: Alfred A. Knopf, 2008). On Mary's travels to New Haven, see HWM to MSAM, December 1, 1848, June 23, 1849, and October 9, 1851, box 3, folder 1, collection 553, Mercer Family Papers, GHS. Edward J. Cashin, *Beloved Bethesda: A History of George Whitefield's Home for Boys, 1740–2000* (Macon, Ga.: Mercer University Press, 2001). *Minutes of the Union Society: Being an Abstract of Existing Records from 1750 to 1858* (Savannah, Ga.: John M. Cooper, 1860), 13. *Proceedings of the 149th Anniversary of the Union Society* (Savannah, Ga.: Morning News Print, 1899), 34; *Proceedings of the Union Society, 1931*, copies at Savannah Public Library. History Revision Committee, *History of St. Andrew's Society, Savannah, Georgia* (n.p., November 1972), 38–39, 44, 100. Although William J. Northen's *Men of Mark in Georgia* (Atlanta, Ga.: A. B. Caldwell, 1912) makes the claim, as does *Savannah Homes and People*, that "he took the law course at the University of Virginia," there is no record of George Anderson Mercer receiving a degree from the institution, although he studied law there, as did his cousin, Edward C. Anderson (grad. 1860); see list of graduates in *Sketch of the History of the University of Virginia, Charlottesville* (n.p., 1880), 28–29. Walter J. Fraser Jr., *Savannah in the Old South* (Athens: University of Georgia Press, 2003), 266–68. The genealogies and papers of the Gordon and Anderson families are at the GHS. George Anderson Gordon married Caroline Steenbergen, whose sister, the young widow Elizabeth "Bessie" Steenbergen Cuyler, took as her second husband General Hugh Weedon Mercer. On the Girl Scouts, see Roger K. Warlick, *As Grain Once Scattered: The History of Christ Church, Savannah, Georgia, 1733–1983* (Columbia, S.C.: State Printing Co., 1987), 142–43; *Savannah Morning News*, November 5, 1937; William

Makepeace Thackeray, letter to Kate Perry, quoted in Patrick Allen, ed., *Literary Savannah* (Athens, GA.: Hill Street Press, 1998), 49.

9. As Hugh Mercer revealed in his letter to his wife, "I wish with all my heart dear wife, I could welcome you to a more stately mansion than the *old castle*—it is indeed an humble dwelling —but if we love each other, can we not be happy even there?" See HWM to MSAM, November 15, 1851, box 3, folder 1, collection 553, Mercer Family Papers, GHS. Wyatt-Brown notes in *Southern Honor* that "property was the key to esteem" because of "the natural association of honor with possessions" (73–74). In 1854, Mary Mercer received six thousand dollars in rents from her half-ownership of the Anderson family wharf lot 4, east of Lincoln Street, with warehouses at 402–10 East Bay Street. The other half of the ownership belonged to her sister, Elizabeth Nicoll, whose son, George Anderson Nicoll, married one of Brodie S. Herndon Sr.'s daughters, Sarah Parker Herndon, from Fredericksburg. Morrison, ed., *Historic Savannah*, 6, 170. Roulhac Toledano, *The National Trust Guide to Savannah* (New York: John Wiley, 1997), 152–54. Architect John S. Norris designed more than two dozen buildings in Savannah, including the 1848 Greek Revival U.S. Custom House, the 1853 Gothic Revival Green-Meldrim House, and the 1860 Italianate Mercer House; similar to the Mercer House, the Italianate Hardee House at 3 West Gordon Street also began in 1860 and remained unfinished until after the war. Other military men who settled in the neighborhood over the century included Joseph Johnston, Henry Rootes Jackson, Lafayette McLaws, and Hugh Comer. Mercer began his house on lots 27 and 28, which combined made the full trust lot, a designation dating back to James Edward Oglethorpe's 1733 design for the city.

10. Adelaide Wilson, *Historic and Picturesque Savannah* (Boston: Boston Photogravure, 1889), 207–10, said of General Mercer that "the soldierly instincts were strong within him; united with them were a chivalrous and dignified courtesy of demeanor, a fund of genial humor, and a ripe scholarship that stamped him a gentleman of the old school in the highest, best acceptation of the term." T. Conn Bryan, *Confederate Georgia* (Athens: University of Georgia Press, 1953), 73, 132–33, 147–48; Fraser, *Savannah in the Old South*, 326–32. HWM to "General" [A. R. Lawton], November 11, 1861; HWM to "My dear Bob" [Robert E. Lee], February 3, 1862; HWM to Captain T. A. Washington, February 16, 1862, all in the Eleanor S. Brockenbrough Library, Museum of the Confederacy, Richmond, Va.

11. Jay Luvaas and Harold W. Nelson, eds., *Guide to the Atlanta Campaign: Rocky Face Ridge to Kennesaw Mountain* (Lawrence: University Press of Kansas, 2008), 1, 43–44, 54. Luvaas and Nelson suggest Johnston's army numbered 64,000, while Bryan finds a force of only 43,000 soldiers; see Bryan's monograph *Confederate Georgia*. Russell K. Brown, *To the Manner Born: The Life of General William H. T. Walker* (Macon, Ga.: Mercer University Press, 2005), 138, 219–50, 260. Preston Russell and Barbara Hines, *Savannah: A History of Her People Since 1733* (Savannah, Ga.: Frederic C. Beil, 1992), 114. Ambitious men used military service to win honor; see Berry, *All That Makes a Man*, 171–73.

12. General Clement A. Evans, *Confederate Military History* (Atlanta, Ga.: Confederate Publishing, 1899), 6:846–47; Charles C. Jones Jr., *The Siege of Savannah in December 1864* (Albany, N.Y.: Joel Munsell, 1874), 85, 113–14, 145–50; Lee Kennett, *Marching through Georgia* (New York: HarperCollins, 1995), 308. Union forces imprisoned General Mercer on murder charges in December 1865, but a military court exonerated him in January 1866. See John H. Eicher and David J. Eicher, *Civil War High Commanders* (Stanford, Calif.: Stanford University Press, 2001), 386; Hermann L. Schreiner, "Gen. Mercer's Grand March" (Macon, Ga.: John C. Schreiner & Son, [1862?]), in the Confederate Imprint collection, Virginia Historical Society, Richmond, Va.; Kimball et al., eds., *Complete Lyrics*, 249.

13. On the problems with the Planter's Bank, see Chatham County deed book 3-X, folio 464–

65, July 10, 1866, Savannah, Ga., and see box 21, folder 509A, and box 22, folder 511, Wayne-Stites-Anderson Papers, collection 846, GHS. On debt and bankruptcy, see Wyatt-Brown, *Southern Honor*, 73–74; for an analysis, see Elizabeth Lee Thompson, *The Reconstruction of Southern Debtors: Bankruptcy after the Civil War* (Athens: University of Georgia Press, 2004). The general sold the mansion to John R. Wilder for fifteen thousand dollars on May 28, 1866; see Chatham County deed book 3-X, folio 353–54; on Jim Williams, see Dorothy Williams Kingery, *More than Mercer House: Savannah's Jim Williams* (Savannah, Ga.: Sheldon Group, 1999), and John Berendt, *Midnight in the Garden of Good and Evil* (New York: Random House, 1994).

14. Lisa Louise Denmark, "At the Midnight Hour: Optimism and Disillusionment in Savannah, 1865–1880," PhD diss., University of South Carolina, 2004. To settle Mary Stites Anderson Mercer's estate, the general surrendered to the children the Old Castle and auctioned off the furniture in 1868; see George Anderson Mercer to "My Dear Sister" [Mary Mercer Walker], November 17, 1868, and H. W. Mercer to "My Dear Daughter" [Mary Mercer Walker], December 1, 1868, collection 553, Mercer Family Papers, GHS; see also the indenture dated January 23, 1869, in Chatham County deed book 4B, folio 429–31. The old general remarried to Bessie, the daughter of John Beale Steenbergen and Mary D. Beirne. She was nearly twenty-five years Mercer's junior and the recent widow of George Anderson Cuyler. They married December 1, 1868, and had a child, Alice Blackford Mercer, whom the Savannah obituary of General Mercer neglects to mention as a survivor (*Savannah Morning News*, June 28, 1877).

15. On the city and the Civil War, see George C. Rable, *Fredericksburg! Fredericksburg!* (Chapel Hill: University of North Carolina Press, 2002). Born in Fredericksburg in 1810, Brodie Strachen Herndon Sr. attended the University of Maryland and returned home in 1843 to practice medicine. During the Civil War, Dr. Herndon served as chief surgeon of hospitals in Richmond while his sons, Brodie Jr., who had married Mary Wallace Gordon of Kenmore and lived in Fredericksburg, and James Carmichael, served in the Army of Northern Virginia as surgeons. After the war, several Herndons relocated to Savannah. In addition to Botts, who died in 1889, three of the Herndons are buried in Bonaventure Cemetery: Brodie Sr. (d. 1886), Lucy (d. 1880), and James, who died while ministering to the sick during a yellow fever epidemic in Fernandina, Florida, in 1877. Dr. Brodie S. Herndon Sr. Diaries, 1847–86, manuscript 2563, University of Virginia, Charlottesville, describes the move to Savannah as well as an 1877 visit to the Blackie Villa, located "on a horseshoe bend of the Lach" outside Glasgow with the observation, "mother and I were entranced." Contemporaries described Robert Blackie, who published art nouveau books and died suddenly in 1896, as "a quiet man of ripe wisdom." His wife, Lucy Herndon, died while in Alexandria, Egypt. His brother, Walter G. Blackie, hired designer Charles Rennie Mackintosh to design the Hill House in 1902. See also Welsh and Cooke, *The Gordons*, 51–57. Stevenson's story published in 1882 pits man's "law of his members warring against the law of his mind," as Jekyll does good and Hyde does evil.

16. On the Baltimore fire that burned the Mercers out of their residence at the corner of Saratoga and Liberty streets, see *Frank Leslie's Illustrated*, August 9, 1873, and the *Baltimore Sun*, July 25, 1973, as well as *Woods' Baltimore City Directory*, 1871. Mercer's death certificate is #108; see *Sterbe-Hauptregister der Stadt, Baden-Baden, Amtgerichts Baden-Baden für das Jahr 1877* (Stadtmuseum/Stadtarchiv, Kuferstrase 3, Baden-Baden); Margaret W. Debolt, "Brigadier General Hugh W. Mercer," *Bonaventure Historical Society Newsletter* 3, no. 2 (November 1996). In 1899, Alice Blackford Mercer married William Henry Ricketts Curtler, later having a son named Hugh Mercer Curtler. Northen, *Men of Mark*, 379–80. Baden-Baden's old Englische Kirche is located at Berthold-Strasse, No. 5. See "Subscriptions for the English Church," kept by the Reverend T. Archibald S. White, who officiated at the general's funeral, also on file at the Kurzführer durch

das Stadtarchiv in Baden-Baden. Clipping of General Hugh W. Mercer's obituary, *Savannah Morning News*, June 28, 1877, located in the George Anderson Mercer Scrapbook, item 6, vol. 6 of box 2, as well as the notes on the Curtler family, collection 553, Mercer Family Papers, GHS. Cemetery records in Baden-Baden show the old grave empty.

17. The George Anderson Mercer family Bible identifies the wedding date and lists the children: Hugh Weedon Mercer (1863–71), Nannie Herndon Mercer (1866–1930), George Anderson Mercer (1868–1940), Lewis Herndon Mercer (1870–1944), Robert Lee Mercer (1871–1957), Edward Clifford Anderson "Ed" or "Ted" Mercer (1873–1943), and Brodie Herndon Mercer (1876–78). All are buried in Savannah. Elite Savannah families retained their interlocking social ties from the antebellum period into the postbellum period. Like their fathers, the sons became close friends, as evident in the 1890 manuscript, "Account of Tramping Trip Taken by W. W. Gordon Jr., R. L. Mercer Jr., George Haskell, and G. A. Gordon through the Mountains of Georgia and North Carolina," collection 318, Gordon Family Papers, GHS. Fraser, *Savannah in the Old South*, 256; Toledano, *National Trust Guide to Savannah*, 171–75. Salvaging the Savannah gray brick, the chiropractor W. R. Griffin demolished George Anderson Mercer's Whitaker Street house in 1963. See the *Savannah Evening Press*, February 14, 1963.

18. The Ogeechee Insurrection, like earlier slave rebellions, demonstrated the ruling class's violent defense of white supremacy; see Jonathan M. Bryant, "'Come Out, You White Sons of Bitches': Constructing the Ogeechee Insurrection by Georgia's Courts, 1868–1870," paper read at the 2002 Southern Historical Association annual meeting. On insurrection and honor, see Wyatt-Brown, *Southern Honor*, 431–34. On Reconstruction Georgia and the effort to restore white supremacy, see Edmund L. Drago, *Black Politicians and Reconstruction in Georgia: A Splendid Failure* (Baton Rouge: Louisiana State University Press, 1982), and on Simms, see Jones, *Saving Savannah*, 389 and passim. For Mercer's legislative activities, see the Georgia Official Records of the General Assembly, microfilm, Georgia Department of Archives and History, Morrow, Ga.; *Savannah News*, October 24, 1907. Frank Wheeler, "'Our Confederate Dead': The Story Behind Savannah's Confederate Monument," *Georgia Historical Quarterly* 82, no. 2 (Summer 1998): 389–90.

19. In the South, the law worked hand in glove with the ideology of honor to regulate society. As a prominent attorney in Savannah, George Anderson Mercer gained esteem through the exercise of power over others; see Wyatt-Brown, *Southern Honor*, 362–64; *Savannah News*, October 24, 1907. After his two terms in the Georgia General Assembly, fellow solons proposed Mercer's name for appointment to the U.S. Congress, but he declined the nomination. Governor William J. Northen convinced Mercer to investigate and help resolve conflicts over the lessees of the State of Georgia Rail Road.

20. *Eleventh Annual Report of the Public Schools of the City of Savannah and County of Chatham for the Year Ending July 16, 1876* (Savannah, Ga.: Morning News Steam Printing House, 1877) and the *Forty-fourth Annual Report of the Public Schools of the City of Savannah and County of Chatham for the Year Ending June 30, 1909* (Savannah, Ga.: Morning News Print, 1910). In 1899, George Anderson Mercer became a trustee of Chatham Academy, a position held by his son, G. A. Mercer, from 1900 to 1932; see *Two Centuries of Educational History in Chatham County* (n.p., n.d.), 129–31, photocopy in the Savannah Schools vertical file, Live Oak Public Library, Bull Street Branch, Savannah, Ga.

21. George Anderson Mercer observed in his will, "my private books have been a source of very great pleasure to me, and it is painful to contemplate their diffusion among strangers." His executor had the library appraised at three thousand dollars and the will specified the children could select six books each with the rest to be sold. At the sale, three of his children, Nannie M. Lang, R. L. Mercer Jr., and G. A. Mercer Jr., bought many of the titles, with most of the rest going to

S. F. Freeman & Company; see his last will, July 8, 1885, and the return on his estate, June 30, 1908, Chatham County Courthouse, Savannah, Ga. *Seventy-fifth Anniversary Report of the Georgia Historical Society* (Savannah, Ga.: Morning News, 1914), 70–73, 103, 104, 107; *Report of the Committee on the Telfair Academy of Arts and Sciences to the Georgia Historical Society, January 2, 1893* (Savannah, Ga.: Morning News Print, 1893); *Savannah News*, October 24, 1907. Diaries kept by George Anderson Mercer from 1851 to 1907 are in the Southern History Collection, University of North Carolina, Chapel Hill, with copies in collection, 553, Mercer Family Papers, GHS.

22. Northen, *Men of Mark in Georgia*; *Proceedings of the 149th Anniversary of the Union Society at Bethesda, Georgia Held on Tuesday, April 25, 1899* (Savannah, Ga.: Morning News Print, 1899), 34. *History of the St. Andrew's Society of the City of Savannah* (Savannah, Ga.: Kennickell, 1950) lists J. M. Lang joining in 1885, G. A. Mercer Jr. joining in 1926, and his sons, Hugh Mercer and G. Walter Mercer, joining in 1926 and 1940 respectively. The 1972 limited edition reprint shows John H. Mercer joining in 1958; *Constitution and By-Laws, Officers and Members of the Oglethorpe Club* (Savannah, Ga., 1909) cites J. M. Lang joining in 1896 and G. A. Mercer joining in 1900 (36). See also Malcolm Bell Jr., *The Oglethorpe Club: The First One Hundred Years* (Savannah, Ga.: n.p., 1970), 7–8, 12. Margaret Stiles and Emma Hamilton Bulloch, *[Savannah] Social Directory 1904*, 2nd ed. (New York: Watkins Press, 1904), cite bachelor Robert Lee Mercer living with his brother, George Anderson Mercer, at 817 Whitaker Street (48).

23. Also outside Savannah during the war, the Confederacy manned Fort Mercer located near Bonaventure Cemetery and staffed Camp Mercer for training purposes. On Savannah families at northern resorts, see Fraser, *Savannah in the Old South*, 266; on White Bluff, see F. D. Lee and J. L. Agnew, *Historical Record of the City of Savannah* (Savannah, Ga.: Morning News Steam-Power Press, 1869), 199–200. A reflection of that shared culture is Charles Colcock Jones Jr., *Gullah Folktales from the Georgia Coast* (Athens: University of Georgia Press, 2000). While his book was originally published in 1888 as *Negro Myths from the Georgia Coast*, Jones wrote down the stories ostensibly related by former slaves in the Gullah-Geechee dialect he learned as a white child growing up on a rice plantation owned by his father, the noted theologian Reverend Dr. Charles Colcock Jones Sr. W. G. Sutlive, "Savannah Yacht Club," *Outing*, February 1899. Other members were the Andersons, Stoddards, Screvens, Joneses, McIntires, and Charltons. The regatta followed a course on the Vernon River from Montgomery to Green Island Sound and back. *Constitution, By-Laws and Sailing Regulations of the Savannah Yacht Club* (Savannah, Ga.: n.p., 1905), 6. See also George Noble Jones, "The Vernon River in the Gay Nineties" (1959), and the history, *Savannah Yacht and Country Club 1869–1966, Bradley Point, Savannah, Georgia*, which lists George Mercer III as a member. Both in Savannah Club vertical file, Live Oak Public Library.

24. Father-son relations kept the patriarchal system intact as Wyatt-Brown explains in *Southern Honor*, 22, 195–98. Mercer wielded his authority by bending the wills of his sons to his wishes. George Anderson Mercer ["Father"] to G. A. Mercer ["My dear boy"], September 12, 1884 (hereafter GAM Sr. to GAM Jr.), box 1, folder 2, collection M002, JM & GM Papers, GSU.

25. GAM Sr. to GAM Jr., September 12, 1884. George Anderson Mercer viewed reasoned self-discipline as the key to the struggle over one's passions. Opposed to masturbation but recognizing the youth's unlikelihood of maintaining celibacy, he recommended in typical southern fashion that when sexual desire grew too strong, "intercourse with a woman, wicked and forbidden though it be, is more decent." Then he added, "if you are ever so unfortunate as to contract venereal disease go at once to the best physician you can reach." In the South, Wyatt-Brown notes, "sexual intercourse was viewed as a natural biological function. For reasons of health, it was simply thought good policy for men to have a reasonably active sex life within marriage or, if necessary outside it. 'Wenching' (as occasion permitted) or having a mistress was strictly a private matter. Illicit male heterosexual activity involved notions of guilt and shame only when it affected reputa-

tion or when it resulted in personal complications or illness." See *Southern Honor*, 309; see also his explanation of shame and how, through "a congruence of social and personal perceptions," it maintained honor or resulted in dishonor (155). Mercer concluded the letter to his son with an image of shame. "When you are tempted to do wrong, think of your dear mother, of her pure love, imagine she sees you and ask yourself what she will think." On the beliefs of Victorians, see Daniel Joseph Singal, *The War Within: From Victorian to Modernist Thought in the South, 1919–1945* (Chapel Hill: University of North Carolina Press, 1982), 4–10 and passim.

26. William C. McDonald, "The True Gentleman: On Robert E. Lee's Definition of the Gentleman," *Civil War History* 32, no. 2 (June 1986): 119–38. On Lee, see Wyatt-Brown, *Southern Honor*, 105–11, who also quoted Lee as writing to his son, Custis, in 1851, "Hold yourself above every mean action. Be strictly honorable in every act, and be not ashamed to do right" (107), themes echoed in Mercer's 1907 obituary.

27. E. C. Mercer, *A Twentieth Century Miracle* (New York: Ferris, 1928), 44. In *Southern Honor*, Wyatt-Brown recognized the importance of maintaining reputation in society: "the internal and external aspects of honor are inalienably connected because honor serves as ethical mediator between the individual and the community by which he is assessed and in which he also must locate himself in relation to others" (14). On the difficulties of living an honorable life, see ibid., 155–56. Johnny quote from the autobiography, box 1, collection MO01, JM Papers, GSU. Savannah held the distinction of being the first city to observe as an annual celebration Robert E. Lee's birthday. As family business partner and friend, Nick Mamalakis observed that all the Mercers lived according to the code of honor; see Nick Mamalakis, oral interview MO34, and William "Bill" Harbach, oral interview M130, both in Popular Music Archives, Georgia State University, Atlanta, Ga.; Kimball et al., eds., *Complete Lyrics*, 138, quote the lines cited here as sung by Fred Astaire in the 1943 film *The Sky's the Limit* as well as the alternate lines used when a woman sings the song: "Could tell you a lot, / But you've got to be true to your code."

28. *The Pandora*, vol. 2 (Augusta, Ga.: Chronicle Book and Publishing, 1887), 67; *The Pandora*, vol. 3 (Augusta, Ga.: Chronicle Book and Publishing, 1888), 24, 65. The men located the two businesses at 124 East Bay Street.

29. Mercer, *Twentieth Century Miracle*. Ed believed "parents should be Christian chums and comrades of their children and tie their boys and girls from infancy to God's Church, and should themselves be loyal to the Church as an example not only to their own, but to all the boys and girls in the community" (19). On honor, he added about his genealogy, the "family background is not mentioned in any spirit of boast or braggadocio but simply to prove the aforestated statement that my refined and cultured and privileged breeding was no guarantee whatsoever for a circumspect moral life, for I went to the very dogs in spite of this splendid heritage and found 'sin no respecter of persons'" (18).

30. Ibid., 24–29. University of Virginia, *Corks and Curls* (1891–92), 26, 118. Wyatt-Brown discusses the links between concepts of honor and excessive drinking, noting that alcohol abuse promoted expressions of masculinity that men respected (*Southern Honor*, 278–80).

31. Mercer, *Twentieth Century Miracle*, 30–37. Wyatt-Brown, *Southern Honor*, explains, "the debt of honor, the gambling debt, was a figurative death; it had to be paid, just as one sacrificed life in battle, heedless of result" (41); he notes that "money in the context of the game or sport served as a means to ratify obligation and deference, not to terminate them, no matter how cheerily the winnings jangled in the pockets of the bettor. The point of play was the distribution of honor and status" (340); see also 339–50. As a 1902 codicil to George Anderson Mercer's will made clear, he gave Ed $5,200 to pay off any debts and begin life over with the stipulation that the amount plus 6 percent interest would be deducted from his estate, and when the final disbursements were made in 1910 an amount of $5,992.30 was subtracted from Ed's share. Yet in support of his conversion,

his brothers and sister donated part of their inheritance so that he might pay off his remaining debts and buy a house in suburban New York. A maternal uncle, Thomas Savage Clay, was the husband of Mollie Herndon Clay, whose sister, Ann Maury Herndon "Nannie" Mercer, was Ed's mother. A devout member of the Fifth Avenue Presbyterian Church, Clay engineered Ed's salvation by surreptitiously introducing him to the mission and then encouraging the conversion through an observation that shamed Ed as explained in the memoir: "He said my dear mother was in Heaven praying for me and that my sinful life was breaking her heart" (37).

32. Mercer, *Twentieth Century Miracle*, 46–47. In 1902, George Anderson Mercer had written to Clay about Ed: "he hoped never again to see my face, and that if I ever took another drink of intoxicating liquor he prayed that it would silence my lips forever." A year after the conversion, news reached George Anderson Mercer of the transformation and he hastened to New York, where in the lobby of the Fifth Avenue Hotel the two were reconciled. Once back in Savannah, the father prepared a news release, writing, "Will the reader attempt to realize the emotions aroused in the breast of a loving parent when in the midst of that goodly company of the reclaimed and redeemed and rescued through its noble ministrations, was seen his own prodigal son, his youngest, who had been almost hopelessly abandoned to the sad company of the loved and lost, in his right mind, with his head erect and clad in the garments of righteousness, and proudly returning to the house of his fathers, crowned with lilies, singing joyous and triumphant song, and bringing with him his fruiting sheaves." In his memoir Ed remembered about his father, "just prior to his death, he wrote me a beautiful letter and told me that my redeemed life had been very helpful to him, and that he desired me to continue my Christian service among young men." In 1905, Ed reunited with his wife, Josephine Peyton Freeland, who also underwent a conversion experience. After the death of an infant girl, they adopted a son, Robert Taylor Mercer, and lived in Flushing, Long Island, and then Salisbury, Connecticut.

33. Ed Mercer's associates included Dr. Henry Sloan Coffin of the Union Theological Seminary, Dr. Ernest M. Stires of St. Thomas Episcopal Church before he became the bishop of New York, and Dr. J. Ross Stevenson of Fifth Avenue Presbyterian Church before he took over Princeton Theological Seminary (Mercer, *Twentieth Century Miracle*, 70–73). Ed might have intervened with Bishop Stires to allow his nephew, Johnny Mercer, and Ginger Meltzer to marry at St. Thomas. *Savannah News*, October 24, 1907.

34. The last will and testament of George Anderson Mercer and the various codicils, all filed together in the Chatham County Courthouse, Savannah, Georgia, stipulated various bequests. He not only paternalistically asked that his children take care of Anna Taliaferro (pronounced in the southern fashion as *Toliver*), but that she be allowed to live with one of them and, if not, that five thousand dollars for her be invested in securities to draw at least twenty dollars monthly for her support. He arranged for the care of his brother, Robert Lee, who lived with him at 817 Whitaker Street and would remain in the house until shortly before his own death on August 29, 1909. To settle the estate, the family sold the house in June 1909 for $14,000 to Ellen McAlpin. The executor sold other properties including — for $3,600 — the wharf lots 4, 5, and west half of 6 east of Lincoln on Bay Street that his mother, Mary Stites Anderson Mercer, had inherited from her father. Family members divided the household goods as specified in the will. The executor placed a final value on the estate of $52,500. *Savannah News*, October 24, 1907.

35. Genealogy notes, collection 553, Mercer Family Papers, GHS. Mary Walter Mercer left an estate valued at eighteen thousand dollars of rental houses on Duffy, Roberts, and Huntington streets and bank stock that together generated two thousand dollars a year to her three sons; see the 1903 Annual Return and the June 13, 1902, Petition of G. A. Mercer Jr., Court of Ordinary, Chatham County, Savannah, Ga. In the 1950s, the Pape School became the Savannah Country Day School. See Paul Presley, "Educating the Daughters of Savannah's Elite: The Pape School, the

Girl Scouts, and the Progressive Movement," *Georgia Historical Quarterly* 80, no. 2 (1996). The architect John S. Norris designed the Massie School in 1856 with wings attached in 1872 and 1886.

36. George Anderson Mercer, Codicils to his Last Will and Testament, July 5, 1901, and July 10, 1902, Chatham County Courthouse, Savannah, Ga. Wyatt-Brown, *Southern Honor*, explains the code: "a gambling debt is a debt of honor, but a debt due a tradesman is not" (345), reflecting the patrician view that honor required deference from people in sales, thereby forcing them into a dependent relationship on others. Hierarchy required that the weak be manipulated. See also Wyatt-Brown's discussion regarding the power of fathers over sons (195–97).

37. The firm stenographer Lillian Ciucevich appears as a witness on the 1902 codicils to the will. The city lowered its flags to half mast and local judges suspended court in honor of the citizen; see *Savannah News*, October 24, 1907; clipping with comment located in box 2, item 6, vol. 6, George Anderson Mercer Scrapbooks, 58–60, GHS. The family delayed the funeral at Christ Church with burial at Bonaventure Cemetery until son Lewis H. Mercer could arrive from New York. After dividing up the colonel's personal property, the heirs placed a value of twenty-five thousand dollars on his rental property that, following the failure of a sale on the courthouse steps in 1910, they divided among themselves in an attempt to settle his estate. See Chatham County deed book 10F, folio 354.

38. To reach the plot in section F, lot 18, visitors to Bonaventure Cemetery may enter the main gate and pass the office traveling down Bonaventure Way, veering to the right on Noble Jones Drive and then to the left on Johnny Mercer Way down to section F and the George Anderson Mercer lot 18. Prior to Bonaventure's opening in 1868, Mercer family members received burial in Laurel Grove Cemetery lots 504 and 506 adjacent to the George Anderson family plot, lot 505. Laurel Grove records suggest Mary Stites Anderson Mercer is buried in lot 686, but that plot is occupied by Confederate officers Colonel Randolph Spalding and Major Joseph L. Locke, and her marker is in lot 504, most likely the actual burial place although this is not in the city records. Yet city records do show the two young sons, Brodie Herndon Mercer and Hugh W. Mercer Jr., as being exhumed from Laurel Grove and reinterred in Bonaventure on February 27, 1879. While it is believed the general's remains were removed from Baden-Baden and reinterred in Savannah, the standard military marker located in the corner of the Herndon plot, section F, lot 19, in Bonaventure signifying a grave for General Hugh Weedon Mercer was not enumerated in the 1938 *Bonaventure Cemetery General Index to Keeper's Record Books* compiled by the Workers of the WPA as Official Project No. 465-34-3-148-1937 and appears to have been added later. Edward C. Anderson Mercer died in 1943 and lies beside Josephine P. Freeland in her family's lot 116 in Laurel Grove. See *Laurel Grove Cemetery, Savannah, Georgia*, vol. 1, *October 12, 1852–November 30, 1861* (Savannah: Georgia Historical Society, 1993), 243. The first family burial in Bonaventure appears to be the December 1880 internment of Lucy H. Herndon followed by the relocation of the remains of her son, Dr. James Carmichael Herndon, from Fernandina, Florida, where he had died fighting the 1877 yellow fever epidemic.

39. G. A. Mercer to Lillian Ciucevich, 1904, and Nannie Mercer Lang to Lillian Ciucevich, November 25, 1906, Mercer Family Collection, AASU. In a quiet ceremony attended by only a handful of guests, the Reverend Francis A. Brown officiated at the marriage of G. A. Mercer to Lillian Barbara Ciucevich in Christ Church on December 8, 1906. In his July 25, 1903, petition to the Court of Ordinary, Chatham County, Savannah, Georgia, G. A. Mercer asked permission to use the proceeds from the estate of Mary Ellis Walter, which he held in trust for their three sons as guardian, "for the maintenance, education and support of said minors with her full knowledge and consent, noting that the petitioner does not earn enough to support said minors in the manner and style in which they have been accustomed to live without the use of said income." As guardian he kept a careful record of the revenues generated by the estate and the expenditures to

keep the three boys at Woodberry Forest School, not surrendering the corpus of the estate to the boys until Hugh had reached the age of twenty-one.

40. The initial birth certificate identified an unnamed white male baby born in Telfair Hospital on November 15, 1909, to "Geo. A. Mercer Jr." and Lillian Mercer and listed the attending family doctor. However, an affidavit filed by Harriet C. [Ciucevich] Clinton and dated June 1, 1942, claimed the original birth certificate had no place for names and that the doctor made a mistake on the birth date, hence the identity of the baby was John Herndon Mercer and the actual birth date was November 18, 1909. Lillian Ciucevich and G. A. Mercer had two other children, Nancy (b. July 11, 1911, d. May 11, 1914) and Juliana (b. August 1, 1915, d. October 8, 2000), who married Henry Gilbert Keith and had one child, Nancy Mercer Keith (Gerard) (b. December 24, 1940, d. May 10, 2013), before divorcing her husband.

41. Katherine Ciucevich O'Leary, "Memories of My Parents," February 1978, copy in author's possession; letter of Francis P. Ciucevich, February 6, 2002, author's possession.

42. U.S. Census 1870, Charleston, S.C. O'Leary, "Memories of My Parents," gives Julia Ann Merritt's birthday as May 1, 1856, in Charlotte, North Carolina. The Charleston city directory lists an H. C. Merritt living in Charleston, 1869–70, while working as the route agent for the Savannah & Charleston (later the Charleston & Savannah) Railroad. The Ciucevich oral histories identify several other Merritt family members living in Charleston such as Julia's sister, Aunt Lenora Merritt Redman, and a former slave named Rachel who would later live with Julia at Five Mile Bend and then in Savannah. The December 6, 1991, oral history of Ann Clinton Staley, the daughter of Harriet Ciucevich Clinton, claimed that Julia's father disowned his daughter when she married the Roman Catholic Austrian and that Julia's mother later lived and died in Charleston. See cathedral records, Office of the Chancery, archives, Roman Catholic Diocese of Charleston, S.C., April 30, 1870, and May 1, 1870. As the great fire of 1861 destroyed the Cathedral of St. John and St. Finbar, the church used a Pro-Cathedral until the dedication of the new building in 1907; see also parish records, Catholic Pastoral Center Diocesan Archives, Roman Catholic Diocese of Savannah, Ga.

43. Chatham County deed book 4-v, folio 52–54, April 3, 1878; Chatham County deed book 7-D, folio 267–68, January 17, 1882; Chatham County deed book 5-C, folio 364, February 7, 1882. On the liquor license, see *Savannah Morning News*, July 15, 1880, and for a conflict between Sarah Ciucevich and the railroad over right-of-way, see *Savannah Morning News*, July 24, 1890. Kimball et al., eds., *Complete Lyrics*, 117.

44. Funeral register of the [Savannah, Ga.] Catholic Church, no. 2520, August 2, 1880, Jno. Francis Ciucevich, age four years, seven months, and no. 2550, October 19, 1880, Antoni Ciucevich, age eight days, both buried in section M, lot 9, cathedral cemetery. When illness threatened the Ciucevich family in 1886, the parents arranged for the Reverend Thomas O'Hara to baptize all the children on June 29. The Roland attack was covered in the *Savannah Morning News*, September 23, October 9, 1888, March 5, 1895. The press also identified him as Dominicia "Mannago" Carish, and family lore says he convinced Julia to call her daughter Lillian because the babe's skin seemed as lovely as a lily.

45. Chatham County deed book A-7, folio 413–14, November 4, 1891. Mills Lane IV later photographed the house before its demolition and a picture of it appears in box 9, folder 4, of the photograph collection 1361, GHS. Estate of Frank Ciucevich, April 1, 1895, Court of Ordinary, Chatham County, Savannah, Ga. Will of Sarah Ciucevich, September 24, 1910, and witnessed by G. A. and Lillian Mercer and Damenco "Manigo" Carcich, Chatham County deed book, 9N, folio 371, July 30, 1907.

46. The city directory in 1902 shows widow Ciucevich living at 909 Jefferson near Bolton Street on the west side of Forsyth Park; her son, Frank, is identified as a farmer. John Ciucevich's January 6, 1899, will, Court of Ordinary, Chatham County, Savannah, Ga. Catholic Diocese of

Savannah records on the Ciucevich family. Cathedral cemetery records give John's death occurring on January 6, 1899, with burial in section O, lot 20. O'Leary, "Memories of My Parents." Photographs of the imposing Romanesque St. Patrick's Church, later demolished after suffering extensive damage during the 1941 hurricane, and the school located at Montgomery and West York streets, which the Chatham County Board of Education managed for a few years before destroying it for the new county courthouse and jail, can be found in Luciana M. Spracher, *Lost Savannah: Photographs from the Collection of the Georgia Historical Society* (Charleston, S.C.: Arcadia, 2002), 59, 63. Willie Jackson cut the storekeeper's throat claiming self-defense, but authorities charged him with murder and armed robbery; see *Savannah Morning News*, August 9, 1914. The Ciuceviches buried Manigo in their family plot at the cathedral cemetery.

47. J. H. Haslam, M. J. Kavannaugh, and R. M. Beytagh to Julia Ciucevich, Chatham County deed book 9T, folio 224–25, October 16, 1908. Morrison, ed., *Historic Savannah*, 138, with photograph number 23.17 on 139. *Savannah Morning News*, April 27, 1929.

48. On Julia Ciucevich creating the trust, see Chatham County deed book 10-D, folio 332–33, February 8, 1910, and folio 456–67, February 25, 1910. Annual Return of G. A. Mercer, Guardian, July 1, 1911, Court of Ordinary, Chatham County, Savannah, Ga. ACME Plumbing kept a shop on the corner of Lincoln and Liberty streets. Frank joined Charles Lamon in purchasing five six-pocket pool tables from the Wagner and Adler Company with cues, balls, and racks, twenty chairs, and assorted barware with which to open the Palace Pool Room in rented space at 335 West Broad Street; see Chatham County deed book 10-3, folio 153–55, February 28, 1910. On prohibition, see John Dittmer, *Black Georgia in the Progressive Era, 1900–1920* (Urbana: University of Illinois Press, 1977), 112–13. On Tybee, see Robert A. Ciucevich, *Tybee Island: The Long Branch of the South* (Charleston, S.C.: Arcadia, 2005), 83, where there is a reproduction of the *Savannah Morning News* May 27, 1916, advertisement of F. J. Ciucevich's Ocean View Hotel.

49. *Savannah City Directories*, 1908–30; O'Leary, "Memories of My Parents."

50. Chatham County deed book 9T, folio 224–25, October 16, 1908. Most of the Ciuceviches remained in Savannah, including Harriet, who married A. V. Clinton in 1918, and Kate (Katherine), who married J. A. O'Leary in 1924. The oldest and youngest sisters moved away, however: having married Ignatius J. Cortina, Mary moved to Tampa, Florida; and, having married F. C. Blowe, Nora moved to Asheville, North Carolina. In 1936, Eddie's son, Johnnie Ciucevich, married Mary Collins and lived on Tybee, where he was joined by the families of Aunt Kate O'Leary and sister Juliana Paige. When in Savannah, Johnny Mercer regularly visited these Ciucevich kinfolk on the island.

Chapter Two. Early Years

The epigraph is from "When the World Was Young (Ah, the Apple Trees)" (1951), with music by M. Philippe-Gerard and original French lyrics by Angele Vannier as the song "Le Chevalier de Paris (Les Pommiers Doux)." See Robert Kimball, Barry Day, Miles Kreuger, and Eric Davis, eds., *The Complete Lyrics of Johnny Mercer* (New York: Alfred A. Knopf, 2009), 196.

1. JM autobiography, box 1, and JM, undated notes on DeSoto Hilton letterhead in box 1, file 14, collection MOOI, JM Papers, GSU.

2. Unidentified newspaper clipping in box 33, file 2, and JM autobiography, box 1, JM Papers, GSU. Henry Kane, *How to Write a Song (as Told to Henry Kane)* (New York: Macmillan, 1962), 76. Not being able to play the piano added to Mercer's mystique as a songwriter, so when asked he might explain as he did in 1963 when talking to Ken Barnard of the *Detroit Free Press*, "Once in a while I fake it for a TV show," adding, "sometimes I do write tunes and pick out the number

with one finger for a musician to write down." Or as the *Savannah Morning News* quoted him in May 24, 1959, "I am not a musician, not being able to play any instrument." He repeated this to jazz pianist Milton Raskin, who noted about Johnny, "He plays no instrument and neither reads nor writes music, but he can with one finger, plunk out a melody for himself on the piano." Raskin then explains Mercer's system, suggesting he could read music because he wrote down the letter of the note with arrows pointing up or down the scale while mentally retaining the rhythm. See *The Newporter* (Newport Beach, Calif.) November 26, 1955.

3. Charles Wesley authored such hymns as "O for a Thousand Tongues to Sing," "Love Divine," and "Jesus Christ Is Ris'n Today," while Lowell Mason wrote or arranged tunes for such hymns as "Blest Be the Tie That Binds" and "Joy to the World!" Since 1906, a vested boys' choir had joined eight men in stalls in the east chancel. Johnny sang with it regularly from 1915 until his departure for Virginia in 1922. Roger K. Warlick, *As Grain Once Scattered: The History of Christ Church Savannah, Georgia, 1733–1983* (Columbia, S.C.: State Printing Co., 1987), 127. One of the Protestant Episcopal Church's great hymnologists, the Reverend F. Bland Tucker, served as rector of Christ Church from 1945 to 1967 and died in Savannah in 1984. He officiated at numerous Mercer family ceremonies. On the links between Jewish music and American popular song, see David Lehman, *A Fine Romance: Jewish Songwriters, American Songs* (New York: Random House, 2009), 86. Lehman said of their music that "it's magic: In my mind the names Mercer and Arlen merge until what is left is Merlin." The two men had grown up surrounded by liturgical music.

4. During Mercer's youth, the Reverend John Durham Wing led the church. Johnny probably participated in the numerous pageants performed at Christ Church in the 1910s, from the Easter and Christmas plays to the Feast of Lights. In the 1920s, a youth group called the Merry Makers performed minstrel shows at the church. Warlick, *As Grain Once Scattered*, 140–42. The instrumental by trumpeter Ziggie Elman called the "Fraelich in Swing" provided the tune for Mercer's 1939 lyrics titled "And the Angels Sing," suggesting the merger of the two ancient Jewish and Anglican traditions. Robert Kimball, Barry Day, Miles Kreuger, and Eric Davis, eds., *The Complete Lyrics of Johnny Mercer* (New York: Alfred A. Knopf, 2009), 83, 124–26, 144. Many other examples of angels and biblical references exist in Mercer's lyrics.

5. Oral interview with Amanda Mercer Neder, January 27, 2010, author's possession; William "Bill" Harbach, oral interview M130, and Barbara Robbins, oral interview M158, both in Popular Music Archives, GSU. Kane, *How to Write a Song*, 78.

6. Songs listed in draft essay ("N.Y. Times Article") and JM undated notes on DeSoto Hilton letterhead. Sir William Schwenck Gilbert lived from 1836 to 1911.

7. Ibid. Johnny would later write such songs as "Mister Meadowlark" and "On Behalf of the Visiting Firemen" with Donaldson. JM autobiography. G. A. Mercer loved poetry, often reading James Whitcomb Riley or Edgar Guest to his sons and sharing verses with his friends. On the musical exposure of jazz musicians in New Orleans, see Samuel Charters, *A Trumpet around the Corner: The Story of New Orleans Jazz* (Jackson: University Press of Mississippi, 2008), 6 and passim.

8. Mercer quoted in *Savannah Morning News*, May 24, 1959. Johnny recognizes Aunt Kate in his autobiography as taking him to performances. Draft essay identified as "N.Y. Times Article." For an excellent evaluation of entertainment in this period, see Charles J. Elmore, *All That Savannah Jazz* (Savannah, Ga.: Savannah State University, 1998), 30–39. One wonders if Mercer observed black vaudevillians at the Palace Theater, ever entered the Pekin Theater, where Georgia's Gertrude "Ma" Rainey sang, or attended one of the tent shows on West Broad Street in Savannah; see also Lynn Abbott and Doug Seroff, *Ragged but Right: Black Traveling Shows, "Coon Songs," and the Dark Pathway to Blues and Jazz* (Jackson: University Press of Mississippi, 2007), 23.

9. Songs listed in draft essay identified as "N.Y. Times Article" and JM undated notes on DeSoto Hilton letterhead. Morgan Pritchard is identified in Ciucevich oral history by Ann

Clinton Staley, the daughter of Harriet Ciucevich Clinton, December 6, 1991, author's possession. Bob Carleton published his surprise hit, "Ja-Da," in 1918.

10. Mercer provides descriptions of the childhood injuries in JM autobiography.

11. Ciucevich oral history by Ann Clinton Staley identifies the cook Rachael; the anecdote is told in JM autobiography. *Atlanta Journal-Constitution Magazine*, August 14, 1955. William Dean Howells, "Savannah Twice Visited," *Harper's Magazine*, 1919, repr. in Patrick Allen, ed., *Literary Savannah* (Athens, GA: Hill Street Press, 1998.

12. Honor relied on hierarchy of class and race; see Bertram Wyatt-Brown, *Southern Honor: Ethics and Behavior in the Old South*, 25th ann. ed. (New York: Oxford University Press, 2007), 369, and on what he calls "white solidarity," 402–3; author's oral interview with Juliana Ciucevich Paige, author's possession. Mercer's views on race — while progressive — nevertheless proved similar to those explored in William H. Chafe, *Civilities and Civil Rights: Greensboro, North Carolina, and the Black Struggle for Freedom* (New York: Oxford University Press, 1980). Never acknowledging the power vested in displays of white supremacy, Mercer nevertheless believed black and white southerners shared a preference for politeness. As he explained to jazz critic Willis Conover in 1970, "We are polite. We believe in saying 'yes sir,' 'yes ma'am.' We take our hats off in elevators. We love colored people but we like them as we knew them when we were first introduced to them. Which is humble and kind. Just like we like humble and kind anybody. I mean we do it ourselves and we expect other people to do it." See Conover interview with Mercer, Special Collections Department, Georgia State University. For a more nuanced analysis of southern race relations, see Jennifer Ritterhouse, *Growing Up Jim Crow: How Black and White Southern Children Learned Race* (Chapel Hill: University of North Carolina Press, 2006). A theoretical framework for considering southern paternalism and deference — in particular, authority and discrimination — may be found in Homi K. Bhabha, *The Location of Culture* (London: Routledge, 1994), where he argues that in the colonial discourse, when "faced with the hybridity of its objects, the presence of power is revealed as something other than what its rules of recognition assert" (112).

13. Mercer genealogy notes, collection 553, Mercer Family Papers, GHS; Savannah city directories, 1909–14. Author's oral interview with Nancy Mercer Keith Gerard, author's possession; Philip Furia, *Skylark: The Life and Times of Johnny Mercer* (New York: St. Martin's Press, 2003), 21, 270–74. Referring to his childhood teachers in a 1930s Christmas card, Johnny recalled "Nina Pape — no teacher's topped her / And that goes for Miss Willhopter."

14. John Ward Motte and G. A. Mercer purchased Burnside Island from G. S. and Lillian E. McAlpin, whose family had owned the three hundred acres since the late antebellum period. See Chatham County deed book 9w, folio 447–48; a plat is recorded in 10F, folio 169. G. A., Robbie, and Nannie all lived in Savannah, so summer houses on the island were practical, while brothers Lewis and Ed, both in metropolitan New York, did not participate. Ann Mercer Klein, FAX to the author, October 27, 1999; Warranty deed between the Burnside Island Development Company, J. W. Motte, president, and Robert L. Mercer, selling lot 6 in block K for $1,500, May 1, 1915, Chatham County Court of Ordinary, Savannah, Ga. The company hired the engineering firm of Gignilliat & Reppard to prepare the site, which included the main roadway down the island, called McAlpin Street, and the Strand pathway across the shoreline front that remained open to all property owners so that any island resident could promenade along the bluff. Johnny recalls in the autobiography that at first there was no pier over the water; other records of land deeds showing the Burnside Island Company's development may be found in the Chatham County General Index to Real Estate, M–N grantee index, 1911–26, and in grantor index L–M, July 1926–44. The 1906 house still stands at 310 McAlpin. For years the Roux family has owned the 1911 G. A. Mercer house, located at 301 McAlpin. The Nannie Mercer Lang house was razed in 1979. The

Torrey family that owned nearby Ossabaw Island purchased the 1911 Robert Lee Mercer house at 306 McAlpin in 1929 for access to the mainland and deeded it to Georgia when it arranged the sale of Ossabaw to the state. The Georgia Department of Natural Resources has allowed the Robert Lee Mercer house to become dilapidated while using the pier as a departure point for boats headed to Ossabaw Island. Nick J. Mamalakis to Lonice W. Barrett, commissioner of the Georgia Department of Natural Resources, September 27, 1999, author's possession.

15. On the Savannah businesses in the 1910s, see the city directories. The Savannah Bank & Trust Company in 1913 also had on its board G. A. Mercer's brother-in-law, the fertilizer merchant Joseph Muir Lang, and his distant kinsman, the banker Jefferson Randolph Anderson. The reorganization of the G. A. Mercer Company allowed him to serve as president for the subsidiary Burnside Island Development Company, which also had C. S. Lebey as treasurer.

16. JM autobiography; Julian K. Quattlebaum, *The Great Savannah Races* (Athens: University of Georgia Press, 1983).

17. Burnside Island Development Company, materials in the M. B. and D. H. Floyd Papers, folder 67, collection 1308, GHS; JM autobiography.

18. Called Gullah in South Carolina and Geechee in Georgia, the distinctively low-country culture with its African retentions is explored in Savannah Unit, Georgia Writers' Project of the Work Projects Administration, *Drums and Shadows: Survival Studies among the Georgia Coastal Negroes* (Athens: University of Georgia Press, 1940). Muriel and Malcolm Bell Jr., who took the photographs included in the volume, were friends of Johnny and his brothers and Walter Rivers.

19. Anne Ciucevich Rivers bought her own bungalow on Lehigh Avenue in Pin Point that fronted Shipyard Creek, a tributary of the Back (Moon) River; she called it Chinquapin Cottage. See the warranty deed between Theodore A. H. Fincken and Anne C. Rivers and Helen Hatch, August 4, 1936, in Walter Rivers Papers, Special Collections, John C. Pace Library, University of West Florida, Pensacola (hereafter UWF). Bob Bach and Ginger Mercer, eds., *Our Huckleberry Friend: The Life, Times, and Lyrics of Johnny Mercer* (Secaucus, N.J.: Lyle Stuart, 1982), 16. In recognition of the centennial of Mercer's birth, family friend Straton Leopold created Huckleberry Cheesecake as a special flavor to sell in the family ice cream parlor.

20. Caroline Couper Lovell, *The Golden Isles of Georgia* (Boston: Little, Brown, 1933). The "Stories from Pin Point" are published in the reprint, Bach and Mercer, eds., *Our Huckleberry Friend*, xxiv–xxxv, with originals in the JM Papers, GSU.

21. Walter Rivers, "Long Search," in Rivers Papers UWF; lyrics for "Any Place I Hang My Hat Is Home" in Kimball et al., eds., *Complete Lyrics*, 159; *The Cadet* (annual, Benedictine Military Institute, Savannah, Ga.), 1924.

22. Walter Rivers letter reprinted in Bach and Mercer, eds., *Our Huckleberry Friend*, 16; *Savannah Morning News*, May 24, 1959. The Ralph Mark Gilbert Civil Rights Museum in Savannah has a collection of photographs of the Easter parade.

23. A description of Brownville, the House of Prayer on Bismark Street, and visits by Daddy Grace appears in the Savannah Unit, *Drums and Shadows*, 46–64; Lenwood G. Davis, ed., *Daddy Grace: An Annotated Bibliography* (Westport, Conn.: Greenwood Press, 1992); James William McIntire, oral interview M148, Popular Music Archives, GSU.

24. JM autobiography; Bach and Mercer, eds., *Our Huckleberry Friend*, 16; Savannah city directories, 1914, 1915, 1916, and 1928. Diagonal to the Langs on the other side of Hall Street lived Savannah mayor Thomas Gamble Jr.; farther down one way lived Abram Minis and down the other lived the transportation magnate George Baldwin and his wife, Lucy, who had started the free kindergarten association in the city.

25. Saxon Pope Bargeron, *The Massie Common School: Historical Sketches* (Savannah, Ga.: Savannah–Chatham County Board of Public Education, 1997). James William McIntire, oral

interview M148, Popular Music Archives, GSU; P. [Pope] Barrow McIntire to Walter Rivers, February 19, 1980, Rivers Papers, UWF; see also "Half Rubber: The Quintessential Savannah Game," in Timothy Daiss, *Rebels, Saints and Sinners: Savannah's Rich History and Colorful Personalities* (Gretna, La.: Pelican, 2002), 73–77.

26. McIntire to Rivers, February 19, 1980, Rivers Papers, UWF; JM autobiography.

27. JM autobiography; on Savannah's Irish population, see David T. Gleeson, *The Irish in the South, 1815–1877* (Chapel Hill: University of North Carolina Press, 2001). A standard recipe for Chatham Artillery Punch involves mixing two parts green tea with three parts light red wine, one part each of rum, brandy, whiskey, and gin, mixed with brown sugar, cherries, oranges, and lemons. The stock ages from two days to a week before serving on ice with three parts champagne.

28. *The Fir Tree* (yearbook, Woodberry Forest School, Orange, Va.), 1917; Elizabeth Copeland Norfleet, *Woodberry Forest School: A Venture in Faith* (New York: Georgian Press, 1955), 74. The school dedicated Anderson Hall in memory of George Wayne Anderson Jr., an honor graduate with Savannah connections killed in the days before the signing of the armistice. Annie's second husband, Morgan Pritchard, ran the ferry to the island, but they divorced and she returned to Savannah, where by 1925 she worked as the city health nurse and lived at 301 East Charlton with son Walter Rivers. On Walter Mercer, see *The Pandora*, 1918, 1919, and the University of Georgia alumni directory (Athens, Ga., 1927).

29. The G. A. Mercer Company provided signed receipts for investors, although its reputation derived from its president, who often received checks from investors with the request that the money be added to an account. As Wyatt-Brown noted in *Southern Honor*, "An oral pledge from a gentleman was thought to be the equivalent of a signed oath, particularly in regard to gaming debts" (56–57). The code of honor promoted speculation as a way to demonstrate imperviousness to the fickle forces of fate while requiring debts of chance to be repaid immediately lest one lose face.

30. *Proceedings of the 149th Anniversary of the Union Society at Bethesda, Georgia, April 25, 1899* (Savannah, Ga.: Morning News Print, 1899); *Proceedings of the Union Society*, 1913. For an analysis of the Savannah Female Asylum that suggests similar motives among the elite, see Betty Wood, *Gender, Race, and Rank in a Revolutionary Age: The Georgia Lowcountry 1750–1820* (Athens: University of Georgia Press, 2000), quotation on 57. Also see Wyatt-Brown, *Southern Honor*, 104–5, on charity and Christian gentility.

31. Edward J. Cashin, *Beloved Bethesda: A History of George Whitefield's Home for Boys, 1740–2000* (Macon, Ga.: Mercer University Press, 2001).

32. Notes on "Mr. George Mercer, Sr." regarding Bethesda, in box 1, folder 25, JM Papers, GSU; in JM autobiography Johnny recalls with fondness the singing around the wassail bowl.

33. Cashin, *Beloved Bethesda*, 211–12; *Proceedings of the Union Society*, 1921, 1922, and in 1922–23, 13. Bethesda sponsored a Boy Scout troop and piano lessons for the musically inclined.

34. Cashin, *Beloved Bethesda*, 212–14, 269; Johnny Mercer to Mr. Burroughs, undated, collection 1205, Ole Wickliff Burroughs Papers, Georgia Historical Society, Savannah, Ga., (hereafter GHS). Christian gentility toyed with the vagaries of life, snatching away from wretchedness a handful of individuals deemed worthy, while the remaining were resigned to the imperviousness of poverty; on fatalism, see Wyatt-Brown, *Southern Honor*, 28–30.

35. James Williams McIntire interview; see also Robbins interview and Robert Rush, oral interview M154, Popular Music Archives, GSU; photograph in the Ole Wickliff Burroughs Papers, GHS. Interview with Nancy Mercer Keith Gerard, author's possession.

36. Savannah city directories, 1921, 1922, 1923. Mary L. Morrison, ed., *Historic Savannah* (Savannah, Ga.: Historic Savannah Foundation, 1979), 234–35 with photo 34.42 on 235. The Reckling family lived at 224 East Gwinnett Street, which was the other half of the duplex. The marker

erected by the Georgia Historical Society identifies 226 East Gwinnett Street as the residence where Mercer grew up; but that distinction actually belongs to 118 East Hall Street. Except for the few months in which Johnny lived as a baby in the row house at 20 East Macon Street, the only other house from his youth in Savannah still standing is 226 East Gwinnett Street. Kimball et al., eds., *Complete Lyrics*, 350.

37. On the history of North Carolina's Scottish immigrants, see Celeste Ray, *Highland Heritage: Scottish Americans in the American South* (Chapel Hill: University of North Carolina Press, 2001); George A. Digges Jr., *Historical Facts Concerning Buncombe County Government* (Asheville, N.C.: n.p., 1935), 216–19; *Asheville Citizen*, July 27, 1952; *The Arrow of Pi Beta Phi*, February 1938, and "Hotel Played Vital Part in History of Old Asheville, ca. 1937, unidentified and undated clipping, in "Asheville, Hotels" vertical file, Pack Memorial Public Library, Asheville, N.C.; *Asheville Citizen-Times*, December 15, 1983. G. A. Mercer to Lillian, June 11, 1923, box 1, folder 7, Mercer Family Collection, AASU.

38. G. A. Mercer to J. C. Walker, October 6, 1922, and July 8, 1924, Norfleet Archives, William H. White Jr. Library, Woodberry Forest School, Orange, Va. (hereafter WFS); "Arthur Murray Taught Me Dancing in a Hurry," words by Johnny Mercer, music by Victor Schertizinger (New York: Famous Music Corporation, 1942); Kathryn Murray to Johnny Mercer, December 5, 1950, box 2, folder 12, JM Papers, GSU.

39. Douglas Swain, *Cabins and Castles: The History and Architecture of Buncombe County, North Carolina* (City of Asheville, Historic Resources Commission of Asheville and Buncombe County), 193; undated clipping, "E. W. Grove Gets Possession Albermarle Park on June 1" and "Asheville Is Fastest Growing Tourist Center in the Country Says Writer after Investigation," clipping dated February 1, 1923, both in vertical file, Pack Memorial Library. Indenture between Anne H. O'Connell, W. L. Jenkins, and the G. A. Mercer Company, July 10, 1923, deed of trust book 178, 74, see also deed of trust book 167, 545–46, Superior Court, Buncombe County, N.C. In 2005, Howard Stafford renovated the Princess Anne at 301 East Chestnut Street into a boutique hotel with sixteen suites (*Atlanta Journal Constitution*, February 5, 2006).

40. *Asheville Citizen*: on the projected opening of the Princess Anne, see June 26, 1923; on the expanding tourist trade, see July 18, 1926. On the attractive neighborhood along Chestnut Street between Merrimon Avenue and Charlotte Street, see Swain, *Cabins and Castles*, 84–85. *Asheville City Directory*, comp. E. H. Miller (Asheville, N.C.: Miller Press, 1923), 356, lists G. A. Mercer as president of Prudential Investment Company; also see the 1924 city directory, 401, which lists the G. A. Mercer Company; list of Asheville Real Estate Board members, including the G. A. Mercer Company in the 1925 city directory. The G. A. Mercer Company owned properties on Delaware Road along Meadow Park and Hendersonville Road near Biltmore. There are perhaps a half-dozen transactions during 1923–24, such as the sale of a corner lot at Merrimon Avenue and Conestee Street, see May 15, 1923, indenture between Charles G. Lee and the G. A. Mercer Company, deed book 272, 282; the August 31, 1923, indenture between the G. A. Mercer Company and G. A. Mercer with Lillian Mercer, deed book 276, 127–28; and the March 7, 1924, indenture between G. A. Mercer with Lillian Mercer and Mattie A. Brown, deed book 282, 116; or the corner of Kimberly and Virginia avenues, see the August 6, 1923, indenture between W. L. Jenkins and G. A. Mercer, deed book 273, 518, and the September 2, 1924, indenture between G. A. Mercer with Lillian Mercer and Charles R. Bailey, deed book 289, 575, all in Buncombe County Superior Court, Asheville, N.C.

41. On Julia Westall Wolfe and Thomas Wolfe, see David Herbert Donald, *Look Homeward: A Life of Thomas Wolfe* (Boston: Little, Brown and Company, 1987); Thomas Wolfe, *You Can't Go Home Again* (New York: The Sun Dial Press, 1942), first quote on 110 and, second quote on 143.

42. G. A. Mercer to "My Little Baby Girl" [Lillian Mercer], June 11, 1923, Mercer Family Collection, AASU; no doubt seeing his parents dancing to jazz inspired Johnny. JM autobiography; Nolan Porterfield, *Jimmie Rodgers: The Life and Times of America's Blue Yodeler* (Urbana: University of Illinois Press, 1979), 12–17, 65–66, 257–60.

43. Porterfield, *Jimmie Rodgers*, 15–74, quotation on 259. Like countless other southern diaspora entertainers, Rodgers and Mercer demonstrated the hybridity of the region's culture as "contestatory subjectivities that are empowered in the act of erasing the politics of binary opposition," to borrow from Bhabha, *The Location of Culture*, 179.

44. Petition of G. A. Mercer Jr., Guardian of George, Walter, Hugh Mercer, July 25, 1903, Court of Ordinary, Chatham County, Savannah, Ga.; Norfleet, *Woodberry Forest School*, quotes Headmaster Carter Walker explaining the school's "two ideals: the value of hard work, regardless of whether the subject matter was hard or easy; and an uncompromising attitude toward honor in work and play" (64). See directory of alumni, Woodberry Forest School. Joe Mercer to Coleman C. Walker, December 11, 1956; G. A. Mercer to J. Carter Walker, November 7, 1906, February 27, August 9, October 29, 1907, March 10, June 12, 1908; J. Carter Walker to G. A. Mercer, November 25, December 2, 1909, all in Norfleet Archives, WFS.

45. The 1914–19 issues of Woodberry's yearbook, *The Fir Tree*, identify the activities of the Mercer brothers, Walter, class of 1917, and Hugh, class of 1919; Alfred Williams to Frank Brown Allen, September 26, 1928, November 1, 1928, Allen Papers, MSS1 AL533 A21-51, Virginia Historical Society, Richmond, Va. (hereafter VHS). F. B. "Brownie" Allen lived in Warrenton, North Carolina, and attended Duke University. Norfleet, *Woodberry Forest School*, 52–53, 64–66, 76–78; *The 1923 Catalogue for Woodberry Forest School*, Norfleet Archives, WFS. The school did not grant leaves for Thanksgiving, which did not become a federal holiday until 1941 and which many southerners viewed as a "Yankee" observance.

46. See Johnny Mercer to Mrs. "T" (Taylor), undated but 1950s, and G. A. Mercer to J. C. Walker, October 6, 1922, Norfleet Archives, WFS; Johnny worked as *The Daily Dope* editor under fellow sixth-form student Malcolm Logan Monroe, who edited *The Fir Tree* in 1927.

47. G. A. Mercer to J. Carter Walker, October 6, 1922, Norfleet Archives, WFS; Norfleet, *Woodberry Forest School*, 58–59, identifies Professor William Leland Lord, who taught at the school from 1916 to 1953 and put up with Mercer's tapping.

48. Johnny Mercer to R. W. D. Taylor, ca. 1953, Norfleet Archives, WFS; Harold I. Donnelly's master's thesis quoted in Norfleet, *Woodberry Forest School*, 14.

49. Norfleet, *Woodberry Forest School*, 61–63, lists many of these "colored friends" such as the headwaiter, Elijah Hopkins, and the porter, Robert Walker, whom the boys called Snow and who "good-naturedly fetched and carried for everybody at Woodberry for 25 years and enjoyed the joshing the boys gave him as much as they enjoyed the sport." Norfleet recalls of Champ Francis, another porter, that "the boys of his time knew Woodberry as well through him as through their other associates" (63).

50. Woodberry Forest School Student Registry, entry for John Mercer, November 5, 1923; Kane, *How to Write a Song*, 79. Mercer said, "It's a boy's name. Always the boy. People who don't know me, when they meet me, somehow, they expect a youngster. Well, the boy grows older. I've been around this game for a quarter of a century." Then grinning, Mercer said to Kane, "It's tough to be a boy all that time." *The Fir Tree* (1926–27), 50, 60, 154. Fellow Savannahians who attended with Johnny included John Wylly and Spencer Jones of the sixth form, Charles Bell of the fifth form, and Frank Papy of the third form. Frederick Hobbs Jr. of Norfolk went by "Hamlin," and his friend Malcolm Monroe of New Orleans went by "Heinie."

51. Alfred Williams to Frank Brown Allen, November 1, 1928, Armistead to Brown, November 12, 1928, in the Allen Papers, VHS.

52. Woodberry Forest School "Football Songs" from 1909 in Charles Ravenscroft Nalle Papers, Mss In 1493A, VHS; Woodberry Forest School student registry, entry for John Mercer, November 5, 1923, Norfleet Archives, WFS. J. Carter Walker's "A Tribute to the Masters" says about Joe Mercer that he arrived at Woodberry Forest School in 1919 "as a little second form boy from Savannah. Five years later he graduated with top honors in scholarship and a reputation of being the best athlete in the School. In 1928 he graduated from the University of Virginia with honors in Spanish." See Norfleet, *Woodberry Forest School*, 70, 103–6. On sport and honor, see Wyatt-Brown, *Southern Honor*, 327–28. Handwritten copy of "Fight for the Orange and Black" with words and music on staff paper by Johnny Mercer, Norfleet Archives, WFS.

53. Johnny Mercer to Mr. Carter, February 25, 1956, and John K. B. Reynolds to Gerald Cooper, July 10, 1976, and the 1927–28 catalogue and announcements for Woodberry Forest School, all in Norfleet Archives, Norfleet Archives, WFS. See also *The Fir Tree* (1927–28 and 1934) for Mercer's "A Study Hall Sonnet." Johnny's friends, Malcolm Monroe and Archie Davis, joined him as chapel assistants.

54. G. A. Mercer to J. Carter Walker, undated but 1924, Norfleet Archives, WFS; JM autobiography.

55. J. C. Walker to G. A. Mercer, October 21, 1925, Norfleet Archives, WFS; *The Fir Tree* (1926–27), 34, 60; Edward S. Northrop to John H. Mercer, February 2, 1945, JM Papers, GSU.

56. *The Fir Tree* (1926–27), 34, 50, 60; *The Fir Tree* (1922–23), 61.

57. The first issue of *The Virginia Reel* appeared on May 15, 1920. In 1921, it began publishing ten times a year. See *The Virginia Reel*, University of Virginia, Charlottesville, copies housed in the VHS. On the locations that sold the magazine, see *The Virginia Reel*, January 1921, 24, and December 1926, 9.

58. As managing editor of *The Oracle*, Mercer would have helped write *The Sorrycle*, which appeared in *The Fir Tree* (1926–27), see 34 for quotation.

· 59. *The Fir Tree* (1926–27), 65, 68; Armistead to Allen, November 12, 1928, November 20, 1928, and January 29, 1929, Allen Papers,VHS.

60. Norfleet, *Woodberry Forest School*, 81; G. A. Mercer to J. C. Walker, February 27, 1907, tried to excuse George's behavior: "he is a boy who is very full of life and animal spirits and impetuous"; see also Walker to Mercer, October 29, 1907; Johnny Mercer to Mrs. R. W. D. Taylor, [1940s], Norfleet Archives, WFS.

61. Clipping of the *Free Press* dated 1963, in box 33, folder 3, *Citizen News*, July 6, 1944, undated notes by JM on the Ambassador letterhead that sketch out the tune for "Dearly Beloved," in box 6, folder 58, and transcript of Sir Michael Parkinson interview with Mercer for the televised program, *Parkinson*, which aired on the BBC, a transcript of which is located with these other documents in JM Papers, GSU.

62. *The Fir Tree* (1926–27), 50. That enthusiasm for music might also be found in his 1936 song for which he wrote both the words and music, "Jamboree Jones"; see also "The Search for Jamboree Jones" from the *Sportscene* 1964; JM autobiography. In the 1934 volume of *The Fir Tree*, in "A Study Hall Sonnet," Johnny wrote "Mister Taylor — with a jerk / That one might almost call berserk / Says 'I could never make him work / For me.' / 'Amo amas amat,' I said / To put it in his silly head; / Instead he put me in my bed / Did he."

63. Mercer quotations are from his autobiography. See Richard M. Sudhalter, *Stardust Melody: The Life and Music of Hoagy Carmichael* (New York: Oxford University Press, 2002), 40–41; Gene Lees, *Cats of Any Color: Jazz Black and White* (New York: Oxford University Press, 1994), 193. Both authors demonstrate the multiracial nature of jazz: Sudhalter recognizes the influence of Louis Armstrong but also the white band leaders Ted Lewis and Paul Whiteman on Carmichael; Lees notes that recordings by the white artists Frank Trumbauer, Jimmy Dorsey, and Bix

Beiderbecke fascinated the black Lester Young. The state displaced many of the black businesses on West Broad Street when the Georgia Department of Transportation bulldozed the area to construct the terminus of Georgia Highway 16. See Luciana M. Spracher, *Lost Savannah: Photographs from the Collection of the Georgia Historical Society* (Charleston, S.C.: Arcadia, 2002), 102, which reprints images of what the area looked like. In Bach and Mercer, eds., *Our Huckleberry Friend*, 226, appears a photograph from the early 1970s of Johnny posed on West Broad Street in front of an old record store in the black business district.

64. O. S. Abrams oversaw the repair department of rental properties, and W. H. Clifton managed the insurance department with Seiler. Savannah city directories, Savannah Board of Trade, *Red Book* (Savannah, Ga.: Review Publishing and Printing, 1924). Ole W. and Henrietta K. Burroughs of Bethesda typified the small investors, squirreling away a thousand dollars; see Ole W. Burroughs to Walter Mercer, May 24, 1925, and Walter Mercer to Burroughs, June 6, 1925, and October 24, 1925, in box 6, folder 55, item 665, Burroughs Papers, GHS; *Savannah Morning News*, July 23, 1926.

65. *Savannah Morning News*, July 23, 1926; Savannah city directories, Savannah Board of Trade, *Red Book* (1926). Henry Flagler developed Palm Beach as a resort community and West Palm Beach as housing for the middle class and area workers who serviced the wealthy, as well as the agricultural countryside. During the 1920s the population of West Palm quadrupled.

66. Nick Wynne and Richard Moorhead, *Paradise for Sale: Florida's Booms and Busts* (Charleston, S.C.: The History Press, 2010) See also Michael Cannon, *Florida: A Short History* (Gainesville: University Press of Florida, 1993), 80–85, with *Nation* quote on 85, and for real estate values see Frank Parker Stockbridge and John Holliday Perry, *Florida in the Making* (Jacksonville, Fla.: de Bower Publishing, 1926), 286–309, which lists $450 million in outside capital invested in 1925 alone.

67. For a history of the collapse of the company, see Alexander R. Lawton to Mr. Diehl of Latham & Watkins, Los Angeles, January 12, 1956; see also the questions posed to George W. Hunt by Pamela Neill of the Reader's Digest Company and Hunt's responses, both located in collection MS 552, JM Papers, GHS.

68. On private matters, see Wyatt-Brown, *Southern Honor*, 310–12. Nancy Mercer Keith Gerard recalled her "Uncle Bubba" Johnny Mercer arriving unannounced in Savannah one day, walking into his mother's house, and interrupting an argument between his sister and her daughter. Disliking such exchanges, he promptly turned around and left; author's oral interview with Nancy Mercer Keith Gerard, author's possession.

69. "Johnny Mercer Kept His Promise," a family oral history, Pearce Hammond Collection, Lane Library, Special Collections, Armstrong Atlantic State University, Savannah, Ga.; *News*, clipping about Mercer and the debt, undated (ca. 1950s), JM Papers, GSU.

70. On resistance to bankruptcy among gentlemen and the ramifications of default, see Wyatt-Brown, *Southern Honor*, 264. Since the speculation served as a gambling debt, G. A. Mercer had little option but to satisfy the original investment entrusted to him, for "the obligation had to be paid so that the relationship between the players could be terminated" (346). Chatham County deed books, grantor indexes L–M, July 1926–44, 49B. The G. A. Mercer Company did a brisk business selling properties in a bid to raise capital to pay the debt. The county records mark the liquidation with the transition to the Mercer Realty Company on May 21, 1927.

71. Payment of Debt, JM Papers, GHS; Family Oral History, Hammond Papers, AASU; undated clipping from *Savannah Morning News*, ca. 1950s, JM Papers, GSU; *Reader's Digest*; Nick Mamalakis, oral interview M034, Popular Music Archives, GSU; Polk's city directories of Savannah.

72. On the Depression and Savannah banks, see *Savannah Morning News*, June 10 and March 10, 1933. Once the bank's resources dropped to $4.67 million in 1930, it required minimum bal-

ances of $100 for all accounts. Shortly thereafter, the bank began issuing script rather than cur-
rency. Not until 1966 would the old Mercer Realty Company be dissolved, when Walter Mercer
merged the rental accounts with Lynes Realty Company. Walter retained control of Mercer Insurance Company; see *Savannah Press Register*, March 10, 1966. Haunted by the loss of other people's
money entrusted to him, G. A. never again felt confident, and he died in 1940. His wife, Lillian,
outlived him by nearly forty years.

73. Envelope with dollars, box 3, folder B, Mercer Family Collection, AASU.

74. Woodberry Forest School Reports of John Herndon Mercer signed by J. Carter Walker,
Head Master, in Norfleet Archives, WFS. See also box 2, folder 5, JM Papers, GHS. The October
23, 1926, report showed grades of 93 on daily recitations and 98 on term examinations in trigonometry, but by December they had dropped to 65 and 87, and then after the news of the financial
difficulties, the grades fell lower as reported on April 23, 1927, to 60 and 35 and on May 21, 1927,
to 50 and 35. The report cards demonstrate that Johnny did not withdraw from the school before
the end of the term as the family has often claimed, for he received his grades in May before the
early June graduation. See also the *Catalogue of Woodberry Forest School, 1926–27*; John to G. A.
Mercer, June 14, 1927, telegram, box 1, folder 4, Mercer Family Collection, AASU.

75. Daniel Joseph Singal, *The War Within: From Victorian to Modernist Thought in the South,
1919–1945* (Chapel Hill: University of North Carolina Press, 1982). According to Singal's definition, Mercer would be a modernist "by the skin of his teeth," for an ambivalent Johnny advanced
into the modern era, trying to retain aspects of a code of honor he admired, while paradoxically
promoting the integration of the region into the rest of the nation and the world. Agents seized
a "fine assortment of liquor," including choice champagne, gin, scotch, and rye packed in four
hundred cases and valued at six thousand dollars from the boat, and while they arrested E. J.
"Eddie" Ciucevich, who served time in the federal penitentiary, his brother, Frank, who sold the
whiskey from the Ocean View Hotel, escaped capture (*Savannah Morning News*, May 8, 1927).
For a description of bootlegging in Savannah see former *Morning News* and *Evening Press* editor
Tom Coffey, "Gambling, Liquor, and Vice," in Allen, *Literary Savannah*, 261–73. On the 1922
banning of jazz in Savannah, see Steve Goodson, *Highbrows, Hillbillies, and Hellfire: Public Entertainment in Atlanta, 1880–1930* (Athens: University of Georgia Press, 2002), 229 n. 25.

76. *Savannah Morning News*, ca. 1950s, JM Papers, GSU.

Chapter Three. New York City

The epigraph is from "The Yodel Blues" (1949), with music by Robert Emmett Dolan. See Robert
Kimball, Barry Day, Miles Kreuger, and Eric Davis, eds., *The Complete Lyrics of Johnny Mercer*
(New York: Alfred A. Knopf, 2009), 176.

1. The *City of Chattanooga* sailed from 1923 to 1942 as a steamship of the Savannah line accord-
ing to Richard E. Price, *Central of Georgia Railway and Connecting Lines* (Salt Lake City, Utah:
Stanway-Wheelwright Printing, 1976), 33. An accomplished sculptor in relief, Joe Mercer joined
Woodberry as a faculty member in 1928 and served as headmaster from 1952 to 1962. He died in
1981; *Savannah Morning News*, May 27, 1981. On the Stiles family, see Caroline Couper Lovell,
The Light of Other Days, intro. by Hugh Stiles Golson and LeeAnn Whites (Macon, Ga.: Mercer
University Press, 1995), 180–83.

2. A statue on River Street recalls Florence Martus, Savannah's famous "waving girl," who
lived in the cottage next to the lighthouse on Elba Island and greeted each ship that passed to and
from the port from 1887 to 1931. Drafts of Johnny Mercer's unfinished autobiography are in box
1, folders 2–14, JM Papers, GSU.

3. *News*, ca. 1950s, [unidentified and undated newspaper clipping], JM autobiography, both in JM Papers, GSU; Gerald Bordman, *American Musical Theatre: A Chronicle* (New York: Oxford University Press, 1992), 422, 424.

4. *Savannah Morning News*, November 7, 1925, July 2, 1926, June 15, 1927, and March 1, 1938.

5. JM autobiography; "Elizabeth's Letter," unidentified and undated newspaper clipping, box 2, folder 20, Mercer Family Collection, AASU. Mercer identifies Peggy Stoddard, the daughter of family friends Margaret S. and the late Edward S. Stoddard; the girl who accompanied her might have been Frances "Fanny" Hargis.

6. Town Theatre program for "Three Original One-Act Plays" for its fourth season, 1927–28. The Pulitzer Prize–winning author Caroline Miller wrote one of the other one-act plays, *Red Calico*, which the troupe performed; 1920s Town Theatre playbills in Ole Wickliff Burroughs Papers, Georgia Historical Society, Savannah, Ga. (hereafter GHS); *Brooklyn-Queens Journal*, March 29, 1932; *Atlanta Journal Constitution Magazine*, April 5, 1964. Although born in the Athens branch of the Barrow family, "Miss Lucy" became one of Savannah's leading citizens, heading the women's division of the Savannah Works Progress Administration and serving as the first Georgia Democratic national committeewoman while helping others to found the Junior League and organize the Historic Savannah Foundation. See the *Savannah Evening Press*, March 16, 1955, and November 6, 1967.

7. O. W. Burroughs to JHM, May 6, 1955, JM Papers, GSU; Philip Furia, *Skylark: The Life and Times of Johnny Mercer* (New York: St. Martin's Press, 2003), 35–36; JM autobiography; *New York Times*, May 12, 1928.

8. JM autobiography; Wright Hunter managed the Henry Hentz & Company from its offices in the Realty Building on Drayton Street in Savannah.

9. Pope Barrow McIntire, oral interview M144, Popular Music Archives, Georgia State University, Atlanta, Ga.; Johnny Mercer to Cornelia McIntire Rivers, undated, Walter Rivers Papers, Special Collections, John C. Pace Library, University of West Florida, Pensacola, Fla.; James N. Gregory, *The Southern Diaspora: How the Great Migrations of Black and White Southerners Transformed America* (Chapel Hill: University of North Carolina Press, 2005), see 23–28, and on Johnny becoming what Gregory calls a diaspora entertainer, see 192–95. Johnny Mercer interview by Willis Conover, January 30, 1970, transcript in Popular Music Archives, Georgia State University, Atlanta, Ga.

10. JM autobiography; Uncle Ed Mercer probably recommended the midtown rooms, which might have been rented by Mrs. Helen D. Drake of 333 East Forty-third Street.

11. JM autobiography; Kenneth T. Jackson, *Encyclopedia of New York City* (New Haven, Conn.: Yale University Press, 1995), 1178; Furia, *Skylark*, 38.

12. Mercer to "Dear Pop," n.d., "Johnny Mercer, Actor, Visitor," newspaper clipping, February 25, 1929, both in box 1, folder 3a, Mercer Family Collection, AASU.

13. Mercer lived with Mansfield at 129 West Eighty-sixth Street. In his autobiography, Johnny discussed the prevalence of gay actors in the theater: "They had, like all good fairies, their water wings on at all times and it was a footrace to get back to the dressing room or pass them in the halls without being manhandled." He admitted, "I had been to a boy's prep school so I knew how to dodge and how to take the advances in the manner in which they were presented . . . lightly and casually . . . and not act as if I were being insulted." He confessed, "Hoping for feminine company, I wanted no more of the sexual discovery nor experimentation that all (or most) young people go through." JM autobiography; Furia, *Skylark*, 40; Mercer to "Fred" [Frederick Hobbs], (ca. spring 1929), JM Papers, GSU.

14. JM autobiography; Joe Laurie Jr., *Vaudeville: From the Honky-Tonks to the Palace* (New York: Henry Holt, 1953), 83–84, 87–89. Years later, Johnny joined Bing Crosby in a tribute to the

Gallagher and Shean Act. With Hoagy Carmichael, Johnny wrote "Queenie, the Quick Change Artist," a song about a female impersonator. Indeed, vaudeville inspired much of Mercer's Broadway production, *Top Banana*, for comic Phil Silvers. Cantor often appeared in blackface. He introduced several of Irving Berlin's songs as well as "Dinah," "Making Whoopie," and "If You Knew Susie," among others. Johnny Mercer to Ole W. Burroughs, on Hotel Arlington (Boston) letterhead, [1930], in which Johnny thanks Burroughs for the address of Frances "Fanny" Hargis and comments on joining a stock company after his traveling show closes; see also Frances to Burroughs, "I was all agog to know what Johnny Mercer said about me," and commenting on Steven Vincent Benét's *John Brown's Body*. All in Burroughs Papers, GHS.

15. The theme of chance appears frequently in Mercer's lyrics; JM autobiography. On the role of fate as part of his cultural heritage and ideology, see Bertram Wyatt-Brown, *Southern Honor: Ethics and Behavior in the Old South*, 25th ann. ed. (New York: Oxford University Press, 2007), 27–32.

16. Bob Bach and Ginger Mercer, eds., *Our Huckleberry Friend: The Life, Times, and Lyrics of Johnny Mercer* (Secaucus, N.J.: Lyle Stuart, 1982), 28–29, 56; JM autobiography; on the original *Garrick Gaieties*, see Armond Fields and L. Marc Fields, *From the Bowery to Broadway* (New York: Oxford University Press, 1993), 431–35; James M. Salem, *A Guide to Critical Reviews*, part 2, *The Musical* (n.p., 1991), 209–10. A native of Cedartown, Georgia, Sterling Holloway gained fame as a character voice for Walt Disney feature animations. *New York Times*, June 5, 1930.

17. JM autobiography; Mercer lived in apartment 6, 21 Jones Street. The Willinghams lived at 85 Barrow Street. *News*, ca. 1950 clipping, JM Papers, GSU.

18. Unlike her son, Lillian Mercer preferred not to cook, employing servants instead. See *Savannah Morning News*, ca. 1950 clipping, JM Papers, GSU; William "Bill" Harbach, oral interview M130, and Jean Bach, oral interview M128, both in Popular Music Archives, GSU.

19. Walter Rivers to "Uncle George," Saturday [1930?], and G. A. Mercer to Walter, October 2, 1930, box 1, folder 2b, Mercer Family Collection, AASU. In the letter, G. A. Mercer explained to Walter, "Of course, you know that I want to do anything I can to help you get started and I will be glad indeed to stake you for $100, $50.00 this month and $50.00 next month." He added the encouragement "Don't give up. Something will take place soon and I will help you all I can. With lots of love."

20. Stanley Green, *Broadway Musicals: Show by Show*, 4th ed. (Milwaukee, Wis.: Hal Leonard, 1994), 67–74; for a critique of the musical in the decade of the 1920s that explains its transformation out of the follies-style revue and into the modern musical, see Ethan Mordden, *Make Believe: The Broadway Musical in the 1920s* (New York: Oxford University Press, 1997).

21. JM autobiography; Jervis Anderson, *This Was Harlem: A Cultural Portrait, 1900–1950* (New York: Farrar Straus & Giroux, 1982), 168–80. Other speakeasies that catered to interracial audiences in Harlem where the hot jazz might be heard included the Yeah Man, the Hotcha, Dickie Wells, and Pod's and Jerry's Log Cabin. See John Hammond with Irving Townsend, *John Hammond on Record* (New York: Summit Books, 1977), 92.

22. JM autobiography; Harms was at 62 West Forty-fifth Street. David A. Jasen, *Tin Pan Alley: The Composers, the Songs, the Performers and Their Times: The Golden Age of American Popular Music from 1886 to 1956* (New York: Donald I. Fine, 1988); Nicholas E. Tawa, *The Way to Tin Pan Alley: American Popular Song, 1866–1910* (New York: Schirmer Books, 1990).

23. Mercer interview by Conover. The plantation melodies, parlor ballads, and comic or protest songs by Stephen Foster and other songwriters in the nineteenth century fueled a publishing industry that marketed what Foster biographer Ken Emerson calls the music of the first chapter in the Great American Songbook. By 1892 and the release of Charles K. Harris's waltz, "After the Ball," a new chapter had begun, as did another chapter with the incorporation of syncopation

into popular song by 1911 with Irving Berlin's "Alexander's Ragtime Band." See Ken Emerson, ed., *Stephen Foster & Co.: Lyrics of America's First Great Popular Songs* (New York: Library of America, 2010), xxii. David Jenness and Don Velsey, *Classic American Popular Song: The Second Half-Century, 1950–2000* (New York: Routledge, 2006), 1–12.

24. Johnny Mercer Song Database, GSU; Robert Kimball, Barry Day, Miles Kreuger, and Eric Davis, eds., *The Complete Lyrics of Johnny Mercer* (New York: Alfred A. Knopf, 2009), 3–4; JM autobiography.

25. JM autobiography; Mordden, *Make Believe*, 173–77.

26. JM autobiography; Walter Rivers to G. A. Mercer, "Saturday," undated, box 1, folder 2b, Mercer Family Collection, AASU; Johnny Mercer to "Ginger honey" [October 6, 1930], and to "Dearest" [Ginger], [October 14, 1930], JM Papers, GSU.

27. Miller Music was located at 62 West Forty-fifth Street in Tin Pan Alley; Johnny Mercer to Mother Sweet, undated, and Johnny Mercer to Dear Pop, April 22 [1931], box 1, folders 3a and 4, Mercer Family Collection, AASU.

28. "While We Danced at the Mardi Gras," words by John Mercer, music by Alfred Opler (New York: Miller Music, 1931); Johnny Mercer to Paul Marks, George Hoffman, Leroy Anderson, Board of Review at ASCAP, November 10, 1962, JM Papers, GSU.

29. Kimball et al., eds., *Complete Lyrics*, 10; Sir Michael Parkinson interview with Johnny Mercer for *Parkinson*, season 2, episode 7, broadcast over the BBC on July 15, 1972, transcript housed in the Popular Music Archives, GSU.

30. JM autobiography; *Brooklyn-Queens Journal*, March 29, 1932. Mrs. Meltzer lived at 1103 Sterling Place.

31. "Meet Johnny Mercer," undated newspaper clipping, as well as "Private Life of Johnny Mercer" from 1945, and telegrams, all in JM Papers, GSU; JM autobiography; Parkinson interview, BBC.

32. St. Thomas Church records identify Ginger's parents as Joseph Meltzer and (apparently incorrectly) Anna Swickel, for her passport and other records indicate her maiden name as Anna Cantor. Claire Meltzer, oral interview M149, and Joyce Pelphrey, oral interview M147, Popular Music Archives, Georgia State University, Atlanta, Ga. Pelphrey is the daughter of Ginger's sister, Deborah Meltzer. Interview with Amanda Mercer Neder, January 27, 2010, author's possession.

33. JM autobiography; *Brooklyn Queens Journal*, March 29, 1932; unidentified clipping "Remarkable Story of Mr. Johnny Mercer," September 12, 1943, and "Meet Johnny Mercer," unidentified and undated, in JM Papers, GSU; Johnny to "Dearest" [Ginger Meehan], postmarked October 14, 1930, and "the Old Mastiff" [Mercer] to "My Darling" [Meehan], postmarked October 27, 1930, box 1, folder 22, JM & GM Papers, GSU. The act of writing Ginger inspired Mercer's "P.S. I Love You." If son Jeff Mercer's recollection as told to Philip Furia (*Skylark*, 265) is correct, Johnny deliberately destroyed his most private papers.

34. Whether the announcement ran first in the Brooklyn paper or if Johnny sent the notice himself to his hometown newspaper is unclear, but his parents read the *Savannah Evening Press*, May 16, 1931, coverage, which described Ginger as "a girl of decided charm, possessing a piquant brunette beauty. She received her education in New York city and abroad," while saying about Johnny that "for the past few years [he] has been making his home in New York where he has made a reputation as a lyricist." The announcement concluded: "The wedding will take place in the near future." Johnny Mercer to "Dear Mother and Father" on Miller Music letterhead, and "Mother Sweet," both undated but April 1931, box 1, folders 3a and 4, Mercer Family Collection, AASU. On the importance of parental involvement in arranging marriages, see Wyatt-Brown, *Southern Honor*, 199–212.

35. Johnny Mercer to "Dear Mother and Father," "Mother Sweet," and "Dear Pop," April 22, 1931, Mercer Family Collection, AASU.

36. Announcements of the wedding in New York and Savannah newspapers contained conflicting information, especially regarding the wedding site, for some accounts erroneously identified the Little Church around the Corner, better known as the Church of the Transfiguration on Twenty-ninth Street between Fifth and Madison avenues that people in show business frequented, as being the location of the ceremony. See the undated and unidentified newspaper clippings in box 6, folder 2, and also Aunt Katherine Mercer to Johnny and Ginger, June 1931, both located in JM & GM Papers, GSU. The St. Thomas Parish lists Rivers and Mrs. Leighton K. Brill as witnesses and identifies Johnny's profession as songwriter while listing no occupation for Ginger. The Manhattan County wedding certificate #12538 is dated June 8, 1931. See also the church history, *St. Thomas Church* (New York: St. Thomas Church, 1965). The former rector at St. Thomas, the Reverend Dr. Ernest M. Stires, had been one of Uncle Ed's associates and served at the time of Johnny's wedding as bishop of Long Island. Bach and Mercer, eds., *Our Huckleberry Friend*, 28–29, 56.

37. *Savannah Evening Press*, December 28, 1931. The Colonial Dames ran the tearoom. Other guests included Mrs. Francis Hunter, Mrs. Joseph Anderson, Mrs. Joseph H. Harrison, Mrs. Rauers Cunningham and her daughter, Frieda, and Augusta Clay.

38. James William McIntire, oral interview M148, and Pope Barrow McIntire, oral interview M144, Popular Music Archives, GSU. Pope was fourteen years younger than Jimmie; his comments reflect hearsay from the community.

39. Johnny Mercer to Lillian Mercer, [1932], box 1, folder 4, Mercer Family Collection, AASU; Mercer interview by Willis Conover, January 30, 1970, collection M82-8, Popular Music Archives, GSU; interview with Amanda Mercer Neder, January 27, 2010, author's possession.

40. Charles Miller to G. A. Mercer, January 15, 1932, box 2, folder 2, JM & GM Papers, GSU.

41. Songs Woodin composed include, among others, "My Raggedy Ann" and "Intermezzo"; see *ASCAP Biographical Dictionary*, 4th ed. (New York: Jacques Cattell Press, 1980), 552; Bach and Mercer, eds., *Our Huckleberry Friend*, 32.

42. Kimball et al., eds., *Complete Lyrics*, 10–11.

43. Harold Meyerson and Ernie Harburg, *Who Put the Rainbow in "The Wizard of Oz"?: Yip Harburg, Lyricist* (Ann Arbor: University of Michigan Press, 1993); Claire Meltzer, oral interview M149, Popular Music Archives, GSU; "Falling Off the Wagon," lyrics by E. Y. Harburg and John Mercer, music by Lewis E. Gensler (New York: Harms Music, 1932). See also Kimball et al., eds., *Complete Lyrics*, 8–9. Mercer and Harburg contributed lyrics to Henry Souvaine's composition, "Lost in the Sun."

44. Meyerson and Harburg, *Who Put the Rainbow in "The Wizard of Oz?"*; Parkinson interview with Mercer, GSU.

45. Edward Jablonski, *Harold Arlen: Rhythm, Rainbows, and Blues* (Boston: Northeastern University Press, 1996); JM autobiography.

46. Jablonski, *Harold Arlen*, 57–58; Kimball et al., eds., *Complete Lyrics*, 9–10.

47. Jablonski, *Harold Arlen*; Meyerson and Harburg, *Who Put the Rainbow in "The Wizard of Oz"?*

48. JM autobiography. Carmichael speculated on where he met Mercer in a letter to Mark Saxton (undated but in 1946) and in undated random notes, box 2, folder 22, Hoagy Carmichael Collection, Archives of Traditional Music, Indiana University, Bloomington, Ind. (hereafter IU).

49. Hoagy Carmichael to Tom, [1933], Carmichael Collection, IU; Richard M. Sudhalter, *Stardust Melody: The Life and Music of Hoagy Carmichael* (New York: Oxford University Press, 2002); John Edward Hasse, *The Classic Hoagy Carmichael* (Indianapolis: Indiana Historical Society, 1988). In a draft version of the manuscript "Jazz Banders" that once published became *The*

Stardust Road (New York: Rinehart, 1946), Carmichael wrote, "with the passing of Bix, my interest in music dropped about 50 percent." See Hoagy Carmichael Collection, IU.

50. Hoagy Carmichael to Mark Saxton (undated but 1946) attributes the lyric "Old Man Harlem" to Johnny Mercer. Original folio sheet music to "Washboard" with Carmichael autograph explaining its connection to "Lazybones" in Carmichael Collection, IU. Carmichael with Stephen Longstreet, *Sometimes I Wonder: The Story of Hoagy Carmichael* (New York: Farrar, Straus & Giroux, 1965), 239–40, 247–48; Carmichael to M. B. "Bass" Yardling, November 12, [1930s], notes they "more or less had to insist on the publisher working on it," which once published kept Southern Music from going under. In a letter to his friend, "Tom," Carmichael wrote, "Just finished a tune with Rudy Vallee —'Old Man Harlem'"— Rudy did the lyrics." He adds, "Just now wrote 'Lazy Bones' all of a sudden like. That's when they're best." Hoagy never mentions the name of Johnny Mercer in the 1933 letter to Tom but does in his 1946 letter to Mark Saxton; Carmichael Collection, IU. Kimball et al., eds., *Complete Lyrics*, 22–23, identify the pair of lines in the middle, "When 'taters need sprayin' / I bet you keep prayin,'" as a comment of a New Jersey farmer whom Mercer overheard when out in the countryside. Yet Mercer identified "Lazybones" as distinctively southern; see Max Wilk, *They're Playing Our Song* (New York: Atheneum, 1973). For an analysis of Tin Pan Alley southern songs see Karen L. Cox, *Dreaming of Dixie: How the South Was Created in American Popular Culture* (Chapel Hill: University of North Carolina Press, 2011).

51. Carmichael with Longstreet, *Sometimes I Wonder*, 247–48; Sudhalter, *Stardust Melody*, 152–57. In his interview with Willis Conover, Mercer recalled that writing "Lazybones" "took forever. Took . . . oh God, it took a long time." He added, "I didn't know much about writing. I learned a lot from him [Carmichael]. I learned a lot *after* that song from other writers."

52. Bach and Mercer, eds., *Our Huckleberry Friend*, 34; Kimball et al., eds., *Complete Lyrics*, 22–23; Sudhalter, *Stardust Melody*, 154–55. Sudhalter asks, "If the young scamp of 'Lazybones' is black, what of it? Does Mercer's lyric endorse, even for a moment, any notion that all black youngsters are layabouts? Certainly not." He adds that nevertheless performers now avoid singing "Lazybones," "Old Man Harlem," and similar songs because of concerns over racial sensitivity. Critics consider the mere suggestion of watermelon as making a demeaning reference to black people although watermelon actually reflects a multiracial South; see the entry by Charles Reagan Wilson in the *Encyclopedia of Southern Culture* (Chapel Hill: University of North Carolina Press, 1989). Similarly, critics attach a black identity to the idea of laziness, an odd outgrowth given the national media's longstanding stereotypical views of white southerners as lazy.

53. Suggesting that societies can be measured by their popular songs, Rowan — who imperfectly remembered the lyrics — wrote about Mercer, "I truly believe that he was telling me something when I sang lines from his 'Lazybones': 'You'll never get your day's work done resting in the morning sun. You'll never get your cornmeal made sleeping in the noonday shade.' Now it seems, Americans learn about the work ethic only from politicians who seek power by berating welfare recipients." Column reprinted in Bach and Mercer, eds., *Our Huckleberry Friend*, 231–32, lyrics on 34. On Hitler, see Sudhalter, *Stardust Melody*, 156–57.

54. James N. Gregory, *The Southern Diaspora: How the Great Migrations of Black and White Southerners Transformed America* (Chapel Hill: University of North Carolina Press, 2005). Gregory notes that in 1920 some 2.7 million southerners lived outside their native region and that the number steadily increased until it peaked in 1980, with 8 million black, 20 million white, and 1 million Latino southerners leaving the region over the course of the century (11–19). Scholars and journalists have emphasized the Great Migration of African Americans at the expense of white and Latino people who also left at the same time for similar reasons.

55. Sheet music for "Down t' Uncle Bill's" and "Moon Country" in JM Papers, GSU. See also

Kimball et al., eds., *Complete Lyrics*, 9, 25–27; Sudhalter, *Stardust Melody*, 161. In his interview with Parkinson for the BBC, Mercer recalled, "When we grew up — Hoagy is ten years older so he grew up in the fields of Indiana that Paul Dresser was writing about Back Home Again on the Wabash. . . . Now down in the South when I write about Moon River and the huckleberries along the banks . . . that's exactly how it used to be. Well, it isn't so much that way now. You drive out on the highway and you see motels and they've got neon signs . . . and the whole world is changing, not only here, not only the high rises in Paris but down South too and in Indiana." In Carmichael, *Sometimes I Wonder*, 10, Hoagy describes his neighbor, the Indiana poet James Whitcomb Riley, lifting him up and carrying him on his shoulders to the grocery store to buy the boy bananas and candy. Riley's poetry played on nostalgia as in *An Old Sweetheart of Mine* (New York: Grosset & Dunlap, 1888).

56. Carmichael, *Sometimes I Wonder*, 230, 247; see also first and second drafts to *Sometimes I Wonder* in which Carmichael said, "About my music I was stubborn, contrary, tenacious, and resolute in the fight, punching away," and see Carmichael to Mark Saxton, undated (1946), both in Carmichael Collection, IU. In his autobiography, Johnny admitted: "Hoagy Carmichael, for whom I had such a hard time writing words in New York, was completely different in Hollywood." He then rhetorically asked, "Have you ever had a tough teacher whom you appreciated later? That's how it was to write with Hoagy. . . . I felt intimidated much of the time and tightened up too much to do my best work." See also André Previn interview by Clint Eastwood and Bruce Ricker, Popular Music Archives, GSU.

57. Composer and sometime Mercer collaborator Robert Emmett Dolan identified Johnny's genius as enabling the collaborations: "it's no accident that he's been able to work with so many great composers," for quotation see Gene Lees, *Portrait of Johnny: The Life of John Herndon Mercer* (New York: Pantheon Books, 2004), 30. Yet Dolan's own correspondence suggests that at times he had difficulties working with Johnny; see his papers in the University of Wyoming, copies in Popular Music Archives, GSU; on composer hopping, see Meyerson and Harburg, *Who Put the Rainbow in "The Wizard of Oz?* 38.

58. *Brooklyn-Queens Journal*, March 29, 1932; Thomas A. DeLong, *Pops: Paul Whiteman, King of Jazz* (Piscataway, N.J.: New Century, 1983), 168–70; Furia, *Skylark*, 67–68. In Bach and Mercer, eds., *Our Huckleberry Friend*, Mercer says that after he performed, "Paul came out and said, 'Who's that piano player?' I said, 'That's Archie Bleyer, the jazz arranger.' Then he said, 'No wonder.' That's probably why I won the contest" (26). Having collaborated in 1932 with Johnny on "Deep South in My Heart" and other songs, Bleyer (who later led Arthur Godfrey's orchestra) also introduced Mercer to Carmichael.

59. DeLong, *Pops*, 170, 184; Lees, *Portrait of Johnny*, 97–98; Bach and Mercer, eds., *Our Huckleberry Friend*, 26. Although Whiteman did not care for the trio that consisted of Johnny, pianist Jack Thompson, and Harold Arlen's brother, Jerry, the bandleader kept Mercer. Neither did Whiteman hire guitarist Dick Hancock when Johnny arranged an audition for his Savannah friend. See JM autobiography.

60. Jay D. Smith and Len Guttridge, *Jack Teagarden: The Story of a Jazz Maverick* (New York: Da Capo Press, 1976).

61. DeLong, *Pops*, 184–85; Kimball et al., eds., *Complete Lyrics*, 24–25. Mercer later thought the comic and high sound Whiteman required of him for the Teagarden duets stunted his singing voice and kept him away from performing ballads; Smith and Guttridge, *Jack Teagarden*, 107–9.

62. Smith and Guttridge, *Jack Teagarden*, 107–9; Furia, *Skylark*, 68; James Lincoln Collier, *Benny Goodman and the Swing Era* (New York: Oxford University Press, 1989), 95–109; Ross Firestone, *Swing, Swing, Swing: The Life and Times of Benny Goodman* (New York: W. W. Norton, 1993), 77–87. At the time of the recording, Goodman dated Holiday; see Stuart Nichol-

son, *Billie Holiday* (Boston: Northeastern University Press, 1995), 130–31, 257; Hammond and Townsend, *John Hammond on Record*, 91–92, 119.

63. Collier, *Benny Goodman*, 108–9; Chilton, *Who's Who of Jazz*, 236, 365; first Mercer quote in Nicholson, *Billie Holiday*, 48–49, second Mercer quote in Donald Clarke, *Wishing on the Moon: The Life and Times of Billie Holiday* (New York: Viking Penguin, 1994), 76. Given that Wesley Wilson wrote the song mentioned by LeRoi Jones, one must wonder which songs the black critic had in mind when he chastised African American writers, saying that "it would be better if such a poet listened to Bessie Smith sing *Gimme a Pigfoot*, or listened to the tragic verse of a Billie Holiday, than be content to imperfectly imitate the bad poetry of the ruined minds of Europe." Although Holiday wrote lyrics to "God Bless the Child" and "Don't Explain," songwriters like Mercer contributed the vast majority of titles in her repertoire. See LeRoi Jones, *Home: Social Essays by LeRoi Jones* (New York: William Morrow, 1966), 113; Leslie Gourse, ed., *The Billie Holiday Companion: Seven Decades of Commentary* (New York: Schirmer Books, 1997), 92, 143. Gourse quotes Holiday's interview by Willis Conover, in which she identifies the influences of Louis Armstrong and Bessie Smith (63); Nicholson, *Billie Holiday*, 47–49, 130–31, 257. Nicholson observes about "Riffin' the Scotch" that the tempo of the recording "allows her a degree of improvisatory manoeuvrability that enables her to stretch and contract lyrics in a way that would become a hallmark of her style, such as between bars thirteen and fifteen of her vocal" (49).

64. *ASCAP Biographical Dictionary*, 211; Nicholson, *Billie Holiday*, identifies January 12, 1938, as the recording date for "When a Woman Loves a Man" on which Gordon Jenkins assisted Hanighen with the music (261); "Here Come the British," Irving Berlin Inc., 1934.

65. *ASCAP Biographical Dictionary*, 319; *Song Hit Folio* (New York: Engel van Wiseman, 1934), 1:7. Other publications designed for the consumer market in which Mercer's lyrics frequently appeared include *Song Hits Magazine* and *Broadcast Songs: Radio, Stage, Screen*. Jack Robbins to Johnny Mercer, April 1, 1936, JM Papers, GSU.

66. DeLong, *Pops*, 177–79; Mercer interview by Conover; Lees, *Portrait of Johnny*, 98; Smith and Guttridge, *Jack Teagarden*, 111; *Newsweek*, January 29, 1945.

67. *Savannah Evening Press*, February 1, 1934.

68. JM autobiography; Herb Sanford, *Tommy and Jimmy: The Dorsey Years* (New Rochelle, N.Y.: Arlington House, 1972), 19–40, McKenzie quote on 40.

69. Alcohol played a key role in male bonding and displays of honor, while drunkenness often led to risky behavior that could result in dishonor; see Wyatt-Brown, *Southern Honor*, 277–81.

70. JM autobiography; Bach and Mercer, eds., *Our Huckleberry Friend*, 29; Kimball et al., eds., *Complete Lyrics*, 43; unidentified (magazine) clipping, "Meet Johnny Mercer" (undated, ca. 1940), JM Papers, GSU.

71. David Shipman, *Judy Garland: The Secret Life of an American Legend* (New York: Hyperion, 1993), 37–41. Jessel appeared on the same bill at the Oriental Theater. Gerald Clarke, *Get Happy: The Life of Judy Garland* (New York: Random House, 2000), 5–22; Gerold Frank, *Judy* (New York: Harper & Row, 1975), 3–17. See also the *Official World's Fair Weekly*, May 21, 27, and June 4, 1933.

72. DeLong, *Pops*, 176–97; Johnny Mercer to Darling [Ginger Mercer], undated, JM Papers, GSU.

73. *Savannah Evening Press*, "Johnny Mercer 'Goes Hollywood,'" April 3, 1935.

74. Bach and Mercer, eds., *Our Huckleberry Friend*.

75. JM autobiography; Nicholson, *Billie Holiday*, 258. These appeared on the Brunswick label as the thirteenth and fourteenth songs she recorded.

76. JM autobiography; Joseph Epstein, *Fred Astaire* (New Haven, Conn.: Yale University Press, 2008), contains errors regarding Astaire's relationship with Mercer. "I'm Building Up to an Awful Let Down," words by Johnny Mercer, music by Fred Astaire. The lyric referenced a popular oper-

etta of the previous decade, *Castles in the Air,* by Percy Wenrich with lyrics by Raymond W. Peck, which in turn refers to flights of fancy that vanish like daydreams.

77. JM autobiography; Mercer interview by Conover. Mercer thought of the words to "Goody Goody" while in the hospital recuperating from jaundice; see *Newsweek,* January 29, 1945. Some accounts suggest the idea for the title came after Mercer read a Chinese menu.

78. JM autobiography; James M. Salem, *A Guide to Critical Reviews,* pt. 2, *The Musical, 1909–1989* (Metuchen, N.J.: Scarecrow, 1991), 366–67; Gerald Bordman, *American Musical Theatre: A Chronicle,* 2nd ed. (New York: Oxford University Press, 1992), 38–39, 486, 514. See also Brian Ward, "Blackbirds in Britain: Florence Mills, Johnny Mercer, and British Imaginings of the American South between the Two World Wars," unpublished paper delivered at the *Popular Music in the Mercer Era, 1910–1970* centennial conference, November 13, 2009, Georgia State University, Atlanta, copy in author's possession.

79. *ASCAP Biographical Dictionary,* 47.

80. "Keep a Twinkle in Your Eye" and "Dixie Isn't Dixie Anymore," words by Johnny Mercer, music by Rube Bloom (London: Compton, 1936); see also Kimball et al., eds., *Complete Lyrics,* 46–47. Mercer wrote Robbins, "You were right about the trip to England. I did make a mountain out of a molehill and although I have been a great deal happier during my lifetime, it wasn't quite as bad as I anticipated." See Mercer to Robbins, July 14, 1936, JM Papers, GSU.

81. Bach and Mercer, eds., *Our Huckleberry Friend,* 69; JM autobiography; *Edinburgh and Leath Post Office Directory* (Edinburgh: Morrison & Gibb, 1936–37). Johnny wrote Robbins, "I am going to Scotland for two weeks rest, where I hope to get rid of a sinus condition which you brought on by sending me over here in the first place"; see Mercer to Robbins, July 14, 1936, JM Papers, GSU.

82. Telegrams and letters between Mercer and Robbins from June 1936 to July 1937, JM Papers, GSU. According to an August 11, 1936, telegram to Mercer from Robbins, Whiting "has been anxious to offer you [Mercer] with thing as team but was turned down by Jack Lavin," and then in a letter dated August 21, 1936, Robbins said, "already everybody knows you will write with Dick [Whiting]." Returning copyright on several lyrics to Johnny, Robbins noted, "Even though Metz [Mercer] isn't writing for me, I still think Metz is tops and I am particularly interested in his work." See Robbins to Mercer, July 21, 1937. Over time the two patched up the relationship and engaged in the occasional business deal; see Barbara Robbins, oral interview M158, Popular Music Archives, GSU. Throughout the correspondence it is clear Mercer wants to live in Hollywood and write with Richard Whiting and the studios.

83. Sudhalter, *Stardust Melody,* 176; Tony Thomas, *Harry Warren and the Hollywood Musical* (Secaucus, N.J.: Citadel Press, 1975), 103. On the fusion of jazz and popular song in the movies, see Henry Pleasants, *Serious Music — and All That Jazz* (New York: Fireside Book, 1969).

84. Although Mercer had been credited with writing the counter remarks in such songs as "Marie," Johnny explained to Willis Conover he might have done something similar on one of his own earlier Decca recordings but that Tommy and the boys came up with such phrases as "Oh, Mama," used to punctuate Dorsey's music. See Mercer interview by Conover. See also Peter J. Levinson, *Tommy Dorsey: A Biography; Livin' in a Great Big Way* (Cambridge, Mass.: Da Capo Press, 2005).

Chapter Four. Hollywood

The epigraph is from "Hooray For Hollywood" (1938), with music by Richard A. Whiting. See Robert Kimball, Barry Day, Miles Kreuger, and Eric Davis, eds., *The Complete Lyrics of Johnny Mercer* (New York: Alfred A. Knopf, 2009), 60.

1. A thorough analysis of the subject may be found in Clive Hirschhorn, *The Hollywood Musical* (New York: Crown, 1981).

2. American Society of Composers, Authors and Publishers, comp., *ASCAP Biographical Dictionary*, 4th ed. (New York: Jacques Cattell Press, 1980), 541; for copies of the contracts, see the Warner Bros. Archive of Historical Papers, Department of Special Collections, Doheny Library, University of Southern California, Los Angeles (hereafter USC).

3. Transcript of Johnny Mercer interview by Willis Conover, January 30, 1970, and William "Bill" Harbach, oral interview M130, Popular Music Archives, Georgia State University, Atlanta, Ga. (hereafter GSU).

4. Margaret Whiting and Will Holt, *It Might as Well Be Spring: A Musical Autobiography* (New York: William Morrow, 1987), 31–33, 37, and passim.

5. Ibid., 31–33; *ASCAP Biographical Dictionary*, 19, 258, 541.

6. Edward Jablonski, *Harold Arlen: Rhythm, Rainbows, and Blues* (Boston: Northeastern University Press, 1996), 196–97; Robert Rush, oral interview M154, and Barbara Robbins, oral interview M158, Popular Music Archives, GSU.

7. Hirschhorn, *Hollywood Musical*, 139; Ken Bloom, *Hollywood Song: The Complete Film and Musical Companion*, 3 vols. (New York: Facts on File, 1995), 1:753–54; Mercer interview by Conover. On *Ready, Willing, and Able*, see box 818, Warner Bros. Archive, USC.

8. Whiteman to Mercer, September 13, 1937, Mercer to Whiteman, September 16, 1937, and Gus Kahn to Johnny Mercer, November 8, 1937, all in box 2, folder 7, JM Papers, GSU.

9. Hirschhorn, *Hollywood Musical*, 147. Hirschhorn said *Hollywood Hotel* marked "the end of an era." See also Peter J. Levinson, *Trumpet Blues: The Life of Harry James* (New York: Oxford University Press, 1999), 45; Whiting and Holt, *It Might as Well Be Spring*, 29. On *Hollywood Hotel*, see boxes 479–81, Warner Bros. Archive, USC.

10. Hirschhorn, *Hollywood Musical*, 147; Mercer interview by Conover; Whiting and Holt, *It Might as Well Be Spring*, 29; Robert Kimball, Barry Day, Miles Kreuger, and Eric Davis, eds., *The Complete Lyrics of Johnny Mercer* (New York: Alfred A. Knopf, 2009), 59–60; Bob Bach and Ginger Mercer, eds., *Our Huckleberry Friend: The Life, Times, and Lyrics of Johnny Mercer* (Secaucus, N.J.: Lyle Stuart, 1982), 61; on fatalism and the code of honor to which Mercer held, see Bertram Wyatt-Brown, *Southern Honor: Ethics and Behavior in the Old South*, 25th ann. ed. (New York: Oxford University Press, 2007), 27–32. For the 1950s lyric, see Doris Day's recording on *Great American Songwriters: Johnny Mercer*, vol. 2 (Los Angeles: Rhino Records, 1993), and for the 1970s version, see Anita O'Day on *Mostly Mercer* (Jackson Heights, N.Y.: Painted Smiles Records, 1989). The film's lyrics go "It makes your dreams come true / Just like the movies do, / Hooray for Hollywood!"

11. Whiting and Holt, *It Might as Well Be Spring*, 38–43; *ASCAP Biographical Dictionary*, 541. On the Age of the Singer, see Henry Pleasants, *Serious Music—and All That Jazz* (New York: Simon & Schuster, 1969), 164–68. Margaret Whiting died on January 10, 2011, at age eighty-six.

12. Bloom, *Hollywood Song*, 190, 316, 339–40; Hirschhorn, *Hollywood Musical*, 149–51; Bob Colonna, *"Greetings, Gate!": The Story of Professor Jerry Colonna* (Albany, Ga.: Bear Manor Media, 2007), 64–65; Mercer interview by Conover. For more information regarding *Gold Diggers in Paris* (boxes 410–12), *Garden of the Moon* (boxes 386–88), *Jezebel* (boxes 534–35), and other films, see Warner Bros. Archive, USC.

13. Hirschhorn, *Hollywood Musical*, 155; transcript of Johnny Mercer interview by Humphrey Lyttleton, BBC *Omnibus*, season 2, episode 19, July 14, 1974, Popular Music Archives, GSU; for more on *Going Places*, see boxes 408–9, Warner Bros. Archive, USC. Also in the movie appeared a young actor named Ronald Reagan.

14. Hirschhorn, *Hollywood Musical*, 161; *Naughty but Nice*, boxes 704–5, Warner Bros.

Archive, USC; "Day In—Day Out" and "Fools Rush In" lyrics in Bach and Mercer, eds., *Our Huckleberry Friend*, 74, 95; see also Kimball et al., eds., *Complete Lyrics*, 83, 97; Mercer interview by Conover. See also Alexander Pope's *Essay on Criticism*, book 1, 625.

15. *ASCAP Biographical Dictionary*, 19. Van Heusen won Oscars for "Swinging on a Star" in 1944 with Johnny Burke, "All the Way" in 1957, "High Hopes" in 1959, and "Call Me Irresponsible" in 1963, all three with lyricist Sammy Cahn, who also won for "Three Coins in the Fountain" in 1954 with Jule Styne. For the lyric sheets to "Blue Rain," "I Thought about You," and "Make with the Kisses," see box 30, folders 1, 4, 6, and for the business correspondence regarding these songs, box 120, folder 36, in the Jimmy Van Heusen Collection, Special Collections, Music Library, University of California, Los Angeles (hereafter UCLA).

16. Mercer interview by Conover. See sketches of "I Thought about You," folder 4, and draft music, box 8, folder 25, in Jimmy Van Heusen Collection, UCLA. Van Heusen's wife apparently disliked Johnny's wild ways and opposed the collaboration. James Van Heusen "Chester" to JHM, n.d. (1974), box 2, folder 23, JM Papers, GSU; Kimball et al., eds., *Complete Lyrics*, 84, 362.

17. Hirschhorn, *Hollywood Musical*, 170, 180, 184, 193; Peter Townsend, *Pearl Harbor Jazz: Change in Popular Music in the Early 1940s* (Jackson: University Press of Mississippi, 2007), 53. Townsend quotes Warren saying that the studios viewed songwriters as "the lowest form of animal life." Among McHugh's songs were "On the Sunny Side of the Street" and "I'm in the Mood for Love." See *ASCAP Biographical Dictionary*, 337; *Navy Blues*, boxes 706–8, Warner Bros. Archive, USC. Harold Arlen, quoted in *New York Times* July 24, 1976.

18. Mandy's husband, Bob Corwin, a jazz pianist who took down Mercer's compositions, recalled, "Johnny *heard* songs. The fact that he was not a professional musician meant absolutely *nothing*. Johnny was a *songwriter*. He heard the melody, he heard the harmonies, he simply didn't know how to write them." See Lees, *Portrait of Johnny*, 231. On ASCAP management, see Russell Sanjek, *Pennies from Heaven: The American Popular Music Business in the Twentieth Century* (New York: Da Capo Press, 1996).

19. Mercer grew up in a patriarchal society that cherished women as ornaments and sexual objects; see Wyatt-Brown, *Southern Honor*, 226–35. "Show Your Linen, Miss Richardson," words by Johnny Mercer, music by Bernie Hanighen (New York: Bourne, 1939), reprinted in Kimball et al., eds., *Complete Lyrics*, 83.

20. "The Week End of a Private Secretary," lyrics by Johnny Mercer, music by Bernie Hanighen (New York: Remick Music, 1938); Hirschhorn, *Hollywood Musical*, 180; Kimball et al., eds., *Complete Lyrics*, 69, 84, 99, 115. "As fresh and as wholesome as the flowers in May," Queenie "hopes to retire to the farm someday, / But you can't buy a farm until you're up in the chips, / So the band plays the polka while she strips!" Even though she's "a peach when she's dressed," "the State Board of Censors / Have declared it a crime, / So she stops—/ And always just in time!" The film censor Joseph L. Breen disliked the idea of a moral striptease so much that he banned the song from the picture. On Crosby's recording of "Personality," after singing "Just tell me how you like my . . . ," Mercer ad-libs "Ruff!" with Bing ending ". . . Personality." JM autobiography.

21. Bach and Mercer, eds., *Our Huckleberry Friend*, 56; Kimball et al., eds., *Complete Lyrics*, 44–45. Cornelia Jackson McIntire married Walter Rivers in Savannah's Cathedral of St. John the Baptist on February 8, 1936. Arnold Shaw, *The Street That Never Slept: New York's Fabled 52d St.* (New York: Coward, McCann & Geoghegan, 1971), 107; Gary Giddins, *Bing Crosby: A Pocketful of Dreams, the Early Years, 1903–1940* (Boston: Little, Brown, 2001), 416–18. As a New Orleans native born of Sicilian parents in the Tremé neighborhood, Prima reflected the hybridity of southern culture; see Bruce Raeburn, "The Sicilian Jazzman," in *Louisiana Endowment for the Humanities*, Summer 2006.

22. Giddins, *Bing Crosby*, quotes Crosby's close friend, Kentuckian Rosemary Clooney, who

suggested that "he did like southerners," going on to say about Crosby, "He loved southern women — it was almost a prerequisite. He wouldn't ask anyone if they were southern, but he got along with southerners very well" (459). Philip Furia, *Skylark: The Life and Times of Johnny Mercer* (New York: St. Martin's Press, 2003), 98, calls "Bob White" "a compendium of big band era musician jive talk." Oddly enough, Kimball et al., eds., *Complete Lyrics*, 64, neglect to include the second refrain whereby the lyrics explain Bob White has jazzed up his trill to the delight of the other birds. After alcoholism claimed Dixie's life, Crosby married Texan Kathryn Grandstaff. The Crosby, Hope, and Mercer children got together at birthday parties according to Amanda Mercer Neder, interview, January 27, 2010, author's possession.

23. The program for the benefit is in box 32, folder 3, JM Papers, GSU; Macfarlane, *Bing Crosby*, 156; Gerald Clarke, *Get Happy: The Life of Judy Garland* (New York: Random House, 2000), 5–22; Gerold Frank, *Judy* (New York: Harper & Row, 1975), 3–17.

24. Barry Ulanov, *The Incredible Crosby* (New York: Whittlesey House, 1948), 141–46; Giddins, *Bing Crosby*, 459–61; materials on the Westwood Marching and Chowder Club located in box 7, folder 17, JM & GM Papers, GSU.

25. Ulanov, *Incredible Crosby*, 146; Giddins, *Bing Crosby*, 462–63; box 7, folder 17, JM & GM Papers, GSU; Joe Laurie Jr., *Vaudeville: From the Honky-tonks to the Palace* (New York: Henry Holt, 1953), 76, 83.

26. Malcolm Macfarlane, *Bing Crosby: Day by Day* (Lanham, Md.: Scarecrow Press, 2001), 175–77, 201, 248. Mercer appeared on the *Kraft Music Hall* on November 17, 1938, and then reflecting his success, on the special holiday broadcasts of July 4, 1940, and December 31, 1942; Bing to Johnny, reprinted in Bach and Mercer, eds., *Our Huckleberry Friend*, 55.

27. Macfarlane, *Bing Crosby*, 167, 174; Wingy Manone and Paul Vandervoort II, *Trumpet on the Wing* (New York: Doubleday, 1948), 163–67; Mercer quoted in Giddins, *Bing Crosby*, 416, 451, as well as Clooney on 515; Crosby quoted in Ulanov, *Incredible Crosby*, 291. Crosby to Mercer, April 13, 1939, box 2, folder 7, JM Papers, GSU. Drinking bonded the two men, too, which might also explain the distance that developed after Bing swore off liquor.

28. Bing, *Day by Day*, 152, 173, 175, 199, 225–26; Gleason quoted in Pleasants, *Serious Music*, 165. Johnny wrote "Mister Meadowlark" with Walter Donaldson. Furia, *Skylark*, describes Mercer throughout as patrician but interprets this to mean a disdain for hard work, something that makes little sense given the success of the man. Mercer's easy-going behavior might have struck Furia as an aversion to labor, something he describes as Johnny's reluctance to break out in a sweat. Yet such genteel behavior does not equate with an unwillingness to work long hours for low pay. Rather, it reflects an attitude toward life and a code of conduct around others. Mercer's relaxed response and in-control appearance underscored a man at ease in his world. It also followed that when alcohol loosened the control of the gentleman, the responding behavior could be most ungentlemanly. This, too, fit the patrician pattern. Bing Crosby identified Louis Armstrong as the greatest singer of the century because of his ability to make a happy song happy and a sad song sad.

29. A special issue of *Palm Springs Life: California's Prestige Magazine*, September 1999, 149–71, celebrated Palm Spring's fifty years as a Hollywood magnet; *Savannah Evening Press*, January 17, 1938. The card appears in the *Savannah Evening Press*, December 28, 1938. In the verse, Johnny writes: "Then there's F for Families / Christmas 'gif' to both of these, / Mother, Mother, Father, too. / Walter, Big and Little Hugh, / Ed and Deborah and Claire. / Polish up the silverware, / Lay the snowy tablespread. / Uncles Lewis, Rob and Ed / Gather 'round, all get clubby, / Meet Elizabeth's new hubby, / George and Bess and George the Third; / Cousin Mamie, cut the bird, / Mercer, Adeline, Aunt K. / Polish off the egg frappe; / Dorothy and Mary Lou, / Joseph and Virginia, too — / Every oldster, every sprout — / Mustn't leave a person out. / Uncle Joe will mix the toddy. / Happy headaches everybody!" Mercer gained fame for his Christmas

greetings, and he occasionally sent them to be published in Savannah; see also the *Savannah Morning News*, December 25, 1969.

30. JHM to "Mother darling," March 4, 1939, box 1, folder 4, Mercer Family Collection, AASU. Mercer rented apartments at 3 East 66th Street and then at 111 East 60th Street, New York.

31. Gerald Bordman, *American Musical Theatre: A Chronicle*, 3rd ed. (New York: Oxford University Press, 1992), 503, 514. *New York Times*, February 13, 1939; James Gavin, *Stormy Weather: The Life of Lena Horne* (New York: Atria Books, 2009), 69–74.

32. Mercer quoted in the *Detroit Free Press*, March 2, 1939. Carmichael had signed with Paramount and shortly thereafter brought his family to California to live. His wife, Ruth Meinardi, a native of Chicago who had matriculated at the Lucy Cobb Institute, a girls' finishing school in Georgia, before attending Indiana University, was quite adept at the Hollywood social life, and the Carmichaels soon became popular guests. Richard M. Sudhalter, *Stardust Melody: The Life and Music of Hoagy Carmichael* (New York: Oxford University Press, 2002), 185–86. Johnny found them "our best parlor entertainers"; see JM autobiography, ch. 12, 7.

33. Bordman, *American Musical Theatre*, 520; Carmichael, *Sometimes I Wonder*, 264–65.

34. Carmichael, *Sometimes I Wonder*, 264–65.

35. Steven Suskin, *Show Tunes: The Songs, Shows, and Careers of Broadway's Major Composers* (New York: Oxford University Press, 2000), 390–91; other songs are "Darn Clever, These Chinee," "Everything Happens to Me," "How Nice for Me," and "What'll They Think of Next"; Larry Hart to Mercer, June 4, 1940, box 2, folder 8, JM Papers, GSU. Mercer quote from JM autobiography. *New York Times*, June 5, 1940. In *Skylark*, Furia suggests: "The same problem with the book for a musical would dog most of Mercer's attempts to have an enduring success on Broadway. Yet he would never attempt what Charlie Miller had told Mercer's father Johnny had to learn to do: write the book, as well as the lyrics, for a Broadway musical" (114–15). Actually, Johnny did try to write the book, lyrics, and music for a couple of musicals, "Beauty from Ashes" and "Mike."

36. Sudhalter, *Stardust Melody*, 215, 227–30; Mercer quoted in Furia, *Skylark*, 82–88, 12. To Furia, in the song "Skylark," Mercer "gave voice to his longing for Judy Garland," with whom he was having a love affair at the time he wrote the song (*Skylark*, 130–31).

37. Original score to "Music Master" with the "hot" notation in Hoagy Carmichael Papers, Lilly Library, Indiana University, Bloomington, Ind. Kimball et al., eds., *Complete Lyrics*, 140; Teagarden and Mercer duet and Will Friedwald, "Johnny Mercer Sings Johnny Mercer: A Centennial Appreciation," liner notes, *Mercer Sings Mercer* (Hollywood: EMI Music Special Markets, 2009).

38. *Newsweek*, January 29, 1945, 85–86; Townsend, *Pearl Harbor Jazz*, 42–52.

39. John Dunning, *Tune In Yesterday: The Ultimate Encyclopedia of Old-time Radio, 1925–1976* (Englewood Cliffs, N.J.: Prentice-Hall, 1976), 25. Perhaps Templeton used "And the Angels Sing" to promote the marriage of "serious" with "popular" music, an outcome later recommended by critic Henry Pleasants in place of the schism that actually occurred; see Pleasants, *Serious Music — and All That Jazz* (New York: Simon & Schuster, 1969), 29; various Warner Bros. *Merrie Melodies* cartoons such as *Daffy Duck and the Dinosaur* and *Have You Got Any Castles* dated from the late 1930s to the early 1940s and may be seen on Looney Tunes Golden Collections V1, V2, V3, V5; "Harold Teen," and other cartoons may be found in JM Papers, GSU.

40. David W. Stowe, *Swing Changes: Big-band Jazz in New Deal America* (Cambridge, Mass.: Harvard University Press, 1994), shows how the interrelated jazz and popular music called swing dominated mass culture and expressed a new inclusive ideology of Americanism. Observing that "popular song recorded before 1955 has not been considered worthy of attention in its own right, *as* popular song rather than as raw material for jazz or another so-called authentic idiom," Townsend sets out to correct the slight. He suggests that for too long "jazz has been seen as

producing its innovations in an internal way, discovering various intervals and tones by a process of pure research." Whereas critics have preferred to keep jazz "separate from popular music; in actuality, however, jazz players spent a lot of time playing nothing but the popular song repertoire. The internal approach of jazz historians holds that the development of harmony in jazz in the early 1940s did not come from outside of jazz music itself—and definitely not from the efforts of popular songwriters like Harold Arlen and Harry Warren." But Townsend then demonstrates otherwise, underscoring the interpenetration of jazz and popular music. See Townsend, *Pearl Harbor Jazz*, 42–52.

41. An exceptional study of the subject is Dave Oliphant, *The Early Swing Era, 1930 to 1941* (Westport, Conn.: Greenwood Press, 2002). John Hammond also promoted Count Basie and His Band, who won acclaim for their playing of swing music; Lewis A. Erenberg, *Swingin' the Dream: Big Band Jazz and the Rebirth of American Culture* (Chicago: University of Chicago Press, 1998), 65–98. Erenberg considers how desegregated groups promoted a liberalization of race relations in the era. Swing music clearly reflected multiracial cooperation, a fact that bothered black music ideologists such as LeRoi Jones, who in 1963 wrote, "Philosophically, swing sought to involve the black culture in a platonic social blandness that would erase it forever, replacing it with the socio-cultural compromise of the 'jazzed-up' popular song: a compromise whose most significant stance was finally catatonia and noncommunication." See LeRoi Jones, *Blues People: Negro Music in White America* (New York: HarperCollins Perennial, 2002), 181.

42. Ross Firestone, *Swing, Swing, Swing: The Life and Times of Benny Goodman* (New York: W. W. Norton, 1993), 178–79; James Lincoln Collier, *Benny Goodman and the Swing Era* (New York: Oxford University Press, 1989), 246. The Palomar stood at Vermont and Second. At the time Johnny worked at RKO. The teenagers cared more for the dance music than the film, *Maid of Salem*, showing at the Paramount.

43. Firestone, *Swing, Swing, Swing*, 190–91; Collier, *Benny Goodman*, 246. For a perceptive analysis of the southern diaspora in California that captures the world of Lionel Hampton, see Douglas Flamming, *Bound for Freedom: Black Los Angeles in Jim Crow America* (Berkeley: University of California Press, 2005), esp. 35–59 and 92–125. On these and other big bands, see Oliphant, *Early Swing Era*. John Hammond tipped Goodman off to the talented Hampton, who played his vibraphone in a Los Angeles dive called the Paradise Cafe. Accompanied by Krupa and the black pianist Teddy Wilson, Goodman and Hampton jammed for a while, then decided to organize the Goodman Quartet. See Benny Goodman, *Benny: King of Swing*, intro. by Stanley Baron (New York: William Morrow, 1979), 33–34, 39.

44. On the role of girl singers, see Firestone, *Swing, Swing, Swing*, 128–29; Collier, *Benny Goodman*, 136–37; Goodman, *Benny*, 50–51.

45. Dunning, *Tune in Yesterday*, 108–9; Kimball et al., eds., *Complete Lyrics, 94*; Goodman, *Benny*, 51.

46. Firestone, *Swing, Swing, Swing*, 206, 214; Collier, *Benny Goodman*, 245–46. The other fraelich Goodman recorded is "Bei Mir Bist du Schön." Furia, *Skylark*, 107–8; Goodman, *Benny*, 51. Baron notes about Goodman's band at this time: "Benny often managed to select musicians of comparable quality. But never again did he succeed in keeping such a redoubtable array for any length of time" (43). The music is credited to Ziggy Elman, while Mercer's lyric is reprinted in Bach and Mercer, eds., *Our Huckleberry Friend*, 70, and in Kimball et al., eds., *Complete Lyrics*, 83. Bing Crosby to "Verseable," April 13, 1939; in a second letter undated but from the same time, Crosby commends Mercer, writing, "your shows have been consistently good." See box 2, folder 7, JM Papers, GSU.

47. Gene Buck to Mercer, April 29, 1940, box 2, folder 8, JM Papers, GSU; for more on the struggle, see the chapter "ASCAP versus the Broadcasters" in Sanjek with Sanjek, *Pennies from*

Heaven, 184–211; John Bush Jones, *The Songs That Fought the War: Popular Music and the Home Front, 1939–1945* (Waltham, Mass.: Brandeis University Press, 2006), 2–4.

48. JHM to "Mother Darling," January 24, 1941, box 1, folder 4, Mercer Family Collection, AASU; "ASCAP on Parade," box 2, folder 8, JM Papers, GSU. See also the *New York Times*, February 1, 1941.

49. Rush oral interview, GSU. Emphasizing how hard Hollywood could be on divorced spouses of celebrities, Rush noted, "The minute they're gone, nobody remembers."

50. On honor, marriage, divorce, and adultery, see the chapter "Status, Law, and Sexual Misconduct," in Wyatt-Brown, *Southern Honor*, 292–324; John Berendt, *Midnight in the Garden of Good and Evil* (New York: Random House, 1994), 154–56.

51. JHM to "Mother Darling," September 17, 1940, Mercer Family Collection, AASU; Lees, *Portrait of Johnny*, 181–82; Furia, *Skylark*, 125, 185, 189. Barbara Robbins, who worked with Johnny at Commander Publishing but had known him for years through her husband Marshall Robbins, recalled talking with her friend, Penny Singleton, about Ginger and her companion, Marc "Red" Cramer. In the 1930s Penny had danced as a chorus girl with Ginger, who, she explained to Barbara, had an affair with Cramer in 1945. See Robbins oral interview, GSU.

52. David Shipman, *Judy Garland: The Secret Life of an American Legend* (New York: Hyperion, 1992), 122; Clarke, *Get Happy*, 146; Frank, *Judy*, 154; Bob Hope with Melville Shavelson, *Don't Shoot, It's Only Me: Bob Hope's Comedy History of the United States* (New York: Putnam, 1990), 54–56; Lees, *Portrait of Johnny*, 175–79; Robert Kimball, ed., *The Complete Lyrics of Cole Porter* (New York: Alfred A. Knopf, 1983), 188. A Decca recording session for Bing Crosby left time for Garland to complete a series of cuts, including the duet with Mercer that the company released as "Friendship" on the A-Side of 3165. See Scott Schechter, *Judy Garland: The Day-by-Day Chronicle of a Legend* (New York: Cooper Square Press, 2002), 65. In his accounting of Garland's activities, Schechter otherwise misses her interactions with Mercer. The first published reference to the Mercer-Garland affair appears to have occurred during Johnny's lifetime in Anne Edwards, *Judy Garland: A Biography* (New York: Simon and Schuster, 1974), 91. Garland biographer Clarke discusses the affair with Mercer; see *Get Happy*, 146.

53. Shipman, *Judy Garland*, 118, quotes Mickey Rooney, "who knew that in the spring of 1941 'she was at last in love with someone who loved her'" (118). Shipman said the man remained a mystery, although he is identified as Mercer in Edwards, *Judy Garland*, 91, and Clarke, *Get Happy*, 145. See also Furia, *Skylark*, 3, 129–30; and Lees, *Portrait of Johnny*, 175–82. Jean Bach identifies Betty Downey, the wife of Mercer's Savannah friend Jimmy Downey and grandmother of actor Robert Downey Jr., as confronting Garland over the affair. Bach describes Mercer as "so smitten that you can't hear when people are talking to you" but adds that given Garland's "self-destructive" behavior "he was lucky to have escaped." Bach is also the source for Clarke's *Get Happy*. See Jean Bach, oral interview M128, Popular Music Archives, GSU.

54. Walter (Rivers) to "Darling" (Cornelia McIntire), undated but referenced to 1935; Dot Wolf to Walter (Rivers), postmarked March 19, 1970; Johnny (Mercer) to "Darling" (Cornelia McIntire Rivers), ca. 1964; all in the Walter Rivers Papers, University of West Florida, Pensacola, Fla. Around 1930, Johnny wrote a friend from his home on Gwinnett Street, "I've stopped falling in love consciously, big boy, and find it much more satisfying. Date more girls & lots more loving." See Mercer to "Fred" Hobbs, n.d., box 3, folder 8, JM & GM Papers, GSU. Furia's critique of Mercer's philandering reflects the era's middle-class morality rather than acknowledging that such behavior was commonplace among elite men of a certain rank and status, especially in the South; see *Skylark*, 53–54, 123–32. An article in *Key: The Weekly Magazine of Southern California Life*, September 1945, 13–20, explained Mercer painted and decorated his house with the watercolors;

see also Wyatt-Brown, *Southern Honor*, 309, and Amanda Mercer Neder oral interview, January 27, 2010, author's possession.

55. Lees, *Portrait of Johnny*, 138–39; Colonna, *"Greetings, Gate!"* 91–92. Other Ciuceviches proved quite prolific. Author's interview with Amanda Mercer Neder, author's collection. Mandy recalled the judge of the juvenile court of Richmond County oversaw the agency managed by Ms. Hamilton. Born May 12, 1939, Mandy learned her birth parents were from Harlem, Georgia, and that the agency "really wanted to place me" and that she danced for Johnny and Ginger, who "just thought I was great." JHM to "Mother Darling," September 17, 1940, Mercer Family Collection, AASU.

56. Leslie Gourse, ed., *The Billy Holiday Companion: Seven Decades of Commentary* (New York: Schirmer Books, 1997), 119, quoting Joachim E. Berendt; Stuart Nicholson, *Billie Holiday* (Boston: Northeastern University Press, 1995), 266. Holiday recorded "Mandy Is Two" with Teddy Wilson's orchestra.

57. JHM to LCM, March 4, 1939, clipping from an unnamed Savannah newspaper, October 1, 1939; G. A. Mercer to Gil Keith, October 4, 1939, all in Mercer Family Collection, AASU. In Lees, *Portrait of Johnny*, 131–37, the breakup of the Keiths' marriage by Lillian Mercer is recounted through the citation of correspondence by family members. Apparently Johnny had no idea of the situation, as a letter to his mother shortly after the birth of Nancy Mercer Keith said, "I can just see Gil snapping pictures at every available opportunity and can imagine Nancy's embarrassment a few years later when he begins showing them to her young gentlemen friends." See JHM to "Mother Darling," January 24, 1941, box 1, folder 4, Mercer Family Collection, AASU.

58. G. A. Mercer "To My Friends," undated card, box 2, folder 8, JM Papers, GSU; JM autobiography. Business associates George W. Hunt and Nick Mamalakis and accountant A. D. Hancock were among the pallbearers at G. A.'s funeral. *Savannah Evening Press*, November 15, 1940; see also the obituary in the *Morning News* and its editorial that stated, "His charitable, philanthropic and religious traits were exemplified by his service in former years as president of the Union Society, his beneficent interest in the Florence Crittenden Home, and his devout adherence to the tenets of the Episcopal Church" (November 15, 1940). "Cast Your Bread upon the Water," words and music by Johnny Mercer (Los Angeles: Commander Publishers, 1963). He used the idea again in an unpublished song lyric titled "Any Blessing Heaven Sends My Way," see Kimball et al, eds., *Complete Lyrics*, 391.

59. Hirschhorn, *Hollywood Musical*, 197, 199; Kimball et al., eds., *Complete Lyrics*, 116.

60. Jablonski, *Harold Arlen*, 153–55; Hirschhorn, *Hollywood Musical*, 199.

61. See Shipman, *Judy Garland*, 84.

62. Jablonski, *Harold Arlen*, 227–28; Meyerson and Harburg, *Who Put the Rainbow in "The Wizard of Oz"?* 219. Just as Johnny would write again with Carmichael, so too, Arlen partnered on and off with Harburg. Kane, *How to Write a Song*, 80–81.

63. Jablonski, *Harold Arlen*, 150, 153–55; Arlen, quoted in the *New York Times*, July 24, 1976; Kimball et al., eds., *Complete Lyrics*, 117.

64. By his own account, Mercer's lyrics derive from the blues he grew up hearing and performing, one might say the definition of authenticity. Mercer interview by Lyttleton; Mercer interview by Conover.

65. Whiting and Holt, *It Might as Well Be Spring*, 63–65. In retelling the story to Max Wilk, Whiting added that Mickey Rooney witnessed the event and repeated, "My God, this is unbelievable!" Garland sang with success "Blues in the Night." See Frank, *Judy*, 154. Kimball et al., eds., *Complete Lyrics*, 117.

66. Jablonski, *Harold Arlen*, 156–57.

67. Alan Lomax, *The Land Where the Blues Began* (New York: Pantheon Books, 1993), ix; Townsend, *Pearl Harbor Jazz*, 62–63, 64, 65. Townsend argues that around this time theorists such as Lomax constructed "normative traditions of jazz and blues" that categorized the music as authentic and explained away the "noncanonical ways" of jazz and blues players who performed popular music as "either parodying" the popular hit, "subverting it," or being forced to make concessions for commercial reasons (64). For a thorough analysis of the issue, see Karl Hagstrom Miller, *Segregating Sound: Inventing Folk and Pop Music in the Age of Jim Crow* (Durham, N.C.: Duke University Press, 2010).

68. Michael Freedland, *Jerome Kern* (New York: Stein & Day, 1978), 149; Mason Wiley and Damien Bona, *Inside Oscar: The Unofficial History of the Academy Awards* (New York: Ballantine, 1986), 121. *Time* magazine editorialized: "Hollywood has its nerve in claiming that nostalgic hit, since it was published without movie sponsorship." While "Blues in the Night" lost out in 1941, Mercer won Oscars for "On the Atchison, Topeka, and the Santa Fe" in 1946, "In the Cool, Cool, Cool of the Evening" in 1951, "Moon River" in 1961, and "Days of Wine and Roses" in 1962.

Chapter Five. War Years

The epigraph is from "I'm Doin' It for Defense (The Jeep Song)" (1942), with music by Harold Arlen. See Robert Kimball, Barry Day, Miles Kreuger, and Eric Davis, eds., *The Complete Lyrics of Johnny Mercer* (New York: Alfred A. Knopf, 2009), 130.

1. JHM to "Mother Darling," September 17, 1940, see also January 24, 1941, in which Mercer writes about letters from Aunt Nell being "too horrible to believe. That paragraph about the dress-maker is blood-curdling." He added, "That one line about Chamberlain improving Churchill so through contact with him, amused me and made me mad at the same time. You'd think the war was being fought on the cricket fields. And I'm sure Churchill is considered rather vulgar because of his American blood. Well, I'm sure they could do with a lot more of his kind about now." See box 1, folder 4, Mercer Family Collection, AASU; JM autobiography.

2. JM autobiography. Loretta Young won the Oscar for Best Actress for her 1947 role in *The Farmer's Daughter*; Harry MacKenzie, *The Directory of Armed Forces Radio Service Series* (Westport, Conn.: Greenwood Press, 1999), xix.

3. Johnny Mercer's personal library contained a copy of Goolrich, *Life of General Hugh Mercer*, which outlines the Patton-Mercer connection. On Walter Rivers, see the Rivers Family Papers, Special Collections, University of West Florida, Pensacola, Fla.

4. Clive Hirschhorn, *The Hollywood Musical* (New York: Crown Publishers, 1981), 214.

5. Edward Mapp, *Directory of Blacks in the Performing Arts* (Metuchen, N.J.: Scarecrow Press, 1978), 8–9; Robert Kimball, Barry Day, Miles Kreuger, and Eric Davis, eds., *The Complete Lyrics of Johnny Mercer* (New York: Alfred A. Knopf, 2009), 129–33. Showing his inclusiveness in "Old Glory," Mercer follows the line "And minutemen and trappers," with Betty Hutton chiming in, "And jitterbugs and flappers!" while Eddie Anderson asks, "And how about Washington? I mean all three — George and Martha, and Booker T." Mercer told Conover about "Dreamland," "I like the song just the way it is"; see interview by Willis Conover, January 20, 1970, transcript in Popular Music Archives, Georgia State University, Atlanta, Ga.

6. David Lehman, *A Fine Romance: Jewish Songwriters, American Songs* (New York: Schocken, 2009), 87; transcript of Johnny Mercer interview by Humphrey Lyttleton, BBC *Omnibus*, season 2, episode 19, July 14, 1974, Popular Music Archives, GSU.

7. Given the response by Rose and knowing the behavior of Garland, one might question the

parentage. Anne Edwards, *Judy Garland: A Biography* (New York: Simon and Schuster, 1974), 79–84; David Shipman, *Judy Garland: The Secret Life of an American Legend* (New York: Hyperion, 1993), 127–28; Gerald Clarke, *Get Happy: The Life of Judy Garland* (New York: Random House, 2000), 162–63. See also Philip Furia, *Skylark: The Life and Times of Johnny Mercer* (New York: St. Martin's Press, 2003), 129–30. Furia's comparison of Garland to Maud Gonne, the muse of Irish poet William Butler Yeats, is apt; yet one might quibble with the extent of the love affair's influence on Mercer's music, for Furia suggests that without Garland, Mercer's "lyrics might be remembered today as clever, vernacular, jazzy evocations of the swing era," but not as the "timeless standards that register romantic agony as poignantly as any songs in the history of American popular music" (130).

8. Margaret Whiting and Will Holt, *It Might as Well Be Spring: A Musical Autobiography* (New York: William Morrow, 1987), 56–58, 220; Whiting's release is Capitol Records 126; Sanjek, *American Popular Music*, 219: Edward Jablonski, *Harold Arlen: Rhythm, Rainbows, and Blues* (Boston: Northeastern University Press, 1996), 157–59. "The words sustain your interest," Arlen said, "make sense, contain memorable phrases, and tell a story. Without the lyric the song would be just another long song" (159). That was high praise from the composer of "Stormy Weather" and "Over the Rainbow," among dozens of other classic jazz standards. Sinatra's version appeared in the 1952 movie, while Davis recorded it for Decca in 1955, Monroe's version appeared in the 1956 film, and Prima and Smith released their recording in 1958.

9. Hirschhorn, *Hollywood Musical*, 204; "I Remember You," words by Johnny Mercer, music by Victor Schertzinger (Paramount Music, 1942); Kimball et al., eds., *Complete Lyrics*, 124; Deems Taylor to John Mercer, June 17, 1942, JM Papers, GSU.

10. Kimball et al., eds., *Complete Lyrics*, 121–25. The songwriters admired each other's art as Mercer said, "I've always loved Porter — those early songs of his were so clever, and later on his melodies became so right and full" (132); Porter telegram in box 2, folder 8, JM Papers, GSU; Mercer interview by Conover.

11. "Tangerine," words by Johnny Mercer, music by Victor Schertzinger (Famous Music, 1942); Kimball et al., eds., *Complete Lyrics*, 122. The film version included the lines "Times when Tangerine / Had the bourgeoisie / Believing she was queen." The lyrics by three years foreshadowed the rise of Evita Perón. On the Jimmy Dorsey Orchestra and "Tangerine," see Dave Oliphant, *The Early Swing Era, 1930–1941* (Westport, Conn.: Greenwood Press, 2002), 121, 123; Mercer interview by Conover.

12. Michael Freedland, *Jerome Kern* (New York: Stein & Day, 1978), 158–59; Kimball et al., eds., *Complete Lyrics*, 126–27; Hirschhorn, *Hollywood Musical*, 215; Alec Wilder, *American Popular Song: The Great Innovators, 1900–1950* (New York: Oxford University Press, 1990), 82–83.

13. Mercer interview by Conover; Kimball et al., eds., *Complete Lyrics*, 125–26.

14. Freedland, *Jerome Kern*, 159; Whiting and Holt, *It Might as Well Be Spring*, 45–46. After hearing him sing "You Were Never Lovelier," Whiting told Kern, "My father would have loved that song. And you brought out the best in Johnny. Oh, it's beautiful. Play it again" (46).

15. "Windmill under the Stars," music by Jerome Kern, lyrics by Johnny Mercer, 1942; Kimball et al., eds., *Complete Lyrics*, 128. During World War I, Colonel John McCrae wrote the poem "In Flanders Fields" (originally entitled "We Shall Not Sleep"), using the poppy to immortalize the dead who fell at the Second Battle of Ypres in 1915. See also Miona Michael, *The Miracle Flower* (Philadelphia: Dorrance and Company, 1941).

16. Richard B. Jewell, *The Golden Age of Cinema: Hollywood, 1929–1945* (Malden, Mass.: Blackwell, 2007), 99–105; Hirschhorn, *Hollywood Musical*, 233, 421; Jablonski, *Harold Arlen*, 169–71; Wilder, *American Popular Song*, 280–81.

17. Jewell, *The Golden Age of Cinema*, 99–105; Hirschhorn, *Hollywood Musical*, 233, 421; Kim-

ball et al., eds., *Complete Lyrics*, 148; Jablonski, *Harold Arlen*, 169–71; Wilder, *American Popular Song*, 280–81; Mercer interview by Conover, 34.

18. John Bush Jones, *The Songs that Fought the War: Popular Music and the Home Front, 1939–1945* (Waltham, Mass.: Brandeis University Press, 2006), 100, 205, 223–24; William H. Young and Nancy K. Young, *Music of the World War II Era* (Westport, Conn.: Greenwood Press, 2008), 16; Kimball et al., eds., *Complete Lyrics*, 121–22, 130, 134.

19. Kimball et al., eds., *Complete Lyrics*, 142–43.

20. Hirschhorn, *Hollywood Musical*, 227; Kimball et al., eds., *Complete Lyrics*, 139; Jablonski, *Harold Arlen*, 160–64.

21. Wilder, *American Popular Song*, 275–77; in his interview with Mercer, Conover quotes Johnny also referencing the play *Shining Hour* by Philip Barrie as "probably unconsciously" influencing his song.

22. Mercer interview by Conover. Lehman observed that "everyone knew that John drank too much and was a nasty drunk, and perhaps only a gentlemanly drunkard with a dark side and a lousy marriage could have written 'One for My Baby, and One More for the Road.'" See *A Fine Romance*, 87; Mercer favored a performance of the song by Peter Hayes; Kimball et al., eds., *Complete Lyrics*, 138.

23. JM autobiography.

24. Kimball et al., eds., *Complete Lyrics*, 8, 97, 294, 400. *New York Times*, 1940. On the reverse of "Visiting Firemen," Crosby and Mercer recorded a duet of Johnny's "Mister Meadowlark," also written in 1940 with music on both songs by Walter Donaldson. For two months around this time, Johnny had tried to write lyrics for a Bob Haggart tune, coming up with "I'm free, free as the birds in the trees," but the lyric failed to click, and Johnny Burke later wrote "What's New?" to the tune that became another Crosby hit. See Giddins, *Bing Crosby*, 542, 579; ad in "The Man Who Writes the Lyrics," *Cosmopolitan* (1946), 48–49, 180–81.

25. Hirschhorn, *Hollywood Musical*, 250; Jablonski, *Harold Arlen*, 166–69; Jones, *Songs That Fought the War*, 223–24; Kimball et al., eds., *Complete Lyrics*, 145.

26. Jablonski, *Harold Arlen*, 166–69; despite the numerous nominations, Arlen and Mercer never shared an Oscar; Whiting and Holt, *It Might as Well Be Spring*, 222; Kimball et al., eds., *Complete Lyrics*, 144; see also Mercer interview by Conover, GSU, and the unidentified clipping from E. H. Morris & Company in the loose newspaper clippings folder of JM Papers, GSU.

27. Mercer quoted in *Ten Minutes of Your Time* interview in JM Papers, GSU; Charles M. Strub to JHM, August 7, 1942, John Shubert to JHM, September 9, 1942, Maurice N. Giezentanner to JHM, November 27, 1942, F. H. Osborn to JHM, December 15, 1942, Bette Davis to JHM, January 12 and March 16, 1943, Terry D. Hunt to JHM, September 17, 1943, M. D. Willcutts to JHM, December 27, 1943, all in box 2, folder 8, JM Papers, GSU. Daughter Mandy recalled accompanying her father when he performed for the USO, see author's interview.

28. MacKenzie, *Directory*, xiii–3.

29. MacKenzie, *Directory*, introduction; Russell Sanjek, *Pennies from Heaven: The American Popular Music Business in the Twentieth Century*, updated by David Sanjek (New York: Da Capo Press, 1996), 218–19; Lewis A. Erenbert, *Swingin' the Dream: Big Band Jazz and the Rebirth of American Culture* (Chicago: University of Chicago Press, 1998), 185.

30. *Command Performance, USA!* March 29, December 24, 1942, copies housed in the Music Archives, Library of Congress, Washington, D.C., henceforth LOC. Frank Sinatra sang "The House I Live In" on the Victory Special that also included Mercer, Lena Horne, Dinah Shore, Bing Crosby, and Jimmy Durante; MacKenzie, *Directory*, 2–3; see also "Armed Forces Radio and Television Service," Museum of Broadcast Communications, http://www.museum.tv/archives/etv/A/htmlA/armedforces/armedforces.htm.

31. *Command Performance, USA!* September 9, 1943, May 20, June 24, August 12, September 13, November 25, 1944, April 5, 1945, copies housed in the Music Archives, LOC.

32. W. F. Tunney to Johnny Mercer, July 30, 1942, box 2, folder 8, JM Papers, GSU; see programs 12 (Shore) and 154 (Crosby) of *Mail Call*; program 619 of *Personal Album*; program 72 of *Yank Swing Session*; program 432 of *Sound Off*; program 81 of *To the Rear March*, June 14, 1944; Thomas H. A. Lewis to Johnny Mercer, November 13, 1944, box 2, folder 9, JM Papers, GSU.

33. Program 1495 of *G.I. Jive*; Mercer wrote the song in late 1943. See Kimball et al., eds., *Complete Lyrics*, 141; Harry P. Warner to John Mercer, March 7, 1945, box 2, folder 10, JM Papers, GSU. On what can be broadcast in wartime, see Jones, *Songs That Fought the War*, 8–14.

34. A favorite of the servicemen and a frequent visitor to the program, the African American singing sensation and pinup Lena Horne appeared on *Jubilee* program 40 (August 1943) and program 150 (October 1, 1945); Erskine Hawkins and Leadbelly on program 107 (October 1944); Sweethearts of Rhythm on program 82 (May 1944); Delta Rhythm Boys on program 52 (October 1943); the King Cole Trio and Ida James on program 51 (October 1943). Crabapple Sound Presents, *Old Time Radio Musical Programs: Jubilee* (cassette recordings RMU-3201 through RMU-3214, containing broadcasts dated between December 25, 1942, and December 1943), Pullen Library, GSU.

35. Lena Horne sang "One for My Baby" on *Jubilee* program 150 (October 1, 1945); the Charioteers performed "G.I. Jive" on program 66 (February 1944); Bing Crosby appeared on program 60 (December 1943); Mercer appeared on program 88 (June 1944).

36. Bob Lee to JHM, January 15, 1943; Livingston Watrous to JHM, February 18, 1943, box 2, folder 8, JM Papers, GSU.

37. Postcard from Bob Hope to JHM, JM Papers, GSU. The card pictured Muslims attending a sermon during Ramadan with a note in Hope's script that read "tough to hear the jokes with those hoods" in a weak attempt at self-depreciating humor. Although having met early in their respective careers, the two men rarely interacted. Perhaps feeling threatened by Mercer's success guest hosting, Hope apparently did not invite the songwriter back for a second stint when next he traveled abroad.

38. Telegrams to JHM from Arthur L. Fishbein, Margaret and Eleanor Whiting, June 22, 1943, box 2, folder 8, JM Papers, GSU; Kimball et al., eds., *Complete Lyrics*, 141; *Metronome* (January 1944).

39. Unidentified clipping headlined "Johnny Mercer," box 31, folder 12; "The Man Who Writes the Lyrics," *Cosmopolitan*, 1946, box 1, folder 15; Berle Adams of the General Amusement Corp. to JHM, June 28, 1943, box 2, folder 8, and in folder 9, the postcard dated August 23, 1944, and signed by Harris Owens, secretary. Mercer treasured the postcard. All in the JM Papers, GSU. See also *New York Times*, March 16, 1971. In his exploration of the postcolonial and postmodern, theorist Homi K. Bhabha discusses cultural hybridity and notes "that this liminal moment of identification — eluding resemblance — produces a subversive strategy of subaltern agency that negotiates its own authority through a process of iterative 'unpicking' and incommensurable, insurgent relinking." See Homi K. Bhabha, *The Location of Culture* (New York: Routledge, 1994), 184–85.

40. Virginia Waring, *Fred Waring and the Pennsylvanians* (Urbana: University of Illinois Press, 1997), 175–77, 185–86, 203; John Dunning, *Tune in Yesterday: The Ultimate Encyclopedia of Old-time Radio, 1925–1976* (Englewood Cliffs, N.J.: Prentice-Hall, 1976), 129; Harry MacKenzie, "The Johnny Mercer Chesterfield Music Shop, with AFRS Additions," NBC Studios, Hollywood, with programs dated from June 12 to December 8, 1944, a Joyce Record Club Publication. A fan of the military-sponsored radio variety programs, Harry MacKenzie inventoried as many of the AFRS programs as he could, including Mercer's *Music Shop*, identifying the stars who appeared and the music performed for each show. A printed copy of the computer database assembled by Mackenzie is located in the Harry MacKenzie Papers, Popular Music Archives, GSU.

41. The barrelhouse roll can be heard on every program. Mercer discusses "Dream" in Bob Bach and Ginger Mercer, eds., *Our Huckleberry Friend: The Life, Times, and Lyrics of Johnny Mercer* (Secaucus, N.J.: Lyle Stuart, 1982), 132. Mercer repeats the story of the song's background, but also confesses he later thought "Dream" sounded like the music to "Whispering," a favorite song from his youth by Malvin Schoenberger, Richard Coburn, and John Schoenberger, see Mercer interview by Conover. Kimball et al., eds., *Complete Lyrics*, 142, quotes Johnny saying about "Dream" that "it's a kind of 'Whispering' sideways.'" The song sat at number one on *Your Hit Parade* for five weeks in 1945.

42. On NBC the *Music Shop* ran from June 12 to December 8, 1944, while on AFRS the rebroadcast ran from June 22 into early 1945. See MacKenzie, "Johnny Mercer Chesterfield Music Shop," which identifies programs 1–96 airing on AFRS up to the December 8 cutoff on NBC, after which programs 97–116 aired Monday through Thursday nights into the New Year. The *New York Times* identifies Stafford "as a female counterpart of Frank Sinatra." In a letter to a colleague, Mercer wrote, "Our program goes off the air this week . . . we have enjoyed these past months very much." JHM to Toronto band leader Jack Allison, December 5, 1944, box 2, folder 9, JM Papers, GSU.

43. MacKenzie, "Johnny Mercer Chesterfield Music Shop." Crabapple Sound Presents, *Old Time Radio Musical Programs: Johnny Mercer (Music Shop)* (cassette recordings of original programs, RMU-3180 through RMU-3187, containing most of the shows between June 26 and November 28, 1944), Popular Music Archives, GSU. Mercer recruited the character Vera Vague played by Barbara Jo Allen from the *Bob Hope Show* and Doodles Weaver from Spike Jones and the City Slickers.

44. Sterling Holloway responded to Mercer's self-effacing lyric with "You know I had thought perhaps that you'd be changed by your success, but no." Mercer can be heard adding, "No, no." Holloway continued, "Instead I am highly gratified to see you still possess that same swelled head." Holloway is best known for his voiceovers for Walt Disney's animations such as *Bambi*, *The Three Caballeros*, *The Jungle Book*, and *Winnie the Pooh*.

45. Janet Blair appeared on *Music Shop* program 40 (August 31, 1944), while Diana Lynn appeared on program 24 (August 3, 1944); Haley also appeared with Judy Garland in her first movie, *Pigskin Parade*. MacKenzie, "Johnny Mercer Chesterfield Music Shop."

46. Roy Rogers appeared on *Music Shop* program 28 (August 10, 1944), which opened with Jo Stafford singing the western star's theme song, "Tumbling Tumbleweeds," followed by Mercer performing "San Fernando Valley."

47. Arthur Treacher appeared on *Music Shop* program 22 (August 1, 1944) and Marlin Hurt on program 18 (July 25, 1944). "The discourse of mimicry is constructed around an ambivalence; in order to be effective, mimicry must continually produce its slippage, its excess, its difference," notes Bhabha, and although Hurt's performance spins the theorist's exploration of "colonial discourse" in a different direction, it nonetheless demonstrates how mimicry uses the idea of the subaltern to decenter social authority. See Bhabha, *The Location of Culture*, 86.

48. Wilder, *American Popular Song*, 280–82, identifies the "misterioso" mood and notes, "It is a very strong song, with splendid support in a John Mercer lyric. Though not typically Arlen in style" (282). For "Out of This World," see *Music Shop* program 27 (August 9, 1944), and for "Minding My Business," see program 24 (August 3, 1944). Kimball et al., eds., *Complete Lyrics*, 148–49; Henry Kane, *How to Write a Song (as Told to Henry Kane)* (New York: Macmillan, 1962), 79, 81.

49. Mercer introduced "Birmingham Bertha" on *Music Shop* program 23 (August 2, 1944) and sang it several times during the six-month run, including on the September 1 and November 7, 1944, programs. Many of these numbers written for radio do not appear among Mercer's collected

songs published in Kimball et al., eds., *Complete Lyrics*. MacKenzie, "Johnny Mercer Chesterfield Music Shop," identifies the military installations where the *Music Shop* recorded on Fridays.

50. *San Pedro Sweepings*, September 21, 1944, clipping in JM Papers, GSU.

51. H. Brewer to JHM, June 3, 1945, box 2, folder 11, JM Papers, GSU.

52. Edward S. "Eddy" Northrop to JHM, February 2, 12, 1945, and Mercer to Northrop, February 8, 1945. Responding to the *Music Shop*'s cancellation, Eddy added, "When are you going back on the air? You are better than a sleeping pill. I find that I have trouble getting my usual rest because I don't hear you any more." Ruffin wrote to ask Mercer how best to break into writing for the movies; see JHM to Peter (Ruffin), February 9, 1945; Pope Barrow McIntire to JHM, November 19, 1975, all in JM Papers, GSU.

53. *Variety*, June 14, 1944; *Johnny Mercer: Sweet Georgia Brown* (Hindsight Records, 1980); a rerelease of a 1949 Capitol record with Paul Weston's orchestra, *The Uncollected Johnny Mercer* derived from the original *Johnny Mercer Chesterfield Music Shop* transcriptions made in 1944.

54. MacKenzie, "Johnny Mercer Chesterfield Music Shop," contains the expense sheet for the week of October 6, 1944, noting that the expenditures ran $14,221.47 against a balance of $13,908.78 ($312.89 over budget).

55. *Judy Garland on Radio: 1936–1944*, vol. 1 (Vintage Jazz Classics, CD, 1993), VJC-1043, with liner notes by David J. Weiner; Gerold Frank, *Judy* (New York: Harper & Row, 1975), 174; the lyrics for "But Not for Me" may be found in Ira Gershwin, *Lyrics on Several Occasions* (New York: Viking, 1973), 234.

56. AFRS, December 25, 1945, copy of broadcast in Popular Music Collection, Georgia State University, Atlanta, Ga.; Kimball et al., eds., *Complete Lyrics*, 149–50. Garland sang Jerome Kern and Ira Gershwin's beautiful song in part because of her filming at MGM the Jerome Kern biopic, *Till the Clouds Roll By*.

57. Jack Price to Mercer, April 26, 1945, with transcript of undated program, *Ten Minutes of Your Time*, box 2, folder 9, JM Papers, GSU; Kenneth E. Palmer, "Musical Moments," 1940; Kane, *How to Write a Song*, 84–85.

58. *Ten Minutes of Your Time*, box 2, folder 9, JM Papers, GSU. Mercer identified Hoagy Carmichael and Mitchell Parish with "Stardust" and George and Ira Gershwin with "I Got Rhythm" as typical entries in the catalogue.

59. *Ten Minutes of Your Time*, box 2, folder 9, JM Papers, GSU; *Variety* (October 4, 1939). For a thorough analysis of the question, see also Jones, *The Songs That Fought the War*, 10–20, 289–91. Also at the top of the wartime charts appeared Eddie Seiler, Sol Marcus, and Bennie Benjamin, "When the Lights Go on Again (All Over the World)." *New York Times*, September 29, 1945.

60. Malcolm Macfarlane, *Bing Crosby: Day by Day* (Lanham, Md.: Scarecrow Press, 2001), 248, 291; Dunning, *Tune in Yesterday*, 73, 470, 664; *Variety*, April 27, 1943; *Radio Review*, June 30, 1943; *Radio Daily*, June 24, 1943; *San Pedro Sweepings*, September 21, 1944; Gene Handsaker, "Hollywood II," Associated Press wire copy, April 30, 1948, *Melody Maker*, November 15, 1969, clippings in box 31, JM Papers, GSU.

61. Dunning, *Tune in Yesterday*, 663–65. The show signed off with "So long to 'Your Hit Parade' and the tunes that you picked to be played"; Jones, *Songs That Fought the War*, 22–23. The combination of record and sheet music sales plus jukebox and broadcast selection provided the figures for the top fifteen. By the 1960s, such a limited ranking expanded when *Variety* evaluated the top fifty. Soon *Billboard* listed the top "Hot 100" songs and 150 albums.

62. Dave Dexter Jr., liner notes for the CD, *Johnny Mercer: Sweet Georgia Brown* (Hindsight Records, 1995); Warren Craig, *Sweet and Lowdown: America's Popular Songwriters* (Metuchen, N.J.: Scarecrow Press, 1978), 346–47; see also the sound recordings of Warren Craig, "Broadway Songbook: Johnny Mercer," that comprise ten "chapters" that offered the first thorough retrospective

of Mercer's career, broadcast originally on KXLU, Los Angeles, California, in the late 1970s after Mercer's death, copies in the holdings of the Georgia Historical Society, Savannah, Ga. Bruce C. Elrod, *Your Hit Parade and American Top 10 Hits* (Ann Arbor, Mich., 1994). During April and May 1942, Mercer's "Tangerine" joined "Skylark," "I Remember You," and "Blues in the Night" as songs rotating in and out of the top ten. A comparison is offered by the Beatles, who set a record by placing songs in all four top spots in 1965. For Martin Block quote, see www.radiocontinuity.com.

63. Mercer interview by Conover, GSU; Gene Lees, *Portrait of Johnny: The Life of John Herndon Mercer* (New York: Pantheon Books, 2004), 168–69; Furia, *Skylark*, 150–51; Michael Feinstein, oral interview by Bruce Ricker, Popular Music Archives, GSU.

64. The discovery section of the legal documents describes the process whereby Mercer saw the movie and created lyrics for the song "Laura." See *John H. Mercer v. Robbins Music Company*, U.S. District Court, Central District of California, no. CV 74-3650-HP, pretrial statement, folder 3, box 5, JM Papers, GSU; Mercer quoted in Kimball et al., eds., *Complete Lyrics*, 148.

65. The lyrics to "Laura" appear in Bach and Mercer, eds., *Our Huckleberry Friend*, 136; see also Kimball et al., eds., *Complete Lyrics*, 148. For years Mercer waged a legal fight with Robbins over his interest in the work and its copyright renewal. Robbins tried to limit Mercer's ownership in the song by denying his collaboration with Raksin on the music and words for the verse, recognizing only his lyric for the refrain. See the legal documents in folder 3, box 5, JM Papers, GSU.

66. Feinstein identifies Porter's and Berlin's desire to have written "Laura." He also notes that Bing Crosby refused to record the song, finding it "too odd, too rangey, too unusual for a pop song. So it's one of those things that through the quality of the music and the lyric it became a standard." Feinstein oral interview, GSU. Of "Arthur Murray Taught Me Dancing in a Hurry," Mercer says, "that one I got a wire from Cole Porter about. Like I did 'Laura' too. He loved 'Laura.' That was his favorite song that he didn't write." See Mercer interview by Conover, 6–7. As Hollywood's top agent, Irving Lazar represented few songwriters. See also Charles Schwartz, *Cole Porter: A Biography* (New York: Dial Press, 1977), 218. The dialogue between Porter and Mercer is recalled by Robert Rush who witnessed the exchange. See Robert Rush, oral interview M154, Popular Music Archives, GSU.

67. Deems Taylor to JHM, June 17, 1942; Sigman noted that Mercer had sold his share of the sheet music company to its co-owner, Buddy Harris, see the correspondence from Carl Sigman to JHM, October 30, 1942, both letters in folder 8, Berle Adams to JHM, October 2, November 4, and Mercer's responses dated October 26 and 30, 1944; Jack Allison to JHM, October 31 and November 21, 1944, and Mercer's December 5 1944, response; and Harry Ruby to JHM, October 23 and November 24, 1944, and Mercer's October 30, 1944 response; J. J. Robbins, Dec. 6, 1944. All in box 2, folder 9, JM Papers, GSU.

68. David Shipman, *Judy Garland: The Secret Life of an American Legend* (New York: Hyperion, 1992), 174–75; Ken Bloom, *Hollywood Song: The Complete Film and Musical Companion*, 3 vols. (New York: Facts on File, 1995), 1:377; Kimball et al., eds., *Complete Lyrics*, 153.

69. "On the Atchison, Topeka, and the Santa Fe," sheet music, JM Papers, GSU.

70. Mercer quoted poet Steven Vincent Benét: "I've fallen in love with American names." Mercer interview by Conover; Mercer interview by Lyttleton.

71. Nine songs competed in 1941, while for the 1946 Oscars Shore also sang "All Through the Day," Dick Haymes sang "I Can't Begin to Tell You," and Andy Russell sang "You Keep Coming Back Like a Song." Mason Wiley and Damien Bona, *Inside Oscar: The Unofficial History of the Academy Awards* (New York: Random House, 1986) 119, 121, 166–67; Sudhalter, *Stardust Melody*, 257.

Chapter Six. Capitol Records

The epigraph is from "Out of This World" (1945), with music by Harold Arlen. See Robert Kimball, Barry Day, Miles Kreuger, and Eric Davis, eds., *The Complete Lyrics of Johnny Mercer* (New York: Alfred A. Knopf, 2009), 148.

1. Russell Sanjek, updated by David Sanjek, *Pennies from Heaven: The American Popular Music Business in the Twentieth Century* (New York: Da Capo Press, 1996), 217–18; *Capitol Records, Fiftieth Anniversary*, undated booklet [1992], box 4, folder 9, collection MOOI, JM Papers, GSU.

2. Willis Conover interview with Johnny Mercer, transcript in Popular Music Archives, Georgia State University, Atlanta, Ga.; "The Man Who Writes the Lyrics," *Cosmopolitan* (ca. 1946), undated clipping in the JM Papers, GSU, also tells the story about Mercer approaching DeSylva to see "if he would let us sell our recordings in the lobby of the Paramount Theatre. Buddy wasn't crazy about the idea but said he'd like to join the business with us. He supplied some of the dough and away we went." Eating dinner at Chasen's and discussing a potential conflict with Liberty Music Shops in New York, Ginger Mercer suggested to the men that the business be called Capitol. See Margaret Whiting with Will Holt, *It Might as Well Be Spring: A Musical Autobiography* (New York: William Morrow, 1987), 48, which quotes Mercer saying to Wallichs, "'How about coming in on a record company with me? Let's try something new.' And Glenn said, 'Fine. You run the company and find the artists.' And Johnny said, 'And you run the business.'" Harry Warren recommended to Ginger that she give Johnny a car radio for his birthday in 1935, which resulted in the introduction between Mercer and Wallichs. At Music City, Wallichs installed and repaired radios, sold releases from the big labels, and had a small recording studio that people could rent to make records for him to sell. In funding the venture, DeSylva later added another $15,000, but Capitol only spent the initial $10,000 plus an additional $5,000 of DeSylva's $25,000 total investment. The May 12, 1947, *Time* presents a slightly different explanation: "As Wallichs was having trouble getting records to sell, why not have Mercer make some for him? Mercer liked the idea but doubted that Wallichs could get any shellac, then one of the shortest of shortages. Wallichs went from house to house collecting old records, melted these down for a starter. Then Wallichs and Mercer persuaded Cinema producer George Gard ('Buddy') DeSylva to invest $50,000 and they launched Capitol Records, Inc."

3. John Bush Jones, *The Songs That Fought the War: Popular Music and the Home Front, 1939–1945* (Waltham, Mass.: Brandeis University Press, 2006), 3–5.

4. Petrillo offered the recording companies the option of paying into the union's unemployment fund a set fee for every record or radio transcription made. Decca caved in to Petrillo's demands in September 1943, and over the next few months Capitol Records and other smaller companies followed suit, but not until November 1944 did the remaining two of the big three, RCA Victor and Columbia, as well as NBC, capitulate to Petrillo's demands. Sanjek, *Pennies from Heaven*, 217–18; Whiting and Holt, *It Might as Well Be Spring*, 59.

5. Wallichs *Downbeat* interview quoted in Peter Townsend, *Pearl Harbor Jazz: Change in Popular Music in the Early 1940s* (Jackson: University Press of Mississippi, 2007), 159; *Capitol News*, June 26, 1943. Capitol used C. P. "Chick" MacGregor's studio. Recognized as a leading sound man with an "uncanny ear coupled with an amazing knowledge of music," Quan later recorded radio shows starring Mercer and others for the military. For their studio appearances, both Billie Holiday and Margaret Whiting earned a flat seventy-five dollars from Capitol; see Stuart Nicholson, *Billie Holiday* (Boston: Northeastern University Press, 1995), 131; Whiting and Holt, *It Might as Well Be Spring*, 57.

6. Thomas A. DeLong, *Pops: Paul Whiteman, King of Jazz* (Piscataway, N.J.: New Century, 1983), 251–52. An anecdote claims that several years later management at MacGregor's painted the

studio walls and inadvertently destroyed the unusual quality of the sound previously captured on the recordings, so Capitol quit using the space.

7. Ibid.; John Chilton, *Who's Who of Jazz: Storyville to Swing Street* (Time-Life Records Special Edition, 1978), 236, 365; Leslie Gourse, ed., *The Billie Holiday Companion* (New York: Schirmer Books, 1997), 92, 143; Robert Kimball, Barry Day, Miles Kreuger, and Eric Davis, eds., *The Complete Lyrics of Johnny Mercer* (New York: Alfred A. Knopf, 2009), 140–41; Nicholson, *Billie Holiday*, 47–49, 130–31; John Chilton, *Billie's Blues: Billie Holiday's Story 1933–1959* (New York: Stein & Day, 1975), 83. Chilton quotes Young saying that after the recording session, "Billie and I went out and spent all the money celebrating, and her mother had to send us the bus fare from California to New York" (83).

8. African American tradition considered as auspicious an infant born with the inner fetal membrane — called a caul or veil — covering the face. Mercer used the same idea with his character Augie in *St. Louis Woman*. See the book that Mercer's friends, Muriel and Malcolm Bell, helped compile for the Savannah Unit of the Georgia Writer's Project of the Work Projects Administration, *Drums and Shadows: Survival Studies among the Georgia Coastal Negroes* (Athens: University of Georgia Press, 1940). Lyrics to "Harlem Butterfly" may be found in Bob Bach and Ginger Mercer, eds., *Our Huckleberry Friend: The Life, Times, and Lyrics of Johnny Mercer* (Secaucus, N.J.: Lyle Stuart, 1982), 145. See also Kimball et al., eds., *Complete Lyrics*, 171. Although Holiday never recorded "Harlem Butterfly," she recorded a number of other Mercer songs, often accompanied by Jimmy Rowles, including "P.S. I Love You," "Day In — Day Out," "I Thought about You," "Come Rain or Come Shine," "Jeepers Creepers," and "One for My Baby," with one of her last four songs recorded being "Too Marvelous for Words" three months before her death on July 15, 1959. Millay's poem reads: "My candle burns at both ends; / It will not last the night; / But ah, my foes, and oh, my friends — / It gives a lovely light!" See Edna St. Vincent Millay, *A Few Figs from Thistles* (New York: Harper & Brothers, 1922), 9.

9. *Capitol Records, Fiftieth Anniversary*, JM Papers, GSU. This publication noted that in its review of the first recordings, *Down Beat* announced under the headline "New Capitol Records Splendid" that "the record situation is upped considerably this week, but not any thanks to the Big Three." Mike Levin wrote the review: "Their first records are excellent. Surface noise and record materials are far better than the general output. The choice is good, with the obvious necessary concessions to commercialism. What gets me, though, is that with everybody else in the business pulling in the shutters, these guys are setting sail full of drive and confidence that they can make a go of it." A native of Dallas, southern diaspora entertainer Ella May Morse first performed with her parents' orchestra before singing at age fifteen with Jimmy Dorsey's orchestra. Whiting and Holt, *It Might as Well Be Spring*, 54. Whiting attended the recording of "Strip Polka" and remembered Jimmy Van Heusen playing the piano with Weston's orchestra. Kay Kyser as well as the Andrews Sisters made popular recordings. See Kimball et al., eds., *Complete Lyrics*, 115.

10. *Capitol Records, Fiftieth Anniversary*, JM Papers, GSU; Whiting and Holt, *It Might as Well Be Spring*, 55.

11. *Capitol News*, June 26, 1943; see also Dave Dexter Jr., *Jazz Cavalcade: The Inside Story of Jazz* (New York: Criterion, 1946), as well as the text that accompanied Capitol's 1964 five-album set, Dave Dexter Jr., *The Jazz Story: From the '90s to the '60s* (Englewood Cliffs, N.J.: Prentice-Hall, 1964).

12. Dave Dexter Jr., *Playback: A Newsman/Record Producer's Hits and Misses from the Thirties to the Seventies* (New York: Billboard Publications, 1976), 85–86.

13. Dexter, *Playback*, 86, 110. Dexter observed that "a stickler of office regimentation despite Mercer's less rigid attitude, Boss Wallichs" nevertheless accepted the informality of the music industry. Likewise, "in deference to Wallichs, I was careful to wear a suit and tie on days when

I had business outside the office." As Dexter realized, "A less understanding company executive might have justifiably sent me back to a newspaper job. Glenn respected creative people. But they puzzled him until the day he died."

14. *Capitol Records, Fiftieth Anniversary,* JM Papers, GSU; Dexter quoted in *Capitol News,* June 26, 1943.

15. *Capitol News,* May 1946; Capitol Records, *Annual Report for the Year Ended December 31, 1946* (Los Angeles: Capitol Records, 1947). The company expanded into the production of phonograph needles and disks for home use. Melvin Brooks, "All Hits Long Runs No Errors," unidentified magazine article, and Johnny Mercer entry, *Current Biography 1948,* 446, unidentified publication, copy in folder 13, box 31, JM Papers, GSU. When Capitol went public it made available 30,000 shares of cumulative preferred stock and 95,000 common shares that later increased to a total of 430,000 common shares.

16. James N. Gregory, *The Southern Diaspora: How the Great Migrations of Black and White Southerners Transformed America* (Chapel Hill: University of North Carolina Press, 2005), statistics on 14, 19, and in appendix A.

17. Gregory, *Southern Diaspora,* 193–94, explores what he calls the "third dimension" that signifies the interaction of black, white, and Latino southerners with a national culture to create something new in such centers of the southern diaspora as Harlem, Los Angeles, and Chicago. He recognized "the cultural production of one almost always referenced the other. Together, the various diaspora cultural enterprises generated models, images, and ideas that contributed to important reformulations of racial identities and southern identities over the course of the twentieth century." Regrettably, Gregory's analysis goes little further than a black blues/jazz and white hillbilly critique.

18. Capitol Records, *Capitol Records: Annual Report for the Year Ended December 31, 1946* (Los Angeles: Capitol Records, Inc., 1947); on the fabrication of "race music," see Karl Hagstrom Miller, *Segregating Sound: Inventing Folk and Pop Music in the Age of Jim Crow* (Durham, N.C.: Duke University Press, 2010).

19. Musicologist Henry Pleasants lays out the argument for jazz interpenetrating popular song: "What many jazz musicians and jazz critics overlook — or choose to forget — is the fact that those who made the post-swing era the Age of the Singer in Popular music — while jazz was moving from swing into bop and from Popular into Art — were, almost without exception, singers who had learned their craft as vocalists with the jazz bands of the swing era: Fitzgerald, Vaughn, Holiday, Sinatra, Lee, Stafford, Shore, Starr, Horne, O'Day, Como, Christy, Connor, Clooney, Eckstine, Haymes and even Bing Crosby, whose apprenticeship was served with the bands of Paul Whiteman and Gus Arnheim." See Henry Pleasants, *Serious Music — and All That Jazz* (New York: Simon & Schuster/Fireside, 1969), 168. This opinion is echoed in "The Singers," in Dave Dexter, *Jazz Story,* 88–104, and in Gene Lees, *Singers and the Song* (New York: Oxford University Press, 1987), and *Singers and the Song II* (New York: Oxford University Press, 1998). Kay Starr and the Dinning Sisters came from Oklahoma; Julia Lee and Johnnie Johnston, Missouri; Martha Tilton, Texas; and Jesse Price, Tennessee.

20. Capitol Records, *Annual Report for the Year Ended December 31, 1946* (Los Angeles: Capitol Records, 1947); Jeffrey J. Lange, *Smile when You Call Me a Hillbilly: Country Music's Struggle for Respectability, 1939–1954* (Athens: University of Georgia Press, 2004), 75 and passim; *Capitol News,* June 26, 1943, copy in JM Papers, GSU.

21. Daniel Mark Epstein, *Nat King Cole* (New York: Farrar, Straus & Giroux, 1999), 14–17, 23–27, and passim. On the significance of Central Avenue in this era, see Douglas Flamming, *Bound for Freedom: Black Los Angeles in Jim Crow America* (Berkeley: University of California Press, 2005).

22. Epstein, *Nat King Cole*, 75–79. On the naming of the trio, Epstein identifies both Bob Lewis and Wesley Prince as possible sources and then observes that "King Cole Trio" came from the nursery rhyme "Old King Cole" and that "the group knew their Mother Goose" (78). At first Cole performed as a jazz pianist, explaining that he had not thought of singing until an inebriated customer had asked him to croon "Sweet Lorraine" at the Sewanee Inn. Cole initially declined the request but the barkeep encouraged him to reconsider given the prominence of the patron. Mercer, who is credited with encouraging Cole to sing, oversaw Cole's Capitol recording of "Sweet Lorraine" and later made his own recording of Jimmie Noone's theme song. Leslie Gourse, *Unforgettable: The Life and Mystique of Nat King Cole* (New York: St. Martin's Press, 1991), 25, 33. About that first recording of Mercer's "Mutiny," Epstein notes, "the simple chords in the left hand, the spare, rippling one-note melody in the treble with only a single triplet for ornamentation. Here is the lightness of touch that would become the pianist's signature" (79). Cole championed the younger Monk; see the definitive Robin D. G. Kelley, *Thelonious Monk: The Life and Times of an American Original* (New York: Free Press, 2009), 131, 139. As Capitol executive Alan Livingston remembered, Cole saw himself as a jazz pianist who did not want to sing, but Mercer kept encouraging Cole. Livingston remembered Johnny told him, "'This can be the biggest vocalist in the country.' And he was the one that pinpointed it." So Johnny worked with Nat to get him to sing; see Alan Livingston, oral interview M138, Popular Music Archives, GSU.

23. Epstein, *Nat King Cole*, 96–100. Epstein suggested, "the musicians are so 'cool' you never feel they are out of control, but the polyrhythms, stop-time, and the liberal chromaticism in the piano solos keep the music on the edge. Bebop, as credited to Charlie Parker, Dizzy Gillespie, and Thelonious Monk, loomed just around the corner, a year and a half away. Yet in Nat's piano — percussive, spare, poetic — you can hear the roots of Monk's technique — the same Monk who had watched in wide-eyed wonder as Nat stroked the keyboard at Kelly's Stables" (97). Musicologist Peter Townsend evaluates the transition from swing to bebop: "In popular song of the late 1930s and the early 1940s, every possible chromatic addition to the diatonic scale had been used: the lowered ninth, the raised fourth, and the raised fifth having been used by writers such as Harry Warren and Hoagy Carmichael" (*Pearl Harbor Jazz*, 50–51). He adds, "The three chromatic alterations mentioned above are also the notes that have been taken to typify the harmonic aspect of bebop. The raised fifth is referred to by theorists as the distinctive element in the bebop scale. The raised fourth (or 'flatted fifth,' as it was called at the time) was for a long time considered a defining feature of the new style; and the lowered ninth note over a dominant chord made frequent appearances in the improvised lines of Charlie Parker, among other bebop players" (50–51). To Townsend, "the development of harmony in jazz of the period exactly parallels the development of harmony in popular songwriting."

24. Epstein, *Nat King Cole*, 110–15. Cole took his lyrics for "Straignten Up and Fly Right" from a sermon by his father, the Reverend Edward James Coles Sr., although it derived from the African American folktale "How the Terrapin was Taught to Fly," first recorded in *Daddy Jake the Runaway*; see Joel Chandler Harris, *The Complete Tales of Uncle Remus* (Boston: Houghton Mifflin, 1955), 435–40. Writing in the early 1960s, Dave Dexter recognized that "Cole is arbitrarily rated a pop singer by jazz fans and is excluded from the 'inner circle' by many. Cole, nevertheless, can sing a jazz vocal unmatched by any man in the world when he wants to. He also can — and sometimes does — rip off a scintillating piano solo equal to anything being played by any jazzman today." Contrasting Cole with the jazz singer Ray Charles, Dexter concluded about Cole, "His appeal is, of course, far more cerebral than Charles' bobbing, weaving, nervous, perspiring approach" (*Jazz Story*, 103).

25. Epstein, *Cole*, 141, 145, 148–49; Amanda Mercer Neder, oral interview M140, Popular Music Archives, GSU.

26. Epstein, *Cole*; see also James Haskins with Kathleen Benson, *Nat King Cole* (New York: Stein & Day, 1984), 46–47.

27. Haskins with Benson, *Nat King Cole*, 63–75, *New York Age* quoted on 70; Epstein, *Cole*, 168–76. After hearing Cole sing "Nature Boy," Irving Berlin tried to buy the rights, but Capitol beat him to the song. A legend surrounds Eden Ahbez, who at the time shared a sleeping bag with his pregnant wife and lived off nuts and fruits. Cole's daughter, Carol, recalled being a little girl standing with her father in front of Wallichs's Music City on the corner of Sunset and Vine being introduced to Ahbez and mistaking the man in robes with long hair for Jesus Christ.

28. Dexter, *Playback*, 88, 95–96.

29. Rivers signed several artists to Capitol, including Miles Davis and the Peruvian Indian Yma Sumac whose nearly five-octave vocal range resulted in several hit records; *Savannah Morning News*, September 15, 1935; April 6, 1947; *Savannah Evening Press*, December 20, 1945; *Town and Village* (New York City), April 26, 1951; Proposed Citation for a Letter of Commendation; *Birmingham Post-Herald*, December 10, 1964; *Birmingham News*, June 9, 1969, all in the Walter Rivers Family Papers, University of West Florida, Pensacola, (hereafter UWF). Back in Savannah, Walter took a job with the old Southern States Iron and Roofing, Co. Cornelia had studied art at Vassar College and the University of Georgia and in France and Mexico as well as with John Koch of the Art Students League in New York around the time Johnny Mercer broke into show business. Having heard Gullah/Geechee in her youth like Mercer, Cornelia enjoyed speaking it with her black cook, Pompey, who had grown up at Pin Point as Johnny and Walter's childhood playmate and who moved with the Rivers to Birmingham in 1957.

30. Author's interview with Amanda Mercer Neder, author's possession. Mandy remembers Jeff's parents came from Augusta. Lees, *Portrait of Johnny*, 174; Philip Furia, *Skylark: The Life and Times of Johnny Mercer* (New York: St. Martin's Press, 2003), 125; "The Man Who Writes the Lyrics," *Cosmopolitan*, April 1945.

31. Alan Livingston, oral interview M138, Popular Music Archives, GSU; Capitol Records, *Annual Report for the Year Ended December 31, 1946* (Los Angeles, 1947). After Mercer and then Wallichs, Livingston became president in 1960 and then chairman of the board at Capitol.

32. Released as *Tales of Uncle Remus for Children*, Capitol CC-40, numbers the three records as 10069–10071; see R. Michael Murray, *The Golden Age of Walt Disney Records, 1933–1988* (Dubuque, Iowa: Antique Trader Books, 1997), 137–38. Livingston oral interview.

33. Mercer's singing on March 20, 1948, marked the third Oscar broadcast that included live performances of the nominated songs. While racism persisted in Hollywood, nevertheless the Academy awarded James Baskett, who had played Uncle Remus and sung the song originally in *Song of the South*, with a "Special Oscar statuette." See Robert Osborne, *50 Golden Years of Oscar: The Official History of the Academy of Motion Picture Arts & Sciences* (La Habra, Calif.: ESE California, 1979). Mercer joined Luana Patten, Bobby Driscoll, Martha Tilton, Billy Gilbert, and the Billy May Orchestra on *Mickey and the Beanstalk*, Capitol CCX-67, records 10098–10100. Murray, *The Golden Age of Walt Disney Records*, 4, 6, 138. In 1957, Mercer collaborated with Jack Marshall on a song called "The Missouri Traveler" for a Disney film by the same name. Not until the 1973 animation *Robin Hood* did Mercer again contribute to a Disney production by writing new lyrics for the traditional song "Bastard King of England."

34. Perhaps Mercer recorded George's song because he recognized how much money the man had lost fighting to protect its copyright, knowing that a fresh recording would provide the author with new income. "My Sugar Is So Refined," released as Capitol 1126 and on the reverse as 1129, "Ugly Chile (You're Some Pretty Doll)." Dexter, *Jazz Cavalcade*, 203. See also *Capitol Records, Fiftieth Anniversary*.

35. Johnny Mercer, interview by Willis Conover, January 30, 1970, transcript in Popular Music Archives, GSU.

36. *Capitol Records, Fiftieth Anniversary.*

37. Ibid.; John Chilton, *Who's Who of Jazz: Storyville to Swing Street* (New York: Time-Life Records Special Edition, 1978), 19–20, 211–12, 299–300; Jay D. Smith and Len Guttridge, *Jack Teagarden: The Story of a Jazz Maverick* (New York: Da Capo Press, 1976), 150–69; Peter Richmond, *Fever: The Life and Music of Miss Peggy Lee* (New York: Henry Holt, 2006), 134–36. Reluctant to participate, Lee asked Dexter about money, and he promised her, "I can get you a hundred dollars for singing two songs, and it will only take an hour" (135). Barbour did not play on Lee's recordings of "Ain't Goin' No Place" and the jazz standard "That Old Feeling." Having previously criticized Lee's voice in a jazz review, Dexter compensated by convincing disc jockeys to play the releases, thereby securing from Barbour and Lee long-term contracts with Capitol.

38. *Capitol Records, Fiftieth Anniversary.*

39. Ibid. See also the chapter "Peg," in Gene Lees, *Singers and the Song* (New York: Oxford University Press, 1987), 116–25. Richmond, *Fever,* 136–37.

40. Richmond, *Fever,* 157, 163, 171–72, Mercer quoted on 143; Lee and Barbour divorced in 1951. Mercer's song "Doctor, Lawyer, Indian Chief," which Betty Hutton sang for Capitol in 1946, lacked the offensiveness of Lee's "Mañana." See also *Capitol Records, Fiftieth Anniversary.* After Mercer stepped down as A&R man at Capitol, Peggy asked to sing the Rodgers and Hart 1933 song "Lover" but met resistance, so when her contract expired she signed with Decca in 1951, where she made a hit of the song.

41. Whiting and Holt, *It Might as Well Be Spring,* 65–67.

42. Ibid.

43. Chilton, *Who's Who of Jazz,* 156, 78, 205; *Capitol Records, Fiftieth Anniversary* quotes Hunt saying, "We did it strictly as a gag, but none of the critics dug that. They were the only ones who accepted it as a serious jazz plate" (39). Manone recorded for Capitol "Besame Mucho" and "Paper Doll," but the company chose not to release the sides; see Wingy Manone and Paul Vandervoort II, *Trumpet on the Wing* (New York: Doubleday, 1964). Manone recalled a running narrative: "Everytime I call up Johnny we have laughs. He comes on with, 'Whacha saaaay, boy?' Naturally I bust out in a big laugh, being so struck by this voice that I got to cut it. To hold him on, I got to rhyme that. 'I'm the man that's jumpin' with joy.' 'Whacha say, man?' Johnny says" (196–97)and the conversation went on from there. Kimball et al., eds., *Complete Lyrics,* 222.

44. John Chilton, *The Song of the Hawk: The Life and Recordings of Coleman Hawkins* (London: Quartet Books, 1990); Chilton, *Who's Who of Jazz,* 136–37.

45. Chilton, *The Song of the Hawk,* 227–28; Chilton, *Who's Who of Jazz,* 214, 242–43. Dexter and McGhee quoted in Ted Gioia, *West Coast Jazz: Modern Jazz in California, 1945–1960* (Berkeley: University of California Press, 1992), 10–11; Dexter, *Playback,* 106.

46. James Lincoln Collier, *The Making of Jazz: A Comprehensive History* (New York: Dell, 1978); Charley Gerard, *Jazz in Black and White: Race, Culture, and Identity in the Jazz Community* (Westport, Conn.: Praeger, 1998); Gene Lees, *Cats of Any Color: Jazz Black and White* (New York: Oxford University Press, 1994); Richard M. Sudhalter, *Lost Chords: White Musicians and Their Contributions to Jazz, 1915–1945* (New York: Oxford University Press, 1999).

47. Many jazz musicians smoked marijuana regularly such as Louis Armstrong, who did so daily. Lewis A. Erenberg, *Swingin' the Dream: Big Band Jazz and the Rebirth of American Culture* (Chicago: University of Chicago Press, 1998), 211–42; see also Townsend, *Pearl Harbor Jazz.* According to Leonard Lyons's newspaper column, Mercer retorted to MGM head L. K. Sidney that he would testify to not being a Communist only if the head of MGM's parent company, Loew's Inc., Nicholas Schenck, did likewise. Mercer never appeared before any investigative committee, nor did he testify against anyone, although he later worked with several people caught up in the Red baiting. Clipping in JM Papers, GSU.

48. Haskins with Benson, *Nat King Cole*, 185; Gioia, *West Coast Jazz*, 18.

49. *Capitol Records, Fiftieth Anniversary*; Gioia, *West Coast Jazz*; Bill Cole, *Miles Davis: A Musical Biography* (New York: William Morrow, 1974), 7–52, 116–21. Cole noted, "during this early period, his tone — not yet matured — didn't sound forceful, let alone aggressive," but it established Davis as "a leader" of the new style of bebop. Cole also suggests that "after bop, Miles slipped briefly, and his dabbling initiated the so-called 'cool' period, which provided a forum for many of its European imitators. However, Miles soon blossomed and became the leading voice of the fifties. Bebop matured also in the fifties and was renamed hard bop. And, as has always been the case throughout the history of African-American music, white musicians created their own watered-down versions of the music called, at various times, 'cool,' 'West Coast,' and 'progressive' jazz" (22–23). A less racial essentialist critique that provides a more detailed and balanced account is provided by Ian Carr, *Miles Davis: A Biography* (New York: William Morrow, 1982), 1–40, quotation on 38; as president, Mercer hired his cousin Walter Rivers as an A & R man for Capitol's New York office, and Rivers is credited along with Stan Kenton's arranger Pete Rugolo with advocating the label sign Davis. It is possible Mercer also attended a performance at the Royal Roost that September 1948, as Johnny traveled constantly in and out of New York. More attuned to the changing sounds of jazz than the recently returned war veteran Rivers, and in the thick of Stan Kenton's studio sessions with Rugolo, it seems likely that Mercer recognized the significance of the Davis Nonet, arranged the contract, and contributed to the studio sessions that list Rivers and Rugolo as producers. For Capitol, Miles Davis and His Orchestra (including Mulligan) recorded on January 21, 1949, "Jeru," "Move," "Godchild," and "Budo"; on April 21, "John's Delight," "What's New," "Heaven's Doors Are Open Wide," and "Focus"; on April 22, "Venus de Milo," "Rouge," Boplicity," and "Israel"; and on March 9, "Deception," "Rocker," "Moon Dreams," and "Darn that Dream." Mercer registered "Moon Dreams" for a copyright in 1941 and recorded it in 1942, with the song being published in January 1944. Johnny wrote hip lyrics in 1959 to a tune by Gene de Paul titled "The Happy Bachelor, or The Courtship of Miles Davis." See also Miles Davis with Quincy Troupe, *Miles, the Autobiography* (New York: Simon & Schuster, 1989), 117–19.

50. Dexter, *Jazz Story*, 126–29, with quotation on 126; for programs of these international concerts, see box 7 of the Edward Kennedy "Duke" Ellington Collection, Library of Congress, Washington, D.C.

51. Firestone, *Swing, Swing, Swing*, 285–86; Bach and Mercer, eds., *Our Huckleberry Friend*, 173; Mercer and the lyrics are quoted in Kimball et al., eds., *Complete Lyrics*, 237. A decade before Mercer had rhymed "Hey, look at that aurora borealis, / That boy must live in Buckingham Palace!" in his song "Sharp as A Tack" for *Star Spangled Rhythm* (see *Complete Lyrics*, 132). Mercer later remarked that the music to "Travelin' Light" "sounds like it doesn't go the way the words do exactly, and the same thing [happens] in the middle of 'Midnight Sun.' I never quite got them straight in my mind time-wise" (Mercer interview by Conover).

52. Mark Tucker, ed., *The Duke Ellington Reader* (New York: Oxford University Press, 1993), 263; Bach and Mercer, eds., *Our Huckleberry Friend*, 181; Kimball et al., eds., *Complete Lyrics*, includes "Blossom," which Mercer and Ellington registered for a copyright on February 5, 1954 (236), and "Satin Doll," which they registered on November 4, 1958, and published on April 13, 1960 (272–73), but the third song seems to be missing unless it is "Take the Mule Train," one of what the editors identify as Johnny's miscellaneous, undated, unpublished songs for whom no composer is identified (415). Don George, *Sweet Man: The Real Duke Ellington* (New York: G. P. Putnam, 1981), 156, 188–89. Mercer interview by Conover; transcript of Johnny Mercer interview by Humphrey Lyttleton, BBC *Omnibus*, season 2, episode 19, July 14, 1974, copy in Popular Music Archive, GSU.

53. William F. Lee, *Stan Kenton: Artistry in Rhythm* (Los Angeles: Creative Press of Los Angeles, 1980), 36, 65; Carol Easton, *Straight Ahead: The Story of Stan Kenton* (New York: William Morrow, 1973), 57–65; Robert A. Ciucevich, *Tybee Island: The Long Branch of the South* (Charleston, S.C.: Arcadia, 2005), 100–101.

54. As early as November 1940, Kenton's band had recorded in Wallichs's Music City Record Shop; see Lee, *Stan Kenton*, 609–616; Easton, *Straight Ahead*, 69, 86–87, quotation on 87. Easton also noted that "Mercer loved 'Eager Beaver,' and was constantly after Stan to record more such melodic — and therefore, he felt, salable — selections. Stan was determined to record what he by God wanted to record, which led to many a pitched battle in Mercer's office with Glenn Wallichs, Paul Weston and Carlos Gastel fruitlessly attempting to mediate" (86).

55. Easton, *Straight Ahead*, 83–89, with quotations on 89; Donald L. Maggin, *Stan Getz: A Life in Jazz* (New York: William Morrow, 1996), 33–36. Just seventeen but already having played professionally with Jack Teagarden, who Stan Getz recalled "taught me a lot, especially about bending my right elbow," the tenor saxophone player gained a reputation with Kenton's band as a showoff. On *City of Glass*, see Gioia, *West Coast Jazz*, 152–66.

56. Gene Lees, *Leader of the Band: The Life of Woody Herman* (New York: Oxford University Press, 1995), 80, 198–99, and passim; Dexter, *Jazz Story*, 128–29, 135; Maggin, *Stan Getz*, 94–95.

57. Julius Hornstein, *Sites and Sounds of Savannah Jazz* (Savannah, Ga.: Gaston Street Press, 1994), speculates that Mercer thought of Tybrisa when writing "Early Autumn" (41). Mercer's quote and the lyrics appear in Bach and Mercer, eds., *Our Huckleberry Friend*, 148; see also Kimball et al., eds., *Complete Lyrics*, 221; Lees quoted in *Leader of the Band*, 202. Recognizing Capitol's "desperate desire to find an audience for the band," Lees cites Herman's wishful quote from *Down Beat* made in November 1950, "There's no doubt the band business is coming back. . . . The public is dance conscious now" (199). In addition to "Early Autumn," popular instrumentals existed for "Laura," "Song of India," and "Satin Doll." Mercer quote from JM autobiography.

58. Lange, *Smile when You Call Me a Hillbilly*, 217–20.

59. Ibid., 227–30. In discussing the California scene, Lange notes that "Capitol Records opened its doors to all types of country music performers from different parts of the country, but their greatest success after the war came with eclectic, California-based acts, such as Hank Thompson, Merle Travis, Tennessee Ernie Ford, Tex Williams, and Jimmy Wakely. These artists surrounded themselves with musicians willing to experiment with different sounds and styles in an effort to create music that appealed to a variety of listeners" (223). He concludes that Capitol "became a stronghold for West Coast performers seeking to distance themselves from hillbilly music, honky-tonk, and even the roots-based country pop produced by southern-bred acts."

60. Andy Babims, *The Story of Paul Bigsby: Father of the Modern Electric Solid Body Guitar* (Savannah, Ga.: F. G. Publishing, 2008), 32–41.

61. *Capitol Records, Fiftieth Anniversary*.

62. Whiting and Holt, *It Might as Well Be Spring*, 52–67; *Capitol Records, Fiftieth Anniversary*. By the early 1950s, Capitol maintained offices at 6362 Hollywood Boulevard. *New York Times*, September 11, 1947. The article noted that Capitol had generated sales nearly thirty percent higher than the figures from the year before.

63. Gene Handsaker, "Hollywood II," AP Newsfeatures, April 30, 1948; *Newsweek*, July 21, 1952; Dexter, *Playback*, 141–43, and Mercer's quote in Dexter's liner notes for the recording, *Johnny Mercer: Sweet Georgia Brown*, with Paul Weston's Orchestra (Burbank, Calif.: Hindsight Records, 1995), recorded in 1949 and previously released as *The Uncollected Johnny Mercer*. As an executive at Capitol, Dave Dexter Jr. later published *The Jazz Story: From the '90s to the '60s* (Englewood Cliffs, N.J.: Prentice-Hall, 1964). June Christy's album *Something Cool* reflects

the continued influence of Mercer at Capitol. Formerly the singer with Stan Kenton's orchestra, Christy recorded twenty-four songs arranged and conducted by Pete Rugolo between 1953 and 1955, including Mercer's "Midnight Sun," "This Time the Dream's on Me," and to a tune by Milt Raskin, "I Never Want to Look into Those Eyes Again." Two others that originally listed the songwriters as unknown, have Merceresque lyrics, "Out of Somewhere" by composer Jimmy Giuffre and "Love Doesn't Live Here Anymore" by composer F. M. Lehman.

64. Barbara Robbins, oral interview M158, and Robert Rush, oral interview M154, Popular Music Archives, GSU; Kimball et al., eds., *Complete Lyrics*, 196.

65. *Capitol Records, Fiftieth Anniversary*; Sanjek, *Pennies from Heaven*, 376.

66. JHM to "Mom," undated [October 8, 1954], Mercer Family Collection, AASU; JHM to "Darling," undated, Walter Rivers Papers, UWF.

Chapter Seven. Broadway

The epigraph is from "Top Banana" (1951), with words and music by Mercer. The opening line is borrowed from Irving Berlin's anthem of the same name from the musical *Annie Get Your Gun*. Mercer crafted an additional set of lyrics for the Broadway anthem that poked fun at Frank Sinatra when performing it as a duet with the crooner on the CBS *Songs by Sinatra* radio show. He later used the lines in the verse to the song "Top Banana." See Robert Kimball, Barry Day, Miles Kreuger, and Eric Davis, eds., *The Complete Lyrics of Johnny Mercer* (New York: Alfred A. Knopf, 2009), 170, 206.

1. *New York Sun*, April 1, 1946. The *New York Journal-American* noted, "the book of 'St. Louis Woman' is its own worst opponent, a tactless tripper-upper." Problems with Bontemps's manuscript are discussed in Edward E. Waldron, *Walter White and the Harlem Renaissance* (Port Washington, N.Y.: Kennikat Press, 1978), 159–60; see also the script to "St. Louis Woman" in the A. W. Bontemps Papers, Collection 82/113c, Bancroft Library, University of California, Berkeley, Calif.

2. *New York Times*, April 1, 1946;, *Variety*, April 3, 1946;, undated clippings from *Variety* [1945] and *New York Post*, all in JM Papers, GSU. On Fredi Washington, who appeared on Broadway in Vincent Youman's *Great Day* (1929) and in *Mamba's Daughters* and on screen with Paul Robeson in *Emperor Jones* (1933) and, in her best role, as the mulatto daughter in *Imitation of Life* (1934), see Charles J. Elmore, *All That Savannah Jazz: From Brass Bands, Vaudeville, to Rhythm and Blues* (Savannah, Ga.: Savannah State University, 1999), 206; Lena Horne and Richard Schickel, *Lena* (New York: Doubleday & Company, Inc., 1965), 187–92. See also the definitive biography by James Gavin, *Stormy Weather: The Life of Lena Horne* (New York: Atria Books, 2009), 115–16, 126, 172–77.

3. *New York Times*, April 1, 1946; *Variety*, April 3, 1946; undated clippings from *Variety* [1945] and *New York Post*, all in JM Papers, GSU; Horne and Schickel, *Lena*, 187–92; Gavin, *Stormy Weather*. Because of an inaccurate report by gossip columnist Walter Winchell, Horne incorrectly believed that Freed and MGM briefly blacklisted her in revenge for her refusing a role in *St. Louis Woman*, but Gavin argues otherwise, noting Louis B. Mayer's response to White's caustic "I'm loath to believe you would permit action of this character" with MGM's response, "We are most anxious for Miss Horne to succeed and that is why we have her under contract" (175). Gavin quotes Bontemps, adding, "Its theme is the struggle of simple people to add a note of grace and beauty to the dark tones of life as they know it. I hope this is still admissible." See also Pearl Bailey, *The Raw Pearl* (New York: Pocket Books, 1971), 58–61.

4. *Variety*, April 3, 1946; liner notes by Mort Goode for *St. Louis Woman*, an Angel Records (ZDM 7 64662 2) 1992 release of the 1946 Capitol Records recording; Edward Jablonski, *Harold Arlen: Rhythm, Rainbows, and Blues* (Boston: Northeastern University Press, 1996), 197–205; feeling snakebit, the producer Ed Gross said he would never undertake "another Negro show"; for a list of reviews, see James M. Salem, *A Guide to Critical Reviews*, part 2, *The Musical, 1909–1989* (n.p., 1991), 568; also see folder 9, box 33, JM Papers, GSU. Comparing *St. Louis Woman* to *Porgy and Bess*, Jablonski blamed the theater critics for unjustly killing the show.

5. Goode liner notes, *St. Louis Woman*, 1992 release; Gavin, *Stormy Weather*, 176; Jablonski, *Harold Arlen*, 204–5, 302–5. *New York Times*, September 3, 1954, December 15, 1959, January 16, February 10, 1960. With *Free and Easy* (the title taken from the opening line of "Any Place I Hang My Hat Is Home"), the producers added instrumentals, lyrics, and whole songs, infuriating Mercer and Arlen. Quincy Jones directed the orchestra as a jazz band, to the detriment of the original music. After a handful of performances the show closed, stranding the actors in Europe. The first black Miss America, Vanessa L. Williams, starred in a 1998 revival of *St. Louis Woman* as a New York City Center's *Encores! Great American Musicals in Concert* that later found release as a cast recording on CD by Decca in 2003. Robert Kimball, Barry Day, Miles Kreuger, and Eric Davis, eds., *The Complete Lyrics of Johnny Mercer* (New York: Alfred A. Knopf, 2009), 158–66.

6. Armed Forces Radio and Television Service materials in Recorded Sound Reference Center of the Music Division, Library of Congress, Washington, D.C.; a useful index is Harry Mackinzie, *The Directory of the Armed Forces Radio Service Series* (Westport, Conn.: Greenwood Press, 1999); *Phonograph Album*, program 13; *Remember*, program 563.

7. John Dunning, *Tune in Yesterday: The Ultimate Encyclopedia of Old-time Radio, 1925–1976* (Englewood Cliffs, N.J.: Prentice-Hall, 1976), 107–8. A play on the company's longstanding marketing slogan, "Call for Philip Morris," the show, *Call for Music* ran for twenty-six weeks, initially broadcasting over CBS on February 13, 1948, and then beginning in April on Tuesday nights over NBC.

8. See Crabapple Sound Presents, Old Time Radio Musical Programs *Call for Music*, cassette tapes numbered RMU 3301–3307, March 26, April 9, and June 1, 1948, copies in the Popular Music Archives, GSU.

9. *Call for Music*, April 9, June 1, 15, and 22, 1948; Vincent Terrace, *The Complete Encyclopedia of Television Programs, 1947–1976*, 2 vols. (South Brunswick, N.J.: A. S. Barnes, 1976), 1:209.

10. Peter J. Levinson, *Trumpet Blues: The Life of Harry James* (New York: Oxford University Press, 1999), 169. See also the March 26, April 9, and June 15, 1948, broadcasts.

11. See *Call for Music*, March 26, June 15, 22, and 29, 1948. Dietz and Schwartz won no Oscars or Tonys over the span of their lengthy careers. They collaborated on "That's Entertainment" and a host of other songs. See American Society of Composers, Authors and Publishers, *ASCAP Biographical Dictionary*, 4th ed. (New York: Jacques Cattell Press, 1980), 126, 450. Mercer performed Dietz's "Dickie Bird Song" on *Call for Music* and made a great recording of Schwartz's "A Gal in Calico." In his study of Broadway, *Show Tunes: The Songs, Shows, and Careers of Broadway's Major Composers* (New York: Oxford University Press, 2000), Steven Suskin notes that "Arthur Schwartz wrote some of the finest theatre music of his time — particularly the haunting minor-key ballads of the thirties ('Dancing in the Dark,' 'Alone Together,' 'You and the Night and the Music') and the later, considerably warmer ones ('Make the Man Love Me,' 'I'll Buy You a Star,' 'Magic Moment'). His skill also displayed itself in outstanding rhythmic work ('I Guess I'll Have to Change My Plan,' the 1953 movie song 'That's Entertainment'). All of which make it difficult to explain Schwartz's record of no successful Broadway book musicals" (147). Suskin volunteers that "not having a full-time lyricist to develop and experiment with was certainly part of it, although Dietz's later lyrics suggest that Schwartz might have done better with, say, Dorothy Fields" (147).

"Back to Dixie" composer Lou Herscher's daughter Ruth Lillian Herscher Grahm wrote the music for "Veronica from Santa Monica." Andrew B. Sterling and Harry Von Tilzer wrote "Wait 'Till the Sun Shines, Nellie," and it was interpolated into *Birth of the Blues*.

12. John Crosby, "Radio in Review" and other clippings, box 31, folder 13, JM Papers, GSU. *New York Times*, April 17, 1948.

13. *ASCAP Biographical Dictionary*, 130; JM autobiography. A novel by Brian Oswald Donn-Byrne provided the text for the book by Robert Nathan and Siegfried "Sig" Herzig that Mercer and Dolan used for *Messer Marco Polo*. See Kimball et al., eds., *Complete Lyrics*, 200, and on 183 the observation that at one point Mercer and Dolan started on a musical tentatively called *Free and Easy* based on a book by Herzig and Milton Lazarus for which they wrote one song, "The Way You Fall in Love," that almost found life in *Texas, Li'l Darlin'*.

14. Gerald Bordman, *American Musical Theatre: A Chronicle* (New York: Oxford University Press, 1992), 571, describes the show as "conventional." Originally built as the Hollywood Theater on West Fifty-first Street, the Hellinger is now home to the Times Square Church. Despite completely different plots, the unfortunate title echoed too closely the 1943 Rodgers and Hammerstein hit *Oklahoma!*

15. Georgia politics are described as the "rule of the rustics" in the classic V. O. Key Jr., *Southern Politics in State and Nation* (New York: Alfred A. Knopf, 1949); for an analysis of the era see Numan V. Bartley, *The New South: 1945–1980: The Story of the South's Modernization* (Baton Rouge: Louisiana State University Press, 1995); Kimball et al., eds., *Complete Lyrics*, 175–82.

16. Gerold Frank, *Judy* (New York: Harper & Row, 1975), 294–95, and passim; David Shipman, *Judy Garland: The Secret Life of an American Legend* (New York: Hyperion, 1993), 263–64, and passim.

17. Shipman, *Judy Garland*, 283–94; Frank, *Judy*, 328–34; Gerald Clarke, *Get Happy: The Life of Judy Garland* (New York: Random House, 2000), 294–95, recounts the Bach anecdote; Jean Bach, oral interview M128, Popular Music Archives, GSU.

18. Kimball et al., eds., *Complete Lyrics*, 384; Bach oral interview. After Johnny's death Ginger gave to Barry Manilow his file of scrap verses to turn into songs; the album *Monica Mancini: The Dreams of Johnny Mercer* (Concord, Calif.: Concord Records, 2000) contains an excellent rendition of "When October Goes." Referring to the lovers, Mandy thought that when their paths crossed, it was as if they said, "Let's go have sex or something." Then thinking about all her father's affairs and the women attracted to his celebrity, she asked, "How do you say no when they stick it in your face?" Author's interview with Amanda Mercer Neder, January 27, 2010, author's possession.

19. Phil Silvers as Jerry Biffle quoted in Kimball et al., eds., *Complete Lyrics*, 209. *Top Banana* cost $250,000 to stage and competed against the previous year's *Call Me Madam*, with Ethel Merman, and *South Pacific* (*Parade*, December 30, 1951). Although he shared a similar sensibility, Mercer did not enjoy the same success writing both music and lyrics as his friend Frank Loesser, whose *Guys and Dolls* and *How to Succeed in Business Without Really Trying* became Broadway blockbusters despite lacking strong melodies.

20. Bordman, *American Musical Theatre*, 581; Kimball et al., eds., *Complete Lyrics*, 205–15.

21. Stanley Green, *Broadway Musicals: Show by Show*, 4th ed. (Milwaukee, Wis.: Hal Leonard, 1994), 150–53; Bordman, *American Musical Theatre*, 523, 581; Kimball et al., eds., *Complete Lyrics*, 206. The absence of a lush musical score and stand-alone songs would plague Mercer's other attempts on Broadway.

22. Clive Hirschhorn, *The Hollywood Musical* (New York: Crown, 1981), 300, 301, 307, 312–15.

23. Richard M. Sudhalter, *Stardust Melody: The Life and Music of Hoagy Carmichael* (New York: Oxford University Press, 2002), 233–40, 275–77; Kimball et al., eds., *Complete Lyrics*, 143;

Bob Bach and Ginger Mercer, eds., *Our Huckleberry Friend: The Life, Times, and Lyrics of Johnny Mercer* (Secaucus, N.J.: Lyle Stuart, 1982), 133. The film includes the immortal lines of Bacall asking Bogart: "You know how to whistle, don't you? You just put your lips together and blow." See Andy Williams, *Moon River and Me: A Memoir* (New York: Viking, 2009), 44–45.

24. *Palm Springs Life*, September 1999, 170; Kimball et al., eds., *Complete Lyrics*, 192–93. Robert Rush, oral interview M154, Popular Music Archives, GSU. On hearing the Oscar announcement, Carmichael mistakenly said, revealing his jealousy, "Naturally I was overjoyed at receiving my Oscar. I'm not sure that my lyricist, Johnny Mercer, was as overjoyed as I because he already had a vulgar display of three Oscars at his home from former years" (Sudhalter, *Stardust Melody*, 276–78). See also Carmichael, *Sometimes I Wonder*, 285. The song beat out the studio favorite "A Kiss to Build a Dream On" by Harry Ruby and Oscar Hammerstein II. It is unclear what joke Carmichael told Mercer, but the basic outline and animal references suggests something out of African American folklore, and vulgar examples regarding the lion and monkey having sex at a party appear in Roger D. Abrahams, *Deep Down in the Jungle: Negro Narrative Folklore from the Streets of Philadelphia* (Chicago: Aldine Publishing, 1970), 70–73, 225–28.

25. Hirschhorn, *Hollywood Musical*, 325, 330, 334. Warren recalled, "I liked the picture even though it was old-fashioned, and it called for a big score, which I also liked. But what Mercer and I liked most was getting twenty-four weeks of work out of it. They kept saying they were having troubles making it, and we kept hoping they would find more and more problems." See Tony Thomas, *Harry Warren and the Hollywood Musical* (Secaucus, N.J.: Lyle Stuart, 1975), 272. JM autobiography. The Astaire scholar Todd Decker argued in his unpublished paper, "'I'm Hep to that Step and I Dig It'" (in the author's possession) that "Johnny Mercer writes for (and with) Fred Astaire," that "Mercer expresses Astaire's quite introverted nature, his devotion to syncopated song and dance, in Mercer's felicitous phrase, his 'footsteps on the sands of rhythm and rhyme.' Astaire was seldom comfortable pointing towards himself or his artistic accomplishments. It's a singular accomplishment that Mercer's restrained, remarkable apt lyric met with Astaire's approval."

26. Hirschhorn, *Hollywood Musical*, 337–40; see the "Modern Version by Johnny Mercer of the Glow-Worm," based on the original words by Lilla Cayley Robinson with music by Paul Lincke, 1902 copyright by Apollo Verlag, Mercer's 1952 copyright by Edward B. Marks Music Corp. Kimball et al., eds., *Complete Lyrics*, 185, 197–98.

27. Robert Rush, oral interview M154, Popular Music Archives, GSU. As Rush puts it, "They wanted to use somebody locally. . . . So I went over and I guess I never left." Neder interview, author's possession. Mandy loved Newport and hated the Hollywood scene: "I can't imagine living in Beverly Hills. They live a fast life," the very life Ginger craved.

28. Polly Ober, oral interview M157, Popular Music Archives, GSU. Recalling her friendship with Johnny, Polly said the real-estate agent introduced the families "and then we started seeing a lot of each other, and I didn't realize, you know, what a terrific guy this gentleman was and how amazing, and all of these things he had written." Amanda Mercer Neder, oral interview M140, Popular Music Archives, GSU.

29. Ober, oral interview M154, Popular Music Archives, GSU.

30. On the accident, see *Los Angeles Times*, October 2 and November 16, 1954, *Los Angeles Daily News*, October 2 and headline November 16, 1954; Rush interview. At the time drunk driving was no more dishonorable than "wenching" or gambling, unless the act generated opprobrium by society that resulted in shame. Getting caught led Johnny to fear being forever labeled a drunkard. Bertram Wyatt-Brown, *Southern Honor: Ethics and Behavior in the Old South*, 25th ann. ed. (New York: Oxford University Press, 2007), 155, explores the connection: "If an honor-centered

person is guilty of some wrong, his or her primary desire is to escape the implications of weakness and inferiority, the lash of contempt." Kimball et al., eds., *Complete Lyrics*, 221.

31. JHM to Juliana Keith, June 28, 1952, and sometime in 1954, JHM to Lillian Mercer, December 12, 1953, folders 5 and 6, box 1, Mercer Family Collection, AASU. To be sure, an occasional Mercer song referenced the islands as in "The Bells of Honolulu" and "Honolulu." For a provocative analysis of the influence of Hawaiian music on American popular culture, see the chapter "Poetry in Motion" in Gary Y. Okihiro, *Island World: A History of Hawai'i and the United States* (Berkeley, Calif.: University of California Press, 2009).

32. Reviews of the show appear in folder 9, box 33, JM Papers, GSU; Livy and Plutarch first recorded the story that appeared as "The Sobbin' Women" in Stephen Vincent Benét, *Twenty-five Short Stories by Stephen Vincent Benét* (Garden City, N.Y.: Sun Dial Press, 1943), 138–61; Hirschhorn, *The Hollywood Musical*, 340–42, quoted on 342. Beth Riedmann to Estate of Johnny Mercer, May 31, 1983, folder 14, box 4, JM Papers, GSU.

33. Robbins Music Corp. published the music from the film; Kimball et al., eds., *Complete Lyrics*, 240–43; Hirschhorn, *Hollywood Musical*, 346.

34. Hirschhorn, *Hollywood Musical*, 353, 356.

35. Undated and unidentified clipping, *New York Times*, September 26, 1953, and Mercer's transcript, "Li'l Abner Revisited," folder 4, box 2, all in JM Papers, GSU. Having choreographed *Finian's Rainbow*, *Guys and Dolls*, and *Can-Can*, Michael Kidd redirected Broadway dance, winning a Tony with *Li'l Abner* (Suskin, *Show Tunes*, 395–96).

36. See "Sadie Hawkins' Day" in Al Capp, *The World of Li'l Abner* (New York: Ballantine Books, 1953), 1–23. See also the critique of such southern stereotypes, Anthony Harkins, *Hillbilly: A Cultural History of an American Icon* (New York: Oxford University Press, 2004). Observing "Capp's portrayal of the community and environs of Dogpatch was equally fantastical and was never intended to be a realistic portrayal of mountain life and conditions," Harkins notes that nevertheless Capp "was widely considered an authority on the southern mountains, despite his own disavowals and all evidence to the contrary" (127). No doubt the storyline resonated with Johnny: just up the river from his hometown in the early 1950s the federal government used eminent domain to remove the entire community of Ellenton, South Carolina, to make way for the nuclear Savannah River Site. In 2007, *The Simpsons Movie* plot took up a notion similar to Capp's, that the government might condemn a community as "the most unnecessary place in the whole U.S.A." See also Suskin, *Show Tunes*, 395–96.

37. Kimball et al., eds., *Complete Lyrics*, 248–59; playbill from the National, "America's First Theatre," and various newspaper clippings in vertical files, Martin Luther King Jr. Public Library, Washington, D.C. Al Capp's General Bullmoose presented a caricature of President Dwight Eisenhower's Secretary of Defense, Charles Erwin Wilson, the former CEO of General Motors, who had famously said, "What was good for the country was good for General Motors and vice versa." Capp wrote Johnny, "My problem from now on will be how can I get the Mercer touch in my strip. Thanks for a splendid job" (Capp to JHM, November. 15, 1956, folder 14, box 2, JM Papers, GSU).

38. Suskin, *Show Tunes*, 395; *Theatre Arts*, January 1957. See also Mercer, BBC interview by Lyttleton. Barbara Robbins, oral interview M158, Popular Music Archives, GSU

39. JHM to Ginger, Jeff, Mandy [October 1955], JHM to "My sweeties" [October 1956], folder 10, box 2, JM Papers, GSU; Suskin, *Show Tunes*, 395–96. During the tryouts on the road, several songs were cut, including "Too Durn Bashful" that Mercer particularly liked because of its use of Capplike punctuation as in "GULP!, SOB!, and SHUDDER!"; Cole Porter to JHM, November 15, and Edith Adams to JHM, November 18, 1955, folder 14, box 2, JM Papers, GSU. In her thank-you note,

Edie added, "Also thanks for the many nice things you did for all of us in the whole company. If it weren't for a guy named Kovacs [the comedian Ernie] I'd fall for you myself!" After the opening, the Mercers attended a blowout cast party hosted by Capp. *New York Times*, November 16, 1956.

40. *Variety*, June 10, 1953; Bing Crosby to JHM, October 11, 1954, JM Papers, GSU. Many of the Armed Forces Radio and Television Service programs are in the Recorded Sound Reference Center, Music Division, Library of Congress, Washington, D.C.

41. Kathryn Murray to JHM, December 5, 1950, Lester Gottlieb to JHM, October 22, 1953; telegram from "The Gang from Prairie Village" in Kansas City, December 9, 1954, to JM; Bill Harbach to JM, December 13, 1954, all in folder 13, box 2, JM Papers, GSU. On the September 3, 1951, broadcast of *The Name's the Same*, see Joan Clarke, Johnny Mercer Collection, M172, Popular Music Archives, GSU. On March 19, 1953, NBC televised the 1952 Academy Awards. Herb Allen to JHM, May 6, 1955; Ernie Ford to JHM, September 6, 1955, box 2, folder 14, JM Papers, GSU; Terrace, *Complete Encyclopedia of Television Programs*, 2:122; *Atlanta Journal and Constitution Magazine*, August 14, 1955.

42. William "Bill" Harbach, oral interview M130, Popular Music Archive, GSU. Years later, Harbach tried to retrieve the film footage of the early *Tonight Shows* but "there was some nut, I understand in New Jersey, who was the head of the [NBC] vaults, and, like, you know, there's not *Milton Berle* shows, those giant *Milton Berle* shows . . . and he said, 'I burned them.' And they said, 'why?' He said, 'well, we needed room for more shows.' I mean, that attitude. It was awesome. There was no control." Allen set one of Johnny's lyrics to a tune he wrote titled "I'm a Man."

43. Terrace, *Complete Encyclopedia of Television Programs*, 2:122. *Musical Chairs* ran on NBC from July 9 to September 17, 1955; Bill Leyden hosted. An effort to revive the concept occurred in 1975 without Mercer's involvement. For the 1955 album, *Bobby Troup Sings Johnny Mercer*, Johnny contributed the lyric to Troup's tune "I'm with You," while in the liner notes, Johnny penned "The Words or Music — Which Came First?" a poem in which he discusses the history of several of the songs on the album. See Kimball et al., eds., *Complete Lyrics*, 243.

44. Terrace, *Complete Encyclopedia of Television Programs*, 2:108, 258, 137; Rosemary Clooney with Joan Barthel, *Girl Singer: An Autobiography* (New York: Doubleday, 1999), 149–52. *The Rosemary Clooney Show*, 1956, and *The Bob Crosby Show*, April 1955, accessed through David Oppenheim and the Friends of Johnny Mercer; Henry Kane, *How to Write a Song (as Told to Henry Kane)* (New York, Macmillan, 1962), 78.

45. James Haskins with Kathleen Benson, *Nat King Cole* (New York: Stein & Day, 1984), 138–41, 143–45. The attack on Cole occurred on April 10, 1956; see Brian Ward, *Just My Soul Responding: Rhythm and Blues, Black Consciousness, and Race Relations* (Berkeley: University of California Press, 1998), 95–105, and Glenn T. Eskew, *But for Birmingham: The Local and National Movements in the Civil Rights Struggle* (Chapel Hill: University of North Carolina Press, 1997), 114; see also *The Nat "King" Cole Show*, 1957. Shocked by her son's appearance on Cole's show, Lillian Mercer registered with Johnny her disapproval of his treating Cole with equality.

46. *The Perry Como Show*, 1962, and *The Andy Williams Show*, 1963, accessed through David Oppenheim and the Friends of Johnny Mercer.

47. Robbins, oral interview. George W. Hunt to "Johnnie," March 11, 1955 and other papers on Mercer's repayment of his father's debt, see Johnny Mercer Correspondence, 1955–1971, collection MS 552, Georgia Historical Society, Savannah, Ga., hereafter GHS. These papers came from Johnny's childhood friend and local banker Malcolm Bell Jr. and document the transaction, including the correspondence between Mercer and Hunt.

48. *Atlanta Journal Constitution*, undated clipping, Hunt to "Johnnie," April 5 and 7, 1955, JM Papers, GSU. "Johnny Mercer Kept His Promise," notes, Mercer Family Collection, AASU; *Savannah Evening Press*, April 13, 1955; AP and UPI wire stories, April 15, 1955, JM Papers, GSU. The *New*

York Times on April 19, 1955, acknowledged, "The Savannah-born songwriter had hoped to keep the transaction secret. But word of it leaked out last week."

49. The AP reporter quoted Mercer's response to the Savannah article of April 13 as "a little premature." He added, "I didn't expect any publicity. Nothing's happened yet." He then suggested the reporters contact his brothers and George Hunt in Savannah for details. Five days later, the *New York Times* quoted Johnny: "I didn't want any publicity. It's just a family affair." AP and UPI wire stories; *New York Times*, April 20, 1955; JHM to George Hunt, [April 1955], JM Correspondence, GHS.

50. Walter Mercer to JHM, April 9, 1955, Lillian Mercer to JHM, May 1, 1955, Aunt Kate to JHM, May 20, 1955, Uncle Robbie to JHM, September 2, 1955. Aunt Nora Ciucevich wrote on April 14, 1955: "You are truly one in a million Johnny — it was a magnificent thing to do & something that will please your father more than anything else." Uncle Robbie, now eighty-three, added, "The wonderful thing you did in putting up all that money in loving memory of your Father, will never be forgotten by hundreds, maybe thousands, of people who were helped out of a debt that was owing [sic] to them." Lillian wrote her son that she had recently taken Robert Mercer to visit the grave of Aunt Katherine in Bonaventure, observing that "he's always been such a good gentle soul." "Uncle Robbie" to "My dear Johnny," April 19, 1955. All letters in JM Papers, GSU.

51. *Lowdown*, October 1955. The *Birmingham News* added, "The act is much more than a gesture. It is the kind of thing a man would not have had to do to keep his own respect, but in the doing, gains him much more of others' respect." See also the *Hartford Courant*; *Memphis Press-Scimitar*, April 21, 1955; *Richmond (Calif.) Independent*, May 21, 1955; a feature in the *Atlanta Journal-Constitution Magazine* "gave me fresh hope for humanity," N. C. Adderley wrote on August 25, 1955; all in box 31, JM Papers, GSU.

52. See the story "Johnny Mercer Repays a Debt" in *Reader's Digest* (February 1956). See J. H. Bemis, March 28, 1956; Fred Waring to JHM, April 26, 1955; William Dozier to JHM, April 20, 1955; Jack Mohr to JHM, April 26, 1955; and Ida M. Stuffler to JHM, May 22, 1955, who added, "It's a great world we live in that produces sons like you — I'm grateful too — to the newspapers for publishing Glad Tidings — we need to hear more of the good deeds." All in box 31, JM Papers, GSU.

53. Nick Mamalakis to JHM and Veda Royall to JHM, September 21, 1955; Malcolm Bell Jr. to JHM, April 29, 1955, JM Papers, GSU.

54. R. W. D. Taylor to JHM, May 26, 1955, JM Papers, GSU. The Savannah attorney A. R. Lawton wrote Mercer on May 3, 1955, to say "what a marvelous thing I think you have done. There are perhaps other men who have wanted to do similar things but never actually do them. Your determination to clear the name of the G. A. Mercer Company and to leave no one who had any claim unsatisfied against it is a splendid thing to have done because there were, of course, many certificate holders who did not know your father personally, as I had the pleasure of knowing him."

55. Chatham Savings Bank Liquidation Agent, April 9, 1957; A. R. Lawton to JHM, November 1, 1957; Minutes to Be Passed by the Directors of Chatham Savings Bank on December 9, 1957; Vernon D. Wood to Chatham Savings Bank, February 25, 1958, all in JM Correspondence, GHS. For "residues" see "The Country's in the Very Best of Hands."

56. *Savannah Evening Press*, November 9, 1956; undated and unidentified clipping headlined "'Abner' Lyricist Mercer Says It's Been a Lot of Fun," JM Papers, GSU. The Mercers previously visited the city at Christmas 1952, when all four of them stayed in the Chatham Apartments (*Savannah Morning News*, December 23, 1952).

57. Charles Ellis Jr. and Marvin G. Davis to JHM, March 28, 1957, box 2, folder 14, JM Papers, GSU. A decade later, when Woodberry convinced Johnny to head a fund-raising appeal, Mercer wrote in a cover letter, "I deplore the endless calls made upon us all for charity these days, but Woodberry was something special to us." See the May 8, 1967, letter and Joe Mercer to Coleman

Walker, December 11, 1956, JHM to Mr. and Mrs. T [Taylor], undated but 1951, and another undated letter to them in which Johnny said he was "trying to keep one jump ahead of the tax man." All in the Norfleet Archives, William H. White Jr., Library, Woodberry Forest School, Orange, Va. Mercer continued to financially support his alma mater until his death.

58. *Savannah Morning News*, July 30, 1957.

59. On December 31, 1957, Hugh Mercer, of the Crovatt-Mercer Realty Company, and Alex A. Lawrence, of the Bouhan, Lawrence, Williams and Levy law firm, closed the $65,000 deal with Gamble, filing the security deed in the Chatham County Superior Court. In purchasing the Gamble home, which has the street address of 514 Moon River Court, brother Hugh secured $5,000 from the funds set aside for the liquidation to use as earnest money for Mrs. Gamble, but Johnny insisted on paying that back so all of his $300,000 donation would be given to the creditors or donated to charity. He wanted to gain nothing from his gift. "Johnny Mercer Kept His Promise," notes, Mercer Family Collection, AASU; see also the *Savannah Evening Press*, December 31, 1957, and the *Savannah News*, January 1, 1958.

60. *Savannah Evening Press*, June 3, 1958; for a description of the house, see the *Savannah Morning News*, August 28, 1986; Nick Mamalakis, oral interview, author's possession. The Emma Kelley Collection at Georgia State University contains a cache of letters written around 1965 between Johnny and the families of his brothers, Walter and Hugh, over the use of the house. They were found in a piece of furniture once in the house and given by Dorothy Mercer to Emma Kelly. More than anything the letters reveal Johnny's generosity with his kinfolk and the frequency of his chatty communications with them. See JHM to Dorothy, JHM to Walter, Hugh to JHM, all undated, now part of the Mercer collections in the Popular Music Archives, GSU.

61. Richard Myers to JHM, August 21, 1958, Peggy to JHM, April 15, 1959, Stanley Gilkey to JHM, February 9, April 14, 1959, folders 15 and 16, box 2, JM Papers, GSU; in box 17, folders 1 and 2, is a copy of the script.

62. *Morning Telegraph*, December 9, 1959; *New York Herald Tribune* and *New York Post*, December 8, 1959. At the outset, Mercer warned Arlen, "If you're going to do *Show Boat*, you're thirty years too late," quoted in Kimball et al., eds., *Complete Lyrics*, 278. Already Hollywood had turned *Show Boat* and *Saratoga Trunk* as well as *Giant* and other Ferber stories into movies.

63. JHM to "Teetie!" dated "Tuesday" but spring 1959, and JHM to "Hi Hearties!" on Ritz Carlton Boston stationery, [October 1959]; in the undated "Dear Jeff," Johnny sent a letter to his son inquiring about his well-being and explaining, "Mandy and Mommy write me letters once in a while so I don't feel so lonesome, and it's nice to know that they're okay." All in box 2, folder 10, JM Papers, GSU. Jablonski, *Harold Arlen*, 294–301. Robbins, oral interview. Commander Publications owned the show.

64. Kimball et al., eds., *Complete Lyrics*, 278–86. In "The Men Who Run the Country," the chorus sings: "We are predatory barons / But in rather hoary shape, / And the only crime we haven't tried / Is statutory rape." Mercer has fun with French in a song dropped from the show, "Bon Appetite." *Philadelphia Inquirer*, October 27, 1959; *New York Journal-American*, December 8, 1958.

65. The show reminded Arlen's biographer, Edward Jablonski, of the "theatrical cliché of leaving a musical humming the scenery"; see Jablonski, *Harold Arlen*, 298. Arlen checked in to the Mount Sinai Hospital. Mercer also composed "The Men Who Run the Country."

66. Nick Mamalakis oral interview M034, Popular Music Archives, GSU. Completed in 1864, the Church of the Transfiguration had the oldest boys' choir in New York City and served as headquarters for the Episcopal Actors Guild. Mercer and Mamalakis might have prayed in the 1908 Mortuary Chapel. See Kenneth T. Jackson, *The Encyclopedia of New York City* (New Haven, Conn.: Yale University Press, 1995), 224.

67. Suskin, *Show Tunes*, 156–57; *New York Mirror* and *New York Times*, December 8, 1959;

Robbins oral interview. In his evaluation, Gerald Bordman notes the show "opened, filled with promise, and closed, a major disappointment, ten weeks later," suggesting that "the fine talents that labored on the new adaption were distressingly uninspired." He argued the "plot seemingly became entangled" in the sets and staging while "Harold Arlen's score, with Johnny Mercer lyrics, was not strong enough to break loose and soar on its own." See Bordman, *American Musical Theatre*, 615. Mercer quoted in Kimball et al., eds., *Complete Lyrics*, 278.

68. Pope Barrow McIntire, oral interview M144, Popular Music Archives, GSU; Shipman, *Judy Garland*, 338; Michael Lomonaco, with Donna Forsman, *The "21" Cookbook: Recipes and Lore from New York's Fabled Restaurant* (New York: Doubleday, 1995), 1–20.

69. The jazz critic Will Friedwald tells the story differently while also quoting Jule Styne. He said Mercer met Williams and "discussed the possibility of collaborating on a musical show, which it goes without saying, would be the great epic of the American south." Williams sent Mercer a rough draft of a script. "A few days later, he came by Mercer's house again to see what he thought. Upon opening the door, Mercer, standing at the top of a flight of stairs, hurled the entire script down at Williams's feet, declaiming in a loud, irritated voice, 'You don't know the first goddamned thing about the South!" See the liner notes to *Great American Songwriters*, vol. 2, *Johnny Mercer* (Rhino Records, 1993); Tennessee Williams, *Three by Tennessee: Sweet Bird of Youth, The Rose Tattoo and The Night of the Iguana* (New York: Signet Classics, 1976); Philip Furia identified the script in question as "The Rose Tattoo"; see *Skylark: The Life and Times of Johnny Mercer* (New York: St. Martin's Press, 2003), 244. Styne wrote scores for *Peter Pan* and *Funny Girl*, too. Gene Lees, *Portrait of Johnny* (New York: Pantheon, 2004), 185, describes Michael Goldsen's request that Mercer contribute lyrics for the movie *Ruby Gentry*; apparently Johnny disliked that script's presentation of the South too and likewise declined the invitation, so Mitchell Parish wrote the words to what became the hit song "Ruby" (244).

70. Johnny Mercer interview by Willis Conover, January 30, 1970, transcript in Popular Music Archives, GSU.

71. Bob Bach worked with the Goodson-Todman Productions agency. Jean Bach interview; Harbach interview.

72. John Lahr, *Notes on a Cowardly Lion: The Biography of Bert Lahr* (Berkeley: University of California Press, 2000); Kimball et al., eds., *Complete Lyrics*, 305; Bordman, *American Musical Theatre*, 634; JM autobiography.

73. Kimball et al., eds., *Complete Lyrics*, 305–19. The producers dropped an abnormally large number of songs from the show, including a sweet duet teaching feminine wiles between Brandy and Celia called "Take It from a Lady" and an equally masculine "Revenge Is Sweet (Opera Number)" sung by Foxy and Doc with the line "You're *Gotterdammerung* right!"

74. Kimball et al., eds., *Complete Lyrics*, 305; Lahr, *Notes on a Cowardly Lion*, 311–25. The *Sun* is quoted in the *New York Times*, July 4, 1962., See also July 26, which explains that operating costs ran $16,000 a week to stage *Foxy* in Canada. In his autobiography, Mercer explained, "*Foxy* I thought was salvageable . . . but I'm sorry I didn't save myself a year or two's worry by just saying 'no.' Working with Bert Lahr was great fun, and I loved everybody in the show, but I just don't get any kick out of spending all that time and effort, getting into backstage politics, bitching and being bitched at, when one song can make me twice the money and never say an unkind word to me."

75. Lahr, *Notes on a Cowardly Lion*, 325. "The failure of Foxy," notes Bordman in his definitive history, "was sad for a number of reasons. First of all, because it was a good show." In particular he cites the "rousing score" by Dolan. See Bordman, *American Musical Theatre*, 634; RCA Victor released the cast recording of *Foxy*.

Chapter Eight. Movie Theme Songs

The epigraph is from "The World of the Heart," with music by Johnny Green, written for the 1966 movie *Johnny Tiger*. See Robert Kimball, Barry Day, Miles Kreuger, and Eric Davis, eds., *The Complete Lyrics of Johnny Mercer* (New York: Alfred A. Knopf, 2009), 331.

1. Henry Pleasants, *Serious Music — and All That Jazz* (New York: Simon & Schuster, 1969), 206–11. Recognizing the potential of the movie soundtrack, Pleasants notes that in such music "is the pulse of jazz, the jazz arranger's skill in the most effective use of a small number of instruments and the virtuosity of the jazz musician in applying the appropriate insinuation to the given phrase or cadence. Inevitably, the composer-arrangers have brought with them to the studios a number of outstanding jazz musicians, who alone know how to read the arranger's 'chart.'"

2. Robert Kimball, Barry Day, Miles Kreuger, and Eric Davis, eds., *The Complete Lyrics of Johnny Mercer* (New York: Alfred A. Knopf, 2009), 260, 266–67; Bob Bach and Ginger Mercer, eds., *Our Huckleberry Friend: The Life, Times, and Lyrics of Johnny Mercer* (Secaucus, N.J.: Lyle Stuart, 1982), 176.

3. Clive Hirschhorn, *The Hollywood Musical* (New York: Crown, 1981), 361, 367, 371. With music by Mark Charlap and lyrics by Carolyn Leigh, *Peter Pan* had opened in late 1954.

4. Kimball et al., eds., *Complete Lyrics*, 274–75; *New York Times*, November 5, 1959; Vincent Terrace, *The Complete Encyclopedia of Television Programs, 1947–1976*, vol. 1 (Cranburty, N.J.: A. S. Barnes, 1976), 29. For only two years *The Addams Family* aired on ABC, from September 18, 1964, to September 2, 1966. Filmways had hired Mizzy to score the show but had declined to pay for a theme song, so Mizzy sang the lyrics while overdubbing himself three times to give the impression of multiple vocals. See www.vicmizzy.com. Author's interview with Amanda Mercer Neder, January 27, 2010, author's possession. Nancy Mercer Keith Gerard confirmed the story regarding Johnny's writing of the theme song lyrics; see author's interview with Nancy Mercer Keith Gerard, July 6, 2012, author's possession.

5. Kimball et al., eds., *Complete Lyrics*, 273, 275, 288, 294–95.

6. Yip Harburg to JHM, May 6, 1959. Mercer's knowledge of his father's correspondence is supported by a letter Johnny received from Mrs. James A. Daly Sr., who as a waitress at W. T. Grant's in Savannah regularly served G. A. Mercer oyster soup and received in return the occasional letter showing concern or support. See box 2, folder 16, JM Papers, GSU.

7. Tony Bennett, with Will Friedwald, *The Good Life* (New York: Pocket Books, 1998), 173. Bennett remembered he introduced the song and that "what a thrill when I found out that Johnny said my version was his favorite interpretation of any song he ever wrote." Sinatra's version competes with Bennett's. See Will Friedwald, *Sinatra! The Song Is You: A Singer's Art* (New York: Scribner, 1995), 206–9, 412–13. Occasionally Mercer sent Sadie notes, often remarking on her appearance and even suggesting she watch her weight. Vimmerstedt wrote a decade later, "received a check from ASCAP $693.91. What a joy! I'll never understand." She added, "I cry a lot because of the happiness you brought into my life." See Vimmerstedt, February 18, 1957, the 1959 thank-you note, and October 19, 1967, in JM Papers, GSU. Mercer's responses are in the Sadie Vimmerstedt Papers, Lane Library Special Collections, Armstrong Atlantic State University, Savannah, Ga. Kimball et al., eds., *Complete Lyrics*, 275, quotes Mercer saying about Vimmerstedt: "She said, 'You've changed my life, Mr. Mercer. People are coming in the store and asking for my autograph. Next week I have to go on the radio in Cleveland.' Two weeks later she said, 'I'm going to Cincinnati, I'm getting to be famous.' Finally, she came to New York and she was on *To Tell the Truth* and then she went to Europe. She said, 'I'm tired, I'm going to get out of show business.'"

8. *Savannah Evening Press*, December 8, 18, and 19, 1959; *Savannah News*, December 24 and 27, 1959. With freezing temperatures in Savannah that year and the carillon of St. John's Episcopal

Church playing carols that echoed in the streets, the mood was very Christmas-like; the New Year's bonfires had been moved from the squares to Thunderbolt and Tybee. For eighty years, from its opening in 1888 to its demolition in 1968, the William Gibbons Preston designed DeSoto Hotel provided Savannahians elegant social space.

9. *Savannah Evening Press*, January 4, 1960, 15; Neder interview, author's possession. The composer of such Disney musicals as *Mary Poppins*, *Winnie the Pooh*, and *The Jungle Book*, Richard Sherman set to music a poem found in Mercer's papers entitled "You're in Savannah," as a new song published for the centennial celebrations in 2009; see www.gpb.org/news/2009/11/18. See also WSAV News 3, November 18, 2009.

10. *Savannah Morning News*, April 19, 1961.

11. In 1958, the Chatham County Board of Education had voted to name the planned school after Johnny's grandfather. Mercer's remarks at the dedication of the school, JM Papers, GSU; *Savannah Evening Press*, October 22, 1962. The *Trenton (N.J.) Sunday Times-Advertiser*, December 17, 1962, identified brother Hugh Mercer, Ginger, Amanda, and Jeff in attendance at the unveiling of the painting by Peggy Peplow Gummere. Johnny had just taped *The Perry Como Show* and after the dedication retired to a bar, where the jukebox played "Bouquet," written by Mercer to music by Percy Faith. When the song ended abruptly, Ginger chirped "just a petal."

12. Carl E. Sanders to JHM, February. 16 and March 11, 1965, JHM to Brandt & Brandt, undated, Carl R. Sullivan of West Virginia to JHM, August, 8, 1962, folder 19, box 2, JM Papers, GSU; *Savannah Evening Press*, May 13, 1965. In 1979, the Georgia General Assembly adopted "Georgia on My Mind" as the new state song and for its first official performance as such arranged for Ray Charles to perform it on March 7 in the state capitol; see Zell Miller, *They Heard Georgia Singing* (Macon, Ga.: Mercer University Press, 1996).

13. Mercer received permission from Benét's widow to use words and phrases from *John Brown's Body* in the lyrics, most notably in the lines "Georgia, Georgia, / Careless yield; / Watermelons ripe in the field." See Stephen Vincent Benét, *Selected Works of Stephen Vincent Benet*, vol. 1, *Poetry* (New York: Farrar and Rinehart, 1942), 23. Even in the title, which quotes Benét, Mercer also references the chorus to "Georgia on My Mind." In addition to JM autobiography, see Kimball et al., eds., *Complete Lyrics*, 332–33; The Reverend Christopher E. Johann, OSB, to JHM, February 15, 1966, Adler's broadside, folder 19, box 2, JM Papers, GSU; *Savannah Evening Press*, March 1, 1966. Referring to a symphonic concert that featured the work, Mercer wrote a letter to the conductor Chauncey Kelly that appeared in the *Savannah Morning News*, February 26, 1966: "through your cooperative efforts, the public accepted the song in the spirit in which it was written. I only wish I could have been there to hear, but accept my thanks, please and congratulations on what obviously was an outstanding program." First Mercer quote in *Savannah Morning News Magazine*, July 1, 1962, second in an undated letter from 1962 that he sent to the *Morning News*. An example of such a lyric is "The Land of My Love," in Kimball, et al., eds. *Complete Lyrics*, 404, and on 422, "You're In Savannah." Mercer's old friend from Savannah, Perry A. Tuten, put Governor Maddox up to it; see Tuten to JHM, March 27, 1968, and Lester Maddox to JHM, March 7, 1968, JM Papers, GSU. Johnny's son-in-law, Bob Corwin, said of the state's rejection that "it was a big heartbreak for him." See Gene Lees, *Portrait of Johnny: The Life of John Herndon Mercer* (New York: Pantheon Books, 2004), 229.

14. JHM to Murray Baker, August 9, 1961, box 2, folder 16, JM Papers, GSU.

15. Barbara Robbins, oral interview M158, Robert Rush, oral interview M154, and William "Bill" Harbach, oral interview M130, Popular Music Archives, GSU. Robbins recalled that Ginger and Rose Gilbert "were very, very close friends for awhile, and then there was a tremendous fall."

16. Harbach, oral interview; unidentified clipping, October 5, 1961; *Sydney (Australia) Daily Telegraph*, September 24, 1964, box 323, folder 15, JM Papers, GSU; Henry Mancini with Gene

Lees, *Did They Mention the Music?* (1989; rprt. New York: Cooper Square Press, 2001), 104. Mancini speculated that Mercer wrote "Moon River" in his studio but given he moved into the Bel Air house after the song's creation, it is more likely he wrote the lyrics elsewhere, perhaps at his Palm Springs house, 282 Camino Carmelita.

17. As late as December 1956, Joe Mercer could write Coleman Walker that Johnny "has no intention, I am sure, of considering it [Woodberry] for his son — which is probably a good thing, as Ginger is too full of educational theories & the idea of letting the child go his own way." Unlike claimed by people quoted by Philip Furia in *Skylark: The Life and Times of Johnny Mercer* (New York: St. Martin's Press, 2003), 186, Mercer contributed to Woodberry throughout the years of Joe Mercer's tenure as headmaster and during the years of his replacement by Headmaster Baker Duncan, including sizeable sums in the 1970s. See Joe Mercer to Coleman Walker, December 11, 1956, Joe Mercer to JHM, January 6, 1961, Coleman C. Walker to JHM, January 18, 1962, Gerald L. Cooper to JHM, May 8, 1967, and March 11, 1968, Emmett Wright to JHM, December 26, 1974, Norfleet Archives, William H. White Jr. Library, Woodberry Forest School, Orange, Va.; JHM to Fred, October 10, 1966, box 2, folder 11, JM Papers, GSU. In addition, Johnny regularly attended meetings of Woodberry alumni in New York and Washington, D.C., remaining committed to his alma mater. Joe Mercer died in May 1981 and after the funeral in the school chapel was buried in Orange, Virginia. On Jeff, see Polly Ober, oral interview M157, and Amanda Mercer Neder, oral interview M140, Popular Music Archives, GSU; see also the "Bel-Airings" column, October 5, 1961; for an insightful analysis, see Amanda Brown, "Dads: A Portrait of Johnny Mercer the Father," GSU student paper in the author's possession.

18. JHM to Mr. Taylor, [ca. 1950s], Norfleet Archives, William H. White Jr. Library, Woodberry Forest School, Orange, Va.; "Bel-Airings" column, October 5, 1961; *Sydney (Australia) Daily Telegraph*, September 24, 1964; Rush oral interview; Amanda Mercer Neder and Jim Corwin, oral interview M140, Popular Music Archives, GSU; Actually born a half-hour into November 19, Jim Corwin nonetheless celebrated his birthday with Johnny on the eighteenth; on Bob Corwin, see Gene Lees, *Portrait of Johnny*, 225–31. Mercer wrote songs with Corwin, including "One Little Evening"; see Kimball et al., eds., *Complete Lyrics*, 325.

19. Furia, *Skylark*, 188–89. Furia quotes Jeff saying, "They got into fights, but you know, I really tried to slough that off. It wasn't my business. I mean, they're the couple." Lees, *Portrait of Johnny*, 223–25, emphasizes the alcoholism of both and the anger expressed in their fights.

20. Neder and Corwin, oral interview; Mercer autobiography.

21. Robbins, oral interview, Ober, oral interview, Rush, oral interview.

22. Joseph Mercer to Coleman Walker, December 11, 1956, Norfleet Archives, William H. White Library, Woodberry Forest School, Orange, Va., Neder and Corwin oral interview; author's interview with Neder, author's possession; Robbins oral interview.

23. A pocket calendar kept by Mercer in 1966 suggests Johnny kept a close eye on costs as he jotted down daily expenses for such mundane items as ice cream, drug prescriptions, and lunch; see box 1, folder 9, JM & GM Papers, GSU. Henry Kane, *How to Write a Song (as Told to Henry Kane)* (New York: Macmillan, 1962), 70; Joseph Mercer to Walker, December 11, 1956, WFS.

24. Ober, oral interview; Robbins, oral interview; Jean Bach, oral interview M128, Popular Music Archives, GSU. On another occasion Arlen disappeared for three days, turning up in Honolulu. See Jablonski, *Harold Arlen*, 227–28; *Newsweek*, January 29, 1945. Jeff's anecdote about Ginger in Lees, *Portrait of Johnny*, 225.

25. Dave Dexter Jr., *Playback: A Newsman/Record Producer's Hits and Misses from the Thirties to the Seventies* (New York: Billboard Publications, 1976), 86. Dexter noted about Mercer: "I found him a tolerant and understanding boss." Kane, *How to Write a Song*, 70–87, quoted on 74.

Barbara Robbins argued Mercer had great control and could separate drinking from working as he explained in the Kane interview. See Robbins, oral interview.

26. Author's interview with Neder, author's possession; Robbins, oral interview; JHM to Lillian Mercer, May 11, 1963, Mercer Family Collection, AASU.

27. André Previn interviewed by Bruce Ricker, Rhapsody Productions; Whiting and Holt, *It Might as Well Be Spring*, 236–37; Lees *Jazzletter* with the essay reprinted as "Roses in the Morning — Johnny Mercer," in Gene Lees, *Singers and the Song* (New York: Oxford University Press, 1987), 44–69, Jo Stafford and Carlos Gastel quoted on 46. Several of Mercer's admirers, such as Gene Lees, say he never turned on them. Rush confirms Ober's opinion regarding the fleeting damage of Mercer's outbursts.

28. Ray Evans and Jay Livingston, oral interview M134, Popular Music Archives, GSU; Lees, *Portrait of Johnny*, 194–200; David Shipman, *Judy Garland: The Secret Life of an American Legend* (New York: Hyperion, 1992), 301–4; Gerald Clarke, *Get Happy: The Life of Judy Garland* (New York: Random House, 2000), 312–13, quotes Mercer's comment to Garland.

29. Johnny Mercer interview by Willis Conover, January 30, 1970, transcript in Popular Music Archives, GSU. Rush attributed the behavior to Mercer's genius, suggesting that "he would take so much of it, and when he would realize" the lack of talent or ignorance of the person would express a critical view in an unfavorable light. See Rush, oral interview.

30. On the 1950s pop sound, see Ken Emerson, *Always Magic in the Air: The Bomp and Brilliance of the Brill Building Era* (New York: Viking, 2005); Dodd Darin, with Maxine Paetro, *Dream Lovers: The Magnificent Shattered Lives of Bobby Darin and Sandra Dee by Their Son* (New York: Warner Books, 1994).

31. Bobby Darin and Johnny Mercer, *Two of a Kind*, with Billy May and His Orchestra (New York: ATCO Records, 1961); Conover interview quoted on Official Bobby Darin website, www .bobbydarin.net/mercerman.html. Both Mercer and Mancini attended Darin's March 1966 sold-out concert at the Coconut Grove. Blood poisoning complicated Darin's heart condition and killed him in 1973.

32. American Society of Composers, Authors and Publishers, comp., *ASCAP Biographical Dictionary*, 4th ed. (New York: Jacques Cattell Press, 1980), 320. Pleasants called Mancini's music for *Peter Gunn* "so original, so skillful and so attractive, and its melodies so striking, that record albums of the *Peter Gunn* music sold more than a million copies." He observed, "The influence of *Peter Gunn* has been felt more recently in the underscores of a number of familiar TV serials — *The Man from U.N.C.L.E.*, *The Girl from U.N.C.L.E.*, *Secret Agent*, *T.H.E. Cat*, *Batman*, *Ironside*, *I Spy* and many more" (*Serious Music*, 207, 212). See the Henry Mancini Collection, Schoenberg Library, University of California, Los Angeles. Blake Edwards recalled, "that was the only time that I suggested something musical to Henry and he had a bongo playing behind it and I suggested that the bongo, I don't know what the meter was at that point but that it should be more excited." Blake Edwards interview by Bruce Ricker, Rhapsody Productions. "To think we even met, I can't believe it yet," go two lines in Mercer's lyric for "Joanna"; see Kimball et al., eds., *Complete Lyrics*, 274.

33. Mancini, *Did They Mention the Music?*, 94–99. Billy May and His Orchestra accompanied Sinatra on the album that also contained Mercer's "Day In, Day Out" and sat on *Billboard*'s top album chart for 140 weeks.

34. On "The Facts of Life," see Kimball et al., eds., *Complete Lyrics*, 291.

35. Mancini, *Did They Mention the Music?*, 94–99.

36. Ibid., 99; Mercer interview by Conover.

37. Mercer interview by Conover; transcript of Johnny Mercer interview by Michael Parkin-

son, BBC *Parkinson*, season 2, episode 7, July 15, 1972, transcript in Popular Music Archives, GSU. About the title, Mancini noted, "there was nothing to prevent John's using it: legally, you cannot copyright a title. But John was reluctant to use 'Blue River.' His kind of honesty has not caught on with many of the young songwriters today." See Mancini, *Did They Mention the Music?*, 99; Kimball et al., eds., *Complete Lyrics*, 293.

38. Mancini, *Did They Mention the Music?*, 99–102; Kimball et al., eds., *Complete Lyrics*, 293; Blake Edwards interview by Ricker. Mercer confirmed the anecdote but used polite language, noting Marty Rackin said, "I'll tell you one thing, that song can go." Hollywood producers tried to strike "Over the Rainbow" from *The Wizard of Oz* too.

39. Kimball et al., eds., *Complete Lyrics*, 293. *Born On the Fourth of July*, directed by Oliver Stone and starring Tom Cruise (Universal City, CA: Universal City Studios, Inc., 1989).

40. In November 1961, *Breakfast at Tiffany's* opened in Japan and Brazil, reaching France, Italy, and the Low Countries by December. In January 1962, it opened in Germany and Austria, reaching Hong Kong by June. American Film Institute, "America's Greatest Music in the Movies," 2005. The number one song, "Over the Rainbow," is followed by "As Time Goes By" and "Singin' in the Rain," with "White Christmas" ranking fifth. Hepburn received the David di Donatello Award in Italy for the Best Foreign Actress, and her iconic image on the film poster remains popular decades later. *New York Times*, October 30, 1963, identifies Harry Warren as sixth, Oscar Hammerstein II as seventh, Lorenz Hart as eighth, George Gershwin as ninth and Jerome Kern as tenth.

41. Mason Wiley and Damien Bona, *Inside Oscar: The Unofficial History of the Academy Awards* (New York: Ballantine, 1986), 337–41, quoted on 339. Mancini also won for Best Score; see Mancini, *Did They Mention the Music?*, 104–7.

42. Mercer interview by Parkinson; Andy Williams, *Moon River and Me: A Memoir* (New York: Viking, 2009), 116–17. Chance played a big role in Williams's relationship with "Moon River." He happened to be in a Los Angeles restaurant where Mercer and Mancini dined after filming Hepburn's singing in the movie. The songwriters told Williams about "Moon River" with Mancini suggesting, "Andy, this would be a great song for you." They gave him a copy of the music. Williams approached his record producer, Johnny's old friend Archie Bleyer, who disliked the "huckleberry friend" line and rejected the number, so the initial recordings went to Mancini as an instrumental and Jerry Butler as a vocal. The success of the music in the movie made it popular, so Williams, who had changed record labels, approached his new producer at Columbia, Bob Mercey, who agreed to title an album *"Moon River" and Other Great Movie Themes*. Over three days, Williams recorded eleven songs, almost running out of time for the last selection, "Moon River." "We had only ten minutes left; it was pretty much one take and that was it," Williams recalled. The luck of the draw paired Williams up with the song to sing during the Academy Awards.

43. Ray Gilbert, telegram to JHM, April 10, 1962, box 2, folder 16, JM Papers, GSU. On the community's response to the success of "Moon River," see *Savannah Morning News*, April 10, 11, 19, 28; May 19, 1962. Chatham County renamed the "Back River from its confluence with Skidaway Narrows and Burnside River to its source." A thankful Mercer said, "If I won't write a ditty about Savannah, the boys will name a river after one already written. Mountain to Mahomet, like. I certainly appreciate the tribute, I do." The Pine River Road address of the house soon changed to 514 Moon River Court. See also Lees, *Portrait of Johnny*, 277. This trip to Hawaii apparently resulted in song ideas, for within a few years Johnny had written "Pineapple Pete" and "Honolulu," and tried to get Don Ho to sing them. See Kimo Wilder McVay to JHM, October 1, 1969, JM Papers, GSU.

44. Mancini, *Did They Mention the Music?*, 111–13. Ernest Dowson's (1867–1900) poem from 1896, *"Vitae Summa Brevis Spem Nos Vetat Incohare Longam,"* was the epigraph for his first vol-

ume of poetry, *Verses*. A member of the Decadent Movement and translator of Balzack and other French novelists, Dowson died at 32, a penniless alcoholic. See Desmond Flower, ed., *The Poetry of Ernest Dowson* (Cranbury, N.J.: Associated University Presses, 1970), 32; to emphasize the ended romance with Lenore, Poe's poem "The Raven" uses "Nevermore." For *Kiss Me, Kate*, Cole Porter had a hit with "Always True to You in My Fashion," using the line, "I have been faithful to thee, Cynara, in my fashion," from Dowson's most popular poem, *Non Sum Qualis Eram Bonae Sub Regno Cynarae*, which also provided Margaret Mitchell with a line to use as the title to her novel, *Gone with the Wind*. Mancini said, "Johnny Mercer was one of the finest demonstrators not only of his songs but anybody's songs. He had a captivating style"(112); Kimball et al., eds., *Complete Lyrics*, 300. British music critic Benny Green said that Mercer "tends to pass all the praise for the exquisite beauty of his lyric to 'Days of Wine and Roses' on to the English fin-de-siècle poet Ernest Dowson, who first conjured up the title phrase. The theory works well enough till you go and take a look at Dowson's original poem, which is not only nothing remotely like Mercer's lyric but is actually not as good." See liner notes to *Johnny Mercer Sings the Songs of Johnny Mercer with the Harry Roche Constellation* (London: Pye Records, 1974).

45. Transcript of Johnny Mercer interview by Humphrey Lyttleton, BBC *Omnibus*, season 2, episode 19, July 14, 1974, transcript in Popular Music Archives, GSU; Mercer interview by Conover.

46. Mancini, *Did They Mention the Music?*, 112–13. *New York Times*, March 19, 1963.

47. Nick Mamalakis, oral interview M034, Popular Music Archives, GSU, and Mamalakis to Mercer telegram, JM Papers, GSU.

48. Robert Osborne, *Fifty Golden Years of Oscar: The Official History of the Academy of Motion Picture Arts and Sciences* (La Habra and Beverly Hills, Calif.: ESE California and Academy of Motion Picture Arts and Sciences, 1979); Mancini, *Did They Mention the Music?* The lyrics appear in Bach and Mercer, eds., *Our Huckleberry Friend*, 202, and Kimball et al., eds., *Complete Lyrics*, 300. Furia, *Skylark*, 239.

49. Osborne, *Fifty Golden Years of Oscar*; Kimball et al., eds., *Complete Lyrics*, 327; Mancini, *Did They Mention the Music?*, 146–49; Barbara Robbins believed Johnny wrote a "purposely terrible lyric," quoting him saying about Mandel that "I wouldn't tell him because that would hinder him in what he's doing" but that there was "just enough of a feel of Arlen" to make Mercer reject the tune; see Robbins, oral interview. But in discussing the effort with Maurice Levine during the New York Ninety-second Street "Y" Series of Lyrics and Lyricists on March 14, 1971, Johnny explains about rejected lyrics: "Would you like to hear about a real new loser? It's like how it was with Buddy DeSylva. I used to play him songs and he'd laugh and say, 'Oh, that's wonderful—can't use it.' That's what happened to the lyric I wrote for the song that became 'The Shadow of Your Smile.' They sent it back and said they couldn't use it. I said, 'Well, get Paul Francis Webster' and they did and had a great big hit." Mercer then sang his lyric to Mandel's tune, see *New York Times*, March 16, 1971, as well as Bach and Mercer, *Our Huckleberry Friend*, 212–13; Furia quotes music publisher Michael Goldsen claiming that a jealous Mercer kept the rejected lyric pinned up by his piano with "You can't win them all" scribbled across the top; see *Skylark*, 240–41; Mercer interview by Conover.

50. Osborne, *Fifty Golden Years of Oscar*; Furia, *Skylark*, 240–41; Mercer interview by Conover; Mercer interview by Parkinson; Kimball et al., eds., *Complete Lyrics*, 323. Paddy Chayefsky wrote the screenplay for *The Americanization of Emily* based on a novel of the same name by William Bradford Huie.

51. Franco Migliacci wrote the words to "Volare" with music by Domenico Modugno. Osborne, *Fifty Golden Years of Oscar*; Mancini, *Did They Mention the Music?*, 137–42, 150. Monica Mancini, *The Dreams of Johnny Mercer* (Concord Records, 2000). As a young kid two decades before, Williams had accompanied his father, who played in the orchestra of Lucky Strike's *Your*

Hit Parade, meeting Mercer when he performed on the program; see Williams interview with Ricker.

52. Mancini, *Did They Mention the Music?*, 167–70; Andrews and Previn interviews by Ricker. The Carpenters consisted of Karen and her brother, Richard, who remains a "Mercer fanatic"; see Previn interview by Ricker.

53. Ken Bloom, *Hollywood Song: The Complete Film and Musical Companion*, 3 vols. (New York: Facts on File, 1995), 1:426. Similar to "Song of India," Mercer describes universal truths: "The sands that blow / Blow over kings as well as slaves, / And there is no diff'rence in their graves," adding, "For we are here for just a little while; / Then we're gone. / But through the summers and the snows / Flows the Nile." See Kimball et al., eds., *Complete Lyrics*, 301; Wiley and Bona, *Inside Oscar*, 363. Earlier Mercer and Green had collaborated on themes for *Everything I Have Is Yours* (1952) and *With You with Me* (1957).

54. Mercer song list, GSU; Cjertrud Smith to JHM, September 24, 1964, box 2, folder 17, JM Papers, GSU.

55. Mercer song list, GSU.

56. Harold Arlen, June 10, 1964, with Arlen's concluding line quoting Rodgers and Hart's "My Funny Valentine"; Harry Ruby to JHM, December 10, 1966, box 2, folders 17 and 18, JM Papers, GSU. Others observed the occasional anti-Semitic remark made by a drunken Mercer. Polly Ober recalled an incident when Mercer brought several Jewish friends to the private Newport Harbor Yacht Club that had extended to the songwriter a guest pass, but the management became incensed at his choice of company. Ober also remembered Ginger being overly sensitive, fearing that others made anti-Semitic remarks about her. See also Jablonski, *Harold Arlen*, 128–29.

57. Jerry Colonna, box 2, folder 17, JM Papers, GSU; Bing Crosby to JHM, December 30, 1970, JM Papers, GSU.

58. Whiting and Holt, *It Might as Well Be Spring*, 236; John Chilton, *Who's Who of Jazz: Storyville to Swing Street* (Philadelphia: Chilton, 1978), passim. Mercer autobiography. Kimball et al., eds., *Complete Lyrics*, 166.

59. David Shipman, *Judy Garland: The Secret Life of an American Legend* (New York: Hyperion, 1992), 506–7; Gerold Frank, *Judy* (New York: Harper & Row, 1975), 510–12, 529–31; Anne Edwards, *Judy Garland: A Biography* (New York: Simon and Schuster, 1974), 208–9; Furia, *Skylark*, 235–37. Furia sees this moment in 1964 as the last effort by Johnny to divorce Ginger and marry Garland. On a renewed discussion about divorce he quotes his interview with Ginger's niece, Joyce Pelphrey, while on the Garland connection he cites earlier essays by Gene Lees that quote Rose Gilbert repeating things she heard from her friend Ginger and her husband, the songwriter Wolfe Gilbert. No doubt the Mercers again considered divorce as Johnny and Judy had rekindled their affair. For details about *The Judy Garland Show*, see Scott Schechter, *Judy Garland: The Day-by-Day Chronicle of a Legend* (New York: Cooper Square Press, 2002), 255–83. See also Kimball et al., eds., *Complete Lyrics*, 321. The day before Garland's funeral, some twenty-thousand mourners passed by her glass-covered casket in the chapel at Eighty-first Street and Madison Avenue. See the *New York Times*, June 28, 1969.

60. JHM to Polly Ober, undated, Polly Ober Papers, Popular Music Archives, GSU.

61. Chilton, *Who's Who of Jazz*; James Gavin, *Stormy Weather: The Life of Lena Horne* (New York: Atria Books, 2009); Kitty Kelley, *His Way: The Unauthorized Biography of Frank Sinatra* (New York: Bantam Books, 1986). See the *New York Times*, January 16, 1962, July 22, 1964; and Richard M. Sudhalter, *Lost Chords: White Musicians and Their Contributions to Jazz* (New York: Oxford University Press, 1999), 688.

62. Mercers' 1966 Christmas card, JM Papers, GSU; "California Melodyland" and "They're

Pavin' California," in Kimball et al., eds., *Complete Lyrics*, 328, 384–85. Rowles arranged the publication of the song in 1988; Neder, oral interview. Harold Arlen had his own reservations about changes in Hollywood; see Harold Arlen to JHM, June 10, 1964, box 2, folder 17, JM Papers, GSU.

63. In *Swing Changes: Big-Band Jazz in New Deal America* (Cambridge, Mass.: Harvard University Press, 1994), David W. Stowe shows how the interrelated jazz and popular music called swing dominated mass culture and expressed a new inclusive ideology of Americanism. Similarly, Lewis A. Erenberg, in his *Swingin' the Dream: Big Band Jazz and the Rebirth of American Culture* (Chicago: University of Chicago Press, 1998), documents the interracial democracy that jazz music promoted during the Depression and war years and that dissipated in the postwar era. Other studies of value include Peter Townsend, *Pearl Harbor Jazz: Change in Popular Music in the Early 1940s* (Jackson: University Press of Mississippi, 2007), and Dave Oliphant, *The Early Swing Era, 1930 to 1941* (Westport, Conn.: Greenwood Press, 2002). See also Gene Lees, *Cats of Any Color: Jazz Black and White* (New York: Oxford University Press, 1994); JHM to Lillian Mercer, [ca. 1965], Mercer Family Collection, AASU. Mercer acknowledged ethnicity, but racist remarks are absent from his papers and correspondence. In a revealing letter to his mother he discussed his need for domestic help like her black assistant, Big Nancy, suggesting his Hispanic maid had quit. "The present one weighs about 350 and would make two of big Nancy. A white girl. Once those Mexicans find out about you, they pass you from hand to hand, like a piñata. They were darling, but I like to choose my own bed-makers, cooks, etc." A product of his time, Mercer joshed with racist friends in Savannah and occasionally made insensitive remarks that were generally acceptable in the dominant popular culture.

64. Lees, *Cats of Any Color*. The unidentified southerner Lees believes was joking is referenced on 243 and Davis on 207. About Davis, he writes, "Miles is often cited as the archetype of the black racist," something that upset him as he explained to Lees: "Gene, why do they call me a racist when my best friend is Gil Evans and my manager is Jack Whittemore?" Lees recognized that "Miles loved saying things for shock value."

65. LeRoi Jones (Amiri Baraka), *Blues People: Negro Music in White America* (New York: William Morrow, 1963). See also his *Black Music* (New York: William Morrow, 1967), where he explains "the first serious white jazz musicians (Original Dixieland Jazz Band, Bix, etc.) sought not only to understand the phenomenon of Negro music but to appropriate it as a means of expression which they themselves might utilize. The success of this 'appropriation' signaled the existence of an American music, where before there was a Negro music" (13). He adds, "The white musician's commitment to jazz, the *ultimate concern*, proposed that the subcultural attitudes that produced the music as a profound expression of human feelings, could be *learned* and need not be passed on as a secret blood rite."

66. Burton W. Peretti, *The Creation of Jazz: Music, Race, and Culture in Urban America* (Urbana: University of Illinois Press, 1992), not only argues that only African Americans play jazz, he also suggests they originated country music too in a fashion that argues racial legitimacy for certain types of music. For a more balanced analysis of the history of jazz, see James Lincoln Collier, *The Making of Jazz: A Comprehensive History* (New York: Dell Publishing Co., Delta Book paperback, 1978). Eric Porter, *What Is This Thing Called Jazz? African American Musicians as Artists, Critics, and Activists* (Berkeley: University of California Press, 2002), uses cultural studies to lay claim to a black nationalism expressed through jazz but then finds a paradox over the music's universalism.

67. Lees, *Cats of Any Color*, 228–41; Ken Burns, *Jazz: A Film by Ken Burns*, 10 episodes (Public Broadcasting System Video, 2000). For a perceptive analysis regarding racial controversies and

jazz music, see Iain Anderson, *This Is Our Music: Free Jazz, the Sixties, and American Culture* (Philadelphia: University of Pennsylvania Press, 2007), and on the jazz at Lincoln Center and jazz documentary, see the epilogue, 182–90.

68. Willie "the Lion" Smith with George Hoefer, *Music on My Mind: The Memoirs of an American Pianist* (London: MacGibbon & Kee, 1965), 241. While suggesting a racial authenticity in jazz, the New York native William Henry Joseph Bonaparte Bertholoff Smith (1897–1973), better known as "Willie the Lion," recognized that "all the composers, lyricists, and arrangers get help or inspiration from each other" regardless of race, so it makes little sense for him to then suggest a racial dynamic behind the instrumentalists who played the music. He helped popularize the stride-piano style of playing and taught black and white jazz musicians, including Artie Shaw. See the *New York Times*, November 21, 1967; Armstrong quoted in Lees, *Cats of Any Color*, 2.

69. Gene Lees, the eminent jazz critic, reprinted the title essay and other essays from his *Jazzletters* as one of his several books. His *Singers and the Song*, revised as *Singers and the Song II* (New York: Oxford University Press, 1998), provides gems of biographical sketches featuring the artists behind the Great American Song. He has also written biographies: *Leader of the Band: The Life of Woody Herman* (New York: Oxford University Press, 1995) and *Portrait of Johnny*, among others. In a thoughtful evaluation of the debate, Charley Gerard similarly contradicts the racial essentialism argument and documents the multiracial nature of the art form; see *Jazz in Black and White: Race, Culture, and Identity in the Jazz Community* (Westport, Conn.: Praeger, 1998).

70. Sudhalter's earlier biographies of Leon "Bix" Beiderbecke and Hoagy Carmichael helped start the revisionist work of scholars currently underway: Richard M. Sudhalter, *Lost Chords: White Musicians and Their Contributions to Jazz, 1915–1945* (New York: Oxford University Press, 1998), and Sudhalter, *Stardust Melody: The Life and Music of Hoagy Carmichael* (New York: Oxford University Press, 2002), Sudhalter with Philip R. Evans, *Bix: Man and Legend* (New York: Arlington, 1974).

71. Eubie Blake to JHM, November 21, 1953, box 2, folder 13, and Bobby Short to Ginger and Johnny, May 5, 1955, box 2, folder 14, JM Papers, GSU. Mercer recalled seeing Louis Armstrong introduce a group of white tap dancers as "The Two Ofays!" See Bach and Mercer, eds., *Our Huckleberry Friend*, 215; Armstrong photograph in JM Papers, GSU. Today the slang words *ophay* and *spade* are considered offensive. See Rush, oral interview.

72. JHM to "Mom," December 24, 1973, JM Papers, GSU. "Trees" reprinted in Bach and Mercer, eds., *Our Huckleberry Friend*, 207. The *New York Times* had reported on April 18, 1969, "Four unusual little trees... produced from a tiny plug of unspecialized non-sexual tree cells, began their existence in a laboratory dish at the Institute of Paper Chemistry in Appleton, Wisconsin, today."

73. Ober, oral interview. Several of the Christmas cards are published in Bach and Mercer, eds., *Our Huckleberry Friend*, and Kimball et al., eds., *Complete Lyrics*, and while the JM Papers at Georgia State University have an assortment of them, no repository has a complete run, although the occasional card appears in a variety of manuscript collections. This undated card is in both the JM Papers and *Complete Lyrics*, 430. "Untitled Poem," reprinted in Bach and Mercer, eds., *Our Huckleberry Friend*, 216. *New York Times*, June 24, 1963; Ed Zahniser of the Wilderness Society rejected Mercer's "Untitled Poem," although he liked the lines: "As for hummingbirds — they're no loss / They're delicious with béarnaise sauce!" See Zahniser to JHM, November 16, 1972, JM Papers, GSU.

74. JM interviewed in the *Trenton (N.J.) Times-Advertiser*, December 17, 1962; Margaret Whiting, essay; Neder interview with Ricker; Mamalakis, oral interview. Mercer parodied the new music with "Swingin' at the Supermart" with its lines "We're gonna rock, / We're gonna

roll, / We're gonna shop, / We're gonna stroll, / And here's the way we're gonna start, / Swingin' at the supermart." See Kimball et al., eds., *Complete Lyrics*, 303.

75. Tony Thomas, *Harry Warren and the Hollywood Musical* (Secaucus, N.J.: Citadel Press, 1975). Warren quoted on 320 and Schwartz quoted on 319.

76. JM to Irving Berlin, September 5, 1973, Irving Berlin Papers, Library of Congress, Washington, D.C.; Lees, *Portrait of Johnny*, 285–87.

77. *New York Times*, March 10, 1971; Abe Olman to JHM, [June 6, 1971], JM Papers; Lees, *Portrait of Johnny*, 288, quotes Sinatra saying, "I love you guys. If it weren't for you, I'd be pushing pencils in Hoboken." See also the Songwriters Hall of Fame website at www.songwritershall offame.com.

78. Irving Berlin Papers, Library of Congress, Washington, D.C.; see also Laurence Bergreen, *As Thousands Cheer: The Life of Irving Berlin* (New York: Viking Press, 1990), 566-67; as well as Philip Furia, *Irving Berlin: A Life in Song* (New York: Schirmer, 1998). *New York Times*, May 17, 1972. Lees, *Portrait of Johnny*, 286–87, describes Berlin as "a formidable egotist" who did not want to be associated with the group because of its name and his belief that "I'm the only songwriter. The fellows who write lyrics are lyric-writers. The fellows who write music are composers. Outside of Cole Porter, I'm the only songwriter." One could quibble because Mercer frequently wrote both words and music and Berlin borrowed heavily from such composers as Scott Joplin. Indeed, the impetus over copyright derived from the expiration of the protection on Berlin's "Alexander's Ragtime Band," which American law secured for only fifty-six years, unlike the European law that protected works for fifty years after the death of the author. Berlin lived until 1989, dying at age 101. Bach, oral interview.

79. JM quoted in *Johnny Mercer: Collectors Series* liner notes (Capitol Records, 1989). Like Mercer, Cahn also won four Oscars: for "Three Coins in the Fountain" (1954), "All the Way" (1957), "High Hopes" (1959), and "Call Me Irresponsible" (1963). Richard Strauss asked in his last opera, *Capriccio*, the eternal question of songwriters: what is more important, the words or the music? In response to a question by fellow singer and songwriter Bobby Troup, Johnny emulated Strauss with his "The Words or Music — Which Came First?" using the lyric to walk through several of his own songs in an effort to answer the question. See Kimball et al., *Complete Lyrics*, 243–44.

80. Yip Harburg to JHM, August 12, 1971; Jimmy McHugh to JHM, May 21, 1968; Richard Rodgers to JHM, August 8, 1968, JM Papers. Like Mercer, Ira Gershwin felt displaced by a Broadway that book-and-lyric writers such as Alan Jay Lerner and Frank Loesser dominated. See Philip Furia, *Ira Gershwin: The Art of the Lyricist* (New York: Oxford University Press, 1996), 231–32. Gershwin died in 1983. The unveiling followed a champaign breakfast attended by Youmans's son and daughter, president of ASCAP Stanley Adams, president of BMI Robert Sour, choreograher Busby Berkeley, and fellow songwriters Dore Schory and Irving Caeser, among others; see the *New York Times*, September 29, 1970.

81. Patricia Nixon to JHM, February 11, 1970, box 2, file 20, JM Papers, GSU; see Mercer's foreword in White House Historical Association, *The White House Record Library* (Washington, D.C.: White House Historical Association, 1973–80), with funding from the Recording Industry Association of America. Johnny happened to be in Savannah with his mother and niece Nancy, whose husband, Steve Gerard, answered the call and, once confirming it was indeed the White House, heard Mercer respond to the invitation by saying, "I don't know if I'm really the one you want to do this." Author's interview with Steve Gerard, July 6, 2012, author's possession.

82. White House Historical Association, *White House Record Library*.

83. Mercer interview by Conover.

84. "Life Is What You Make It," lyric by Johnny Mercer, music by Marvin Hamlisch (AMPICO

Music, 1971). Kimball et al., *Complete Lyrics*, 356; also see JM autobiography on Mercer's view of people blaming the system: "But don't complain about the establishment to me. Hell, without the establishment, you wouldn't even be here. None of you — black or white, or polka-dotted."

85. *New York Times*, March 16, 1971.

86. *New York Times*, March 16, 1971; Mercer recognized the validity of Wilson's criticism and addressed the questions when writing the last chapters of his autobiography in which he discusses the process of writing songs with composers.

87. *New York Times*, and the local *Washington Square Journal*, March 16, 1971; *Variety*, March 17, 1971, includes the comment about Mercer, "He remains on the side of talent and integrity, praising the talents of James Taylor, whom he believes to be sincere, and 'that singer from Blood, Sweat & Tears' [David Clayton Thomas]." Hadassah B. Markson to JHM, March 15, 1971, box 2, file 21, JM Papers, GSU.

Chapter Nine. Global Southerner

The epigraph is from "Summer Wind," with music by Henry Mayer and original German words by Hans Bradtke. See Robert Kimball, Barry Day, Miles Kreuger, and Eric Davis, eds., *The Complete Lyrics of Johnny Mercer* (New York: Alfred A. Knopf, 2009), 328.

1. Robert Kimball, Barry Day, Miles Kreuger, and Eric Davis, eds., *The Complete Lyrics of Johnny Mercer* (New York: Alfred A. Knopf, 2009), 69, 72, 122.

2. Karen L. Cox, "Dixie Lullaby: Songs of the South from Tin Pan Alley," delivered at the "Popular Music in the Mercer Era, 1910–1970" conference, November 13, 2009, Georgia State University, Atlanta, Ga., unpublished paper, author's possession.

3. Kimball et al., eds., *The Complete Lyrics*, 46–47. A positive review of the show appeared in the *Times* (London), July 10, 1936.

4. Henry Kane, *How to Write a Song (as Told to Henry Kane)* (New York: Macmillan, 1962), 82–83; Herb Sanford, *Tommy and Jimmy: The Dorsey Years* (New Rochelle, N.Y.: Arlington House, 1972), 101; Roland L. Bessette, *Mario Lanza: Tenor in Exile* (Portland, Ore.: Amadeus Press, 1999), 146; Mel Tormé, *My Singing Teachers* (New York: Oxford University Press, 1994), 52.

5. The definition by Stephen Vertovec that describes transnationalism as "multiple ties and interactions linking people or institutions across the borders of nation-states" seems to fit the argument here well. See his essay "Conceiving and Researching Transnationalism," *Ethnic and Racial Studies* 22, no. 2 (March 1999), with quotation on 447. For an insightful analysis that explains the global aspirations that accompanied the development of the music industry, see the chapter "Talking Machine World" in Karl Hagstrom Miller, *Segregating Sound: Inventing Folk and Pop Music in the Age of Jim Crow* (Durham, N.C.: Duke University Press, 2010). Stephen Foster "Americanized" a number of European popular songs.

6. Kimball et al., eds., *The Complete Lyrics*, 22, 240; "C-A-T Spells Cat," Sheet Music Collection, Popular Music Archives, GSU.

7. Joseph Kosma studied music in Budapest and Berlin before emigrating in 1933 to Paris, where he began composing for films. He befriended many artists, including Jacques Prevert, whose 1945 publication of *Paroles* marked him as the nation's leading poet. As a Jew, Kosma experienced persecution by the Nazis and suffered the murders of family members, a palpable sense of loss evident in his music. Director Marcel Carne used songs by Kosma and Prevert in several films, including *Les Portes de la Nuit*. Enoch et Cie published "Les feuilles mortes" in 1947, with Mercer's English lyrics under the title "Autumn Leaves" copyrighted in 1950; Kimball et al., eds., *Complete Lyrics*, 188; Bob Bach and Ginger Mercer, eds., *Our Huckleberry Friend: The Life, Times, and Lyrics of*

Johnny Mercer (Secaucus, N.J.: Lyle Stuart, 1982), 159, 163, 201. Despite "the greatest stars of our time on one big program" being introduced on *The Big Show* by Tallulah Bankhead every Sunday night, NBC Radio lost a million dollars and surrendered to television in 1952. John Dunning, *Tune In Yesterday: The Ultimate Encyclopedia of Old-Time Radio, 1925–1976* (Englewood Cliffs, N.J.: Prentice-Hall, 1976), 66–67. See also Carolyn Burke, *No Regrets: The Life of Edith Piaf* (New York: Alfred A. Knopf, 2011), quoted on 150. Aldrich also directed *What Ever Happened to Baby Jane?* and *The Dirty Dozen.*

8. Prévert's version opens with "Oh! Je voudrais tant que tu te souviennes / Des jours heureux ou nous etions amis, / En ce temps-la la vie etait plus belle, / Et le soleil plus brulant qu'aujourd'hui." Then the song continues, "Les feuilles mortes se ramassent a la pelle, / Les souvenirs et les regrets aussi / Et le vent du nord les emporte / Dans la nuit froide de l'oubli." Kimball et al., eds., *Complete Lyrics*, 188; see also Johnny Mercer interview by Willis Conover, January 30, 1970, transcript in Popular Music Archives, GSU.

9. Born in 1924, M. Philippe-Gerard became a refugee in Paris during the war and following liberation gained recognition when Edith Piaf selected one of his songs to sing and placed others in movies starring Yves Montand. The Britanny poet Angele Marie Therese Vannier is best known for *Le Sang Des Nuits.* The song "Le Chevalier de Paris" opens with "Ah! Les pommiers doux, / Rondes et ritournelles. / J'ai pas peur des loups, / Chantonnait la belle. / Ils ne sont pas mechants / Avec les enfants / Qu'ont le Coeur fidele / Et les genoux blancs."

10. Mercer interview by Conover; Kimball et al., eds., *Complete Lyrics*, 196–97.

11. As teenagers in Occupied Paris, Barclay, a native of the city whose parents owned a café, and Marnay, a native of Algiers who worked as a scriptwriter in the French film industry, illegally listened to jazz recordings during the war. Legrand joined his collaborators as habitués of the postwar Parisian jazz scene. Barclay composed few songs such as "La Valse des Lilas," while Marnay wrote over four thousand lyrics, including "Les Amants de Paris" popularized by Edith Piaf, the title song for Charlie Chaplin's 1957 film *A King for New York*, a French translation of Barbra Streisand's "Evergreen," and most of the French songs sung by Celine Dion. See the *Los Angeles Times*, January 6, 2003. See also the 2005 biographical entry in Radio France International, www.rfimusic.com/artist/jazz/michel-legrand/biography. Jean Bach, oral interview M128, Popular Music Archives, GSU.

12. A friend recalled Mabel Mercer spent "all this time trying to shape this one line, and I kept thinking I wonder why Mercer used this line . . . until finally she did it, with that laugh that she could do. And suddenly, you knew what she was trying to say." See James Haskins, *Mable Mercer: A Life* (New York: Atheneum, 1987), 66, 175–76; Kimball et al., eds., *Complete Lyrics*, 298; Mercer interview by Conover. For Habib's quotation, see the liner notes to *Great American Songwriters: Johnny Mercer* (Hollywood, Calif.: Laserlight Digital, Stanyan Records, 1994), which includes "Autumn Leaves" sung by Ertha Kitt, with Rod McKuen singing the other two. Illuminating the transnationality of music, Homi Bhabha argues this "Third Space of enunciation, which makes the structure of meaning and reference an ambivalent process, destroys this mirror of representation in which cultural knowledge is customarily revealed as an integrated, open, expanding code." Rather than see culture as a "homogenizing, unifying force," "authenticated by the originary Past" and the people, the Third Space "constitutes the discursive conditions of enunciation that ensure that the meaning and symbols of culture have no primordial unity or fixity; that even the same signs can be appropriated, translated, rehistoricized, and read anew." Bhabha suggests a "split-space of enunciation may open the way to conceptualizing an international culture, based not on exoticism of multiculturalism or the diversity of cultures, but on the inscription and articulation of culture's hybridity." See Homi K. Bhabha, *The Location of Culture* (London, Routledge, 1994), 36-39.

13. Ibid.; Joshua Berrett, *The Louis Armstrong Companion: Eight Decades of Commentary* (New York: Schirmer Books, 1999), 179–80; Stuart Nicholson, *Ella Fitzgerald: A Biography of the First Lady of Jazz* (New York: Charles Scribner's Sons, 1993), 161–62, 170. Armstrong left the stage cursing the organizer of the Newport festival, George Wein.

14. Nicholson, *Ella Fitzgerald*, 13, 157–61, 189–91; from 1925 to 1936 the Boswell Sisters made recordings as a group; then Connie — who later changed the spelling to Connee — Boswell enjoyed a solo career. *The Complete Ella in Berlin: Mack the Knife* (Verve, 1960); *Ella Fitzgerald: The Johnny Mercer Songbook* (Verve, 1964), liner notes in 1984 Polygram Records release. The other recordings in the Songbook series include *The Harold Arlen Songbook*, 2 vols.; *The Irving Berlin Songbook*, 2 vols.; *The Duke Ellington Songbook*, 2 vols.; *The George and Ira Gershwin Songbook*; *The Jerome Kern Songbook*; *The Cole Porter Songbook*, 2 vols.; *The Rodgers and Hart Songbook*, 2 vols.; Mercer quoted in agreement with Ellington on Ella Fitzgerald in the *San Diego Union*, January 22, 1967; Dave Dexter called Ella Fitzgerald "the most gifted musician I ever recorded," and having followed her career since first hearing her in 1937, he picked up the Verve account for Capitol Records in 1966. See Dave Dexter Jr., *Playback: A Newsman/Record Producer's Hits and Misses from the Thirties to the Seventies* (New York: Billboard Publications, Inc., 1976), 194–95. Leslie Gourse, ed., *The Ella Fitzgerald Companion: Seven Decades of Commentary* (New York: Schirmer Books, 1998), 101.

15. Johnny might have also gotten the idea from Ira and George Gershwin's comic song, "The Lorelei," although his version is truer to the myth of the siren; Marvin E. Paymer, ed., *Facts behind the Songs: A Handbook of American Popular Music from the Nineties to the '90s* (New York: Garland, 1993), 9; see also the "Modern Version by Johnny Mercer of the Glow-Worm," based on the original words by Lilla Cayley Robinson with music by Paul Lincke (Apollo Verlag, 1902), Mercer's 1952 copyright by Edward B. Marks Music Corp. Johnny had his own hit recording of the song for Capitol in 1953. A decade later, he added special lyrics written especially for Bing Crosby to sing on a 1962 Christmas show: "Glow, little glow worm, and remember / Once, on a long-ago December, / There came to earth a tiny stranger / Who lit a dark and lonely manger." See Kimball et al., eds., *Complete Lyrics*, 221. The death of brother John Jr., in 1936 and his replacement by father John Sr., allowed the remaining three Mills Brothers — Herbert, Harry, and Donald — to remain a quartet, and their recording of "Glow Worm" reached *Billboard's* No. 1 spot.

16. Mercer and Weill, "The Bilbao Song," published by Harms Music, 1961. See also Kimball et al., eds., *Complete Lyrics*, 293.

17. Bach and Mercer, eds., *Our Huckleberry Friend*, 206; Kimball et al., eds., *Complete Lyrics*, 328; Nancy Sinatra, *Frank Sinatra: An American Legend* (Santa Monica, Calif.: General Publishing Group, 1995), 147; undated clipping headlined "Mercer Paid Off Old Debt," JM Papers, GSU. Sinatra's "Summer Wind" reached *Billboard's* No. 1 spot and is the background theme music for the movie *The Pope of Greenwich Village*; Friedwald notes in *Sinatra!* that "Summer Wind" remains the favorite of Sinatra insiders (272).

18. Mercer wrote other songs in Spanish, including "Que le vaya bien," or "May Things Go Well," music by Fabian Andre and lyrics by Mercer (Commander Publisher, n.d.), although the American Andre is better known for his "Dream a Little Dream of Me"; "Quiéreme y verás," or "Every Now and Then," music by José Antonio Méndez with lyrics by Johnny Mercer (Southern Music Co., 1954). See also Kimball et al., eds., *Complete Lyrics*, 26, 107, 236, 412; "The Rumba Jumps!" lyrics by Johnny Mercer, music by Hoagy Carmichael (New York: Mercer & Morris, 1939), for the musical *Three after Three*. The Glenn Miller Orchestra made a popular recording of it in 1940. See also Kimball et al., eds., *Complete Lyrics*, 93, 434–35, 438; John Storm Roberts, *The Latin Tinge: The Impact of Latin American Music on the United States* (New York: Oxford University Press, 1979), 113. Mercer owned several volumes in the Music series published by the Pan American Union, including Gilbert Chase, *Partial List of Latin American Music Obtainable*

in the United States, 1942; Gustavo Duran, *Recordings of Latin American Songs and Dances: An Annotated Selected List of Popular and Folk Music*, 1942; and *14 Traditional Spanish Songs from Texas*, 1942; Albert T. Luper, *The Music of Argentina*, 1942; *The Music of Brazil*, 1943, all published in Washington, D.C., by the Music Division of the Pan American Union.

19. Ruy Castro, *Bossa Nova: The Story of the Brazilian Music That Seduced the World*, trans. Lysa Salsbury (Chicago: A Cappella Books, 2000), 7–18, and passim. The Bossa Nova simply demonstrates Homi Bhabha's point that there is "no inherent purity and originality of cultures." The idea of how the exchange of products changes lives is explored in Robert R. Alvarez Jr., *Mangos, Chiles and Truckers: The Business of Transnationalism* (Minneapolis: University of Minnesota Press, 2005).

20. Charles A. Perrone and Christopher Dunn, eds., *Brazilian Popular Music and Globalization* (Gainesville: University Press of Florida, 2001), 16–18; Castro, *Bossa Nova*, xi–xii. Loti (the pseudonym of Charlie Lots), Pagano (the pseudonym of Victor Ingeveldt), and Madinez (the pseudonym of Gaston Bogaert) performed as the Latin soul band the Chakachas that in 1972 produced the disco hit "Jungle Fever"; "Brasilia," words by Johnny Mercer, music by Pagano-Loti-Madinez (Cromwell Music and Editora Musical Essex, Édiciones Musicales Novel, 1961); Kimball et al., eds., *Complete Lyrics*, 292, 437–38.

21. Perrone and Dunn, *Brazilian Popular Music and Globalization*, 16–18; Castro, *Bossa Nova*, 147; Ken Bloom, *Hollywood Song: The Complete Film and Musical Companion*, 3 vols. (New York: Facts on File, 1995), 3:1136–37.

22. Chris McGowan and Ricardo Pessanha, *The Brazilian Sound: Samba, Bossa Nova, and the Popular Music of Brazil* (Philadelphia: Temple University Press, 1998), 55–73; Castro, *Bossa Nova*, 230–42, 256–58. The Portuguese version, "Garota de Ipanema," had been around a year before the Verve recording in New York, which followed a famous concert on November 21, 1962, in Carnegie Hall featuring Gilberto, Jobim, and others. Perhaps Johnny Mercer joined the three thousand in attendance who included Tony Bennett, Miles Davis, Dizzy Gillespie, and Peggy Lee. Astrud Gilberto made recordings of several Mercer songs, including, "Once Upon a Summertime."

23. John Storm Roberts, *Latin Jazz: The First of the Fusions, 1880s to Today* (New York: Schirmer Books, 1999), 123–24; "Old Guitaron," words by Johnny Mercer, music by Laurindo Almeida (Commander Publications, 1964). Joanie Sommers made a lovely recording of "Old Guitaron." "Love Like Yours," words by Johnny Mercer, music by Luiz Bonfá (1964). See also Kimball et al., eds., *Complete Lyrics*, 339.

24. Castro, *Bossa Nova*, 306–7. Willis Conover interview with Mercer, January 30, 1970, collection M82-8, Popular Music Archives, GSU. In 1972, the two songwriters apparently revisited the idea of collaboration. Mercer received a curious telegram from Antonio Carlos Jobim dated April 5, 1972, that read: "DEAR JOHNNY ALL MY SONGS ARE AVAILABLE FOR YOU LETTER FOLLOWS LOVE JOBIM." There is no additional letter in the folder. See box 2, folder 22, JM Papers, GSU.

25. Gene Lees, *Portrait of Johnny: The Life of John Herndon Mercer* (New York: Pantheon Books, 2004), 3–9, 307–9; Lees worked with the arranger, Claus Ogerman, who constructed the scores for the Sinatra recordings; Leonard Mustazza, ed., *Frank Sinatra and Popular Culture: Essays on an American Icon* (Westport, Conn.: Praeger, 1998); William "Bill" Harbach, oral interview M130, Popular Music Archives, GSU.

26. In such a letter he describes life at Vernon View; see *Savannah Morning News*, May 19, 1962; JHM to "Darling Mom," undated but ca. late 1960s, Mercer Family Collection, AASU.

27. *Savannah Morning News*, March 13, 1967.

28. Xerox of typed manuscript dated "Wed. 4-26-67, Ossabaw Island, Savannah, Ga.," and included in a letter to Cornelia McIntire Rivers, Walter Rivers Papers, University of West Florida, Pensacola, Fla.

29. Linda Orr King, "'The Fourth Day of the Windy Moon': Ossabaw Island, Georgia as a

Context for the Interpretation of Historical, Cultural, and Environmental Change," Georgia State University dissertation manuscript in author's possession; Eleanor Torrey West, "Personal Story about Johnny Mercer," undated typescript, Georgia Historical Society, Savannah, Ga.

30. Johnny Mercer's "Mike," collection M210, box 1, Popular Music Archives, GSU; the script for "Mike" is dated March 1967; see folder 6, box 20, and folders 1 and 2, box 21, JM Papers, GSU; Kimball et al., ed., *Complete Lyrics*, 323, 342–48.

31. *Savannah Evening Press*, July 8, and August 18, 1967.

32. The former president of the Great Dane Trailer Company, which he had incorporated in 1958 and sold to U.S. Freight Company in 1968, George Anderson Mercer died at age seventy-five; see the *Savannah Morning News*, September 10, 1968. Mercer's note of condolence to his niece read: "Your Dad was one of my lifelong inspirations, both because of his sense of humor and his really lightninglike mind. That doesn't even take in his darling personality and all the other cute things about him." JHM to Elizabeth Hammond, January 3, 1969, courtesy of George Anderson Mercer Hammond. Muriel Bell to Cornelia McIntire, postmarked May 14, 1969; JHM to "Darling" (Cornelia Rivers), [spring 1969]. Mercer added, "Thank you for your painting — and for the letter — and for inviting me to your birthday party (age 4?). I've always felt like one of the family since." See also Walter Rivers to JHM, May 28, 1968, W [Walter Rivers] to "Hi Folks," [Johnny and Ginger Mercer], no date, and "jm" undated response, all in Rivers Papers, Special Collections, John Pace Library, University of West Florida, Pensacola, Fla. Cornelia died June 9, 1969, with burial adjacent to Bonaventure in Greenwich Cemetery lot 30 N, block B, section 8, while Walter died on November 13, 1982, leaving his body to the University of Alabama in Birmingham Medical School, an odd outcome given a 1963 letter Johnny wrote to his mother referring to "vital organs — the kind Walter Rivers blanches at when confronted with them at the dining table." See Cornelia McIntire Rivers's obituary in the *Birmingham News*, June 9, 1969, and Paul Walter Rivers's obituary in the *Birmingham Post-Herald*, November 16, 1982.

33. John Berendt, *Midnight in the Garden of Good and Evil* (New York: Random House, 1994), 78–94, recounts Emma Kelly's story in the chapter "The Lady of Six Thousand Songs." With slight variation it appears in the extended obituary, *Savannah Morning News*, January 18, 2001. The lines went: "If you were mine, / I could be a ruler of kings; / And if you were mine, / I could do such wonderful things! / I'd say to a star, / 'Stop where you are, / Light up my lover's way,' / And ev'ry star above you / Would obey." Kimball et al., ed., *Complete Lyrics*, 39.

34. Mary Skinner, "Singing Savannah: The Musical Relationship of Johnny Mercer and Emma Kelly," April 29, 1999, Georgia State University, unpublished student paper, author's possession.

35. Skinner, "Singing Savannah"; *Savannah Morning News*, January 18, 2001; Emma Kelly Papers, collection M183, Popular Music Archives, GSU.

36. Bloom, *Hollywood Song*, 1267. Moving to Hollywood in 1966, Legrand enjoyed a successful career writing movie theme songs for the studios, often with lyrics by the Bergmans, such as *Ode to Billy Joe* (1976) and the James Bond thriller, *Never Say Never Again* (1983); he also scored the Billie Holiday biopic *Lady Sings the Blues* (1972) and Barbra Streisand's *Yentl* (1983), as well as *Dingo* with Miles Davis (1991) and *Madeline* (1998). Written in 1969, "Les Petits Oiseaux" appeared in the 1970 film *Darling Lili* directed by Blake Edwards and starring Julie Andrews. French children sing the song, including the lyric "Ho, ho, e-cout-ons la melodie des can-a-ris. / Oui, oui trills the tiny chickadee. / It's my turn now." In the verses that follow, the old birder enumerates a variety of feathered friends, including the titmouse, thrush, rooster, cuckoo, and scarlet tanager. See collection M001, box 6, folder 61, JM Papers, GSU.

37. JHM to "Poll," postcard, postmarked November 3, 1969, and undated letter that refers to the Mercer's return date of September 22, 1969, both in Ober Family Papers, collection M157, Popular Music Archives, GSU. There are actually four nymphs on the bridge, but the postcard pictured

only one. Nancy Keith Mercer Gerard recalls the painting, which she said Ginger gave to Lidia and her husband Osvaldo Giovannini, the housekeepers and caregivers who looked after Ginger in her final months of life while suffering from Alzheimer's, interview with Gerard.

38. JM autobiography includes Mercer's evaluation: "Michel LeGrand has a big future also, in my estimation, as he composes like turning on a faucet. Melody springs from him as from a bird, and with luck, which we all need, he will be one of our great composers in the future, as will Antonio Carlos Jobim"; *Melody Maker*, November 15, 1969; Mercer interview by Conover.

39. Hugh Fordin, oral interview M010, Popular Music Archives, GSU; *Melody Maker*, November 15, 1969; JHM to Polly Ober, undated letter in Ober Family Papers, collection M157, Popular Music Archives, GSU. Apparently when traveling Mercer allowed others to use his residences, as suggested by a letter from author Ray Bradbury, who with his wife stayed in the Palm Springs house. See Ray Bradbury to Mercer, July 6, 1971, JM Papers, GSU.

40. JHM to Lillian Mercer, February 28, 1974, and JHM to Katherine Ciucevich O'Leary, May 25, 1972, Mercer Family Collection, AASU; William H. Ford to JHM, February 21, 1972, box 2, folder 22, JM Papers, GSU. Ford writes: "Your father's reputation, as the most important man in the history of the Union Society of Savannah, is well known. He is responsible for most of the endowments which help operate Bethesda to-day." Explaining the orphanage received no government or civic agency support, Ford added, "the fact that we do not have to depend on these sources is a tribute to your father." JHM to Peter Rawley, August 15, 1972, folder 22, box 2, JM Papers GSU.

41. Kane, *How to Write a Song*, 70, 73. During a visit to Savannah while drinking in the Exchange on River Street, Mercer gave his Greek hat to the bartender, K. "Ken" Medernach.

42. Notes on the 1972 trip to Europe; separately filed sheet music by Salve D'Esposito with Mercer's notes, box 6, folder 61, and Giuseppe Gramitto Ricci to JHM, August 29, 1972, box 2, folder 22, both in JM Papers, GSU.

43. Paul (McCartney) to Bruce (Ricker), February 25, 2009, Bruce Ricker, personal collection; Mandy Neder interview by Bruce Ricker; Mercer interview by Conover. *Savannah Morning News*, August 16, 1973.

44. Mercer interviewed in the *Trenton (N.J.) Times-Advertiser*, December 17, 1962; Margaret Whiting's telling of the anecdote appears in an unpublished essay and in oral interviews. Whiting on the opinions of family about the Beatles in Margaret Whiting and Will Holt, *It Might as Well Be Spring: A Musical Autobiography* (New York: William Morrow, 1987), 201–2, 208–9. She recalls that her mother, Eleanor Whiting, had long blamed the Beatles for destroying popular music in America, but that her daughter, Debbie, liked the British group.

45. "The Long Goodbye," lyrics by Johnny Mercer, music by John Williams (New York: Unart Music Corp., 1973). Friends with Henry Mancini and André Previn, the jazz pianist Dave Grusin served as music director for Andy Williams until 1964, when he began to score films, including the Academy Award nominees *Heaven Can Wait*, *On Golden Pond*, *Tootsie*, and *The Fabulous Baker Boys*, as well as such television sitcoms as *Maude* and *St. Elsewhere*. Blossom Dearie sang "Mother Necessity," "Figure Eight," and "Unpack Your Adjectives" on *Schoolhouse Rock!* while Sheldon sang "Conjunction Junction," "I'm Just a Bill," and "Them Not-So-Dry Bones" and other songs for the program produced by Michael Eisner, the vice president of ABC's children's programming.

46. "I'm Shadowing You" with words by Johnny Mercer and music by Blossom Dearie and "My New Celebrity Is You," words and music by Johnny Mercer (Hollywood: Mercer Music, 1978); in some ways the latter's lyrics parallel "Anything Goes" by Cole Porter. Bach and Mercer, eds., *Our Huckleberry Friend*, 219, 224–25. Kimball et al., ed., *Complete Lyrics*, 382,.

47. Ellen C. Nathan, October 5, 1970, box 2, folder 20, and Jobim to JHM, April 5, 1972, box 2, folder 22, JM Papers, GSU.

48. Dave Dexter to JHM, October 31, 1973, box 2, folder 23, JM Papers, GSU.

49. Philip Furia, *Skylark: The Life and Times of Johnny Mercer* (New York: St. Martin's, 2003), 257; Fordin, oral interview.

50. Savannah *Daily News*, January 12, 1973; *New York Times*, January 12, 1973; Mercer received but did not fulfill an invitation to come back in 1974. See Candace Leeds to JHM, January. 12, 1973, box 2, folder 23, JM Papers, GSU; see "Face" to "Dada," undated, Hoagy Carmichael Collection, Archives of Traditional Music, Indiana University, Bloomington, Ind.

51. Lawrence Kasha to JHM, August 13, 1965; O'Malley's Book Store to JHM, July 1, 1968; Frank Loesser to JHM, August 20, 1962. All in JM Papers, GSU. As Johnny's contemporary having been born in 1910, Loesser had landed several Broadway blockbusters such as *Guys and Dolls* in 1950 and *The Most Happy Fella* in 1956. The writer of both words and music (often with book writer Abe Burrows), Loesser had a knack for putting together a show featuring everyday people singing in the vernacular. While Duke, the Anglicized name of the Russian Vladimir Dukelsky, had gone on to write for the *Ziegfeld Follies* with E. Y. "Yip" Harburg and Ira Gershwin, his last Broadway success had been the 1940 *Cabin in the Sky*, written with lyricist John Latouche. JHM to Vernon Duke, June 18, 1966; Duke to JHM, October 1, 1966; JHM to Duke, [fall 1968]; Duke to JHM, July 12, 1968, all in Vernon Duke Collection, Library of Congress, Washington, D.C. Mercer and Duke had written "Yours for Keeps" in 1954. Duke's testiness in his letters to Mercer makes it apparent why Johnny chose not to collaborate with the composer: "Much as I would like to work with you, I'm long past the stage of wooing lyricists; I'm interested in an enthusiastic collaborator who would like things I like and instantly reject properties found unsuitable — the way we both said 'no' to Hodshire on 'Wee Gordie.'" Ephron worked on *Carousel, Take Her, She's Mine*, and *There's No Business Like Show Business*, see *New York Times*, September 30, 1971; See also John Whedon to JHM and Bobby [Dolan], January 5, 1972, and Bing Crosby to JHM, October 31, 1972; Don Devendorf to JHM, February 18, 1971, includes the curious line, "I'm anxious to hear what Irving comes up with, and to see your lyrics." See also September 14, 1971; Michel Legrand to JHM, November 17, 1971, all in box 2, folders 21, 22, JM Papers, GSU. On *The Pig War*, Kimball et al., eds., *Complete Lyrics*, 421, reprints the only known lyric still extant, that of "Without Benefit of Clergy," which General Winfield Scott was to sing to an "attractive British spy," as he worked to avert the near calamity.

52. American Society of Composers, Authors and Publishers, comp., *ASCAP Biographical Dictionary*, 4th ed. (New York: Jacques Cattell Press, 1980), 403; Martin Bookspan and Ross Yockey, *André Previn: A Biography* (New York: Doubleday, 1981); Dave Dexter Jr., *Playback: A Newsman/Record Producer's Hits and Misses from the Thirties to the Seventies* (New York: Billboard Publications, 1976), 111; André Previn to JHM, November 23, 1970, and January 8, 1971, JM Papers, GSU.

53. André Previn to JHM, November 23, 1970, and January 8, 1971, box 2, folders 20, 21, JM Papers, AASU. The editors of *Complete Lyrics* quote Philip Furia's assertion in *Skylark* (256) that Mercer proposed the *Little Women* idea, but Previn's correspondence to Mercer clearly demonstrates otherwise. See also André Previn interview by Bruce Ricker, Rhapsody Productions, on file at Georgia State University. Kimball et al., eds., *Complete Lyrics*, 365, 378, 389.

54. J. B. Priestley, *The Good Companions* (New York: Harper & Brothers, 1929). The novel sold a million copies. The opening verse of the song reads: "Although it lies outside of my dominion, / If you should ask me for my opinion, / When out with good companions / And voices ring, / There comes a time before the party's closing, / Perhaps the old ones have started dozing, / When one toast needs proposing, / I raise my glass and sing: / Here's to my lady." See Kimball et al., ed., *Complete Lyrics*, 196. Bookspan and Yockey, *André Previn*.

55. Andre Previn to JHM, undated but spring 1972, JHM to Previn, April 5, 1972; JHM to J. B. Priestley, August 16, 1972, box 2, folders 21, 22, JM Papers, GSU.

56. JM to Andre, January 8, and Previn to JHM, February 19, 1973, in box 2, folder 23, JM Papers, GSU: Bookspan and Yockey, *André Previn*, 255, 277. The London Symphony Orchestra prospered during these years under Previn's baton. Bach and Mercer, eds., *Our Huckleberry Friend*, 191; Previn interview by Ricker; Jean Bach suggested that "Johnny didn't get along with him [Previn] too well" (Jean Bach, oral interview M128, Popular Music Archives, GSU); yet Johnny made both Previn and Mia Farrow subjects in his song written for Blossom Dearie called "My New Celebrity Is You," with the lines "I've swooned at Mia Farrow, / Angular and narrow, / Drove her Pierce Arrow / To a *Gatsby* preview" and "Her husband André Previn — / Absolutely heaven. / Even Herman Levin / Wants to hire him too." See Kimball et al., eds., *Complete Lyrics*, 382–83.

57. Priestley, *The Good Companions*. Kimball et al., eds., *Complete Lyrics*, 364–78; see also the *Sunday Times* (London), and other clippings in the Mercer Family Collection, AASU. The original actress to play Susie, Celia Bannerman, quit the production when it reached Manchester, leaving the understudy, Marti Webb, to play the part before the audience. Judi Dench recalled a notice in the paper by Braham Murray that gave the cast a "dressing-down," leading Dench to say to the director, "You must be joking if you think any of us wouldn't be working hard, you must be *joking*, Braham, if you think that we were all pulling back and not doing our best, with an understudy on playing the lead!" See John Miller, *Judi Dench: With a Crack in her Voice* (New York: Welcome Rain Publishers, 2000), 136.

58. *Times* (London), July 12 and 14, 1974, UPI wire copy dated July 12, 1974; *Observer*, review, July 14, 1974. Mercer first used the rhymes of English place names found in "And Points Beyond" in the lyrics for "Bon Vivant" in the 1964 show *Foxy*: "Manchester and Dorchester / And Chichester and Perth." See Kimball et al., eds., *Complete Lyrics*, 309, 372.

59. Upon reflection, Mills wrote in his autobiography, "I shall always look back on those 250 performances we played at Her Majesty's Theatre as one of the happiest times I have ever spent in a show. There is a magic back-stage in musicals that one never feels in the legitimate theatre. The atmosphere is terrific." John Mills, *Up in the Clouds, Gentlemen Please* (New Haven, Conn.: Ticknor & Fields, 1981), 268–69; Miller, *Judi Dench*, 135–37.

60. The *Standard*, the *Guardian*, and the *Mail* on July 14, 1974, had the critical headlines; Furia, *Skylark*, 261, documents the Irish Republican Army attacks and quotes scriptwriter Ronnie Harwood noting, "we were doing rather well" but that "we were not a big enough hit to survive." Shortly after the show, Previn resigned his post as conductor of the London Symphony Orchestra to take up the baton at the Pittsburgh Symphony Orchestra. See also Bach and Mercer, eds., *Our Huckleberry Friend*, 221–23.

61. *Johnny Mercer Sings the Songs of Johnny Mercer with the Harry Roche Constellation* (London: Pye Records, 1974).

62. Benny Green liner notes for *Johnny Mercer Sings the Songs of Johnny Mercer.*

63. Malcolm Macfarlane, *Bing Crosby: Day by Day* (Lanham, Md.: Scarecrow Press, 2001), 620. Back at Chappells Studios in London in February 1975, Ken Barns added in the orchestrations to the duets and recorded the rest of the album with Crosby and Pete Moore and His Orchestra. Kimball et al., eds., *Complete Lyrics*, 368–70. Like his contemporary, Harry Lauder, Will Fyffe gained fame as a popular Scottish entertainer. Bing Crosby later used "The Pleasure of Your Company" as a theme song for charitable benefits; see Crosby to Ginger Mercer, February 17, 1976, JM Papers, GSU.

64. Furia quotes Previn in *Skylark*, 259; R. W. Montgomery to J. Mercer, June 5, 1974, and note in Mercer's hand, [winter 1975?], box 2, folder 23, JM Papers, GSU; Harbach, oral interview.

65. Whiting and Holt, *It Might as Well Be Spring*, 238.

66. JHM to Liz, JHM to Frannie, [January 1975], JHM to Andre [Previn], January 8, 1973, John Gibson to JHM, December 1, 1974, box 2, folder 23, JM Papers, GSU.

67. Nancy Mercer Keith Gerard, interview by the author; Lees, *Portrait of Johnny*, 306–7; Furia, *Skylark*, 263–64. Almonds contain a derivative called laetrile that in the 1970s some people thought would cure cancer. When Nancy tried to repay Johnny for his financial support over the years he said to her, "No sweetiepie, I don't expect you to do that," but then added, "will you do something for me? When I'm down and out, will you pass the hat for me?" Author's interview with Nancy Mercer Keith Gerard, July 6, 2012, author's possession.

68. *Savannah Morning News*, September 17 and 22, 1975; Lee Adler, "Johnny Mercer — Savannah's Song Writing Genius," undated and unpublished paper presented to the Madeira Club, author's possession; John Berendt quotes Jim Williams saying that Johnny offered to buy Mercer House, but no evidence supports this claim, and it appears unlikely given Mercer's modesty and his ownership already of a house on Burnside Island. See John Berendt, *Midnight in the Garden of Good and Evil: A Savannah Story* (New York: Random House, 1994), 13. *Mike Douglas Show*, season 14, episode 44, October 30, 1975. Reynolds's stuntman Dick Ziker also appeared on that show. Previously Mercer appeared on season 6, episode 55, which aired on November 17, 1967, and season 6, episode 97, which aired on January 16, 1968.

69. Nick Mamalakis, oral interview M034, Popular Music Archives, GSU. Julie Paige interview by the author. Her brother, John, had married Mary Collins.

70. *Variety*, March 16 and July 30, 1976; September 2, 7, and 30, 1977, clippings in the Margaret Herrick Library, Academy of Motion Pictures Arts and Sciences, Los Angeles, Calif.

71. "In Memoriam: Theodore Kurze, MD," *Bulletin of the American Association of Neurological Surgeons* 11, no. 3 (Fall 2002); *Variety*, October 29, 1975, listed Mercer "in fair condition after undergoing brain surgery." Robbins, oral interview; Furia, *Skylark*, 265–67; Lees, *Portrait of Johnny*, 310–14. Bill Harbach later talked with Kurze about the operation and the surgeon confessed, "I opened him up, and I said, 'Oh, God.'" Harbach, oral interview. Barbara Robbins questions Harbach's testimony because "Billy Harbach, I know, went around telling people he was out of it completely. And Billy Harbach says he saw him, and he never did." She added that Harbach "may have seen Ginger at the house."

72. Amanda Mercer Neder and Jim Corwin, oral interview M140, Robbins and Harbach, oral interviews, all in Popular Music Archives, GSU; Whiting and Holt, *It Might as Well Be Spring*, 238.

73. Neder and Corwin, oral interview, and Robbins, oral interview; Henry Mancini to Ginger Mercer, Jenkins Boys Club, both letters in box 3, JM Papers, GSU.

74. *Variety*, July 30, 1976; September 2, 7, and 30, 1977; Lees, *Portrait of Johnny*, 305–16; JM obituary, *Savannah Morning News*, June 26, 1976; Neder and Corwin, oral interview; Robbins, oral interview; Harbach, oral interview. Harbach figured that nursing care over the year cost about $350,000. He also observed that Ginger's sometime lover, Marc Cramer, hung around the house at that time, too, a claim disputed by Johnny's grandson, James "Jim" Corwin, author's interview with Corwin, March 22, 2011, notes in author's possession.

75. The initial obituary by Al Martinez in the *Los Angeles Times*, June 25, 1976, called Mercer the "lazy-voiced lyricist" who was "one of the most talented and prolific of the nation's composers" and who "was a giant in the music world, writing alone and collaborating with the top names in his business to produce memorable tunes." Zan Thompson quoted in a July 1976 editorial; *New York Times*, June 26, 1976. Bing Crosby to Ginger Mercer, September 24, 1976; Pearl Bailey to Mrs. Georgia [sic] Mercer, June 28, 1976; undated statement of Gerald R. Ford, all in JM Papers, GSU. *Times* (London), June 28, 1976.

76. *Savannah Morning News–Evening Press* Combined Sunday Edition, June 27, 1976. Berendt, *Midnight in the Garden of Good and Evil*, 33.

77. Nancy Mercer Keith Gerard recalled the family members in attendance, the Mercer and

Hammond families and the Ciucevich and O'Leary families. Aunt Katie had joined her sister, Lillian, at the Tybee nursing home. Juliana also attended the graveside service.

78. Ober, oral interview; eulogy for Johnny Mercer by Mike Ober, dated June 3, 1976 (actually July 3, 1976), Ober Family Papers, collection M157, box 1, folder 4, Popular Music Archives, GSU.

79. The stones read, "John Herndon Mercer (Johnny) November 18, 1909, June 25, 1976, 'And the Angels Sing'" and "Elizabeth Meltzer Mercer (Ginger), Beloved wife of John Herndon Mercer, June 25, 1909, October 21, 1994, 'You Must Have Been a Beautiful Baby.'"

80. *Los Angeles Times*, July 2 and 19, 1976, see also obituary, June 27, 1976; *Hollywood Reporter*, July 1, 16, and 23, 1976; *Variety*, June 28, July 30, 1976. Variety identified $1,500 as the quarterly payment going first to Lillian and then upon her death to Juliana, and $750 quarterly to Ann Meltzer, with Ginger receiving the balance of ASCAP royalty payments. It also identified his real estate as valued in excess of two hundred thousand dollars.

81. Hugh had died four months before his brother Johnny.

Conclusion

The epigraph is from "Hello Out There, Hello" (1952), with music by Wingy Manone. See Robert Kimball, Barry Day, Miles Kreuger, and Eric Davis, eds., *The Complete Lyrics of Johnny Mercer* (New York: Alfred A. Knopf, 2009), 222.

1. *Savannah Evening Press*, June 26, 1976, March 6 and April 30, 1977; Roulhac Toledano, *The National Trust Guide to Savannah* (New York: John Wiley and Sons, 1997), 83.

2. Mills B. Lane to JHM, February 25, 1972, folder 22, box 2, JM Papers, GSU.

3. *Savannah Morning News–Evening Press*, May 28, 1978; Margaret Whiting and Will Holt, *It Might as Well Be Spring: A Musical Autobiography* (New York: William Morrow, 1987), 273. Proclamation of the city of Savannah by Mayor John P. Rousakis, May 25, 1978, JM Papers, GSU.

4. *Savannah Morning News–Evening Press*, May 28, 1978.

5. The early literature on the Johnny Mercer Foundation suggests it contributed to charities that help children with hearing problems. In time the mission changed to "preserving and celebrating the American Popular Song in the tradition of Johnny Mercer" as well as Ginger's pet charities, including leukemia research and public television. Ginger had taken up again with an old lover, Marc "Red" Cramer, who Barbara Robbins said "took very good care of her." Robbins quotes Penny Singleton saying of Ginger and Cramer, "They had a thing in 1945." For several years, Cramer accompanied Ginger on extended trips to Europe, with Baden-Baden, Germany being a favorite destination. To control her and her wealth, Cramer tried to alienate Ginger from "everybody, her sisters, Mandy and Jeffrey," but he failed to shut out Rush because, as Bobby said, "I got there first. I had known her, and I had precedence over anyone and anybody that came afterward. And I had keys to the house." See Barbara Robbins oral interview M158 and Robert Rush oral interview M154, Popular Music Archives, GSU. On the foundation, see also JM & GM Papers, GSU and Gene Lees, *Portrait of Johnny: The Life of John Herndon Mercer* (New York: Pantheon Books, 2004), 324–26.

6. Gene M. Gressley to JHM, October 2, 1969, box 20, folder 2, Adolph Deutsch to JHM, October 1, 1972, box 2, folder 22, JM Papers, GSU. On Mills B. Lane's donation, see the *Morning News*, September 16, 1976. See also the *Georgia Historical Society Archives Minute Book*, 1972–1981, which references the September 10, 1976, Board of Curators meeting with its announcement of the donation. A new director, Anthony R. Dees, conducted the conversations regarding the donation of the Mercer Papers. In his director's report for the society's annual meeting on April 17, 1982, he describes the organization's longstanding problem of space, noting, "we are still trying to

accession the Hartridge Collection" and that "our large Central of Georgia Collection had to be moved last September, and I sincerely hope its next move is into a facility owned by the Georgia Historical Society."

7. On the JM Papers, see *Savannah News-Press*, July 26, 1981, and April 11, 1982.

8. Bob Bach to JHM, undated, folder 20, and Merrill Pollack to JHM, August 1, December 5, 1973, and Fess Williams to JHM, January 29, 1974, both in box 2, folder 23, JM Papers, GSU; Mercer had signed copies of many of these books in his personal library. See Irving Berlin, *Songs by Irving Berlin* (New York: printed by author, 1969), signed "For Johnny Mercer, with my best always"; E. Y. Harburg, *Rhymes for the Irreverent* (New York: Grovesman Publishers, 1965), signed "Glad to see you both looking so fit"; Hoagy Carmichael with Stephen Longstreet, *Sometimes I Wonder: The Story of Hoagy Carmichael* (New York: Farrar Straus & Giroux, 1966); Ira Gershwin, *Lyrics on Several Occasions* (New York: Viking Press, 1959); Fred Astaire, *Steps in Time: An Autobiography* (New York: Perennial Library, 1959); Bing Crosby, *Call Me Lucky, by Bing Crosby as Told to Pete Martin* (New York: Simon and Schuster, 1953); Bob Hope, *The Last Christmas Show*; and in Edward Jablonski, *Harold Arlen: Happy with the Blues* (New York: Doubleday, 1961), Mercer's collaborator wrote: "For John — memorable days they were and still are, thanks to you." Max Wilk, *They're Playing Our Song* (New York: Atheneum, 1973). Sidney Carroll, "Yes, Mr. Mercer," *Esquire*, September 1942. The drafts of Mercer's autobiography are located in box 1, JM Papers, GSU.

9. Ginger Mercer to Irving Berlin, August 18, 1981, Irving Berlin Papers, Library of Congress, Washington, D.C. Bob Bach and Ginger Mercer, eds., *Our Huckleberry Friend: The Life, Times, and Lyrics of Johnny Mercer* (Secaucus, N.J.: Lyle Stuart, 1982). A division of Lyle Stuart, Citadel published similar heavily illustrated titles about entertainers such as Tony Thomas, *Harry Warren and the Hollywood Musical* (Secaucus, N.J.: Citadel, 1975). Lees later published Mancini's autobiography as Henry Mancini with Gene Lees, *Did They Mention the Music?* (1989; rprt. New York: Cooper Square Press, 2001).

10. JM autobiography; *Western Union Mailgram*, June 26, 1976; see also the Berlin Collection; Bach and Mercer, eds., *Our Huckleberry Friend*.

11. Fordin, oral interview, Popular Music Archives, Georgia State University, Atlanta, Ga.; Nancy Mercer Keith Gerard interview, author's possession.

12. Warren Craig, *Sweet and Lowdown: America's Popular Songwriters* (Metuchen, N.J.: Scarecrow Press, 1978), 345–47. Mercer remains one of the four top Oscar winners for Best Original Song. As collaborators, the composer Jimmy Van Heusen and lyricist Sammy Cahn won three of their four Oscars for "All the Way" (1957), "High Hopes" (1959), and "Call Me Irresponsible" (1963), with Cahn's fourth for "Three Coins in the Fountain" with Jule Styne (1954) and Heusen's fourth for "Swinging on a Star" with Johnny Burke (1944). Of a new generation, Alan Menken won his four Best Song Oscars writing for Disney movies *The Little Mermaid* (1989) and *Beauty and the Beast* (1991), both with Howard Ashman; *Aladdin* with Tim Rice (1992); and *Pocahontas* with Stephen Schwartz (1995). When considering the Oscars he also won for the scores to these movies, Menken holds the record for the most Oscars won by anybody with eight, while Cahn holds the record for the most nominations for Best Song with twenty-six.

13. Robbins, oral interview, Rush, oral interview; Henry Kane, *How to Write a Song (as Told to Henry Kane)* (New York: Macmillan, 1962), 86–87.

14. Dave Dexter Jr., *Jazz Cavalcade: The Inside Story of Jazz* (New York: Da Capo Press, 1977, ca. 1946), 190.

15. John Egerton, *The Americanization of Dixie: The Southernization of America* (New York: Harper and Row, 1974); Peter Applebome, *Dixie Rising: How the South Is Shaping American Values, Politics, and Culture* (New York: Random House, 1996). In his chapter on Nashville,

Applebome explores how country music "Took Over America." Fifty years before, the same could be said for jazz. See also James N. Gregory, *The Southern Diaspora: How the Great Migrations of Black and White Southerners Transformed America* (Chapel Hill: University of North Carolina Press, 2005), in which Gregory questions the extent of Egerton's subtitle (and Applebome's echo of it in his first chapter, "The Southernization of America"), noting that what is often attributed to diaspora southerners in the North and West — racism and reactionary politics — are problems expressed by nonsoutherners too, as these problems are not native to one region. James C. Cobb provides a more thorough critique, exploring how the South is used to dismiss the nation's ills in *The South and America Since World War II* (New York: Oxford Univesity Press, 2010). See also Cobb, *Redefining Southern Culture: Mind and Identity in the Modern South* (Athens: University of Georgia Press, 1999).

16. Dr. John (Malcolm John Rebennack Jr.), *Mercernary*, 2006; *The Color Purple*, a musical presented by Oprah Winfrey, music and lyrics by Brenda Russell, Allee Willis, Stephen Bray, with book by Marsha Norman based on the novel by Alice Walker, had its world premier in Atlanta, Georgia, in 2004 before moving to Broadway in 2005.

17. *Music Week*, August 25, 1984; Whiting and Holt, *It Might as Well Be Spring*, 222–23; Manilow quoted in *New York Times*, October 14, 1991, 35. Other Manilow-Mercer titles include "At Last," "Can't Teach My Old Heart New Tricks," "If It Can't Be You," and "Just Remember." Nancy Wilson, *With My Lover Beside Me* (Columbia, 1991). In the liner notes, Manilow observed "Mercer is to songwriters what Picasso is to painters," and Wilson, who "felt" Mercer's presence in the recording sessions, said, "to be the first to interpret the poetry of Johnny Mercer is quite a thrill and an honor." The most poignant lyrics recall lost love, such as "I Can't Teach My Old Heart New Tricks" and "Heart of Mine, Cry On"; Monica Mancini, *The Dreams of Johnny Mercer* (Concord Records, 2000).

18. Will Friedwald, *Sinatra! The Song Is You: A Singer's Art* (New York: Scribner, 1995), 40–41, 350–51, 468; Kimball et al., *Complete Lyrics*, 362; James Van Heusen to JHM, n.d. (1974), box 2, folder 23, JM Papers, GSU. The Gordon Jenkins arrangement of "Empty Tables" saw release in the United States as a 45 but was dropped from the American album *Ol' Blue Eyes Is Back,* while being added to the Italian release. The *Complete Lyrics* neglects to include "A Kiss from You." For the Benny Carter and Billy Eckstine recording, see the *Trav'lin' Light* volume of the *Verve Johnny Mercer Songbook.*

19. Jewly Hight, "Moon River: The Geography of a Timeless Song," *Georgia Music Magazine*, Fall 2009; *The Simpsons*; Andy Williams singing "Moon River" can be heard on "Bart on the Road," episode 3F17, originally aired March 31, 1996; the spoof of "Days of Wine and Roses" appeared as "Days of Wine and D'oh'ses," episode BABF14, originally aired April 9, 2000; Frank Sinatra singing "Summer Wind" can be heard on "Bart of Darkness," Episode 1F22, originally aired September 4, 1994. See "The Simpsons Archive" at www.snpp.com/episodes; Bach and Mercer, *Our Huckleberry Friend*, 123; Gary Larsen, *The Far Side*, December 3, 1975.

20. Bach and Mercer, *Our Huckleberry Friend: The Life, Times and Song Lyrics of Johnny Mercer*, reprint edition (Marietta, Ga.: Cherokee Publishing Company, 2009), 255–72.

21. Ibid., 273–78.

22. *Savannah Morning News*, January 18, 2001.

23. John Berendt, *Midnight in the Garden of Good and Evil* (New York: Random House, 1994). See also Kristine F. Anderson, "A Conversation with John Berendt," *The Writer* (January 1998); *Midnight in the Garden of Good and Evil: Music from and Inspired by the Motion Picture* (Warner Brothers, 1997).

24. Clint Eastwood and Bruce Ricker, *Johnny Mercer: "The Dream's on Me"* (Rhapsody Productions, 2009). The Emmy nomination was under the Outstanding Nonfiction Special category.

Becky Marshall had produced such Georgia documentaries as *America's First Gold Rush*, which won a Telly Award in 2008.

25. Eastwood and Ricker, *Johnny Mercer: "The Dream's on Me."* Just days after Mercer's death, Crosby recorded his Christmas special in July 1976; see Malcolm Macfarlane, *Bing Crosby: Day by Day* (Lanham, Md.: Scarecrow Press, 2001), 642; JM to Jack [unidentified], October 15, 1973, box 2, folder 23, JM Papers, GSU; Studs Terkel, "Tribute to Johnny Mercer," recorded August 18, 1976, for broadcast over WFMT, Studs Terkel Program Collection, Chicago History Museum Research Center, Chicago, Ill. In his September 17, 1976, *New York Times* review, John S. Wilson identified Mercer and McPartland's "Twilight World" as "a virtually unknown Mercer gem;" Warren Craig, *Sweet and Lowdown: America's Popular Songwriters* (Metuchen, N.J.: Scarecrow Press), 346–47.

26. See the www.johnnymercercentennial.com website; "Johnny Mercer: Too Marvelous for Words," Special Commemorative Supplement, *Savannah Magazine* (2009); The Friends of Johnny Mercer, Inc., and the City of Savannah, "The 2009 Centennial Birthday Tribute to Johnny Mercer" program, November 15, 2009.

27. The November 13–14, 2009, conference at Georgia State University, "Popular Music in the Mercer Era, 1910–1970," featured academic talks by scholars Karen Cox, Brian Ward, Mary Montgomery Wolf, Samuel Charters, Michael T. Bertrand, Frank A. Salamone, Patrick Huber, Kirby Pringle, Steve Goodson, Joshua Berrett, Todd Decker, Cynthia J. Miller, and Kyle Barnett. See www.johnnymercerfoundation.com.

28. See www.youtube.com/user/JohnnyMercer100; *New York Times*, November 15, 2009.

29. *New York Times*, December 8, 1959; *Newsweek*, January 29, 1945, 85–86.

PERMISSIONS TO QUOTE LYRICS

For the assistance he has received in gaining permission to quote song lyrics, the author would like to thank John Marshall and Alvin Deutsch of the Johnny Mercer Foundation and the heirs of Johnny Mercer, Amanda Mercer Neder and John J. Mercer, as well as Michael Worden of Alfred Music Publishing, Julie McDowell of Hal Leonard Corporation, Delda Sciurba of Criterion Music Corporation, Marco Berrocal of Bourne Music Corporation, Monica Corton of Next Decade Entertainment, and Lacey R. Chemsak of Sony/ATV.

For all lyrics quoted: © All Rights Reserved. International Copyright Secured. Used by Permission.

Bourne Music Publishers

"There's Nothing Like a College Education" © 1935 Bourne Music Publishers. Lyrics by Johnny Mercer. Music by Lewis E. Gensler.
"Personality" Music and lyrics by Johnny Burke and Jimmy Van Heusen.

Criterion Music Corporation

"When the World Was Young (Ah, the Apple Trees)" © 1951 Criterion Music Corp. Original French lyrics by Angele Vannier as "Le Chevalier de Paris (les Pommiers Doux)." English lyrics by Johnny Mercer. Music by M. Philippe-Gerard Bloch.
"Save the Bones for Henry Jones" by Daniel Barker, Michael H. Goldsen, and Henry McCoy Jones.

Hal Leonard

"Ac-Cent-Tchu-Ate the Positive" © 1944 Harwin Music Co. (MPL Music Publishing Inc.) Lyrics by Johnny Mercer. Music by Harold Arlen.
"Dearly Beloved" © 1942 PolyGram Music Publishing (Universal Music Publishing Group). Lyrics by Johnny Mercer. Music by Jerome Kern.
"Emily" © 1964 CBS Inc. (Hal Leonard). Lyrics by Johnny Mercer. Music by Johnny Mandel.
"Harvey, the Victory Garden Man" © 1943 Harwin Music Co (MPL Music Publishing Inc.) Lyrics by Johnny Mercer. Music by Harold Arlen.
"I'm Old Fashioned" © 1942 PolyGram Music Publishing (Universal Music Publishing Group). Lyrics by Johnny Mercer. Music by Jerome Kern.
"Life Is What You Make It" © 1971, 1972 MCA (Universal Music Publishing Group). Lyrics by Johnny Mercer. Music by Marvin Hamlisch.
"Long Goodbye, The" © 1973 CBS Inc. (Hal Leonard). Lyrics by Johnny Mercer. Music by John Williams.
"Man's Favorite Sport" © 1964 All Nations Music Publishing Ltd. (Universal Music Publishing Group). Lyrics by Johnny Mercer. Music by Henry Mancini.
"My Shining Hour" © 1943 Harwin Music Co. (MPL Music Publishing Inc.) Lyrics by Johnny Mercer. Music by Harold Arlen.

"On the Atchison, Topeka, and the Santa Fe" © 1943, 1945 CBS Inc. (Hal Leonard). Lyrics by Johnny Mercer. Music by Harry Warren.

"Once upon a Summertime" © 1962 MCA (Universal Music Publishing Group). Original French lyric by Eddie Marnay as "La Valse des Lilas." English lyric by Johnny Mercer. Music by Michel Legrand and Eddie Barclay.

"One for My Baby (and One More for the Road)" © 1943 Harwin Music Co. (MPL Music Publishing Inc.) Lyrics by Johnny Mercer. Music by Harold Arlen.

"Out of This World" © 1945 MPL Music Publishing Inc. Lyrics by Johnny Mercer. Music by Harold Arlen.

"There's a Fella Waiting in Poughkeepsie" © 1944 Harwin Music Co. (MPL Music Publishing Inc.) Lyrics by Johnny Mercer. Music by Harold Arlen.

"Whistling Away the Dark" © 1969, 1970, 1971 All Nations Music Publishing Ltd. (Universal Music Publishing Group). Lyrics by Johnny Mercer. Music by Henry Mancini.

Next Decade Entertainment

"Addams Family Theme" by Vic Mizzy. Published by Unison Music Company (ASCAP). Administered by Next Decade Entertainment Inc., All Rights Reserved. Used by Permission.

Sony/ATV Music Publishing

"Arthur Murray Taught Me Dancing in a Hurry" © 1942 Famous Music (Sony/ATV Music Publishing). Lyrics by Johnny Mercer. Music by Victor Schertzinger.

"Fleet's In, The" © 1942 Famous Music (Sony/ATV Music Publishing). Lyrics by Johnny Mercer. Music by Victor Schertzinger.

"I'm Doin' It for Defense!" © 1942 Famous Music (Sony/ATV Music Publishing). Lyrics by Johnny Mercer. Music by Harold Arlen.

"In the Cool, Cool, Cool of the Evening" © 1951 Famous Music (Sony/ATV Music Publishing). Lyrics by Johnny Mercer. Music by Hoagy Carmichael.

"I Remember You" © 1942 Famous Music (Sony/ATV Music Publishing). Lyrics by Johnny Mercer. Music by Victor Schertzinger.

"Moon River" © 1961 Famous Music (Sony/ATV Music Publishing). Lyrics by Johnny Mercer. Music by Henry Mancini.

"Old Glory" © 1942 Famous Music (Sony/ATV Music Publishing). Lyrics by Johnny Mercer. Music by Harold Arlen.

"Old Music Master, The" © 1943 Famous Music (Sony/ATV Music Publishing). Lyrics by Johnny Mercer. Music by Hoagy Carmichael.

"Sharp as a Tack" © 1942 Famous Music (Sony/ATV Music Publishing). Lyrics by Johnny Mercer. Music by Harold Arlen.

"Tangerine" © 1942 Famous Music (Sony/ATV Music Publishing). Lyrics by Johnny Mercer. Music by Victor Schertzinger.

"That Old Black Magic" © 1942 Famous Music (Sony/ATV Music Publishing). Lyrics by Johnny Mercer. Music by Harold Arlen.

"Waiter and the Porter and the Upstairs Maid, The" © 1941 Famous Music (Sony/ATV Music Publishing). Lyrics and music by Johnny Mercer.

Warner Chappell Music Inc.

"Afterbeat, The" © 1959 Warner-Chappell Music Inc. Words and music by Johnny Mercer and Fred Astaire.

"Air-Minded Executive, The" © 1940 Warner-Chappell Music Inc. Lyrics by Johnny Mercer. Music by Bernie Hanighen.

"And Points Beyond" © 2009 Warner-Chappell Music Inc. Lyrics by Johnny Mercer. Music by Andre Previn.

"And the Angels Sing" © 1939 Warner-Chappell Music Inc. Lyrics by Johnny Mercer. Music by Ziggy Elman.

"Any Place I Hang My Hat Is Home" © 1946 Warner-Chappell Music Inc. Lyrics by Johnny Mercer. Music by Harold Arlen.

"Any Way the Wind Blows" © 2009 Warner-Chappell Music Inc. Lyrics and music by Johnny Mercer.

"At the Jazz Band Ball" © 1950 Warner-Chappell Music Inc. Music and original lyrics circa 1917 by D. J. "Nick" LaRocca, Larry Shields, and possibly Edwin B. Edwards, Henry Ragas, and Tony Spago. New lyrics by Johnny Mercer.

"Autumn Leaves" © 1950 Warner-Chappell Music Inc. Original French lyrics by Jacques Prevert as "Les Feuilles Mortes." English lyrics by Johnny Mercer. Music by Joseph Kosma.

"Bernardine" © 1957 Warner-Chappell Music Inc. Lyrics and music by Johnny Mercer.

"Big Movie Show in the Sky, The" © 1949 Warner-Chappell Music Inc. Lyrics by Johnny Mercer. Music by Robert Emmett Dolan.

"Bilbao Song, The" © 1961 Warner-Chappell Music Inc. Original German lyrics by Bertolt Brecht with free adaptation by Johnny Mercer. Music by Kurt Weill.

"Blue Rain" © 1939 Warner-Chappell Music Inc. Lyrics by Johnny Mercer. Music by Jimmy Van Heusen.

"Blues in the Night" © 1941 Warner-Chappell Music Inc. Lyrics by Johnny Mercer. Music by Harold Arlen.

"Bob White" © 1937 Warner-Chappell Music Inc. Lyrics by Johnny Mercer. Music by Bernie Hanighen.

"Brasilia" (subtitled "Serenata Negra" or "Black Serenade") © 1961 Warner-Chappell Music Inc. Music and Portuguese lyrics by Vico Pagano, Carlos Loti, and Tito Madinez with English lyrics by Johnny Mercer.

"California's Melodyland" © 1965 Warner-Chappell Music Inc. Lyrics and music by Johnny Mercer.

"Captains of the Clouds" © 1942 Warner-Chappell Music Inc. Lyrics by Johnny Mercer. Music by Harold Arlen.

"Cast Your Bread upon the Water" © 2009 Warner-Chappell Music Inc. Lyrics and music by Johnny Mercer.

"C-A-T Spells Cat" © 1954 Warner-Chappell Music Inc. Lyrics and music by Johnny Mercer.

"Charade" © 1963 Warner-Chappell Music Inc. Lyrics by Johnny Mercer. Music by Henry Mancini.

"Day In — Day Out" © 1939 Warner-Chappell Music Inc. Lyrics by Johnny Mercer. Music by Rube Bloom.

"Days of Wine and Roses" © 1962 Warner-Chappell Music Inc. Lyrics by Johnny Mercer. Music by Henry Mancini.

"Dixie Isn't Dixie Anymore" © 1936 Warner-Chappell Music Inc. Lyrics by Johnny Mercer. Music by Rube Bloom.

"Dixieland Band, The" © 1935 Warner-Chappell Music Inc. Lyrics by Johnny Mercer. Music by Bernie Hanighen.

"Dog Eat Dog" © 1959 Warner-Chappell Music Inc. Lyrics by Johnny Mercer. Music by Harold Arlen.

"Dream" © 1944, 1945 Warner-Chappell Music Inc. Lyrics and music by Johnny Mercer.

"Duration Blues" © 1944 Warner-Chappell Music Inc. Lyrics and music by Johnny Mercer.

"Early Autumn" © 1952 Warner-Chappell Music Inc. Lyrics by Johnny Mercer. Music by Ralph Burns and Woody Herman.

"Empty Tables" © 1974, 1976 Warner-Chappell Music Inc. Lyrics by Johnny Mercer. Music by Jimmy Van Heusen.

"Equivalent of a Haa-vud Education, The" © 2009 Warner-Chappell Music Inc. Lyrics and music by Johnny Mercer.

"Facts of Life, The" © 1960 Warner-Chappell Music Inc. Lyrics and music by Johnny Mercer.

"Falling Off the Wagon" © 2009 Warner-Chappell Music Inc. Lyrics by Johnny Mercer and E. Y. "Yip" Harburg. Music by Lewis E. Gensler. Originally published 1932.

"Fare-Thee-Well to Harlem" © 1933, 1934 Warner-Chappell Music Inc. Lyrics by Johnny Mercer. Music by Bernie Hanighen.

"Finale (from *Foxy*)" © 1978, 2009 Warner-Chappell Music Inc. Lyrics by Johnny Mercer. Music by Robert Emmett Dolan.

"Fools Rush In" © 1940 Warner-Chappell Music Inc. Lyrics by Johnny Mercer. Music by Rube Bloom.

"Friendship" © 1939 Warner-Chappell Music Inc. Music and lyrics by Cole Porter.

"Game of Poker" © 1959 Warner-Chappell Music Inc. Lyrics by Johnny Mercer. Music by Harold Arlen.

"Georgia, Georgia" © 1966 Warner-Chappell Music Inc. Lyrics and music by Johnny Mercer.

"G. I. Jive" © 1943, 1944 Warner-Chappell Music Inc. Lyrics and music by Johnny Mercer.

"Girlfriend of the Whirling Dervish, The" © 1938 Warner-Chappell Music Inc. Lyrics by Al Dubin and Johnny Mercer. Music by Harry Warren.

"Glow Worm" © 1952 Warner-Chappell Music Inc. Music by Paul Lincke. Original German lyrics by Heinz Bolten-Backers in 1902 as "Glühwürmchen." Original English lyric by Lilla Cayley Robinson in 1907. New English lyrics by Johnny Mercer.

"Good Companions" © 1974 Warner-Chappell Music Inc. Lyrics by Johnny Mercer. Music by Andre Previn.

"Goody Goody" © 1935, 1936 Warner-Chappell Music Inc. Lyrics by Johnny Mercer. Music by Matt Malneck.

"Goose Never Be a Peacock" © 1959 Warner-Chappell Music Inc. Lyrics by Johnny Mercer. Music by Harold Arlen.

"Harlem Butterfly" © 1948, 1956 Warner-Chappell Music Inc. Lyrics and music by Johnny Mercer.

"Hello Out There, Hello" © 1952 Warner-Chappell Music Inc. Lyrics by Johnny Mercer. Music by Wingy Manone.

"He Loved Me Till the All-Clear Came" © 1942 Warner-Chappell Music Inc. Lyrics by Johnny Mercer. Music by Harold Arlen.

"Here Come the British, Bang! Bang!" © 1934 Warner-Chappell Music Inc. Lyrics by Johnny Mercer. Music by Bernie Hanighen.

"Here's to My Lady" © 1951 Warner-Chappell Music Inc. Lyrics by Johnny Mercer. Music by Rube Bloom.

"History of the Beat, The" © 2009 Warner-Chappell Music Inc. Lyrics and music by Johnny Mercer.

"Hooray for Hollywood" © 1937 Warner-Chappell Music Inc. Lyrics by Johnny Mercer. Music by Richard A. Whiting.

"How Little We Know" © 1944 Warner-Chappell Music Inc. Lyrics by Johnny Mercer. Music by Hoagy Carmichael.

"Human Race Is Human after All, The" © 2009 Warner-Chappell Music Inc. Lyrics by Johnny Mercer. Music by Robert Emmett Dolan.

"I Fought Every Step of the Way" © 1950 Warner-Chappell Music Inc. Lyrics and music by Johnny Mercer.

"I Had Myself a True Love" © 1946 Warner-Chappell Music Inc. Lyrics by Johnny Mercer. Music by Harold Arlen.

"I Happen To Like New York" © 1930 Warner-Chappell Music Inc. Music and Lyrics by Cole Porter.

"I'm an Old Cowhand (From the Rio Grande)" © 1936 Warner-Chappell Music Inc. Music and lyrics by Johnny Mercer.

"I'm Building Up to an Awful Letdown" © 1935 Warner-Chappell Music Inc. Lyrics by Johnny Mercer. Music by Fred Astaire.

"I'm Shadowing You" © 1973 Warner-Chappell Music Inc. Lyrics by Johnny Mercer. Music by Blossom Dearie.

"In Loving Memory" © 1978, 2009 Warner-Chappell Music Inc. Lyrics by Johnny Mercer. Music by Robert Emmett Dolan.

"I Thought about You" © 1939 Warner-Chappell Music Inc. Lyrics by Johnny Mercer. Music by Jimmy Van Heusen.

"It's Always Darkest Just Before the Dawn" © 1974 Warner-Chappell Music Inc. Lyrics by Johnny Mercer. Music by Andre Previn.

"It's a Woman's Prerogative" © 1946, 1950 Warner-Chappell Music Inc. Lyrics by Johnny Mercer. Music by Harold Arlen.

"It's Great to Be Alive" © 1949, 1950 Warner-Chappell Music Inc. Lyrics by Johnny Mercer. Music by Robert Emmett Dolan.

"I Wanna Be Around" © 1959, 1963 Warner-Chappell Music Inc. Lyrics by Johnny Mercer and Sadie Vimmerstedt. Music by Johnny Mercer.

"I Wanna Be In Love Again" © 1964 Warner-Chappell Music Inc. Music and lyrics by Johnny Mercer.

"Jubilation T. Cornpone" © 1956 Warner-Chappell Music Inc. Lyrics by Johnny Mercer. Music by Gene de Paul.

"Keep a Twinkle in Your Eye" © 1936 Warner-Chappell Music Inc. Lyrics by John Mercer. Music by Rube Bloom.

"Larceny and Love" © 1962 Warner-Chappell Music Inc. Lyrics by Johnny Mercer. Music by Robert Emmett Dolan.

"Laura" © 1945 Warner-Chappell Music Inc. Lyrics by Johnny Mercer. Music by David Raksin.

"Lazybones" © 1953 Warner-Chappell Music Inc. Words and Music by Johnny Mercer and Hoagy Carmichael.

"Love in the Afternoon" © 1957 Warner-Chappell Music Inc. Lyrics by Johnny Mercer. Music by Matt Malneck.

"Love Like Yours" © 1969 Warner-Chappell Music Inc. Music and lyrics by Johnny Mercer and Luiz Bonfa.

"Make with the Kisses" © 1939 Warner-Chappell Music Inc. Lyrics by Johnny Mercer. Music by Jimmy Van Heusen.

"Mandy Is Two" © 1941, 1942 Warner-Chappell Music Inc. Lyrics by Johnny Mercer. Music by Fulton McGrath.

"Satin Doll" © 1958, 1960 Warner-Chappell Music Inc. Lyrics by Johnny Mercer. Music by Duke Ellington and Billy Strayhorn.

"Show Your Linen, Miss Richardson" © 1939 Warner-Chappell Music Inc. Lyrics by Johnny Mercer. Music by Bernie Hanighen.

"Skylark" © 1941, 1942 Warner-Chappell Music Inc. Lyrics by Johnny Mercer. Music by Hoagy Carmichael.

"Sobbin' Women" © 1953, 1954 CBS Inc. (Alfred MP). Lyrics by Johnny Mercer. Music by Gene de Paul.

"Something's Gotta Give" © 1954, 1955 Warner-Chappell Music Inc. Lyrics and music by Johnny Mercer.

"Song of India" © 1953 Warner-Chappell Music Inc. Lyrics by Johnny Mercer. Music by Nikolai Rimsky-Korsakov.

"Strip Polka" © 1942 Warner-Chappell Music Inc. Lyrics and music by Johnny Mercer.

"Summer Wind, The" © 1965 Warner-Chappell Music Inc. Original German lyrics by Hans Bradtke as "Der Sommerwind" with English lyrics by Johnny Mercer. Music by Henry Mayer.

"Swing into Spring" © 1959 Warner-Chappell Music Inc. Lyrics by Johnny Mercer. Music by Bob Swanson.

"Tailgate Ramble" © 1944 Warner-Chappell Music Inc. Lyrics by Johnny Mercer. Music by Wingy Manone.

"Talk to Me, Baby" © 1963 Warner-Chappell Music Inc. Lyrics by Johnny Mercer. Music by Robert Emmett Dolan.

"Take a Crank Letter" © 1949 Warner-Chappell Music Inc. Lyrics by Johnny Mercer. Music by Robert Emmett Dolan.

"Taste" © 1978, 2009 Warner-Chappell Music Inc. Lyrics by Johnny Mercer. Music by Andre Previn.

"Texas Li'l Darlin'" © 1949 Warner-Chappell Music Inc. Lyrics by Johnny Mercer. Music by Robert Emmett Dolan.

"Thanksgivin'" © 1932 Warner-Chappell Music Inc. Lyrics by Johnny Mercer. Music by Hoagy Carmichael.

"These Orchids" © 1956 Warner-Chappell Music Inc. Lyrics by Johnny Mercer. Music by Jerome Kern.

"This Time the Dream's on Me" © 1941 Warner-Chappell Music Inc. Lyrics by Johnny Mercer. Music by Harold Arlen.

"Too Marvelous for Words" © 1937 Warner-Chappell Music Inc. Lyrics by Johnny Mercer. Music by Richard A. Whiting.

"Top Banana" © 1950, 1951 Warner-Chappell Music Inc. Lyrics and music by Johnny Mercer.

"Travelin' Light" © 1943 Warner-Chappell Music Inc. Lyrics by Johnny Mercer. Music by Jimmy Mundy and Trummy Young.

"Trees" © 1978, 2009 Johnny Mercer Foundation, A. M. Neder, J. J. Mercer. Poem by Johnny Mercer.

"Turn Out the Lights (and Call the Law)" © 1978, Warner-Chappell Music Inc. Lyrics by Johnny Mercer. Music by Arthur Schwartz.

"Two of a Kind" © 1980 Warner-Chappell Music Inc. Lyrics by Johnny Mercer. Music by Bobby Darin.

"Weekend of a Private Secretary, The" © 1938 Warner-Chappell Music Inc. Lyrics by Johnny Mercer. Music by Bernie Hanighen.

INDEX

Note: J.M. indicates Mercer, Johnny; G.M. indicates Mercer, Ginger.